Social and Communica
Following Traumatic B.

Traumatic brain injury (TBI) can seriously disrupt the social and communication skills that are basic requirements for everyday life. It is the loss of these interpersonal skills that can be the most devastating for people with TBI and their families. Although there are many books that focus upon TBI, none focus on social and communication skills specifically. This important book fills this gap in the literature and provides information ranging from a broad overview of the nature of pathology following TBI and its effects on cognition and behaviour, through to the latest evidence about ways to assess and treat social and communication disorders.

Much has changed in the field of communication disorders and TBI since the first edition of this book was published in 1999. There have been advances in neuroimaging, providing a more accurate understanding of how the brain is damaged in TBI, and also insights into its repair. There has been a burgeoning interest in social cognition, and advances in how communication is conceptualized, with a particular focus on how context facilitates or impedes communicative ability. Most importantly, much has changed in the arena of rehabilitation. There is now a growing evidence base for treatments aimed at improving communication problems following TBI, new resources for accessing this information and renewed interest in different kinds of methods for demonstrating treatment effects.

Bringing together a range of expert international researchers interested in understanding the nature and treatment of TBI, this book covers topics from understanding how brain damage occurs, how it affects social and communication skills and how these problems might be treated. As such it will be of great interest to clinicians, postgraduate and undergraduate students, and researchers in neuropsychology and speech and language pathology.

Skye McDonald is Professor of Clinical Neuropsychology at the University of New South Wales. She leads a Centre of Research Excellence in psychosocial rehabilitation following traumatic brain injury and is Associate Editor of the *Journal of the International Neuropsychological Society.*

Leanne Togher is Professor of Communication Disorders following Traumatic Brain Injury, Senior Research Fellow of the National Health and Medical Research Council and Principal Research Fellow of the University of Sydney. Togher serves on a number of editorial boards, including the *Journal of Rehabilitation Medicine, Aphasiology, Brain Impairment* and *Brain Injury.*

Chris Code is a Fellow of the Royal College of Speech and Language Therapists, and the British Psychological Society. He is a Professorial Research Fellow in Psychology at the University of Exeter, Foundation Professor of Communication Sciences and Disorders (Hon) at the University of Sydney and co-founding Editor of *Aphasiology.*

Brain, Behaviour and Cognition

Series editors
Chris Code and Glyn W. Humphreys

Milestones in the History of Aphasia
Theories and protagonists
Juergen Tesak and Chris Code

Anomia
Theoretical and clinical aspects
Matti Laine and Nadine Martin

Neuropsychology of Art
Neurological, cognitive and evolutionary perspectives
Dahlia W. Zaidel

Classic Cases in Neuropsychology, Volume II
Chris Code, Yves Joanette, André Roch Lecours and Claus-W. Wallesch

Category Specificity in Brain and Mind
Emer M. E. Forde and Glyn W. Humphreys

Neurobehavioural Disability and Social Handicap Following Traumatic Brain Injury
Rodger Ll. Wood and Tom M. McMillan

Developmental Neuropsychology
A clinical approach
Vicki Anderson, Julie Hendy, Elisabeth Northam and Jacquie Wrennall

Developmental Disorders of the Frontostriatal System
Neuropsychological, neuropsychiatric and evolutionary perspectives
John L. Bradshaw

Clinical and Neuropsychological Aspects of Closed Head Injury
John T. E. Richardson

Communication Disorders Following Traumatic Brain Injury
Skye McDonald, Leanne Togher and Chris Code

Transcortical Aphasias
Marcelo Berthier

Spatial Neglect
A clinical handbook for diagnosis and treatment
Ian H. Robertson and Peter W. Halligan

Social and Communication Disorders Following Traumatic Brain Injury

Second Edition

Edited by
**Skye McDonald, Leanne Togher
and Chris Code**

Ψ Psychology Press
Taylor & Francis Group
LONDON AND NEW YORK

Second edition published 2014
by Psychology Press
27 Church Road, Hove, East Sussex BN3 2FA

and by Psychology Press
711 Third Avenue, New York, NY 10017

Psychology Press is an imprint of the Taylor & Francis Group, an informa business

© 2014 McDonald, Togher and Code

First edition published 1999 by Psychology Press

British Library Cataloguing in Publication Data
A catalogue record for this book is available from the British Library

Library of Congress Cataloging in Publication Data
Social and communication disorders following traumatic brain injury /
[edited by] Skye McDonald, Leanne Togher, and Chris Code.
pages cm
Revision of: Communication disorders following traumatic brain injury.
1999.
ISBN 978-1-84872-129-6 (hb) -- ISBN 978-1-84872-135-7 (pb) 1. Brain
damage--Patients--Rehabilitation. 2. Brain--Wounds and injuries--
Complications. 3. Communicative disorders. I. McDonald, Skye. II.
Togher, Leanne. III. Code, Christopher, 1942- IV. Title.
RC387.5.C648 2014
617.4'81044--dc23
2013010634

ISBN: 978-1-84872-129-6 (hbk)
ISBN: 978-1-84872-135-7 (pbk)
ISBN: 978-0-20355-719-8 (ebk)

Typeset in Times New Roman
by Saxon Graphics Ltd, Derby

Contents

List of figures   vii
List of tables   viii
List of contributors   x
Series preface   xi
About the editors   xii

1 **Social and communication disorders following traumatic
   brain injury**   1
   LEANNE TOGHER, SKYE McDONALD AND CHRIS CODE

2 **Traumatic brain injury: basic features**   26
   SKYE McDONALD, LEANNE TOGHER AND CHRIS CODE

3 **The nature of cognitive deficits and psychosocial function
   following TBI**   48
   SKYE McDONALD, LEANNE TOGHER AND CHRIS CODE

4 **Cognitive communication disability following TBI: examining
   discourse, pragmatics, behaviour and executive function**   89
   LEANNE TOGHER, SKYE McDONALD, CARL A. COELHO AND
   LINDSEY BYOM

5 **Disorders of social cognition and social behaviour following
   severe TBI**   119
   SKYE McDONALD, CYNTHIA HONAN, MICHELLE KELLY,
   LINDSEY BYOM AND JACQUELINE RUSHBY

6 **A theoretical approach to understanding social dysfunction
   in children and adolescents with TBI**   160
   VICKI ANDERSON, MIRIAM BEAUCHAMP, STEFANIE ROSEMA
   AND CHERYL SOO

7 **Issues in the assessment and treatment of cognitive communication disorders in children with TBI**   190
LINDSEY BYOM, KRISTEN M. ALLISON AND
LYN S. TURKSTRA

8 **Dysarthria in children and adults with TBI**   218
ANGELA MORGAN

9 **Higher-level cognitive–communication approaches in chronic TBI to harness brain plasticity**   258
LORI G. COOK, ASHA VAS AND SANDRA B. CHAPMAN

10 **Evidence-based practice and cognitive rehabilitation therapy**   282
MARY R.T. KENNEDY

11 **Communication and social skills training**   307
CYNTHIA BRADEN

12 **Training communication partners of people with TBI: communication really is a two way process**   336
LEANNE TOGHER

13 **Using single-case methodology to treat social–pragmatic communication disorders**   361
ROBYN L. TATE, VANESSA AIRD AND CHRISTINE TAYLOR

Subject index   389
Name index   394

Figures

2.1 Diffusion Tensor Imaging depicting the loss of white matter
    fibres in a Caucasian male in his early twenties with a severe
    TBI (initial GCS below 8) compared to the normal fibre tracts
    of a healthy adult Asian male in his early thirties   27
2.2 Comparison of a (CT) scan taken on the day of injury (DOI)
    compared to a (MRI) scan taken 20 months later for a patient
    with severe TBI   28
6.1 The social brain network   164
7.1 Model of pragmatic skills   195
7.2 Classification of health outcomes   198
8.1 Aerophone II airflow measurement system   234
8.2 Respiratory spirometer   234
8.3 Respitrace system for kinematic assessment of speech breathing   235
8.4 Acrylic electropalatography plate with imbedded touch sensors   236
8.5 Client fitted with AG500 system   237
8.6 Nasometer   238
9.1 Preliminary findings for adolescent TBI group mean scores
    for gist reasoning and memory for text details before and after
    SMART training   271
10.1 Evidence-based practice (EBP) represented in a Venn diagram
    of four overlapping features considered within a therapeutic
    context   283
12.1 Example of communication problem solving form from *TBI
    Express* for working through difficult communication situations   352
13.1 Schematic representation of the Model for Assessing Treat
    Effect (MATE)   380

Tables

2.1	Glasgow Coma Scale	32
2.2	Classification of severity of head injury according to depth of coma or length of period of altered consciousness	34
3.1	Summary of attentional deficits commonly experienced following TBI including frequently used tests and qualitative features	54
3.2	Areas of memory impairment, common tests and qualitative features	60
3.3	Areas of executive impairment, common tests and qualitative features	65
4.1	Levels of discourse analysis	91
4.2	Some examples of assessment instruments for measuring communication after TBI	106
5.1	Some common measures of social cognition	133
5.2	Some common instruments for measuring emotion and behaviour dysregulation	142
7.1	Some common measures of paediatric language	201
7.2	Some paediatric measures of social cognition	203
8.1	Reported prevalence of dysarthria associated with traumatic brain injury in children and adults	219
8.2	Perceptually detected clinical features of dysarthria associated with traumatic brain injury in children and adults	225
8.3	Comprehensive perceptual motor speech assessment battery applicable to TBI	231
8.4	Physiological instrumentation utilized in the assessment of dysarthria following TBI	232
8.5	Example approaches for treatment of dysarthria associated with traumatic brain injury in children and adults	242
10.1	Levels of evidence, clinical recommendations and evidence requirements for recommendations	291
10.2	Levels of evidence, requirements of the evidence as specified by the National Health and Medical Research Council (NHMRC, 1999) using PEDro-P scores (PsycBITE; www.psycbite.com) to rate the evidence from group trials	294

10.3	A summary of practice standards and guidelines made by authors of CRT systematic reviews and organized by cognitive domain	295
11.1	Topics for treatment sessions during Group Interactive Structured Treatment (GIST)	316
11.2	Evidence for treatment of social communication, pragmatics, social skills impairments in TBI	321
12.1	Contextual dimensions for a service encounter (ordering pizza over the phone	340
12.2	Examples of exchange types	346
12.3	Elements of service encounters according to generic structure analysis	349
12.4	Ingredients for successful collaboration in conversation	353
12.5	Types of collaboration	354
12.6	Examples of exchange types	355
13.1	Summary of single-case studies on interventions for social–pragmatic communication disorders	366

Contributors

Vanessa Aird, BApp Sc
Cortex Communication Partners, Sydney

Kristen M. Allison, MA, CCC-SLP
University of Wisconsin-Madison

Vicki Anderson, PhD
Murdoch Children's Research
    Institute, Melbourne

Miriam Beauchamp, PhD
University of Montreal

**Cynthia Braden MA, CCC, CPHQ,
    FACRM**
Craig Hospital, Colorado

Lindsey Byom, MS
University of Wisconsin-Madison

Sandra B. Chapman, PhD
Center for BrainHealth®, University
    of Texas at Dallas

Chris Code, PhD
University of Exeter

Carl A. Coelho, PhD
University of Connecticut

Lori G. Cook, PhD, CCC-SLP
University of Texas at Dallas

Cynthia Honan, PhD
Moving Ahead: Centre of Research
    Excellence in Brain Recovery

Michelle Kelly, PhD
Specialist Mental Health Services for
    Older People (SMHSOP)

Mary R.T. Kennedy, PhD, CCC-SLP
College Program for Students with
    Brain Injury, UMN

Skye McDonald, PhD
University of New South Wales

Angela Morgan PhD
University of Melbourne

Stefanie Rosema
Murdoch Children's Research
    Institute, Melbourne

Jacqueline Rushby, PhD
University of New South Wales

Cheryl Soo
Murdoch Children's Research
    Institute, Melbourne

Robyn L. Tate, PhD
University of Sydney

Christine Taylor, BAppSc
Cortex Communication Partners,
    Sydney

Leanne Togher, PhD
University of Sydney

Lyn S. Turkstra, PhD, Professor
University of Wisconsin-Madison

Asha Vas, PhD
University of Texas at Dallas

Series preface

From being an area primarily on the periphery of mainstream behavioural and cognitive science, neuropsychology has developed in recent years into an area of central concern for a range of disciplines. We are witnessing not only a revolution in the way in which brain–behaviour–cognition relationships are viewed, but also a widening of interest concerning developments in neuropsychology on the part of a range of workers in a variety of fields. Major advances in brain-imaging techniques and the cognitive modelling of the impairments following brain injury promise a wider understanding of the nature of the representation of cognition and behaviour in the damaged and undamaged brain.

Neuropsychology is now centrally important for those working with brain-damaged people, but the very rate of expansion in the area makes it difficult to keep up with findings from the current research. The aim of the *Brain, Behaviour and Cognition* series is to publish a wide range of books that present comprehensive and up-to-date overviews of current developments in specific areas of interest.

These books will be of particular interest to those working with the brain-damaged. It is the editors' intention that undergraduates, postgraduates, clinicians and researchers in psychology, speech pathology and medicine will find this series a useful source of information on important current developments. The authors and editors of the books in the series are experts in their respective fields, working at the forefront of contemporary research. They have produced texts that are accessible and scholarly. We thank them for their contribution and their hard work in fulfilling the aims of the series.

Chris Code and Glyn W. Humphreys
University of Exeter, UK and University of Birmingham, UK
Series Editors

About the editors

Skye McDonald *(right)* is Professor of Clinical Neuropsychology at the University of New South Wales. She is an experienced clinical neuropsychologist and a senior researcher specializing in disorders of communication, social cognition and emotion following traumatic brain injury. McDonald has over 100 peer reviewed research studies focusing on these topics. She leads a Centre of Research Excellence in psychosocial rehabilitation following traumatic brain injury and is Associate Editor of the *Journal of the International Neuropsychological Society*.

Leanne Togher *(middle)* is Professor of Communication Disorders following Traumatic Brain Injury, Senior Research Fellow of the National Health and Medical Research Council and Principal Research Fellow of the University of Sydney. Togher is widely known for her work characterizing discourse and communication disorders post-TBI. Togher has published over 80 peer reviewed journal articles and serves on a number of editorial boards, including the *Journal of Rehabilitation Medicine, Aphasiology, Brain Impairment* and *Brain Injury*.

Chris Code *(left)* is a Fellow of the Royal College of Speech and Language Therapists, and the British Psychological Society. He trained as a speech–language pathologist–therapist with degrees in psychology and linguistics. He is a Professorial Research Fellow in Psychology at the University of Exeter, Foundation Professor of Communication Sciences and Disorders (Hon) at the University of Sydney and co-founding Editor of *Aphasiology*. Research interests include the neuropsychology of language and speech, psychosocial consequences, recovery and treatment of aphasia.

1 Social and communication disorders following traumatic brain injury

Leanne Togher, Skye McDonald and Chris Code

Traumatic brain injury (TBI) is the most common form of brain injury in the modern Western world. While TBI is sustained in people of all ages, the peak incidence is during early adulthood resulting in devastating disabilities for many young adults without any truncation of lifespan. These disabilities span physical, emotional, and cognitive and behavioural domains of function. Impairments in communication and social functioning may be a consequence of disabilities within and across these domains and collectively represent a unique area of investigation for clinicians and researchers alike. The past four decades have seen a major evolution in the way in which such disorders have been described and this chapter will provide an overview and introduction to the various approaches used.

Definitions

The term traumatic brain injury refers to brain injury caused by trauma rather than disease, vascular accidents, alcohol, etc. Traumatic brain injury is a consequence of a head injury of sufficient severity to cause damage to the brain beneath and can be either penetrating or blunt. Penetrating or open head injuries are an uncommon cause of traumatic brain injury, with the exception of war-wounds. Penetrating injuries occur when a missile, such as a bullet, pierces the skull and traverses the brain tissue. High velocity missile wounds cause catastrophic focal and diffuse damage and are usually fatal while low velocity missiles or missile fragments produce focal lesions restricted to the area of direct damage (Grafman & Salazar, 1987). Loss of consciousness is relatively uncommon following such injuries (Salazar *et al.*, 1986) and the functional sequelae often closely resemble that of other kinds of focal neurological lesions often leading to discrete and specific kinds of cognitive impairment (Grafman & Salazar, 1987). Research into aphasia following penetrating head injuries has been important in the development of theoretical approaches to aphasia and aphasia classification. Unfortunately, wars provided the circumstances for the first detailed studies of traumatic brain injury. For instance, Goldstein (1942) developed hospital treatment for brain-injured soldiers in Frankfurt during the First World War where he assessed and treated over 2,000 patients. This work influenced his theoretical approach, although he also had extensive experience with vascular lesions. Russell and Espir (1961) studied the records of 1,166 brain-injured patients examined in Oxford during the Second World War. They estimated that about 60 per cent of left hemisphere damaged patients had aphasia of some degree. Perhaps the most well-known neuropsychologist whose approach to aphasia is influenced by his experience with penetrating head injury is Luria. His famous book, *Traumatic Aphasia* (Luria, 1970), was first published in Russia in 1947 and details his theoretical approach which developed during his work with Russian soldiers during the Second World War.

More recently, the wars in Iraq and Afghanistan has resulted in a different type of TBI arising from exposure to improvised explosive device (IED) explosions with up to 60 per cent of returned service personnel sustaining brain injuries (Warden *et al.*, 2005). These blast injuries create a sudden increase in air pressure by heating and accelerating air molecules and, immediately thereafter, a sudden decrease in pressure that produces intense wind. These rapid pressure shifts can injure the brain directly, producing concussion or contusion. Air emboli can also form in blood vessels and travel to the brain, causing cerebral infarcts. In addition, blast waves and wind can propel fragments, bodies, or even vehicles with considerable force, causing head injuries by any of these mechanisms (Bell *et al.*, 2009; Summers *et al.*, 2009). Even so, the majority of moderate to severe blast injuries are associated with penetrating fragments (Masel *et al.*, 2012).

Blunt head injuries are by far the most common type of head injury in peacetime (Grafman & Salazar, 1987). Most of these are caused by the rapid acceleration and deceleration of the head such as occurs during motor vehicle accidents, falls or sporting injuries. This kind of injury produces multi-focal pathology in the brain, is associated with altered consciousness in the acute stages and generally causes widespread deficits quite unlike penetrating head injuries. Henceforth the term TBI in this book will refer to traumatic brain injury caused by blunt head injuries. It should also be noted that the term head injury is sometimes used interchangeably, since both this and the more specific term 'closed head injury' has had wide usage in the TBI literature.

It is now well recognized that communication problems following a TBI are distinctly different to those subsequent to a more focal lesion such as occurs in a cerebrovascular accident (or a penetrating head injury) and these require different approaches to assessment and remediation. This has come from the recognition that, due to the multi-focal nature of TBI, there is a complex interplay of cognitive, emotional, linguistic, physical, behavioural and organic psychosocial factors which may contribute to the communication difficulties experienced. These may include anything from word finding problems and impoverished output to excessive talkativeness, poor turn taking and repetitiveness (Snow *et al.*, 1998). In turn, communication problems can have a significant effect on psychosocial outcomes. The ability to communicate successfully is crucial to being able to maintain relationships and to establishing vocational and leisure activities. Overall, loss of communicative competence presents a major obstacle to reintegration into the community because it makes the person more taxing and less rewarding to interact with socially (Bond & Godfrey, 1997). Friends, carers and family begin avoiding them and this generally limits their ability to maintain pre-injury relationships (Elsass & Kinsella, 1987; Tate *et al.*, 1989). In addition, they often misjudge social situations, for example they may appear to be overly familiar with potential acquaintances thus interfering with their ability to establish new relationships.

As a result of diminished communication and interpersonal skills, people with TBI become socially isolated, have reduced opportunities for employment and may even require caregivers to help them with everyday tasks such as shopping or pursuing leisure options. But even with caregivers, the poor communication skills of people with TBI are problematic. Caring for people with TBI is stressful, with high levels of caregiver burden and depression (Hanks *et al.*, 2007; Knight *et al.*, 1998; Lefebvre & Levert, 2012; Wedcliffe & Ross, 2001). The main sources of this stress have been identified as problems communicating with the person with TBI (MAA, 1998), behavioural disturbance (Knight *et al.*, 1998) and the level of cognitive processing difficulties and poor insight of the person with TBI (Prigatano *et al.*, 2005; Wallace *et al.*, 1998).

Approaches to assessing communication disorders after traumatic brain injury

The complexity of communication and social problems following TBI has resulted in a range of approaches from varied theoretical backgrounds, including neuropsychology, psychosocial outcomes, pragmatics, sociolinguistics, social skills, discourse analysis and neurophysiology. This chapter will provide a brief overview of these different and often confusing perspectives and will refer the reader to the relevant chapters within the book.

Language assessment from the perspective of aphasia

In the 1970s it was recognized that communication problems following TBI were unique (Groher, 1977; Halpern *et al.*, 1973) differing from those experienced by patients with other types of neurological disorders. Communication was described as being confused (Groher, 1977), confabulatory (Hagan, 1982), tangential (Hagan, 1982; Levin *et al.*, 1979; Thomsen, 1975), full of empty phrases (Heilman *et al.*, 1971) and failing to display logico-sequential relationship between thoughts (Hagan, 1982). While recovery of language function was demonstrated at below the sentence level, it was frequently observed that TBI subjects did not manage at conversational levels (Groher, 1977; Halpern *et al.*, 1973; Levin *et al.*, 1982).

In the absence of appropriate measurement tools, researchers were only able to provide a superficial description of the way in which people with TBI communicated. Use of aphasia test batteries failed to delineate the problems which were observed in day-to-day communication leading to the creation of new definitions such as 'subclinical aphasia' (Sarno, 1980) and subsequent debates as to what constitutes aphasic impairment (Holland, 1984). In aphasia the patient has problems which can be described in terms of representational linguistic levels of phonology, morphology, syntax and lexical semantics (Code, 1991). Certainly it was recognized that a TBI might well result in aphasic disturbances. Indeed, early descriptions of language impairment following TBI suggested that aphasia occurred in 2 per cent of 750 cases and 14 per cent of 50 cases respectively (Heilman *et al.*, 1971; Levin *et al.*, 1976). But in addition, while Sarno and colleagues (Sarno, 1980; Sarno & Levita, 1986) indicated that 32 per cent of their TBI subjects evidenced frank aphasia, they also argued that many subjects suffered a form of subclinical aphasia, defined as 'evidence of linguistic processing deficits on testing in the absence of manifestations of clinical impairment' (Sarno, 1980: 687). The linguistic deficits in the subclinical aphasia group included difficulties with visual naming, word fluency and impaired performance on the Token Test, when compared with a matched dysarthric group. These results have been replicated in later studies with evidence of specific word finding difficulties on naming and word fluency tasks being the most common finding when people with TBI are evaluated on tests of traditional language functioning (Adamovich & Henderson, 1984; Levin *et al.*, 1981; Lohman *et al.*, 1989).

Difficulty with naming appears to be one of the most reported persisting communication problems following TBI. Thomsen's (1975) study of 50 patients with severe TBI found persistent oral expression impairment in half of the subjects when they were examined, on average, 33 months post-injury. Groher (1977) assessed a group of 14 severe TBI patients at monthly periods following resolution of coma. Patients demonstrated intact confrontation naming on the Porch Index of Communicative Abilities (Porch, 1967) four months after regaining consciousness; however their communication was described as lacking in conversational content. Levin *et al.* (1976) found in their sample of 50 severe TBI patients of varying severity that 40 per cent evidenced impaired naming on the Multilingual Aphasia Examination (Benton, 1967). In a follow-up study of 21 subjects who had been acutely aphasic, Levin *et al.* (1981) found that 12 showed persistent naming impairments.

Naming impairments have also been investigated in children (Jordan *et al.*, 1992; Jordan *et al.*, 1990) and adults with TBI (Kerr, 1995) using an information processing approach to assessment in the tradition of Coltheart (1987) and Shallice (1987). The advantage of a psycholinguistic perspective is the control it allows over the context in which language production occurs. The sophistication of this approach, widely used in aphasia therapy in describing the nature of naming impairments, holds some promise for word level analysis with TBI patients. Sentence level processing also appears to be affected by brain injury, so that, for example, complex syntactic processing has been associated with increased pause time (Ellis & Peach, 2009).

The information processing approach to word finding impairments has been applied in treatment (Hillis, 1998) to successfully remediate both semantic and phonological impairments (Leemann *et al.*, 2011; Vitali *et al.*, 2007; Wambaugh & Wright, 2007; Yeung & Law, 2010). Recent advances in brain imaging have demonstrated that remediation of naming is associated with re-activation of language brain areas (Vitali *et al.*, 2007) lending support to the use of principles of experience dependent neuroplasticity which is revolutionizing rehabilitation processes worldwide (Kleim & Jones, 2008).

Frank aphasic and specific naming deficits in TBI have been conventionally assessed using standard aphasia batteries such as the Western Aphasia Battery (Kertesz, 1982), The Boston Diagnostic Aphasia Examination (Goodglass & Kaplan, 1972) and the Multilingual Aphasia Examination (Benton *et al.*, 1994) supplemented by specific tests of naming such as the Boston Naming Test (Kaplan *et al.*, 1983) and comprehension e.g. the Revised Token Test (McNeil & Prescott, 1978). The development of the psycholinguistic approach to language assessment has culminated in the production of assessment instruments based upon these principles such as the Psycholinguistic Assessment of Language Processing in Aphasia (Kay *et al.*, 1992) and more recently, the Northwestern Assessment of Verbs and Sentences (NAVS: Cho-Reyes & Thompson, 2012; Thompson, 2012). However, while these instruments may be sensitive to basic linguistic deficits following TBI, such instruments inadequately capture the spectrum of communication deficits experienced in TBI. Nor do they take socially mediated aspects of language functioning into account.

Recognizing the influence of other cognitive disorders

Sarno's term 'subclinical aphasia' precipitated a debate regarding the terminology researchers and clinicians should be using when describing language impairment following TBI. Holland (1984) argued that language disorders following TBI are not aphasia but are second to cognitive and memory impairments. She objected to Sarno's term 'subclinical aphasia' as inappropriate labelling. Braun and Baribeau (1987) further criticized Sarno for not reporting nonverbal psychological functions which they felt precluded the differentiation between generalized intellectual dysfunction and aphasia. This foreshadowed the interest which was to follow in the relationship between cognitive impairments and communication.

By the middle to late 1980s increasing awareness of the interplay between cognition and language led to the introduction of the term *cognitive-language disorder* (Hagan, 1984; Kennedy & DeRuyter, 1991). Researchers began to investigate the relationship between the cognitive disturbances that frequently follow TBI and psycholinguistic aspects of language. For example, Hagan (1984) described the relationship between impairments of attention, memory, sequencing, categorization and associative abilities and impaired capacity to organize and structure incoming information, emotional reactions and the flow of thought. Such cognitive impairments, Hagan argued, cause a disorganization of language processes. Cognitive disorganization is reflected through language use which is characterized by irrelevant utterances which may not make sense, difficulty inhibiting inappropriate utterances, word-finding difficulties and problems ordering words and propositions.

Prigatano *et al.* (1985) described nonaphasic language disturbances following TBI including problems of talkativeness, tangentiality and fragmented thought processes. Some attempt was made to compare eight TBI subjects who were described by relatives as 'Talkative' on the Katz-R Adjustment Scale (Katz & Lyerly, 1963) with 40 TBI subjects who were described as 'Non-Talkative' on their respective neuropsychological status (e.g. on the Vocabulary, Block Design and Digit Symbol subtests of the Wecshler Adult Intelligence Scale-Revised: Wechsler, 1981) but no differences were found between the two groups. In addition, Prigatano *et al.* (1985) described an individual with TBI who was subjectively noted to be tangential in a written text and who was found to evidence difficulty with short-term memory and with shifting cognitive set (as measured on the Trail Making Test: Reitan, 1958). The only 'language' problems noted were difficulties naming pictures, repeating sentences and rapidly retrieving names on a word fluency task although these deficits were not reported to be 'obvious' in casual conversation. Prigatano and colleagues therefore argued that this tangential output was the result of the association of core neuropsychological impairments with tangential thinking and communication.

In recent times, the term *cognitive–communication disorder* (Hartley, 1995) has become the most common descriptor of the kinds of communication difficulties experienced by those with severe TBI. The focus on cognition arose from an examination of the underlying pathophysiology of TBI (described in detail in Chapter 2) which commonly results in multifocal cerebral damage with a preponderance of injury to the frontal lobes. Cognition can be broadly described as 'mental activities or operations involved in taking in, interpreting, encoding, storing, retrieving and making use of knowledge or information and generating a response' (Ylvisaker & Szekeres, 1994: 548). Examples of cognitive processes attributed to the frontal lobes include ability to focus attention to stimuli, remembering and learning, organizing information, reasoning and problem solving. In addition to specific cognitive processes, the frontal lobes appear to mediate executive control of thought and behaviour (see Chapter 3). Such executive functions include goal setting, planning and sequencing, goal oriented behaviour, initiation and evaluation of performance (Lezak *et al.*, 2004). It became increasingly obvious to researchers that it was impossible to assess language functioning without taking neuropsychological functioning into account.

Tacit recognition that TBI communication disturbances are likely to reflect other cognitive deficits has influenced everyday clinical assessment procedures. Clinicians often rely upon the more difficult of conventional language tasks that appear to have an additional cognitive load in order to gain an indication of the presence of communication disturbances experienced by their TBI clientele. For example, verbal fluency, so often noted to be impaired in TBI, and attributed to subclinical aphasia by Sarno (1980), is a task independently recognized as having additional cognitive demands. The Controlled Oral Word Association Test

(COWAT), which forms part of the Multilingual Aphasia Examination (Benton *et al.*, 1994), the Neurosensory Centre Comprehensive Examination for Aphasia (Spreen & Benton, 1969) and the Delis-Kaplan Executive Function System (Delis *et al.*, 2001) requires generativity of words in rapid succession according to specific rules. This task demands speed, productivity and flexibility in addition to linguistic competence and is impaired in many forms of brain damage including frontal lobe dysfunction and specifically in people with TBI (Kave *et al.*, 2011; Strong *et al.*, 2011). Poor COWAT performance is also correlated to relatives' perception of communication difficulties as rated using the Latrobe Communication Questionnaire (Douglas, 2010; Douglas *et al.*, 2000). Failure to perform on this task, in the absence of clear linguistic deficits on other parts of standard aphasia batteries, can therefore be taken to indicate the presence of cognitive deficits which are *impacting* upon language performance.

Other verbal tasks with an emphasis on abstraction skills, such as the decoding of metaphor in the Right Hemisphere Language Battery (Bryan, 1989), proverbs in the earlier and more recent Wechsler Adult Intelligence Scales (Wechsler, 2008) and other figurative language in the Test of Language Competence – Expanded Edition (Wiig & Secord, 1989) can also give an indication of impaired language *performance* which can frequently be observed independent of linguistic deficits *per se*. More complex and difficult sentence structures such as those used in the Wiig-Semel Test of Linguistic Concepts (Wiig & Semel, 1976) or the Test for Reception of Grammar (Bishop, 1983) may elicit difficulties for TBI patients who perform relatively normally on the simpler tests of comprehension. Finally, the ability to extract and convey the gist of complex verbal material is thought to be a reflection of the close interaction of language based skills and executive function. It is a skill that is extremely sensitive to TBI (Brookshire *et al.*, 2000; Gamino *et al.*, 2009) providing another avenue for assessment and also remediation (Vas *et al.*, 2011). The exploration of gist based assessment and remediation is detailed in Chapter 9.

While impaired performance on cognitively demanding language tasks may alert the clinician to the presence of communication disturbances, such assessment procedures fall short of providing accurate, comprehensive or ecologically relevant measures of impaired communication skills in TBI. How does the inability to think of words beginning with 'f' translate into communication competence in the workplace, the home and the general community? Obviously, in the case of Prigatano *et al.* (1985) above, such deficits did not appear to translate at all.

Approaches to language assessment and treatment with a focus on communication

By the end of the 1980s, researchers were focusing their attention less on isolated language functions and more on the impact of linguistic impairments on discourse functioning (e.g. Penn & Cleary, 1988), discourse being defined as a unit of language which conveys a message (Ulatowska & Bond Chapman,

1989). There are different types of discourse tasks which have also been referred to as different discourse *genres*. A genre is a particular text-type, which has its own structure and sequence. Some examples of discourse genres include narrative (or recounting a story), procedural (a set of instructions for doing something), expository (giving an opinion or discussing a topic in detail) and conversation. This change in focus represented a significant shift in the way communication problems following TBI were viewed. Developments in discourse analysis were related to a proliferation of interest across a number of disciplines including sociology (Hymes, 1986; Labov, 1970), psychology (Mandler & Johnson, 1977), artificial intelligence (Schank & Abelson, 1977) and linguistics (Grimes, 1975; van Dijk, 1977). Particular techniques in discourse analyses have been derived from both the psycholinguistic and sociolinguistic perspectives. The psycholinguistic analyses include measures of syntax (Chapman *et al.*, 1992; Glosser & Deser, 1991; Liles *et al.*, 1989), productivity (Hartley & Jensen, 1991; Mentis & Prutting, 1987) and content (Hartley & Jensen, 1991). On the other hand, sociolinguistic techniques include cohesion analysis (Coelho *et al.*, 1991; Hartley & Jensen, 1991; McDonald, 1993; Mentis & Prutting, 1987), analysis of coherence (Chapman *et al.*, 1992; Ehrlich & Barry, 1989; McDonald, 1993), analysis of topic (Mentis & Prutting, 1991) and compensatory strategies (Penn & Cleary, 1988). The practical application of these new methodologies to brain-injured populations has proven to be fruitful as a means to exemplify communication disorders not apparent in traditional testing.

Discourse analysis

Discourse analysis was initially used to describe the communication of people with aphasia following stroke (Bottenberg *et al.*, 1985; Ulatowska *et al.*, 1981) which led to descriptions of treatment using discourse level tasks (Armstrong, 1993; Ulatowska & Bond Chapman, 1989). Examining discourse as an index of communication following TBI occurred for the following reasons: a) to address the need for scientific verification of clinical impressions of the discrepancy between TBI subjects' performance on traditional language tests and their impaired communicative functioning in social contexts; b) to examine the relationship between language and cognition in connected speech tasks; and c) to address the need for assessments to form the basis for treatment of communication in real life contexts taking into consideration the impact of communication impairment on activity and participation. The application of discourse analysis in adults with TBI is discussed in Chapter 4 with further consideration of children and adolescents in Chapter 7. Chapter 4 provides an overview of microlinguistic discourse analysis (i.e. examining discourse at the word or sentence levels, e.g. phonological, lexical and syntactic processes) and macrolinguistic discourse analyses (i.e. examining discourse across sentences and/or at the level of the entire text, e.g. cohesion, story structure) as well as other measures of productivity and content of TBI discourse.

Pragmatics

Embodied within the broader field of discourse analysis is the study of the pragmatic nature of interactions. Pragmatics is concerned with the way language is used and the context of its use rather than the forms language takes (Levinson, 1983). As communication problems following TBI have been described as a difficulty with language use rather than form (Holland, 1984) it is not surprising that the tenets of pragmatics have been applied to this population.

The application of pragmatics and its relationship to cognitive processing in adults with TBI is also described in Chapter 4 and its application to children and adolescents is considered in Chapter 7. In Chapter 4 an overview is provided of key concepts applied to characterizing communication problems following TBI. These include the role of politeness in communication, the application of Grice's maxims of quantity, quality, relevance and manner (Grice, 1975) to characterize failures of communication and the sensitivity of indirect speech acts (such as sarcasm) as a means to elicit problems with understanding implied conversational meanings post-TBI.

The importance of context

Since the early discourse studies (Mentis & Prutting, 1987; Mentis & Prutting, 1991) there has been increased attention to different types of discourse genres and an array of approaches has emerged to measure them. Most of these approaches have been borrowed from the disciplines of behavioural psychology, pragmatics and sociolinguistics. With the development of these approaches there has been an increasing recognition of the complexity of language functioning as it occurs within social contexts. One approach emerging from sociolinguistics was Systemic Functional Linguistics (Halliday, 1985). This is a theory of language use based within a sociocultural framework. The language produced in an interaction is viewed as being interdependent with the contextual features of that situation. One of these contextual features is the relationship between the participants (also called the *tenor*). For example, it is proposed that factors such as familiarity and social status will directly influence the language which is produced. To evaluate the way in which language is influenced by the context in which it occurs, the use of analyses from Systemic Functional Linguistics are also overviewed in Chapter 4. Communication problems following TBI have been described as interactional in nature (Hartley, 1995), and the use of Systemic Functional Linguistics in Chapter 4 focuses on the way interactions unfold according to who is involved. The two-way nature of interactions is also reflected in this analysis with data being reported on the language produced from both TBI and control speakers and their communication partners.

The role of the communication partner

This interest in context and specifically in the ways in which the communication partner may impact on the communication of the person with TBI has been developing since the 1990s (Bond & Godfrey, 1997; Coelho *et al.*, 1991; Mentis & Prutting, 1991). The common observation from these studies is that the communication partner (i.e. the research assistant or speech pathologist) was required to take responsibility for maintaining the conversation as evidenced by increased frequency of question asking, prompting and requesting clarification and interpretation. Similarly, communication partners have been reported to talk for a significantly shorter time to people with TBI than they do with control participants, possibly because they were less likely to find a topic of common interest with the person with TBI. They may also have been given few opportunities to speak or not encouraged to keep talking by their conversational partner with TBI. Interactions of people with TBI have therefore been judged to be less rewarding, interesting and appropriate when compared with control interactions (Bond & Godfrey, 1997). If we examine the relationship between the people with TBI and their partners and the type of talking activity they were being asked to complete, these results may have been expected. If partners are in a therapist–patient relationship, the roles they can assume during a conversation are predetermined and quite different to other relationships the person with TBI might have. Their interactions with friends and family, for example, will look and sound quite different to their interactions with therapists or even strangers in the clinic or research setting. Therefore, it is important to examine with whom the person with TBI is talking when we study their interactions. Taking the relationship between speakers into account is a critical feature of the research presented in Chapter 4.

This increasing focus on functional communication, (i.e. communication in natural environments) has led to assessment procedures which can be used to describe a person with TBI's communication outside the clinical environment. Thus both relative and self-report questionnaires have an important role in characterizing communication difficulties in everyday settings. The La Trobe Communication Questionnaire (Douglas *et al.*, 2000), for example, was specifically designed for this purpose based upon Grice's maxims. Rating scales have also been developed or adapted to provide detailed ratings of specific communicative behaviours in naturalistic settings focusing upon either the person with TBI themselves (e.g. the Behavioural Referenced Index of Social Skills (Revised) (BRISS-R), Farrell *et al.*, 1985) or their communication partner (e.g. the Adapted Measure of Support in Togher *et al.*, 2010). Another approach has been the development of naturalistic material to assess comprehension of meanings in everyday language samples. The Awareness of Social Inference Test (TASIT) (McDonald *et al.*, 2003) uses video vignettes to assess comprehension of irony while The Functional Assessment of Verbal Reasoning and Executive Strategies (FAVRES) (MacDonald & Johnson, 2005) utilizes a range of everyday activities such as planning an event, developing a work schedule and deciding upon a gift. Different assessment resources for adults are overviewed in Chapter 4 and also Chapter 11 while assessments for children and adolescents are detailed in Chapter 7.

The relevance of social cognition to understanding communication disorders

While the 1980s and 1990s saw the innovative application of discourse theories to characterize communication disorders following TBI, the 2000s have seen the rapid development of another highly relevant field, that of social cognition. Social cognition refers to the cognitive processes that are engaged in making sense of interpersonal and social cues in order to predict the behaviour of others and to communicate with them. Interest in social cognition in general, and social neuroscience in particular, is growing rapidly. There are many facets to social cognition including the capacity to recognize emotions in others, gauge what they might be thinking and also what they are intending by their behaviour/communication. The notion that people with TBI might have difficulty recognizing the feelings, thoughts and intentions of others was intimated in early characterizations of personality change post TBI. For example, Lezak (1978) described a disorder of social perceptiveness as a key feature of the altered personality seen after TBI. Research that has used relatives' report has also highlighted problems with self-centredness (Kinsella *et al.*, 1991), insensitivity (Brooks & McKinlay, 1983), disinterest and childishness (Elsass & Kinsella, 1987; Thomsen, 1984) that suggest a failure to pick up on interpersonal cues.

Although two papers were published in the 1980s that documented deficits in emotion perception following TBI (Jackson & Moffat, 1987; Prigatano & Pribram, 1982), there was no further real interest in this field until the 2000s. There is now a steady stream of research that attests to problems in social cognition following severe TBI including two recent meta-analyses (Babbage *et al.*, 2011; Martin-Rodriguez & Leon-Carrion, 2010). Impaired social cognition has direct implications for communication. Not only do emotional expressions provide important feedback in any interpersonal communication but, as conversation is often indirect (Gibbs & Mueller, 1988), listeners need to make judgements about what speakers intend by what they say. Indeed, when it comes to tasks that assess the ability to make such mental judgements (i.e. Theory of Mind), tasks that use indirect speech acts such as sarcasm yield the largest effect sizes differentiating people with TBI from those without (Martin-Rodriguez & Leon-Carrion, 2010). Disorders of social cognition in adults with TBI are examined in detail in Chapter 5 and in children in Chapters 6 and 7.

The role of emotion regulation in communication

Emotional and behavioural regulation is frequently disturbed following TBI, often characterized as under-arousal (a loss of drive) or conversely, excitability and disinhibition (poor control) (Kinsella *et al.*, 1991). These kinds of problems also impact negatively upon interpersonal relationships (Wood *et al.*, 2005) and are, again, directly relevant to communication competence. The impoverishment of verbal output contrasting with the excessive talkativeness previously described following TBI (Snow *et al.*, 1998) may well reflect these different disorders of regulation. However, the role of emotion regulation in communication is yet to be examined in detail. Advancement in this field has been partly limited by the lack of reliable ways to measure emotion regulation. However, recent research using psychophysiological techniques that can index arousal and emotional valence (McDonald *et al.*, 2011a; McDonald *et al.*, 2011b) hold promise for new inroads into understanding the relation between emotion and communication including empathic communication. Indeed, the umbrella term 'cognitive–communication disorder' may soon be challenged by clearer characterization of disorders of 'affective-communication'. These issues are explored in Chapter 5.

Dysarthria

In addition to the social communication difficulties we have described, TBI can result in physical impairments which may interfere with speech production mechanisms. The resulting speech disorder, named dysarthria, may leave the TBI patient with a mild articulation difficulty so that occasional words need to be repeated or a listener needs to strain to understand, or in its severest case, the person may be completely unable to communicate verbally. Given the heterogeneous nature of TBI, a single pattern of dysarthric impairments has not been reported. The assessment and treatment of dysarthric impairments therefore provides the clinician with the challenge of identifying the nature of the disorder by taking into account its perceptual, acoustic and physiological features. Discussion of dysarthric impairments and their treatment following TBI is given in Chapter 8.

Understanding the psychosocial and developmental context of TBI

Understanding the nature of a TBI and how this might impact upon cognition, language, emotion and behaviour provides some inroads into assessment and remediation of cognitive communication disorders, but certainly not all. It is well recognized that psychosocial deficits following a TBI arise from a number sources. A recent model proposed by Beauchamp and Anderson (2010), further explored in Chapter 6, provides a good overview of these. Their model emphasizes the role of internal factors which include not only impairment in brain structures and function (e.g. loss of executive function) and the concomitant loss of skills, but also pre-existing factors such as personality and indirect effects such as anxiety and depression. Importantly, they also reflect external factors, such as the quality and nature of local support networks (e.g. the family) and broader social opportunities for participation (including the skill of everyday communication partners).

When a brain injury occurs in a child, there are additional complications as the neural substrate for later developing skills may be damaged. Children who experience TBI may thus be doubly disadvantaged as they not only experience impairments to existing abilities but are limited in their capacity to develop new ones in the course of normal maturation. Thus maturational factors are critical to understanding pediatric TBI. Studies that examine social outcomes of pediatric TBI are mixed in their findings, emphasizing the complex relationship between developmental, neuropathological and environmental influences. These issues are explored in detail in Chapters 6 and 7.

The conceptual approach to understanding the broader context of TBI in this book fits with the World Health Organization's International Classification of Function, Disability, and Health (ICF; World Health Organization, 2001). According to the ICF, there are different levels by which difficulties as a result of a health condition can be conceptualized. These include impairments in particular functions (e.g. aphasia, emotion perception), activity limitation (e.g. poor social skills) and, finally, restricted participation in social roles (for further discussion see Chapter 7). Taking this broader perspective it is clear that assessment of social and cognitive communication disorders need to address all ICF levels. As discussed above, assessments of both cognitive communication disorders and disorders of social cognition are expanding to address these different levels and these issues are considered further in Chapters 4, 5 and 11 (adult TBI) and Chapters 6, 7 and 9 (children and adolescents with TBI).

Remediation and rehabilitation

One of the great challenges in rehabilitation is what to do about social and communication problems following TBI. With the increasing array of assessment approaches available to us, it is often difficult to isolate practical goals for therapy which are objective and from which we can demonstrate change. The ability to communicate is obviously crucial to maintaining intact social and vocational networks, and therefore communication impairments will significantly affect a TBI individual's ability to reintegrate into these networks after their injury. Identifying appropriate treatment methodologies to facilitate this process is intricately linked with a successful return to these networks. Treatment usually commences very soon after the occurrence of the injury and may extend for many years. Traditionally, however, clinicians have had relatively few resources to guide their treatment choices. This is changing. There are a number of major research thrusts in recent times that have the potential to significantly improve rehabilitation. The increasing sophistication in the way in which communication disorders following TBI are characterized and assessed provides new targets and techniques for remediation. In addition, there have been rapid developments in the neurosciences providing renewed vigour for remediation research and increasing understanding of the importance of evidence based practice. These issues are the focus of the latter chapters of this book.

Remediating impairment

One important impetus in recent times comes from a renewed interest in the direct remediation of impaired processes. Aphasia treatment has traditionally focused upon careful, repetitive exercises aimed at re-building skills in a hierarchical fashion. Recent neuroscientific evidence that the brain can reorganize and regenerate following injury provides renewed optimism for this kind of treatment (Cornelissen *et al.*, 2003). The dominant view in past decades was that brain injury is permanent and, therefore, the best that can be hoped for compensatory training (Ogden, 2000). However, emerging research shows that processes can be re-established following brain injury, provided remediation targets are highly specific, attention is focused on relevant stimuli or behaviour and target processes are practiced repeatedly (Robertson & Murre, 1999). Constrained Induced Movement Therapy, for example, has shown that attention to the paretic limb and carefully targeted, graduated practice improves movement (Liepert *et al.*, 2001). This is accompanied by a use-dependent expansion of the cortical representation of the affected limb indicating brain plasticity and recovery at a neural level. Importantly, the combination of attention to and massed practice of specific processes also produces significant improvements in not only aphasia (Cornelissen *et al.*, 2003) but other perceptual and cognitive disorders including cortical blindness (Pleger *et al.*, 2003), sustained attention (Longoni *et al.*, 2000), unilateral neglect (Pizzamiglio *et al.*, 1998) and dyslexia (Temple *et al.*, 2003). In each case, use-dependent expansion of the cortical areas subserving these processes was reported.

This approach to remediation is useful for targeting specific deficits that interfere with cognitive–communication abilities. For example, direct remediation of emotion perception abilities following TBI has shown to have some success (Bornhofen & McDonald, 2008a, 2008b) (for further details see Chapter 11). Another approach is to target gist based reasoning as a means to stimulate and develop top-down, higher order processing of verbal information. This approach has been used successfully with adults with TBI (Vas *et al.*, 2011) and is currently being trialled with youth with TBI. The rationale and findings of gist based remediation are explored in detail in Chapter 9.

Retraining skills

Basic remediation research aims to ameliorate the *impairment* of damaged neural, cognitive, emotional processes. Another approach to remediation is to apply techniques that arise from the social skills literature to address the next level of the ICF framework, i.e. *activity limitation* by training skills. The underlying basis of social skills training, developed essentially from the general psychology literature, is an understanding of what normal social skills entail. A somewhat similar approach, developed within the context of speech and language therapy, is known as the functional treatment approach to communication deficits. Such functional approaches are seen to bridge the gap between the medical setting and the social world in post-acute stages of rehabilitation, so that patients can achieve the highest level of functioning in living, social, work and academic activities (Malkmus, 1989). As an intervention strategy, functional approaches employ a top-down path, where the desired outcomes, based on adult roles and activities, are identified first and competencies needed for those outcomes are then the targets for intervention (Hartley, 1995). In addition, it is important to tailor remediation to personalized contexts. This ensures the relevance of the training, the motivation for the participant and social opportunities to practise new skills (Ylvisaker *et al.*, 2005). There have been a number of well-controlled treatment trials of social skills training for adults with TBI and these are discussed in Chapter 11.

Providing opportunities to participate

At another level, interventions to improve social and cognitive–communication function in people with TBI can address the extent to which they are able to adopt social roles, i.e. the third level of the ICF: *participation*. Such interventions may not directly address the deficits of the person with TBI but may target those within their immediate community. For example, Johnson and Davis (1998) trialled an intervention focusing upon supporting community members to facilitate social opportunities for people with TBI. Struchen and colleagues involved others with a TBI as peer mentors to improve social participation (Struchen *et al.*, 2011). On a somewhat different tack, remediation can focus upon improving the skills of those who interact with people with TBI. Specifically, it has been demonstrated that communication partners of people with TBI (e.g. their mothers, friends, health professionals) can either ameliorate or exacerbate the communication problems that the person with TBI demonstrates. Condescending and patronizing interactional styles, or failure to provide the person with TBI adequate opportunity to respond in conversation can have the effect of disempowering and forestalling communication efforts (Togher *et al.*, 1997). Conversely, training communication partners how to structure conversations to equalize input and provide scaffolding, where needed, can be very effective and mutually beneficial. The issues underpinning communication partner training are addressed in detail in Chapter 12.

Understanding the evidence base for remediation

The fact that there is now a base of research emerging that addresses social and communication deficits at the levels of impairment, activity and participation after TBI is highly encouraging. This was not the case when the first edition of this book was published (McDonald *et al.*, 1999). With advances in the conceptual basis of remediation there has also been a growing sophistication in understanding what entails proper evidence that a specific remediation strategy is effective. One of the most authoritative sources in the area is the Oxford Centre of Evidence Based Medicine (http://www.cebm.net/index.aspx?o=5653) which provides a hierarchy of levels of evidence. According to this, the highest level of evidence has traditionally been that provided by a systematic review of eligible empirical studies of a given treatment. Following this, randomized controlled trials are considered the gold standard for evaluating a given treatment within a single trial. Group comparisons that do not entail randomization are seen as providing weaker evidence and so on. It is imperative that clinicians are aware of the differences between stronger and weaker levels of evidence and can critically evaluate the evidence for the treatments they choose. Indeed, an alarmingly high proportion of clinicians do not consult the literature at all when choosing a treatment for their client with brain injury (Perdices *et al.*, 2006).

Fortunately, there are now a range of Internet resources available to assist both clinicians and researchers to access the literature. PsycBITE (http://www. psycbite.com) is a freely available database that has collated all the studies ever published in English that provide evidence for non-pharmaceutical treatments for the psychological consequences of acquired brain impairment. SpeechBITE (http://www.speechbite.com) is the sister database to PsycBITE and provides access to all studies that attest to treatments for disorders of communication and swallowing disorders. A unique feature of both databases is that all group treatment studies are rated for their methodological rigour using the PEDro-P scale (adapted from Moher *et al.*, 2001). Thus, clinicians and researchers alike can use PsycBITE and SpeechBITE to access treatments for a particular condition at the touch of a button and also access information about the quality of the trials that emerge. Specific information about how to use such information is explored in detail in Chapter 10.

Given the small but growing evidence base for treatments addressing aspects of communication and social and interpersonal skills it is timely that we review the evidence to date and that is a specific purpose of Chapters 11 and 13 both of which provide a different focus. Chapter 11 provides an overview of research into treatments for social and interpersonal skills after TBI. It focuses upon RCTs, group comparison studies and multiple baseline studies that provide evidence for practice guidelines or practice options. Here the particular clinical techniques and approaches are fleshed out based on this evidence. Chapter 13 commences with a similar constellation of studies but extends this to focus upon single case experimental designs (SCEDs) in detail. As argued by the authors, single case experimental designs provide a flexible, practical and scientifically rigorous alternative to group studies in the evaluation of specific disorders in social and communicative skills. They enable focus on very specific kinds of problems and well-characterized treatment approaches. The value of the SCED has been recognized by its inclusion in the top level of scientific evidence in the most recent edition of the Oxford Centre of Evidence Based Medicine (2011) alongside systematic reviews.

Although SCEDs can be scientifically rigorous by the use of appropriate design, adequate sampling etc., there is, in reality, a great deal of variability in the methodological quality amongst those in the published literature. In order to address this both PsycBITE and SpeechBITE provide ratings of the methodological quality of SCEDs in the same way as group comparisons are rated using the PEDro-P scale. There are a number of scales that have been developed for this purpose including the Risk of Bias in N-of-1 Trials (RoBiN-T) Scale and its predecessor, the Single-Case Experimental Design (SCED) Scale (Tate *et al.*, 2008). In Chapter 13, clear guidelines are provided for designing single case studies whether these are for the purposes of publishing research into treatment effects or for upgrading the manner in which treatments are implemented and evaluated in the clinic.

Conclusions

Outcome studies of people with severe TBI over the past 40 years have repeatedly painted a picture of significant long term disability encompassing personal, social and vocational difficulties (Anson & Ponsford, 2006; Levin *et al.*, 1979; Oddy *et al.*, 1985; Ponsford & Schönberger, 2010; Tate *et al.*, 1989a; Willer *et al.*, 1993). The occurrence of a TBI results in a range of physical, cognitive, communication, emotional and psychosocial problems, that result in a loss of friends, reduction in work options and breakup of the family unit with resulting social isolation and secondary problems of depression, anxiety and poor emotional functioning in both the person with TBI (Anson & Ponsford, 2006) and family members (Schönberger *et al.*, 2010) (see Chapter 3 for further discussion). The ability to communicate is critical to maintaining social and vocational networks, and therefore communication impairments will significantly affect a TBI individual's ability to reintegrate into these networks after their injury. Communication and social disorders are, thus, core obstacles to successful rehabilitation.

Since early characterization of the communication problems experienced by people with TBI, there has been growing interest in elucidating how, where and why such problems manifest. While early research saw the problem as one of language, more recent approaches view communication from the perspective of cognition (e.g. memory, attention and executive processes), social processing (e.g. emotion perception and ToM) and available social contexts (e.g. communication partners and social opportunities). With this broadening of the definition of communication comes new insight into approaches to assessments that are sensitive to the actual problems that people with TBI experience in their everyday function. Such broadening of focus also provides the opportunity to reconsider targets for remediation and the best approaches by which these can be achieved. These issues are the central focus of this book.

References

Adamovich, B. L. B. & Henderson, J. A. (1984). Can we learn more from word fluency measures with aphasic, right brain injured and closed head trauma patients? In R. H. Brookshire (Ed.), *Clinical Aphasiology Conference Proceedings* (vol. 14, pp. 124–131). Minneapolis: BRK Publishers.

Anson, K. & Ponsford, J. (2006). Coping and emotional adjustment following traumatic brain injury. *Journal of Head Trauma Rehabilitation, 21*(3), 248–259.

Armstrong, E. M. (1993). Aphasia rehabilitation: a sociolinguistic perspective. In A. L. Holland & M. M. Forbes (Eds), *Aphasia Treatment: World Perspectives* (pp. 263–290). San Diego, CA: Singular.

Babbage, D. R., Yim, J., Zupan, B., Neumann, D., Tomita, M. R. & Willer, B. (2011). Meta-analysis of facial affect recognition difficulties after traumatic brain injury. *Neuropsychology, 25*(3), 277–285.

Beauchamp, M. & Anderson, V. (2010). SOCIAL: an integrative framework for the development of social skills. *Psychological Bulletin, 136*, 39–64.

Bell, R. S., Vo, A. H., Neal, C. J., Tigno, J., Roberts, R., Mossop, C., Dunne, J. R. & Armonda, R. A. (2009). Military traumatic brain and spinal column injury: a 5-year study of the impact blast and other military grade weaponry on the central nervous system. *Journal of Trauma-Injury Infection & Critical Care, 66*(4 Suppl), S104–111.

Benton, A. L. (1967). Problems of test construction in the field of aphasia. *Cortex, 3,* 32–58.

Benton, A. L., Hamsher, K. & Sivan, A. B. (1994). *Multilingual Aphasia Examination.* Iowa City: AJA Associates.

Bishop, D. V. M. (1983). *Test for Reception of Grammar.* Cambridge, UK: Medical Research Council.

Bond, F. & Godfrey, H. P. D. (1997). Conversation with traumatically brain-injured individuals: a controlled study of behavioural changes and their impact. *Brain Injury, 11 (5),* 319–329.

Bornhofen, C. & McDonald, S. (2008a). Comparing strategies for treating emotion perception deficits in traumatic brain injury. *Journal of Head Trauma Rehabilitation, 23,* 103–115.

——(2008b). Treating deficits in emotion perception following traumatic brain injury. *Neuropsychological Rehabilitation, 18*(1), 22–44.

Bottenberg, D. E., Lemme, M. L. & Hedberg, N. L. (1985). Analysis of oral narratives of normal and aphasic adults. In R. H. Brookshire (Ed.), *Clinical Aphasiology Conference Proceedings* (pp. 241–247). Minneapolis, MN: BRK Publishers.

Braun, C. M. J. & Baribeau, J. M. C. (1987). Subclinical aphasia following closed head injury: a response to Saino, Buonaguro & Levita. *Clinical Aphasiology, 17,* 326–333.

Brooks, D. N. & McKinlay, W. (1983). Personality and behavioural change after severe blunt head injury – a relative's view. *Journal of Neurology, Neurosurgery & Psychiatry, 46*(4), 336–344.

Brookshire, B. L., Chapman, S. B., Song, J. & Levin, H. S. (2000). Cognitive and linguistic correlates of children's discourse after closed head injury: a three-year follow-up. *Journal of the International Neuropsychological Society, 6*(7), 741–751.

Bryan, K. L. (1989). *The Right Hemisphere Language Battery.* Kibworth: Far Communications.

Chapman, S. B., Culhane, K. A., Levine, H. S., Harward, H., Mendelsohn, D., Ewing-Cobbs, L., Fletcher, J. M. & Bruce, D. (1992). Narrative discourse after closed head injury in children and adolescents. *Brain and Language, 43,* 42–65.

Cho-Reyes, S. & Thompson, C. K. (2012). Verb and sentence production and comprehension in aphasia: Northwestern Assessment of Verbs and Sentences (NAVS). *Aphasiology, 26*(10), 1250–1277.

Code, C. (1991). Symptoms, syndromes, models: the nature of aphasia. In C. Code (Ed.), *The Characteristics of Aphasia* (pp. 1–22). Hove: Lawrence Erlbaum Associates.

Coelho, C. A., Liles, B. Z. & Duffy, R. J. (1991). The use of discourse analysis for the evaluation of higher level traumatically brain injured adults. *Brain Injury, 5,* 381–392.

Coltheart, M. (1987). Functional architecture of the language processing system. In M. Coltheart, G. Sartori & R. Job (Eds), *The Cognitive Neuropsychology of Language* (pp. 1–26). Hillsdale, NJ: Erlbaum.

Cornelissen, K., Laine, M., Tarkiainen, A., Jaervensivu, T., Martin, N. & Salmelin, R. (2003). Adult brain plasticity elicited by anomia treatment. *Journal of Cognitive Neuroscience, 15*(3), 444–461.

Delis, D. C., Kaplan, E. & Kramer, J. H. (2001). *Delis-Kaplan Executive Function System (D-KEFS).* New York: Harcourt Assessment: The Psychological Corporation.

Douglas, J. M. (2010). Relation of executive functioning to pragmatic outcome following severe traumatic brain injury. *Journal of Speech, Language, and Hearing Research, 53*(2), 365–382.

Douglas, J. M., O'Flaherty, C. A. & Snow, P. C. (2000). Measuring perception of communicative ability: the development and evaluation of the La Trobe communication questionnaire. *Aphasiology, 14*(3), 251–268.

Ehrlich, J. & Barry, P. (1989). Rating communication behaviours in the head injured. *Brain Injury, 3,* 193–198.

Ellis, C. & Peach, R. (2009). Sentence planning following traumatic brain injury. *NeuroRehabilitation, 24*(3), 255–266.

Elsass, L. & Kinsella, G. (1987). Social interaction following severe closed head injury. *Psychological Medicine, 17*(1), 67–78.

Farrell, A. D., Rabinowitz, J. A., Wallander, J. L. & Curran, J. P. (1985). An evaluation of two formats for the intermediate-level assessment of social skills. *Behavioral Assessment, 7*(2), 155–171.

Gamino, J. F., Chapman, S. B. & Cook, L. G. (2009). Strategic learning in youth with traumatic brain injury: evidence for stall in higher-order cognition. *Topics in Language Disorders, 29*(3), 224–235.

Gibbs, R. W. & Mueller, R. A. (1988). Conversational sequences and preferences for indirect speech acts. *Discourse Processes, 11*(1), 101–116.

Glosser, G. & Deser, T. (1991). Patterns of discourse production among neurological patients with fluent language disorders. *Brain and Language, 40*(1), 67–88.

Goldstein, K. (1942). *After-effects of Brain Injuries in War.* New York: Grune and Stratton.

Goodglass, H. & Kaplan, E. (1972). *The Assessment of Aphasia and Related Disorders.* Philadelphia: Lea & Febiger.

Grafman, J. & Salazar, A. M. (1987). Methodological considerations relevant to the comparison of recovery from penetrating and closed head injuries. In H. S. Levin, J. Grafman & H. M. Eisenberg (Eds), *Neurobehavioural Recovery from Head Injury.* New York: Oxford University Press.

Grice, H. P. (1975). Logic and conversation. In P. Cole & J. Morgan (Eds), *Syntax and Semantics: Speech Acts* (Vol. 3). New York: Academic Press.

Grimes, J. (1975). *The Thread of Discourse.* The Hague: Mouton.

Groher, M. (1977). Language and memory disorders following closed head trauma. *Journal of Speech and Hearing Research, 20,* 212–223.

Hagan, C. (1982). Language-cognitive disorganisation following closed head injury: a conceptualization. In L. Trexler (Ed.), *Cognitive Rehabilitation Conceptualization and Intervention* (pp. 131–151). New York: Plenum Press.

——(1984). Language disorders in head trauma. In A. Holland (Ed.), *Language Disorders in Adults.* San Diego: College Hill Press.

Halliday, M. A. K. (1985). *An Introduction to Functional Grammar.* Australia: Edward Arnold.

Halpern, H., Darley, F. L. & Brown, J. R. (1973). Differential language and neurologic characteristics in cerebral involvement. *Journal of Speech and Hearing Disorders, 38*(2), 162–173.

Hanks, R. A., Rapport, L. J. & Vangel, S. (2007). Caregiving appraisal after traumatic brain injury: the effects of functional status, coping style, social support and family functioning. *NeuroRehabilitation – An Interdisciplinary Journal, 22*(1), 43–53.

Hartley, L. L. (1995). *Cognitive-communicative Abilities Following Brain Injury: A Functional Approach.* San Diego, CA: Singular.

Hartley, L. L. & Jensen, P. J. (1991). Narrative and procedural discourse after closed head injury. *Brain Injury, 5,* 267–285.

Heilman, K. M., Safran, A. & Geschwind, N. (1971). Closed head trauma and aphasia. *Journal of Neurology, Neurosurgery & Psychiatry, 34,* 265–269.

Hillis, A. E. (1998). Treatment of naming disorders: new issues regarding old therapies. *Journal of the International Neuropsychological Society, 4,* 648–660.

Holland, A. L. (1984). When is aphasia aphasia? The problem of closed head injury. In R. W. Brookshire (Ed.), *Clinical Aphasiology* (vol. 4, pp. 345–349). Minneapolis: BRK Publishers.

Hymes, D. (1986). Models of the interaction of language and social life. In J. J. Gumperz & D. Hymes (Eds), *Directions in Sociolinguistics. The Ethnography of Communication* (pp. 35–71). Basil Oxford: Blackwell.

Jackson, H. F. & Moffat, N. J. (1987). Impaired emotional recognition following severe head injury. *Cortex, 23,* 293–300.

Johnson, K. & Davis, P. K. (1998). A supported relationships intervention to increase the social integration of persons with traumatic brain injuries. *Behaviour Modification, 22*(4), 502–528.

Jordan, F. M., Ozanne, A. E. & Murdoch, B. E. (1990). Performance of closed head injured children on a naming task. *Brain Injury, 4,* 27–32.

Jordan, F. M., Cannon, A. & Murdoch, B. E. (1992). Language abilities of mildly closed head injured (CHI) children 10 years post-injury. *Brain Injury, 6*(1), 39–44.

Kaplan, E., Goodglass, H., Weintraub, S. & Segal, O. (1983). *Boston Naming Test.* Philadelphia: Lea & Febiger.

Katz, M. M. & Lyerly, S. B. (1963). Methods for measuring adjustment and social behavior in the community: I. Rationale, description, discriminative validity and scale development. *Psychological Reports, 13*(2 (Mono Suppl No 4–V13)), 503–535.

Kave, G., Heled, E., Vakil, E. & Agranov, E. (2011). Which verbal fluency measure is most useful in demonstrating executive deficits after traumatic brain injury? *Journal of Clinical and Experimental Neuropsychology, 33*(3), 358–365.

Kay, J., Lesser, R. & Coltheart, M. (1992). *Psycholinguistic Assessment of Language Performance in Aphasia.* Hove, East Sussex, UK: Lawrence Erlbaum.

Kennedy, M. R. T. & DeRuyter, F. (1991). Cognitive and language bases for communication disorders. In D. R. Beukelman & K. M. Yorkston (Eds), *Communication Disorders Following Traumatic Brain Injury: Management of Cognitive, Language and Motor Impairments* (pp. 123–190). Texas, TX: Pro-Ed.

Kerr, C. (1995). Dysnomia following traumatic brain injury: an information-processing approach to assessment. *Brain Injury, 9*(8), 777–796.

Kertesz, A. (1982). *Western Aphasia Battery.* New York, NY: Grune & Stratton.

Kinsella, G., Packer, S. & Olver, J. (1991). Maternal reporting of behaviour following very severe blunt head injury. *Journal of Neurology, Neurosurgery & Psychiatry, 54*(5), 422–426.

Kleim, J. A. & Jones, T. A. (2008). Principles of experience-dependent neural plasticity: Implications for rehabilitation after brain damage. *Journal of Speech, Language, and Hearing Research, 51*(1), S225–S239.

Knight, R., Devereux, R. & Godfrey, H. (1998). Caring for a family member with traumatic brain injury. *Brain Injury, 12*(6), 467–481.

Labov, W. (1970). The study of language in its social context. *Studium Generale, 23,* 30–87.

Leemann, B., Laganaro, M., Chetelat-Mabillard, D. & Schnider, A. (2011). Crossover trial of subacute computerized aphasia therapy for anomia with the addition of either levodopa or placebo. *Neurorehabilitation and Neural Repair, 25*(1), 43–47.

Lefebvre, H. & Levert, M.-J. (2012). The close relatives of people who have had a traumatic brain injury and their special needs. *Brain Injury, 26*(9), 1084–1097.

Levin, H. S., Grossman, R. G. & Kelly, P. J. (1976). Aphasic disorders in patients with closed head injury. *Journal of Neurology, Neurosurgery and Psychiatry, 39,* 1062–1070.

Levin, H. S., Grossman, R. G., Rose, J. E. & Teasdale, G. (1979). Long term neuropsychological outcome of closed head injury. *Journal of Neurosurgery, 50,* 412–422.

Levin, H. S., Grossman, R. G. & Sarwar, M. (1981). Linguistic recovery after closed head injury. *Brain and Language, 12,* 360–374.

Levin, H. S., Benton, A. L. & Grossman, R. G. (1982). *Neurobehavioural Consequences of Closed Head Trauma.* New York: Oxford University Press.

Levinson, S. C. (1983). *Pragmatics.* London: Cambridge University Press.

Lezak, M. D. (1978). Living with the characterologically altered brain-injured patient. *Journal of Clinical Psychology, 39,* 592–598.

Lezak, M. D., Howieson, D. B. & Loring, D. W. (2004). *Neuropsychological Assessment* (4th edn). Oxford: Oxford University Press.

Liepert, J., Bauder, H., Miltner, W. H. R., Taub, E. & Weiller, C. (2001). Motor cortex plasticity during forced-use therapy in stroke patients: a preliminary study. *Journal of Neurology, Neurosurgery & Psychiatry, 284,* 315–321.

Liles, B. Z., Coelho, C. A., Duffy, R. J. & Zalagens, M. R. (1989). Effects of elicitation procedures on the narratives of normal and closed head injured adults. *Journal of Speech and Hearing Disorders, 54,* 356–366.

Lohman, T., Ziggas, D. & Pierce, R. S. (1989). Word fluency performance on common categories by subjects with closed head injuries. *Aphasiology, 3*(8), 685–693.

Longoni, F., Sturm, W., Weis, S., Holtel, C., Specht, K., Herzog, H. *et al.* (2000). Functional reorganization after training of alertness in two patients with right-hemisphere lesions. *Zeitschrift für Neuropsychologie, 11,* 250–261.

Luria, A. R. (1970). *Traumatic Aphasia.* The Hague: Mouton.

MAA. (1998). *Training Needs of Attendant Carers.* Sydney: Motor Accidents Authority.

MacDonald, S. & Johnson, C. J. (2005). Assessment of subtle cognitive–communication deficits following acquired brain injury: a normative study of the functional assessment of verbal reasoning and executive strategies (FAVRES). *Brain Injury, 19*(11), 895–902.

Malkmus, D. D. (1989). Community reentry: cognitive-communicative intervention within a social skill context. *Topics in Language Disorders, 9,* 50–66.

Mandler, J. A. & Johnson, N. S. (1977). Remembrance of things parsed: story structure and recall. *Cognitive Psychology, 9,* 111–151.

Martin-Rodriguez, J. F. & Leon-Carrion, J. (2010). Theory of mind deficits in patients with acquired brain injury: a quantitative review. *Neuropsychologia, 48,* 1181–1191.

Masel, B. E., Bell, R. S., Brossart, S., Grill, R. J., Hayes, R. L., Levin, H. S., Rasband, M. N., Ritzel, D. V., Wade, C.E. & DeWitt, D. S. (2012). Galveston Brain Injury Conference 2010: clinical and experimental aspects of blast injury. *Journal of Neurotrauma, 29*(12), 2143–2171.

McDonald, S. (1993). Pragmatic language skills after closed head injury: ability to meet the informational needs of the listener. *Brain and Language, 44*(1), 28–46.

McDonald, S., Togher, L. & Code, C. (Eds). (1999). *Communication Disorders Following Traumatic Brain Injury*. Hove, UK: Psychology Press.

McDonald, S., Flanagan, S., Rollins, J. & Kinch, J. (2003). TASIT: a new clinical tool for assessing social perception after traumatic brain injury. *Journal of Head Trauma Rehabilitation, 18*, 219–238.

McDonald, S., Li, S., De Sousa, A., Rushby, J., Dimoska, A., James, C. & Tate, R. L. (2011a). Impaired mimicry response to angry faces following severe traumatic brain injury. *Journal of Clinical and Experimental Neuropsychology, 33*(1), 17–29.

McDonald, S., Rushby, J., Li, S., de Sousa, A., Dimoska, A., James, C., Tate, R. & Togher, L. (2011b). The influence of attention and arousal on emotion perception in adults with severe traumatic brain injury. *International Journal of Psychophysiology, 82*(1), 124–131.

McNeil, M. R. & Prescott, T. E. (1978). *Revised Token Test*. Baltimore, MD: University Park Press.

Mentis, M. & Prutting, C. A. (1987). Cohesion in the discourse of normal and head-injured adults. *Journal of Speech and Hearing Research, 30*, 583–595.

——(1991). Analysis of topic as illustrated in a head-injured and a normal adult. *Journal of Speech and Hearing Research, 34*, 583–595.

Moher, D., Schulz, K. F. & Altman, D. G. (2001). The CONSORT statement: revised recommendations for improving the quality of reports of parallel-group randomised trials. *Lancet, 357*, 1191–1194.

Oddy, M., Coughlan, T., Tyerman, A. & Jenkins, D. (1985). Social adjustment after closed head injury: a further follow-up seven years after injury. *Journal of Neurology, Neurosurgery & Psychiatry, 48*(6), 564–568.

Ogden, J. A. (2000). Neurorehabilitation in the third millenium: new roles for our environment, behaviors, and mind in brain damage and recovery? *Brain & Cognition, 42*(1), 110–112.

Penn, C. & Cleary, J. (1988). Compensatory strategies in the language of closed head injured patients. *Brain Injury, 2* (1), 3–17.

Perdices, M., Schultz, R., Tate, R. L., McDonald, S., Togher, L., Savage, S., Winders, K. & Smith, K. (2006). The evidence base of neuropsychological rehabilitation in acquired brain impairment (ABI): how good is the research? *Brain Impairment, 7*, 119–132.

Pizzamiglio, L., Perani, D., Cappa, S. F., Vallar, G., Paolucci, S., Grassi, F., Paulesu, E. & Fazio, F. (1998). Recovery of neglect after right hemispheric damage: H2(15)O positron emission tomographic activation study. *Archives of Neurology, 55*(4), 561–568.

Pleger, B., Foerster, A. F., Widdig, W., Henschel, M., Nicolas, V., Jansen, A., Frank, A., Knecht, S., Schwenkreis, P. & Tegenthoff, M. (2003). Functional magnetic resonance imaging mirrors recovery of visual perception after repetitive tachistoscopic stimulation in patients with partial cortical blindness. *Neuroscience Letters, 335*, 192–196.

Ponsford, J. & Schönberger, M. (2010). Family functioning and emotional state two and five years after traumatic brain injury. *Journal of the International Neuropsychological Society, 16*(2), 306–317.

Porch, B. E. (1967). *Porch Index of Communicative Ability*. Palo Alto, CA: Consulting Psychologists Press.

Prigatano, G. P. & Pribram, K. H. (1982). Perception and memory of facial affect following brain injury. *Perceptual and Motor Skills, 54*, 859–869.

Prigatano, G. P., Roueche, J. R. & Fordyce, D. J. (1985). Nonaphasic language disturbances after closed head injury. *Language Sciences, 7*, 217–229.

Prigatano, G., Borgaro, S., Baker, J. & Wethe, J. (2005). Awareness and distress after traumatic brain injury: a relative's perspective. *Journal of Head Trauma Rehabilitation* *20*(4), 359–367.

Reitan, R. M. (1958). Validity of the Trail Making Test as an indicator of organic brain damage. *Perceptual and Motor Skills, 8*, 271–276.

Robertson, I. H. & Murre, J. M. J. (1999). Rehabilitation of brain damage: brain plasticity and principles of guided recovery. *Psychological Bulletin, 125*(5), 544–575.

Russell, W. R. & Espir, M. L. E. (1961). *Traumatic Aphasia.* Oxford, UK: Oxford University Press.

Salazar, A. M., Grafman, J., Vance, S. C., Weingarter, H., Dillon, J. D. & Ludlow, C. (1986). Consciousness and amnesia after penetrating head injury: neurology and anatomy. *Neurology, 36*, 178–187.

Sarno, M. T. (1980). The nature of verbal impairment after closed head injury. *The Journal of Nervous and Mental Disease, 168*, 682–695.

Sarno, M. T. & Levita, E. (1986). Characteristics of verbal impairment in closed head injured patients. *Archives of Physical Medicine Rehabilitation, 67*, 400–405.

Schank, R. & Abelson, R. (1977). *Scripts, Plans, Goals and Understanding.* Hillsdale, NJ: Lawrence Erlbaum.

Schönberger, M., Ponsford, J., Olver, J. & Ponsford, M. (2010). A longitudinal study of family functioning after TBI and relatives' emotional status. *Neuropsychological Rehabilitation, 20*(6), 813–829.

Shallice, T. (1987). Impairments of semantic processing; multiple dissociations. In M. Coltheart, G. Sartori & R. Job (Eds), *The Cognitive Neuropsychology of Language* (pp. 111–127). London, UK: Erlbaum.

Snow, P., Douglas, J. & Ponsford, J. (1998). Conversational discourse abilities following severe traumatic brain injury: a follow up study. *Brain Injury, 12*(11), 911–935.

Spreen, O. & Benton, A. L. (1969). *Neurosensory Center Comprehensive Examination For Aphasia.* Victoria: British Columbia: Neuropsychology Laboratory, University of Victoria.

Strong, C.-A. H., Tiesma, D. & Donders, J. (2011). Criterion validity of the Delis-Kaplin Executive Function System (D-KEFS) fluency subtests after traumatic brain injury. *Journal of the International Neuropsychological Society, 17*(2), 230–237.

Struchen, M. A., Pappadis, M. R., Sander, A. M., Burrows, C. S. & Myszka, K. A. (2011). Examining the contribution of social communication abilities and affective/behavioral functioning to social integration outcomes for adults with traumatic brain injury. *The Journal of Head Trauma Rehabilitation, 26*(1), 30–42.

Summers, C. R., Ivins, B. & Schwab, K. A. (2009). Traumatic brain injury in the United States: an epidemiologic overview. *Mount Sinai Journal of Medicine, 76*(2), 105–110.

Tate, R. L., Lulham, J. M., Broe, G. A., Strettles, B. & Pfaff, A. (1989). Psychosocial outcome for the survivors of severe blunt head injury: the results from a consecutive series of 100 patients. *Journal of Neurology, Neurosurgery, and Psychiatry, 52*, 1128–1134.

Tate, R. L., McDonald, S., Perdices, M., Togher, L., Schultz, R. & Savage, S. (2008). Rating the methodological quality of single-subject designs and n-of-1 trials: introducing the Single-case Experimental Design (SCED) Scale. *Neuropsychological Rehabilitation, 18*(4), 385–401.

Temple, E., Deutsch, G. K., Poldrack, R. A., Miller, S. L., Tallal, P., Merzenich, M. M. & Gabrieli, J. D. (2003). Neural deficits in children with dyslexia ameliorated by behavioral remediation: evidence from functional MRI. *Proceedings of the National Academy of Sciences of the United States of America, 100*, 2860–2865.

Thompson, C. (2012). *The Northwestern Assessment of Verbs and Sentences (NAVS)*. Evanston, IL.

Thomsen, I. V. (1975). Evaluation and outcome of aphasia in patients with severe closed head trauma. *Journal of Neurology, Neurosurgery & Psychiatry, 38*, 713–718.

——(1984). Late outcome of very severe blunt head trauma: a 10–15 year second follow-up. *Journal of Neurology, Neurosurgery & Psychiatry, 47*(3), 260–268.

Togher, L., Hand, L. & Code, C. (1997). Analysing discourse in the traumatic brain injury population: telephone interactions with different communication partners. *Brain Injury, 11*(3), 169–189.

Togher, L., McDonald, S., Tate, R., Power, E. & Rietdijk, R. (2010). Measuring the social interactions of people with traumatic brain injury and their communication partners: the adapted Kagan scales. *Aphasiology, 24*(6–8), 914–927.

Ulatowska, H. K. & Bond Chapman, S. (1989). Discourse considerations for aphasia management. In R. S. Pierce & M. J. Wilcox (Eds), *Seminars in Speech and Language. Aphasia and Pragmatics* (vol. 10, pp. 298–314). New York: Thieme Medical Publishers.

Ulatowska, H. K., North, A. J. & Macaluso-Haynes, S. (1981). Production of narrative and procedural discourse in aphasia. *Brain and Language, 13*, 345–371.

van Dijk, T. A. (1977). *Text and Context: Explorations in the Semantics and Pragmatics of Discourse*. London: Longman.

Vas, A. K., Chapman, S. B., Cook, L. G., Elliott, A. C. & Keebler, M. (2011). Higher-order reasoning training years after traumatic brain injury in adults. *Journal of Head Trauma Rehabilitation, 26*(3), 224–239.

Vitali, P., Abutalebi, J., Tettamanti, M., Danna, M., Ansaldo, A.-I., Perani, D., Joanette, Y. & Cappa, S. F. (2007). Training-induced brain remapping in chronic aphasia: a pilot study. *Neurorehabilitation and Neural Repair, 21*(2), 152–160.

Wallace, C., Bogner, J., Corrigan, J., Clinchot, D., Mysiw, W. & Fugate, L. (1998). Primary caregivers of persons with brain injury: life changes 1 year after injury. *Brain Injury, 12*(6), 483–493.

Wambaugh, J. L. & Wright, S. (2007). Improved effects of word-retrieval treatments subsequent to addition of the orthographic form. *Aphasiology, 21*(6–8), 632–642.

Warden, D. L., Ryan, L. M., Helmick, K. M., Schwab, K., French, L. M. & Lu, W. C. (2005). War neurotrauma: the Defense and Veterans Brain Injury Center (DVBIC) experience at Walter Reed Army Medical Center (WRAMC). *Journal of Neurotrauma, 22*, 1178.

Wechsler, D. (1981). *Wechsler Adult Intelligence Scale – Revised (WAIS-R)*. New York: The Psychological Corporation.

——(2008). *Wechsler Adult Intelligence Scale* (4th edn). New York: Pearson Assessment.

Wedcliffe, T. & Ross, E. (2001). The psychological effects of traumatic brain injury on the quality of life of a group of spouses/partners. *South African Journal of Communication Disorders – die Suid-Afrikaanse Tydskrif vir Kommunikasieafwykings, 48*, 77–99.

Wiig, E. H. & Semel, E. M. (1976). *Language Disabilities in Children and Adults*. Columbus, OH: Merrill.

Wiig, E. H. & Secord, W. (1989). *Test of Language Competence–Expanded Edition*. San Antonio, TX: Psychological Corporation.

Willer, B., Rosenthal, M., Kreutzer, J. S., Gordon, W. A. & Rempel, R. (1993). Assessment of community integration following rehabilitation for traumatic brain injury. *Journal of Head Trauma Rehabilitation, 8*, 75–87.

Wood, R. L., Liossi, C. & Wood, L. (2005). The impact of head injury neurobehavioural sequelae on personal relationships: preliminary findings. *Brain Injury, 19*(10), 845–851.

World Health Organization (2001). *International Classification of Functioning, Disability and Health.* Geneva: Switzerland.

Yeung, O. & Law, S.-P. (2010). Executive functions and aphasia treatment outcomes: data from an ortho-phonological cueing therapy for anomia in Chinese. *International Journal of Speech-Language Pathology, 12*(6), 529–544.

Ylvisaker, M. & Szekeres, S. F. (1994). Communication disorders associated with closed head injury. In R. Chapey (Ed.), *Language Intervention Strategies in Adult Aphasia* (3rd edn, pp. 546–568). Baltimore, MD: Williams & Wilkins.

Ylvisaker, M., Turkstra, L. S. & Coelho, C. A. (2005). Behavioral and social interventions for individuals with traumatic brain injury: a summary of the research with clinical implications. *Seminars in Speech & Language, 26*(4), 256–267.

2   Traumatic brain injury

Basic features

Skye McDonald, Leanne Togher and Chris Code

As described in Chapter 1, communication disorders following traumatic brain injury are complex and heterogeneous reflecting the influences of a variety of neurophysical and neuropsychological impairments. In order to appreciate the spectrum of these disorders and to understand the different assessment and remediation approaches discussed in this book, it is necessary to be familiar with the basic features of TBI. This chapter provides a general overview including neuropathology, classification of severity, incidence, clinical course and outcome of TBI.

Neuropathology

Traumatic brain injuries reflect brain damage due to external forces including penetrating objects (e.g. bullets), direct impact, acceleration-deceleration or blast waves from an explosion, the damage caused reflecting the nature, direction and intensity of forces on the whole brain (Maas *et al.*, 2008). A traumatic brain injury may be either closed where the skull and/or the dura, the membrane covering the brain, remain intact, or open, in which case additional injury may occur because the skull is fractured and the cerebrum is penetrated by bony fragments.

Diffuse axonal injuries

In high velocity injuries, the fibres constituting the white matter of the cerebrum are often stretched, compressed and rotated by the force of the injury leading to diffuse axonal injury (DAI) that is apparent within one hour of the injury and may continue to develop for up to 72 hours (Bigler, 2001; Maas *et al.*, 2008). This can range from transient disruption of action potentials along axons due to disrupted transfer of ions across the axonal cell membrane, through to enlargement and swelling of axons, or more severe again, to structural and irrevocable damage leading to micro-lesions in white matter tracts and shearing at the white-grey matter juncture. Secondary deterioration of axons can occur weeks and months following the injury as a result of localized pathology and deterioration of neighbouring axons (Bigler & Maxwell, 2011). The corpus callosum appears to be consistently vulnerable to DAI (Viano *et al.*, 2005). Diffusion tensor imaging (DTI) techniques provide extremely clear views of the white matter tracts in the brain and are very useful for detecting DAI (see Figure 2.1).

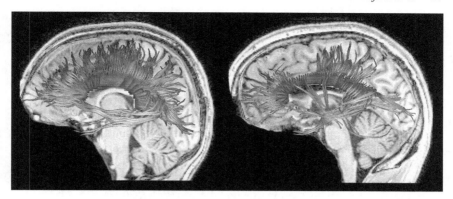

Figure 2.1 Diffusion Tensor Imaging depicting, on the *right*, the loss of white matter fibres in a Caucasian male in his early twenties with a severe TBI (initial GCS below 8) compared to, on the *left*, the normal fibre tracts of a healthy adult Asian male in his early thirties (images courtesy of Professor Erin D. Bigler and Trevor Wu)

Intracranial bleeding and ischemia

Intracranial bleeding is seen in almost half of all people presenting with TBI (Perel *et al.*, 2009) and can be extradural, subdural or intracerebral, single or multiple leading to numerous, often microscopic, areas of haemorrhage throughout the cerebrum. In addition, later ischemic changes have been reported in up to 91 per cent of people who died as a result of TBI (Graham *et al.*, 1978). While diffuse ischemic changes are associated with cardiac arrest or status epilepticus, focal ischemic lesions are thought to arise from a critical reduction in regional blood flow as might occur with increased intracranial pressure and selective arterial compression and/or systemic hypotension/hypoxia due to blood loss, airway obstruction, etc. Ischemic lesions are more common in the hippocampus (81 per cent) and basal ganglia (79 per cent) than the cerebral cortex (46 per cent) and cerebellum (44 per cent) (Graham *et al.*, 1978).

Skull fractures

Skull fractures are common in TBI and are an added complication. In some cases they may represent a protective factor as much of the force of the injury may be absorbed by the skull resulting in a depressed skull fracture and relatively superficial brain injury (Maas *et al.*, 2008). A significant minority of those with depressed skull features do not experience loss of consciousness, reflecting the focal nature of the injury (Jennett, 1976). However, depending on severity, there may be additional complications such as torn dura mater and infiltration of brain tissue.

Contusions

Contusions are a major source of brain damage in TBI reflecting localized areas of bruising and laceration at the point of impact and also contrecoup injuries at distant points due to the brain ricocheting against the bony protuberances of the skull (see Figure 2.2). The orbital and ventral surfaces of the frontal lobes and ventromedial surfaces of the temporal lobes are particularly vulnerable to such injury due to their proximity to the bony shelves of the anterior and middle fossae. While the rough, bony pockets of the anterior and middle fossae are well designed to cradle the temporal and frontal lobes of the brain safely during normal activity and even minor blows, their rough surfaces and sharp edges cause serious abrasions in high impact injuries consistent with the preponderance of frontotemporal lesions seen in this population (Bigler, 2007).

In the axial scan on the DOI there is clear evidence of an epidural haematoma in the left temporoparietal region suggesting coup injury as there is an underlying skull fracture and a large amount of extracranial soft-tissue swelling indicating the point of impact from a fall of approximately 20 feet. Also, note that the haematoma has produced effacement of the left lateral ventricle reflecting associated oedema, most readily visible in the coronal image. Note that the left temporal horn is not identifiable, indicating the massive degree of brain compression. Twenty months later a large area of cortical loss is apparent in the right frontal lobe consistent with the effects of contrecoup injury. Importantly, the 20-month post-injury scan now shows that marked temporal horn dilation

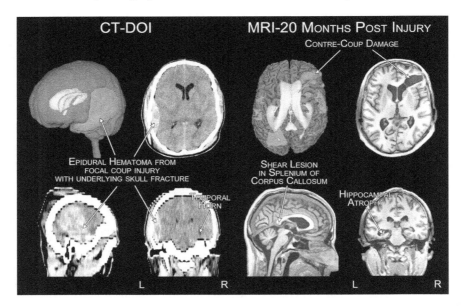

Figure 2.2 Comparison of (CT) scan taken on the day of injury (DOI) compared to (MRI) scan taken 20 months later for a patient with severe TBI

associated with left hippocampal atrophy has occurred in the temporal lobe compressed by the haematoma. Also note the shear injury in the posterior corpus callosum (see arrow in the splenium). The coup contrecoup effects place large shear forces across the corpus callosum. The three-dimensional (3-D) images depict the location of the epidural haematoma on the surface of the dura mater (top left) where the red depicts the haematoma and the aquamarine, the ventricle and the dorsal 3-D view (top right) shows the dilated ventricular system indicating generalized atrophy as well as where focal brain loss (encephalomalacia) occurred as indicated in red, including the right frontal region that sustained the contrecoup injury (images courtesy of Professor Erin D. Bigler).

Secondary effects

While significant damage occurs instantaneously with a traumatic brain injury, secondary problems rapidly cascade and exacerbate the initial condition. Neuronal depolarization is associated with increased release of excitatory neurotransmitters such as glutamate (Choi, 2003) which occurs for days after the injury, stimulating astrocyte swelling, exacerbating intracranial pressure, further increasing the imbalance of ion transfer across axonal membranes and facilitating the influx of calcium and free radicals which are a major cause of neuronal necrosis. Inflammatory responses within hours to days of the injury, while necessary to manage the removal of debris and stimulate repair (Molina-Holgado & Molina-Holgado, 2010), further increase intracranial pressure. The release of cytokines mediate both necrotic and apoptotic (programmed) cell death (Maas *et al.*, 2008). Raised intracranial pressure also impedes blood flow increasing the risk of ischemia (Ghajar, 2000).

Infection where the brain has become exposed due to skull fracture or neurosurgical intervention is also a frequent consequence. Finally, air or fat emboli from other injuries may further complicate the condition (Levin *et al.*, 1982).

The evolving pattern of biochemical cascades, increasing and subsiding intracranial pressure, ischemia, progressive cell death and macrophagic removal of debris makes it extremely difficult to anticipate the extent of brain damage from initial scans. Sixteen per cent or more of patients with diffuse injuries deteriorate, with the majority of these developing mass lesions (Servadei *et al.*, 2000a). Around 40–50 per cent of patients suffer expansion of initial contusions during the early phases (Chang *et al.*, 2006; Servadei *et al.*, 2000a; Servadei *et al.*, 2000b). Wallerian degeneration involves the deterioration of downstream structures that become disconnected to structures at lesion sites and further complicates the picture. Indeed, it has been suggested that it may take weeks or months for the pathology associated with traumatic brain injury to fully develop (Bigler & Maxwell, 2011).

Stabilization and recovery

Gradually, homeostasis is re-established and oedema resolves, enabling the patient to stabilize. There are many additional processes of recovery that occur in the traumatically injured brain most of which are poorly understood. On the positive side, recent research suggests that there is greater plasticity and potential for neuronal regeneration in the brain than traditionally believed. There are a plethora of neurogenerative and growth hormones that are secreted into the cerebrospinal fluid following injury that stimulate neuronal repair (Johanson *et al.*, 2011). Neurons can, at least partially, regenerate severed axons and are capable of collateral sprouting. To date, however, there is little evidence that such regeneration is of functional significance although identification of inhibitory and facilitatory factors is rapidly accruing (Sun & He, 2010). Adult neural stem cells are being increasingly researched for their potential role in recovery. For example, it is believed that neuroimflammatory cytokines may play a role in stimulating endogenous stem cells to differentiate into neurons and migrate to the areas of damaged tissue (Johanson *et al.*, 2011; Mathieu *et al.*, 2010; Molina-Holgado & Molina-Holgado, 2010).

Clinical events

Several clinical features are important indicators to establish a TBI has occurred. These include: (1) any period of altered consciousness; (2) any loss of memory for the events immediately before or after the injury; (3) the presence of neurological deficits, such as weakness, language impairment etc.; and/or (4) any alteration in mental state such as slowed thinking, confusion etc., at the time of injury (Menon *et al.*, 2010). Although co-existing factors such as intoxication, shock etc. may produce some similar features, this does not preclude the presence of a brain injury and the possibility of a TBI needs to be teased out carefully. Increasingly, management of a patient with a moderate-severe TBI follows standardized protocols according to international guidelines (e.g. see Maas *et al.*, 2008). TBI is always associated with alteration of consciousness at the time of impact and the more seriously injured patients are usually comatosed. In such cases, the immediate focus of care following the TBI is upon the prevention of hypoxia and hypotension by intubation and fluid resuscitation if required. Detection of lesions that require neurosurgery, based upon initial scans and/or observation of neurological deterioration is the next priority. CT scans based upon older, conventional X-ray technology remain common but provide more grainy, less detailed images than imaging based upon magnetic resonance imaging (MRI) (see Figure 2.1 for comparison). Neurosurgery may be necessary to debride brain tissue of bone and other debris, stop bleeding or relieve intracranial pressure. Once stabilized, the cardiorespiratory function, temperature, nutrition, glycemic levels and intracranial pressure of the unconscious patient are carefully monitored. Sedation and artificial ventilation may be introduced to reduce brain swelling. Prophylactic anti-epileptic medication may commence.

When the patient emerges from coma they enter into the state of post-traumatic amnesia (PTA) which requires quite different management techniques. While PTA is so named because of the characteristic amnesia for ongoing events, there are additional behavioural changes. There may be inappropriate and disturbed behaviour ranging from restless agitation to noisy shouting, verbal aggression and occasionally assaultive behaviour (Eames, 1990). During this time the patient may be mobile and restless, requiring special attention and supervision to prevent him or her coming to any harm. Emergence from PTA is usually gradual, characterized by increasing periods of lucidity, until the patient is noted to be consistently oriented in time and place and laying down memories of daily events.

In the weeks and months following PTA the patient usually demonstrates significant spontaneous improvement in physical and cognitive functions but this levels off within the second year of injury (Lezak, 1995). Active rehabilitation programmes for TBI sufferers usually commence once the patient has emerged from PTA. Severe TBI patients may require many months of inpatient therapy followed, in many cases, by additional therapy as outpatients. Despite improvements in rehabilitation services for the TBI population in recent years, long-term outcome studies have shown that the majority of severely injured patients continue to experience debilitating impairments, especially in cognitive function and behaviour, years after their injury (Brooks *et al.*, 1987; Conzen *et al.*, 1992; Kaplan, 1993; Levin *et al.*, 1979a; Oddy *et al.*, 1985; Thomsen, 1984).

Assessing the severity of the injury

For some the brain injury is reflected in a few minutes of disorientation with rapid recovery while for others the injury may lead to a protracted period of deep unconsciousness followed by a poor trajectory of recovery and lifelong disabilities. The severity of the injury is usually calibrated with reference to the depth and duration of altered consciousness.

Initial level of consciousness

In general, an important index of severity is the extent of altered consciousness experienced immediately following the head injury. This may vary from transient disorientation to deep coma. Depth of altered consciousness is usually quantified by giving the patient a score between 3 and 15 on the Glasgow Coma Scale (GCS) (Table 2.1) (Teasdale & Jennett, 1976). On this broadly used scale, points are gained in three categories: eye opening (ranging from 4 points for spontaneous eye opening to 1 point for nil), best motor response (ranging from 6 points for obeying commands through to 1 point for nil) and best verbal response (ranging from 5 points for oriented through to 1 point for nil). In the mildest injuries the patient may be awake and cooperative but confused (GCS 13–15) whereas in the most severe the patient may make no eye, verbal or motor response at all (GCS of 3).

Table 2.1 Glasgow Coma Scale

Eye opening response	Spontaneous	4 points
	Opens to verbal command, speech, or shout	3 points
	Opens to pain, not applied to face	2 points
	None	1 point
Verbal response	Oriented	5 points
	Confused conversation, but able to answer questions	4 points
	Inappropriate responses, words discernible	3 points
	Incomprehensible speech	2 points
	None	1 point
Motor response	Obeys commands for movement	6 points
	Purposeful movement to painful stimulus	5 points
	Withdraws from pain	4 points
	Abnormal (spastic) flexion, decorticate posture	3 points
	Extensor (rigid) response, decerebrate posture	2 points
	None	1 point

The Ranchos Los Amigos Levels of Cognitive Functioning Scale (Hagan *et al.*, 1972) has also commonly been used as a rapid measure of cognitive function where clinicians make a judgement as to what level best describes a patient with 8 levels ranging from I: No response through V: confused, inappropriate and non-agitated to VIII: purposeful and appropriate. Despite its widespread use in the USA, there are concerns about the instrument, including its failure to discriminate between subtle changes in consciousness and poor psychometric properties relative to other scales (Gouvier *et al.*, 1987). The JFK Coma Recovery Scale-Revised (CRC-R) (Giacino *et al.*, 2004) is a newer scale carefully developed to differentiate between vegetative states, minimum consciousness and emergence from minimum consciousness (Tate, 2010) with good psychometric properties, endorsed by the American Congress of Rehabilitation Medicine (American Congress of Rehabilitation Medicine *et al.*, 2010).

Length of altered consciousness

Another important index is the length of time the patient experienced altered consciousness, either coma or a state of confusion. In severe cases the patient may remain in coma for hours, days, weeks or longer and in very severe cases may never resume full consciousness. In such a case a persistent vegetative state is diagnosed. The majority of patients do, however, gradually regain consciousness (usually defined as commencing when the patient is able to follow commands) whereupon they are disorientated and confused. It is also common for patients to experience a period of confusion and disorientation in the absence of documented loss of consciousness. This period of confusion immediately following coma is known as post-traumatic amnesia (PTA) and is considered to be ended when the patient becomes rational, oriented and able to lay down continuous memories for ongoing events (Russell & Smith, 1961). While Russell and Smith argued that the end of PTA is apparent in a qualitative shift in orientation and awareness, the clinician's capacity to identify this shift from observation is limited (Tate *et al.*, 2006b).

Alternatively, emergence from PTA can be monitored prospectively by the use of purpose designed scales such as the Galveston Orientation and Amnesia Test (GOAT) (Levin *et al.*, 1979b), the modified Oxford PTA scale (MOPTAS) (Fortuny *et al.*, 1980) or the Westmead PTA Scale (WPTAS) (Shores *et al.*, 1986). By using such scales it is apparent the emergence from PTA is gradual rather than abrupt, although different scales vary in the demands placed upon the patient and this leads to differing estimations of the end of PTA. The GOAT requires the patient to answer autobiographical and orientation questions. The MOPTAS and WPTAS ask questions about orientation and also include an episodic memory task whereby the patient is required to learn three pictures and recall or recognize them among distractors. Accordingly, it has been found that emergence from PTA is earlier when assessed by the GOAT than the MOPTAS and WPTAS (Tate *et al.*, 2006b) and that emergence is more protracted on the WPTAS where the episodic memory task is complex (i.e. once three items to be learned are mastered, they become foils and foils become new items to be learned) than on the MOPTAS which involves a simpler version of picture learning. Interestingly, people emerging from PTA can demonstrate quite different trajectories in the resolution of disorientation and new learning (Tate *et al.*, 2006b). Furthermore, it can often be difficult to differentiate amnesia due to PTA from ongoing cognitive impairment making the end-point of PTA difficult to ascertain based on learning scores. For this reason, it has been recommended that the end of PTA on scales such as the WPTAS and MOPTAS should be marked by the first occasion of a perfect score rather than the traditional criterion of three perfect scores in a row (Tate *et al.*, 2006b).

Prior to the systematic use of prospective PTA scales the duration of PTA was often estimated retrospectively by detailed questioning of the patient to determine when ongoing memories commenced. This continues to be the only option when assessing patients who were not prospectively monitored.

Other neurological signs

While the extent and duration of altered consciousness is an important index of severity of brain insult, there are many other factors that affect the picture. The presence of skull fractures, depressed or linear, penetration of the cerebral tissue, infection, bleeding and focal neurological signs may all influence the extent of damage sustained (Jennett, 1976; Stein & Spettell, 1995).

Classification of the severity of the injury

For diagnostic and research purposes there is a need to categorize patients along the spectrum of severity from mild, moderate to severe and very severe although opinion differs as to where each of these boundaries are set, or how they are defined. Depth of initial coma and period of altered consciousness (including coma and post-traumatic amnesia) have both been used to define the severity of the brain injury although the GCS has not been particularly reliable. One of the problems for the GCS is that patients may not be assessed immediately post-trauma for their level of GCS. Alternatively, consciousness may fluctuate resulting in variable GCS scores depending on when the measure was taken. Other clinical variables such as intoxication, sedation and shock may further complicate the picture.

Consequently, altered consciousness, specifically PTA, has consistently been proven to be the better indicator of outcome (Brown *et al.*, 2005; Jennett, 1976; Sherer *et al.*, 2008). According to the influential work by Russell and Smith (1961) a brain injury is mild if associated with PTA of less than 1 hour, moderate if 1–24 hours, severe if 1–7 days and very severe if greater than 7 days and extremely severe if greater than 4 weeks. However, there has been a move towards classifying a mild traumatic brain injury as associated with up to 24 hours of altered consciousness (Esselman & Uomoto, 1995; Kay *et al.*, 1993) provided loss of consciousness is less than 30 minutes and GCS after regaining consciousness is 13–15. Focal neurological signs may also accompany the mild brain injury. Using this metric, a moderate injury is defined as associated with PTA of 1–7 days, or GCS of 9–12 while a severe TBI is diagnosed if the patient has an initial GCS of 3–8 and is in PTA for longer than 7 days (Williamson *et al.*, 1996). Duration of coma has also been used as an index of severity (Corrigan *et al.*, 2010; Rimel *et al.*, 1982) (see Table 2.2).

While the length of altered consciousness remains the most robust indicator of severity of injury, changing criteria over recent years have meant that patients defined as sustaining mild, moderate or severe injuries in past literature do not necessarily equate to those with mild, moderate and severe injuries in more contemporary work. Decisions to change classifications of severity are mainly based upon research into how duration of altered consciousness relates to outcome in large prospective studies (Nakase-Richardson *et al.*, 2011; Sherer *et al.*, 2008; Walker *et al.*, 2010). Indeed, such prospective studies have argued for

Table 2.2 Classification of severity of head injury according to depth of coma or length of period of altered consciousness

Severity	GCS	Loss of consciousness	PTA
Mild	13–15	<30 mins	<1 day
Moderate	9–12	30mins–24 hours	1–7 days
Severe	3–8	>24 hours	>7 days

the stretching of the severity scale to classify those with injuries associated with durations of PTA of 4 weeks or longer as severe and PTA of 8–10 weeks or more reflecting the very severe end of the spectrum in which good recovery is unlikely (Nakase-Richardson *et al.*, 2011; Walker *et al.*, 2010).

This approach to classification is not universally accepted as it has been argued that such an approach conflates estimates of initial injury severity with outcome. Simply because a person makes a good recovery, this cannot be taken to imply their injury was not severe (Jennett, 1976). Furthermore, even those who make a good recovery in terms of standard indicators (such as return to work, level of independence) may continue to suffer impairment and reduced quality of life.

Incidence and prevalence

The general incidence of head injury is difficult to calculate as definitions of brain injury vary as do hospital codes for diagnosis. Overall, it has been estimated that in Western countries such as the USA, Australia and Finland, 100–200 people per 100,000 of the population suffer a traumatic brain injury leading to either immediate death (around 18 per 100,000: Corrigan *et al.*, 2010; Rutland-Brown *et al.*, 2006) or hospitalization (Kraus & McArthur, 1996; Tate *et al.*, 1998; Winqvist *et al.*, 2007) while countries such as China report lower rates (e.g. 55–65/100,000: Wang *et al.*, 1986). For every five people admitted to hospital, another 27 or so may be seen in emergency departments and released (Kraus & McArthur, 1996) and there are many others who do not seek medical attention (McKinlay *et al.*, 2008). Those who do not seek medical attention or are released the same day from emergency departments are most likely to suffer milder forms of injury. Indeed, it has been estimated that 70–90 per cent of cases admitted to hospitals with head injuries were actually mild and either resulted in no brain injury per se or at most very mild brain injury (Cassidy *et al.*, 2004; Kraus *et al.*, 1984; Winqvist *et al.*, 2007). The figures for moderate or severe traumatic brain injury are much fewer and have been estimated between 12–14/100,000 and 15–20/100,000 population per annum respectively (Kraus *et al.*, 1984; Tate *et al.*, 1998).

While the annual incidence of medically treated TBI world-wide is huge (estimated in 1990 as 9.5 million: Corrigan *et al.*, 2010), the number of people who are likely to sustain such an injury in their lifetime (prevalence) is many magnitudes greater. In a large population study in Finland (Winqvist *et al.*, 2007), excluding those with mild injuries, it was estimated that by age 34, 269/100,000 had experienced a TBI with ongoing effects. The economic costs of such injuries are immense, for example, in the USA alone, costs of medically treated TBI cases in the year 2000 were $51.2 billion, including medical costs and loss of productivity but not including the costs of extended rehabilitation and long-term support (Corrigan *et al.*, 2010).

Brain injuries are not equally distributed in the community. Overall, TBI is most common in the very young (0–4 years) and the elderly (65+). Falls are a common reported cause in these groups (32 per cent) as are sporting injuries (18 per cent) (especially in school aged children) (Rutland-Brown *et al.* 2006; Tate *et al.*, 1998). However, more serious brain injuries show a different distribution. In this case, males outnumber females 2:1 and the highest incidence occurs in the 15–24 year age group. Motor vehicle accidents are by far the most common cause of serious traumatic brain injury in general and specifically in the peak (18–25) age group (Kalsbeek *et al.*, 1980; Kraus *et al.*, 1984; McKinlay *et al.*, 2008; Myburgh *et al.*, 2008). There is also variation in the relative proportion of different causal factors which relate to the cultures examined. For example, there is a high incidence of brain injury as a result of violence and falls in the Bronx (Cooper *et al.*, 1983) and bicycle accidents in China (Wang *et al.*, 1986). US military involvement in Iraq and Afghanistan over the past 10 years has resulted in a high proportion of blast injuries in military personnel with TBI (Bell *et al.*, 2009; Summers *et al.*, 2009).

Outcome of traumatic brain injury

Presence of impairment

Mild brain injuries are not usually associated with lasting impairment (Tate *et al.*, 1998). Such injuries lead to changes in cell metabolism and axonal function in the acute stages (Niogi & Mukherjee, 2010; Vagnozzi *et al.*, 2010; Wilde *et al.*, 2008) but this tends to normalize from 3–15 days afterwards (Vagnozzi *et al.*, 2010), provided a second injury during this vulnerable time is not incurred. Subtle white matter changes and volume loss can still be apparent after 6 to 12 months (Kraus *et al.*, 2007; Levine *et al.*, 2008) suggesting that even mild TBI can have long-lasting neuropathological sequelae although neuropsychological symptoms do not usually persist. A post-concussional syndrome of poor attention, slowed information processing, dizziness, headaches and fatigue is reported in a small proportion of mild injuries (Bohnen *et al.*, 1995; Leininger *et al.*, 1990) but this usually dissipates over the ensuing months (Dikmen *et al.*, 1986; Rohling *et al.*, 2011). Ongoing symptoms beyond this time are thought to reflect the impact of additional psychological factors (Gronwall, 1991; Williams *et al.*, 2010). Mild-moderate injuries (PTA up to 24 hours) are also infrequently associated with lasting impairment (Tate *et al.*, 1998). On the other hand, moderate to severe head injuries are almost always associated with some form of lasting impairment.

It has been estimated that 75 per cent of patients with severe TBI have ongoing physical impairments arising from the brain injury (Jennett *et al.*, 1981; Thomsen, 1984) although in 40 per cent these are subtle and not apparent to the casual observer and only 10–20 per cent are of clinical significance (Tate *et al.*, 1989a; Tate *et al.*, 2006a). Similarly, approximately 67 per cent of patients have ongoing neuropsychological problems defined as impairment on a range of tasks tapping cognitive abilities (e.g. memory, concept formation) and psychosocial parameters (e.g. loss of drive, loss of control) (Tate *et al.*, 1989a) that are apparent many years post-injury (Draper & Ponsford, 2008) and can, in fact, deteriorate as time goes by (Senathi-Raja *et al.*, 2010). Only 8 per cent of patients escape clinically significant deficits in either neurophysical or neuropsychological functioning and even these cases may have subtle impairments as a result of the TBI (Tate *et al.*, 1989a). The incidence of impairment increases as the severity of the injury increases (duration of PTA: Draper & Ponsford, 2008; Tate *et al.*, 2006a; time to follow commands [coma]: Dikmen *et al.*, 1995). It is those with severe injuries that have come under scrutiny for their poor communication skills.

Psychosocial and functional outcome

There have been a number of studies that have followed up survivors of severe TBI in order to determine their level of functional outcome. It has been generally found that the majority of such patients examined had achieved independence in terms of activities of daily living (Ponsford *et al.*, 1995; Tate *et al.*, 1989b) but had much poorer outcomes in terms of psychosocial function. For example, almost 50 per cent of patients suffering a severe TBI have been found to have limited or no social contacts and few leisure interests one year or more later (Tate *et al.*, 1989b; Weddell *et al.*, 1980), while between 64–68 per cent were found to rely more on their parents or spouse for emotional support than prior to the injury (Ponsford *et al.*, 1995) and to have substantial difficulty forming new social relationships (Tate *et al.*, 1989b). Only 30–40 per cent or less of TBI patients previously employed find themselves in full-time employment (Brooks *et al.*, 1987; McMordie *et al.*, 1990; Tate *et al.*, 1989b) and the majority of these either have a drop in occupational status or maintain their previous level only with difficulty (Tate *et al.*, 1989b; van Velzen *et al.*, 2009).

There is significant variability within those who have sustained even severe brain injuries. Two thirds of people with injuries at the 'milder' end of the severe spectrum (1–4 weeks PTA) experienced a reasonable recovery with no, mild or only partial disability 18 months later. In contrast, up to 75 per cent of those with very severe injuries (PTA greater than 4 weeks) experienced persisting significant disability (Tate *et al.*, 2006a) with two-thirds failing to resume employment, education or home-making duties (Nakase-Richardson *et al.*, 2011).

Psychosocial outcome is related to, but not synonymous with, degree of brain damage. In general terms, the severity and breadth of impairments experienced will have direct consequences for the capacity of the patient to resume his/her previous lifestyle. But the nature and constellation of these impairments has a complex relationship to outcome with some kinds of impairment having greater consequence than others. Despite the fact that neurophysical and neuro-psychological impairments occur at similar frequencies in the TBI population, it is the neuropsychological aspects, particularly those affecting personality and behaviour, that are most strongly related to poor social outcome (Bond, 1975, 1976; Tate, 1991) and relative stress (Brooks *et al.*, 1986; Kinsella *et al.*, 1991; Thomsen, 1984). It is important to note that a number of factors, other than the injury itself, are also associated with poorer outcomes. These include older age at injury, pre-injury unemployment, pre-injury substance abuse and poorer functioning at rehabilitation discharge (Senathi-Raja *et al.*, 2010; Willemse-van Son *et al.*, 2007).

Incidence of dysarthria

Dysarthria refers to a group of speech disorders resulting from disturbances in muscular control which may be characterized by weakness, slowness or incoordination of the speech mechanism due to damage to the central or peripheral nervous system or both. The term encompasses coexisting neurogenic disorders of several or all of the basic processes of speech: respiration, phonation, resonance, articulation and prosody (Wertz, 1985). Estimates of the incidence of dysarthria following severe TBI vary widely but probably affect around one-third of adults (Safaz *et al.*, 2008; Thomsen, 1984) and children (Morgan *et al.*, 2010). Dysarthria following TBI has been reported to be one of the most persistent of communication impairments, resulting in a significant impact on the person with TBI's ability to regain functional independence (Beukelman & Yorkston, 1991). Dysarthric impairments following TBI differ in terms of type (e.g. ataxic, spastic and mixed dysarthria) and severity (e.g. mild through to severe) and recovery may continue over a period of years (Enderby & Crow, 1990). The perceptual, acoustic and physiological features associated with dysarthria following TBI are described in detail in Chapter 8. While there is a paucity of research examining dysarthria treatment for people with TBI instrumentation may be useful in assessment and treatment (Theodoros & Murdoch, 1994) and awareness that recovery of dysarthric impairments may be possible over the period of several years.

Incidence of aphasia

As discussed in Chapter 1, the incidence of aphasia has been estimated from between 2 per cent (750 cases: Heilman *et al.*, 1971) to roughly 30 per cent (56–125 patients: Sarno, 1980, 1984, 1988; Sarno & Levita, 1986). Anomic aphasia is reported to be the most prevalent in adults (Heilman *et al.*, 1971; Levin *et al.*, 1976; Thomsen, 1975) while non-fluent aphasias (Global and Broca-like) are more prevalent in children and adolescents (Basso & Scarpa, 1990). For a proportion of these patients such aphasic deficits resolve over the ensuing months (Grosswasser *et al.*, 1997; Thomsen, 1975, 1984) although few completely regain premorbid language abilities (Basso & Scarpa, 1990; Thomsen, 1984).

Although not classified as aphasic, many other TBI patients perform lower than expected on aphasia battery subtests e.g. confrontation naming, word finding or verbal associative tasks as well as structured tests of comprehension (Coppens, 1995; Gruen *et al.* 1990; Levin *et al.*, 1976; Levin *et al.*, 1979a; Sarno, 1988). As we canvassed in Chapter 1, opinion has differed as to whether such deficits reflect a 'subclinical aphasia' not apparent in casual conversation (Sarno, 1988) or other cognitive deficits including attention and memory disorders rather than linguistic impairment per se (Holland, 1984; Sohlberg & Mateer, 1989). In contemporary work such disorders are often referred to as cognitive–

communication disorders, reflecting the now widely held view that they represent deficits in the complex interplay of language and other cognitive functions (see Chapters 4 and 7 for further discussion).

Incidence of neuropsychological sequelae

Non-linguistic cognitive impairments may or may not be responsible for poor performance on aphasia battery subtests. There can be no doubt, however, that effective communication skills rely upon the integrity of a range of cognitive and psychosocial abilities and that this integrity is frequently disrupted in the severe TBI population. Given the complexity of neuropathology associated with severe TBI it is unsurprising that the population is heterogeneous with respect to both nature and severity of neuropsychological impairments. Nevertheless, certain deficits are more common than others. In a consecutive series of severe TBI patients assessed six years post-injury (Tate *et al.*, 1991) it was found that 56.5 per cent suffered a disorder of memory and learning, 34 per cent having a material specific learning problem (either verbal or nonverbal) while 22 per cent had generalized learning difficulties. Other reports have confirmed that poor memory is the most common complaint reported in at least 50 per cent of those with moderate to severe TBI (Dikmen *et al.*, 1993; Ponsford *et al.*, 1995; Tate *et al.*, 2006a). Slowed information processing was apparent in 34 per cent, while in this study basic neuropsychological functions such as orientation, visual perception, ideomotor apraxia, constructional apraxia and aphasic disorders accounted for only 16 per cent of the deficits seen. Finally, executive disorders of either drive (inflexibility) or control (disinhibition) were seen in 40 per cent. These latter deficits were apparent upon formal neuropsychological tests but also have implications for psychosocial function (Tate *et al.*, 1991).

Children and traumatic brain injury

This chapter has focused on the nature and sequelae of traumatic brain injury as it affects the adult population, with particular emphasis on young adults because TBI is common in this age group. Brain injury is the leading cause of death and disability in children and adolescents, however (Faul *et al.*, 2010), and differences in causes, mortality and morbidity make this group a particular at-risk population. Causes of TBI in children and adolescents include those common in adults – such as motor vehicle accidents, falls and assault, particularly for older adolescents. For children, causes vary by age, with falls more common at younger ages and sports injuries more common in school-age children (Keenan & Bratton, 2006). Intentional injury (child abuse) also is a common cause of brain injury, particularly in young children (Faul *et al.*, 2010). The sequelae for children differ from those of adults for a variety of mechanistic and developmental reasons (Giza *et al.*, 2007). As a general rule, children have lower mortality, fewer residual sensorimotor impairments and more severe long-term neuropsychological impairments than do adults with similar injury severity (Faul *et al.*, 2010).

Sequelae for children also vary as a function of age at injury (e.g. social withdrawal may be more common in younger children who are injured vs. aggressive behaviours in older children [Geraldina *et al.*, 2003]). Children under one year of age have the highest morbidity and mortality, in part because the brain is so incompletely developed (Bonnier *et al.*, 2007). A critical consideration for children is injury to the substrate of later-developing cognitive skills, such as executive functions and working memory, which continue to develop throughout the adolescent years. These cognitive developments underlie later communication developments, such as the use of figurative language, sophisticated pragmatic functions like persuasion and debate, and the ability to produce and understand complex syntactic constructions. As a result of this protracted developmental time course, the full morbidity of childhood brain injury may not be evident until years after the injury (Gamino *et al.*, 2009). It should also be noted that psychosocial implications of injury are different for children, who are still dependent on their families for most of life's activities and are still actively learning, usually within a formal educational system. Rehabilitation of children with TBI thus often employs a model of supported *inter*-dependence rather than independence, with a particular focus on educational re-integration. Communication outcomes for children and adolescents with TBI will be considered in more detail in Chapters 6 and 7.

References

American Congress of Rehabilitation Medicine, Brain Injury Interdisciplinary Special Interest Group: Disorders of Consciousness Task Force: Seel, R. T., Sherer, M., Whyte, J., Katz, D. I., Giacino, J. T., Rosenbaum, A. M., Hammond, F. M., Kalmar, K., Pape, T. L., Zafonte, R., Biester, R. C., Kaelin, D., Kean, J. & Zasler, N. (2010). Assessment scales for disorders of consciousness: evidence-based recommendations for clinical practice and research. *Archives of Physical Medicine & Rehabilitation, 91*(12), 1795–1813.

Basso, A. & Scarpa, M. T. (1990). Traumatic aphasia in children and adults: a comparison of clinical features and evolution. *Cortex, 26*(4), 502–514.

Bell, R. S., Vo, A. H., Neal, C. J., Tigno, J., Roberts, R., Mossop, C., Dunne, J. R. & Armonda, R. A. (2009). Military traumatic brain and spinal column injury: a 5-year study of the impact blast and other military grade weaponry on the central nervous system. *Journal of Trauma-Injury Infection & Critical Care, 66*(4 Suppl), S104–111.

Beukelman, D. R. & Yorkston, K. M. (1991). Traumatic brain injury changes the way we live. In D. R. Beukelman & K. M. Yorkston (Eds), *Communication Disorders Following Traumatic Brain Injury* (pp. 1–13). Austin: Pro-Ed.

Bigler, E. D. (2001). The lesion(s) in traumatic brain injury: implications for clinical neuropsychology. *Archives of Clinical Neuropsychology, 16*(2), 95–131.

——(2007). Anterior and middle cranial fossa in traumatic brain injury: relevant neuroanatomy and neuropathology in the study of neuropsychological outcome. *Neuropsychology, 21*(5), 515–531.

Bigler, E. D. & Maxwell, W. L. (2011). Neuroimaging and neuropathology of TBI. *NeuroRehabilitation, 28*, 1–12.

Bohnen, N. I., Jolles, J., Twijnstra, A., Mellink, R. & Wijen, G. (1995). Late neurobehavioural symptoms after mild head injury. *Brain Injury, 9*, 27–33.

Bond, M. R. (1975). *Assessment of the Psychosocial Outcome After Severe Head Injury.* Paper presented at the Outcome of Severe Damage to the Central Nervous System: CIBA Foundation Symposium, 34, Amsterdam.

——(1976). Assessment of the psychosocial outcome of severe head injury. *Acta Neurochir, 34,* 57–70.

Bonnier, C., Marique, P., Van Hout, A. & Potelle, D. (2007). Neurodevelopmental outcome after severe traumatic brain injury in very young children: role for subcortical lesions. *Journal of Child Neurology, 22*(5), 519–529.

Brooks, D. N., Campsie, L., Symington, C., Beattie, A. & McKinlay, W. (1986). The five year outcome of severe blunt head injury: a relative's view. *Journal of Neurology, Neurosurgery & Psychiatry, 49*(7), 764–770.

Brooks, D. N., McKinlay, W., Symington, C., Beattie, A. & Campsie, L. (1987). Return to work within the first seven years of severe head injury. *Brain Injury, 1,* 5–19.

Brown, A. W., Malec, J. F., McClelland, R. L., Diehl, N., Englander, J. & Cifu, D. X. (2005). Clinical elements that predict outcome after traumatic brain injury: a prospective multicenter recursive partitioning (decision-tree) analysis. *Journal of Neurotrauma, 22,* 1040–1051.

Cassidy, J. D., Carroll, L. J., Peloso, P. M., Borg, J., von Holst, H., Holm, L., Kraus, J., Coronado, V. G. (2004). Incidence, risk factors and prevention of mild traumatic brain injury: results of the WHO Collaborating Centre Task Force on Mild Traumatic Brain Injury. *Journal of Rehabilitation Medicine, Supplement*(43), 28–60.

Chang, E. F., Meeker, M. & Holland, M. C. (2006). Acute traumatic intraparenchymal hemorrhage: risk factors for progression in the early post-injury period. *Neurosurgery, 58*(4), 647–655.

Choi, D. W. (2003). Calcium mediated neurotoxicity: relationship to specific channel types and role in ischemic damage. *Trends in Neuroscience, 11,* 465–469.

Conzen, M., Ebel, H., Swart E., Skreczek, W. & Oppel, F. (1992). Long term neuropsychological outcome after severe head injury with good recovery. *Brain Injury, 6*(1), 45.

Cooper, K. D., Tabaddor, K., Hauser, A., Shulman, K. & Feiner, C. (1983). The epidemiology of head injury in the Bronx. *Neuroepidemiology, 2,* 70–88.

Coppens, P. (1995). Subpopulations in closed-head injury: preliminary results. *Brain Injury, 9*(2), 195–208.

Corrigan, J. D., Selassie, A. W. & Orman, J. A. L. (2010). The epidemiology of traumatic brain injury. *Journal of Head Trauma Rehabilitation, 25*(2), 72–80.

Dikmen, S. S., McLean, A. & Temkin, N. R. (1986). Neuropsychological and psychosocial consequences of minor head injury. *Journal of Neurology, Neurosurgery and Psychiatry, 49*(11), 1227–1232.

Dikmen, S. S., Machamer, J. E. & Temkin, N. R. (1993). Psychosocial outcome in patients with moderate-severe head injury: 2 year follow up. *Brain Injury, 7,* 113–124.

Dikmen, S. S., Machamer, J. E., Winn, H. R. & Temkin, N. R. (1995). Neuropsychological outcome at 1-year post head injury. *Neuropsychology, 9*(1), 80–90.

Draper, K. & Ponsford, J. (2008). Cognitive functioning ten years following traumatic brain injury and rehabilitation. *Neuropsychology, 22*(5), 618–625.

Eames, P. (1990). Organic bases of behavioural disorders after traumatic brain injury. In R. L. Wood (Ed.), *Neurobehavioural Sequalae of Traumatic Brain Injury.* Bristol, Pennsylvania: Taylor & Francis.

Enderby, P. & Crow, E. (1990). Long-term recovery patterns of severe dysarthria following head injury. *British Journal of Disorders of Communication, 25,* 341–354.

Esselman, P. C. & Uomoto, J. C. (1995). Classification of the spectrum of mild traumatic brain injury. *Brain Injury, 9*, 417–424.

Faul, M., Xu, L., Wald, M. M. & Coronado, V. G. (2010). *Traumatic Brain Injury in the United States: Emergency Department Visits, Hospitalizations and Deaths 2002–2006*. Atlanta (GA): Centers for Disease Control and Prevention, National Center for Injury Prevention and Control.

Fortuny, A. I., Briggs, L. M., Newcombe, F., Ratcliffe, G. & Thomas, C. (1980). Measuring the duration of post-traumatic amnesia. *Journal of Neurology, Neurosurgery, and Psychiatry, 43*, 879–882.

Gamino, J., Chapman, S. B. & Cook, L. G. (2009). Strategic learning in youth with traumatic brain injury: evidence for stall in higher-order cognition. *Topics in Language Disorders, 29*(3), 224–235.

Geraldina, P., Mariarosaria, L., Annarita, A., Susanna, G., Michela, S., Alessandro, D., Sandra, S. & Enrico, C. (2003). Neuropsychiatric sequelae in TBI: a comparison across different age groups. *Brain Injury, 17*(10), 835–846.

Ghajar, J. (2000). Traumatic brain injury. *Lancet, 356*, 923–929.

Giacino, J. T., Kalmar, K. & Whyte, J. (2004). The JFK Coma Recovery Scale-Revised: measurement characteristics and diagnostic utility. [Research Support, Non-U.S. Gov't Validation Studies]. *Archives of Physical Medicine & Rehabilitation, 85*(12), 2020–2029.

Giza, C. C., Mink, R. B. & Madikians, A. (2007). Pediatric traumatic brain injury: not just little adults. *Current Opinion in Critical Care, 13*(2), 143–152.

Gouvier, W. D., Blanton, P. D., LaPorte, K. K. & Nepomuceno, C. (1987). Reliability and validity of the Disability Rating Scale and the Levels of Cognitive Functioning Scale in monitoring recovery from severe head injury. [Research Support, Non-U.S. Gov't]. *Archives of Physical Medicine & Rehabilitation, 68*(2), 94–97.

Graham, D. I., Adams, J. H. & Doyle, D. (1978). Ischaemic brain damage in fatal non-missile head injuries. *Journal of the Neurological Sciences, 39*(2–3), 213–234.

Gronwall, D. (1991). Minor head injury. *Neuropsychology, 5*(4), 253–265.

Grosswasser, Z., Mendelson, L., Stern, M. J., Schecter, L. & Najenson, T. (1997). Re-evaluation of prognostic factors in rehabilitation after head injury. *Scandinavian Journal of Rehabilitation Medicine, 9*, 147–149.

Gruen, A. K., Frankle, B. C. & Schwartz, R. (1990). Word fluency generation skills of head-injured patients in an acute trauma centre. *Journal of Communication Disorders, 23*, 163–170.

Hagan, C., Malkmus, D. & Durham, M. S. (1972). *The Ranchos Los Amigos Levels of Cognitive Functioning Scale*. Downey, CA: Ranchos Los Amigos Hospital.

Heilman, K. M., Safran, A. & Geschwind, N. (1971). Closed head trauma and aphasia. *Journal of Neurology, Neurosurgery & Psychiatry, 34*, 265–269.

Holland, A. L. (1984). When is aphasia aphasia? The problem of closed head injury. In R. W. Brookshire (Ed.), *Clinical Aphasiology* (vol. 14, pp. 345–349). Minneapolis: BRK Publishers.

Jennett, B. (1976). Assessment of severity in head injury. *Journal of Neurology, Neurosurgery and Psychiatry 39*, 647–655.

Jennett, B., Snoek, J., Bond, M. R. & Brooks, D. N. (1981). Disability after severe head injury: observations on the use of the Glasgow Coma Scale. *Journal of Neurology, Neurosurgery and Psychiatry, 44*, 285–293.

Johanson, C., Stopa, E., Baird, A. & Sharma, H. (2011). Traumatic brain injury and recovery mechanisms: peptide modulation of periventricular neurogenic regions by the choroid plexus–CSF nexus. *Journal of Neural Transmission, 118*(1), 115–133.

Kalsbeek, W. D., McLauren, R., Harris, B. S. H. & Miller, J. D. (1980). The national head and spine injury survey: major findings. *Journal of Neurology, Neurosurgery & Psychiatry, 53*, S19–S31.

Kaplan, S. P. (1993). Five-year tracking of psychosocial changes in people with severe traumatic brain injury. *Rehabilitation Counseling Bulletin, 36*(3), 151–159.

Kay, T., Harrington, D. E., Adams, R., Anderson, T., Berrol, S., Cicerone, K., Dahlberg, C., Gerber, D., Goka, R., Harley, P., Hilt, J., Horn, L., Lehmkuhl, D. & Malec, J. (1993). Definition of mild traumatic brain injury. *Journal of Head Trauma Rehabilitation, 8*, 86–87.

Keenan, H. T. & Bratton, S. L. (2006). Epidemiology and outcomes of pediatric traumatic brain injury. *Developmental Neuroscience, 28*(4–5), 256–263.

Kinsella, G., Packer, S. & Olver, J. (1991). Maternal reporting of behaviour following very severe blunt head injury. *Journal of Neurology, Neurosurgery & Psychiatry, 54*(5), 422–426.

Kraus, J. F. & McArthur, D. L. (1996). Epidemiologic aspects of brain injury. *Neurologic Clinics, 14*(2), 435–450.

Kraus, J. F., Black, M. A., Hessol, N., Ley, P., Rokaw, W., Sullivan, C., Bowers, S., Knowlton, S. & Marshall, L. (1984). The incidence of acute brain injury and serious impairment in a defined population. *American Journal of Epidemiology, 119*, 186–201.

Kraus, M. F., Susmaras, T., Caughlin, B. P., Walker, C. J., Sweeney, J. A. & Little, D. M. (2007). White matter integrity and cognition in chronic traumatic brain injury: a diffusion tensor imaging study. *Brain: A Journal of Neurology, 130*(10), 2508–2519.

Leininger, B. E., Gramling, S. E., Farrell, A. D., Kreutzer, J. S. & Peck, E. A. (1990). Neuropsychological deficits in symptomatic minor head injury patients after concussion and mild concussion. *Journal of Neurology, Neurosurgery and Psychiatry, 53*, 293–296.

Levin, H. S., Grossman, R. G. & Kelly, P. J. (1976). Aphasic disorders in patients with closed head injury. *Journal of Neurology, Neurosurgery and Psychiatry, 39*, 1062–1070.

Levin, H. S., Grossman, R. G., Rose, J. E. & Teasdale, G. (1979a). Long term neuropsychological outcome of closed head injury. *Journal of Neurosurgery, 50*, 412–422.

Levin, H. S., O'Donnell, V. M. & Grossman, R. G. (1979b). The Galveston Orientation and Amnesia Test: A practical scale to assess cognition after head injury. *The Journal of Nervous and Mental Disease, 167*(11), 675–684.

Levin, H. S., Benton, A. L. & Grossman, R. G. (1982). *Neurobehavioural Consequences of Closed Head Trauma*. New York: Oxford University Press.

Levine, B., Kovacevic, N., Nica, E. I., Gao, F., Schwartz, M. L. & Black, S. E. (2008). The Toronto traumatic brain injury study: injury severity and quantified MRI. *Neurology, 70*(10), 771–778.

Lezak, M. D. (1995). *Neuropsychological Assessment* (3rd edn) (Vol. xviii). New York: Oxford University Press.

Maas, A. I. R., Stocchetti, N. & Bullock, R. (2008). Moderate and severe traumatic brain injury in adults. *The Lancet Neurology, 7*(8), 728–741.

Mathieu, P., Battista, D., Depino, A., Roca, V., Graciarena, M. & Pitossi, F. (2010). The more you have, the less you get: the functional role of inflammation on neuronal differentiation of endogenous and transplanted neural stem cells in the adult brain. *Journal of Neurochemistry, 112*(6), 1368–1385.

McKinlay, A., Grace, R. C., Horwood, L. J., Fergusson, D. M., Ridder, E. M. & MacFarlane, M. R. (2008). Prevalence of traumatic brain injury among children, adolescents and young adults: prospective evidence from a birth cohort. *Brain Injury, 22*(2), 175–181.

McMordie, W. R., Barker, S. L. & Paolo, T. M. (1990). Return to work (RTW) after head injury. *Brain Injury, 4*, 57–90.

Menon, D. K., Schwab, K., Wright, D. W. & Maas, A. I. (2010). Position statement: definition of traumatic brain injury. *Archives of Physical Medicine and Rehabilitation, 91*(11), 1637–1640.

Molina-Holgado, E. & Molina-Holgado, F. (2010). Mending the broken brain: neuroimmune interactions in neurogenesis. *Journal of Neurochemistry, 114*(5), 1277–1290.

Morgan, A. T., Mageandran, S. D. & Mei, C. (2010). Incidence and clinical presentation of dysarthria and dysphagia in the acute setting following paediatric traumatic brain injury. *Child: Health, Care and Development, 36*(1), 44–53.

Myburgh, J. A., Cooper, D. J., Finfer, S. R., Venkatesh, B., Jones, D., Higgins, A., Bishop, N. & Higlett, T. (2008). Epidemiology and 12-month outcomes from traumatic brain injury in Australia and New Zealand. *Journal of Trauma-Injury Infection & Critical Care, 64*(4), 854–862.

Nakase-Richardson, R., Sherer, M., Seel, R. T., Hart, T., Hanks, R., Arango-Lasprilla, J. C., Yablon, S. A., Sander, A. M., Barnett, S. D., Walker, W. C. & Hammond, F. (2011). Utility of post-traumatic amnesia in predicting 1-year productivity following traumatic brain injury: comparison of the Russell and Mississippi PTA classification intervals. *Journal of Neurology, Neurosurgery & Psychiatry, 82*, 494–499.

Niogi, S. N. & Mukherjee, P. (2010). Diffusion tensor imaging of mild traumatic brain injury. *The Journal of Head Trauma Rehabilitation, 25*(4), 241–255.

Oddy, M., Coughlan, T., Tyerman, A. & Jenkins, D. (1985). Social adjustment after closed head injury: a further follow-up seven years after injury. *Journal of Neurology, Neurosurgery & Psychiatry, 48*(6), 564–568.

Perel, P., Roberts, I., Bouamra, I., Woodford, M., Mooney, M. & Lecky, F. (2009). Intracranial bleeding in patients with traumatic brain injury: a prognostic study. *BMC Emergency Medicine, 9*, 15.

Ponsford, J., Olver, J. H. & Curran, C. (1995). A profile of outcome: two years after traumatic brain injury. *Brain Injury, 9*(1), 1–10.

Rimel, R., Giordani, B., Barth, J. & Jane, J. (1982). Moderate head injury: completing the clinical spectrum of brain trauma. *Neurosurgery, 11*, 344–351.

Rohling, M. L., Binder, L. M., Demakis, G. J., Larrabee, G. J., Ploetz, D. M. & Langhinrichsen-Rohling, J. (2011). A meta-analysis of neuropsychological outcome after mild traumatic brain injury: re-analyses and reconsiderations of Binder *et al.* (1997), Frencham *et al.* (2005), and Pertab *et al.* (2009). *The Clinical Neuropsychologist, 25*(4), 608–623.

Russell, W. & Smith, A. (1961). A post-traumatic amnesia in head injury. *Archives of Neurology, 5*, 16–29.

Rutland-Brown, W., Langlois, J. A., Thomas, K. E. & Xi, Y. L. (2006). Incidence of traumatic brain injury in the United States, 2003. *Journal of Head Trauma Rehabilitation, 21*(6), 544–548.

Safaz, I., Alaca, R., Yasar, E., Tok, F. & Yilmaz, B. (2008). Medical complications, physical function and communication skills in patients with traumatic brain injury: a single centre 5-year experience. *Brain Injury, 22*(10), 733–739.

Sarno, M. T. (1980). The nature of verbal impairment after closed head injury. *The Journal of Nervous and Mental Disease, 168,* 682–695.

——(1984). Verbal impairment after closed head injury: report of a replication study. *Journal of Nervous and Mental Diseases, 172,* 475–479.

——(1988). 1. Head injury: language and speech defects. *Scandinavian Journal of Rehabilitation. (Med. Suppl.), 17,* 55–64.

Sarno, M. T. & Levita, E. (1986). Characteristics of verbal impairment in closed head injured patients. *Archives of Physical Medicine Rehabilitation, 67,* 400–405.

Senathi-Raja, D., Ponsford, J. & Schönberger, M. (2010). Impact of age on long-term cognitive function after traumatic brain injury. *Neuropsychology, 24*(3), 336–344.

Servadei, F., Murray, G. D., Penny, K., Teasdale, G. M., Dearden, M., Iannotti, F., Lapierre, F., Maas, A. J., Karimi, A., Ohman, J., Persson, L., Stocchetti, N., Trojanowski, T. & Unterberg, A. (2000a). The value of the 'worst' computed tomographic scan in clinical studies of moderate and severe head injury. *Neurosurgery, 46*(1), 70–77.

Servadei, F., Nasi, M. T., Giuliani, G., Cremonini, A. M., Cenni, P., Zappi, D. & Taylor, G. S. (2000b). CT prognostic factors in acute subdural haematomas: the value of the 'worst' CT scan. *British Journal of Neurosurgery, 14*(2), 110–116.

Sherer, M., Struchen, M. A., Yablon, S. A., Wang, Y. & Nick, T. G. (2008). Comparison of indices of traumatic brain injury severity: Glasgow Coma Scale, length of coma and post-traumatic amnesia. *Journal of Neurology, Neurosurgery & Psychiatry, 79*(6), 678–685.

Shores, A., Marosseky, J. E., Sandanam, J. & Batchelor, J. (1986). Preliminary validation of a clinical scale for measuring the duration of post-traumatic amnesia. *Medical Journal of Australia, 114,* 569–582.

Sohlberg, M. M. & Mateer, C. A. (1989). *Introduction to Cognitve Rehabilitation: Theory and Practice.* New York: The Guilford Press.

Stein, S. C. & Spettell, C. (1995). The Head Injury Severity Scale (HISS): a practical classification of closed head injury. *Brain Injury, 9,* 437–444.

Summers, C. R., Ivins, B. & Schwab, K. A. (2009). Traumatic brain injury in the United States: an epidemiologic overview. *Mount Sinai Journal of Medicine, 76*(2), 105–110.

Sun, F. & He, Z. (2010). Neuronal intrinsic barriers for axon regeneration in the adult CNS. *Current Opinion in Neurobiology, 20*(4), 510–518.

Tate, R. L. (1991). Impairments after severe blunt head injury: their consequences for rehabilitation and psychosocial reintegration. In W. R. Levick, B. G. Frost, M. Watson & H. P. Pfister (Eds), *Brain Impairment: Advances in Applied Research. Proceedings of the 15th Annual Conference of the Australian Society for the Study of Brain Impairment* (pp. 219–227). Newcastle: University of Newcastle.

——(2010). *A Compendium of Tests, Scales and Questionnaires: The Practitioner's Guide to Measuring Outcomes After Acquired Brain Impairment.* Hove, UK: Psychology Press.

Tate, R. L., Broe, G. A. & Lulham, J. (1989a). Impairment after severe blunt head injury: the results from a consecutive series of 100 patients. *Acta Neurologica Scandinavica, 79*(2), 97–107.

Tate, R. L., Lulham, J., Broe, G. A., Strettles, B. & Pfaff, A. (1989b). Psychosocial outcome for the survivors of severe blunt head injury: the results from a consecutive series of 100 patients. *Journal of Neurology, Neurosurgery and Psychiatry, 52,* 1128–1134.

Tate, R. L., Fenelon, B., Manning, M. & Hunter, M. (1991). Patterns of neuropsychological impairment after severe blunt head injury. *Journal of Nervous and Mental Disease, 179*(3), 117–126.

Tate, R. L., McDonald, S. & Lulham, J. M. (1998). Incidence of hospital-treated traumatic brain injury in an Australian community. *Australian & New Zealand Journal of Public Health, 22*(4), 419–423.

Tate, R. L., Harris, R. D., Cameron, I. D., Myles, B. M., Winstanley, J. B., Hodgkinson, A. E., Baguley, I. J., Harradine, P. G. & Brain Injury Outcomes Study (BIOS) Group (2006a). Recovery of impairments after severe traumatic brain injury: findings from a prospective, multicentre study. *Brain Impairment, 7*(1), 1–15.

Tate, R. L., Pfaff, A., Baguley, I. J., Marosszeky, J. E., Gurka, J. A., Hodgkinson, A. E., King, C., Lane-Brown, A. T. & Hanna, J. (2006b). A multicentre, randomised trial examining the effect of test procedures measuring emergence from post-traumatic amnesia. *Journal of Neurology, Neurosurgery & Psychiatry, 77*(7), 841–849.

Teasdale, G. & Jennett, B. (1976). Assessment and prognosis of coma after head injury. *Acta Neurochirurgica, 34*, 45–55.

Theodoros, D. G. & Murdoch, B. E. (1994). Laryngeal dysfunction in dysarthric speakers following severe closed-head injury. *Brain Injury, 8*(8), 667–684.

Thomsen, I. V. (1975). Evaluation and outcome of aphasia in patients with severe closed head trauma. *Journal of Neurology, Neurosurgery & Psychiatry, 38*, 713–718.

——(1984). Late outcome of very severe blunt head trauma: a 10–15 year second follow-up. *Journal of Neurology, Neurosurgery & Psychiatry, 47*(3), 260–268.

Vagnozzi, R., Signoretti, S., Cristofori, L., Alessandrini, F., Floris, R., Isgrò, E., Ria, A., Marziale, S., Zoccatelli, G., Tavazzi, B., Del Bolgia, F., Sorge, R., Broglio, S. P., McIntosh, T. K. & Lazzarino, G. (2010). Assessment of metabolic brain damage and recovery following mild traumatic brain injury: a multicentre, proton magnetic resonance spectroscopic study in concussed patients. *Brain: A Journal of Neurology, 133*(11), 3232–3242.

van Velzen, J. M., van Bennekom, C. A. M., Edelaar, M. J. A., Sluiter, J. K. & Frings-Dresen, M. H. W. (2009). How many people return to work after acquired brain injury? A systematic review. *Brain Injury, 23*(6), 473–488.

Viano, D. C., Casson, I. R., Pellman, E. J., Zhang, E. J., King, A. I. & Yang, K. H. (2005). Concussion in professional football: brain responses by finite element analysis: part 9. *Neurosurgery, 57*, 891–916.

Walker, W. C., Ketchum, J. M., Marwitz, J. H., Chen, T., Hammond, F., Sherer, M. & Meythaler, J. (2010). A multicentre study on the clinical utility of posttraumatic amnesia duration in predicting global outcome after moderate-severe traumatic brain injury. *Journal of Neurology, Neurosurgery & Psychiatry, 81*, 87–89.

Wang, C.-C., Schoenberg, B. S., Li, S.-C., Yang, Y.-C., Cheng, X.-M. & Bolis, L. (1986). Brain injury due to head trauma: epidemiology in urban areas of the People's Republic of China. *Archives of Neurology, 43*, 570–572.

Weddell, R., Oddy, M. & Jenkins, D. (1980). Social adjustment after rehabilitation: a two year follow-up of patients with severe head injury. *Psychological Medicine, 10*(2), 257–263.

Wertz, R. T. (1985). Neuropathologies of speech and language: an introduction to patient management. In D. F. Johns (Ed.), *Clinical Management of Neurogenic Communicative Disorders* (2nd Edn, pp. 1–96). Boston: Little, Brown & Company.

Wilde, E. A., McCauley, S. R., Hunter, J. V., Bigler, E. D., Chu, Z., Wang, Z. J., Hanten, G. R., Troyanskaya, M., Yallampalli, R., Li, X., Chia, J. & Levin, H. S. (2008). Diffusion tensor imaging of acute mild traumatic brain injury in adolescents. *Neurology, 70*(12), 948–955.

Willemse-van Son, A. H. P., Ribbers, G. M., Verhagen, A. P. & Stam, H. J. (2007). Prognostic factors of long-term functioning and productivity after traumatic brain injury: a systematic review of prospective cohort studies. *Clinical Rehabilitation, 21*(11), 1024–1037.

Williams, W. H., Potter, S. & Ryland, H. (2010). Mild traumatic brain injury and Postconcussion Syndrome: a neuropsychological perspective. *Journal of Neurology, Neurosurgery and Psychiatry, 81*, 1116–1122.

Williamson, D. J. G., Scott, J. G. & Adams, R. L. (1996). Traumatic brain injury. In R. L. Adams, O. A. Parsons, J. L. Culbertson & S. J. Nixon (Eds), *Neuropsychology for Clinical Practice: Etiology, Assessment, and Treatment of Common Neurological Disorders* (pp. 9–64). Washington, DC: American Psychological Association.

Winqvist, S., Lehtilahti, M., Jokelainen, J., Luukinen, H. & Hillbom, M. (2007). Traumatic brain injuries in children and young adults: a birth cohort study from Northern Finland. *Neuroepidemiology, 29*(1–2), 136–142.

3   The nature of cognitive deficits and psychosocial function following TBI

Skye McDonald, Leanne Togher and Chris Code

In Chapter 2, the incidence of various neuropsychological impairments following severe TBI, especially those affecting learning, processing speed and executive function was described. Attentional deficits are also commonly arising, possibly reflecting impaired processing speed, executive dysfunction or both. In this chapter we shall discuss the nature of these particular cognitive impairments in TBI as these are integral to psychosocial outcome in general and communication abilities in particular. We will focus on disorders of attention and processing speed, memory, executive function and social cognition. In each section, clinical features will be described, followed by a consideration of underpinning mechanisms and neuroanatomical correlates and finally issues to do with their assessment. Following this, we will discuss psychosocial factors which have implications for communication skills. Organic personality change will be explored as well as other contributing factors to post-traumatic psychosocial function.

Attention and information processing speed

Clinical features

Slow processing, poor attention and impaired concentration are common complaints throughout the spectrum of severity of TBI although notably more frequent and persistent after severe TBI (Dikmen *et al.*, 1995; Draper *et al.*, 2007; McKinlay *et al.*, 1983; McKinlay *et al.*, 1981; Oddy *et al.*, 1985; Oddy *et al.*, 1978; Tate *et al.*, 2006b; van Zomeren & van den Burg, 1985). Poor attention is manifested in a variety of ways. Firstly, many people with severe TBI are slow to process information spanning simple motor tasks to complex problem solving (Dikmen *et al.*, 1995) and become easily overwhelmed when presented with too much information or too quickly. Secondly, they have great difficulty attending to two tasks at once, such as watching television while performing a domestic task. Relatedly, people with severe TBI are frequently extremely distractible. They may, for example, drop the task at hand in order to engage in conversation with a stranger who enters the therapy area or may cease responding to an instruction in physiotherapy in order to pick up a trivial object from the floor.

The tendency to abandon one task for another again highlights the incapacity to attend to more than one thing at a time. Thirdly, therapists frequently complain that patients make mistakes due to lapses of attention (Ponsford & Kinsella, 1991). Finally, they can have difficulty dealing with complex tasks that are routinely carried out in everyday life. For example, it may be necessary to break down the planning of a bus trip into the component parts (getting a timetable, determining the fare, working out travel time, etc.) in order for the person to complete this successfully.

Attention for demanding tasks: the role of working memory

In an effort to examine the nature of attentional problems after TBI, researchers have turned to the cognitive psychology literature for a framework.[1] One model of cognitive processes describes attentional phenomena using the concept of working memory (Baddeley, 1990). This model is particularly useful as a perspective from which to consider problems attending to complex information following TBI. According to this approach, conscious attention, or working memory, is required whenever the task at hand is novel or demanding. Many quite complex tasks (e.g. driving a car) can be dealt with at a semi-automatic level and thus require little conscious attentional resources, certain cues strongly prompting the habitual response. Such tasks can often be performed simultaneously with other more (attention) demanding tasks with little interference between the two (Schneider & Shiffrin, 1977). On the other hand, novel tasks require working memory in order to: (1) selectively focus on the task at hand; (2) juggle cognitive resources in order to perform more than one task simultaneously; (3) suppress habitual responses which might interfere with the generation of new ways of responding; and (4) guide cognitive activity in a goal directed fashion. In working memory the 'central executive' (Baddeley, 1990) or 'supervisory attentional system' (Norman & Shallice, 1986) utilizes information which is temporarily stored in an unspecified number of sub-systems, including a 'phonological loop' and 'visuospatial scratch pad'.

Both the sub-systems (verbal/visual scratchpads) and the central executive have limited capacity. While the sub-systems only hold a finite amount of information, the central executive is limited in both in terms of the amount of information it can process at one time and also the speed with which this occurs. If its limits are exceeded, for example by increasing the amount of information it has to process, then the rate with which tasks are performed decreases accordingly (Baddeley, 1986; Baddeley & Hitch, 1974). If the demands are increased further errors begin to occur, and these typically reflect failure to inhibit habitual or stereotyped responses that are not appropriate in the given context (Baddeley, 1966). This model of attention and the roles that it plays fits well with clinical descriptions of TBI subjects who are slow to respond and inaccurate in their performance on demanding tasks.

Evidence for impaired processing speed and poor divided attention

Meta-analyses have indicated that, in general, people with severe TBI are typically one standard deviation slower than their peers on both simple and complex reaction time tasks. Further, they have been consistently shown to have a reduced attentional span (Mathias & Wheaton, 2007) limiting 'scratchpad capacity'.[2] Processing speed impacts upon working memory (Kennedy *et al.* 2003). Consistent with this, severe TBI is typically associated with working memory impairments especially related to slowed responses rather than inaccuracy per se. For example, people with severe TBI, while as accurate on the Stroop test as matched controls, were slow under neutral conditions (simple focused attention) as well as conditions requiring the suppression of competing responses (Ponsford & Kinsella, 1992; Stuss *et al.*, 1985). Divided attention tasks including choice reaction time tasks have repeatedly demonstrated that severe TBI subjects are no less accurate than their matched controls although they are significantly slower (Ponsford & Kinsella, 1992; Shum *et al.*, 1990; Stuss *et al.*, 1989; van Zomeren, 1981) with a disproportionate increase in reaction time, relative to controls, as the complexity of the task increases (Anderson & Knight, 2010; Ponsford & Kinsella, 1992; van Zomeren, 1981; van Zomeren & Brouwer, 1987).

Problems of accuracy do, however, emerge when such patients are faced with tasks requiring divided attention which are paced in a manner that they cannot control, e.g. the Paced Auditory Serial Addition Test (Gronwall & Sampson, 1974) or N-back tasks with fixed presentation rates (Asloun *et al.*, 2008).[3] In such cases participants with severe TBI are significantly less accurate than controls (Asloun *et al.*, 2008; Ponsford & Kinsella, 1992). Ponsford and Kinsella (1992) concluded from their series of experiments that TBI subjects perform less efficiently on a variety of attentional tasks than non-brain-damaged controls because their speed of information processing is reduced. Where possible they trade off speed in order to maintain accuracy but when this cannot occur errors emerge.

Evidence of poor inhibitory control

An additional component of working memory is inhibitory control, i.e. the capacity to stop a habitual course of action that is made inappropriate by changing circumstance. One way of measuring this is by examining how well people can inhibit an activated motor response (such as when responding regularly to frequent stimuli, the response must be inhibited to infrequent stimuli). Commonly used paradigms include the Go/Nogo task (e.g. Roche *et al.*, 2004), Stop-signal task (Logan, 1994), the Sustained Attention to Response Task (SART) (Robertson *et al.*, 1997) and some versions of the Continuous Performance Task (CPT) (Duncan *et al.*, 2005). Each of these tasks measures an overt, effortful, suppression of an activated motor response (Nigg, 2000) and has shown clear deficits in groups with moderate to severe TBI. Inefficient response inhibition may occur because inhibition fails to activate or is too slow to activate, or if the response process is too fast or too variable (Logan, 1994). In general, it appears that deficits in inhibition control following TBI are independent of response speed, suggesting they arise due to a failure or slowing of the process of inhibition itself (Dimoska *et al.*, 2011).

Inhibition of cognitive processes (rather than motor responses: often referred to as interference control) is also theoretically important to working memory. While in theory, interference control would be expected to be impaired following severe TBI, studies using the Stroop colour word interference score as a measure of interference control have not consistently demonstrated a deficit once response speed has been controlled (Dimoska *et al.*, 2011), again suggesting that information processing speed may be the major contributor to poor performance (Felmingham *et al.*, 2004).

Neuroanatomical correlates of working memory

Slowed information processing following TBI may reflect diffuse injury from shearing of long nerve fibres that constitute the white matter (van Zomeren & Brouwer, 1987), resulting in neuronal cell loss, and consequently circuitous transmission, myelin damage and/or reduced dendritic sprouting (Felmingham *et al.*, 2004). Patients with TBI who have more indicators of diffuse axonal injury evidence greater slowing than those who have less (Felmingham *et al.*, 2004). Recent scanning techniques, specifically diffusion tensor imaging (DTI) which visualizes white matter tracts (see Figure 2.1) tend to confirm these observations. For example, reduced working memory following TBI has been reportedly associated with damage to long fibre tracts including the superior longitudinal fasiculus, the corpus callosum, the arcuate fasiculus and the fornix (Palacios *et al.*, 2011).

The notion that working memory impairments reflect diffuse pathology also fits with animal, cerebral blood flow and computer simulation studies, all of which suggest that working memory reflects a parallel distributed network that is not centralized and therefore not strongly localized. Instead, such models describe working memory as a set of dynamic associations between representations of goals, environmental stimuli and stored knowledge (Kimberg & Farah, 1993). In turn, these representations are mediated by a specific constellation of sub-systems spread across the human cortex, the particular sub-systems activated being dependent on the given task (Goldman-Rakic & Freedman, 1991). Accordingly, slowed information processing will have an effect that is not specific to task, but is disruptive to all demands on working memory.

Inhibitory and interference control, while also affected by processing speed, possibly entail some specific neural pathways including the right dorsolateral and medial prefrontal cortices: (Aron & Poldrack, 2005; Bush *et al.*, 1999; Cabeza *et al.*, 1997). There also appear to be non-overlapping neural regions supporting these two facets of control: inhibitory control – right thalamus and parietal lobe; interference control – left inferior frontal gyrus (Wager *et al.*, 2005).

Maintenance of attention over time

An aspect of attentional control that is not directly incorporated in the working memory thesis is the ability to maintain arousal and attention over an extended period. This has been termed *tonic* arousal (van Zomeren, 1981) and related to the brain stem reticular formation and its connections to the frontal lobes (Gronwall, 1987), although it will also be vulnerable to diffuse white matter injury. Given the propensity for damage to occur in these areas in TBI it might be expected that many TBI patients suffer from loss of tonic arousal and therefore ability to maintain arousal, particularly in the context of long and monotonous tasks. Clinically, this is certainly noticeable (Ponsford & Kinsella, 1991) but has been difficult to demonstrate. Experimental studies of people with TBI (of varying degrees of severity from mild to very severe) performing vigilance tasks have demonstrated generally impaired performances (Mathias & Wheaton, 2007) but no differential changes in performance over time in comparison to controls (Belmont *et al.*, 2009; Brouwer & Van Wolffelaar, 1985; Ponsford & Kinsella, 1992; van Zomeren & Brouwer, 1987; Whyte *et al.*, 2006). One clue to this may lie in the finding that while people with severe TBI can sustain performance on vigilance tasks this comes at a cost compared to their non-injured counterparts as seen in an association between subjective ratings of mental effort and errors (Belmont *et al.*, 2009) and increasing diastolic blood pressure over the duration of the task which, in turn, was associated with increased subjective fatigue (Ziino & Ponsford, 2006). It may also be that decrements in performance are more obvious on more cognitively demanding tasks. For example, when people with severe TBI have been asked to repeat complex cognitive tests over a number of hours their speed was maintained but accuracy decreased, in direct contrast to control participants who showed benefits of practice on both speed and accuracy (Ashman *et al.*, 2008). In this study they also complained of increased fatigue although there was no association between this and task performance.

Attention to important or novel events

Finally, *phasic* arousal is defined as those transient states of arousal that are stimulated by significant environmental or internal events (van Zomeren, 1981). Impaired phasic arousal has been suggested to underlie impaired selective attention and concomitant distractibility (Trexler & Zappala, 1988). It has been suggested that this reflects a failure to inhibit the salience of irrelevant stimuli secondary to damage to the dorsolateral prefrontal cortex (Knight, 1991). Given that distractibility is commonly reported after TBI (Ponsford & Kinsella, 1991) and the prefrontal lobes are frequently implicated (Lezak, 1995), the possibility exists that phasic arousal is specifically disturbed in TBI. However, investigation of the ability of severe TBI patients to benefit from warnings in a reaction time task suggest that, as a group, their phasic awareness was unimpaired (Ponsford & Kinsella, 1992; Whyte *et al.*, 1997).

Overview of attentional deficits following TBI

In summary, attentional deficits are frequently reported following severe TBI but are unlikely to reflect uniform impairment. A common finding is that of slowed information processing which limits both the amount of information that can be attended to and the time taken to perform complex tasks. Where possible speed is traded for accuracy but when this is not possible errors emerge. Slowed information processing has been attributed to diffuse axonal injury. In addition, TBI patients have been observed to suffer under-arousal and lapses in attention on extended tasks and this has been attributed to loss of tonic arousal associated with frontomedial brain stem dysfunction. Experimental evidence has not, at this stage, confirmed these observations. Finally, distractible behaviour is commonly associated with TBI and has been attributed to diminished phasic arousal secondary to dorsolateral frontal lesions, but this too awaits experimental verification.

It is interesting that, on the whole, TBI patients have performed better than expected in most experimental studies of attention. Nevertheless, it is important to recognize that complex unstructured situations as commonly occur in everyday life are more demanding of attention than the controlled experimental tasks described here (Ponsford *et al.*, 1995). Failure to elicit impaired attention on experimental tasks cannot, therefore, be taken as evidence of an absence of attentional deficit particularly in the light of such frequent clinical observation to the contrary. The challenge remains to produce measures that are sensitive to observed attentional deficits which clearly elucidate their nature and which are able to characterize these in a way that can be meaningfully translated into everyday behaviour.

Assessment of attention and information processing

Attention and concentration problems may be patently apparent when the TBI patient is faced with any task that is complex, demanding or sustained or which must be performed in a noisy or otherwise busy environment. Neuropsychological testing does not always capture such problems because it is usually conducted in a quiet room free from distractions. Where attentional problems are sufficiently severe to interfere with neuropsychological testing these can be seen on standard tests that are sensitive to the needs of processing speed and working memory. The widely used Wechsler Adult Intelligence Test – fourth edition (WAISIV: Wechsler, 2008a) – yields both a Processing Speed Index (comprising two subtests: Symbol Search and Coding) and a Working Memory Index (comprising Digit Span and Arithmetic). Other tests specifically designed to tap working memory type skills include the Paced Auditory Serial Addition Test (PASAT) (Gronwall, 1977), the Trail Making Test (TMT) (Reitan, 1958), the Stroop test (Trenerry *et al.*, 1989) and various measures of complex reaction time (e.g. van Zomeren & Brouwer, 1987) (see Table 3.1). A more comprehensive, behavioural approach to the assessment of attention is also provided by the Test for Everyday Attention

(TEA) (Robertson *et al.*, 1994) with subtests focused on selective attention, divided attention, sustained attention and attentional switching. Some aspects of the assessment of attention overlap with the way in which executive function is conceptualized and measured (see section on Executive Function).

Table 3.1 Summary of attentional deficits commonly experienced following TBI including frequently used tests and qualitative features. Note some tests are sensitive to a range of cognitive impairments.

Cognitive area	Common neuro-psychological tests	Qualitative features
Processing speed	Reaction time tests; WAISIV: Processing Speed Index (Symbol Search, Coding); TMT Part A	Slowed responses and processing
Attention span	WAISIV: Digit Span, word and reading span tasks	Reduced attention span
Focused/selective attention	WAISIV: Digit Symbol, Symbol Search, Trail Making Test Parts A and B; Stroop Colour and Word Test; TEA: Map Search	Tendency to sacrifice speed for accuracy
Divided attention/ attentional switching	Reaction time dual tasks; PASAT; N-back tasks; TMT Part B; TEA: Telephone Directory; Elevator Counting	Loss of accuracy with paced tasks; difficulty in maintaining and altering direction of sequenced information
Inhibitory control	Go, Nogo tests, SART, Stop-Signal	Failure to inhibit activated motor response
Interference control	Stroop Colour and Word Test	Failure to inhibit automatic cognitive process evident in errors and generally slowed performance
Sustained attention	CPT; SART; cancellation tasks; TEA: Elevator Counting and Lottery; other vigilance tasks	Maintenance of performance in vigilance tasks but changes in physiological and subjective measures of fatigue and mental effort. Increasing errors over time for complex tasks

Key: WAISIV – Wechsler Adult Intelligence Scale (fourth edition); PASAT – Paced Auditory Serial Addition Test; SART – Sustained Attention to Response Test; CPT – Continuous Performance Test; TEA – Test of Everyday Attention; TMT – Trail Making Test.

Memory

Clinical features

Severe TBI is always associated with some period of amnesia comprising the period of post-traumatic amnesia. In addition, many TBI patients experience limited problems recalling events from the immediate past prior to the injury. There is inevitably a loss of recall for the moments immediately prior to the injury but in addition there may be a substantial loss of important autobiographical information such as all events in the weeks before, the last birthday prior to the accident, a wedding or the birth of a child. In addition, it is common to see substantive difficulties recalling ongoing events. Thus, such patients may be forgetful of instructions, messages and phone calls while on the ward. They may get lost returning from the bathroom to their bed or when attempting to find their way to therapy. They may be unreliable in attending therapy without prompting and may fail to carry through information from one session to the next. Once at home, such memory problems can be extremely disabling. Shopping may be impossible without a list and driving may be seriously impeded by frequent wrong turns and episodes of disorientation. Appointments may be remembered only with the assistance of a diary. Work may be disrupted due to failure to recall names, information or new procedures and the capacity to pass school or university tests may be severely impaired regardless of the amount of study and preparation. Poor memory also has a direct impact upon communication and social skills. It is very difficult for a patient with poor ongoing memory to engage in social conversation and chat which often revolves around 'gossip' or 'small talk' involving free exchange of a copious number of details concerning recent events. Retrograde amnesia and ongoing new learning difficulties appear to represent distinct phenomena and will be discussed separately.

Retrograde amnesia and autobiographical memory

Retrograde amnesia, i.e. loss of memory for events preceding the trauma, can range from seconds to days, weeks or even months prior to the injury and often shrinks as the patient recovers although some brief period of permanent amnesia usually remains (Baddeley, 1990; Squire, 1987). The pervasiveness of retrograde amnesia varies in the TBI population as it does in other clinical groups (see Baddeley, 1990; Squire, 1987 for review). In some patients, particularly those still in PTA, retrograde amnesia may extend for decades with relative preservation of early, personally salient, memories (Levin *et al.*, 1985). Once out of PTA, retrograde amnesia does tend to shrink to a time limited period immediately preceding the injury (e.g. Barbizet, 1970). Absolute loss of memories immediately prior to the injury does appear to reflect disruption of consolidation of memories secondary to impaired hippocampal functioning (Mattioli *et al.*, 1996). However, even after PTA has resolved some patients with severe TBI may continue to experience faulty autobiographical knowledge extending decades pre-injury

(Hunkin *et al.*, 1995; Levin *et al.*, 1985) and also ongoing. This appears to reflect a particular loss of the ability to retrieve episodic (time and spatial context) details about the past (Coste *et al.*, 2011; Markowitsch *et al.*, 1993). For example, Knight and O'Hagan (2009) demonstrated that while people with severe TBI were able to recognize famous faces from pre-injury and post-injury periods, they were unable to recall any details about them. People with severe TBI are also unable to mentally transport themselves back to the past in order to re-experience the sensory quality of past events (Levine *et al.*, 1998; Piolino *et al.*, 2007). They are also impacted by intrusions and confabulation when attempting to recall (Baddeley, 1990; Baddeley *et al.*, 1987). These more pervasive failures in autobiographical memory may represent impairment of working memory and/or executive functions (Piolino *et al.*, 2007) and have been specifically associated with difficulties updating working memory and poor interference control (Coste *et al.*, 2011). It is these problems accessing specific, detailed, autobiographical memories that make social contact, interpersonal relations and communication difficult because the person with TBI cannot share past experiences. Poor autobiographical memory will also impede the ability to solve everyday problems as the person is unable to call upon past memories of similar situations that might point to a solution (Knight & O'Hagan, 2009).

Learning new information

Ongoing impairment in the capacity to learn new information is a salient feature of severe TBI, presenting as a specific learning disorder for either verbal learning, reflecting damage to the left hemisphere, nonverbal learning implicating the right hemisphere, or, in fewer cases, a non-specific learning disorder reflecting bilateral cerebral pathology. Deficits in the ability to recall new information can range from mild and inconvenient to severe and debilitating. There is also variability in the type of learning process affected.

For some, there is a problem of acquisition of new information, i.e. the memory is not stored or consolidated and therefore can neither be recalled nor recognized at a later stage. Such memory disorders are similar to those seen following damage to the hippocampus and associated structures, right in the case of visuospatial learning impairment, left in the case of verbal learning impairment and both in the case of generalized learning impairment.

In many cases, the TBI patient may have faulty or imperfect learning. In general, there are a number of factors that may contribute, including a low attention span, limiting the amount of information that can be processed and inefficient learning due to disorganized or passive learning strategies (Blackstein *et al.*, 1993; DeJong & Donders, 2009; Millis & Ricken, 1994). Accurate recall may be diminished and contaminated by irrelevant intrusions (DeJong & Donders, 2009; Haut, 1992; Millis & Ricken, 1994). In many such cases the TBI patient may have difficulty spontaneously retrieving information but have adequate recall when provided with specific cues. Thus recognition of material previously encountered far outweighs spontaneous recall (Wilde *et al.*, 1995). In addition to problems recalling isolated facts, severe TBI patients have been found to have additional difficulty recalling the temporal sequence of the information (Cooke & Kauslen, 1995).

These characteristics of imperfect learning have sometimes been thought to reflect a learning problem that reflects frontal lobe disruption causing a failure to use context effectively to facilitate encoding and retrieval (Lezak, 1995; Squire, 1987), a problem that is qualitatively distinct from the 'classic' amnesias secondary to medial temporal lesions in which there is poor acquisition and retention of information. However, equally, such problems may reflect degrees of severity in combination with other cognitive impairment (Baddeley *et al.*, 1987; DeLuca & Diamond, 1995). General executive impairment has been thought to cause learning deficits (Stuss & Benson, 1986; Walsh, 1987) but there is little relation between tests of memory and general measures of executive function in TBI (Vanderploeg *et al.*, 1994). Alternatively, there is some evidence that impaired working memory and susceptibility to interference do influence poor verbal learning (Vanderploeg *et al.*, 1994).

Procedural learning

In some cases it has also been demonstrated that TBI patients are impaired in the acquisition of skills and procedures (Baddeley *et al.*, 1987). Poor procedural learning has been associated with lesions specifically to the basal ganglia and is thought to reflect a quite distinct kind of memory problem (Mishkin & Appemzeller, 1987) although it is also seen with significant frontal cortical lesions (Beldarrain *et al.*, 1999). Conversely, the ability to learn new procedures can be intact in people with poor episodic memory – to the point that they may improve on a procedural task with practice despite poor conscious recall of the process of learning (Kime *et al.*, 1996; Turkstra & Bourgeois, 2005).

Prospective memory

Prospective memory (PM) refers to the ability to remember, at some point in the future, to perform a particular task. Prospective memory is involved when remembering to take medicine with dinner, to attend a dentist's appointment on Friday, or to pick up some milk on the way home from work. It is this kind of memory that we rely upon continuously in everyday life and it is this kind of memory that appears to be particularly concerning for people with severe TBI and their relatives (Mateer *et al.*, 1987; Shum *et al.*, 2011). It is generally believed that prospective memory is comprised of two components, a retrospective component, i.e. remembering what task needs to be performed and when, and a prospective component, i.e. self-cueing that it is time to execute the task. With respect to the latter, there are two kinds of cues; remembering to perform a task when a particular event occurs (e.g. taking medicine when dinner is finished), known as event based PM, and remembering to perform an intention at a particular time, e.g. attending a dentist at 2 pm or taking the cake out of the oven after 30 minutes, known as time based PM. In addition, habitual PM tasks (e.g. taking medicine every evening) are less difficult than those that arise sporadically (remembering to pick up a medical script on the way home). Although it is generally believed that event based PM tasks are less difficult than time based, overall people with TBI fare poorly on both, with no apparent difference between the two (Shum *et al.*, 2011).

Theoretical accounts of event based PM suggest that strategic processing is needed to monitor events in the environment especially when the task is demanding (McDaniel & Einstein, 2000; McDaniel *et al.*, 2005), although simply maintaining the intention may also require ongoing cognitive resources (Smith & Bayen, 2004). People with TBI do allocate attention to monitoring when faced with event PM tasks, although not as much as controls (Pavawalla *et al.*, 2011). They also have difficulties recognizing when an event cue has occurred, despite being able to remember the nature of the cue, possibly suggestive of a failure of retrospective memory processes (Pavawalla *et al.*, 2011). In time based PM tasks there are no explicit external cues and people must self-cue when the intention is to be realized. This requires active monitoring of the passage of time and this is another area where people with TBI are found to be impaired, specifically due to an underestimation of how much time has passed (Schmitter-Edgecombe & Rueda, 2008), although this does recover (Anderson & Schmitter-Edgecombe, 2011). Time estimation has been associated with time based PM in functional terms (McFarland & Glisky, 2009) and also as related to areas of brain damage, specifically the right polar frontal region (Volle *et al.*, 2011).

In summary, PM is an everyday area of memory that is often disrupted following TBI. If people with TBI suffer from poor learning (and therefore have poor recall, i.e. retrospective memory) they will fail to perform PM tasks as they will not remember what needs doing or when. But even in the absence of retrospective memory failure, people with TBI may have poor PM function because they cannot actively monitor time or develop strategies to remind themselves when the intention is to be realized. Both event based and time based PM tasks appear to require additional cognitive resources over and above learning (Shum *et al.*, 2011); however, arguably, event based PM is more reliant upon retrospective memory and time based PM is more reliant upon working memory and executive function (Kinch & McDonald, 2001; Potvin *et al.*, 2011).

Neuroanatomical correlates of poor memory

The neuroanatomical underpinnings of poor memory following TBI are likely to be complex, reflecting the diffuse and multifocal nature of injuries. In general, damage to the hippocampi, fornix, anterior cingulate and interhemispheric connectivity have been associated with poor associative learning in TBI (de la Plata *et al.*, 2011; Kinnunen *et al.*, 2011) with similar regions, including ventral frontal cortex and underlying white matter implicated in retrograde memory loss (Levine *et al.*, 1998; Markowitsch *et al.*, 1993; Mattioli *et al.*, 1996). Dorsolateral and ventral frontal pathology are also specifically implicated in the prospective aspect of prospective memory (Umeda *et al.*, 2011). In addition, characteristics of inefficient learning, such as impaired use of organizational strategies, susceptibility to interference and poor temporal and contextual memory, have been reported following frontal lobe lesions from other etiologies (e.g. Della Rocchetta & Milner, 1993; Janowsky *et al.*, 1989; Milner, 1971; Petrides, 1991; Shimamura *et al.*, 1990; Stuss *et al.*, 1994), as well as diencephalic lesions in Korsakoff's disease (Squire, 1987) and damage to the basal forebrain and striate secondary to anterior communicating artery aneurysm (DeLuca & Diamond, 1995). Given the propensity for damage to be sustained in the orbitomedial frontal areas in TBI it is likely that these features of learning impairment in TBI also arise from damage to frontal cortex and adjacent subcortical systems.

Assessment of memory

Assessment of retrograde memory loss has frequently been performed via interview and questioning of the patient on autobiographical details with collaboration from family members and friends. There are also structured tests such as the Autobiographical Memory Interview (Kopelman *et al.*, 1991). Assessment of the ability to acquire information can occur with numerous tests and procedures specifically developed for this purpose. Such assessment is a complex procedure which takes into account modality, level of complexity, structure available when encoding and availability of cues in recall. Commonly used tests (see Table 3.2) include the Wechsler Memory Scales, e.g. the fourth edition (WMS IV) (Wechsler, 2008b), the Rey Auditory Verbal Learning Test (Taylor, 1959) and Californian Verbal Learning Test – first and second editions (Delis *et al.*, 1987; Delis *et al.*, 2000) and the Rey Osterrieth Complex Figure (Osterrieth, 1944). The Rivermead Behavioural Memory Test – Third Edition (RBMT-3) (Wilson *et al.*, 2008) provides a simple, practical assessment of everyday memory function that is particularly useful for more severe memory impairments. Research into prospective memory is relatively recent so there are few standardized instruments available. The Cambridge Test of Prospective Memory (CAMPROMPT) (Wilson *et al.*, 2005), the Memory for Intentions Screening test (Raskin, 2009) and the Royal Prince Alfred Prospective Memory Test (RPA-ProMem) (Radford *et al.*, 2011) are all designed specifically to measure PM while the RBMT includes some items for screening.

Table 3.2 Areas of memory impairment, common tests and qualitative features.

Cognitive area	Common neuropsychological tests	Qualitative features
Autobiographical memory	Autobiographical Memory Interview	Loss of memory of personal events prior to injury and possibly ongoing
Informational learning – verbal	WMS IV – verbal subtests, RAVLT, CVLT, RBMT	Failure to acquire new memories, inaccurate recall, intrusions in recall, sometimes better recognition than spontaneous recall. May have differential difficulty with verbal versus visuospatial material
Informational learning – visuospatial	WMS IV – visual subtests, Rey Figure Recall, RBMT	As above but may have differentially poor learning for visuospatial information compared to verbal
Procedural learning		Failure to learn new motor tasks
Prospective memory	CAMPROMPT, MIST, RPAProMem, RBMT	Failure to remember to do tasks at an allocated time, or in response to specific events, despite sometimes remembering what the task is

Key: WMS IV – Wechsler Memory Scale (fourth edition); RAVLT – Rey Auditory Verbal Learning Test; CVLT – Californian Verbal Learning Test; RBMT – Rivermead Behavioural Memory Test; CAMPROMPT – Cambridge Test of Prospective Memory; MIST – Memory for Intentions Screening Test; RPAProMem – Royal Prince Alfred Prospective Memory Test

Executive function

Executive functions are those which mediate and regulate other cognitive activities and behaviour in a purposeful and goal directed fashion. Loss of executive control thus results in failure to problem solve effectively and to adapt to changing circumstances. Executive deficits have been considered the most disruptive to successful rehabilitation (Lezak, 1995). Unfortunately, of all neuropsychological sequelae of TBI, executive impairment has also been estimated to be, on average, the most severely disturbed of cognitive functions when premorbid intelligence is controlled for (Johnstone *et al.*, 1995).

Clinical features

Having said this, the severity and degree to which executive impairment manifests from one individual to the next varies enormously, influenced not only by the severity of the injury but also premorbid intelligence, motivation and the nature of the task (Shallice & Burgess, 1991; Sloan & Ponsford, 1995). In less severe cases, routine behaviour previously learnt may be carried out normally and basic skills retained. However, there may be a disruption of the capacity to focus attention voluntarily and to deal with novel situations adaptively. When deficits are more pervasive all behaviour may be disrupted.

Drive and control

Many aspects of executive impairment can be described as representing either a loss of drive or a loss of control. Impaired drive will result in an uncontrolled apathy or inertia, rigidity, inflexibility and perseveration. Such patients may have difficulty initiating any behaviour unprompted, or in less severe cases may be restricted to behaviour that is stereotypic, repetitive and stimulus bound. A disorder of control is characterized by poor response inhibition and/ or interference control. These patients are impulsive, disinhibited and distractible. Disorders of drive and control are dissociable, representing distinct pathological processes, as evidenced by the finding that they manifest both separately and in co-existence in a significant minority of severe TBI patients (Tate *et al.*, 1991).

Problem solving

Problem solving behaviour is fundamentally disrupted. Patients may be unable to anticipate a situation, or analyse it critically. They may focus on concrete or superficial aspects of their environment, being unable to shift their attention and failing to assume a more abstract attitude. Alternatively they may be disorganized and fragmented when formulating a plan of action and have difficulty maintaining a stable intention when carrying it out.

Metacognition: self-reflection

The capacity to self-reflect, also known as metacognition (the ability to think about cognitive processes), is frequently impaired. Metacognition is considered by some to be an integral facet of executive function as it provides the capacity to ponder larger goals and the means by which these may be achieved (Fernandez-Duque *et al.*, 2000). It also provides the means by which the patient can evaluate his/her progress towards a goal critically and modify it in light of feedback. Poor error detection and correction is common after severe TBI (Hart *et al.*, 1998; O'Keeffe *et al.*, 2007) suggestive of metacognitive impairment. Despite this, metacognition does not appear to be an all or nothing phenomenon. People with TBI can have varying levels of metacognition across different kinds of tasks (Chiou *et al.*, 2011).

Cognitive regulation of behaviour

Finally, executive impairment may result in failure to regulate behaviour with an internal command producing the curious dissociation between 'knowing' and 'doing' whereby the patient can verbalize an instruction or intention while being unable to use that intention to guide behaviour (Walsh, 1985).

Cognitive explanations of executive dysfunction

The focus of contemporary cognitive models of executive function has been on the development of a unified account for the mechanisms underlying executive control. According to such models, executive control is mediated by a diffuse network of operations which fits with the neuroanatomical evidence for more diffuse pathology underlying executive dysfunction in TBI. For example, according to the influential model proposed by Shallice (1988) the symptoms seen in the dysexecutive syndrome are thought to reflect the impairment of a 'supervisory attentional system' (Norman & Shallice, 1986) which has access to all other cognitive processes and which over-rides routine and habitual responses to enable novel responses to occur. This conceptualization suggests that behaviour such as perseveration, stimulus-bound responding and distractibility are reflections of habitual responses triggered automatically and in an uncontrolled manner by internal or external events (Duncan, 1986; Shallice, 1988). This type of explanation also places working memory as central to executive control (Baddeley, 1990; Daigneault *et al.*, 1992; Fuster, 1991; Goldman-Rakic & Freedman, 1991; Kimberg & Farah, 1993) because it is here that representations of perceptual information, memory, actions and goals are activated and maintained and irrelevant associations inhibited so that purposeful plans can be formed and behaviour monitored to ensure the desired goal is achieved.

Disruption of working memory as an explanation for impaired executive function in TBI is consistent with observation of impaired working memory on other kinds of tasks as described in our discussion of attentional disorders. Furthermore, it has been demonstrated that people with severe TBI who are poor at recognizing and utilizing errors have impaired sustained attention (McAvinue *et al.*, 2005) reinforcing the idea that metacognition and executive processing are linked. Whether all attributes of executive impairment in TBI can be usefully described using this rubric has, however, been questioned (e.g. van Zomeren & Brouwer, 1987). It is certainly the case that executive processes are not uniformly affected by TBI nor do they demonstrate a consistent relationship to awareness (McAvinue *et al.*, 2005) further suggesting that executive functions are multi-faceted. Nevertheless, the model is useful for addressing the regulation of ongoing behaviour and the control of cognitive processes engaged in goal directed behaviour.

Emotional contributions to executive dysfunction

It is becoming increasingly recognized that high level cognitive processes are influenced by somatic and emotional factors. In the 1990s, Bechara and colleagues argued that 'somatic markers' may guide decision making in cognitive domains (Bechara *et al.*, 1994; Bechara *et al.*, 2000; Bechara *et al.*, 1997; Damasio *et al.*, 1991) where anticipation of complex response contingencies can be associated with somatic responses even prior to conscious awareness of those contingencies (Bechara *et al.*, 1997). This has most frequently been examined via the Iowa Gambling Task. Using this task it has been shown that healthy adults learn over trials to play the more advantageous decks and experience somatic changes when choosing from risky decks even before they are able to articulate which decks are the risky ones. Patients with (ventromedial) frontal damage do not learn these contingencies and, reportedly, do not show somatic changes (Bechara *et al.*, 1994; Bechara *et al.*, 2000; Fellows & Farah, 2005). People with TBI also perform poorly on the Iowa Gambling Task (Fujiwara *et al.*, 2008; Levine *et al.*, 2005) suggestive of similar somatic deficits. This issue is pursued in more detail in Chapter 5.

Neuroanatomical correlates of executive dysfunction

Executive function has been traditionally associated with the frontal lobes, in particular the prefrontal regions which have been attributed with the activation, programming, regulation and verification of other cognitive activity (Luria, 1973; Luria, 1976). The dorsolateral aspects of the prefrontal lobes with their rich connections to sensory and motor functional systems mediate the intellectual regulation of behaviour and cognition while the orbitomedial and basal aspects with their rich limbic connections have been associated with control and regulation of internal drives and emotion (Alexander *et al.*, 1989; Eslinger, 2008).

However, the idea that focal frontal lesions are required to produce executive impairment has been challenged. It has been shown experimentally that the severity and pervasiveness of intellectual disturbance ascribed to frontal lobe pathology is often a result of frontal lobe pathology in association with more global cerebral dysfunction (Canavan *et al.*, 1985). Patients with more circumscribed lesions may escape many of the deficits described (Drewe, 1974). In the case of TBI, there is strong argument that many features of the 'frontal lobe syndrome' are, in fact, produced by diffuse pathology (Anderson *et al.*, 1995). Thus, 'frontal lobe' deficits may not necessarily reflect disruption to a 'centre' in the frontal lobes but, rather, result from lesions to frontal distributed networks and/or subcortical relay stations and associated connections (Mesulam, 1990). In support of this diffuse tensor imaging has revealed correlation between poor scores on executive measures following TBI and damage to fronto-parietal cortex (Warner *et al.*, 2010), overall white matter loss (Kraus *et al.*, 2007), inter and intrahemisphere frontal white matter (Kinnunen *et al.*, 2011) and damage to thalamo-cortical pathways (Kinnunen *et al.*, 2011; Little *et al.*, 2010).

Assessment of executive dysfunction

Patients with executive impairment may not demonstrate deficit on standardized tests of intelligence such as the Wechsler adult intelligence scales (e.g. Shallice & Burgess, 1991) or other tests that rely on well-learned or familiar routines. There is, however, enormous variability in the severity and pervasiveness of executive dysfunction exhibited and in severe cases, performance on even the most basic tasks can be disrupted due to disorganized, concrete or perseverative responding. For example, patients who are confined to extremely concrete responses may perform abnormally on the Wechsler subtest Vocabulary because they interpret part of the word without reference to its entirety (e.g. interpreting 'fortitude' as referring to a fort [Walsh, 1987]). In less severe cases, standard tests that rely on well-learned knowledge (such as vocabulary) may be performed adequately by patients with executive disorders whereas tasks that require novel inference or simple problem solving may be below premorbid expectations. Thus, using the WAIS, it is not uncommon to see subtests such as Block Design and Similarities performed poorly by frontally damaged patients compared to subtests tapping general knowledge such as Vocabulary and Information (Lezak, 1995). There is of course, enormous normal variation in the capacity to perform on such tests and interpretation of abnormal performance needs to be made with care, taking into consideration the psychometric properties of the tests as well as the appropriate normative data.

Where the patient with TBI is well educated, highly intelligent and/or has relatively subtle executive impairments there may be no evidence of difficulty on such tasks and problems will only be apparent on more difficult and taxing tests (see Table 3.3). Thus the Controlled Oral Word Association Test (COWAT) (Benton, 1973), the Wisconsin Card Sorting Test (WCST) (Heaton *et al.*, 1993), the Five-point test (Goebel *et al.*, 2009), the Rey-Osterrieth Complex Figure (Osterrieth, 1944), the Halstead Category Test (DeFillipis *et al.*, 1979) and the Tower of London (Shallice, 1982) have each become known as 'frontal lobe tests'. This term is misleading because such tests can be failed for a variety of reasons and are therefore susceptible to the effects of many types of cognitive impairment as well as generalized cerebral dysfunction. Only in cases where there is no evidence of basic cognitive disturbance can impaired performance on such tests be reasonably attributed to executive dysfunction. In such cases quantitative scores are frequently in the abnormal range. In addition there may be qualitative features of test performance that point to executive disturbance. For example, perseveration, rule breaking and failure to maintain attentional set are often observed and are indicative of disorders of drive and control respectively. Many tasks described in the assessment of attentional problems (Stroop Colour and Word Test, Trail Making Test, Go-Nogo Tests, etc.) are also sensitive to difficulties with disinhibition, perseveration, etc. The WCST and the Five-point Test also enable such behaviour to be scored and compared to available normative data (Goebel *et al.*, 2009; Heaton *et al.*, 1993). The Delis-Kaplan Executive Functions System (Delis *et al.*, 2001) is a battery designed to measure executive functions

Table 3.3 Areas of executive impairment, common tests and qualitative features.

Cognitive area	Common neuropsychological tests	Qualitative features
Higher order inference	WAISIV: Similarities and Matrix Reasoning; WCST; Halstead Category Test	Concrete responses; failure to report/act upon conceptual relationships
Flexibility/fluency	WCST; TMT Part B; COWAT; Five-point Test; Halstead Category Test	Reduced number of categories and low COWAT score; failure to change categories; perseveration; poor generativity; slow responses on Trails B
Inhibition of motor/ cognitive processes	Haylings Sentence Completion; Stroop Colour and Word Test; Go, Nogo tests; SART; Stop-Signal	Inability to control automatic responding
Strategy formation/ planning	ROCFT; BADS: Key Search; Tower of London	Disorganized, ineffective, piecemeal strategy
Decision making	BADS: 6 Modified Six Elements; Iowa Gambling Task (experimental only)	Failure to prioritize tasks; failure to learn to make advantageous decisions
Self-evaluation		Poor awareness of performance
Error utilization	Many tests (e.g. COWAT, WCST, Trails B; Five-point Test) that require explicit rule compliance	Numerous errors that break/ ignore rules despite awareness of rules

Key: WAIS-V – Wechsler Adult Intelligence Test (fourth edition); BADS – Behavioural Assessment of the Dysexecutive Syndrome; COWAT – Controlled Oral Word Association Test; ROCFT – Rey-Osterrieth Complex Figure Test; TMT – Trail Making Test; WCST – Wisconsin Card Sorting Test.

that encompasses versions of many of the standard tests already mentioned which also attempts to isolate executive dysfunction from more basic processes (word reading, psychomotor speed, etc.) (although for psychometric critique see Crawford *et al.*, 2008).

Finally, there is a significant proportion of patients who appear to suffer executive dysfunction and may, indeed, have demonstrable pathology on CT scan who do not exhibit deficits at all on standardized tests (e.g. Eslinger & Damasio, 1985; Shallice & Burgess, 1991). In such cases impairment of frontal control systems is mainly apparent in behaviour in everyday life. For example, despite normal or even superior ability on most neuropsychological tests, frontal lobe dysfunction has been associated with a profound disorganization of daily activities, irresponsibility and indecision on the most trivial matters, sometimes of sufficient severity to prohibit return to work and independent living (e.g. Saver & Damasio, 1991; Shallice & Burgess, 1991). It is patients like these who have motivated the search for more ecologically sensitive executive assessments. One such test designed to directly assess behavioural manifestations of dysexecutive function is the Behavioural Assessment of the Dysexecutive Syndrome (BADS) (Wilson *et al.*, 1996) in which subtests attempt to emulate everyday problems (developing a strategy to find a lost set of car keys in a field; balancing the need to complete a number of tasks in a set time). In particular, the BADS 6 elements test attempts to instate the kinds of decision making faced in everyday life where the tasks themselves are not inherently difficult, but there are numerous potential solutions and a need to juggle a number of priorities (Shallice & Burgess, 1991).

Social cognition

It is increasingly accepted that the processing of social information (e.g. emotional expressions, intentions and beliefs) is distinct from the processing of non-social cognition both in functional and neuroanatomical terms. For example, patients with brain lesions can be relatively unimpaired on standard neuropsychological tests and yet fail to understand social information or vice versa. The ventromedial surfaces of the frontal lobes, along with the network of frontotemporal limbic structures, have been implicated in social cognition and are also very vulnerable to severe TBI. It is, therefore, no surprise that deficits in many facets of social cognition have been reported in this group. For example, people with severe TBI have been found to have difficulty recognizing emotional expressions in both face and voice (Milders *et al.*, 2003) and difficulty inferring what another person is thinking (Bibby & McDonald, 2005) or intimating in their conversation (Channon & Watts, 2003). They also have problems with empathy (Wood & Williams, 2008) and judging morality (Blair & Cipolotti, 2000). Social cognition is directly relevant to communication and social skills and is addressed more fully in Chapters 5, 6 and 7.

Personality change

Up to 60–80 per cent of family members report that their person with TBI has experienced personality change (Brooks *et al.*, 1986; Jennett *et al.*, 1981; McKinlay *et al.*, 1981; Thomsen, 1975; Weddell & Leggett, 2006). It is also a problem that persists in the majority of these patients as indicated by similar prevalence figures many years later (Brooks *et al.*, 1986; Oddy *et al.*, 1985; Thomsen, 1984) and must be considered a significant contributing factor to reduction of psychosocial functioning observed in this group.

Personality change on personality inventories

In an effort to characterize the nature of personality change following TBI, a number of studies have used general personality measures such as the Personality Assessment Inventory (PAI) (Demakis *et al.*, 2007; Till *et al.*, 2009; Velikonja *et al.*, 2010) or the Minnesota Multiphasic Personality Inventory-2 (MMPI-2)

(Warriner *et al.*, 2003) on people with a wide spectrum of severity of TBI. Similar to relative report, the proportion of people reporting personality profiles that are indistinguishable from normal is around 25–50 per cent (Demakis *et al.*, 2007; Velikonja *et al.*, 2010; Warriner *et al.*, 2003). Among the remainder, psychiatric distress (depression, anxiety, somatic complaints) is frequent (Demakis *et al.*, 2007; Velikonja *et al.*, 2010; Warriner *et al.*, 2003), as is confused thinking (Demakis *et al.*, 2007; Till *et al.*, 2009). A significant proportion have also reported profiles indicative of emotional dysregulation, including impulsivity and substance abuse (13–19 per cent) and mania, irritability and severe externalizing behaviours (14–16 per cent) (Demakis *et al.*, 2007; Warriner *et al.*, 2003).

Only a few studies have attempted to examine personality change relative to premorbid levels. Using the Eysenck Personality Questionnaire-Revised with a group of individuals with severe TBI, Tate reported increases in emotional instability and a trend for decreased extroversion relative to estimates of premorbid personality on the same measure (Tate, 2003). A similar, albeit small, reduction in extroversion post-injury was reported on the Neo Personality Inventory – revised in one study (Kurtz *et al.*, 1998) but not another (Rush *et al.*, 2006). It is unclear whether the variability in findings using these personality measures post-TBI reflects a lack of sensitivity of the personality inventories to brain related changes, or whether it speaks to the relative stability of personality even in the face of serious neuropathology. It is important to note that, for the studies by Rush *et al.* and Kurtz *et al.*, data was available for less than 50 per cent of the cohort who agreed to be involved, raising questions as to the nature of experiences for those families who did not return the forms. Certainly, relative reports of the high incidence of personality change noted above suggest that perceived personality change is very real and further, that this is a source of great emotional distress for family members (Kinsella *et al.*, 1991; Weddell & Leggett, 2006).

Disorders of emotional regulation

A major limitation of established personality inventories is that these were not designed to examine changes to personality as a result of insult to brain structures and they are often difficult to interpret or cross-compare for this reason. Arguably a more fruitful approach is to examine behaviour change using purpose designed questionnaires and interviews that are completed by the person with TBI, their relative or both. According to this research, irritability and fatigue are the most common complaints (Brooks *et al.*, 1986; Dikmen *et al.*, 1993; Kaitaro *et al.*, 1995; Kinsella *et al.*, 1991; Thomsen, 1984; Weddell *et al.*, 1980). To some extent, personality change can be attributed to loss of regulation of emotional behaviour similar to the dysexecutive syndrome affecting intellectual processes. In general, two clusters of behavioural change are seen after severe TBI: loss of emotional control on the one hand and loss of motivation (arousal) on the other (Kinsella *et al.*, 1991), each encompassing a range of behavioural changes. These problems can occur independently, but also together in the one patient and are indicative of an overall problem with emotional regulation.

Disorders of control

Using the purpose designed Current Behaviour Scale (CBS) (Elsass & Kinsella, 1987), Kinsella and colleagues identified short temper, quarrelsomeness, aggression, emotional lability, self-centredness and impulsiveness as reflecting a loss of emotional control (Kinsella *et al.*, 1991). In addition, childishness and sexually disinhibited behaviour have been frequently reported (Brooks *et al.*, 1986; Lezak, 1978; Thomsen, 1984) and would seem to belong to this constellation of problems. Prevalence of problems with dyscontrol following severe TBI are high, reported in up to 34–67 per cent of people with severe TBI in the first year of injury (Brooks *et al.*, 1987; Kim *et al.*, 1999). Further, they remain stable over time (Brooks *et al.*, 1987; Oddy *et al.*, 1985). Irritability is one of the most common behavioural complaints made by people with TBI and their families (Denmark & Geneinhardt, 2002; Hanks *et al.*, 1999; McKinlay *et al.*, 1981) with clinically significant levels of irritability and aggression continuing in approximately 12 per cent of individuals with severe TBI at 18 months post-trauma (Tate *et al.*, 2006). Problems with emotion regulation, i.e. mood swings, are also a significant predictor of relationship breakdown post-TBI (Wood *et al.*, 2005).

Disorders of emotional arousal (drive)

Equally common after TBI are complaints of a relative reduction of emotionality and arousal. Decreased initiative, fatigue, loss of spontaneity, disinterest and socially inappropriate behaviour have been frequently observed (Kaitaro *et al.*, 1995; Kinsella *et al.*, 1991; Thomsen, 1984) and emerge as a single factor representing loss of motivation or drive as measured by the CBS (Kinsella *et al.*, 1991; Tate, 1999). Like disorders of control, prevalence rates for apathy are high, estimated to affect 43–78 per cent of those with severe TBI (Kant *et al.*, 1998; Lane-Brown & Tate, 2009; Oddy *et al.*, 1985) with clinically significant apathy occurring in 15 per cent at 18 months post-trauma (Tate *et al.*, 2006). While depression can masquerade as apathy, the two disorders are independent (Lane-Brown & Tate, 2009; Levy *et al.*, 1998), with apathy more strongly related to reduced cognitive function (Kant *et al.*, 1998). While disorders of drive and control occur independently, they also occur together in roughly equal proportions (Tate *et al.*, 1991). Further, clear changes in both drive and control relative to pre-injury levels have been documented using the CBS (Tate, 2003). Poor emotion regulation and motivation is a significant predictor of poor social outcome (Cattran *et al.*, 2011).

Contribution of cognitive deficits to personality change

It is not only behaviour change that is reflected in personality post-TBI but also thinking styles. Lezak, in her oft cited description of the characterologically altered person following TBI (Lezak, 1978), suggests that stimulus bound behaviour, rigidity, poor planning and organizational skills and a failure to profit from experience characterize many TBI patients. Translated into the psychosocial sphere these deficits have major ramifications for adequate social function.

Firstly, stimulus bound behaviour and rigidity may result in poor judgement, the tendency to be 'black and white' in the appraisal of social information and perseverative, rigid and uncompromising when responding in social contexts. Rigidity may also directly impact upon the ability to perceive the viewpoint of others. The notion that there is a loss of empathy has been empirically supported by the finding that a group of TBI patients were incapable of filling out a personality questionnaire 'as though they were someone else' (Spiers *et al.*, 1994) and also by the related finding that loss of flexibility is associated with measures of empathy (Eslinger & Grattan, 1993) and more general estimates of social skill (Marsh & Knight, 1991).

Secondly, poor planning, organization and self-regulation results in a failure to successfully plan, initiate and complete projects, often despite proclaimed schemes and assurances to the contrary. This kind of behaviour was perhaps most vividly described by Dr Harlow of his celebrated patient Phineas Gage:

> impatient of restraint and advice when it conflicts with his desires, at times perniciously obstinate yet capricious and vacillating, devising many schemes for future operation which no sooner are arranged than they are abandoned in turn for others seeming more feasible.
>
> (as cited in Walsh, 1987, p. 117)

In less extreme cases, projects may be commenced only to be abandoned before completion, or the patient may experience difficulty juggling priorities in order to maximize the use of time and resources (Shallice & Burgess, 1991).

In addition, impaired social cognition is likely to have a direct effect on psychosocial functioning impairing the individual's capacity to interpret social signals accurately or use social feedback to guide behaviour. There is also evidence that poor empathy following TBI is associated with changes in arousal to emotional stimuli (de Sousa *et al.*, 2010). These issues are explored in depth in Chapter 4.

Lack of insight

An important and frequent observation is that many TBI patients are unrealistic in self-appraisal and suffer from a lack of insight (Flanagan *et al.*, 1995; Levin *et al.*, 1991; Lezak, 1978; Lishman, 1990). Thus, plans for the future may be unrealistically optimistic as the patient continually fails to take their newly acquired deficits into account. For example, a young man with severe TBI seen by these authors was insistent that he could return to his trade as an electrician despite massive damage to his eyes and consequent total blindness. Even when this was pointed out, he insisted that he could return, relying on a work mate to tell him the colours of the wires. Empirical studies have demonstrated that a proportion of severe TBI subjects consistently under-estimate memory impairments (Boake *et al.*, 1995), their ability to do a variety of simple and complex tasks (Fordyce & Roueche, 1986; Prigatano & Altman, 1990) and their intellectual and behavioural limitations (Godfrey *et al.*, 1993). Fleming and colleagues have argued that there are three levels at which impaired insight is manifest. Loss of awareness can reduce ability to recognize that there are physical, social and cognitive deficits arising from the brain injury, can limit ability to appraise the functional implications of these, or can impede the capacity to make realistic decisions and set goals in accordance with such knowledge (Fleming *et al.*, 1996). Lack of awareness increases with injury severity and the number of brain lesions (Sherer *et al.*, 2005) and is related to poorer social outcomes (Ownsworth & Fleming, 2005; Ownsworth *et al.*, 2007).

Lack of insight is a complex phenomenon and may encompass organic deficit culminating in a loss of self-reflection (Lezak, 1978), combined with the acute effects of adjustment to altered physical and mental abilities (e.g. denial and anger) (Crossen, 1987). Insight improves over time (Bond, 1984; Fordyce *et al.*, 1983; Godfrey *et al.*, 1993) perhaps as continual exposure to the consequences of his or her impairments provides the patient with feedback concerning these. Furthermore, there is some evidence that insight is not uniformly diminished. For example, while concern about lack of insight has resulted in the avoidance of self-report measures in earlier studies of emotional and behavioural consequences of TBI (e.g. Brooks & McKinlay, 1983; Oddy & Humphrey, 1980; Thomsen, 1975, 1984) it has been demonstrated that TBI patients are capable of reliably reporting emotional changes both in the short and longer term, i.e. 6 months or less and 5 years or more respectively (Elsass & Kinsella, 1987; Kinsella *et al.*, 1988). Not only this but there is reasonable correlation between self-report of emotional and personality variables and ratings provided by a 'close other' (Elsass & Kinsella, 1987; Fordyce *et al.*, 1983; Kinsella *et al.*, 1988; Rush *et al.*, 2006) providing additional validation for the stability of the self-report of people with TBI regarding their emotional state. The extent to which such self-ratings of emotion reflect accurate self-appraisal in a broader sense is unclear. For example, such patients, while able to report that they had fewer opportunities for social contact than premorbidly, were not less satisfied with this state of affairs (Elsass & Kinsella, 1987).

Neuroanatomical correlates of personality change

Although research into the neural underpinnings of emotion regulation are yet to be fully understood, there does appear to be differentiation of different regulatory processes. Damage to the orbitomedial and orbitobasal aspects of the prefrontal lobes, thought to mediate emotional control, is particularly prevalent in TBI and has been associated with descriptions of personality change in TBI (Levin *et al.*, 1991) and frontal lobe injury from other etiologies (DeLuca & Diamond, 1995; Girgis, 1971; Lishman, 1990; Saver & Damasio, 1991). More specifically, it has been argued that the ventromedial cortex with close connections to the amygdala, insula, ventral striatum and ventral anterior cingulate underpins both many facets of social cognition and automatic emotion regulation (Phillips, 2003) including self-initiation and sustained behaviour (arousal) (Andrewes, 2001; Darby & Walsh, 2005; Eslinger, 2008; Luria, 1973; Stuss *et al.*, 1992) while the orbitobasal cortex mediates the flexible control of excitation and inhibition of emotional behaviour (control) (Luria, 1973; Walsh, 1985). A dorsal system, including the hippocampus, dorsal aspects of the anterior cingulate gyrus and dorsolateral prefrontal cortex (Phillips *et al.*, 2003) is argued to mediate effortful processing and the engagement of cognitive processes via connections to other cortical regions (executive function). Given the complex interplay of frontal systems that are both functionally intimate and in close proximity, it is not surprising that the blunt forces that result in TBI lead to variable and often overlapping constellations of deficits in emotional behaviour as well as executive dysfunction. The ventral, medial and orbitobasal frontal regions, regions specifically related to emotion regulation, are especially vulnerable. During acceleration-deceleration trauma the brain is mechanically abraded by the surfaces of the middle and cranial fossae leading to contusion along the ventral surface of the frontal and temporal lobes (Bigler, 2007).

The inability to critically self-reflect with concomitant lack of insight has also been attributed to the prefrontal systems of the brain (Alexander *et al.*, 1989; Stuss & Benson, 1986) and has been associated with relatively more extensive lesions in TBI, particularly affecting the frontal and parietal lobes (Prigatano & Altman, 1990). Finally, it has been suggested that explosive outbursts of anger may reflect temporal lobe abnormalities (Eames, 1990).

Psychological reactions

In addition to organic personality change there are normal psychological reactions to acute disablement and its chronic effects. Psychological distress is a very real and frequent ongoing companion to brain injury. Large scale studies report that around 50–75 per cent of people with brain injuries report some level of distress with clinically significant levels of depression, anxiety and/or concern about somatic complaints in at least 40–50 per cent (Velikonja *et al.*, 2010; Warriner *et al.*, 2003). Post-traumatic stress disorder is also now recognized as one of the many emotional sequelae of TBI (McMillan *et al.*, 2003). The incidence of mood disorders appears to be consistent regardless of the severity of injury suggestive that non-neurological factors underpin these emotional disturbances (Bowen *et al.*, 1998; Demakis *et al.*, 2007; Rush *et al.*, 2006). Even so, it is important to note that many symptoms of depression and anxiety, including poor concentration, psychomotor slowing, fatigue and sleep disturbance, may also reflect organic brain changes (Fleminger *et al.*, 2003). Thus, cross sectional studies may confound differences in mood disorders across severity. For example, those with greater insight associated with milder injuries may report more symptoms as may those with more severe injuries who demonstrate organic features that may be mistaken for depression.

Of concern is the general trend for mood disorders to increase with time. For example, where depression has been examined within the first year post-injury, the incidence rate has been estimated at around 25 per cent (Bombardier *et al.*, 2010; Demakis *et al.*, 2007; Jorge *et al.*, 1993; Kersel *et al.*, 2001) but this rises to 40–50 per cent or more in studies that include people who have had their injuries for several years (Kreutzer *et al.*, 2001; Velikonja *et al.*, 2010). Premorbid psychiatric disturbance is an important risk factor for later disturbance, but in the majority of cases anxiety and depression emerge as new disorders following the injury (Gould *et al.*, 2011; Whelan-Goodinson *et al.*, 2010).

Denial and anger may masquerade as, or else exacerbate, lack of insight and loss of emotional control in the acute stages (Crossen, 1987). However, anxiety and depression at 1 year post are clearly predicted by the extent of disability experienced at 6 months (Schönberger *et al.*, 2011) and these increase as insight improves (Godfrey *et al.*, 1993; Wallace & Bogner, 2000), conversely, with higher rates of disability, there may be reduced anxiety and depression, suggestive of the ongoing protective effects of anasognosia (Demakis *et al.*, 2010). Emotional distress is a serious concern for those who survive severe TBI, especially for those who do not have any close confidants (Kinsella *et al.*, 1988). Depression is a significant predictor of functional outcome (Bowen *et al.*, 1998; Malec *et al.*, 2004; Rush *et al.*, 2006) and, indeed, presages a high incidence of suicide relative to the general community (Fleminger *et al.*, 2003; Simpson & Tate, 2007).

Premorbid personality

The premorbid personality of people with TBI will obviously influence the manner in which they present post-trauma. Pre-existing psychiatric conditions, personality difficulties or lack of social skills will create additional obstacles to successful rehabilitation and reintegration. Nevertheless, it is important not to overstate the extent to which premorbid factors account for post-traumatic personality problems. For example, it has been argued that youth at risk of TBI tend to have poor social adjustment premorbidly, as evidenced by learning difficulties, criminal behaviour and drug and alcohol abuse (Bond, 1984; Brooks, 1994; Levin *et al.*, 1982; Rimel *et al.*, 1982). However, studies that have attempted to examine pre-injury personality variables (e.g. by asking a significant other to complete a personality inventory regarding their injured relative's premorbid personality as close to the time of injury as possible: Kurtz *et al.*, 1998; Malec *et al.*, 2004; Rush *et al.*, 2006; Tate, 2003) have uniformly indicated that the profile of the TBI group under examination was essentially within normal limits. Similarly, incidence estimates of maladjustment vary widely but are not clearly inflated relative to community estimates. For example, estimates of the incidence of levels of hazardous drinking pre-injury in young adults (the peak group for sustaining severe TBI) have been variously estimated between 18 and 66 per cent (Corrigan, 1995; Hall *et al.*, 1994; Ponsford *et al.*, 2007; Rimel *et al.*, 1982) which is similar to the general population in this age group (40–65 per cent) (Australian Institute of Health and Welfare, 2011; Substance Abuse and Mental Health

Services Adminstration, 2010). Between 9 and 36 per cent of head-injured subjects have used illicit drugs pre-injury (Kreutzer *et al.*, 1991; Ponsford *et al.*, 2007) which is, again, consistent with population based estimates. Furthermore, when compared to a demographically matched control group, no differences in the incidence of drug and alcohol abuse in people with TBI has been found (Ponsford *et al.*, 2007). Between 9–30 per cent of people with TBI have been reported to have criminal convictions or reported delinquency (Hall *et al.*, 1994; Kreutzer *et al.*, 1995; Tate, 1998). The incidence of these behaviours in the comparable cohort for these patients have not been reported but risk-taking behaviour is generally high in this particular age group as evidenced by the finding that two-thirds of the general population with criminal convictions are under the age of 30 (Zawitz, 1988; as cited in Kreutzer *et al.*, 1995).

Thus it can be safely stated that while a minority of TBI subjects have premorbid social adjustment difficulties and pre-existing psychiatric conditions that put them at risk for ongoing difficulties post-TBI, this does not account for the extent of personality problems seen post-morbidly. Indeed, attempts to establish a relationship between premorbid personality variables and either post-traumatic behaviour change or psychosocial outcome have been unsuccessful (Tate, 1997, 2003). In addition, efforts to dismiss post-morbid personality change on the basis of premorbid characteristics are greatly diminished by the finding that when appropriate matched control groups are used, e.g. sibling controls (Tate *et al.*, 1991); orthopedic controls (Snow, 1995); vocation and education matched controls (McDonald, 1992, 1993; McDonald & Van Sommers, 1993) group differences in facets of personality and social communicative behaviour emerge strongly.

As another slant on the role of premorbid personality in the post-traumatic picture, it has been suggested that post-traumatic personality change, particularly the less severe forms, reflects an exaggeration of premorbid personality (e.g. Crossen, 1987; Jarvie, 1954; Lishman, 1990) but, once again, investigation of post-traumatic personality change indicates qualitative rather than quantitative differences (Kurtz *et al.*, 1998; Tate, 2003).

Communication disorders

Although aphasia is infrequent in severe TBI, loss of communication skills is not. Unlike many aphasic patients who are observed to communicate better than they can talk, TBI patients appear to have problems in the reverse (Holland, 1984). Communication problems following TBI are variable. Firstly, many people with TBI have been described as over talkative (Hagan, 1984; Milton *et al.*, 1984; Milton & Wertz, 1986) but inefficient (Hartley & Jensen, 1992) drifting from topic to topic (Snow *et al.*, 1986), making tangential and irrelevant comments (Prigatano *et al.*, 1986).

Alternatively, some patients are impoverished in the amount and variety of language produced (Chapman *et al.*, 1992; Ehrlich, 1988; Hartley & Jensen, 1991; Hartley & Jensen, 1992), their conversational style characterized by slow, frequently incomplete responses, numerous pauses and a reliance on set expressions (Thomsen, 1975). Comprehension of conversational language may also be affected, particularly long or complex utterances (Thomsen, 1975) or conversational inference and innuendo (McDonald, 1992, 1993; McDonald & Pearce, 1995, 1996; McDonald & Van Sommers, 1993; Pearce *et al.*, 1998). Conversational style may fail to acknowledge important social requirements as suggested by insensitivity to others, self-focused conversation without interest in other people, immature or inappropriate humour, frequent interruptions, blunt manner, overly familiar and disinhibited remarks or advances and inappropriate levels of self-disclosure (Crossen, 1987; Flanagan *et al.*, 1995; Milton & Wertz, 1986; Prigatano, 1986).

Cognitive and psychosocial sequelae of TBI play a major role in the manifestation of these disorders and are implicated in their remediation. Having reviewed the nature of these neuropsychological and psychosocial parameters in this chapter, we are now well placed to examine different approaches to the assessment and management of communication disorders after TBI and this is the focus of the remainder of this book.

Notes

1 For those interested in this topic, a comprehensive account of experimental approaches to attentional processes can be found in Baddeley (1990) and specifically as this relates to head injury in Anderson & Knight (2010); Ponsford & Kinsella (1992); van Zomeren & Brouwer (1987).
2 It is frequently assumed that Digit Span Backwards, i.e. the ability to repeat a series of digits in reverse order to that presented, is an accurate reflection of working memory. However, Digit Span Backwards does not readily discriminate people with TBI from those without, whereas Digit Span total score (forward and backwards) appears to be a good index of span and is sensitive to TBI (Mathias & Wheaton, 2007).
3 In N-back tasks the participant is presented with a temporal stream of stimuli and is required to make a decision as to whether a given stimulus matches a target in events prior.

References

Alexander, M. P., Benson, D. F. & Stuss, D. T. (1989). Frontal lobes and language. *Brain and Language, 37*, 656–691.
Anderson, C. V., Bigler, E. D. & Blatter, D. D. (1995). Frontal lobe lesions, diffuse damage and neuropsychological functioning in traumatic brain-injured patients. *Journal of Clinical and Experimental Neuropsychology, 17*(6), 900–908.
Anderson, J. W. & Schmitter-Edgecombe, M. (2011). Recovery of time estimation following moderate to severe traumatic brain injury. *Neuropsychology, 25*(1), 36–44.
Anderson, T. M. & Knight, R. G. (2010). The long-term effects of traumatic brain injury on the coordinative function of the central executive. *Journal of Clinical and Experimental Neuropsychology, 32*(10), 1074–1082.
Andrewes, D. (2001). *Neuropsychology: From Theory to Practice*. Hove and New York: Psychology Press.

Aron, A. R. & Poldrack, R. A. (2005). The cognitive neuroscience of response inhibition: relevance for genetic research in attention-deficit/hyperactivity disorder. *Biological Psychiatry, 57*(11), 1285–1292.

Ashman, T. A., Cantor, J. B., Gordon, W. A., Spielman, L., Egan, M., Ginsberg, A., Engmann, C., Dijkers, M. & Flanagan, S. (2008). Objective measurement of fatigue following traumatic brain injury. *The Journal of Head Trauma Rehabilitation, 23*(1), 33–40.

Asloun, S., Soury, S., Couillet, J., Giroire, J. M., Joseph, P. A., Mazaux, J. M. & Azouvi, P. (2008). Interactions between divided attention and working-memory load in patients with severe traumatic brain injury. *Journal of Clinical and Experimental Neuropsychology, 30*(4), 481–490.

Australian Institute of Health and Welfare (2011). *2010 National Drug Strategy Household Survey Report*. Drug statistics series no. 25. Cat. no. PHE 145. Canberra: AIHW.

Baddeley, A. (1966). The capacity for generating information by randomisation. *Quarterly Journal of Experimental Psychology, 18*, 119–129.

——(1986). *Working Memory*. Oxford: Oxford University Press.

——(1990). *Human Memory. Theory and Practice*. Hove and London: Lawrence Erlbaum Associates.

Baddeley, A. & Hitch, G. (1974). Working memory. In G. Bower (Ed.), *Recent Advances in Learning and Motivation* (Vol. 8). New York: Academic Press.

Baddeley, A., Harris, J., Sunderland, A., Watts, K. P. & Wilson, B. A. (1987). Closed head injury and memory. In H. S. Levin, J. Grafman & H. M. Eisenberg, (Eds), *Neurobehavioural Recovery from Head Injury*. New York: Oxford University Press.

Barbizet, J. (1970). *Human Memory and Its Pathology*. San Francisco, CA: Freeman.

Bechara, A., Damasio, A., Damasio, H. & Anderson, S. W. (1994). Insensitivity to future consequences following damage to human prefrontal cortex. *Cognition, 50*(1–3), 7–15.

Bechara, A., Damasio, H., Tranel, D. & Damasio, A. R. (1997). Deciding advantageously before knowing the advantageous strategy. *Science, 275*(5304), 1293–1294.

Bechara, A., Damasio, H. & Damasio, A. R. (2000). Emotion, decision making and the orbitofrontal cortex. *Cerebral Cortex, 10*(3), 295–307.

Beldarrain, M. G., Grafman, J., Pascual-Leone, A. & Garcia-Monco, J. C. (1999). Procedural learning is impaired in patients with prefrontal lesions. *Neurology, 52*(9), 1853–1860.

Belmont, A., Agar, N. & Azouvi, P. (2009). Subjective fatigue, mental effort, and attention deficits after severe traumatic brain injury. *Neurorehabilitation and Neural Repair, 23*(9), 939–944.

Benton, A. (1973). The measurement of aphasic disorders. In A. Caceres Velasquez (Ed.), *Aspectos patologicos del lengage*. Lima: Centro Neuropsicologico.

Bibby, H. & McDonald, S. (2005). Theory of mind after traumatic brain injury. *Neuropsychologia, 43*(1), 99–114.

Bigler, E. D. (2007). Anterior and middle cranial fossa in traumatic brain injury: relevant neuroanatomy and neuropathology in the study of neuropsychological outcome. *Neuropsychology, 21*(5), 515–531.

Blackstein, H., Valkil, E. & Hoofien, D. (1993). Impaired learning in patients with closed head injuries: an analysis of components of the acquisition process. *Neuropsychology, 7*(4), 530–535.

Blair, R. J. R. & Cipolotti, L. (2000). Impaired social response reversal: a case of 'acquired sociopathy'. *Brain, 123*, 1122–1141.

Boake, C., Freelands, J. C., Ringholz, G. M., Nance, M. L. & Edwards, K. E. (1995). Awareness of memory loss after severe closed head injury. *Brain Injury, 9*(3), 273–283.

Bombardier, C. H., Fann, J. R., Temkin, N. R., Esselman, P. C., Barber, J. & Dikmen, S. S. (2010). Rates of major depressive disorder and clinical outcomes following traumatic brain injury. *JAMA: Journal of the American Medical Association, 303*(19), 1938–1945.

Bond, M. R. (1984). The psychiatry of closed head injury. In N. Brooks (Ed.), *Closed Head Injury.* Oxford: Oxford University Press.

Bowen, A., Neumann, V., Conner, M., Tennant, A. & Chamberlain, A. (1998). Mood disorders following traumatic brain injury: identifying the extent of the problem and the people at risk. *Brain Injury, 12*, 177–190.

Brooks, D. N. (1994). *Closed Head Injury: Psychological, Social and Family Consequences.* Oxford: Oxford University Press.

Brooks, D. N. & McKinlay, W. (1983). Personality and behavioural change after severe blunt head injury – a relative's view. *Journal of Neurology, Neurosurgery & Psychiatry, 46*(4), 336–344.

Brooks, D. N., Campsie, L., Symington, C., Beattie, A. & McKinlay, W. (1986). The five year outcome of severe blunt head injury: a relative's view. *Journal of Neurology, Neurosurgery & Psychiatry, 49*(7), 764–770.

Brooks, N., Campsie, L., Symington, C., Beattie, A. & McKinlay, W. (1987). The effects of severe head injury on patient and relative within seven years of injury. *Journal of Head Trauma Rehabilitation, 2*(3), 1–13.

Brouwer, W. H. & Van Wolffelaar, P. C. (1985). Sustained attention and sustained effort after closed head injury. *Cortex, 21*, 111–119.

Bush, G., Frazier, J. A., Rauch, S. L., Seidman, L. J., Whalen, P. J., Jenike, M. A., Rosen, B. R. & Biederman, J. (1999). Anterior cingulate cortex dysfunction in attention-deficit/hyperactivity disorder revealed by fMRI and the counting stroop. *Biological Psychiatry, 45*(12), 1542–1552.

Cabeza, R., Grady, C. L., Nyberg, L., McIntosh, A. R., Tulving, E., Kapur, S., Jennings, J. M., Houle,S. & Craik, F. I. M. (1997). Age-related differences in neural activity during memory encoding and retrieval: a positron emission tomography study. *Journal of Neuroscience, 17*(1), 391–400.

Canavan, A., Janota, I. & Schurr, P. H. (1985). Luria's frontal lobe syndrome: psychological and anatomical considerations. *Journal of Neurology, Neurosurgery and Psychiatry, 48*, 1049–1053.

Cattran, C. J., Oddy, M., Wood, R. L. & Moir, J. F. (2011). Post-injury personality in the prediction of outcome following severe acquired brain injury. *Brain Injury, 25*(11), 1035–1046.

Channon, S. & Watts, M. (2003). Pragmatic language interpretation after closed head injury: relationship to executive functioning. *Cognitive Neuropsychiatry, 8*(4), 243–260.

Chapman, S. B., Culhane, K. A., Levine, H. S., Harward, H., Mendelsohn, D., Ewing-Cobbs, L. Fletcher, J. M. & Bruce, D. (1992). Narrative discourse after closed head injury in children and adolescents. *Brain and Language, 43*, 42–65.

Chiou, K. S., Carlson, R. A., Arnett, P. A., Cosentino, S. A. & Hillary, F. G. (2011). Metacognitive monitoring in moderate and severe traumatic brain injury. *Journal of the International Neuropsychological Society, 17*(4), 720–731.

Cooke, D. L. & Kauslen, D. H. (1995). Content memory and temporal memory for actions in survivors of traumatic brain injury. *Journal of Clinical and Experimental Neuropsychology, 17*(1), 90–99.

Corrigan, J. D. (1995). The nature and extent of substance abuse problems in persons with traumatic brain injury. *The Journal of Head Trauma Rehabilitation, 10*(3), 29–46.

Coste, C., Agar, N., Petitfour, E., Quinette, P., Guillery-Girard, B., Azouvi, P. & Piolino, P. (2011). Exploring the roles of the executive and short-term feature-binding functions in retrieval of retrograde autobiographical memories in severe traumatic brain injury. *Cortex: A Journal Devoted to the Study of the Nervous System and Behavior, 47*(7), 771–786.

Crawford, J. R., Sutherland, D. & Garthwaite, P. H. (2008). On the reliability and standard errors of measurement of contrast measures from the D-KEFS. *Journal of the International Neuropsychological Society, 14*, 1069–1073.

Crossen, B. (1987). Treatment of interpersonal deficits for head-trauma patients in inpatient rehabilitation settings. *The Clinical Neuropsychologist, 1*(4), 335–352.

Daigneault, S., Braun, C. M. J. & Whitaker, H. A. (1992). An empirical test of two opposing theoretical models of prefrontal lobe function. *Brain and Cognition, 19*, 48–71.

Damasio, A. R., Tranel, D. & Damasio, H. (1991). Somatic markers and the guidance of behavior: theory and preliminary testing. In H. S. Levin, H. M. Eisenberg & A. L. Benton (Eds), *Frontal Lobe Function and Dysfunction* (pp. 217–229). New York: Oxford University Press, Inc.

Darby, D. & Walsh, K. W. (2005). *Walsh's Neuropsychology: A Clinical Approach* (5th edn). Edinburgh: Elsevier.

de la Plata, C. D. M., Garces, J., Kojori, E. S., Grinnan, J., Krishnan, K., Pidikiti, R., Spence, J., Devous Sr., M. D., Moore, C., McColl, R., Madden, C. & Diaz-Arrastia, R. (2011). Deficits in functional connectivity of hippocampal and frontal lobe circuits after traumatic axonal injury. *Archives of Neurology, 68*(1), 74–84.

de Sousa, A., McDonald, S., Rushby, J., Li, S., Dimoska, A. & James, C. (2010). Why don't you feel how I feel? Insight into the absence of empathy after severe Traumatic Brain Injury. *Neuropsychologia, 48*, 3585–3595.

DeFillipis, N. A., McCampbell, E. & Rogers, P. (1979). Development of a booklet form of a category test: normative and validity data. *Journal of Experimental and Clinical Neuropsychology, 1*, 339–342.

DeJong, J. & Donders, J. (2009). A confirmatory factor analysis of the California Verbal Learning Test – Second Edition (CVLT-II) in a traumatic brain injury sample. *Assessment, 16*(4), 328–336.

Delis, D. C., Kramer, J. H., Kaplan, E. & Ober, B. A. (1987). *Californian Verbal Learning Test: Adult Version*. San Antonia, TX: The Psychological Corporation.

Delis, D. E., Kramer, J. H., Kaplan, E. & Ober, B. E. (2000). *The Californian Verbal Learning Test – Second Edition*. New York: Pearson.

Delis, D. C., Kaplan, E. & Kramer, J. H. (2001). *Delis-Kaplan Executive Function System (D-KEFS)*. New York: Harcourt Assessment: The Psychological Corporation.

Della Rocchetta, A. I. & Milner, B. (1993). Strategic search and retrieval inhibition: the role of the frontal lobes. *Neuropsychologia, 31*, 503–524.

DeLuca, J. & Diamond, B. J. (1995). Aneurysm of the anterior communicating artery: a review of neuroanatomical and neuropsychological sequelae. *Journal of Clinical and Experimental Neuropsychology, 17*(1), 100–121.

Demakis, G. J., Hammond, F., Knotts, A., Cooper, D. B., Clement, P., Kennedy, J. & Sawyer, T. (2007). The Personality Assessment Inventory in individuals with Traumatic Brain Injury. *Archives of Clinical Neuropsychology, 22*(1), 123–130.

Demakis, G. J., Hammond, F. M. & Knotts, A. (2010). Prediction of depression and anxiety 1 year after moderate-severe traumatic brain injury. *Applied Neuropsychology, 17*(3), 183–189.

Denmark, J. & Geneinhardt, M. (2002). Anger and its management for survivors of acquired brain injury. *Brain Injury, 16*, 91–108.

Dikmen, S. S., Machamen, J. E. & Temkin, N. R. (1993). Psychosocial outcome in patients with moderate-severe head injury: 2 year follow up. *Brain Injury, 7*, 113–124.

Dikmen, S. S., Machamer, J. E., Winn, H. R. & Temkin, N. R. (1995). Neuropsychological outcome at 1-year post head injury. *Neuropsychology, 9*(1), 80–90.

Dimoska, A., McDonald, S., Kelly, M., Tate, R. L. & Johnstone, S. (2011). A meta-analysis of performance in inhibitory control paradigms in adults with traumatic brain injury (TBI). *Journal of Clinical and Experimental Neuropsychology, 33*, 471–485.

Draper, K., Ponsford, J. & Schönberger, M. (2007). Psychosocial and emotional outcomes 10 years following traumatic brain injury. *Journal of Head Trauma Rehabilitation, 22*(5), 278–287.

Drewe, E. A. (1974). The effect of type and area of brain lesions on Wisconsin Card Sorting Test. *Cortex, 10*(2), 159–170.

Duncan, C. C., Kosmidis, M. H. & Mirsky, A. F. (2005). Closed head injury-related information processing deficits: an event-related potential analysis. *International Journal of Psychophysiology, 58*(2–3), 133–157.

Duncan, J. (1986). Disorganisation of behaviour after frontal lobe damage. *Cognitive Neuropsychology, 3*, 271–290.

Eames, P. (1990). Organic bases of behavioural disorders after traumatic brain injury. In R. L. Wood (Ed.), *Neurobehavioural sequelae of traumatic brain injury*. Bristol, Pennsylvania: Taylor & Francis.

Ehrlich, J. S. (1988). Selective characteristics of narrative discourse in head-injured and normal adults. *Journal of Communication Disorders, 21*, 1–9.

Elsass, L. & Kinsella, G. (1987). Social interaction following severe closed head injury. *Psychological Medicine, 17*(1), 67–78.

Eslinger, P. J. (2008). The frontal lobes: executive, emotional and neurological functions. In P. Marien & J. Abutalebi (Eds), *Neuropsychological Research: A Review*. New York: Psychology Press.

Eslinger, P. J. & Damasio, A. R. (1985). Severe disturbance of higher cognitive function after bilateral frontal ablation: patient EVR. *Neurology, 35*, 1731–1741.

Eslinger, P. J. & Grattan, L. M. (1993). Frontal lobe and frontal-striatal substrates for different forms of human cognitive flexibility. *Neuropsychologia, 31*(1), 17–28.

Fellows, L. K. & Farah, M. J. (2005). Different underlying impairments in decision-making following ventromedial and dorsolateral frontal lobe damage in humans. *Cerebral Cortex, 15*(1), 58–63.

Felmingham, K. L., Baguley, I. J. & Green, A. M. (2004). Effects of diffuse axonal injury on speed of information processing following severe traumatic brain injury. [Comparative Study]. *Neuropsychology, 18*(3), 564–571.

Fernandez-Duque, D., Baird, J. A. & Posner, M. I. (2000). Executive attention and metacognitive regulation. *Consciousness and Cognition, 9*, 288–307.

Flanagan, S., McDonald, S. & Togher, L. (1995). Evaluating social skills following traumatic brain injury: the BRISS as a clinical tool. *Brain Injury, 9*(4), 321–338.

Fleming, J. M., Strong, J. & Ashton, R. (1996). Self-awareness of deficits in adults with traumatic brain injury: how best to measure? *Brain Injury, 10*, 1–15.

Fleminger, S., Oliver, D. L., Williams, W. H. & Evans, J. (2003). The neuropsychiatry of depression after brain injury. *Neuropsychological Rehabilitation, 13*, 65–87.

Fordyce, D. J. & Roueche, J. R. (1986). Changes in perspectives of disability among patients, staff and relatives during rehabilitation of brain injury. *Rehabilitation Psychology, 31*, 217–219.

Fordyce, D. J., Roueche, J. R. & Prigatano, G. P. (1983). Enhanced emotional reactions in chronic head trauma patients. *Journal of Neurology, Neurosurgery & Psychiatry, 46*(7), 620–624.

Fujiwara, E., Schwartz, M. L., Gao, F., Black, S. E. & Levine, B. (2008). Ventral frontal cortex functions and quantified MRI in traumatic brain injury. *Neuropsychologia, 46*(2), 461–474.

Fuster, J. M. (1991). Role of prefrontal cortex in delay tasks: evidence from reversible lesion and unit recording in the monkey. In H. S. Levin, H. M. Eisenberg & A. L. Benton (Eds), *Frontal Lobe Function and Dysfunction* (pp. 59–71). New York: Oxford University Press.

Girgis, M. (1971). The orbital surface of the frontal lobe of the brain. *Acta Psychiatrica Scandinavica, Supplementum, 222*, 1–58.

Godfrey, H. P., Partridge, F. M., Knight, R. G. & Bishara, S. N. (1993). Course of insight disorder and emotional dysfunction following closed head injury: a controlled cross-sectional follow-up study. *Journal of Clinical and Experimental Neuropsychology, 15*(4), 503–515.

Goebel, S., Fischer, R., Ferstl, R. & Mehdorn, H. M. (2009). Normative data and psychometric properties for qualitative and quantitative scoring criteria of the Five-point Test. *The Clinical Neuropsychologist, 23*(4), 675–690.

Goldman-Rakic, P. & Freedman, H. (1991). The circuitry of working memory revealed by anatomy and metabolic imaging. In H. S. Levin, H. M. Eisenberg & A. L. Benton (Eds), *Frontal Lobe Function and Dysfunction* (pp. 72–91). New York: Oxford University Press.

Gould, K. R., Ponsford, J. L., Johnston, L. & Schönberger, M. (2011). The nature, frequency and course of psychiatric disorders in the first year after traumatic brain injury: a prospective study. *Psychological Medicine: A Journal of Research in Psychiatry and the Allied Sciences, 41*(10), 2099–2109.

Gronwall, D. (1977). Paced auditory serial-addition task: a measure of recovery from concussion. *Perceptual and Motor Skills, 44*, 367–373.

——(1987). Advances in the assessment of attention and information processing after head injury. In H. S. Levin, J. Grafman & H. M. Eisenberg (Eds), *Neurobehavioural Recovery from Head Injury* (pp. 355–371). Oxford: Oxford University Press.

Gronwall, D. & Sampson, H. (1974). *The Psychological Effects of Concussion*. Auckland: University Press/Oxford University Press.

Hagan, C. (1984). Language disorders in head trauma. In A. Holland (Ed.), *Language Disorders in Adults*. San Diego: College Hill Press.

Hall, K., Karzmark, P., Stevens, M., Englander, J., O'Hare, P. & Wright, J. (1994). Family stressors in traumatic brain injury: a two year follow-up. *Archives of Physical Medicine and Rehabilitation, 75*, 876–884.

Hanks, R. A., Temkin, N., Machamer, J. & Dikmen, S. S. (1999). Emotional and behavioural adjustment after traumatic brain injury. *Archives of Physical Medicine and Rehabilitation, 80*, 991–997.

Hart, T., Giovannetti, T., Montgomery, M. W. & Schwartz, M. F. (1998). Awareness of errors in naturalistic action after traumatic brain injury. *Journal of Head Trauma Rehabilitation, 13*, 16–28.

Hartley, L. L. & Jensen, P. J. (1991). Narrative and procedural discourse after closed head injury. *Brain Injury, 5*, 267–285.

——(1992). Three discourse profiles of closed-head-injury speakers: theoretical and clinical implications. *Brain Injury, 6*, 271–282.

Haut, M. W. & Shutty, M.S. (1992). Patterns of verbal learning after closed head injury. *Neuropsychology, 6*, 51–58.

Heaton, R. K., Chelune, G. J., Talley, J. L., Kay, G. G. & Curtiss, G. (1993). *Wisconsin Card Sorting Test*. Philadelphia: Psychological Assessment Resources.

Holland, A. L. (1984). When is aphasia aphasia? The problem of closed head injury. In R. W. Brookshire (Ed.), *Clinical Aphasiology* (Vol. 14, pp. 345–349). Minneapolis: BRK Publishers.

Hunkin, N. M., Parkin, A.J., Bradley, V.A., Burrows, E. H., Aldich, F. K., Jansain, A. & Burdon-Cooper, C. (1995). Focal retrograde amnesia following closed head injury: a case study and theoretical account. *Neuropsychologia, 33*(4), 509–523.

Janowsky, J. S., Shimamura, A. P. & Squire, L. R. (1989). Source memory impairment on patients with frontal lobe lesions. *Neuropsychologia, 27*(8), 1043–1056.

Jarvie, H. F. (1954). Frontal lobe wounds causing disinhibition. A study of six cases. *Journal of Neurology, Neurosurgery and Psychiatry, 17*, 14–32.

Jennett, B., Snoek, J., Bond, M. R. & Brooks, D. N. (1981). Disability after severe head injury: observations on the use of the Glasgow Coma Scale. *Journal of Neurology, Neurosurgery and Psychiatry, 44*, 285–293.

Johnstone, B., Hexum, C. & Ashkanazi, G. (1995). Extent of cognitive decline in traumatic brain injury based on an estimate of premorbid intelligence. *Brain Injury, 9*, 377–384.

Jorge, R. E., Robinson, R. G. & Arndt, S. (1993). Are there symptoms that are specific for depressed mood in patients with traumatic brain injury? *Journal of Nervous & Mental Disease, 181*, 91–99.

Kaitaro, T., Koskinen, S. & Kaipio, M. L. (1995). Neuropsychological problems in everyday life: a 5 year follow up study of young severely closed head injured patients. *Brain Injury, 9*(7), 713–727.

Kant, R., Duffy, J. D. & Pivovarnik, A. (1998). Prevalence of apathy following head injury. *Brain Injury, 12*(1), 87–92.

Kennedy, J. E., Clement, P. F. & Curtiss, G. (2003). WAIS-III processing speed index scores after TBI: the influence of working memory, psychomotor speed and perceptual processing. *The Clinical Neuropsychologist, 17*(3), 303–307.

Kersel, D. A., Marsh, N. V., Havill, J. H. & Sleigh, J. W. (2001). Psychosocial functioning during the year following severe traumatic brain injury. *Brain Injury, 15*(8), 683–696.

Kim, S. H., Manes, F., Kosier, T., Baruah, S. & Robinson, R. G. (1999). Irritability following traumatic brain injury. *Journal of Nervous and Mental Disease, 187*, 327–335.

Kimberg, D. & Farah, M. (1993). A unified account of cognitive impairment following frontal lobe damage: the role of working memory in complex, organised behaviour. *Journal of Experimental Psychology: General, 122*, 411–428.

Kime, S. K., Lamb, D. & Wilson, B. (1996). Use of a comprehensive programme of external cueing to enhance procedural memory in a patient with dense amnesia. *Brain Injury, 10*(1), 17–25.

Kinch, J. & McDonald, S. (2001). Traumatic brain injury and prospective memory: an examination of the influences of executive function and retrospective memory. *Brain Impairment, 2*, 119–130.

Kinnunen, K. M., Greenwood, R., Powell, J. H., Leech, R., Hawkins, P. C., Bonnelle, V., Patel, M. C., Counsell, S. J. & Sharp, D. J. (2011). White matter damage and cognitive impairment after traumatic brain injury. *Brain: A Journal of Neurology, 134*(2), 449–463.

Kinsella, G., Moran, C., Ford, B. & Ponsford, J. (1988). Emotional disorder and its assessment within the severe head-injured population. *Psychological Medicine, 18*, 57–63.

Kinsella, G., Packer, S. & Olver, J. (1991). Maternal reporting of behaviour following very severe blunt head injury. *Journal of Neurology, Neurosurgery & Psychiatry, 54*(5), 422–426.

Knight, R. G. & O'Hagan, K. (2009). Autobiographical memory in long-term survivors of severe traumatic brain injury. *Journal of Clinical and Experimental Neuropsychology, 31*(5), 575–583.

Knight, R. T. (1991). Evoked potential studies of attention capacity in human frontal lobe lesions. In H. S. Levin, H. M. Eisenberg & A. L. Benton (Eds), *Frontal Lobe Function and Dysfunction*. New York: Oxford University Press.

Kopelman, M., Wilson, M. & Baddeley, A. (1991). *The Autobiographical Memory Interview*. Suffolk, England: Thames Valley Test Company.

Kraus, M. F., Susmaras, T., Caughlin, B. P., Walker, C. J., Sweeney, J. A. & Little, D. M. (2007). White matter integrity and cognition in chronic traumatic brain injury: a diffusion tensor imaging study. *Brain: A Journal of Neurology, 130*(10), 2508–2519.

Kreutzer, J. S., Wehlman, P. H., Harris, J. A., Burns, C. T. & Young, H. F. (1991). Substance abuse and crime patterns among persons with traumatic brain injury referred for supported employment. *Brain Injury, 5*, 177–187.

Kreutzer, J. S., Marwitz, J. H. & Witol, A. D. (1995). Inter-relationship between crime substance abuse and aggressive behaviours among persons with traumatic brain injury. *Brain Injury, 9*(8), 757–768.

Kreutzer, J. S., Seel, R. T. & Gourley, E. (2001). The prevalence and symptom rates of depression after traumatic brain injury: a comprehensive examination. *Brain Injury, 15*, 563–576.

Kurtz, J. E., Putnam, S. H. & Stone, C. (1998). Stability of normal personality traits after traumatic brain injury. *Journal of Head Trauma Rehabilitation, 13*, 1–14.

Lane-Brown, A. T. & Tate, R. L. (2009). Measuring apathy after traumatic brain injury: psychometric properties of the Apathy Evaluation Scale and the Frontal Systems Behavior Scale. *Brain Injury, 23*, 999–1007.

Levin, H. S., Benton, A. L. & Grossman, R. G. (1982). *Neurobehavioural Consequences of Closed Head Trauma*. New York: Oxford University Press.

Levin, H. S., High, W. M., Jr., Meyers, C. A., Von Laufen, A., Hayden, M. E. & Eisenberg, H. M. (1985). Impairment of remote memory after closed head injury. *Journal of Neurology, Neurosurgery & Psychiatry, 48*, 556–563.

Levin, H. S., Goldstein, F. C., Williams, D. H. & Eisenberg, H. M. (1991). The contribution of frontal lobe lesions to the neurobehavioral outcome of closed head injury. In H. S. Levin & H. M. Eisenberg (Eds), *Frontal Lobe Function and Dysfunction*. (pp. 318–338). London: Oxford University Press.

Levine, B., Black, S. E., Cabeza, R., Sinden, M., McIntosh, A. R., Toth, J. P., Tulving, E. & Stuss, D. T. (1998). Episodic memory and the self in a case of isolated retrograde amnesia. *Brain: A Journal of Neurology, 121*(10), 1951–1973.

Levine, B., Black, S. E., Cheung, G., Campbell, A., O'Toole, C. & Schwartz, M. L. (2005). Gambling task performance in traumatic brain injury: relationships to injury severity, atrophy, lesion location, and cognitive and psychosocial outcome. *Cognitive and Behavioral Neurology, 18*(1), 45–54.

Levy, M. L., Cummings, J. L., Fairbanks, L. A., Masterman, D., Miller, B. L., Craig, A. H., Paulsen, J. S. & Litvan, I. (1998). Apathy is not depression. *The Journal of Neuropsychiatry and Clinical Neurosciences, 10*(3), 314–319.

Lezak, M. D. (1978). Living with the characterologically altered brain-injured patient. *Journal of Clinical Psychology, 39,* 592–598.

——(1995). *Neuropsychological Assessment* (3rd edn) (Vol. xviii). New York: Oxford University Press.

Lishman, W. A. (1990). *Organic Pyschiatry.* Oxford: Blackwell Scientific Publications.

Little, D. M., Kraus, M. F., Joseph, J., Geary, E. K., Susmaras, T., Zhou, X. J., Pliskin, N. & Gorelick, P. B. (2010). Thalamic integrity underlies executive dysfunction in traumatic brain injury. *Neurology, 74*(7), 558–564.

Logan, G. D. (1994). *On The Ability to Inhibit Thought and Action: A Users' Guide to the Stop Signal Paradigm.* San Diego, CA: Academic Press.

Luria, A. R. (1973). *The Working Brain.* London: Allen Lane: The Penguin Press.

——(1976). *Higher Cortical Functions in Man.* London: Basic Books.

Malec, J. F., Brown, A. W. & Moessner, A. M. (2004). Personality factors and injury severity in the prediction of early and late traumatic brain injury outcomes. *Rehabilitation Psychology, 49,* 55–61.

Markowitsch, H. J., Calabrese, P., Liess, J., Haupts, M., Durwen, H. F. & Gehlen, W. (1993). Retrograde amnesia after traumatic injury of the fronto-temporal cortex. *Journal of Neurology, Neurosurgery & Psychiatry, 56*(9), 988–992.

Marsh, N. V. & Knight, R. G. (1991). Behavioral assessment of social competence following severe head injury. *Journal of Clinical and Experimental Neuropsychology, 13*(5), 729–740.

Mateer, C. A., Sohlberg, M. M. & Crinean, J. (1987). Focus on clinical research: perceptions of memory function in individuals with closed-head injury. *Journal of Head Trauma Rehabilitation, 2,* 74–84.

Mathias, J. L. & Wheaton, P. (2007). Changes in attention and information-processing speed following severe traumatic brain injury: a meta-analytic review. *Neuropsychology, 21,* 212–223.

Mattioli, F., Grassi, F., Perani, D., Cappa, S. F., Miozzo, A. & Fazio, F. (1996). Persistent post-traumatic retrograde amnesia: a neuropsychological and (18F)FDG PET study. *Cortex: A Journal Devoted to the Study of the Nervous System and Behavior, 32*(1), 121–129.

McAvinue, L., O'Keeffe, F., McMackin, D. & Robertson, I. H. (2005). Impaired sustained attention and error awareness in traumatic brain injury: implications for insight. *Neuropsychological Rehabilitation, 15*(5), 569–587.

McDaniel, M. A. & Einstein, G. O. (2000). Strategic and automatic processes in prospective memory retrieval: a multiprocess framework. *Applied Cognitive Psychology, 14,* S127–S144.

McDaniel, M. A., Guynn, M. J., Einstein, G. O. & Breneiser, J. (2005). Cue-focused and reflexive-associative processes in prospective memory retrieval. *Journal of Experimental Psychology: Learning, Memory, and Cognition, 30,* 605–614.

McDonald, S. (1992). Differential pragmatic language loss after closed head injury: ability to comprehend conversational implicature. *Applied Psycholinguistics, 13*(3), 295–312.

——(1993). Pragmatic language skills after closed head injury: ability to meet the informational needs of the listener. *Brain and Language, 44*(1), 28–46.

McDonald, S. & Van Sommers, P. (1993). Pragmatic language skills after closed head injury: ability to negotiate requests. *Cognitive Neuropsychology, 10*(4), 297–315.

McDonald, S. & Pearce, S. (1995). The 'dice' game: a new test of pragmatic language skills after closed-head injury. *Brain Injury, 9*(3), 255–271.

——(1996). Clinical insights into pragmatic theory: frontal lobe deficits and sarcasm. *Brain and Language, 53*(1), 81–104.

McFarland, C. P. & Glisky, E. L. (2009). Frontal lobe involvement in a task of time-based prospective memory. *Neuropsychologia, 47*(7), 1660–1669.

McKinlay, W. W., Brooks, D. N., Bond, M. R., Martinage, D. P. & Marshall, M. M. (1981). The short-term outcome of severe blunt head injury as reported by relatives of the injured persons. *Journal of Neurology, Neurosurgery & Psychiatry, 44*(6), 527–533.

McKinlay, W. W., Brooks, D. N. & Bond, M. R. (1983). Post-concussional symptoms, financial compensation and outcome of severe blunt head injury. *Journal of Neurology, Neurosurgery & Psychiatry, 46*(12), 1084–1091.

McMillan, T. M., Williams, W. H. & Bryant, R. (2003). Post-traumatic stress disorder and traumatic brain injury: a review of causal mechanisms, assessment, and treatment. *Neuropsychological Rehabilitation, 13*(1–2), 149–164.

Mesulam, M. M. (1990). Large scale neurocognitive networks and disrupted processing for attention, language and memory. *Annals of Neurology, 28*, 597–613.

Milders, M., Fuchs, S. & Crawford, J. R. (2003). Neuropsychological impairments and changes in emotional and social behaviour following severe traumatic brain injury. *Journal of Clinical & Experimental Neuropsychology, 25*(2), 157–172.

Millis, S. R. & Ricken, J. H. (1994). Verbal learning patterns in moderate and severe traumatic brain injury. *Journal of Clinical and Experimental Neuropsychology, 16*(4), 498–507.

Milner, B. (1971). Interhemispheric differences in the localisation of psychological processes in man. *British Medical Bulletin, 27*, 272–277.

Milton, S. B. & Wertz, R. T. (1986). Management of persisting communication deficits in patients with traumatic brain injury. In B. P. Uzzell & Y. Gross (Eds), *Clinical Neuropsychology of Intervention*. Boston: Martinus Nijhoff Publishing.

Milton, S. B., Prutting, C. A. & Binder, G. M. (1984). Appraisal of communication competence in head injured adults. In R. W. Brookshire (Ed.), *Clinical Aphasiology* (Vol. 14, pp. 114–123). Minneapolis: BRK Publishers.

Mishkin, M. & Appemzeller, T. (1987). The anatomy of memory. *Scientific American, 256*, 62–71.

Nigg, J. T. (2000). On inhibition/disinhibition in developmental psychopathology: views from cognitive and personality psychology and a working inhibition taxonomy. *Psychological Bulletin, 126*(2), 220–246.

Norman, D. & Shallice, T. (1986). Attention to action: willed and automatic control of behaviour. In R. Davidson, G. Schwartz & D. Shapiro (Eds), *Consciousness and Self-regulation. Advances in Research and Theory* (Vol. 4, pp. 1–18). New York: Plenum Press.

O'Keeffe, F., Dockree, P., Moloney, P., Carton, S. & Robertson, I. (2007). Characterising error-awareness of attentional lapses and inhibitory control failures in patients with traumatic brain injury. *Experimental Brain Research, 180*(1), 59–67.

Oddy, M., Humphrey, M. & Uttley, D. (1978). Stresses upon the relatives of head-injured patients. *British Journal of Psychiatry, 133*, 507–513.

Oddy, M. & Humphrey, M. (1980). Social recovery during the year following severe head injury. *Journal of Neurology, Neurosurgery and Psychiatry, 43*, 798–802.

Oddy, M., Coughlan, T., Tyerman, A. & Jenkins, D. (1985). Social adjustment after closed head injury: a further follow-up seven years after injury. *Journal of Neurology, Neurosurgery & Psychiatry, 48*(6), 564–568.

Osterrieth, P. (1944). Le test de copie d'une figure complexe. *Archives de Psychologie, 30*, 206–356.

Ownsworth, T. & Fleming, J. (2005). The relative importance of metacognitive skills, emotional status, and executive function in psychosocial adjustment following acquired brain injury. *Journal of Head Trauma Rehabilitation, 20*(4), 315–332.

Ownsworth, T. L., Fleming, J., Strong, J., Radel, M., Chan, W. & Clare, L. (2007). Awareness typologies, long-term emotional adjustment and psychosocial outcomes following acquired brain injury. *Neuropsychological Rehabilitation, 17*, 129–150.

Palacios, E. M., Fernandez-Espejo, D., Junque, C., Sanchez-Carrion, R., Roig, T., Tormos, J. M., Bargallo, N. & Vendrell, P. (2011). Diffusion tensor imaging differences relate to memory deficits in diffuse traumatic brain injury. *BMC Neurology, 11*.

Pavawalla, S. P., Schmitter-Edgecombe, M. & Smith, R. E. (2011). Prospective memory after moderate-to-severe traumatic brain injury: a multinomial modeling approach. *Neuropsychology, 26*(1), 91–101.

Pearce, S., McDonald, S. & Coltheart, M. (1998). Interpreting ambiguous advertisements: the effect of frontal lobe damage. *Brain and Cognition, 38*(2), 150–164.

Petrides, M. (1991). Learning impairments following excisions of the primate frontal cortex. In H. S. Levin, H. M. Eisenberg & A. L. Benton (Eds), *Frontal Lobe Function and Dysfunction.* (pp. 256–274). New York: Oxford University Press.

Phillips, M. L. (2003). Understanding the neurobiology of emotion perception: implications for psychiatry. *British Journal of Psychiatry, 182*(3), 190–192.

Phillips, M. L., Drevets, W. C., Rauch, S. L. & Lane, R. D. (2003). Neurobiology of emotion perception I: the neural basis of normal emotion perception. *Society of Biological Psychiatry, 54*, 504–514.

Piolino, P., Desgranges, B., Manning, L., North, P., Jokic, C. & Eustache, F. (2007). Autobiographical memory, the sense of recollection and executive functions after severe traumatic brain injury. *Cortex: A Journal Devoted to the Study of the Nervous System and Behavior, 43*(2), 176–195.

Ponsford, J. & Kinsella, G. (1991). The use of a rating scale of attentional behaviour. *Clinical and Experimental Neuropsychology, 14*, 822–838.

——(1992). Attention deficits following closed-head injury. *Journal of Clinical and Experimental Neuropsychology, 14*(5), 822–838.

Ponsford, J., Sloan, S. & Snow, P. C. (1995). *Traumatic Brain Injury: Rehabilitation for Everyday Adaptive Living.* Hove: Lawrence Erlbaum Associates.

Ponsford, J., Whelan-Goodinson, R. & Bahar-Fuchs, A. (2007). Alcohol and drug use following traumatic brain injury: a prospective study. *Brain Injury, 21*(13–14), 1385–1392.

Potvin, M. J., Rouleau, I., Audy, J., Charbonneau, S. & Giguère, J. F. (2011). Ecological prospective memory assessment in patients with traumatic brain injury. *Brain Injury, 25*(2), 192–205.

Prigatano, G. P. (1986). Personality and psychosocial consequences of brain injury. In G. P. Prigatano, D. J. Fordyce, H. K. Zeiner, J. R. Roueche, M. Pepping & B. Casewood (Eds), *Neuropsychological Rehabilitation after Brain Injury* (pp. 29–50). Baltimore: John Hopkins University Press.

Prigatano, G. P. & Altman, I. W. (1990). Impaired awareness of behavioural limitations after traumatic brain injury. *Archives of Physical Medication and Rehabilitation, 71*, 1058–1064.

Prigatano, G. P., Roueche, J. R. & Fordyce, D. J. (1986). *Neuropsychological Rehabilitation after Brain Injury.* Baltimore: John Hopkins University Press.

Radford, K. A., Lah, S., Say, M. J. & Miller, L. A. (2011). Validation of a new measure of prospective memory: the Royal Prince Alfred Prospective Memory Test. *The Clinical Neuropsychologist, 25*(1), 127–140.

Raskin, S. (2009). Memory for intentions screening test: psychometric properties and clinical evidence. *Brain Impairment, 10,* 23–33.

Reitan, R. M. (1958). Validity of the Trail Making Test as an indicator of organic brain damage. *Perceptual and Motor Skills, 8,* 271–276.

Rimel, R., Giordani, B., Barth, J. & Jane, J. (1982). Moderate head injury: completing the clinical spectrum of brain trauma. *Neurosurgery, 11,* 344–351.

Robertson, I. H., Ward, T., Ridgeway, V. & Nimmo-Smith, I. (1994). *The Test of Everyday Attention.* Suffolk, England: The Thames Valley Test Company.

Robertson, I. H., Manly, T., Andrade, J., Baddeley, B. T. & Yiend, J. (1997). 'Oops!': performance correlates of everyday attentional failures in traumatic brain injured and normal subjects. *Neuropsychologia, 35*(6), 747–758.

Roche, R. A., Dockree, P. M., Garavan, H., Foxe, J. J., Robertson, I. H. & O'Mara, S. M. (2004). EEG alpha power changes reflect response inhibition deficits after traumatic brain injury (TBI) in humans. *Neuroscience Letters, 362*(1), 1–5.

Rush, B. K., Malec, J. F., Brown, A. W. & Moessner, A. M. (2006). Personality and functional outcome following traumatic brain injury. *Rehabilitation Psychology, 51*(3), 257–264.

Saver, J. L. & Damasio, A. R. (1991). Preserved access and processing of social knowledge in a patient with acquired sociopathy due to ventromedial frontal damage. *Neuropsychologia, 29,* 1241–1249.

Schmitter-Edgecombe, M. & Rueda, A. (2008). Time estimation and episodic memory following traumatic brain injury. *Journal of Clinical and Experimental Neuropsychology, 30,* 1–12.

Schneider, R. & Shiffrin, R. (1977). Controlled and automatic information processing. I: detection, search and detection. *Psychological Review, 84,* 1–66.

Schönberger, M., Ponsford, J., Gould, K. R. & Johnston, L. (2011). The temporal relationship between depression, anxiety, and functional status after traumatic brain injury: a cross-lagged analysis. *Journal of the International Neuropsychological Society, 17*(5), 781–787.

Shallice, T. (1982). Specific impairments of planning. *Philosophical Transactions of the Royal Society of London, 298,* 199–209.

——(1988). *From Neuropsychology to Mental Structure.* New York: Cambridge University Press.

Shallice, T. & Burgess, P. W. (1991). Deficits in strategy application following frontal damage in man. *Brain, 114,* 727–741.

Sherer, M., Hart, T., Whyte, J., Nick, T. G. & Yablon, S. A. (2005). Neuroanatomic basis of impaired self-awareness after traumatic brain injury: findings from early computed tomography. *The Journal of Head Trauma Rehabilitation, 20*(4), 287–300.

Shimamura, A. P., Janowsky, J. S. & Squire, L. R. (1990). Memory for the temporal order of events in patients with frontal lobe lesions and amnesic patients. *Neuropsychology, 28,* 803–813.

Shum, D., McFarland, K., Bain, J. D. & Humphreys, M. S. (1990). Effects of closed head injury on attentional processes: an information processing stage model. *Journal of Clinical and Experimental Neuropsychology, 12,* 247–264.

Shum, D., Levin, H. S. & Chan, R. C. K. (2011). Prospective memory in patients with closed head injury: a review. *Neuropsychologia, 49*(8), 2156–2165.

Simpson, G. K. & Tate, R. L. (2007). Suicidality in people surviving a traumatic brain injury: prevalence, risk factors and implications for clinical management. *Brain Injury, 21*(13–14), 1335–1351.

Sloan, S. & Ponsford, J. (1995). Assessment of cognitive difficulties following TBI. In J. Ponsford, S. Sloan & P. Snow (Eds), *Traumatic Brain Injury: Rehabilitation for Everyday Adaptive Living.* Hove, East Sussex: Lawrence Erlbaum Associates.

Smith, R. E. & Bayen, U. J. (2004). A multinomial model of event-based prospective memory. *Journal of Experimental Psychology: Learning, Memory, and Cognition, 30*, 756–777.

Snow, P. C. (1995). Presidential Address: discourse assessment following traumatic brain injury. In J. Fonez & N. Page (Eds), *Treatment issues and Long Term Outcomes: Processings of the 18th Annual BIC.* Hobart, Australia: Australian Academic Press on behalf of ASSBI.

Snow, P. C., Lambier, J., Parson, C., Mooney, L., Couch, D. & Russell, J. (1986). *Conversational Skills Following Closed Head Injury: Some Preliminary Findings.* Paper presented at the Brain Impairment: Proceedings of the Eleventh Annual Brain Impairment Conference.

Spiers, M. V., Pouk, J. A. & Santoro, J. M. (1994). Examining perspective-taking in the severely head injured. *Brain Injury, 8*, 463–473.

Squire, L. R. (1987). *Memory and Brain.* New York: Oxford University Press.

Stuss, D. T. & Benson, D. F. (1986). *The Frontal Lobes.* New York: Raven Press.

Stuss, D. T., Hugenholtz, H., Richard, M., LaRochelle, S., Poirier, C. A. & Bell, I. (1985). Subtle neuropsychological deficits in patients with good recovery after closed head injury. *Neurosurgery, 17*, 41–47.

Stuss, D. T., Stethem, L. L., Hugenholtz, H., Picton, T., Pivik J. & Richard, M. T. (1989). Reaction time after head injury: fatigue, divide and focused attention and consistency of performance. *Journal of Neurology, Neurosurgery & Psychiatry, 52*, 742–748.

Stuss, D. T., Alexander, M. P., Palumbo, C. L., Buckle, L., Sayer, L. & Pogue, J. (1994). Organisational strategies of patients with unilateral or bilateral frontal lobe injury in word learning tasks. *Neuropsychology, 8*(3), 355–373.

Stuss, D. T., Gow, C. A. & Hetherington, C. (1992). 'No longer gage': frontal lobe dysfunction and emotional changes. *Journal of Consulting and Clinical Psychology, 60*(3), 349–359.

Substance Abuse and Mental Health Services Administration (2010). *Results from the 2009 National Survey on Drug Use and Health: Volume I. Summary of National Findings* (Office of Applied Studies, NSDUH Series H-38A, HHS Publication No. SMA 10-4586Findings). Rockville, MD.

Tate, R. L. (1998). 'It is not only the kind of injury that matters, but the kind of head': the contribution of premorbid psychosocial factors to rehabilitation outcomes after severe traumatic brain injury. *Neuropsychological Rehabilitation, 9*, 1–15.

——(1999). Executive dysfunction and characterological changes after traumatic brain injury: two sides of the same coin? *Cortex, 35*(1), 39–55.

——(2003). Impact of pre-injury factors on outcome after severe traumatic brain injury: does post-traumatic personality change represent an exacerbation of premorbid traits? *Neuropsychological Rehabilitation, 13*(1–2), 43–64.

Tate, R. L., Fenelon, B., Manning, M. & Hunter, M. (1991). Patterns of neuropsychological impairment after severe blunt head injury. *Journal of Nervous and Mental Disease, 179*(3), 117–126.

Tate, R. L., Harris, R. D., Cameron, I. D., Myles, B. M., Winstanley, J. B., Hodgkinson, A. E., Baguley, I. J., Harradine, P. G. & Brain Injury Outcomes Study (BIOS) Group (2006). Recovery of impairments after severe traumatic brain injury: findings from a prospective, multicentre study. *Brain Impairment*, *7*, 1–15.

Taylor, E. M. (1959). *Psychological Appraisal of Children with Cerebral Defects*. Harvard, Mass: Harvard University Press.

Thomsen, I. V. (1975). Evaluation and outcome of aphasia in patients with severe closed head trauma. *Journal of Neurology, Neurosurgery & Psychiatry*, *38*, 713–718.

——(1984). Late outcome of very severe blunt head trauma: a 10–15 year second follow-up. *Journal of Neurology, Neurosurgery & Psychiatry*, *47*(3), 260–268.

Till, C., Christensen, B. K. & Green, R. E. (2009). Use of the Personality Assessment Inventory (PAI) in individuals with traumatic brain injury. *Brain Injury*, *23*(7–8), 655–665.

Trenerry, M., Crossen, B., DeBoa, J. & Leber, W. (1989). *Stroop Neuropsychological Screening Test*. Odessa, FL: Psychological Assessment Resources.

Trexler, L. E. & Zappala, G. (1988). Neuropathological determinants of acquired attention disorders in traumatic brain injury. *Brain and Cognition*, *8*, 291–302.

Turkstra, L. S. & Bourgeois, M. (2005). Intervention for a modern day HM: errorless learning of practical goals. *Journal of Medical Speech-Language Pathology*, *13*(3), 205–212.

Umeda, S., Kurosaki, Y., Terasawa, Y., Kato, M. & Miyahara, Y. (2011). Deficits in prospective memory following damage to the prefrontal cortex. *Neuropsychologia*, *49*(8), 2178–2184.

van Zomeren, A. H. (1981). *Reaction Time After Closed Head Injury*. Lisse: Swets Publishing Services.

van Zomeren, A. H. & van den Burg, W. (1985). Residual complaints of patients two years after severe head injury. *Journal of Neurology, Neurosurgery and Psychiatry*, *48*(1), 21–28.

van Zomeren, A. H. & Brouwer, W. H. (1987). Head injury and concepts of attention. In H. S. Levin, J. Grafman & H. M. Eisenberg (Eds), *Neurobehavioural Recovery From Head Injury*. (pp. 398–415). Oxford: Oxford University Press.

Vanderploeg, R., Schinka, J. A. & Retzlaff, P. (1994). Relationship between measures of auditory verbal learning and executive firing. *Journal of Clinical and Experimental Neuropsychology*, *16*(2), 243–252.

Velikonja, D., Warriner, E. & Brum, C. (2010). Profiles of emotional and behavioral sequelae following acquired brain injury: cluster analysis of the Personality Assessment Inventory. *Journal of Clinical and Experimental Neuropsychology*, *32*(6), 610–621.

Volle, E., Gonen-Yaacovi, G., de Lacy Costello, A., Gilbert, S. J. & Burgess, P. W. (2011). The role of rostral prefrontal cortex in prospective memory: a voxel-based lesion study. *Neuropsychologia*, *49*(8), 2185–2198.

Wager, T. D., Sylvester, C.-Y. C., Lacey, S. C., Nee, D. E., Franklin, M. & Jonides, J. (2005). Common and unique components of response inhibition revealed by fMRI. *Neuroimage*, *27*(2), 323–340.

Wallace, C. A. & Bogner, J. (2000). Awareness of deficits: emotional implications for persons with brain injury and their significant others. *Brain Injury*, *14*, 549–562.

Walsh, K. W. (1985). *Understanding Brain Damage: A Primer or Neuropsychological Evaluation*. Edinburgh: Churchill Livingstone.

——(1987). *Neuropsychology: A Clinical Approach* (2nd Edn). Edinburgh: Churchill Livingston.

Warner, M. A., de la Plata, C. M., Spence, J., Wang, J. Y., Harper, C., Moore, C., Devous, M. & Diaz-Arrastia, R. (2010). Assessing spatial relationships between axonal integrity, regional brain volumes, and neuropsychological outcomes after traumatic axonal injury. *Journal of Neurotrauma, 27*(12), 2121–2130.

Warriner, E. M., Rourke, B. P., Velikonja, D. & Metham, L. (2003). Subtypes of emotional and behavioral sequelae in patients with traumatic brain injury. *Journal of Clinical and Experimental Neuropsychology, 25,* 904–917.

Warriner, E. M., Rourke, B. P., Velikonja, D. & Metham, L. (2003). Subtypes of emotional and behavioural sequelae in patients with traumatic brain injury. *Journal of Clinical and Experimental Neuropsychology, 25,* 904–917.

Wechsler, D. (2008a). *Wechsler Adult Intelligence Scale* (fourth edition). New York: Pearson.

——(2008b). *Wechsler Memory Scale – fourth edition*. New York: Pearson.

Weddell, R. A. & Leggett, J. A. (2006). Factors triggering relatives' judgements of personality change after traumatic brain injury. *Brain Injury, 20*(12), 1221–1234.

Weddell, R., Oddy, M. & Jenkins, D. (1980). Social adjustment after rehabilitation: a two year follow-up of patients with severe head injury. *Psychological Medicine, 10*(2), 257–263.

Whelan-Goodinson, R., Ponsford, J. L., Schönberger, M. & Johnston, L. (2010). Predictors of psychiatric disorders following traumatic brain injury. *The Journal of Head Trauma Rehabilitation, 25*(5), 320–329.

Whyte, J., Fleming, M., Polansky, M., Cavallucci, C. & Coslett, H. B. (1997). Phasic arousal in response to auditory warnings after traumatic brain injury. *Neuropsychologia, 35*(3), 313–324.

Whyte, J., Grieb-Neff, P., Gantz, C. & Polansky, M. (2006). Measuring sustained attention after traumatic brain injury: differences in key findings from the sustained attention to response task (SART). *Neuropsychologia, 44*(10), 2007–2014.

Wilde, M. C., Boake, C. & Sherer, M. (1995). Do recognition-free recall discrepancies detect retrieval deficits in CHI? An exploratory analysis with the CVLT. *Journal of Clinical and Experimental Neuropsychology, 17*(6), 849–855.

Wilson, B. A., Alderman, N., Burgess, P. W., Emslie, H. & Evans, J. J. (1996). *The Behavioural Assessment of the Dysexecutive Syndrome*. New York: Pearson.

Wilson, B. A., Greenfield, E., Clare, L., Baddeley, A., Cockburn, J., Watson, P., Tate, R., Sopena, S., Nannery, R. & Crawford, J. (2008). *The Rivermead Behavioural Memory Test – Third Edition*. New York: Pearson.

Wilson, B. A., Emslie, H., Foley, J., Shiel, A., Watson, P., Hawkins, K., Groot, Y. & Evans, J. J. (2005) *The Cambridge Prospective Memory Test (CAMPROMPT)*, London: Harcourt Assessment

Wood, R. L., Liossi, C. & Wood, L. (2005). The impact of head injury neurobehavioural sequelae on personal relationships: preliminary findings. *Brain Injury, 19*(10), 845–851.

Wood, R. L. & Williams, C. (2008). Inability to empathize following traumatic brain injury. *Journal of the International Neuropsychological Society, 14,* 289–296.

Ziino, C. & Ponsford, J. (2006). Vigilance and fatigue following traumatic brain injury. *Journal of the International Neuropsychological Society, 12*(1), 100–110.

4 Cognitive communication disability following TBI

Examining discourse, pragmatics, behaviour and executive function

Leanne Togher, Skye McDonald, Carl A. Coelho and Lindsey Byom

The nature of communication difficulties after TBI

Observational studies in the 1970s (Levin *et al.*, 1979; Thomsen, 1975) described communication difficulties following severe TBI that did not easily fit within the conventional rubric of aphasia. Aphasia was reported in few people (2–30 per cent) with TBI (Heilman *et al.*, 1971; Sarno, 1980; Sarno & Levita, 1986). On the other hand, relatives described a range of deficits in the sphere of communication. Their family member with TBI was described as slow and hesitant, without initiative in social settings and restricted to a limited repertoire of stereotypic expressions, or otherwise tangential, inappropriate and over-talkative (Levin *et al.*, 1979; Thomsen, 1975). Initially, it was suggested that these difficulties might represent a sub-clinical aphasic language disorder (Sarno, 1980; Sarno & Levita, 1986) but it is now widely accepted that these kinds of difficulties reflect underlying cognitive impairment rather than language per se.

In general, it is apparent that most adults with severe TBI who experience communication difficulties do so not because they lack the language skills required, but rather because they are unable to apply their language skills adaptively and flexibly to meet everyday conversational requirements. In an effort to capture the nature of these difficulties researchers have taken a more contextual approach to the characterization of language skills, envisaging these in terms of: (1) aspects of social behaviour more broadly defined (e.g. McFall, 1982); (2) larger language units, e.g. discourse (Halliday, 1985); or (3) how language is used in context to impart meaning (pragmatics) (Searle, 1976). They have also become increasingly aware of how deficits in executive functioning, working memory and new learning impact upon communication. In this chapter we will cover each of these topics.

Behavioural approaches to understanding communication deficits

One way of conceptualizing communication disorders that emerge after TBI is from the point of view of social behaviour or social skills (McFall, 1982). There are a number of checklists and rating scales based on this framework. These vary in focus from global measures of verbal and nonverbal behaviour e.g. 'social performance' (Newton & Johnson, 1985; Rousseaux *et al.*, 2010; Spence *et al.*, 1993) to intermediary measures e.g. 'partner directed behaviour' (Flanagan *et al.*, 1995; McDonald *et al.*, 2004) and 'turn-taking' (Coelho *et al.*, 2002; Drummond & Boss, 2004) to measures of specific and discrete attributes of communication e.g. 'frequency of questions' (Godfrey *et al.*, 1989).

Using this approach people with severe TBI have been reported to be generally less interesting, less rewarding and more effortful to interact with than control speakers (Bond & Godfrey, 1997; Godfrey *et al.*, 1991). They also elicit higher rates of verbal facilitation from their conversational partner (Coelho *et al.*, 2002; Godfrey *et al.*, 1989) and are found to be generally unskilled in response to their partner's questions (Spence *et al.*, 1993). They have also been noted to be egocentric in their discussion and fail to actively involve their conversational partner, e.g. by asking questions or supporting them with the use of verbal reinforcers (Bond & Godfrey, 1997; Flanagan *et al.*, 1995; Marsh & Knight, 1991; McDonald *et al.*, 2004).

Discourse analyses

Discourse analysis focuses upon regularities within the flow of language that reflect the nature of social interactions. Discourse analysis is concerned with the text as a whole, across the conventional boundaries of clauses and sentences, focusing upon its continuity and organization and the relation between structure and meaning. Discourse was described as a unit of language which conveys a message (Ulatowska & Bond Chapman, 1989). As the analysis of discourse does not simply focus on studying a sequence of clauses but upon meanings that occur beyond the clause (Martin & Rose, 2003), it has provided a way of examining the cognitive communication abilities of people with TBI. It provides a way of studying how social activity unfolds through the texts that are produced within each activity. For example, a shopping encounter of a person with TBI can be examined through the language produced by the person with TBI and the shop assistant during that activity. Examining social discourse also gives insight into the culture in which it manifests. People with TBI may be inappropriate in their discourse production during a shopping expedition, and shop assistants may be uncomfortable or lack confidence in these interactions as a result. Examining the language during this type of interaction can shed light on how brain injury has affected the unfolding of this social activity. It can also provide direction for intervention and training; both for the person with TBI and also their communication partner. Therefore, studying the discourse of people with TBI offers a way of examining how they and their communication partners are making meanings during their everyday activities, and provides direction on how to improve these interactions to enable social participation (Togher *et al.*, 1996).

The term 'discourse' covers a broad range of speaking tasks, also referred to as discourse *genres*. A genre is a particular text-type, which has its own structure and sequence (Halliday & Hasan, 1985). Discourse genres include narrative (or recounting a story), procedural (a set of instructions for doing something), expository (giving an opinion or discussing a topic in detail) and conversation. Discourse genres can be monologic (i.e. non-interactive) or dialogic, such as a conversation or a service encounter. In addition to this variety of discourse types, there are different levels of analysis that can be used to examine each sample of text.

Levels of discourse analysis

Four levels of discourse analysis have been proposed including microlinguistic, microstructural, macrostructural and superstructural approaches to the assessment of discourse of people with TBI (Coelho, 2007) (see Table 4.1).

Microlinguistic analyses or within-sentence analyses include productivity measures (e.g. words per T-unit), grammatical complexity (e.g. subordinate clauses per T-unit) or tallies of propositions and content units (such as the Utterance with New Information or UNI or Correct Information Unit or CIU). Microstructural or across sentence analyses involve measures of cohesion and

Table 4.1 Levels of discourse analysis

Level of analysis (Coelho 2007)	Analysis
Microlinguistic (within sentence measures)	Productivity (e.g. Number of words, number of T-units* per narrative, words per minute, moves per minute) Grammatical complexity (e.g. subordinate clauses per T-unit, ratio of agrammatical T-units to total T-units) Tallies of propositions and content units
Microstructural (across sentence measures)	Cohesion Cohesive adequacy
Macrostructural analysis	Local and global coherence Content units (e.g. correct information units/minute, Utterances with New Information) Exchange structure analysis Speaker-initiator vs. speaker responder analysis
Superstructural analysis	Story grammar (e.g. episode analysis consisting of initiating event, attempt and direct consequence) Analysis of topic Generic structure analysis (e.g. narrative, procedural, casual conversation, structured interview, service encounter)

* T-unit is defined as an independent clause plus any dependent clauses associated with it (Hunt, 1970)

cohesive adequacy (Halliday & Hasan, 1976). This provides insight into the degree to which the speaker uses lexical items across a text to create a cohesive story (Armstrong, 1987; Davis & Coelho, 2004). Macrostructural analyses involve measures of local and global coherence which are indicators of thematic unity of a narrative (Glosser & Deser, 1991). Global coherence refers to the relationship of the meaning or content of an utterance to the general topic of the story while local coherence examines the relationship of the meaning or content of an utterance to that of a preceding utterance. Other measures at this level include exchange structure analysis which provides an indication of information giving, information requesting and receiving, and the amount of negotiation needed for the messages to be conveyed (dynamic moves) (Togher *et al.*, 1997a). Coelho, Youse & Le (2002) proposed a discourse analysis procedure where the middle 6 minutes of a 15 minute conversation is transcribed and analysed according to whether the person is a speaker-initiator or speaker-responder. A speaker-initiator's utterances are evaluated according to their 'summoning power' where those that clearly summon or demand a response are designated obliges, while those that do not are comments. The utterances of the speaker-responder are evaluated according to their appropriateness or adequacy within the interaction: adequate plus, adequate or inadequate. Finally, superstructural analyses encompass the overall organization of content or information and include the analysis of story grammar, topic maintenance (Coelho, 2007) and generic structure potential analysis (Hasan 1985; Togher *et al.*, 1997b).

Another way to classify discourse analysis is to examine the theoretical underpinnings of the measurement approach. Broadly, analysts have used either psycholinguistic approaches or sociolinguistic perspectives. Psycholinguistic approaches to evaluating language arise from an intrapsychological framework where the breakdown is seen as a disruption to the linguistic rule system within the individual or in a blockage of access to particular modules for that individual (Nickels, 2002). The psycholinguistic analyses include measures of syntax (Chapman *et al.*, 1992; Ellis & Peach, 2009; Ewing-Cobbs *et al.*, 1998; Glosser & Deser, 1991; Liles *et al.*, 1989), content (Hartley & Jensen, 1991) including propositional analysis (Coelho *et al.*, 2005) and productivity or efficiency analysis (Hartley & Jensen, 1991; Jorgensen & Togher, 2009; Mentis & Prutting, 1987).

Efficiency of discourse can be conceptualized as either the rate of speech or the amount of information imparted in the words produced. Confirming observational accounts of slow, hesitant speech, adults and adolescents with TBI have been found to speak more slowly (Hartley & Jensen, 1991; Stout *et al.*, 2000), produce fewer meaningful words (Brookshire *et al.*, 2000; Chapman *et al.*, 1992; Chapman *et al.*, 1995; Hartley & Jensen, 1991), produce more incomplete, ambiguous or uninterpretable utterances (Body & Perkins, 2004; Hartley & Jensen, 1991; Stout *et al.*, 2000), as well as shorter information units (C-units) (Hartley & Jensen, 1991), provide less information overall (Biddle *et al.*, 1996), and less efficiently delivered information (per minute, or per C unit)

(Coelho, 2002; Coelho *et al.*, 2005; Erlich, 1988; Stout *et al.*, 2000; Wilson *et al.*, 2002).

Syntactic aspects of discourse have been investigated using measures such as the percentage of T units containing dependent clauses (Chapman *et al.*, 1992), embeddedness of subordinate clauses (Glosser & Deser, 1991) and subordinate clauses per T unit (Liles *et al.*, 1989), with no differences being found between TBI and control participants. Glosser and Deser (1991) found that their TBI participants made significantly more grammatical errors than control participants (such as omissions of the subject, main verb and other grammatical morphemes), even though they demonstrated an adequate range of grammatical constructions in their spontaneous speech. While useful in explaining the reduced complexity of TBI discourse, psycholinguistic analyses at word level failed to delineate these problems and therefore researchers trialled analyses examining sentence level processing (Ellis & Peach, 2009) and the connectedness of TBI participants' discourse.

Sociolinguistic perspectives to discourse analysis differ from psycholinguistic approaches because, rather than focusing on the forms of language, there is an emphasis on language in use (Halliday, 1994). Language is seen as a semantic, rather than a grammatical unit, which must be examined within the context it occurs. Context encompasses the situation in which the language has occurred, the purpose of the language use and the people involved within the situation. Context is interdependent with the text that occurs, so that, for example, the purpose of a text (which might be telling a story) realizes or leads to the use of particular words, phrases, sentences and genres. From this viewpoint, language analysis is always interpreted with the underlying context in mind.

Sociolinguistic analyses used to examine TBI discourse have included cohesion analysis (Coelho, 2002; Coelho *et al.*, 1991a, 1991b; Davis & Coelho, 2004; Hartley & Jensen, 1991; McDonald, 1993; Mentis & Prutting, 1987), analysis of coherence (Chapman *et al.*, 1992; McDonald, 1993), story structure (Cannizzaro & Coelho, 2002), analysis of topic (Mentis & Prutting, 1991) and generic structure analysis (Togher & Hand, 1999; Togher *et al.*, 1997).

Cohesion analysis

Cohesion analysis has provided mixed results in the delineation of discourse deficits of individuals with TBI. The analysis of cohesion (Halliday & Hasan, 1976) examines the components of the linguistic system that enables a text to function as a single meaningful whole. The semantic relations that function to achieve cohesion are expressed partly through the vocabulary and partly through the grammar. According to this analysis, various types of meaning relations described as cohesive markers or ties join sentences. Thus cohesion is created by the interdependence of linguistic items across separate clauses in a text (such as a pronoun in one clause linked to its referent in another) (Halliday, 1985; Halliday & Hasan, 1985; Hasan, 1984; Hasan, 1985). Because adults with TBI are frequently insufficiently informative, it makes sense to examine the cohesive adequacy of their discourse, focusing upon monologues. In a seminal study, Mentis and Prutting (1987) compared three TBI participants with three uninjured speakers using an analysis of cohesion during conversational and narrative samples with a familiar partner. While syntax was relatively well preserved in all three TBI participants, qualitative and quantitative differences in the TBI participants' cohesion abilities were reported including the use of fewer cohesive ties in the narrative tasks. Davis & Coelho (2004) recorded eight participants with TBI and compared them to eight control participants on a sample of six stories with tasks of cartoon elicited storytelling and auditory-oral retelling. Deficits were found in the clinical group with respect to referential cohesion, logical coherence and accuracy of narration. Interestingly, the occurrence of deficits depended on the condition of narrative production and, as previously reported by Liles and colleagues (1989), on the particular story or elicitation task used. Impairment of referential cohesion and accuracy was found with picture elicitation, whereas impairment of logical coherence occurred during retelling. This suggested that both the discourse feature being studied and the processing demands of the task should be considered when studying TBI discourse. The importance of the elicitation task was confirmed by Jorgensen & Togher (2009) who found that their ten participants with TBI had fewer cohesive ties in a monologue picture narrative task compared to a matched control group, but no significant differences in a jointly produced narrative task.

This kind of approach has revealed that adults with TBI can vary the amount and type of cohesion they use appropriately, depending on the type of discourse task (e.g. narrative, procedural, conversational, etc.) (Coelho, 2002; Davis & Coelho, 2004; Hartley & Jensen, 1991; Jorgensen & Togher, 2009; Liles *et al.*, 1989; Mentis & Prutting, 1987). However, whether the quality of cohesion is affected is disputed. In some studies TBI speakers have been found to use less cohesive ties than non-brain-damaged control subjects (Carlomagno *et al.*, 2011; Davis & Coelho, 2004; Hartley & Jensen, 1991; Marini *et al.*, 2011; Mentis & Prutting, 1987) but other studies have not found this (Coelho, 2002; Galski *et al.*, 1998; Hough, 1990; Jordan *et al.*, 1991; Van Leer & Turkstra, 1999; Wilson *et al.*, 2002). Similarly, there is disagreement as to whether or not TBI speakers produce more incomplete references where the source for interpretation of a given linguistic unit is missing or ambiguous (Hartley & Jensen, 1991; Hough & Barrow, 2003; Liles *et al.*, 1989; McDonald, 1993; Mentis & Prutting, 1987; Van Leer & Turkstra, 1999).

There are several potential reasons for this variability, including the inherent heterogeneity of communication disorders in the population, differences in the way in which local coherence is calculated (Davis & Coelho, 2004) and the nature of the comparison group, who should be matched for both verbal ability and socio-cultural factors but sometimes are not (Brookshire *et al.*, 2000; Coelho, 2002; Snow & Douglas, 2000; Snow *et al.*, 1997b). Additionally, this approach to measuring linguistic cohesion does not appear to correspond to subjective impressions concerning the coherence of the discourse (Glosser & Deser, 1991; McDonald, 1993).

Coherence

The coherence of discourse refers its semantic continuity (Patry & Nespoulous, 1990) either at a local (between adjacent propositions) or global (discourse structure) level which can vary systematically with different kinds of discourse tasks (Coelho *et al.*, 1991a, 1991b; Patry & Nespoulous, 1990). Coherence ratings reveal how well an individual maintains and conveys the overall theme of a narrative. Arguably, global coherence is a more sensitive measure than local coherence, i.e. the structure of the discourse as revealed in the nature and sequence of the propositional content (Kintsch & van Dijk, 1978; van Dijk & Kintsch, 1983). For example, in stories, the propositional structure can be defined according to its depiction of a sequence of events with defined beginnings, middles and ends (Brookshire *et al.*, 2000; Chapman *et al.*, 1992; Jordan *et al.*, 1991; Liles *et al.*, 1989; Mortensen, 2005). In procedural narratives, propositions are identified as to whether they represent essential, non-essential, ambiguous or irrelevant information and whether they are sequenced appropriately according to the sequence of the procedure (Galski *et al.*, 1998; McDonald, 1993; McDonald & Pearce, 1995; Snow *et al.*, 1995; Snow *et al.*, 1997b; Turkstra *et al.*, 1996).

Research examining global coherence is also variable. On the one hand, children and adults with TBI have been found to produce as many essential propositions as control speakers (Jordan *et al.*, 1991; Liles *et al.*, 1989; Snow *et al.*, 1997b; Van Leer & Turkstra, 1999). On the other, it has been reported that they provide less essential information (Brookshire *et al.*, 2000; Chapman *et al.*, 1992; Coelho, 2002; Coelho & Duffy, 1995; Le *et al.*, 2011b; Liles *et al.*, 1989; Mozeiko *et al.*, 2011) and a disrupted sequence of explanation, including irrelevant and ambiguous material (McDonald, 1993; McDonald & Pearce, 1995; Turkstra *et al.*, 1996). Raters' impressions of procedural texts produced by TBI speakers support notions of disrupted global coherence by suggesting they are confused and disorganized (McDonald, 1993). Recent findings indicate that global rather than local coherence is more compromised following TBI, particularly individuals with damage to the dorsolateral prefrontal cortex (Coelho *et al.*, 2012).

Such psycholinguistic and sociolinguistic approaches reinforce the findings from behavioural assessments, i.e. speakers with TBI elicit a greater number of questions and prompts from their partners (Coelho *et al.*, 1991). They have difficulty initiating conversation (Coelho *et al.*, 2002; Drummond & Boss, 2004; Ehrlich & Barry, 1989; Godfrey *et al.*, 1989) and maintaining a topic (Angeleri *et al.*, 2008; Dardier *et al.*, 2011; Drummond & Boss, 2004; Erlich, 1988; Milton *et al.*, 1984) and tend to provide information in an inefficient and disorganized manner (Brookshire *et al.*, 2000; Coelho *et al.*, 2005; Mentis & Prutting, 1987; Snow *et al.*, 1997a, 1998).

Analysis of topic

Mentis and Prutting (1991) employed an elaborate multidimensional classification system for studying topic management in their study of conversational and monologue samples of a TBI subject. In this procedure the basic unit for analysing topic and subtopic maintenance was the intonation unit as described by Chafe (1987). Chafe defines an intonation unit as 'a sequence of words combined under a single, coherent intonation contour, usually preceded by a pause' (p. 22). According to Chafe, each intonation unit expresses only one new concept at a time. Therefore, the intonation unit may be used as a measure of the amount of information conveyed within a single topic as well as the individual contributions of each of the participants in a conversation to topic maintenance. Mentis and Prutting categorized intonation units as ideational (i.e. which carry propositional, ideational information), and textual or interpersonal (i.e. which serve a primarily textual or interpersonal function in a conversation). The ideational units were further classified into four categories based on the extent to which each participant contributes to the development of a conversation by adding novel or relevant information: (1) new information; (2) no new information; (3) side sequence units; and (4) problematic. Findings indicated that topic management abilities of their TBI subject were impaired. Specific difficulties included non-coherent topic changes as well as the production of ambiguous, unrelated and incomplete ideational units. These resulted in a decrease in continuity of topic development. Reduction in the TBI speaker's topic management abilities was evident in his production of fewer new information units than the normal control. In addition, the speaker with TBI did not maintain discourse topics through the addition of novel information to the same extent as the normal speaker also studied. According to Mentis and Prutting (1991) in order for discourse to be coherent, topic changes and all ideational units need to be structured so as to reveal thematic relevance and informational salience. The failure of the speaker with a TBI to structure discourse was evident in his production of non-coherent topic changes and his ambiguous, unrelated and incomplete ideational units. Ambiguity of the TBI speaker's ideational units was primarily the result of his reference to items that were absent from the text and not identifiable from the context. Given that this TBI individual was also aphasic, the observed problems with topic management cannot be attributed to cognitive deficits alone.

Story grammar

Story grammar knowledge refers to the purported regularities in the internal structure of stories that guide an individual's comprehension and production of the logical relationships between people and events (e.g. temporal and causal). Descriptions of story grammars differ, but the episode unit is central to virtually all models proposed by many investigators (e.g. see Stein & Glenn, 1979). Analysis at the story grammar level generally consists of looking at the number of 'complete' episodes in each story. An episode (as described by Stein & Glenn) is judged to be complete only if it contains all three components: (a) an initiating event that causes a character to formulate a goal-directed behavioural sequence; (b) an action; and (c) a direct consequence marking attainment or non-attainment of the goal. In addition, these three components must be logically related.

Analysis of story structure has been undertaken in a variety of investigations of the discourse of TBI individuals. Chapman *et al.* (1992) observed that their group of children and adolescents with severe TBI showed a reduction in essential story components, failing to signal new episodes with setting information, and often omitted essential action information in a story retelling task. These authors noted that the finding of disrupted story structure in their participants with TBI subjects was unexpected, in that story structure develops relatively early and is more resistant to disruption than intersentential structures in aphasic individuals. They further observed that it is unclear whether this difficulty was a reflection of an underlying impairment in internal story schema or difficulty implementing story schema during discourse production.

Speakers with TBI and normal speakers produced a comparable number of episodes in story retelling (presented via filmstrip), as reported by Liles *et al.* (1989). In story generation (generating a story depicted in a single picture), however, three of the four TBI speakers produced no episodes. The greater difficulty with story structure in the generation task demonstrated by Liles *et al.*'s (1989) speakers, was related to Blank, Rose and Berlin's (1978) notion of cognitive reordering. Adequate story development requires a speaker to transpose a static representation of the depicted events (in a picture) to a dynamic representation (a story). Blank *et al.* (1978) refer to such a disparity between the context and required language use as cognitive reordering. The TBI speakers' apparent inability to use episode structure in the story generation task, in spite of having been able to produce complete episodes in the story retelling task, suggested that the story generation task required an interaction of cognition and language use, a capacity the TBI speakers could not consistently engage. Further, the interactions among sentential grammar, intersentential cohesion and story structure required to produce a story may place a communicative load on TBI individuals' performance, which may reveal problems not observable in other forms of discourse.

These findings have subsequently been supported by two large studies of TBI, one with individuals post-closed head injury (CHI; $N=55$) and the second with survivors of penetrating head injury (PHI; $N=167$). In both studies the participants with brain injuries demonstrated significant difficulty with story grammar (Coelho, 2002; Coelho *et al.*, 2012). The finding that the PHI group's discourse performance, characterized by difficulty with the discourse measures focused on macro-organization (i.e. story grammar and completeness), was consistent with what has been observed for individuals with CHI was interesting considering the differences in the mechanism of injury. The PHI group had relatively focal injuries while the CHI group presented with primarily diffuse damage. This suggests that discourse performance, macrostructural components in particular, may be disrupted at any point along a cognitive-linguistic network.

Story goodness

Facility at relating information through well-formed stories is critical to successful communication (Le *et al.*, 2011a; Mar, 2004). As noted above, individuals with TBI consistently demonstrate difficulty organizing semantic content of story narratives (i.e. story grammar). However, organization does not completely describe what constitutes a meaningful story. The content within a story needs to be complete to fully explicate messages. Story content has been noted to be lacking in individuals with TBI (Chapman *et al.*, 2001; Hartley & Jensen, 1992; McDonald & Pearce, 1995). To determine completeness Le and colleagues (2011) conducted an inventory of the key components (events and characters) of a story used to elicit story retellings from 46 members of a non-brain-injured (NBI) comparison group (Le *et al.*, 2011b). When pooled across participants in a matrix, these actions and events clustered into distinct components of the story. A total of seven components were identified. Components that were mentioned by 80 per cent or more of the normative group were considered to be critical to the story. Of the seven components, two were produced by approximately 65 per cent of the comparison group and did not meet the criterion for inclusion. The remaining five components were produced by more than 80 per cent of the participants (range: 83–98 per cent). All narratives from both normative and brain-injured groups were then reviewed for the presence of the five components. This analysis generated the completeness score, which was the total number of critical components produced in each participant's story retelling. Story retellings from two groups, 46 NBI and 171 with TBI, were analysed for story grammar and story completeness. The two scores were plotted as coordinates, completeness on the horizontal axis and story grammar on the vertical axis, which enabled quantification of what the authors termed 'story goodness'. Results indicated that the participants' scores fell into four distinct categories of story goodness which discriminated the groups. For example, 82 per cent (N=38) of the participants' scores from the NBI group fell into quadrant 2 (complete and well-organized stories) while only 54 per cent (N=93) of participants with TBI fell into quadrant 2. For quadrant 3 (incomplete and poorly organized stories), 9 per cent (N=3) of the participants who were NBI and 19 per cent (N=32) of the participants with TBI were noted. These findings indicate that the story goodness measure is sensitive for individuals with TBI and is a useful supplement to standard discourse analyses.

Generic structure analysis

Communication during everyday activities can be described according to the superstructural analysis of generic structure analysis (Hasan, 1985). The focus here is on the genre in which communication partners are engaged, whether it be casual conversation (Ventola, 1979), a service encounter in a shop (Hasan, 1985), during a phone call (Togher *et al.*, 1997) or a problem solving discussion (Kilov *et al.*, 2009). In each of these situations the language produced is viewed as a social process which unfolds step by step, according to the context of the situation and the core structural elements expected in that particular type of interaction. For example, the essential elements of a service encounter where a customer makes a phone call to order a pizza include:

Greeting:	A: Hello Pizza Pizzazz
	B: Hello
Service initiation:	A: What can I do for you today?
Service request:	B: I was wanting to order a large supreme pizza to pick up please
Service enquiry:	A: What is your name and phone number?
	B: My name is Judy and my number is 425 330 2298
Service compliance:	A: No problem – it will be ready in 20 minutes
Close:	B: OK thanks very much – I'll see you soon
Goodbye:	A: OK see you then, Bye.

A more thorough description of this analysis can be found in Togher *et al.* (1997), but it is useful to examine one aspect of this analysis to demonstrate its value. This study examined the telephone conversations of five participants with severe TBI and compared them to five control participants who were the brothers of the TBI participants. Each of the ten participants made phone calls to a range of communication partners, including police officers, bus timetable call centre operators, their mothers and a therapist. The first two of these conditions constituted service encounters, as the participants were telephoning to find out information. Generic structure analysis showed that the elements in TBI service encounters differed in length and composition to those of control interactions. There were difficulties with the opening sequences of TBI interactions, as well as with the main *service request*. Repeated and inappropriate elements were present in TBI samples, whereas they did not occur in the control samples. There were also significant differences between the bus timetable call centre condition and the police interactions. In the control-police interactions, the *greeting* sequences were short and quickly followed by a clear succinct service request and the *close/goodbye* sequences were significantly longer than in the bus condition. In contrast, the TBI subject-police interactions evidenced long greeting sequences and short close/goodbye elements. Opening and closing elements reflect the development of interpersonal relationships, by initially establishing credibility and, finally, by confirming the success of the encounter, as well as encouraging future contact. In all control interactions, the police officer encouraged subjects to call again. The interpersonal relationship was therefore reinforced by a longer closure than in the TBI interactions. In short, generic analysis provided a new lens to evaluate the social relationships between participants during their interactions.

Pragmatic theoretical approaches

Pragmatics is consistent with sociolinguistic theoretical approaches in that it is also concerned with the meanings that arise from language use in context. While sociolinguistics is mainly concerned about discourse, pragmatic approaches have focused not only upon extended language samples but also smaller units known as speech acts. Each instance of language can be conceptualized as a behavioural event, i.e. a speech *act* that is intended to influence the recipient in some way, to persuade, inform, request cooperation etc. Speech acts may be direct, in that the speaker states what is on his or her mind directly, e.g. *'Help me lift this'*, or indirect although clearly transparent, e.g. *'I was wondering if you would be able to help me lift this'* whereby the speaker asks about the listener's ability rather than making a direct request. In both cases the speaker wishes the listener to respond; however the approach is more tentative in the latter example, distancing the speaker from the content of the request. Such tentative signals are thought to convey an unwillingness to impinge on the listener, i.e. an unwillingness to threaten their 'negative face' (Brown & Levinson, 1978). An alternative strategy is to use jokes, slang, compliments, e.g. *'Give us a hand honey!'* to indicate friendship and inclusion, i.e. appealing to the listener's 'positive face'. The manner in which speech acts are formulated varies systematically depending on the familiarity and status of the recipient as well as the import of the message. When negotiating a delicate social situation where diplomacy is paramount, speech acts may be so indirect as to be opaque in their meaning (*'This is so heavy!'*). On the other hand, when dealing with routine matters, with equals and with highly familiar others, positive politeness may be the preferred strategy.

The speaker's choice of utterance (e.g. the level of indirectness, use of slang) reflects their appraisal of the social situation and perception of their relationship towards their co-conversant. The converse also holds true, i.e. the choice of utterance used by a speaker will inform the listener about how they are viewed by the speaker. Indeed, people can be very sensitive to how subtle changes in the surface forms of the same underlying request (*'Do you know where Jordan Hall is?'* *'Could you tell me where I might find Jordan Hall?'* etc.) systematically vary the degree of indirectness and hesitancy they signal (Clark & Schunk, 1980). Competent communication requires the ability to use different kinds of devices appropriately depending on the social context. Thus a familiar, jokey request with a superior at work will be viewed poorly, as will an overly stiff and formally polite exchange with a close friend or relative.

Viewing language, specifically speech acts, from this perspective is useful for addressing communication impairments in people with TBI for two reasons. Firstly, it suggests that, in order to be adept at understanding the social nuances of language, listeners must be able to use politeness signals such as hesitancy, slang, etc. They must also have the means to produce speech acts that convey their intended meanings via inference. Such skill goes beyond basic competence in semantics, syntax and phonology. Secondly, it suggests that there must be some means by which opaque indirect speech acts (*'This is so heavy!'*) are decoded for the speaker's intended meaning. People with severe TBI have been described as both blunt and insensitive in their language use and concrete and literal in their general responses and understanding of information (Crosson, 1987; Milton & Wertz, 1986; Prigatano, 1986). Thus, a pragmatic approach to assessment of communication following TBI has a number of advantages in terms of both assessing language production and language comprehension.

Pragmatic language production

Politeness theory

As described above, one aspect of pragmatics refers to the use of linguistic devices to moderate politeness. At a basic level, adults with TBI appear to have an intact repertoire of polite strategies (e.g. use of modal verbs, 'would' rather than 'will', use of honorifics etc.: McDonald & van Sommers, 1992) although they may be less able to use these flexibly across different contexts than non-injured speakers (Togher & Hand, 1998). They have greater difficulty when the need for diplomacy is high. For example, they can find it very difficult to hint, and tend to directly state what is on their mind (McDonald & van Sommers, 1992). They have also been shown to make comments when making requests that were counter-productive to their desired outcome (McDonald & Pearce, 1998). Younger speakers with TBI also have difficulties producing appropriate speech acts to meet contextual constraints (Dennis & Barnes, 2000).

Grice's maxims

An alternative, complementary framework to assess language production after TBI is that based upon Grice's maxims of cooperative communication (Grice, 1975). According to Grice, speakers assume cooperation from each other and to this end trust that whatever is said is sufficient (maxim of quantity), accurate (maxim of quality), relevant (maxim of relevance) and imparted in an orderly fashion (maxim of manner). If there is a patent disregard for one of these maxims, (e.g. saying something that is clearly untrue), the listener may recognize this transgression as occurring deliberately, e.g. saying the opposite of what is true to be sarcastic. On the other hand, accidental transgressions of these maxims will confuse the listener and render the communication ineffective.

The general characterization of communication difficulties post-TBI would suggest that there are difficulties adhering to Grice's implicit maxims. Discourse is characterized as reflecting a lack of initiative, relying on set expressions and generally impoverished in the amount and variety of language produced (Chapman *et al.*, 1992; Erlich, 1988; Hartley & Jensen, 1991; Hartley & Jensen, 1992) or else over-talkative (Hagan, 1984; Milton *et al.*, 1984), tangential and inappropriate (e.g. Marini *et al.*, 2011; Prigatano *et al.*, 1986).

There have also been a number of tasks developed using Grice's maxims to look specifically at discourse production following TBI. For example, adults with TBI have been found to have difficulty conforming to these expectations when providing instructions about how to play a simple board game. They omitted essential information, included irrelevant and therefore misleading information, repeated information and failed to sequence important steps in their correct chronological sequence (McDonald & Pearce, 1995). When blind raters were given the transcriptions, they rated the TBI productions as transgressing the maxim of quantity (i.e. overly repetitive, insufficiently detailed) and the maxim of manner (i.e. unclear, disorganized and ineffective), clearly differentiating them from the productions of demographically matched peers (McDonald, 1993). Similar problems have been found on different procedural tasks (Galski *et al.*, 1998; Prince *et al.*, 2002; Snow *et al.*, 1999). Conversations have also been reportedly repetitive (Body & Parker, 2005) and narratives providing insufficient essential content and/or inaccuracies (Body & Perkins, 1998; Brookshire *et al.*, 2000; Davis & Coelho, 2004; Marini *et al.*, 2011; Snow *et al.*, 1999). Finally, checklists and questionnaires using Grice's maxims as a framework to focus on communicative competence either in observed conversation (Prutting & Kirchner, 1987) or impressions of everyday function (Douglas *et al.*, 2007b) have also proven sensitive to discourse difficulties.

Pragmatic understanding

The comprehension of indirect language after TBI has also been the focus of a number of studies in recent years with a particular interest in sarcasm and irony. When being sarcastic, the speaker commonly says something that is literally the reverse, or at least different from, what they mean, for example *'What a great haircut'* spoken to suggest the reverse. In the absence of language deficits, many adults and children with severe traumatic brain injury have great difficulty comprehending irony and sarcasm (Angeleri *et al.*, 2008; Channon & Crawford, 2010; Channon *et al.*, 2005; Channon & Watts, 2003; Dennis *et al.*, 2001; McDonald, 1992; McDonald & Flanagan, 2004; McDonald *et al.*, 2003; McDonald & Pearce, 1996; Shamay-Tsoory *et al.*, 2005; Turkstra *et al.*, 1996).

Cognitive contributions to communication disorders

It is now widely accepted that communication disorders following TBI are likely to emerge due to underlying cognitive deficits. Indeed, the term 'cognitive–communication disorder' has become increasingly accepted as the most apt descriptor for this cluster of difficulties. There are several facets of cognitive processes that have relevance for communicative competence, in particular, executive functions, processing speed, working memory and possibly new learning.

Executive functions

Executive functions mediate and regulate other cognitive activities and behaviour in a purposeful and goal directed fashion. In general, executive dysfunction significantly impairs problem-solving capacity. Individuals may experience reduced attention (working memory), fail to reason at an abstract level (draw inferences), fail to develop effective plans, or monitor and regulate behaviour. They also fail to learn from mistakes (Darby & Walsh, 2005). Executive dysfunction can often be conceptualized as representing either a loss of drive resulting in apathy and inertia, rigidity, inflexibility and perseveration or a loss of control leading to impulsivity, disinhibition and distractibility. Slowed information processing speed exacerbates these difficulties. As it has been argued that most communication requires planning, perspective taking (flexibility), regulation of output and the capacity to make inferences, it is clear that executive dysfunction will impact upon communication.

Evidence for this emerges from examination of a widely used self-report questionnaire of communicative competence following TBI, the La Trobe Communication Questionnaire (LCQ). Factor analysis revealed that, while originally conceptualized along the lines of Grice's maxims, the LCQ appeared to cluster somewhat differently (Douglas *et al.*, 2007a). Two factors appeared to represent 'quantity'. On the one hand there appeared to be a constellation reflecting 'too much' suggesting the impact of disinhibition. On the other there was too little, i.e. dysfluencies such as word finding problems, hesitancies and failure to provide sufficient information suggesting a role for loss of drive and initiative. Another factor that emerged reflected attentional difficulties, that is, losing track when conversing and becoming sidetracked. Yet another reflected the problem solving, planning and monitoring aspect of executive function, i.e. the ability to manage the task of communication, by selecting accurate information to meet the listener's needs, keeping track of main details, putting ideas together logically, self-monitoring, adapting conversational style to different situations and knowing when to talk and when to listen.

These results suggest that Grice's maxims, while useful for highlighting the role of speaker expectations in communication, do not map directly onto psychological processes involved in effective discourse. On the other hand, discourse difficulties do appear to correspond to aspects of executive dysfunction after TBI and this is also seen in some empirical research that relates specific language tasks to measures of neuropsychological performance.

Firstly, there is some evidence that measures of conceptual thought, generativity and problem solving are related to discourse structure, specifically the capacity to produce sufficient essential information in discourse (Brookshire *et al.*, 2000; Le *et al.*, 2012; McDonald & Pearce, 1995; Mozeiko *et al.*, 2011) or to identify macrostructure in written texts (Chapman *et al.*, 2004). Thus, it appears that deficits in the ability to reason flexibly and readily may interfere with the orderly identification and transmission of information. Furthermore, certain kinds of discourse tasks may be more taxing of executive abilities than others. Story generation tasks, for example, wherein the speaker has no template for the structure and flow of information are likely to be more challenging for those with executive disorders than story recall based on prior exposure to an oral or pictorial story. In general, it appears that story generation tasks are more demanding for adult speakers, whether with or without TBI (Coelho, 2002).

Secondly, it is reasonable to suggest that the generation of appropriately polite utterances will also depend upon executive control. Consistent with this, poor performance in the production of effective requests has been found to be correlated to indices of disinhibition on formal neuropsychological tests (McDonald & Pearce, 1998).

Thirdly, it can be argued that comprehension, especially the capacity to understand pragmatic inference, will be impacted by executive dysfunction. There is a clear link between frontal injury in TBI and poor inferential reasoning (Dennis *et al.*, 2001; Ferstl *et al.*, 2002) and also frontal injury and sarcasm comprehension (Shamay-Tsoory *et al.*, 2005). It is possible, therefore, that pragmatic inferential reasoning represents a particular application of generic inferential reasoning skills. In support of this, measures of general inference making have been linked to poor pragmatic understanding in people with TBI (Martin & McDonald, 2005; McDonald *et al.*, 2006). Furthermore, impulsivity (poor control) has also been found to contribute to poor comprehension of sarcasm (Channon & Watts, 2003).

Working memory

At a more refined level, it is interesting to question what particular aspects of executive dysfunction contribute to discourse deficits. Working memory is an important candidate. Coherent discourse requires continuous monitoring of verbal output in order to, for example, ensure that each pronominal reference used has an unambiguous source, and that ideas are inserted logically and effectively into the language flow. This is an on-line processing task that will depend upon good working memory capacity. Empirical evidence supports a relationship between impaired working memory and estimates of low efficiency and cohesion (Hartley & Jensen, 1991), complexity of clauses within T-Units (Youse & Coelho, 2005), story grammar and completeness (Le *et al.*, 2012).

Barnes and Dennis (2001) have argued that the problem with inferential reasoning may also be specifically to do with the working memory demands of integrating discourse meaning and world knowledge in real time rather than the computational aspects of inferencing. By a careful reduction of working memory demands, they demonstrated that deficits in inferential reasoning could be correspondingly reduced in children with TBI. Independent studies have also reported correlations between poor working memory capacity and poor inferential reasoning (Dennis & Barnes, 1990) including the ability to understand sarcasm (McDonald *et al.*, 2006). Slowed information processing is linked to working memory deficits and has, similarly, been associated with poor pragmatic understanding (Martin & McDonald, 2005; McDonald *et al.*, 2006).

New learning

The capacity to learn and recall information will also interfere with successful communication. The ability to relate a narrative in a coherent order will depend upon the ability to recall the events to be narrated as well as the events of the narration that have already unfolded. Consistent with this, linguistic cohesion and coherence are more affected by poor new learning capacity when the task requires retelling a previously heard story than generating one on the basis of a stimulus that remains in front of them (Brookshire *et al.*, 2000; Youse & Coelho, 2005).

New learning will also affect pragmatic understanding as contextual information that is relevant to the conversational exchange may have occurred some time earlier. Consistent with this standard, measures of new learning are associated with poor understanding of sarcastic inference (McDonald *et al.*, 2006).

In sum, common cognitive sequelae of severe traumatic brain injury, including slowed information speed and working memory, rigidity and impulsivity, poor problem solving and regulation and poor new learning may interfere with effective communication. Despite this, they are unlikely to be the total explanation. Indeed, correlations between communication performance and neuropsychological test scores are modest at best (Channon & Watts, 2003; McDonald *et al.*, 2006; Muller *et al.*, 2010). As an alternative it is important to consider the role that impairment in social cognition and emotional regulation may play in disrupting interpersonal functioning, including communication, following TBI. Social cognition and emotional regulation are discussed in Chapter 5.

Assessment of communication deficits

The different theoretical approaches to describing communication deficits have fostered a variety of assessment instruments that have utility in the characterization of communication problems and also the assessment of remediation approaches (see Chapter 11 for further discussion in relation to treatment). Table 4.2 provides a summary of several commonly used assessment instruments.

Rating scales

A number of rating scales have been developed that are based on behavioural and/or discourse/pragmatic theories regarding communication skills. Both the Pragmatic Protocol (Prutting & Kirchner, 1987) and the Profile of Pragmatic Functional Impairment in Communication (PFIC) (Linscott *et al.*, 1996) have been developed to rate videotaped social behaviours and identify both behavioural aspects of social interactions and the nature of language used, using Grice's maxims as a framework. The Pragmatic Protocol is used mainly as a checklist while the PFIC produces quantitative scores and has reportedly moderate to good inter-rater reliability (Dahlberg *et al.*, 2006) (see Chapter 11 for further discussion).

The Behavioural Referenced Index of Social Skills (Revised) (BRISS-R: Farrell et al., 1985)

The BRISS-R is a set of rating scales that focuses on social behaviour, usually a videotaped interaction, with some facets that are particularly useful for assessment of people with TBI including a scale that examines partner directed behaviour (including subscales examining the use of reinforcers, self-centred

Table 4.2 Some examples of assessment instruments for measuring communication after TBI

Name of instrument	Nature of response	Scored by	Level of analysis	Normative information
Behavioural Referenced Index of Social skills (Farrell et al., 1985)	Rating of social behaviour on scales with behavioural referents ranging from 1 (very inappropriate) to 7 (very appropriate)	Independent raters	Based upon social skills theory BRISS-R has 6 scales, 2 of which are sensitive to pragmatics, i.e. Personal Conversational Style including: 1) self-disclosure; 2) use of humour; 3) social manners and Partner Directed behaviour (including 1) Use of reinforcers; 2) partner focused behaviour and 3) self centred behaviour.	Descriptive TBI data for pre- and post-treatment available (N = 51, mean ages/SD = 33.1–36.3/ 10.7–11.7) (McDonald et al., 2008).
The Awareness of Social Inference Test (McDonald et al., 2011)	Presentation of videoed vignettes following which participant responds to questions that probe understanding of videoed vignettes	Clinician	Comprehension of: (1) basic emotion; (2) social emotions; (3) theory of mind including speaker beliefs and intentions; and (4) pragmatic inferences contrasting sincere exchanges with sarcasm and lies.	Normative data available for older children and adults aged 14–60 years (N = 134 for Part 1; N = 253 for Parts 2 & 3) (McDonald et al., 2011).
Adapted Kagan Scales (Togher et al., 2010)	10–15 minute video of interaction is rated for participation of the person with TBI (MPC scales) and the support provided by the communication partner (MSC scales) on a 9-point scale from 0 (no participation/support) to 4 (full)	Clinician	Measure of Participation in Conversation has 9-point scales with descriptors and anchors: Interaction and Transaction. The Measure of Support in Conversation has 2 scales: Acknowledging and Revealing Competence. The latter is divided into 3 subscales: (a) Ensuring the adult understands; (b) Ensuring the adult has a means of responding; and (c) Verification.	N/A

Measure	Task	Rater	Description	Normative data
Pragmatic Protocol (Prutting & Kirchner, 1987)	Checklist of behaviours judged to be 'appropriate'/'not appropriate' on the basis of a 15 minute video recording of a conversation.	Clinician	Descriptive taxonomy of 30 aspects of pragmatic competence (e.g. turn taking, topic selection and maintenance).	N/A
The Profile of Pragmatic Impairment in Communication (Linscott et al., 2003)	A 15 minute videotape is rated for presence of specific communication impairments each rated from 0 normal to 5 very severely impaired.	Independent raters	84 specific communication behaviours categorized into 10 subscales: (1) Logical Content; (2) General Participation; (3) Quantity; (4) Quality; (5) Internal Relation; (6) External Relation; (7) Clarity of Expression; (8) Social Style; (9) Subject Matter; (10) Aesthetics.	Limited descriptive data on TBI sample available (N = 20, age range 15–44) (Linscott et al., 1996).
La Trobe Communication Questionnaire (Douglas et al., 2000)	Questions regarding frequency of communicative behaviours over preceding months answered from 1 (never) to 4 (usually)	Person with TBI and/or significant other	30 questions based upon Grice's maxims as well as some additional questions tapping communication problems arising from cognitive deficits (such as word retrieval, distractibility and impulsivity).	Normative data for self (N = 147, mean age 21.2, age range 16–39) and close other ratings available (Douglas et al., 2000). Descriptive TBI data for self (N = 88, mean age/SD = 37.89/13.41) and close others ratings also available (Douglas et al., 2007b).
Functional Assessment of Verbal Reasoning and Executive Strategies (MacDonald & Johnson, 2005)	Reading, interpreting and integrating text in 4 tasks representing everyday type tasks: scheduling a work day, planning an event, making a complaint	Clinician	Tasks are designed to tap complex communication skills, verbal reasoning and executive functioning. Scores focus on efficiency (time), accuracy and quality of rationale (latter two ranging from 0 poor to 5 good).	Descriptive data for acquired brain injury sample (N = 52, mean age/SD = 34.56/13.33) and control samples (N = 101, mean age/SD = 38.59/14.41) available (MacDonald & Johnson, 2005).

behaviour and partner directed behaviour) and a scale examining personal conversational style, including social manners, use of humour and self-disclosure. The BRISS-R has been used in a number of studies of people with TBI (Flanagan *et al.*, 1995; McDonald *et al.*, 2004; McDonald *et al.*, 2008). The problem with the BRISS-R is that it requires extensive rater training, and even then, good inter-rater reliability is difficult to achieve.

Adapted Kagan Scales (Togher et al., 2010)

There is relative paucity of measurement instruments which evaluate the contributions of both the person with TBI and their communication partner during everyday interactions. To address this issue, two new scales were published in 2010 with the aim of developing sensitive outcome measures for a clinical trial which aimed to improve the communication of everyday communication partners and their friend or relative with TBI. The first of these measures examines the contributions to interactions by the person with TBI, the Adapted Measure of Participation in Conversation (MPC). The second set of scales, the Adapted Measure of Support in Conversation (MSC) is particularly innovative because they evaluate the contributions of the communication partner to the interaction (Togher *et al.*, 2010).

The Adapted Measure of Participation in Conversation (MPC) measures the person with TBI's level of participation in conversation in terms of his/her ability to interact or socially connect with a partner and to respond to and/or initiate specific content. It uses a nine point Likert scale, presented as a range of zero to four with 0.5 levels for ease of scoring. The scale ranges from 0 (no participation) through to 2 (adequate participation) to 4 (full participation in conversation). Within the MPC, there are two subscales encompassing Interaction and Transaction.

Using the Adapted Measure of Support in Conversation (MSC) raters can measure the degree of support provided by the communication partner on a nine point scale from 0–4 with 0.5 increments similar to the MPC. The MSC has two subscales including Acknowledging Competence and Revealing Competence. The Revealing Competence subscale is, in turn, composed of three elements which are scored separately and averaged to give the score for this subscale. The elements are: (a) Ensuring the adult understands; (b) Ensuring the adult has a means of responding; and (c) Verification.

Inter-rater reliability for both the Adapted MPC and the MSC scales is excellent ranging from ICC = 0.84 for the Adapted MPC Interaction and Transaction scales to ICC = 0.97 for the Adapted MSC Acknowledge Competence scale (Togher *et al.*, 2010). Intra-rater agreement was also strong (MSC: ICC = 0.80–0.90; MPC: = 0.81–0.92). Over 90 per cent of all ratings scored within 0.5 on the nine point scale. Importantly, both scales are sensitive outcome measures for communication partner training where the partners were paid carers (Behn *et al.*, 2012) and family and friends (Togher *et al.*, 2013).

Assessment tools

The Awareness of Social Inference Test

Arguably, our test, the Awareness of Social Inference Test (TASIT) (McDonald *et al.*, 2011), represents the most extensively developed instrument to date by which to measure both social cognition (see Chapter 5 for more detailed discussion) and the ability to interpret pragmatic inference in people with TBI. It uses videotaped vignettes of professional actors and has three parts, each with alternate forms. TASIT 1 is mainly an assessment of social cognition with a particular focus on emotion perception. It comprises 28 video vignettes representing four examples of each of the six basic emotions (happiness, sadness, anger, fear, revulsion (disgust) and surprise as well as neutral). All scripts are ambiguous monologues or dialogues and are enacted by actors trained in a Method style of acting that requires the actor to elicit a real emotion in him or herself. Thus, the vignettes depict dynamic, complex but naturalistic emotions. Recognition is assessed by selecting one of seven possible emotion labels.

TASIT 2 and 3 specifically assess the ability to comprehend pragmatic inference. TASIT 2 comprises 15 vignettes in which speakers enact ambiguous scripts either sincerely or sarcastically. As there are no verbal cues as to the real meaning of the exchange, listeners must base their interpretation on the demeanour and emotional expressions of the actors. TASIT 3 comprises 16 vignettes in which there is a counterfactual exchange that is either a lie (to conceal the true state of affairs or otherwise minimize the truth) or sarcastic. In TASIT 3 there is additional information provided as to the true state of affairs, e.g. showing a full dinner plate as the parents discuss whether their son has eaten his dinner. In TASIT 2 and 3, comprehension of each vignette is assessed by asking four questions that tap understanding of the speakers' emotions, their beliefs, their intentions and what they mean by what they say.

There is normative adult data for TASIT (McDonald *et al.*, 2003) and limited norms for adolescents (McDonald *et al.*, 2011). It has moderate to high test-retest reliability (McDonald *et al.*, 2006). The material in TASIT is complex and dynamic, so, not unsurprisingly, performance is associated with deficits in information processing, working memory, the ability to learn and retain information and the ability to think flexibly (executive function) as well as overall IQ (McDonald *et al.*, 2006). TASIT is sensitive to deficits post-TBI (McDonald & Flanagan, 2004; McDonald *et al.*, 2004; McDonald *et al.*, 2003; McDonald & Saunders, 2005). In each group studied, the people with TBI were more variable than the matched non-clinical control group. This is expected given that TBI is a heterogeneous condition and not all speakers with TBI are expected to suffer deficits in social perception and pragmatic inference. It also indicates that TASIT is potentially sensitive to a range of competencies in communicative understanding in this clinical group.

Functional Assessment of Verbal Reasoning and Executive Strategies

The Functional Assessment of Verbal Reasoning and Executive Strategies (FAVRES) (MacDonald & Johnson, 2005) takes a somewhat different approach by providing the participants with complex text that mirrors the mixture of texts that might potentially be found in everyday tasks, e.g. scheduling a work day or making a complaint. The participant must select information, make inferences and develop reasoned arguments to complete the task. The FAVRES, as the name implies, is designed to challenge executive function and verbal reasoning and is sensitive to TBI.

Questionnaires

Questionnaires provide the opportunity to gain an overview of how difficulties in communication manifest in everyday life. Grice's maxims have also guided the development of a questionnaire designed for both relatives and people with TBI. As mentioned previously, the LCQ (Douglas *et al.*, 2000) consists of 30 questions based upon Grice's maxims as well as some additional questions tapping particular communication problems arising from cognitive deficits (such as word retrieval, distractibility and impulsivity). The questionnaire has been found to be sensitive to discourse difficulties in people with TBI (Douglas, 2010; Douglas *et al.*, 2007a; Douglas *et al.*, 2007b; Watts & Douglas, 2006).

Summary

Communication is a complex activity that occurs naturally in our everyday lives. Typically, as communicators, we are unaware of the multi-level processing that occurs to ensure that we produce the right words in the right context most of the time. However, a severe traumatic brain injury can disrupt this processing leading to a breakdown in effective discourse for these individuals. To measure this complexity and treat discourse deficits the clinician requires an understanding of the microlinguistic, microstructural, macrostructural and superstructural features of language. Discourse analysis can be guided by psycholinguistic approaches that conceptualize communication impairment as reflecting deviations from linguistic rules or sociolinguistic and pragmatic approaches that view communication difficulties as reflecting problems in how language is used and understood in context. There is also recognition of the need to evaluate the person in dyadic exchanges with their everyday communication partners. Another paradigm shift in our conceptualization of communication disorders arises from understanding more about the relationship between executive functioning and language.

While the complexity of these approaches can appear daunting, there are now a number of sensitive measures which have been developed in response to the need for appropriate cognitive–communication evaluation. Clearly, the assessment of communication disorders following TBI is expanding to include new frontiers in the application of sociolinguistic and pragmatic theories in interaction with neuropsychological considerations. Yet another major consideration is the influence of disorders that affect social cognition (such as the perception of another's emotional and mental state) and emotional behaviour. These issues are rapidly attracting attention as critical variables that influence communication and interpersonal behaviour and these are discussed in detail in Chapter 5.

References

Angeleri, R., Bosco, F. M., Zettin, M., Sacco, K., Colle, L. & Bara, B. G. (2008). Communicative impairment in traumatic brain injury: a complete pragmatic assessment. *Brain and Language, 107*(3), 229–245.

Armstrong, E. (1987). Cohesive harmony in aphasic discourse and its significance to listener perception of coherence. *Clinical Aphasiology Conference Proceedings.* R. H. Brookshire. Minneapolis: BRK Publishers.

Barnes, M. A. & Dennis, M. (2001). Knowledge-based inferencing after childhood head injury. *Brain and Language, 76*(3), 253–265.

Behn, N., Togher, L., Power, E. & Heard, R. (2012). Evaluating communication training for paid carers of people with traumatic brain injury. *Brain Injury, 26,* 1702–1715.

Biddle, K. R., McCabe, A. & Bliss, L. S. (1996). Narrative skills following traumatic brain injury in children and adults. *Journal of Communication Disorders, 29*(6), 446–469.

Blank, M., Rose, S. A. & Berlin, L. J. (1978). *The Language of Learning: The Preschool Years.* New York: Grune and Stratton.

Body, R. & Perkins, M. R. (1998). Ecological validity in assessment of discourse in traumatic brain injury: ratings by clinicians and non-clinicians. *Brain Injury, 12*(11), 963–976.

——(2004). Validation of linguistic analyses in narrative discourse after traumatic brain injury. *Brain Injury, 18*(7), 707–724.

——(2005). Topic repetitiveness after traumatic brain injury: an emergent, jointly managed behaviour. *Clinical Linguistics & Phonetics, 19*(5), 379–392.

Bond, F. & Godfrey, H. P. (1997). Conversation with traumatically brain-injured individuals: a controlled study of behavioural changes and their impact. *Brain Injury, 11,* 319–329.

Brookshire, B. L., Chapman, S. B., Song, J. & Levin, H. S. (2000). Cognitive and linguistic correlates of children's discourse after closed head injury: a three-year follow-up. *Journal of the International Neuropsychological Society, 6*(7), 741–751.

Brown, P. & Levinson, S. (1978). Universals in language usage: politeness phenomena. In E. N. Goody (Ed.), *Questions and Politeness: Strategies in Social Interaction.* Melbourne: Cambridge University Press.

Cannizzaro, M. S. & Coelho, C. A. (2002). Treatment of story grammar following traumatic brain injury: a pilot study. *Brain Injury, 16*(12), 1065–1073.

Carlomagno, S., Giannotti, S., Vorano, L. & Marini, A. (2011). Discourse information content in non-aphasic adults with brain injury: a pilot study. *Brain Injury, 25*(10), 1010–1018.

Channon, S. & Watts, M. (2003). Pragmatic language interpretation after closed head injury: relationship to executive functioning. *Cognitive Neuropsychiatry, 8*(4), 243–260.

Channon, S., Pellijeff, A. & Rule, A. (2005). Social cognition after head injury: sarcasm and theory of mind. *Brain and Language, 93*(2), 123–134.

Channon, S. & Crawford, S. (2010). Mentalising and social problem-solving after brain injury. *Neuropsychological Rehabilitation, 20*(5), 739–759.

Chapman, S. B., Culhane, K. A., Levin, H. S., Harward, H., Mendelsohn, D., Ewing-Cobbs, L. & Bruce, D. (1992). Narrative discourse after closed head injury in children and adolescents. *Brain and Language, 43*, 42–65.

Chapman, S. B., Levin, H. S., Matejka, J., Harward, H. & Kufera, J. A. (1995). Discourse ability in children with brain injury: correlations with psychosocial, linguistic and cognitive factors. *Journal of Head Trauma Rehabilitation, 10*(5), 36–54.

Chapman, S. B., Sparks, G., Levin, H. S., Dennis, M., Roncadin, C., Zhang, L. & Song, J. (2004). Discourse macrolevel processing after severe pediatric traumatic brain injury. *Developmental Neuropsychology, 25*(1–2), 37–60.

Clark, H. H. & Schunk, D. H. (1980). Polite responses to polite requests. *Cognition, 8*(2), 111–143.

Coelho, C. (2002). Story narratives of adults with closed head injury and non-brain-injured adults: influence of socioeconomic status, elicitation task, and executive functioning. *Journal of Speech, Language, & Hearing Research., 45*(6), 1232–1248.

——(2007). Management of discourse deficits following traumatic brain injury: progress, caveats, and needs. *Seminars in Speech & Language, 28*(2), 122–135.

Coelho, C., Liles, B. Z. & Duffy, R. J. (1991a). Discourse analysis with closed head injured adults: evidence for differing patterns of deficits. *Archives of Physical Medicine and Rehabilitation, 72*, 465–468.

——(1991b). The use of discourse analysis for the evaluation of higher level traumatically brain injured adults. *Brain Injury, 5*, 381–392.

——(1995). Impairments of discourse abilities and executive functions in traumatically injured adults. *Brain Injury, 9*, 471–477.

Coelho, C. A., Youse, K. M. & Le, K. N. (2002). Conversational discourse in closed-head-injured and non-brain-injured adults. *Aphasiology, 16*(4–6), 659–672.

Coelho, C., Grela, B., Corso, M., Gamble, A. & Feinn, R. (2005). Microlinguistic deficits in the narrative discourse of adults with traumatic brain injury. *Brain Injury, 19*(13), 1139–1145.

Coelho, C., Le, K., Mozeiko, J., Hamilton, M., Tyler, E., Krueger, F. & Grafman, J. (2012). *Characterizing Discourse Deficits Following Penetrating Head Injury.* Paper presented at the Clinical Aphasiology Conference, Lake Tahoe, CA.

Coelho, C., Le, K., Mozeiko, J., Krueger, F. & Grafman, J. (2012). Discourse production following injury to the dorsolateral prefrontal cortex. *Neuropsychologia, 50*, 3564–3572.

Crosson, B. (1987). Treatment of interpersonal deficits for head-trauma patients in inpatient rehabilitation settings. *The Clinical Neuropsychologist, 1*(4), 335–352.

Dahlberg, C., Hawley, L., Morey, C., Newman, J., Cusick, C. P. & Harrison-Felix, C. (2006). Social communication skills in persons with post-acute traumatic brain injury: three perspectives. *Brain Injury, 20*(4), 425–435.

Darby, D. & Walsh, K. W. (2005). *Walsh's Neuropsychology: A Clinical Approach* (5th ed.). Edinburgh: Elsevier.

Dardier, V., Bernicot, J., Delanov, A., Vanberten, M., Fayada, C., Chevignard, M. & Dubois, B. (2011). Severe traumatic brain injury, frontal lesions, and social aspects of language use: a study of French-speaking adults. [doi: 10.1016/j.jcomdis.2011.02.001]. *Journal of Communication Disorders, 44*(3), 359–378.

Davis, G. & Coelho, C. (2004). Referential cohesion and logical coherence of narration after closed head injury. *Brain and Language, 89*(3), 508–523.

Dennis, M. & Barnes, M. A. (1990). Knowing the meaning, getting the point, bridging the gap, and carrying the message: aspects of discourse following closed head injury in childhood and adolescence. *Brain and Language, 39*, 428–446.

——(2000). Speech acts after mild or severe childhood head injury. *Aphasiology, 14*(4), 391–405.

Dennis, M., Guger, S., Roncadin, C., Barnes, M. A. & Schachar, R. (2001). Attentional-inhibitory control and social-behavioral regulation after childhood closed head injury: do biological, developmental, and recovery variables predict outcome? *Journal of the International Neuropsychological Society, 7*(6), 683–692.

Dennis, M., Purvis, K., Barnes, M. A., Wilkinson, M. & Winner, E. (2001). Understanding of literal truth, ironic criticism, and deceptive praise following childhood head injury. *Brain and Language, 78*, 1–16.

Douglas, J. M. (2010). Using the La Trobe Communication Questionnaire to measure perceived social communication ability in adolescents with traumatic brain injury. *Brain Impairment, 11*(2), 171–182. doi: 10.1375/brim.11.2.171

Douglas, J. M., O'Flaherty, C. A. & Snow, P. C. (2000). Measuring perception of communicative ability: the development and evaluation of the La Trobe communication questionnaire. *Aphasiology, 14*(3), 251–268.

Douglas, J. M., Bracy, C. A. & Snow, P. C. (2007a). Exploring the factor structure of the La Trobe Communication Questionnaire: insights into the nature of communication deficits following traumatic brain injury. *Aphasiology, 21*(12), 1181–1194.

Douglas, J. M., Bracy, C. A. & Snow, P. C. (2007b). Measuring perceived communicative ability after traumatic brain injury: reliability and validity of the La Trobe Communication Questionnaire. *Journal of Head Trauma Rehabilitation, 22*(1), 31–38.

Drummond, S. S. & Boss, M. R. (2004). Functional communication screening in individuals with traumatic brain injury. *Brain Injury, 18*(1), 41–56.

Ehrlich, J. & Barry, P. (1989). Rating communication behaviours in the head injured. *Brain Injury, 3*, 193–198.

Ellis, C. & Peach, R. (2009). Sentence planning following traumatic brain injury. *NeuroRehabilitation, 24*(3), 255–266.

Erlich, J. S. (1988). Selective characteristics of narrative discourse in head-injured and normal adults. *Journal of Communication Disorders, 21*, 1–9.

Ewing-Cobbs, L., Brookshire, B., Scott, M. & Fletcher, J. (1998). Children's narratives following traumatic brain injury: linguistic structure, cohesion and thematic recall. *Brain and Language, 61*, 395–419.

Farrell, A. D., Rabinowitz, J. A., Wallander, J. L. & Curran, J. P. (1985). An evaluation of two formats for the intermediate-level assessment of social skills. *Behavioral Assessment, 7*(2), 155–171.

Ferstl, E. C., Guthke, T. & von Cramon, D. Y. (2002). Text comprehension after brain injury: left prefrontal lesions affect inference processes. *Neuropsychology, 16*(3), 292–308.

Flanagan, S., McDonald, S. & Togher, L. (1995). Evaluating social skills following traumatic brain injury: the BRISS as a clinical tool. *Brain Injury, 9*(4), 321–338.

Galski, T., Tompkins, C. & Johnston, M. V. (1998). Competence in discourse as a measure of social integration and quality of life in persons with traumatic brain injury. *Brain Injury, 12*(9), 769–782.

Glosser, G. & Deser, T. (1991). Patterns of discourse production among neurological patients with fluent language disorders. *Brain and Language, 40*(1), 67–88.

Godfrey, H. P., Knight, R. G., Marsh, N. V., Moroney, B. & Bishara, S. N. (1989). Social interaction and speed of information processing following very severe head-injury. *Psychological Medicine, 19*(1), 175–182.

Godfrey, H. P., Knight, R. G. & Bishara, S. N. (1991). The relationship between social skill and family problem-solving following very severe closed head injury. *Brain Injury, 5*(2), 207–211.

Grice, H. P. (1975). Logic and conversation. In P. Cole & J. Morgan (Eds.), *Syntax and Semantics: Speech Acts* (Vol. 3). New York: Academic Press.

Hagan, C. (1984). Language disorders in head trauma. In A. Holland (Ed.), *Language Disorders in Adults*. San Diego: College Hill Press.

Halliday, M. A. K. (1985). *An Introduction to Functional Grammar*. Australia: Edward Arnold.

——(1994). *An Introduction to Functional Grammar* (2nd edn). London: Edward Arnold.

Halliday, M. A. K. & Hasan, R. (1985). *Language, Context and Text: Aspects of Language in a Social-Semiotic Perspective*. Melbourne: Deakin University Press.

Hartley, L. & Jensen, P. (1991). Narrative and procedural discourse after closed head injury. *Brain Injury, 5 (3)*, 267–285.

——(1992). Three discourse profiles of closed-head-injury speakers: theoretical and clinical implications. *Brain Injury, 6*, 271–282.

Hasan, R. (1984). Coherence and cohesive harmony. In J. Flood (Ed.), *Understanding Reading Comprehension*.

——(1985). The texture of a text. In M. A. K. Halliday & R. Hasan (Eds.), *Language, Context, and Text: Aspects of Language in a Social-semiotic Perspective*. Victoria: Deakin University Press.

Heilman, K. M., Safran, A. & Geschwind, N. (1971). Closed head trauma and aphasia. *Journal of Neurology, Neurosurgery & Psychiatry, 34*, 265–269.

Hough, M. S. (1990). Narrative comprehension in adults with right and left hemisphere brain damage: theme organisation. *Brain and Language, 38*, 253–277.

Hough, M. S. & Barrow, I. (2003). Descriptive discourse abilities of traumatic brain-injured adults. *Aphasiology, 17*(2), 183–191.

Hunt, K. (1970). Syntactic maturity in school children and adults. *Monographs of the Society for Research in Child Development, 35* (134), 1–67.

Jordan, F. M., Murdoch, B. E. & Buttsworth, D. L. (1991). Closed-head-injured children's performance on narrative tasks. *Journal of Speech & Hearing Research, 34*(3), 572–582.

Jorgensen, M. & Togher, L. (2009). Narrative after traumatic brain injury: a comparison of monologic and jointly-produced discourse. *Brain Injury, 23*(9), 727–740.

Kilov, A. M., Togher, L. & Grant, S. (2009). Problem solving with friends: discourse participation and performance of individuals with and without traumatic brain injury. *Aphasiology, 23*(5), 584–605.

Kintsch, W. & van Dijk, T. A. (1978). Toward a model of text comprehension and production. *Psychological Review, 85*, 363–394.

Le, K., Coelho, C., Mozeiko, J. & Grafman, J. (2011a). Measuring goodness of story narratives. *Journal of Speech, Language & Hearing Research, 54*, 118–126.

Le, K., Coelho, C., Mozeiko, J., Krueger, F. & Grafman, J. (2011b). Measuring goodness of story narratives: implications for traumatic brain injury. *Aphasiology, 25*(6–7), 748–760.

——(2012). Predicting story goodness performance from cognitive measures following traumatic brain injury. *American Journal of Speech-Language Pathology, 21*, S115–S125.

Levin, H. S., Grossman, R. G., Rose, J. E. & Teasdale, G. (1979). Long term neuropsychological outcome of closed head injury. *Journal of Neurosurgery, 50*, 412–422.

Liles, B. Z., Coelho, C. A., Duffy, R. J. & Zalagens, M. R. (1989). Effects of elicitation procedures on the narratives of normal and closed head injured adults. *Journal of Speech and Hearing Disorders, 54*, 356–366.

Linscott, R. J., Knight, R. G. & Godfrey, H. P. (1996). The profile of functional impairment in communication (PFIC): a measure of comunication impairment for clinical use. *Brain Injury, 10*, 397–412.

———(2003). *Profile of Pragmatic Impairment in Communication (PPIC).* Unpublished manuscript, University of Otago, Dunedin.

MacDonald, S. & Johnson, C. J. (2005). Assessment of subtle cognitive–communication deficits following acquired brain injury: a normative study of the functional assessment of verbal reasoning and executive strategies (FAVRES). *Brain Injury, 19*(11), 895–902.

Mar, R. (2004). The neuropsychology of narrative: story comprehension, story production and their interrelation. *Neuropsychologia, 42*(10), 28–46.

Marini, A., Galetto, V., Zampieri, E., Vorano, L., Zettin, M. & Carlomagno, S. (2011). Narrative language in traumatic brain injury. [doi: 10.1016/j.neuropsychologia.2011.06.017]. *Neuropsychologia, 49*(10), 2904–2910.

Marsh, N. V. & Knight, R. G. (1991). Behavioral assessment of social competence following severe head injury. *Journal of Clinical and Experimental Neuropsychology, 13*(5), 729–740.

Martin, I. & McDonald, S. (2005). Evaluating the causes of impaired irony comprehension following traumatic brain injury. *Aphasiology, 19*(8), 712–730.

Martin, J. R. & Rose, D. (2003). *Working With Discourse: Meaning Beyond the Clause.* London: Continuum.

McDonald, S. (1992). Differential pragmatic language loss after closed head injury: ability to comprehend conversational implicature. *Applied Psycholinguistics, 13*(3), 295–312.

———(1993). Pragmatic language skills after closed head injury: ability to meet the informational needs of the listener. *Brain and Language, 44*(1), 28–46.

McDonald, S. & van Sommers, P. (1992). Differential pragmatic language loss following closed head injury: ability to negotiate requests. *Cognitive Neuropsychology, 10*, 297–315.

McDonald, S. & Pearce, S. (1995). The 'dice' game: a new test of pragmatic language skills after closed-head injury. *Brain Injury, 9*(3), 255–271.

———(1996). Clinical insights into pragmatic theory: frontal lobe deficits and sarcasm. *Brain and Language, 53*(1), 81–104.

———(1998). Requests that overcome listener reluctance: impairment associated with executive dysfunction in brain injury. *Brain and Language, 61*, 88–104.

McDonald, S. & Flanagan, S. (2004). Social perception deficits after traumatic brain injury: interaction between emotion recognition, mentalizing ability, and social communication. *Neuropsychology, 18*(3), 572–579.

McDonald, S. & Saunders, J. C. (2005). Differential impairment in recognition of emotion across different media in people with severe traumatic brain injury. *Journal of the International Neuropsychological Society, 11*(4), 392–399.

McDonald, S., Flanagan, S., Rollins, J. & Kinch, J. (2003). TASIT: a new clinical tool for assessing social perception after traumatic brain injury. *Journal of Head Trauma Rehabilitation, 18*, 219–238.

McDonald, S., Flanagan, S., Martin, I. & Saunders, C. (2004). The ecological validity of TASIT: test of social perception. *Neuropsychological Rehabilitation, 14*, 285–302.

McDonald, S., Bornhofen, C., Shum, D., Long, E., Saunders, C. & Neulinger, K. (2006). Reliability and validity of 'The Awareness of Social Inference Test' (TASIT): a clinical test of social perception. *Disability and Rehabilitation, 28*, 1529–1542.

McDonald, S., Tate, R. L., Togher, L., Bornhofen, C., Long, E., Gertler, P. & Bowen, R. (2008). Social skills treatment for people with severe, chronic acquired brain injuries: a multicenter trial. [Article]. *Archives of Physical Medicine and Rehabilitation, 89*(9), 1648–1659. doi: 10.1016/j.apmr.2008.02.029

McDonald, S., Flanagan, S. & Rollins, J. (2011). *The Awareness of Social Inference Test (Revised).* Sydney, Australia: Pearson Assessment.

McFall, R. M. (1982). A review and reformulation of the concept of social skills. *Behavioral Assessment, 4*(1), 1–33.

Mentis, M. & Prutting, C. A. (1987). Cohesion in the discourse of normal and head-injured adults. *Journal of Speech and Hearing Research, 30*, 583–595.

———(1991). Analysis of topic as illustrated in a head-injured and a normal adult. *Journal of Speech and Hearing Research, 34*, 583–595.

Milton, S. B. & Wertz, R. T. (1986). Management of persisting communication deficits in patients with traumatic brain injury. In B. P. Uzzell & Y. Gross (Eds.), *Clinical Neuropsychology of Intervention.* Boston: Martinus Nijhoff Publishing.

Milton, S. B., Prutting, C. A. & Binder, G. M. (1984). Appraisal of communication competence in head injured adults. In R. W. Brookshire (Ed.), *Clinical Aphasiology* (Vol. 14, pp. 114–123). Minneapolis: BRK Publishers.

Mortensen, L. (2005). Written discourse and acquired brain impairment: evaluation of structural and semantic features of personal letters from a Systemic Functional Linguistic perspective. *Clinical Linguistics & Phonetics, 19*(3), 227–247.

Mozeiko, J., Le, K. N., Coelho, C. A., Krueger, F. & Grafman, J. (2011). The relationship of story grammar and executive function following TBI. *Aphasiology, 25*(6–7), 826–835.

Muller, F., Simion, A., Reviriego, E., Galera, C., Mazaux, J.-M., Barat, M. & Joseph, P.-A. (2010). Exploring theory of mind after severe traumatic brain injury. *Cortex: A Journal Devoted to the Study of the Nervous System and Behavior, 46*(9), 1088–1099.

Newton, A. & Johnson, D. A. (1985). Social adjustment and interaction after severe head injury. *British Journal of Clinical Psychology, 24*, 225–234.

Nickels, L. (2002). Therapy for naming disorders: Revisiting, revising, and reviewing. *Aphasiology, 16*(10–11), 935–979.

Patry, R. & Nespoulous, J.-L. (1990). Discourse analysis in linguistics: historical and theoretical background. In Y. Joanette & H. H. Brownell (Eds.), *Discourse Ability and Brain Damage: Theoretical and Empirical Perspectives.* New York: Springer-Verlag.

Prigatano, G. P. (1986). Personality and psychosocial consequences of brain injury. In G. P. Prigatano, D. J. Fordyce, H. K. Zeiner, J. R. Roueche, M. Pepping & B. Casewood (Eds), *Neuropsychological Rehabilitation after Brain Injury* (pp. 29–50). Baltimore: John Hopkins University Press.

Prigatano, G. P., Fordyce, D. J., Zeiner, H. K., Roueche, J. R., Pepping, M. & Casewood, B. (Eds) (1986). *Neuropsychological Rehabilitation after Brain Injury.* Baltimore: John Hopkins University Press.

Prince, S., Haynes, W. O. & Haak, N. J. (2002). Occurrence of contingent queries and discourse errors in referential communication and conversational tasks: a study of college students with closed head injury. *Journal of Medical Speech Language Pathology, 10*(1), 19–39.

Prutting, C. A. & Kirchner, D. M. (1987). A clinical appraisal of the pragmatic aspects of language. *Journal of Speech & Hearing Disorders, 52*, 105–119.

Rousseaux, M., Verigneaux, C. & Kozlowski, O. (2010). An analysis of communication in conversation after severe traumatic brain injury. *European Journal of Neurology*, *17*(7), 922–929.

Sarno, M. T. (1980). The nature of verbal impairment after closed head injury. *The Journal of Nervous and Mental Disease*, *168*, 682–695.

Sarno, M. T. & Levita, E. (1986). Characteristics of verbal impairment in closed head injured patients. *Archives of Physical Medicine Rehabilitation*, *67*, 400–405.

Searle, J. (1976). A classification of illocutionary acts. *Language in Society*, *5*(1), 1–23.

Shamay-Tsoory, S. G., Tomer, R. & Aharon-Peretz, J. (2005). The neuroanatomical basis of understanding sarcasm and its relationship to social cognition. *Neuropsychology*, *19*, 288–300.

Snow, P. C. & Douglas, J. M. (2000). Conceptual and methodological challenges in discourse assessment with TBI speakers: towards an understanding. *Brain Injury*, *14*(5), 397–415.

Snow, P. C., Douglas, J. M. & Ponsford, J. (1995). Discourse assessment following traumatic brain injury: a pilot study examining some demographic and methodological issues. *Aphasiology*, *9*(4), 365–380.

——(1997a). Conversational assessment following traumatic brain injury: a comparison across two control groups. *Brain Injury*, *11*(6), 409–429.

——(1997b). Procedural discourse following traumatic brain injury. *Aphasiology*, *11*(10), 947–967.

——(1998). Conversational discourse abilities following severe traumatic brain injury: a follow-up study. *Brain Injury*, *12*(11), 911–935.

——(1999). Narrative discourse following severe traumatic brain injury: a longitudinal follow-up. *Aphasiology*, *13*(7), 529–551.

Spence, S., Godfrey, H. P., Knight, R. G. & Bishara, S. N. (1993). First impressions count: a controlled investigation of social skill following closed head injury. *British Journal of Clinical Psychology Vol 32(3) Sep 1993*, 309–318.

Stein, N. L. & Glenn, C. G. (1979). An analysis of story comprehension in elementary school children. In R. Freedle (Ed.), *New Directions in Discourse Processing.* Vol. 2. Hillsdale, N.J.: Ablex.

Stout, C. E., Yorkston, K. M. & Pimentel, J. I. (2000). Discourse production following mild, moderate, and severe traumatic brain injury: a comparison of two tasks. *Journal of Medical Speech Language Pathology*, *8*(1), 15–25.

Thomsen, I. V. (1975). Evaluation and outcome of aphasia in patients with severe closed head trauma. *Journal of Neurology, Neurosurgery & Psychiatry*, *38*, 713–718.

Togher, L. & Hand, L. (1998). Use of politeness markers with different communication partners: an investigation of five subjects with traumatic brain injury. *Aphasiology*, *12*(7–8), 755–770.

——(1999). The macrostructure of the interview: are traumatic brain injury interactions structured differently to control interactions? *Aphasiology*, *13*(9–11), 709–723.

Togher, L., Hand, L. & Code, C. (1996). A new perspective in the relationship between communication impairment and disempowerment following head injury in information exchanges. *Disability and Rehabilitation*, *18 (11)*, 559–566.

——(1997a). Analysing discourse in the traumatic brain injury population: telephone interactions with different communication partners. *Brain Injury*, *11 (3)*, 169–189.

——(1997b). Measuring service encounters in the traumatic brain injury population. *Aphasiology*, *11 (4/5)*, 491–504.

Togher, L., McDonald, S., Tate, R., Power, E. & Rietdijk, R. (2010). Measuring the social interactions of people with traumatic brain injury and their communication partners: the adapted Kagan scales. *Aphasiology, 24*(6–8), 914–927.

Togher, L., McDonald, S., Tate, R., Power, E. & Rietdijk, R. (2013). Training communication partners of people with severe traumatic brain injury improves everyday conversations: a multicenter single blind clinical trial. *Journal of Rehabilitation Medicine, 45,* 637–645.

Turkstra, L. S., McDonald, S. & Kaufmann, P. M. (1996). Assessment of pragmatic communication skills in adolescents after traumatic brain injury. *Brain Injury, 10*(5), 329–345.

Ulatowska, H. K. & Bond Chapman, S. (1989). Discourse considerations for aphasia management. In R. S. Pierce & M. J. Wilcox (Eds), *Seminars in Speech and Language. Aphasia and pragmatics* (November edn, vol. 10 (4), pp. 298–314). New York: Thieme Medical Publishers.

van Dijk, T. & Kintsch, W. (1983). *Strategies of Discourse Comprehension.* New York: Academic Press.

Van Leer, E. & Turkstra, L. S. (1999). The effect of elicitation task on discourse coherence and cohesion in adolescents with brain injury. *Journal of Communication Disorders, 32*(5), 327–349.

Ventola, E. (1979). The structure of casual conversation in English. *Journal of Pragmatics, 3,* 267–298.

Watts, A. J. & Douglas, J. M. (2006). Interpreting facial expression and communication competence following severe traumatic brain injury. *Aphasiology, 20*(8), 707–722.

Wilson, B. M., Proctor, A., Wilson, B. M. & Proctor, A. (2002). Written discourse of adolescents with closed head injury. *Brain Injury, 16*(11), 1011–1024.

Youse, K. M. & Coelho, C. A. (2005). Working memory and discourse production abilities following closed-head injury. *Brain Injury, 19*(12), 1001–1009.

5 Disorders of social cognition and social behaviour following severe TBI

Skye McDonald, Cynthia Honan, Michelle Kelly, Lindsey Byom and Jacqueline Rushby

Social cognition refers to the capacity to attend to, recognize and interpret interpersonal cues that enable us to understand and predict the behaviour of others, to share experiences and communicate effectively. It has been argued that social cognition has a privileged status in human brain evolution as humans live in communities and, thus, must both compete and cooperate in order to survive (Adolphs, 2003). Developmental disorders such as Asperger syndrome (preserved IQ and impaired social cognition) and Williams syndrome (impaired IQ and preserved social cognition) (Karmiloff-Smith *et al.*, 1995) provide evidence for the dissociation between social and non-social cognition. So too does research accounts of individuals with focal frontal lesions from trauma or other pathology who have relatively preserved intellectual skills in the context of impaired social functioning (e.g. Blair & Cipolotti, 2000; Cicerone & Tanenbaum, 1997; Eslinger & Damasio, 1985; Tranel *et al.*, 2002). There is also a neuroanatomical distinction between social and non-social cognitive processes. Social cognition appears to engage structures in the orbito-ventral and medial frontal lobes while dorsal regions of the lateral and medial prefrontal cortex mediate integration with non-social cognitive functions (Adolphs, 2009; Phillips *et al.*, 2003).

Pathology after severe TBI is concentrated in the ventrolateral and orbital frontal lobes and the ventromedial temporal lobes due to abrasion against the anterior and middle fossa of the skull (Bigler, 2007; Courville, 1945; Gentry *et al.*, 1988; Hadley *et al.*, 1988). Additional medial frontal damage arises as these surfaces are compressed against the dorsal bone and collide with the cerebral falx (Bigler, 2007). This, along with Wallerian degeneration and diffuse axonal injury to the brainstem, corpus callosum and the grey-white matter junctions of the cerebral cortex, will further impair functional connections in this region (Adams *et al.*, 1989; Meythaler *et al.*, 2001; Viano *et al.*, 2005) and make deficits in social cognition highly likely following severe TBI.

Clinicians have long been aware that people with a severe TBI are frequently insensitive to others. In 1978 Lezak argued that a disorder of social perceptiveness was a core component of the 'characterological changes' seen following severe TBI (Lezak, 1978). To date, deficits in social cognition have been characterized as mainly deficits in either: (1) emotional processing, including emotion perception and empathy (Decety & Meyer, 2008; Phillips *et al.*, 2003); or (2) mental judgements, i.e. the ability to infer the beliefs and intentions of others (theory of mind) and to see things from another's perspective (Baron-Cohen *et al.*, 1994).

Emotion

Research that commenced in the 1980s (Jackson & Moffatt, 1987; Prigatano & Pribam, 1982) has now established that people with acute and chronic severe TBI are impaired in the recognition of photographic images of facial expressions (Borgaro *et al.*, 2004; Croker & McDonald, 2005; Green *et al.*, 2004; Ietswaart *et al.*, 2008; Knox & Douglas, 2009; McDonald & Saunders, 2005; Milders *et al.*, 2003; Milders *et al.*, 2008; Spell & Frank, 2000). A meta-analysis of 296 people with TBI from 13 studies (Babbage *et al.*, 2011) confirmed the presence of emotion perception deficits with a relatively large effect size (1.1 SD). Overall, up to 39 per cent of people with severe TBI in convenience samples experienced deficits in recognizing emotions from static presentations of facial expressions.

Although emotion perception is typically assessed using static photographs, naturally occurring facial expressions are dynamic and evolve rapidly from one emotion to another. This increases processing speed demands. It also provides additional cues from facial movement that have been shown to facilitate recognition in normal adults (Bassili, 1978). People with TBI find dynamic displays difficult (Knox & Douglas, 2009; McDonald & Saunders, 2005), although there can be dissociations such that some have more difficulty with dynamic than static faces (McDonald & Saunders, 2005) and vice versa (Knox & Douglas, 2009). Dynamic facial movement is processed by dorsal frontal-parietal zones in contrast to static expressions which appear to be mediated by ventral frontal-temporal systems (Adolphs *et al.*, 2003). Ventral frontal damage is more common following TBI than parietal lobe damage and consistent with this, we have found that fewer people with TBI have deficits in dynamic expressions compared to static (McDonald & Saunders, 2005). Even so, other cognitive deficits especially slowed processing speed and flexible attention will impact upon the ability to process dynamic expressions where the information is transient and changing. Both processing speed and flexibility have been found to be associated with poor emotion perception in people with TBI (Ietswaart *et al.*, 2008; McDonald & Saunders, 2005).

Vocal emotion

It is not just perception of facial expressions that is impaired following TBI. Recognition of vocal emotions is also affected (Dimoska *et al.*, 2010; Hornak *et al.*, 1996; Marquardt *et al.*, 2001; McDonald & Pearce, 1996; McDonald & Saunders, 2005; Milders *et al.*, 2003; Milders *et al.*, 2008; Spell & Frank, 2000). Deficits in facial and vocal perception recognition can co-occur (Ietswaart *et al.*, 2008) but can also appear independently (Hornak *et al.*, 1996; McDonald & Saunders, 2005). Once again, such dissociations may reflect different underlying neural pathology. It has been argued that emotional prosody engages orbitofrontal, frontoparietal and temporal brain systems (especially right hemisphere) which overlap but do not entirely coincide with those engaged in facial expressions (Adolphs *et al.*, 2002). However, there are also cognitive demands that may explain vocal expression deficits. As emotions in voice are conveyed by two sources – speech content and quality – processing vocal emotion is a dual processing task and may be affected by slow processing speed, attentional flexibility etc. Even so, in one study to examine this by experimentally reducing the semantic content, it was found that the problems processing vocal tone were amplified. This suggests that there are genuine problems processing the tonal quality *per se* (Dimoska *et al.*, 2010) although it remains possible that there are other cognitive contributors, such as the fact that facial expressions are more readily verbalisable (Hornak *et al.*, 2003).

Research into the functional significance of emotion perception deficits following TBI is limited and variable but, in general, supports the proposition that poor emotion recognition is a source of interpersonal difficulty. Patients with TBI with impaired emotion perception have been judged by hospital staff as likely to misinterpret the mood of others (Hornak *et al.*, 1996), rated by relatives as having poor pragmatic communication (Milders *et al.*, 2008; Watts & Douglas, 2006) and low social integration (Knox & Douglas, 2009), and rated by independent observers as lacking humour in a spontaneous interaction (McDonald *et al.*, 2004).

Relative impairment with negative emotions

Not all emotional expressions are equally poorly recognized following TBI. There is consistent evidence that there is greater impairment for negative emotional expressions (fear, disgust, sadness and anger) (Callahan *et al.*, 2011; Croker & McDonald, 2005; Hopkins *et al.*, 2002; Jackson & Moffat, 1987; McDonald *et al.*, 2003; Prigatano & Pribam, 1982) although not always (Hornak *et al.*, 2003; Ietswaart *et al.*, 2008; McDonald & Saunders, 2005). This fits with the notion that the ventromedial frontal and limbic structures, frequently damaged in TBI, form a circuit that is primed for the early, rapid detection of ambiguous events in the environment that have emotional salience, but especially if there is potential threat (Adolphs, 2001). Amygdala lesions impair recognition of fear, sadness and anger (Adolphs, 2002; Adolphs *et al.*, 1999; Adolphs & Tranel, 2004; Graham *et al.*, 2007; Sato *et al.*, 2002). Orbitofrontal activation is found in normal adults when viewing angry faces (Blair *et al.*, 1999) and, conversely, is slowed down significantly, if orbitofrontal function is temporarily disrupted using transcranial magnetic stimulation (Harmer *et al.*, 2001).

Interestingly, this ventromedial frontal circuit not only enables rapid orientation to (especially negative) emotionally significant events, but also mediates autonomic responses to these events even prior to conscious awareness (Phillips *et al.*, 2003). This suggests that people with TBI may also have impaired orientation and arousal to negative emotional events and, indeed, there is growing evidence that this is the case. Firstly, a minority of people with severe TBI self-report a blunting of emotional experience (Croker & McDonald, 2005; Hornak *et al.*, 1996). Secondly, objective physiological recording, including the startle reflex, skin conductance levels and facial reactivity has demonstrated reduced arousal and reactivity to negatively valenced pictures and films (de Sousa *et al.*, 2012; de Sousa *et al.*, 2010; Sánchez-Navarro *et al.*, 2005; Saunders *et al.*, 2006; Soussignan *et al.*, 2005). Although this has been reported for both positive and negative stimuli (de Sousa *et al.*, 2012; Sánchez-Navarro *et al.*, 2005; Soussignan *et al.*, 2005), it has also been found to be specific to negatively valenced materials (Angrilli *et al.*, 1999; de Sousa *et al.*, 2010; Saunders *et al.*, 2006). In some cases the participants with TBI not only demonstrated low reactivity to emotional materials, but also self-reported that they did not find them arousing (de Sousa *et al.*, 2012; de Sousa *et al.*, 2010; Saunders *et al.*, 2006) but this has not always been found (Sánchez-Navarro *et al.*, 2005; Soussignan *et al.*, 2005).

The role of simulation in emotion perception following TBI

These changes in physiological reactivity, combined with accounts of poor emotion perception, lead us to consider the role of simulation in emotion recognition (Goldman & Sripada, 2005; Neidenthal *et al.*, 2001). It has been argued that by simulating another person's emotion we have a congruent emotional experience that helps identify the emotion we are observing (Goldman & Sripada, 2005). Indeed, evidence for simulation is well established in the normal adult literature. Adults experience faint facial mimicry (Dimberg & Lundquist, 1990; Dimberg & Petterson, 2000; Dimberg & Thunberg, 1998), changes in skin conductance (Merckelbach *et al.*, 1989; Vrana & Gross, 2004) and subjective experience (Hess & Blairy, 2001; Wild *et al.*, 2001) when they are viewing facial expressions. Facial movements can also alter emotional experience (Adelman & Zajonc, 1989; Levenson *et al.*, 1990) and the emotional state of the observer influences recognition of emotional states in others (Neidenthal *et al.*, 2001).

While the ventromedial system mediates some physiological responses to emotional events, there has been growing interest in a 'mirror neuron' system in the premotor cortex. The inferior frontal lobule is activated when observing the actions of others (Fadiga *et al.*, 1995). Furthermore, motor networks normally engaged in the production of facial movements are activated when viewing facial expressions (Carr *et al.*, 2003; Kilts *et al.*, 2003). Somatosensory activation may also accompany emotion perception, providing the viewer with sensory cues 'as if' the expression were their own. Lesions in the somatosensory cortices (SI and SII) produce specific deficits in emotion recognition (Adolphs *et al.*, 2000).

The possibility that people with TBI have deficits in their capacity to simulate emotions in others is worth considering. Damage to the ventral frontal system will impair the physiological reactivity while diffuse axonal injury may disrupt connections to motor and sensory systems (Green *et al.*, 2004). A specific deficit in the mimicry of angry expressions but not happy has been reported (McDonald *et al.*, 2011b) along with reduced skin conductance changes (Blair & Cipolotti, 2000; de la Plata *et al.*, 2011; Hopkins *et al.*, 2002). This suggests that simulation is impaired but only for negative expressions. Interestingly however, researchers to date have been unable to establish a correlation between mimicry and/or skin conductance and emotion perception accuracy in either people with TBI (McDonald *et al.*, 2011a; McDonald *et al.*, 2011b) or normal adults (Blairy *et al.*, 1999; Hess & Blairy, 2001). This opens up further questions as to the role of mimicry. It may be that mimicry has less to do with specific accuracy in emotional perception and more to do with an empathic response to others. In such a case, the mimicked expression serves two purposes – to convey an understanding of the other person's situation and also to engender a similar, shared experience via body feedback (McIntosh, 1996). The following section will consider deficits in emotional empathic understanding following TBI.

Emotional empathy

Sixty to seventy per cent of people with severe TBI report that they experience little to no emotional empathy compared to 30 per cent of demographically matched adult control participants (de Sousa *et al.*, 2012; de Sousa *et al.*, 2010; de Sousa *et al.*, 2011; Williams & Wood, 2010; Wood & Williams, 2008). Consistent with the body feedback hypothesis, there is a significant relationship between self-report of low emotional empathy and impaired emotional mimicry to negative facial expressions (de Sousa *et al.*, 2010). It is also the case that people with TBI show less negative (specifically, sad) emotion both spontaneously and when asked to pose this expression (Dethier *et al.*, 2012) suggesting a lowering of emotional expressivity, specific to negative emotions. They also report experiencing less congruent mood changes when adopting a body posture consistent with an angry or sad emotional state compared to happy (Dethier *et al.*, 2013). Each of these features, (1) low mimicry, (2) low expressivity and (3) low mood change when adopting an expression, would impair the empathic process by impeding the explicit communication of empathy and by reducing the vicarious sharing of the emotion.

Self-awareness and self-regulation are also important in the empathic process so as to recognize the difference between oneself and others and to regulate the empathic reaction (Decety & Meyer, 2008). TBI not only leads to a lack of reactivity to emotions in others but may also impair recognition of physiological changes that do occur. For example, people with severe TBI have been shown to fail to accurately monitor their own heartbeat (Hynes *et al.*, 2011). Many people with TBI (32–58 per cent) self-report problems with alexithymia, i.e. difficulties identifying and describing their emotions and physiological reactions (Henry *et al.*, 2006b; Koponen *et al.*, 2005; Williams *et al.*, 2001; Wood & Williams, 2007) in comparison to the minority (7–15 per cent) seen in the non-clinical population (Koponen *et al.*, 2005; Pasini *et al.*, 1992). Furthermore, alexithymia has been associated with lowered emotional empathy in TBI (Williams & Wood, 2010). Finally, disorders of emotion regulation, i.e. apathy (disorder of drive) and/or poor frustration tolerance and disinhibition (disorders of control) are common following TBI (Kinsella *et al.*, 1991; Tate, 1999). One study to date has examined the relation between impaired empathy and emotion dysregulation. This found an association between lowered motivation (as reported by relatives) and reduced self-reported empathy with a similar trend for heightened dyscontrol and *heightened* empathy (de Sousa *et al.*, 2012).

Theory of mind

The capacity to attribute mental states, such as thoughts, beliefs, desires and intentions, i.e. having a Theory of Mind (ToM), is considered pivotal to understand and predict the behaviour of others and to make sense of communication. Cognitive empathy is a related construct and refers to an individual's capacity to consider another person's perspective (as opposed to emotional empathy which refers to engaging with their feelings). ToM has been thought to underpin the communicative disorders seen in autism. Many individuals with high functioning autism or Asperger syndrome have normal IQ and are fluent and articulate but, nonetheless, are pedantic and over-literal (Happe & Frith, 1996), fail to interact normally in conversation, often talk at length on obscure or inappropriate topics (Ozonoff & Miller, 1996), have inappropriate nonverbal communication and poor adherence to social rules (Bowler, 1992). They also fail to appreciate how utterances are used to convey information in a socially appropriate manner (Surian *et al.*, 1996) and misinterpret both metaphor and irony (Happe, 1993; Kaland *et al.*, 2011).

Similar deficits in social reasoning and social communication are reported in adults with TBI, i.e. they have been described as egocentric, self-focused, lacking interest in other people, displaying inappropriate humour, frequent interruptions, a blunt manner, overly familiar and disinhibited remarks or advances and inappropriate levels of self-disclosure (Byom & Turkstra, 2012; Crosson, 1987; Flanagan *et al.*, 1995; Levin *et al.*, 1979; McDonald *et al.*, 2004; McDonald & Pearce, 1998; McDonald & van Sommers, 1992). They also self-report reduced cognitive empathy (de Sousa *et al.*, 2010; Grattan & Eslinger, 1989; Wells *et al.*, 2005) with approximately 50 per cent of individuals with TBI self-reporting impaired cognitive empathy compared to 18 per cent of matched controls (de Sousa *et al.*, 2010; Grattan & Eslinger, 1989).   .

They also appear to have specific impairment in judgements that require mentalizing, such as filling in a questionnaire as though they were somebody else (Spiers *et al.*, 1994), identifying the source of interpersonal conflict or the meaning of behaviour in social interactions (Channon & Crawford, 2010; Hynes *et al.*, 2011; Kendall *et al.*, 1997; Turkstra, 2008) and interpreting nonverbal interpersonal interactions (Bara *et al.*, 2001; Cicerone & Tanenbaum, 1997).

Many tasks designed to assess ToM rely upon comprehension of stories, cartoons and photos. Using such tasks it has been reported that adults and children with TBI are impaired in their understanding of complex stories that require knowing that one of the protagonists is operating on a false belief or has committed a faux pas (Bibby & McDonald, 2005; Geraci *et al.*, 2010; Milders *et al.*, 2003; Milders *et al.*, 2006; Milders *et al.*, 2008; Spikman *et al.*, 2012; Stone *et al.*, 1998; Turkstra *et al.*, 2008). They do not understand jokes that are pivoted upon understanding the character's thoughts (Bibby & McDonald, 2005; Milders *et al.*, 2006; Milders *et al.*, 2008; Spikman *et al.*, 2012), cannot predict the intentions of characters in cartoon sequences (Havet-Thomassin *et al.*, 2006; Muller *et al.*, 2010) or a person's mental states based upon the eye region of the face (Geraci *et al.*, 2010; Havet-Thomassin *et al.*, 2006; Henry *et al.*, 2006a; Turkstra *et al.*, 2008). ToM judgements based upon more realistic video vignettes of social interactions are also impaired (McDonald & Flanagan, 2004; Turkstra *et al.*, 2004).

The extent to which poor performance on these tasks reflects specific problems with mental state judgements rather than more generic cognitive skills is difficult to ascertain. Different ToM tasks (e.g. stories versus photographs) rely differentially upon cognitive skills such as visual attention and language. They also vary in complexity, making disparate demands upon cognitive processes such as flexibility, working memory, learning and abstract reasoning, abilities that are often compromised as a result of TBI. Some studies have failed to find any association between ToM tasks and cognitive processes, especially executive function (Havet-Thomassin *et al.*, 2006; Muller *et al.*, 2010; Spikman *et al.*, 2012) whereas other have (Bibby & McDonald, 2005; Channon & Crawford, 2010; Dennis *et al.*, 2009; Havet-Thomassin *et al.*, 2006; Henry *et al.*, 2006a; Milders *et al.*, 2006; Turkstra, 2008). Even if ToM tasks are correlated with non-social tasks this does not preclude the possibility that they require additional, specialized skills. For example, Bibby and McDonald (2005) found that while more complex, second order ToM tasks were reliant upon working memory and general inferencing capacity, simple first order ToM was not, suggesting that the latter may be tapping into a particular mentalizing impairment.

In general, it would appear that there are common processes required for social and non-social tasks, depending upon the medium and response requirements (spoken, written etc.), but there may also be unique requirements called into play when making ToM judgements. Whether ToM represents a modular function that is differentially impaired in TBI, or a higher order ability reliant upon generic executive skills, it is clearly related to impaired pragmatic understanding. Furthermore, it is important to note that low ToM (i.e. cognitive empathy) is associated with high distress in care-givers (Wells *et al.*, 2005) highlighting the importance of social cognition to interpersonal relationships.

Social knowledge and moral reasoning

Another facet of social cognition that is slowly emerging is that of social knowledge. It is commonly assumed that people with TBI have access to previously acquired social knowledge but have difficulty applying this adaptively (Darby & Walsh, 2005). However, social neuroscience research is providing new evidence that suggests that social knowledge is also vulnerable to localized brain damage. In particular, automatic social cognitions such as making assessments of physical attractiveness, dominance and sexual orientation activate the medial prefrontal cortex (Ishai, 2007; Kampe *et al.*, 2001; Karafin *et al.*, 2004; O'Doherty *et al.*, 2003) while the amygdala appears to be involved in judgements of 'trustworthiness' based on facial characteristics (Adolphs *et al.*, 1998; Winston *et al.*, 2002). Judgements of extroversion, warmth, neuroticism, reliability and adventurousness based upon the movements of light points on a walking figure are impaired in people with focal brain lesions, with the relevant cortical region localized to the left frontal opercular cortices (Heberlein *et al.*, 2004). No research to date has examined this in TBI although there does appear to be some disruption to the extent to which people with TBI are influenced by social stereotypes. Whether this reflects a loss of access (Milne & Grafman, 2001) or dysregulation (Barker *et al.*, 2004; McDonald *et al.*, 2011d) is not clear and awaits further research in this field.

Finally, moral reasoning has also been attracting interest in social neuroscience although there has been no work specifically with people with TBI. Moral reasoning refers to the ability to follow ethical and accepted rules and norms (Blair & Cipolotti, 2000) and is of clear relevance to TBI given that these groups are frequently described as disinhibited and inappropriate. Paradoxically, normal adults are reluctant to push a stranger off a footbridge in front of an oncoming trolley in order to save five people on the main track but would take a similar course (sacrifice one person in order to save five) if this involved pulling a lever to divert a run-away tram. The difference is thought to arise from the emotional engagement with physically sending a person to their death. People with fronto-temporal dementia (Mendez *et al.*, 2005) and focal ventromedial damage (Koenigs *et al.*, 2007) show less reluctance to take action in the trolley car scenario than their non-injured counterparts. It has been hypothesized that this reflects impaired emotional responsiveness. Research into this area with people with TBI is yet to be developed.

Contribution of deficits in social cognition to communication

Social cognition has clear relevance to communication. Being able to judge the emotional state of the listener will be important when deciding what to say and how to say it. Conversely, understanding the emotional stance of the speaker should provide important cues in terms of interpreting the meaning behind their utterance. Sarcasm, for example, is almost always associated with a scornful attitude. There has been little research examining the role of emotion perception in specific language production tasks but a correlation has been reported between emotion perception and difficulties with pragmatic aspects of communication as reported by relatives (Milders *et al.*, 2008; Watts & Douglas, 2006) and also the appropriate use of humour in spontaneous conversations (McDonald *et al.*, 2004). An association between the ability to recognize emotions and the ability to understand sarcasm in people with TBI when using scripted sarcasm stories has been supported in one study (Shamay-Tsoory *et al.*, 2005) but not another (McDonald & Pearce, 1996). Interestingly, no relation was found between emotion perception and sarcasm as depicted in realistic videoed vignettes

(McDonald & Flanagan, 2004). Conversely, a relationship was found using the same vignettes with adults with fronto-temporal dementia (Kipps *et al.*, 2009), another clinical population with similar social cognitive deficits.

ToM also bears a clear potential relation to communication skills. As described in Chapter 4, speakers need to be able to consider the listener's perspective when formulating their communication in order to adhere to Grice's maxims of relevance, quality, quantity and manner. They also need to be able to judge the social relationship between themselves and their conversational partner accurately when selecting an appropriately polite utterance. Research is scant as to the effects of ToM deficits upon these aspects of discourse production. Interestingly, another facet of mentalizing is the ability to use mental state terms (e.g. think, want, believe) appropriately. Adolescents with TBI who scored poorly on a measure of ToM also used fewer words that reflected mental states than either adolescents without injuries or their peers with TBI who had normal ToM performance (Stronach & Turkstra, 2008). Men with severe TBI have also been found to have trouble adjusting mental state terms in their language to accommodate the topic of intimacy in conversation with a friend (Byom & Turkstra, 2012).

ToM is directly implicated in the comprehension of pragmatic inference and there is some research that supports this. Specifically, those who experience difficulties understanding second order ToM inferences (i.e. what one person wants another person to believe) or report impaired cognitive empathy are also those most likely to experience problems understanding the meaning of sarcastic exchanges (Channon *et al.*, 2005; McDonald & Flanagan, 2004; Shamay-Tsoory *et al.*, 2005; Shamay *et al.*, 2002) and hints (Muller *et al.*, 2010).

Assessment of social cognition

In many clinical settings, deficits in social cognition are often inferred on the basis of neuropsychological test performance in domains such as processing speed, attention, working memory, long-term memory and executive functioning. However, while dysfunction in these areas may undermine an individual's ability to perform in social settings, they do not account for all the difficulties experienced (Bibby & McDonald, 2005; McDonald *et al.*, 2006; Struchen *et al.*, 2008). In view of the high incidence of social dysfunction following TBI, and its detrimental long-term effects (e.g. unemployment, social withdrawal), the use of specific social cognition assessment tools is increasingly being seen as an integral part of the neuropsychological testing regime. Selected measures (summarized in Table 5.1) are reviewed below.

Assessment of emotion perception and processing

Emotion perception and processing is fundamental to communication and social cognition (Johnston *et al.*, 2008; Knox & Douglas, 2009; McDonald, 2000; Watts & Douglas, 2006). Ekman and Friesen's (1976) Pictures of Facial Affect, a series of black and white photographs of faces depicting the six basic emotions of fear, disgust, anger, happiness, sadness and surprise, have formed the basis of many tests (e.g. *emotion identification tasks, matching facial expression tasks*, and *labelling morphed facial expression tasks*) that aim to assess 'context-free' aspects of emotion perception and processing. Research consistently indicates that individuals with TBI perform worse than normal control participants on these types of tasks (Croker & McDonald, 2005; Henry *et al.*, 2006a; Ietswaart *et al.*, 2008; Milders *et al.*, 2008). A commercially available package of tests containing Ekman and Friesen's series of faces is the *Facial Expression of Emotion: Stimuli and Tests* (FEEST; Young *et al.*, 2002). The package contains: *The Ekman60 Faces Test*, an emotion identification task that uses 60 randomly presented images of facial expressions; and *The Emotion Hexagon Test*, an alternative emotion identification task that uses 30 images of morphed (i.e. of graded difficulty) facial expressions. Split-half reliabilities for these tests are 0.62 and 0.92, respectively. Both tests are moderately-strongly correlated with each other and percentage correct scores correlate well with the original Ekman and Friesen's (1976) Pictures of Facial Affect (Young *et al.*, 2002). The package also contains more than 1,000 images of facial expressions that can be tailored for assessment and development purposes.

The Florida Affect Battery (FAB; Bowers *et al.*, 1991a) examines two elemental components of social cognition: facial expressions and tone of voice. Although the battery was originally designed as a research tool to examine perceptual disturbances and understanding of nonverbal communicative signals of emotions in neurological or psychiatric disorders, it is a promising tool to screen for 'lower-order' social cognition deficits in adults with TBI. The FAB is based on a theoretically driven cognitive model of affect processing (Bowers *et al.*, 1993; Bowers *et al.*, 1991b), which suggests that evaluations of affective faces and voices (otherwise termed the 'nonverbal affect lexicon') are both modular and dissociative. The FAB comprises 10 subtests involving face and sound affect discrimination, naming, comprehension and selection, matching, or conflict detection (i.e. whether semantic content and prosody conflict). Cross-modal subtests requiring affect matching across facial and prosodic domains are also included. The five core emotions of happiness, sadness, anger, fear and neutral, are assessed across these subtests.

FAB prosody subtests have been used in prior TBI research with the results indicating that individuals with TBI are significantly more impaired than controls in their ability to verbally label affective prosody and judge inconsistent prosody, but not in their ability to discriminate emotion tone of voice and detect spoken sentences with consistent semantic content and prosody (Ietswaart *et al.*, 2008; Milders *et al.*, 2003; Milders *et al.*, 2008). The FAB reportedly has excellent test–retest reliability (Bowers *et al.*, 1991a), although details of its internal consistency and validity are lacking.

The Diagnostic Assessment of Nonverbal Affect-2 (DANVA2; Nowicki, 2010) is a promising tool to assess emotion identification ability in individuals with TBI. It consists of a collection of tests that contain emotions displayed by multicultural adults and children in various domains of nonverbal behaviour including facial expressions, voice and posture. While some research to validate its use in normative adult and TBI populations has been undertaken (e.g. Baum & Nowicki, 1998; Pitterman & Nowicki, 2004; Spell & Frank, 2000), this is largely still in development. Internal and test–retest reliabilities for the DANVA2 subtests are adequate and scores on most subtests are discriminant from measures of intelligence (Nowicki, 2010).

The Advanced Clinical Solutions (ACS; NCS Pearson Inc, 2009) Social Cognition battery comprises three subtests: Social Perception, Faces and Names. Social Perception contains three tasks including Affect Naming, Prosody-Face Matching and Prosody-Pair Matching. In Affect Naming, examinees are asked to name the emotion expressed in different faces by selecting one from a list of alternatives (happy, sad, angry, afraid, surprised, disgusted and neutral). In Prosody-Face Matching, examinees are asked to select a face with an emotion (amongst six alternatives) that best matches the emotional tone of a spoken statement. In Prosody-Pair Matching, examinees are asked to select a picture of two people interacting from four alternative pictures, which best matches the emotional tone of a spoken statement, and to identify the emotion. The Faces and Names subtests measures an individual's ability to learn and recall (following a 10–15 minute delay) faces and their spatial locations on a 4x4 grid, and face-name associations (i.e. matching a face to their favourite activity). The ACS Social Cognition tests maintain acceptable internal, test-retest and inter-rater reliabilities and it correlates minimally with other measures of cognition and memory (NCS Pearson Inc, 2009). However, although it is a well normed test, owing to its recent development, there are no published studies of its ability to detect dysfunction in individuals with TBI. In a recent pilot study in individuals with Asperger syndrome, schizophrenia and control participants, the Social Perception subtest demonstrated moderate convergent validity with measures of emotional processing including The Ekman60 test and the Reading the Mind in the Eyes Test – Revised (Kandalaft *et al.*, 2012). The ACS Social Perception subtest was most divergent from Abell *et al.*'s (2000) Social Perception Task, a ToM measure that uses animated shapes to elicit attributions of actions, interactions and mental states, and the Mayor-Salovey-Caruso Emotional Intelligence Test-Managing Emotion Subtest (MSCEIT-ME; Mayer *et al.*, 2000), a measure of openness to feelings and ability to modulate them in oneself and others.

Assessing ToM and cognitive empathy

There are numerous tests that aim to assess ToM or cognitive empathy. One such measure is the *Reading the Mind in the Eyes* test. Both the original (Baron-Cohen *et al.*, 1997) and revised version (Baron-Cohen *et al.*, 2001) of this test purport to assess an individual's ability to infer other people's mental states by visually examining photographs of the eye region. Whereas the original version comprises 25 pictures with two opposing mental state terms (e.g. 'concerned' or 'unconcerned'), the revised version comprises 36 pictures with four mental state response options (e.g. 'jealous', 'panicked', 'arrogant' or 'hateful'). The revised version was developed to improve the psychometric properties of the original version (e.g. variability and ceiling effects). Unlike the original version, it does not include items that focus on attention due to the belief that eye gaze direction makes judgements about a person's mental state too easy. There is reportedly no correlation between this measure and intelligence (Baron-Cohen *et al.*, 2001).

Research indicates that individuals with TBI perform significantly worse than controls on the revised version of the Mind in the Eyes test (Havet-Thomassin *et al.*, 2006; Henry *et al.*, 2006a; Muller *et al.*, 2010), although no differences between individuals with severe TBI and controls have been detected using the original version (Milders *et al.*, 2003). Several limitations concerning the validity of the Reading the Mind in the Eyes test have also been reported (Johnston *et al.*, 2008) and it is important to bear these in mind when using this measure to assess an individual's ability to make inferences about mental states. In brief, these limitations include: the provision of no contextual information and depiction of unknown actual psychological states, the assumption that the 'appropriate word' will be evident even though this was determined by consensus through a panel of judges, the inherent assumption that psychological state can be inferred by the eye region even though facial expressions are not necessarily linked to affective experiences (e.g. smiling when not happy or not frowning when angry), the assumption that specific psychological states (e.g. 'fantasizing', 'cautious') are uniquely specified by static information of the eye region even though this can often only be determined through the provision of additional contextual cues (e.g. an upturned mouth) and in at least half the items, the correct response option can be identified merely because the word is 'the odd one out'.

The *Faux Pas Recognition Test* (Stone *et al.*, 1998) is another ToM task comprising 20 short vignettes (10 containing a social faux pas and 10 containing no social faux pas). A faux pas is an unintentional statement that should not have been made (i.e. an insult or awkward remark). Written vignettes are placed in front of examinees whilst the examiner reads them aloud. Several questions concerning detection of the faux pas (or its absence), understanding of the intentions and beliefs of the characters and general comprehension of the non-faux pas vignettes, are answered. Studies indicate that individuals with TBI or bilateral damage to the orbitofrontal cortex are sometimes more impaired than individuals with dorsolateral prefrontal cortex lesions or normal controls in detecting faux pas (Milders *et al.*, 2003; Stone *et al.*, 1998) or correctly rejecting non-faux pas (Milders *et al.*, 2006). However, questions involving understanding of intentions in the faux pas appear to best discriminate individuals with TBI from normal controls (Milders *et al.*, 2008; Milders *et al.*, 2006). Information on the test's reliability and validity is lacking, however, split-half reliabilities (0.44–0.55) have been reported for individuals with bipolar disorder (Harari *et al.*, 2010).

Happè *et al.*'s (1999) *Cartoon task* was originally developed to detect ToM deficits in patients with a history of right hemispheric stroke. The task consists of 12 cartoons (sourced from magazines) depicting humorous situations. Half contain jokes that require inferences to be made about a character's beliefs, intentions or focus of attention and half contain jokes that are based on physical anomalies or violation of a social norm. Examinees are asked to explain why each cartoon is funny. Information on the test's reliability and validity is lacking; however, one study reports that males perform significantly better on this task than women (Russell *et al.*, 2007). Individuals with TBI are also significantly impaired relative to normal controls on both the 'mental' and 'physical' components of this task (Milders *et al.*, 2008; Milders *et al.*, 2006) indicating problems with the construct validity of the tool. However, Bibby and McDonald (2005) demonstrated an emergence of deficits specific to mental state inferences once the effects of working memory are taken into account. Future research to further delineate the usefulness of this type of task in TBI populations is required.

One promising ToM test that is yet to be validated in a TBI population is the Hinting Task (Corcoran *et al.*, 1995). This test comprises of ten verbally presented short stories involving an interaction between two characters. Each story concludes with one of the characters dropping a very obvious hint. For example, 'Simon is enjoying an evening out at the pub with his friend Gareth. Gareth is about to buy some more drinks when Simon says: "I have a very busy day tomorrow, and I need to be at my best".' The examinee is asked to state what the character really meant. If a correct response is not given, a second more direct hint is given. The Hinting Task is a reliable and well-validated tool for use in people with schizophrenia and maintains good psychometric properties (Corcoran *et al.*, 1995; Fiszdon *et al.*, 2007; Greig *et al.*, 2004; Marjoram *et al.*, 2005).

Ecologically valid measures of social cognition

Tests of ecological validity are designed to predict social and functional abilities relevant to real world settings. TASIT (McDonald *et al.*, 2011a), described in detail in Chapter 4, is a clinically sensitive and reliable tool that assesses higher-level social perception deficits in individuals with TBI. Due to the limitations posed by traditional emotion recognition measures that use static displays (e.g. photographs) of emotional expressions, TASIT was specifically developed to assess the complex spontaneous displays of emotion encountered in everyday social interactions via audiovisual vignettes, thus making it a highly ecologically valid measure. TASIT has three parts; TASIT 1 measures emotion perception focusing upon speakers engaged in ambiguous conversations, TASIT 2 and 3 measure the ability to identify the thoughts, intentions and feelings of speakers along with the ability to interpret their conversational meanings as sincere, sarcastic, or deceptive. Performance on TASIT also correlates with real world social performance in people with TBI (McDonald *et al.*, 2004).

Self-report questionnaires

Self-report measures of social cognition are also available. The Balanced Emotional Empathy Scale (BEES; Mehrabian, 2000) is an internally reliable and valid 30-item measure of emotional empathy (i.e. the ability to experience the feelings expressed by others). Emotional empathy is a domain of social cognition that is affected by a large proportion of individuals with TBI (de Sousa *et al.*, 2010; de Sousa *et al.*, 2011; Williams & Wood, 2010; Wood & Williams, 2008), thus its measurement is important. Responses on the BEES are made on a 9-point Likert scale, ranging from 'very strong disagreement' to 'very strong agreement'.

The Interpersonal Reactivity Index (Davis, 1980; Davis, 1983) is an alternative reliable and valid self-report measure comprising 28 items that assesses various dimensions of emotional empathy and cognitive empathy (i.e. the ability to adopt another person's point of view). Items are rated on a 5-point Likert scale with response options ranging from 'does not describe me well' to 'describes me very well'. There are four subscales: Empathetic Concern (EC) – assesses an individual's capacity to feel warmth, compassion and concern for others; Personal Distress (PD) – assesses an individual's ability to feel discomfort in response to the misfortunes of others; Perspective Taking (PT) – assesses the tendency to spontaneously adopt the psychological point of view of others; and Fantasy (FS) – assesses the tendency to transpose oneself imaginatively into the feelings and actions of fictional characters in books, movies and plays. Whereas EC and PD are thought to tap into emotional empathy, PT and FS are thought to tap into the cognitive elements of empathy. Evidence on the IRI's ability to detect empathy difficulties in individuals with TBI is mixed with one study reporting that individuals with TBI score lower than normal controls on the emotional empathy and cognitive empathy subscale types (de Sousa *et al.*, 2010) and another study reporting no such differences (Muller *et al.*, 2010). An alternative scale measuring both the affective and cognitive dimensions of empathy is the 40-item Empathy Quotient (EQ; Baron-Cohen & Wheelwright, 2004) scale. Although normative information for this scale is not available, it has adequate psychometric properties (Allison *et al.*, 2011; Muncer & Ling, 2006), and both dimensions of the scale discriminate individuals with TBI from normal controls (de Sousa *et al.*, 2010).

Emotional and behavioural dysregulation

While interpersonal skills will be impacted by poor understanding of social cues, many people with TBI experience additional difficulties in the regulation of their emotions and their behaviour. Such difficulties are highlighted by relatives as causing the most distress for family members (Kinsella *et al.*, 1991) and are predictive of relationship breakdown post-TBI (Wood *et al.*, 2005). As overviewed in Chapter 3, there are two main clusters of behavioural disorders that are typically seen post-TBI.

The first is a disorder of control, manifest in poor self-monitoring, impulsivity and emotional lability, including poor frustration tolerance, aggression, irritability, childishness and sexual disinhibition (Brooks *et al.*, 1986; Demark & Gemeinhardt, 2002; Hanks *et al.*, 1999; Kinsella *et al.*, 1991; Lezak, 1978; McKinlay *et al.*, 1981; Tate, 1999; Thomsen, 1984). The second is a disorder of drive characterized by apathy, loss of initiative and spontaneity and poor

Table 5.1 Some common measures of social cognition

Name of instrument	Nature of response	Scored by	Level of analysis	Normative information
Facial Expression of Emotion: Stimuli and Tests (Young et al., 2002)	Identification of basic emotions shown in photographs of faces displayed on a computer	Clinician	Contains 2 tests of emotion identification 1) *The Ekman 60 Faces Test* and 2) *The Emotion Hexagon Test.* Total scores in each test are assessed.	Normative data for The Ekman 60 Faces Test (N = 227, ages 20–70 years) and the Emotion Hexagon Test (N = 125, ages 20–75) are available (Young *et al.*, 2002).
Reading the Mind in the Eyes – Revised (Baron-Cohen et al., 2001)	Selection of 'emotional' mental state terms (amongst 4 alternatives) depicted by photographs of the eye region	Clinician	Total scores based on 36 items.	Normative data stratified by gender available (N = 122, mean age/SD = 46.5/16.9) (Simon Baron-Cohen *et al.*, 2001). Descriptive TBI (*n* = 16, mean age/SD = 44.4/13.36, age range 20–61) and control data (*n* = 11) also available (Henry *et al.*, 2006a).
Faux Pas Recognition Test (Stone et al., 1998)	Aurally presented vignettes following which the examinee answers questions that probe detection and understanding of social faux pas	Clinician	Detection and explanation of faux pas in vignettes containing either a faux pas (20 items) or no faux pas (20 items).	Descriptive TBI data (*n* = 36, mean age/SD = 37.5/16.1) and orthopaedic control data (*n* = 34, mean age/SD = 35.6/13.1) available (Milders *et al.*, 2006).
Cartoon task (Happè et al., 1999)	Explanation of humorous situations depicted in cartoons	Clinician	Correct explanation of jokes that require inferences about a character's beliefs, intentions, or focus of attention (6 mental cartoons) or that contain jokes based on physical anomalies (6 physical cartoons).	Limited normative data available stratified by gender (Males: *n* = 40, mean age/SD = 34.4/10.58; Females: *n* = 40, mean age/SD = 30.35/9.39) (Russell *et al.*, 2007). Descriptive TBI (*n* = 36, mean age/SD = 37.5/16.1) and orthopaedic control data (*n* = 34, mean age/SD = 35.6/13.1) available (Milders *et al.*, 2006).

Table 5.1 continued

Name of instrument	Nature of response	Scored by	Level of analysis	Normative information
Hinting task (Corcoran et al., 1995)	Response to questions asking about the intended meaning of statements contained in aurally presented interactions between two people	Clinician	Correct identification of intended meaning in 10 short stories involving the interactions; whether an additional hint is required is reflected in overall score.	Control data available (n = 30, mean age/SD = 31.2/10.0) (Corcoran et al., 1995).
Florida Affect Battery (Bowers et al., 1993; Bowers et al., 1991a)	Face or sound identity and affect discrimination, naming, comprehension and selection, matching, and conflict detection using various formats	Clinician	10 modality specific subtests including: (1) Facial Identity Discrimination; (2) Facial Affect Discrimination; (3) Facial Affect Naming; (4) Facial Affect Selection; (5) Facial Affect Matching; (6) Nonemotional Prosody Discrimination; (7) Emotional Prosody Discrimination; (8) Name the Emotional Prosody/Conflicting Emotional Prosody; (9) Match Emotional Prosody to an Emotional Face; (10) Match Emotional Face to the Emotional Prosody.	Normative data available (N = 164, ages 18–85 years) (Bowers, et al., 1991b).
Advanced Clinical Solutions Social Cognition tests (NCS Pearson Inc, 2009)	Various response formats are required including affect discrimination and matching, recalling spatial locations of faces on a grid, and recalling face/name associations	Clinician	3 subtests are included: (1) Social Perception includes three tasks: Affect Naming, Prosody-Face Matching, and Prosody-Pair Matching; (2) Faces include spatial learning and recall of faces; (3) Names include learning and recall of name-face associations.	Normative data available for adolescents and adults aged 16–90 years (N = 800) (NCS Pearson Inc, 2009).

Measure	Rater	Description	Normative data
Diagnostic Assessment of Nonverbal Accuracy 2 (DANVA-2) (Nowicki & Carton, 1993; Nowicki & Duke, 1994)	Clinician	Identification of basic emotions depicted in pictures of faces and body posture, and voices	Recognition of emotions displayed by children and adults in the domains of: (1) faces; (2) voices; and (3) posture.	Normative data available for most age groups (N > 2,000) (Nowicki, 2010).
TASIT (McDonald et al., 2011a)	Clinician	Presentation of videoed vignettes following which participant responds to questions that probe understanding of videoed vignettes	Comprehension of: (1) basic emotion; (2) social emotions; (3) ToM including speaker beliefs and intentions; and (4) pragmatic inferences contrasting sincere exchanges with sarcasm and lies.	Normative data available for adolescents and adults aged 14–60 years (N = 134 for part 1; N = 253 for Parts 2 & 3) (McDonald et al., 2011a).
Balanced Emotional Empathy Scale (Mehrabian, 2000)	Clinician	Self-ratings of emotional empathy with referents ranging from –4 (very strong disagreement) to 4 (very strong agreement)	Total emotional empathy scores based on 30 items are analysed.	Normative data stratified by gender is available from manual (Mehrabian, 2000). Community data stratified by gender (N = 127, ages 25–45 years) (Toussaint & Webb, 2005) and descriptive TBI sample (n = 64, mean age/SD = 35.84/13.33) with control data (n = 64, mean age/SD = 36.09/14.24) also available (Williams & Wood, 2010).
Interpersonal Reactivity Index (Davis, 1980; Davis, 1983)	Clinician	Self-ratings of emotional and cognitive empathy with referents ranging from A (does not describe me well) to E (describes me very well)	28 items covering four subscales including; two relate to emotional empathy (Empathetic Concern and Personal Distress subscales) and two relate to the cognitive elements of empathy (Perspective Taking and Fantasy subscales).	Normative data based on college students stratified by gender available (N = 1,161) (Davis, 1980). Descriptive TBI data (n = 20, mean age/SD = 47.4/10.0) and control data (n = 22, mean age/SD = 36.1/12.6) also available (de Sousa et al., 2010).
Empathy Quotient (Baron-Cohen & Wheelwright, 2004)	Clinician	Ratings of emotional and cognitive empathy with referents ranging from 'strongly agree' to 'strongly disagree'	40 items covering the affective and cognitive dimensions of empathy.	Control data stratified by gender is available (Males: n = 71, mean age/SD = 38.8/13.7; Females: n = 126, mean age/SD = 39.5/12.8, age range 17–73) (Baron-Cohen & Wheelwright, 2004).

cognitive flexibility (Kinsella *et al.*, 1991; Tate, 1999) that may occur independently, or in conjunction with a disorder of control (Tate *et al.*, 1991). Disorders of control and drive are often conceptualized as impairments/deficits of executive function, but they also play a particular role in the regulation of emotional behaviour and also behavioural decision making.

Similar neural systems to those already discussed in relation to social cognition are implicated in emotion regulation, i.e. the medial cortex is implicated in self-initiation and sustained behaviour (Andrewes, 2001; Darby & Walsh, 2005; Eslinger, 2008; Luria, 1973; Stuss *et al.*, 1992), the orbitobasal frontal lobes are associated with the flexible control of excitation, inhibition and emotional control of behaviour (Walsh, 1985) and a dorsal system that entails the hippocampus, dorsal aspects of the anterior cingulate gyrus and dorsolateral prefrontal cortex (Phillips *et al.*, 2003) are involved in the effortful regulation of automatic processing and the engagement of cognitive processes via connections to other cortical regions. In the following sections disorders of control and drive will be overviewed.

Disorders of control

Disinhibition across behavioural, cognitive and emotional domains is prevalent following severe TBI. For example, there may be inability to inhibit impulsive and habitual behaviour leading to inappropriate touching and verbal disinhibition (Rao & Lyketsos, 2000). There are different kinds of inhibition, including the overt suppression of an activated motor response (inhibitory control) and the ability to inhibit an automatic response in favour of another (interference control: e.g. the Stroop effect) (Nigg, 2000). Meta-analyses of studies examining overall inhibitory control deficits in people with TBI, ranging from mild to very severe, suggest a small-to-moderate impairment (Dimoska *et al.*, 2011; Mathias & Wheaton, 2007), especially for response inhibition. Although reduced frontal activation has been seen in people with mild through to severe TBI when performing tasks that require cognitive control (Christodoulou *et al.*, 2001; McAllister *et al.*, 1999; McAllister *et al.*, 2001; Perlstein *et al.*, 2004), focal frontal lesions are unlikely to be the only culprit. Effective control relies on efficient transmission of inhibitory neural signals along prefrontal-subcortical thalamic circuits (Rubia *et al.*, 2001). Slowed information processing is prevalent following TBI (Frenchmen *et al.*, 2005; for a review see Mathias & Wheaton, 2007; Ponsford & Kinsella, 1992), probably due to diffuse axonal injury leading to a shearing of interconnections between networks (Felmingham *et al.*, 2004). Slow information processing will also cause poor inhibitory control (Mathias & Wheaton, 2007; Ponsford & Kinsella, 1992), whereby slow or delayed activation of the inhibition process may result in a failure to inhibit (Logan, 1994).

Although effortful inhibitory control is important for the deliberate regulation of both cognition and socio-emotional behaviour (Zelazo & Cunningham, 2007), it is not clear whether the same inhibitory processes are common to both. Some studies do suggest a relationship. For example, it has been reported that errors on standard neuropsychological measures were associated with relative reports of difficulties in emotional control (irritability, restlessness, aggression) (Tate, 1999; Tate & Broe, 1999) and social integration (Odhuba *et al.*, 2005). We have also directly manipulated emotional responses in people with severe TBI. In this study people with severe TBI were asked to self-rate their emotions after watching film clips chosen to elicit feelings of anger (McDonald *et al.*, 2010). Those who demonstrated poorer inhibition in terms of a greater number of errors on tests were those who self-reported more angry responses to these provocative films.

Disorders of drive

Medial and dorsal frontal pathology is thought to give rise to disorders of drive (Andrewes, 2001; Darby & Walsh, 2005; Eslinger, 2008; Luria, 1973; Stuss *et al.*, 1992) although these are not unitary and appear to fall into three clusters: (1) indifference to external and internal states; (2) aspontaneity, i.e. inability to self-initiate activity in the absence of external stimulation; and (3) adynamia, i.e. lowered ability to engage/disengage cognition and behaviour flexibly (Tate, 1999).

Indifference

Indifference refers to a failure to engage with and respond to emotionally salient information. In our work using anger inducing films (McDonald *et al.*, 2010) we found that a minority (6/34) of our group of people with severe TBI (and 2/34 control participants) self-reported very little emotional reaction to the films. This concurs with the research into emotional responsivity reported above, i.e. many people with TBI demonstrate reduced physiological reactions to emotionally evocative materials (de Sousa *et al.*, 2011; Hopkins *et al.*, 2002; Sánchez-Navarro *et al.*, 2005; Saunders *et al.*, 2006; Soussignan *et al.*, 2005) including a muted orientation response (skin conductance response) when passively viewing emotional material (McDonald *et al.*, 2011c). Interestingly, explicit instructions to attend to the stimuli may overcome this. In two studies, one of people with TBI (McDonald *et al.*, 2011c) and one of people with focal frontal lesions (Damasio *et al.*, 1990) when participants were given explicit instructions to attend to the emotional images, in order to answer questions, they demonstrated normal skin conductance responses. This suggests that their indifference could be ameliorated with a deliberate attentional strategy.

Decreased responsivity to environmental events will diminish the emotional experience of the individual. It may also impact upon complex decision making in cognitive domains. Bechara and colleagues have argued that physiological responses provide a 'somatic marker' as to risky choices (Bechara *et al.*, 1994; Bechara *et al.*, 2000; Bechara *et al.*, 1997; Damasio *et al.*, 1991). This research is based upon reports of patients with damage to the prefrontal cortex who made inappropriate and risky decisions in their everyday lives, despite having an intact knowledge of social norms. An orbitofrontal lesion patient, EVR, was famed for having an above-average intellect and memory, and scoring in the average range on various neuropsychological tests, while displaying impaired social conduct. Damasio and colleagues claimed that sociopathy associated with damage to the prefrontal cortex was the consequence of impaired activation of the somatic states required to comprehend the implications of poor social decisions (Damasio *et al.*, 1990).

The Iowa Gambling Task

The majority of work examining the somatic marker hypothesis has focused upon the Iowa Gambling Task (IGT). This is a card game whereby participants need to select cards from four decks in order to win money. Two decks are disadvantageous as they yield large gains, but are associated with even larger losses and will yield a small profit over time. The two advantageous decks yield smaller gains, but also smaller losses, and selecting cards from these two decks will lead to a larger profit in the long term. Damasio and colleagues propose that anticipation of complex response contingencies is associated with somatic responses even prior to conscious awareness of those contingencies, that is, prior to conscious knowledge of the best decks (Bechara *et al.*, 1997). In support of this healthy adults learn over trials to play the advantageous decks whereas patients with ventromedial damage do not (Bechara *et al.*, 1994; Bechara *et al.*, 2000; Fellows & Farah, 2005). Further, whereas, normal adults exhibit changes in skin conductance in anticipation of their choice, even before they can verbalize the rules (see Maia & McClelland, 2004 for counter argument), people with ventromedial damage do not, suggesting they are deprived of this somatic signal (Bechara *et al.*, 1997; Bechara *et al.*, 1996; Naccache *et al.*, 2005). Although the majority of research on the somatic marker hypothesis has been conducted in patients with focal lesions, some work has also been conducted on people with TBI. Levine *et al.* (2005) found that the IGT was sensitive to TBI in general; however, contrary to predictions performance was not associated with the severity of TBI. Fujiwara *et al.* (2008) found that people with TBI started out in the task more conservatively than controls, however, they required longer to identify the advantageous strategy. While the authors of the IGT claim that task performance is reliant upon subconscious somatic markers, evidence for the necessity of conscious knowledge of deck contingencies was provided by Garcia-Molina *et al.* (2007) that is, those with greater reportable knowledge of the card game made better decisions.

The Iowa Gambling Task has been heralded as a useful measure of poor decision making that may be more closely aligned to social outcomes than conventional neuropsychological tests. However, concerns regarding the reliability and validity of the IGT have been raised (Buelow & Suhr, 2009). Indeed there is little evidence that performance on the IGT is indicative of real-world social outcomes, thus questioning whether it is a socially relevant task.

As discussed throughout this chapter, successful social interaction requires the synthesis of social knowledge and feedback from the environment, including remaining sensitive to social cues such as emotional expressions, retrieval of social knowledge, inferring the intent of others and adapting behaviour appropriately (Corrigan, 1997). The ability to look to the environment for social feedback and use this feedback to guide ongoing social exchanges is therefore essential. One facet of this is the ability to register social signals that indicate whether one is being included or excluded in social situations, i.e. responsivity to internal and external cues that signal the likelihood of future interactions. Recently a novel task was developed within our lab to examine this.

The Social Decision Making Task

The Social Decision Making Task (SDMT; Kelly *et al.*, Submitted) is a pseudo online game of catch-and-throw where the participant is required to use social feedback provided within the task to guide future decisions aimed at increasing the likelihood of future interactions in the game. Participants need to learn who the 'friendly' people are and throw the ball to those players in order to increase their inclusion in the game. Initial findings demonstrated that adults with severe TBI make poorer social decisions when compared with healthy control participants, that is, they are less able to learn who the friendly players are (Kelly *et al.*, Submitted). This finding was replicated even when they were given twice as many trials with which to learn. Performance on the SDMT was associated with reversal learning and drive (motivation/initiation) (Kelly *et al.*, Submitted). Whilst more exploration using this novel task is required to support these findings, the associations observed highlight the importance of being able to use feedback from the social environment in order to guide future pro-social behaviour.

Results presented above, along with evidence that social isolation or exclusion are common following TBI (Annoni *et al.*, 1992; Marsh *et al.*, 1998; Struchen *et al.*, 2011), led researchers in our lab to examine the psychological effects of social exclusion (ostracism) in adults with brain injury. The Cyberball paradigm (Williams *et al.*, 2000) provides a method for examining this phenomenon. In this game participants play the same internet ball-throwing game reported above (SDMT); however, this original version includes the real participant in the game for only the first few throws and then excludes them thereafter. Research in normal adults has demonstrated that ostracism has detrimental effects on one's sense of self-esteem, control, meaningful existence and belonging (Williams & Sommer, 1997). Research from our lab (Kelly & McDonald, Submitted) demonstrated that adults with TBI were less affected by ostracism than non-injured adults. That is, while they were aware that they were being excluded, they reported less severe psychological consequences than did normal adults. This finding poses problems for adults with TBI. Firstly, it is possible that the threat to psychological needs is necessary for 'driving' strategies that will result in re-engagement with the group. Secondly, threats to these needs are thought to promote social attentiveness such as mimicry (Lakin & Chartrand, 2003) and memory for socially relevant information (Gardner *et al.*, 2000). Failure to engage in compensatory strategies aimed at increasing the likelihood of future inclusion, no doubt, will lead to further social isolation.

Aspontaneity (apathy)

Disorders of drive may also be manifest in the failure to spontaneously self-initiate behaviour, a condition known as apathy (Cummings, 1985) or pseudodepression (Blumer & Benson, 1975). The medial and dorsal frontal systems that mediate arousal and effortful regulation of emotional responses are extensively connected to the thalamus and mesencephalic reticular formation (Heilman, 2000; Phillips *et al.*, 2003) and may be specifically involved. Unlike skin conductance responses that index orientation and attention, skin conductance levels (SCL) index relatively slow changes in arousal (Barry *et al.*, 2005; Critchley *et al.*, 2002; Rushby & Barry, 2007). Using SCL it has been shown that people with severe TBI show unusual levels of habituation to emotional materials (McDonald *et al.*, 2011c). Instructions to attend to the stimuli did not alter these arousal profiles in the TBI participants suggesting that their problems rested with self-initiated arousal. These findings are consistent with Russian work from the 1960s. Homskaya and her colleagues performed a series of studies (summarized in Luria, 1973) that used physiological measures to demonstrate that frontal (especially ventromedial) lesions lead to unstable intention and rapid habituation. She also reported that those with dorsolateral lesions were able to increase their attention temporarily given verbal instruction but this was poorly sustained.

Adynamia

Another dimension of drive/arousal is the ability to engage and disengage from cognitive tasks. Such flexibility requires not only sufficient activation, but also inhibitory control in order to inhibit the prepotent response (Dimoska *et al.*, 2011), so may well reflect the balance between arousal and control. It has been suggested that orbitobasal frontal systems mediate this flexible control (Walsh, 1985). In support of this Crowe (1992) found that while disinhibited errors on the Controlled Oral Word Association Test (COWAT) were seen in patients with specific orbitofrontal lesions (surmised to mediate disinhibition), total word production was affected by lesions in the medial and dorsal cortex (thought to mediate apathy) as well as orbitofrontal lesions.

Adynamia is important, not only for cognitive tasks but also emotional and social behaviour. In her seminal paper, Lezak (1978) described some of the characterological changes seen following severe TBI as reflecting rigid, inflexible thinking, the tendency to be 'black and white' in the appraisal of social information and perseverative, rigid and uncompromising when responding in social contexts. This rigidity of thinking has clear implications for social interaction where it is important to negotiate social goals and encompass other points of view.

Contribution of emotional and behavioural dysregulation to communication

There has been very little research examining the specific impact of disorders of drive and control on communication. As mentioned in Chapter 4, lack of control will impact upon the ability to use language diplomatically and to this end, disinhibition on neuropsychological tests has correlated with the ability to produce effective requests (McDonald & Pearce, 1998). In general, however, the relation between loss of emotional control and disorders of communication and interpersonal behaviour are yet to be examined.

Some problems with loss of drive have been operationalized using psychophysiological measures as we have described above. These have revealed impairment in response to processing emotionally evocative materials including facial expressions, although the extent to which loss of responsivity impairs emotion recognition is not clear. In addition, adynamia or rigid thinking will impede the kind of perspective taking that is necessary to make ToM judgements, as well as the capacity to have cognitive empathy (Eslinger & Grattan, 1993; Grattan & Eslinger, 1989). Loss of drive is also likely to underpin the inert, sparse communication pattern that is so often reported by relatives, but empirical evidence for this is yet to be established.

Assessment of emotional and behavioural dysregulation

Research that uses specific decision making tasks such as the IGT and the SDMT in conjunction with psychophysiological measures has the potential to provide objective measures of disorders in emotion regulation. These measures, however, are not developed to the point that they can be regarded as clinically reliable indicators for individual patients. On the other hand, measures of inhibitory or interference control (see Chapter 2) are often used in clinical practice to infer behaviour and emotion regulation difficulties in TBI populations. However, how a person performs in these artificial testing environments does not always translate to the types of regulation difficulties that may occur in everyday life, particularly in complex social settings (Chaytor & Schmitter-Edgecombe, 2003). Consequently, the assessment of emotional and behavioural dysregulation in people with TBI continues to rely largely upon the ratings of either the patient themselves, or someone who knows them.

Some of the most commonly used rating measures of emotional and behavioural dysregulation in individuals with TBI are summarized in Table 5.2. In general, these measures require either the individual with the injury or a significant other to report the frequency of occurrence of several itemized behaviours on a Likert scale. The Frontal Systems Behavior Scale (FrSBe; Grace & Malloy, 2001), for example, is a reliable and valid (Grace & Malloy, 2001; Velligan *et al.*, 2002) 46-item questionnaire available in both self- and relative-report format, which aims to measure the frequency of various 'frontal-type' behaviours (apathy, disinhibition and executive dysfunction) on a scale from 1

Table 5.2 Some common instruments for measuring emotion and behaviour dysregulation

Name of instrument	Nature of response	Completed by	Level of analysis	Normative information
Current Behaviour Scale (Elsass & Kinsella, 1987)	Questionnaire with 25 bipolar adjectives rated on a 7 point scale	Relative	Items classified as representing either a Loss of Emotional Control or a Loss of Motivation.	Descriptive TBI (Males only, $n = 40$, mean age/SD = 27.0/4.4) and control data ($n = 40$, mean age/SD = 24.0/5.3) available (Kinsella *et al.*, 1991). More recent descriptive TBI data also available (N = 28, mean age/SD = 26.82/8.79) (Tate, 2003).
Social Performance Survey Schedule (SPSS) (Lowe & Cautela, 1978)	Questionnaire with 100 questions each rated from 0 (not at all) to 4 (very much)	Relative	Items are classified as positive or negative behaviours.	Normative data based on college students stratified by gender available (N = 303) (Lowe & Cautela, 1978). Australian normative data ($n = 190$, mean age/SD = 28.2/12.6) with descriptive TBI data also available ($n = 49$, mean age/SD = 35.0/11.2) (Long *et al.*, 2008).
Frontal Systems Behavior Scale (FrSBe) (Grace & Malloy, 2001)	Questionnaire with 46 items rated from 1 (almost never) to 5 (almost always). This questionnaire can be used to rate current as well as premorbid function.	Relative and Self forms available	Emotional and behavioural consequences of brain injury classified in three scales: (1) Apathy; (2) Disinhibition; and (3) Executive.	Normative data (N = 436, mean age 48.1, age range 18–95) stratified by gender, age, and education, and limited descriptive data for TBI sample (Grace & Malloy, 2001).
Neuropsychological Behaviour and Affect profile (Nelson et al., 1994)	Questionnaire with 106 items each rated as 'agree' (i.e. occurs typically or often) and 'disagree' (i.e. occurs seldom or hardly at all)	Relative and Self forms available	Emotional and behavioural consequences of acquired brain injury defined in five subscales: (1) Indifference; (2) Inappropriateness; (3) Prognosia; (4) Depression; (5) Mania.	Descriptive TBI data ($n = 48$, mean age/SD = 33.11/16.08) and control data ($n = 129$, mean age/SD = 37.93/15.17) for informant ratings available (Nelson *et al.*, 1998). Descriptive TBI data (N = 28, mean age/SD = 36.8/15.8) for both self and informant ratings also available (Cannon, 2000).

Measure	Format	Form	Description	Normative/Descriptive data
Katz Adjustment Scale –Revised (Goran & Fabiano, 1993)	Questionnaire with 79 statements each item rated from 1 (almost never) to 4 (almost always)	Relative	Emotional and behavioural changes post-TBI categorized into 10 subscales (belligerence, apathy, social irresponsibility, orientation, antisocial behaviour, speech/cognitive dysfunction, bizarre acts or beliefs, paranoid ideas, verbal expansiveness, emotional sensitivity).	Descriptive TBI data available (N = 88; mean age = 27.2, age range 16–65 years) (Goran & Fabiano, 1993).
Dysexecutive Questionnaire (Wilson et al., 1996)	Questionnaire with 20 items rated from 0 (never) to 4 (always).	Relative and self forms available	Behavioural and emotional characteristics categorized into emotional, behavioural and cognitive subscales.	Descriptive data available for neurological sample (N = 78; mean age/SD = 38.8/15.7) (Wilson et al., 1996). Descriptive TBI data (n = 45, mean age/SD = 41.2/11.1) with control data (n = 21, mean age/SD = 42.4/13.1) also available (Anderson & Knight, 2010).
Behavior Rating Inventory of Executive Function – Adult version (Roth et al., 2005)	Questionnaire with 75 items with ratings of 'never', 'sometimes' or 'often'	Relative and self forms available	Nine subscales and two summary index scales including: (1) Behavioral Regulation Index (inhibition, shifting, emotional control, and self-monitoring); and (2) The Metacognition Index (initiation, working memory, planning/organizing, task monitoring, and organizing materials).	Normative data available for self-report form (N = 1,050, ages 19–81 years) and informant-report form (N = 1,215, 26–89 years).

Table 5.2 continued

Name of instrument	Nature of response	Completed by	Level of analysis	Normative information
Overt Behaviour Scale (Kelly et al., 2006)	Severity ratings on various categories of common challenging behaviours	Clinician	Challenging behaviour clusters, level, and total weighted severity analyzed based on nine categories: (1) verbal aggression; (2) aggression against objects; (3) aggression against self; (4) aggression against people; (5) inappropriate sexual behaviour; (6) perseveration/repetition; (7) wandering/absconding; (8) inappropriate social behaviour (9) Lack of initiation.	Descriptive TBI data available (N = 30; mean age/*SD* = 31.5/13.2) (Kelly et al., 2006).
Agitated Behavior Scale (Corrigan, 1989)	Scale with 14 items rated from 1 (absent) to 4 (present to an extreme degree)	Clinician	Total scores indicate clinically significant degree of agitation.	Descriptive TBI data with cut-off score available (N = 35, mean age = 28.2) (Corrigan, 1989).

(almost never) to 5 (almost always). Two clinician-rated measures are the Overt Behaviour Scale (OBS; Kelly *et al.*, 2006) and the Agitated Behavior Scale (ABS; Corrigan, 1989). Whereas behavioural ratings on the OBS may be based either on observation or patient history and it is designed for use with people living in the community, the ABS is an observational scale designed for use in acute TBI settings to facilitate improved patient assessment and management (Tate, 2010).

Conclusions

In conclusion, social cognition is pivotal to successful interpersonal interactions, providing cues and information regarding the emotions, attitudes and intentions of others. The possibility that emotion recognition, ToM judgements and social attitudes are uniquely represented in the frontal systems of the brain and processed differently from non-social information opens a whole new avenue of research. While there has been some research into how social cognition impairments (especially ToM) contribute to impoverished communication skills after TBI, there is clearly a need to understand this in greater detail and this is a challenge for future research.

Furthermore, recent research has seen a growing sophistication in our understanding of how emotion dysregulation is manifest following TBI and how loss of appropriate emotional responsivity may play a role in good social decision making. Once again, the role that emotional regulation plays in communication disorders is yet to be established empirically. While these inter-relationships are the subject for future research, it is clear that communication skills, social cognition and emotion regulation are key to interpersonal functioning following TBI. To this end, we have overviewed some of the more common, clinically useful instruments in the field. We recommend that assessment of these constructs should be a core aspect of management of psychosocial impairments following TBI.

References

Abell, F., Happè, F. & Frith, U. (2000). Do triangles play tricks? Attribution of mental states to animated shapes in normal and abnormal development. *Cognitive Development, 15*, 1–16.

Adams, J. H., Doyle, D., Ford, I., Gennarelli, T. A., Graham, D. I. & McLellan, D. R. (1989). Diffuse axonal injury in head injury: definition, diagnosis and grading. *Histopathology, 15*(1), 49–59.

Adelman, P. & Zajonc, R. (1989). Facial efference and the experience of emotion. *Annual Review of Psychology 40*, 249–280.

Adolphs, R. (2001). The neurobiology of social cognition. *Current Opinion in Neurobiology, 11*, 231–239.

——(2002). Neural systems for recognizing emotion. *Current Opinion in Neurobiology, 12*(2), 169–177.

——(2003). Cognitive neuroscience of human social behaviour. *Nature Reviews Neuroscience, 4*(3), 165–178.

——(2009). The social brain: neural basis of social knowledge. *Annual Review of Psychology, 60,* 693–716.

Adolphs, R., Tranel, D. & Damasio, A. R. (1998). The human amygdala in social judgment. *Nature, 393*(6684), 470–474.

Adolphs, R., Russell, J. A. & Tranel, D. (1999). A role for the human amygdala in recognizing emotional arousal from unpleasant stimuli. *Psychological Science, 10*(2), 167–171.

Adolphs, R., Damasio, H., Tranel, D., Cooper, G. & Damasio, A. R. (2000). A role for somatosensory cortices in the visual recognition of emotion as revealed by three-dimensional lesion mapping. *Journal of Neuroscience, 20*(7), 2683–2690.

Adolphs, R., Damasio, H. & Tranel, D. (2002). Neural systems for recognition of emotional prosody: a 3-D lesion study. *Emotion, 2*(1), 23–51.

Adolphs, R., Tranel, D. & Damasio, A. R. (2003). Dissociable neural systems for recognizing emotions. *Brain & Cognition, 52*(1), 61–69.

Adolphs, R. & Tranel, D. (2004). Impaired judgments of sadness but not happiness following bilateral amygdala damage. *Journal of Cognitive Neuroscience, 16*(3), 453–462.

Allison, C., Baron-Cohen, S., Wheelwright, S. S. J., Stone, M. H. & Muncer, S. J. (2011). Psychometric analysis of the Empathy Quotient (EQ). *Personality and Individual Differences, 51,* 829–835.

Anderson, T. M. & Knight, R. G. (2010). The long-term effects of traumatic brain injury on the coordinative function of the central executive. *Journal of Clinical and Experimental Neuropsychology, 32,* 1074–1082.

Andrewes, D. (2001). *Neuropsychology: From Theory to Practice.* Hove and New York: Psychology Press.

Angrilli, A., Palomba, D., Cantagallo, A., Maietti, A. & Stegagno, L. (1999). Emotional impairment after right orbitofrontal lesion in a patient without cognitive deficits. *Neuroreport, 10*(8), 1741–1746.

Annoni, J. M., Beer, S. & Kesselring, J. (1992). Severe traumatic brain injury – epidemiology and outcome after 3 years. *Disability and Rehabilitation, 14* (1), 23–26.

Babbage, D. R., Yim, J., Zupan, B., Neumann, D., Tomita, M. R. & Willer, B. (2011). Meta-analysis of facial affect recognition difficulties after traumatic brain injury. *Neuropsychology, 25*(3), 277–285.

Bara, B. G., Cutica, I. & Tirassa, M. (2001). Neuropragmatics: extralinguistic communication after closed head injury. *Brain and Language, 77*(1), 72–94.

Barker, L. A., Andrade, J. & Romanowski, C. A. J. (2004). Impaired implicit cognition with intact executive function after extensive bilateral prefrontal pathology: a case study. *Neurocase, 10*(3), 233–248.

Baron-Cohen, S., Ring, H., Moriarty, J., Schmitz, B., Costa, D. & Ell, P. (1994). The brain basis of theory of mind: the role of the orbito-frontal region. *British Journal of Psychiatry, 165,* 640–649.

Baron-Cohen, S., Jolliffe, T., Mortimore, C. & Robertson, M. (1997). Another advanced test of theory of mind: evidence from very high functioning adults with autism or Asperger Syndrome. *Journal of Child Psychology & Psychiatry & Allied Disciplines, 38*(7), 813–822.

Baron-Cohen, S., Wheelwright, S., Hill, J., Raste, Y. & Plumb, I. (2001). The 'Reading the Mind in the Eyes' test revised version: a study with normal adults with Asperger syndrome or high-functioning autism. *Journal of Child Psychology and Psychiatry, 42,* 241–251.

Baron-Cohen, S. & Wheelwright, S. (2004). The empathy quotient: an investigation of adults with Asperger syndrome or high functioning autism and norm sex differences. *Journal of Autism and Developmental Disorders, 34*, 163–175.

Barry, R. J., Clarke, A. R., McCarthy, R., Selikowitz, M. & Rushby, J. A. (2005). Arousal and activation in a continuous performance task: an exploration of state effects in normal children. *Journal of Psychophysiology, 19*(2), 91–99.

Bassili, J. N. (1978). Facial motion in the perception of faces and of emotional expression. *Journal of Experimental Psychology: Human Perception and Performance, 4*, 373–379.

Baum, K. M. & Nowicki, S. (1998). Perception of emotion: measuring decoding accuracy of adult prosodic cues varying in intensity. *Journal of Nonverbal Behavior, 22*, 89–107.

Bechara, A., Damasio, A., Damasio, H. & Anderson, S. W. (1994). Insensitivity to future consequences following damage to human prefrontal cortex. *Cognition, 50*(1–3), 7–15.

Bechara, A., Tranel, D., Damasio, H. & Damasio, A. (1996). Failure to respond autonomically to anticipated future outcomes following damage to prefrontal cortex. *Cereb. Cortex, 6*(2), 215–225. doi: 10.1093/cercor/6.2.215

Bechara, A., Damasio, H., Tranel, D. & Damasio, A. R. (1997). Deciding advantageously before knowing the advantageous strategy. *Science, 275*(5304), 1293–1294.

Bechara, A., Damasio, H. & Damasio, A. R. (2000). Emotion, decision making and the orbitofrontal cortex. *Cerebral Cortex, 10*(3), 295–307.

Bibby, H. & McDonald, S. (2005). Theory of mind after traumatic brain injury. *Neuropsychologia, 43*(1), 99–114.

Bigler, E. D. (2007). Anterior and middle cranial fossa in traumatic brain injury: relevant neuroanatomy and neuropathology in the study of neuropsychological outcome. *Neuropsychology, 21*(5), 515–531.

Blair, R. J. R. & Cipolotti, L. (2000). Impaired social response reversal: a case of 'acquired sociopathy'. *Brain, 123*, 1122–1141.

Blair, R. J. R., Morris, J. S., Frith, C. C., Perrett, D. I. & Dolan, R. J. (1999). Dissociable neural responses to facial expressions of sadness and anger. *Brain, 122*(5), 883–893.

Blairy, S., Herrera, P. & Hess, U. (1999). Mimicry and the judgment of emotional facial expressions. *Journal of Nonverbal Behavior, 23*(1), 5–41.

Blumer, D. & Benson, D. F. (1975). Personality changes with frontal and temporal lobe lesions. In D. F. Benson & D. Blumer (Eds.), *Psychiatric Aspects of Neurologic Disease* (pp. 151–170). New York: Grune & Stratton.

Borgaro, S. R., Prigatano, G. P., Kwasnica, C., Alcott, S. & Cutter, N. (2004). Disturbances in affective communication following brain injury. *Brain Injury, 18*(1), 33–39.

Bowers, D., Blonder, L. X. & Heilman, K. M. (1991a). *Florida Affect Battery*. Gainsville, FL.: Centre for Neuropsychological Studies, University of Florida.

Bowers, D., Blonder, L. X., Feinberg, T. & Heilman, K. M. (1991b). Differential impact of right and left hemisphere lesions on facial emotion and object imagery. *Brain, 114*, 2593–2609.

Bowers, D., Bauer, R. M. & Heilman, K. M. (1993). The nonverbal affect lexicon: theroretical perpectives from neuropsychological studies of affect perception. *Neuropsychology, 7*, 433–444.

Bowler, D. M. (1992). 'Theory of mind' in Asperger's Syndrome. *Journal of Child Psychology and Psychiatry, 33*, 877–893.

Brooks, D. N., Campsie, L., Symington, C., Beattie, A. & McKinlay, W. (1986). The five year outcome of severe blunt head injury: a relative's view. *Journal of Neurology, Neurosurgery & Psychiatry, 49*(7), 764–770.

Buelow, M. T. & Suhr, J. A. (2009). Construct validity of the Iowa Gambling Task. *Neuropsychology Review, 19*(1), 102–114.

Byom, L. J. & Turkstra, L. S. (2012). Effects of social cognitive demand on Theory of Mind in conversations of adults with traumatic brain injury. *International Journal of Language and Communication Disorders, 47*(3), 310–321. doi: 10.1111/ j.1460–6984.2011.00102.x [doi]

Callahan, B. L., Ueda, K., Sakata, D., Plamondon, A. & Murai, T. (2011). Liberal bias mediates emotion recognition deficits in frontal traumatic brain injury. *Brain and Cognition, 77*(3), 412–418.

Cannon, B. J. (2000). A comparison of self- and other-rated forms of the Neuropsychology Behavior and Affect Profile in traumatic brain injury population. *Archives of Clinical Neuropsychology, 15*, 327–334.

Carr, L., Iacoboni, M., Dubeau, M.-C., Maxzziotta, J. C. & Lenzi, G. L. (2003). Neural mechanisms of empathy in humans: a relay from neural systems for imitation to limbic areas. *Proceedings of the National Academy of Science: USA, 100*, 5487–5502.

Channon, S. & Crawford, S. (2010). Mentalising and social problem-solving after brain injury. *Neuropsychological Rehabilitation, 20*(5), 739–759.

Channon, S., Pellijeff, A. & Rule, A. (2005). Social cognition after head injury: sarcasm and theory of mind. *Brain and Language, 93*(2), 123–134.

Chaytor, N. & Schmitter-Edgecombe, M. (2003). The ecological validity of neuropsychological tests: a review of the literature on everyday cognitive skills. *Neuropsychology Review, 13*, 181–197.

Christodoulou, C., DeLuca, J., Ricker, J. H., Madigan, N. K., Bly, B. M., Lange, G. & Ni, A. C. (2001). Functional magnetic resonance imaging of working memory impairment after traumatic brain injury. *Journal Neurology Neurosurgery Psychiatry, 71*(2), 161–168. doi: 10.1136/jnnp.71.2.161

Cicerone, K. D. & Tanenbaum, L. N. (1997). Disturbance of social cognition after traumatic orbitofrontal brain injury. *Archives of Clinical Neuropsychology, 12*, 173–188.

Corcoran, R., Mercer, G. & Frith, C. D. (1995). Schizophrenia, symptomology and social inference: investigating 'theory of mind' in people with schizophrenia. *Schizophrenia Research, 17*, 5–13.

Corrigan, J. D. (1989). Development of a scale for assessment of agitation following traumatic brain injury. *Journal of Clinical and Experimental Neuropsychology, 11*, 261–277.

Corrigan, P. W. (1997). The social perceptual deficits of schizophrenia. *Psychiatry, 60*, 309–326.

Courville, C. B. (1945). *Pathology of the Nervous System* (2nd Edn) Mountain View, CA: California Pacific Press.

Critchley, H. D., Melmed, R. N., Featherstone, E., Mathias, C. J. & Dolan, R. J. (2002). Volitional control of autonomic arousal, a functional magnetic resonance study. *NeuroImage, 16*, 909–912.

Croker, V. & McDonald, S. (2005). Recognition of emotion from facial expression following traumatic brain injury. *Brain Injury, 19*, 787–789.

Crosson, B. (1987). Treatment of interpersonal deficits for head-trauma patients in inpatient rehabilitation settings. *The Clinical Neuropsychologist, 1*(4), 335–352.

Crowe, S. F. (1992). Dissociation of two frontal lobe syndromes by a test of verbal fluency. *Journal of Clinical and Experimental Neuropsychology, 14*(2), 327–339. doi: 10.1080/01688639208402832

Cummings, J. L. (1985). *Clinical Neuropsychiatry.* New York: Grune & Stratton.

Damasio, A. R., Tranel, D. & Damasio, H. (1990). Individuals with sociopathic behavior caused by frontal damage fail to respond autonomically to social stimuli. *Behavioural Brain Research, 41*(2), 81–94.

Damasio, A. R., Tranel, D. & Damasio, H. (1991). Somatic markers and the guidance of behavior: theory and preliminary testing. In H. S. Levin, H. M. Eisenberg & A. L. Benton (Eds.), *Frontal Lobe Function and Dysfunction* (pp. 217–229). New York: Oxford University Press, Inc.

Darby, D. & Walsh, K. W. (2005). *Walsh's Neuropsychology: A Clinical Approach* (5th edn). Edinburgh: Elsevier.

Davis, M. H. (1980). A multidimensional approach to individual differences in empathy. *JSAS Catalog of Selected Documents in Psychology, 10*, 85.

——(1983). Measuring individual differences in empathy: evidence for a multidimensional approach. *Journal of Personality and Social Psychology, 44*(1), 113–126. doi: 10.1037/0022-3514.44.1.113

de la Plata, C. D. M., Garces, J., Kojori, E. S., Grinnan, J., Krishnan, K., Pidikiti, R., & Diaz-Arrastia, R. (2011). Deficits in functional connectivity of hippocampal and frontal lobe circuits after traumatic axonal injury. *Archives of Neurology, 68*(1), 74–84. doi: 10.1001/archneurol.2010.342

de Sousa, A., McDonald, S., Rushby, J., Li, S., Dimoska, A. & James, C. (2010). Why don't you feel how I feel? Insight into the absence of empathy after severe traumatic brain injury. *Neuropsychologia, 48*, 3585–3595.

de Sousa, A., McDonald, S., Rushby, J., Li, S., Dimoska, A. & James, C. (2011). Understanding deficits in empathy after traumatic brain injury: the role of affective responsivity. *Cortex, 47*(5), 526–535.

de Sousa, A., McDonald, S. & Rushby, J. (2012). Changes in emotional empathy, affective responsivity and behaviour following severe traumatic brain injury. *Journal of Clinical and Experimental Neuropsychology 34*(6), 606–623. doi: http://dx.doi.org/10.1080/13803395.2012.66706

Decety, J. & Meyer, M. (2008). From emotional resonance to empathic understanding: a cortical developmental neuroscience account. *Development and Psychopathology, 20*, 1053–1080.

Demark, J. & Gemeinhardt, M. (2002). Anger and its management for survivors of acquired brain injury. *Brain Injury, 16*(2), 91–108. doi: 10.1080/02699050110102059

Dennis, M., Agostino, A., Roncadin, C. & Levin, H. S. (2009). Theory of mind depends on domain-general executive functions of working memory and cognitive inhibition in children with traumatic brain injury. *Journal of Clinical and Experimental Neuropsychology, 31*(7), 835–847. doi: 10.1080/13803390802572419

Dethier, M., Blairy, S., Rosenberg, H. & McDonald, S. (2012). Spontaneous and posed emotional facial expressions following severe traumatic brain injury. *Journal of Clinical and Experimental Neuropsychology, 34* (9), 936–947.

Dethier, M., Blairy, S., Rosenberg, H. & McDonald, S. (2013). Deficits in processing feedback from emotional behaviours following severe TBI. *Journal of the International Neuropsychological Society, 19* (4), 367–379.

Dimberg, U. & Lundquist, L.-O. (1990). Gender differences in facial reaction to facial expressions. *Biological Psychology, 30*, 151–159.

Dimberg, U. & Thunberg, M. (1998). Rapid facial reactions to emotional facial expressions. *Scandinavian Journal of Psychology, 39*, 39–45.

Dimberg, U. & Petterson, M. (2000). Facial reactions to happy and angry facial expressions: Evidence for right hemisphere dominance. *Psychophysiology, 37*, 693–696.

Dimoska, A., McDonald, S., Pell, M. C., Tate, R. L. & James, C. M. (2010). Recognising vocal expressions of emotion following traumatic brain injury: is the 'what' more important than the 'how'? *Journal of the International Neuropsychological Society, 16*, 369–382.

Dimoska, A., McDonald, S., Kelly, M. A., Tate, R. & Johnstone, S. (2011). A meta-analysis of performance in inhibitory control paradigms in adults with traumatic brain injury (TBI). *Journal of Clinical and Experimental Neuropsychology, 33*, 471–485.

Ekman, P. & Friesen, W. (1976). *Pictures of Facial Affect*. Palo Alto, CA: Consulting Psychological Press.

Elsass, L. & Kinsella, G. (1987). Social interaction following severe closed head injury. *Psychological Medicine, 17*(1), 67–78.

Eslinger, P. J. (2008). The frontal lobes: executive, emotional and neurological functions. In P. Marien & J. Abutalebi (Eds), *Neuropsychological Research: A Review*. New York: Psychology Press.

Eslinger, P. J. & Damasio, A. R. (1985). Severe disturbance of higher cognitive function after bilateral frontal ablation: patient EVR. *Neurology, 35*, 1731–1741.

Eslinger, P. J. & Grattan, L. M. (1993). Frontal lobe and frontal-striatal substrates for different forms of human cognitive flexibility. *Neuropsychologia, 31*(1), 17–28.

Fadiga, L., Fogassi, L., Pavesi, G. & Rizzolaati, G. (1995). Motor facilitation during action observation: a magnetic simulation study. *Journal of Neurophysiology, 73*, 2608–2611.

Fellows, L. K. & Farah, M. J. (2005). Different underlying impairments in decision-making following ventromedial and dorsolateral frontal lobe damage in humans. *Cerebral Cortex, 15*(1), 58–63.

Felmingham, K. L., Baguley, I. J., & Green, A. M. (2004). Effects of diffuse axonal injury on speed of information processing following severe traumatic brain injury. [Comparative Study]. *Neuropsychology, 18*(3), 564–571.

Fiszdon, J. M., Richardson, R., Greig, T. & Bell, M. D. (2007). A comparison of basic and social cognition between schizophrenia and schizoaffective disorder. *Schizophrenia Research, 91*(1–3), 117–121. doi: 10.1016/j.schres.2006.12.012

Flanagan, S., McDonald, S. & Togher, L. (1995). Evaluating social skills following traumatic brain injury: the BRISS as a clinical tool. *Brain Injury, 9*(4), 321–338.

Frenchmen, K. A., Fox, A. M. & Mayberry, M. T. (2005). Neuropsychological studies of mild traumatic brain injury: a meta-analytic review of research since 1995. *Journal of Clinical and Experimental Neuropsychology, 27*, 334–351.

Fujiwara, E., Schwartz, M. L., Gao, F., Black, S. E. & Levine, B. (2008). Ventral frontal cortex functions and quantified MRI in traumatic brain injury. *Neuropsychologia, 46*(2), 461–474.

Garcia-Molina, A., Roig-Rovira, T., Ensenat-Cantallops, A., Sanchez-Carrion, R., Pico-Azanza, N. & Pena-Casanova, J. (2007). Examination of decision-making processes in patients with traumatic brain injury. *Neurologia, 22*(4), 206–212.

Gardner, W. L., Pickett, C. L. & Brewer, M. B. (2000). Social exclusion and selective memory: how the need to belong influences memory for social events. *Personality and Social Psychology Bulletin, 26*, 486–496.

Gentry, L. R., Godersky, J. C. & Thompson, B. (1988). MR imaging of head trauma: review of the distribution and radiopathologic features of traumatic lesions. *American Journal of Roentgenology, 150*, 663–672.

Geraci, A., Surian, L., Ferraro, M. & Cantagallo, A. (2010). Theory of mind in patients with ventromedial or dorsolateral prefrontal lesions following traumatic brain injury. *Brain Injury, 24*(7–8), 978–987. doi: 10.3109/02699052.2010.487477

Goldman, A. I. & Sripada, C. S. (2005). Simulationist models of face-based emotion recognition. *Cognition, 94*, 193–213.

Goran, D. A. & Fabiano, R. J. (1993). The scaling of the Katz Adjustment Scale in a traumatic brain injury rehabilitation sample. *Brain Injury, 7*, 219–229.

Grace, J. & Malloy, P. F. (2001). *FrSe, Frontal Systems Behavior Scale: Professional manual.* Lutz: FL: Psychological Assessment Resources, Inc.

Graham, R., Devinsky, O. & LaBar, K. S. (2007). Quantifying deficits in the perception of fear and anger in morphed facial expressions after bilateral amygdala damage. *Neuropsychologia, 45*(1), 42–54.

Grattan, L. M. & Eslinger, P. J. (1989). Higher cognition and social behavior: changes in cognitive flexibility and empathy after cerebral lesions. *Neuropsychology, 3*(3), 175–185.

Green, R. E. A., Turner, G. R. & Thompson, W. F. (2004). Deficits in facial emotion perception in adults with recent traumatic brain injury. *Neuropsychologia, 42*, 133–141.

Greig, T. G., Nicholls, S. S., Wexler, B. E. & Bell, M. D. (2004). Test-retest stability of neuropsychological testing and individual differences in variability in schizophrenia outpatients. *Psychiatry Research, 129*(3), 241–247. doi: 10.1016/j.psychres.2004.09.006

Hadley, D. M., Teasdale, G. M., Jenkins, A., Condon, B., MacPherson, P., Patterson, J. & Rowan, J. O. (1988). Magnetic resonance imaging in acute head injury. [Comparative Study Research Support, Non-U.S. Gov't]. *Clinical Radiology, 39*(2), 131–139.

Hanks, R. A., Temkin, N., Machamer, J. & Dikmen, S. S. (1999). Emotional and behavioural adjustment after traumatic brain injury. *Archives of Physical Medication and Rehabilitation, 80*, 991–997.

Happè, F. (1993). Communicative competence and theory of mind in autism: a test of relevance theory. *Cognition*(48), 101–119.

Happè, F. & Frith, U. (1996). The neuropsychology of autism. *Brain, 119*(4), 1377–1400.

Happè, F., Brownell, H. & Winner, E. (1999). Acquired 'theory of mind' impairments following stroke. *Cognition, 70*, 211–240.

Harari, H., Shamay-Tsoory, S. G., Ravid, M. & Levkovitz, Y. (2010). Double dissociation between cognitive and affective empathy in borderline personality disorder. *Psychiatry Research, 175*(3), 277–279. doi: 10.1016/j.psychres.2009.03.002

Harmer, C. J., Thilo, K. V., Rothwell, J. C. & Goodwin, G. M. (2001). Transcranial magnetic stimulation of medial-frontal cortex impairs the processing of angry facial expressions. *Nature Neuroscience, 4*, 17–18.

Havet-Thomassin, V., Allain, P., Etcharry-Bouyx, F. & Le Gall, D. (2006). What about theory of mind after severe brain injury? *Brain Injury, 20*(1), 83–91.

Heberlein, A. S., Adolphs, R., Tranel, D. & Damasio, H. (2004). Cortical regions for judgments of emotions and personality traits from point-light walkers. *Journal of Cognitive Neuroscience, 16*, 1143–1158.

Heilman, K. M. (2000). Emotional experience: a neurological model. In R. D. Lane & L. Nadel (Eds), *Cognitive Neuroscience of Emotions* (pp. 328–344). Oxford: Oxford University Press.

Henry, J. D., Phillips, L. H., Crawford, J. R., Ietswaart, M. & Summers, F. (2006a). Theory of mind following traumatic brain injury: the role of emotion recognition and executive dysfunction. *Neuropsychologia, 44*(10), 1623–1628.

Henry, J. D., Phillips, L. H., Crawford, J. R., Theodorou, G. & Summers, F. (2006b). Cognitive and psychosocial correlates of alexithymia following traumatic brain injury. *Neuropsychologia, 44*, 62–72.

Hess, U. & Blairy, S. (2001). Facial mimicry and emotional contagion to dynamic emotional facial expressions and their influence on decoding accuracy. *International Journal of Psychophysiology, 40*(2), 129–141.

Hopkins, M. J., Dywan, J. & Segalowitz, S. J. (2002). Altered electrodermal response to facial expression after closed head injury. *Brain Injury, 16*, 245–257.

Hornak, J., Rolls, E. & Wade, D. (1996). Face and voice expression identification in patients with emotional and behavioural changes following ventral frontal lobe damage. *Neuropsychologia, 34*(4), 247–261.

Hornak, J., Bramham, J., Rolls, E., Morris, R., O'Doherty, J., Bullock, P. & Polkey, C. (2003). Changes in emotion after circumscribed surgical lesions of the orbitofrontal and cingulate cortices. *Brain: A Journal of Neurology, 126*(7), 1691–1712.

Hynes, C. A., Stone, V. E. & Kelso, L. A. (2011). Social and emotional competence in traumatic brain injury: new and established assessment tools. *Social Neuroscience, 6*(5–6), 599–614. doi: 10.1080/17470919.2011.584447

Ietswaart, M., Milders, M., Crawford, J. R., Currie, D. & Scott, C. L. (2008). Longitudinal aspects of emotion recognition in patients with traumatic brain injury. *Neuropsychologia, 46*, 148–159.

Ishai, A. (2007). Sex, beauty and the orbitofrontal cortex. *International Journal of Psychophysiology, 63*(2), 181–185. doi: 10.1016/j.ijpsycho.2006.03.010

Jackson, H. F. & Moffatt, N. J. (1987). Impaired emotional recognition following severe head injury. *Cortex, 23*(2), 293–300.

Johnston, L., Miles, L. & McKinlay, A. (2008). A critical review of the Eyes Test as a measure of social-cognitive impairment. *Australian Journal of Psychology, 60*, 135–141.

Kaland, N., Mortensen, E. L. & Smith, L. (2011). Social communication impairments in children and adolescents with Asperger syndrome: slow response time and the impact of prompting. *Research in Autism Spectrum Disorders, 5*(3), 1129–1137.

Kampe, K. K. W., Frith, C. D., Dolan, R. J. & Frith, U. (2001). Reward value of attractiveness and gaze. *Nature, 413*, 589.

Kandalaft, M. R., Didehbani, N., Cullum, C. M., Krawczyk, D. C., Allen, T. T., Tamminga, C. A. & Chapman, S. B. (2012). The Wechsler ACS Perception subtest: A preliminary comparison with other measures of social cognition. *Journal of Psychoeducational Assessment, 30*, 455–465.

Karafin, M. S., Tranel, D. & Adolphs, R. (2004). Dominance attributions following damage to the ventromedial prefrontal cortex. *Journal of Cognitive Neuroscience, 16*, 1796–1804.

Karmiloff-Smith, A., Klima, E., Bellugi, U., Grant, J. & Baron-Cohen, S. (1995). Is there a social module? Language, face processing, and theory of mind in individuals with Williams syndrome. *Journal of Cognitive Neuroscience, 7*(2), 196–208.

Kelly, G., Todd, J., Simpson, G., Kremer, P. & Martin, C. (2006). The overt behaviour scale (OBS): a tool for measuring challenging behaviours following ABI in community settings. *Brain Injury, 20*, 307–319.

Kelly, M. & McDonald, S. (Submitted). The psychological effects of social exclusion following brain injury.

Kelly, M., McDonald, S. & Kellett, D. (Submitted). Development of a novel task for investigating decision making in a social context following traumatic brain injury.

Kendall, E., Shum, D., Halson, D., Bunning, S. & Teh, M. (1997). The assessment of social problem solving ability following traumatic brain injury. *Journal of Head Trauma Rehabilitation, 12*, 68–78.

Kilts, C. D., Egan, G., Gideon, D. A., Ely, T. A. & Hoffman, J. F. (2003). Dissociable neural pathways are involved in the recognition of emotion in static and dynamic facial expressions. *NeuroImage, 18*, 156–168.

Kinsella, G., Packer, S. & Olver, J. (1991). Maternal reporting of behaviour following very severe blunt head injury. *Journal of Neurology, Neurosurgery & Psychiatry, 54*(5), 422–426.

Kipps, C. M., Nestor, P. J., Acosta-Cabronero, J., Arnold, R. & Hodges, J. R. (2009). Understanding social dysfunction in the behavioural variant of frontotemporal dementia: the role of emotion and sarcasm processing. *Brain, 132*, 592–603.

Knox, L. & Douglas, J. (2009). Long-term ability to interpret facial expression after traumatic brain injury and its relation to social integration. *Brain and Cognition, 69*, 442–449.

Koenigs, M., Young, L., Adolphs, R., Tranel, D., Cushman, F., Hauser, M. & Damasio, A. (2007). Damage to the prefontal cortex increases utilitarian moral judgements. *Nature, 446*(7138), 908–911.

Koponen, S., Taiminen, T., Honkalampi, K., Joukamaa, M., Viinamäki, H., Kurki, T., Portin, R., Himanen, L., Isoniemi, H., Hinkka, S. & Tenovuo, O. (2005). Alexithymia after traumatic brain injury: its relation to magnetic resonance imaging findings and psychiatric disorders. *Psychosomatic Medicine, 67*(5), 807–812.

Lakin, J. L. & Chartrand, T. L. (2003). Using nonconscious behavioral mimicry to create affiliation and rapport. *Psychological Science, 14*(4), 334–339.

Levenson, R. W., Ekman, P. & Friesen, W. V. (1990). Voluntary facial action generates emotion-specific autonomic nervous system activity. *Psychophysiology 27*(4), 363–384.

Levin, H. S., Grossman, R. G., Rose, J. E. & Teasdale, G. (1979). Long term neuro-psychological outcome of closed head injury. *Journal of Neurosurgery, 50*, 412–422.

Levine, B., Black, S. E., Cheung, G., Campbell, A., O'Toole, C. & Schwartz, M. L. (2005). Gambling task performance in traumatic brain injury: relationships to injury severity, atrophy, lesion location, and cognitive and psychosocial outcome. *Cognitive and Behavioral Neurology. Vol, 18*(1), 45–54.

Lezak, M. D. (1978). Living with the characterologically altered brain-injured patient. *Journal of Clinical Psychology, 39*, 592–598.

Logan, G. D. (1994). On the ability to inhibit thought and action: a users' guide to the stop signal paradigm. Inhibitory processes in attention, memory, and language. In D. Dagenbach & T. H. Carr (Eds.), *Inhibitory Processes in Attention, Memory, and Language* (pp. 189–239). San Diego, CA: Academic Press.

Long, E., McDonald, S., Tate, R., Togher, L. & Bornhofen, C. (2008). Assessing social skills in people with very severe traumatic brain injury: validity of the Social Performance Survey Schedule (SPSS). *Brain Impairment, 9*, 274–281.

Lowe, M. R. & Cautela, J. R. (1978). A self-report measure of social skill. *Behaviour Therapy, 9*, 535–544.

Luria, A. R. (1973). *The Working Brain*. London: Allen Lane: The Penguin Press.

Maia, T. V. & McClelland, J. L. (2004). From the cover: a reexamination of the evidence for the somatic marker hypothesis: what participants really know in the Iowa gambling task. *Proceedings of the National Academy of Sciences, 101*(45), 16075–16080. doi: 10.1073/pnas.0406666101

Marjoram, D., Gardner, C., Burns, J., Miller, P., Lawrie, S. & Johnstone, E. (2005). Symptomatology and social inference: a theory of mind study of schizophrenia and psychotic affective disorder. *Cognitive Neuropsychiatry, 10*(5), 347–359. doi: 10.1080/13546800444000092

Marquardt, T. P., Rios-Brown, M., Richburg, T., Seibert, L. K. & Cannito, M. P. (2001). Comprehension and expression of affective sentences in traumatic brain injury. *Aphasiology, 15*(10–11), 1091–1101.

Marsh, N. V., Kersel, D. A., Havill, J. H. & Sleigh, J. W. (1998). Caregiver burden at 1 year following severe traumatic brain injury. *Brain Injury, 12*(12), 1045–1059.

Mathias, J. L. & Wheaton, P. (2007). Changes in attention and information-processing speed following severe traumatic brain injury: a meta-analytic review. *Neuropsychology, 21*(2), 212–223.

Mayer, J. D., Salovey, P. & Caruso, D. R. (2000). *Mayer–Salovey–Caruso Emotional Intelligence Test (MSCEIT) User's Manual*. Toronto, Ontario: MHS Publishers.

McAllister, T. W., Saykin, A. J., Flashman, L. A., Sparling, M. B., Johnson, S. C., Guerin, S. J., Yanofsky, N. (1999). Brain activation during working memory one month after mild traumatic brain injury: a functional MRI study. *Neurology, 12*, 1300–1308.

McAllister, T. W., Sparling, M. B., Flashman, L. A., Guerin, S. J., Mamourian, A. C. & Saykin, A. J. (2001). Differential working memory load effects after mild traumatic brain injury. *NeuroImage, 14*(5), 1004–1012.

McDonald, S. (2000). Putting communication disorders in context after traumatic brain injury. *Aphasiology, 14*(4), 339–347.

McDonald, S. & van Sommers, P. (1992). Differential pragmatic language loss following closed head injury: ability to negotiate requests. *Cognitive Neuropsychology, 10*, 297–315.

McDonald, S. & Pearce, S. (1996). Clinical insights into pragmatic theory: frontal lobe deficits and sarcasm. *Brain and Language, 53*(1), 81–104.

——(1998). Requests that overcome listener reluctance: impairment associated with executive dysfunction in brain injury. *Brain and Language, 61*, 88–104.

McDonald, S. & Flanagan, S. (2004). Social perception deficits after traumatic brain injury: interaction between emotion recognition, mentalizing ability, and social communication. *Neuropsychology, 18*(3), 572–579.

McDonald, S. & Saunders, J. C. (2005). Differential impairment in recognition of emotion across different media in people with severe traumatic brain injury. *Journal of the International Neuropsychological Society, 11*(4), 392–399.

McDonald, S., Bornhofen, C., Shum, D., Long, E., Saunders, C. & Neulinger, K. (2006). Reliability and validity of The Awareness of Social Inference Test (TASIT): a clinical test of social perception. *Disability Rehabilitation, 28*(24), 1529–1542.

McDonald, S., Flanagan, S., Rollins, J. & Kinch, J. (2003). TASIT: a new clinical tool for assessing social perception after traumatic brain injury. *Journal of Head Trauma Rehabilitation, 18*, 219–238.

McDonald, S., Flanagan, S., Martin, I. & Saunders, C. (2004). The ecological validity of TASIT: a test of social perception. *Neuropsychological Rehabilitation, 14*, 285–302.

McDonald, S., Hunt, C., Henry, J. D., Dimoska, A. & Bornhofen, C. (2010). Angry responses to emotional events: the role of impaired control and drive in people with severe traumatic brain injury. *Journal of Clinical and Experimental Neuropsychology, 32*, 855–864.

McDonald, S., Flanagan, S. & Rollins, J. (2011a). *The Awareness of Social Inference Test (Revised)*. Sydney, Australia: Pearson Assessment.

McDonald, S., Li, S., de Sousa, A., Rushby, J., Dimoska, A., James, C. & Tate, R. L. (2011b). Impaired mimicry response to angry faces following severe traumatic brain injury. *Journal of Clinical and Experimental Neuropsychology, 33*(1), 17–29.

McDonald, S., Rushby, J., Li, S., de Sousa, A., Dimoska, A., James, C., Togher, L. (2011c). The influence of attention and arousal on emotion perception in adults with severe traumatic brain injury. *International Journal of Psychophysiology, 82*(1), 124–131. doi: 10.1016/j.ijpsycho.2011.01.014

McDonald, S., Saad, A. & James, C. (2011d). Social dysdecorum following severe traumatic brain injury: Loss of implicit social knowledge or loss of control? *Journal of Clinical and Experimental Neuropsychology, 33*(6), 619–630.

McIntosh, D. N. (1996). Facial feedback hypotheses: Evidence, implications and directions. *Motivation and Emotion, 20*, 121–145.

McKinlay, W. W., Brooks, D. N., Bond, M. R., Martinage, D. P. & Marshall, M. M. (1981). The short-term outcome of severe blunt head injury as reported by relatives of the injured persons. *Journal of Neurology, Neurosurgery & Psychiatry, 44*(6), 527–533.

Mehrabian, A. (2000). *Manual for the Balanced Emotional Empathy Scale (BEES).* Available from Albert Mehrabian, 1130 Alta Mesa Road, Montery, CA 93040.

Mendez, M. F., Anderson, E. & Shapira, J. S. (2005). An investigation of moral judgement in frontotemporal dementia. *Cognitive and Behavioral Neurology, 18*, 193–197.

Merckelbach, H., van Hout, W., van den Hout, M. A. & Mersch, P. P. (1989). Psychophysiological and subjective reactions of social phobics and normals to facial stimuli. *Behaviour Research and Therapy 27*, 289–294.

Meythaler, J. M., Peduzzi, J. D., Eleftheriou, E. & Novack, T. A. (2001). Current concepts: diffuse axonal injury-associated traumatic brain injury. [Review] [107 refs]. *Archives of Physical Medicine & Rehabilitation, 82*(10), 1461–1471.

Milders, M., Fuchs, S. & Crawford, J. R. (2003). Neuropsychological impairments and changes in emotional and social behaviour following severe traumatic brain injury. *Journal of Clinical and Experimental Neuropsychology, 25*, 157–172.

Milders, M., Ietswaart, M., Crawford, J. R. & Currie, D. (2006). Impairments in theory of mind shortly after traumatic brain injury and at 1-year follow-up. *Neuropsychology, 20*(4), 400–408.

Milders, M., Ietswaart, M., Crawford, J. R. & Currie, D. (2008). Social behavior following traumatic brain injury and its association with emotion recognition, understanding of intentions, and cognitive flexibility. *Journal of the International Neuropsychological Society, 14*, 318–326.

Milne, E. & Grafman, J. (2001). Ventromedial prefrontal cortex lesions in humans eliminate implicit gender stereotyping. *Journal of Neuroscience, 21*(12), 1–6.

Muller, F., Simion, A., Reviriego, E., Galera, C., Mazaux, J.-M., Barat, M. & Joseph, P.-A. (2010). Exploring theory of mind after severe traumatic brain injury. *Cortex, 46*, 1088–1099.

Muncer, S. J. & Ling, J. (2006). Psychometric analysis of the empathy quotient (EQ) scale. *Personality and Individual Differences, 40*, 1111–1119.

Naccache, L., Dehaene, S., Cohen, L., Habert, M.-O., Guichart-Gomez, E., Galanaud, D. & Willer, J.-C. (2005). Effortless control: executive attention and conscious feeling of mental effort are dissociable. *Neuropsychologia, 43*(9), 1318–1328.

NCS Pearson Inc. (2009). *Advanced Clinical Solutions for WAIS-IV and WMS-IV: Administration and Scoring Manual.* San Antonio, TX: Author.

Neidenthal, P. M., Brauer, M., Halberstadt, J. B. & Innes-Ker, Å. H. (2001). When did her smile drop? Facial mimicry and the influences of emotional state on the detection of change in emotional expression. *Cognition & Emotion, 15*(6), 853–864. doi: 10.1080/02699930143000194

Nelson, L., Satz, P. & D'Elia, L. (1994). *Manual of the Neuropsychology Behavior and Affect Profile*. Palo Alto, CA: Mind Garden Press.

Nelson, L., Drebing, C., Satz, P. & Uchiyama, C. L. (1998). Personality change in head trauma: a validity study of the Neuropsychology Behavior and Affect Profile. *Archives of Clinical Neuropsychology, 13*, 549–560.

Nigg, J. T. (2000). On inhibition/disinhibition in developmental psychopathology: views from cognitive and personality psychology and a working inhibition taxonomy. *Psychological Bulletin, 126*(2), 220–246.

Nowicki, S. (2010). *Manual for the Receptive Tests of the Diagnostic Analysis of Nonverbal Accuracy 2 (DANVA2)*. Atlanta, GA: Available from Dr Stephen Nowicki, Jr., Department of Psychology, Emory University.

Nowicki, S. & Carton, J. (1993). The measurement of emotional intensity from facial expressions. *Journal of Social Psychology, 133*, 749–750.

Nowicki, S. & Duke, M. P. (1994). Individual differences in the nonverbal communication of affect: the diagnostic analysis of nonverbal accuracy. *Journal of Nonverbal Behavior, 18*, 9–35.

O'Doherty, J., Winston, J., Critchley, H., Perrett, D., Burt, D. & Dolan, R. (2003). Beauty in a smile: the role of medial orbitofrontal cortex in facial attractiveness. *Neuropsychologia, 41*(2), 147–155.

Odhuba, R. A., van den Broek, M. D. & Johns, L. C. (2005). Ecological validity of measures of executive functioning. *British Journal of Clinical Psychology, 44*(2), 269–278.

Ozonoff, S. & Miller, G. A. (1996). An explanation of right hemisphere contributions to the pragmatic impairments of autism. *Brain and Language, 52*, 411–434.

Pasini, A., Chiale, D. & Serpia, S. (1992). Alexithymia as related to sex, age and educational level: results of the Toronto Alexithymic Scale in 417 normal subjects. *Comprehensive Psychiatry, 33*, 42–46.

Perlstein, W. M., Cole, M. A., Demery, J. A., Seignourel, P. J., Dixit, N. K., Larson, M. J. & Briggs, R. W. (2004). Parametric manipulation of working memory load in traumatic brain injury: behavioral and neural correlates. *Journal of the International Neuropsychological Society, 10*(05), 724–741. doi: doi:10.1017/S1355617704105110

Phillips, M. L., Drevets, W. C., Rauch, S. L. & Lane, R. D. (2003). Neurobiology of emotion perception I: the neural basis of normal emotion perception. *Society of Biological Psychiatry, 54*, 504–514.

Pitterman, H. & Nowicki, S. (2004). A test of the ability to identify emotion in human standing and sitting postures: the Diagnostic Analysis of Nonverbal Accuracy-2 Posture Test (DANVA2–POS). *Genetic, Social, and General Psychology Monographs, 130*, 146–162.

Ponsford, J. & Kinsella, G. (1992). Attentional deficits following close head injury. *Journal of Clinical and Experimental Neuropsychology, 14*(5), 822–838.

Prigatano, G. P. & Pribam, K. H. (1982). Perception and memory of facial affect following brain injury. *Perceptual and Motor Skills, 54*(3), 859–869.

Rao, V. & Lyketsos, C. (2000). Neuropsychiatric sequelae of traumatic brain injury. *Psychosomatics, 41*(2), 95–103. doi: 10.1176/appi.psy.41.2.95

Roth, R. M., Isquith, P. K. & Gioia, G. A. (2005). *BRIEF-A: Behavior Rating Inventory of Executive Function – Adult version*. Lutz, FL: Psychological Assessment Resources, Inc.

Rubia, K., Russell, T., Overmeyer, S., Brammer, M. J., Bullmore, E. T., Sharma, T., Simmons, A., Williams, S. C., Giampietro, V., Andrew, C. M. & Taylor, E. (2001).

Mapping motor inhibition: conjunctive brain activations across different versions of go/no-go and stop tasks. *NeuroImage 13*, 250–261.

Rushby, J. A. & Barry, R. J. (2007). Event-related potential correlates of phasic and tonic measures of the orienting reflex. *Biological Psychology, 75*(3), 248–259.

Russell, T. A., Tchanturia, K., Rahman, Q. & Schmidt, U. (2007). Sex differences in theory of mind: a male advantage on Happè's 'cartoon' task. *Cognition and emotion, 21*, 1554–1564.

Sánchez-Navarro, J. P., Martínez-Selva, J. M. & Román, F. (2005). Emotional response in patients with frontal brain damage: effects of affective valence and information content. *Behavioural Neuroscience, 119*, 87–97.

Sato, W., Kubota, Y., Okada, T., Murai, T., Yoshikawa, S. & Sengoku, A. (2002). Seeing happy emotion in fearful and angry faces: qualitative analysis of facial expression recognition in a bilateral amygdala-damaged patient. *Cortex: A Journal Devoted to the Study of the Nervous System and Behavior, 38*(5), 727–742.

Saunders, J. C., McDonald, S. & Richardson, R. (2006). Loss of emotional experience after traumatic brain injury: findings with the startle probe procedure. *Neuropsychology, 20*(2), 224–231.

Shamay, S. G., Tomer, R. & Aharon-Peretz, J. (2002). Deficit in understanding sarcasm in patients with prefrontal lesion is related to impaired empathic ability. *Brain and Cognition 48*(2–3), 558–563.

Shamay-Tsoory, S. G., Tomer, R. & Aharon-Peretz, J. (2005). The neuroanatomical basis of understanding sarcasm and its relationship to social cognition. *Neuropsychology, 19*, 288–300.

Soussignan, R., Ehrle, N., Henry, A., Schaal, B. & Bakchine, S. (2005). Dissociation of emotional processes in response to visual and olfactory stimuli following frontotemporal damage. *Neurocase, 11*, 114–128.

Spell, L. A. & Frank, E. (2000). Recognition of nonverbal communication of affect following traumatic brain injury. *Journal of Nonverbal Behavior, 24*(4), 285–300.

Spiers, M. V., Pouk, J. A. & Santoro, J. M. (1994). Examining perspective-taking in the severely head injured. *Brain Injury, 8*, 463–473.

Spikman, J. M., Timmerman, M. E., Milders, M. V., Veenstra, W. S. & van der Naalt, J. (2012). Social cognition impairments in relation to general cognitive deficits, injury severity, and prefrontal lesions in traumatic brain injury patients. *Journal of Neurotrauma, 29*(1), 101–111.

Stone, V., Baron-Cohen, S. & Knight, R. T. (1998). Frontal lobe contributions to theory of mind. *Journal of Cognitive Neuroscience, 10*(5), 640–656.

Stronach, S. T. & Turkstra, L. S. (2008). Theory of mind and use of cognitive state terms by adolescents with traumatic brain injury. *Aphasiology, 22*(10), 1054–1070. doi: 10.1080/02687030701632187

Struchen, M. A., Clark, A. N., Sander, A. M., Mills, M. R., Evans, G. & Kurtz, D. (2008). Relation of executive functioning and social communication measures to functional outcomes following traumatic brain injury. *NeuroRehabilitation, 23*, 185–198.

Struchen, M. A., Pappadis, M. R., Sander, A. M., Burrows, C. S. & Myszka, K. A. (2011). Examining the contribution of social communication abilities and affective/behavioral functioning to social integration outcomes for adults with traumatic brain injury. *The Journal of Head Trauma Rehabilitation, 26*(1), 30–42.

Stuss, D. T., Gow, C. A. & Hetherington, C. (1992). 'No longer gage': frontal lobe dysfunction and emotional changes. *Journal of Consulting and Clinical Psychology, 60*(3), 349–359.

Surian, L., Baron-Cohen, S. & Van der Lely, H. (1996). Are children with autism deaf to Gricean maxims? *Cognitive Neuropsychiatry, 1*(1), 55–71.

Tate, R. L. (1999). Executive dysfunction and characterological changes after traumatic brain injury: two sides of the same coin? *Cortex, 35*(1), 39–55.

——(2003). Impact of pre-injury factors on outcome after severe traumatic brain injury: does post-traumatic personality change represent an exacerbation of premorbid traits? *Neuropsychological Rehabilitation, 13*(1–2), 43–64.

——(2010). *A Compendium of Tests, Scales and Questionnaires: The Practitioner's Guide to Measuring Outcomes After Acquired Brain Impairment.* Hove, UK: Psychology Press.

Tate, R. L. & Broe, G. A. (1999). Psychosocial adjustment after traumatic brain injury: what are the important variables? *Psychological Medicine, 29*(3), 713–725.

Tate, R. L., Fenelon, B., Manning, M. & Hunter, M. (1991). Patterns of neuropsychological impairment after severe blunt head injury. *Journal of Nervous and Mental Disease, 179*(3), 117–126.

Thomsen, I. V. (1984). Late outcome of very severe blunt head trauma: a 10–15 year second follow-up. *Journal of Neurology, Neurosurgery & Psychiatry, 47*(3), 260–268.

Toussaint, L. & Webb, J. R. (2005). Gender differences in the relationship between empathy and forgiveness. *Journal of Social Psychology, 145*, 673–685.

Tranel, D., Bechara, A. & Denburg, N. L. (2002). Asymmetric functional roles of right and left ventromedial prefrontal cortices in social conduct, decision making and emotional processing. *Cortex, 38*(4), 589–612.

Turkstra, L. S. (2008). Conversation-based assessment of social cognition in adults with traumatic brain injury. *Brain Injury, 22*(5), 397–409. doi: 10.1080/02699050802027059

Turkstra, L. S., Dixon, T. M. & Baker, K. K. (2004). Theory of Mind and social beliefs in adolescents with traumatic brain injury. *NeuroRehabilitation, 19*(3), 245–256.

Turkstra, L. S., Williams, W., Tonks, J. & Frampton, I. (2008). Measuring social cognition in adolescents: implications for students with TBI returning to school. *NeuroRehabilitation, 23*(6), 501–509.

Velligan, D. I., Ritch, J. L., Sui, D., DiCocco, M. & Huntzinger, C. D. (2002). Frontal Systems Behavior Scale in schizophrenia: relationships with psychiatic symtomatology, cognition and adaptive function. *Psychiatry Research, 113*(3), 227–236.

Viano, D. C., Casson, I. R., Pellman, E. J., Zhang, E. J., King, A. I. & Yang, K. H. (2005). Concussion in professional football: brain responses by finite element analysis: part 9. *Neurosurgery, 57*, 891–916.

Vrana, S. R. & Gross, D. (2004). Reactions to facial expressions: effects of social context and speech anxiety on responses to neutral, anger, and joy expressions. *Biological Psychology, 66*, 63–78.

Walsh, K. W. (1985). *Understanding Brain Damage: A Primer or Neuropsychological Evaluation.* Edinburgh: Churchill Livingstone.

Watts, A. J. & Douglas, J. M. (2006). Interpreting facial expression and communication competence following severe traumatic brain injury. *Aphasiology, 20*(8), 707–722.

Wells, R., Dywan, J. & Dumas, J. (2005). Life satisfaction and distress in family caregivers as related to specific behavioural changes after traumatic brain injury. *Brain Injury, 19*(13), 1105–1115.

Wild, B., Erb, M. & Bartels, M. (2001). Are emotions contagious? Evoked emotions while viewing emotionally expressive faces: quality, quantity, time course and gender differences. *Psychiatry Research, 102*, 109–124.

Williams, C. & Wood, R. L. (2010). Alexithymia and emotional empathy following traumatic brain injury. *Journal of Clinical and Experimental Neuropsychology, 32*(3), 259–267.

Williams, K. D. & Sommer, K. L. (1997). Social ostracism by coworkers: does rejection lead to loafing or compensation? *Personality and Social Psychology Bulletin, 23*(7), 693–706. doi: 10.1177/0146167297237003

Williams, K. D., Cheung, C. K. T. & Choi, W. (2000). Cyberostracism: effects of being ignored over the Internet. *Journal of Personality and Social Psychology, 79*(5), 748–762. doi: 10.1037/0022-3514.79.5.748

Williams, K. R., Galas, J., Light, D., Pepper, C., Ryan, C., Kleinmann, A. E., Donovick, P. (2001). Head injury and alexithymia: implications for family practice care. *Brain Injury, 15*(4), 349–356.

Wilson, B. A., Alderman, N., Burgess, P. W., Emslie, H. & Evans, J. J. (1996). *The Behavioural Assessment of the Dysexecutive Syndrome.* New York: Pearson.

Winston, J. S., Strange, B. A., O'Doherty, J. & Dolan, R. J. (2002). Automatic and intentional brain responses during evaluation of trustworthiness of faces. *Nature Neuroscience, 5*(3), 277–283.

Wood, R. L. & Williams, C. (2007). Neuropsychological correlates of organic alexithymia. *Journal of the International Neuropsychological Society, 13*, 471–479.

Wood, R. L. & Williams, C. (2008). Inability to empathize following traumatic brain injury. *Journal of the International Neuropsychological Society, 14*, 289–296.

Wood, R. L., Liossi, C. & Wood, L. (2005). The impact of head injury neurobehavioural sequelae on personal relationships: preliminary findings. *Brain Injury, 19*(10), 845–851.

Young, A., Perret, D., Calder, A., Sprengelmeyer, R. & Ekman, P. (2002). *Facial Expression of Emotion-stimuli and Tests (FEEST).* Bury St Edmunds, England: Thames Valley Test Company.

Zelazo, P. D. and Cunningham, W. A. (2007). Executive function: mechanisms underlying emotion regulation. In J. J. Gross (ed.) *Handbook of Emotion Regulation,* pp. 135–158. New York: Guilford.

6 A theoretical approach to understanding social dysfunction in children and adolescents with TBI

Vicki Anderson, Miriam Beauchamp,
Stefanie Rosema and Cheryl Soo

Introduction

The manner in which a child operates within a social environment, by relying on social skills and interacting with others, is fundamental to the development and formation of lasting relationships and to effective participation within the community (Beauchamp & Anderson, 2010; Blakemore, 2010; Cacioppo, 2002). While children's social interactions appear to take place quite naturally they are, in fact, highly complex processes. They require the involvement of a distributed neural network, the activation of a range of neurocognitive skills, as well as reference to the child's environment and life experiences.

Disruptions in social skill development can result in psychological distress, social isolation and reduced self-esteem, all of which have major implications for quality of life. While still in its infancy, social neuroscience, which focuses on social cognitive processes (i.e. social cognition) and the neural substrates thought to underpin them, offers an opportunity to establish a conceptual foundation for better understanding the social domain. However, biological models alone are likely to be insufficient to fully understand the complexities of social development. The critical importance of environment and experience for social skills must also be considered in moving towards a comprehensive model of social function (Belsky & de Haan, 2011; Bos *et al.*, 2009; Bowlby, 1962; Masten *et al.*, 1999). Despite advances in both of these domains, many aspects of social function and social cognition remain poorly understood – prevalence, predictors, psychological and biological bases, and developmental pathways are largely unknown.

The impact of disruption as a result of early brain insult is even less well understood, but is likely to have dramatic effects as these skills are developing and emerging during childhood and adolescence. Such disruption in early life may interfere with the child's capacity to acquire and develop social skills. An example of such 'disruption' is provided by childhood traumatic brain injury (TBI), where it is well established that injury can result in physical dysfunction, cognitive and communication deficits, behavioural problems and poor academic performance (Anderson *et al.*, 2009). Minimal research has examined the impact of such insults on social function; however, given that many social skills are rapidly emerging through childhood, it is highly likely that victims of such insults will also experience comprised social development.

This chapter aims to review the current literature examining social outcomes from TBI sustained in childhood and adolescence, and then to interpret these findings within a theoretical framework. We begin with a summary of key definitions and the epidemiology of social skills within the developmental domain and then highlight conceptual models which incorporate the brain, environment and developmental dimensions. Within this framework we will review the literature examining social outcomes following TBI occurring within childhood and adolescence. We will also explore empirical findings relating to the influence of brain and environmental factors on social skills in the context of child TBI. Finally, intervention approaches for the remediation of social dysfunction will be addressed.

Social skills: definitions and epidemiology

The term 'social skills' incorporates a range of components. For the purposes of this discussion, we have chosen to employ three specific elements: social competence, social interaction and social adjustment. *Social competence* we define as the ability to achieve personal goals in social interaction while simultaneously maintaining positive relationships with others over time and across situations. *Social interaction* refers to the social actions and reactions between individuals or groups modified to their interaction partner(s), while *social adjustment* represents the capacity of individuals to adapt to the demands of their social environment (Anderson & Beauchamp, 2012; Beauchamp & Anderson, 2010; Bedell & Dumas, 2004).

The development of social skills is precarious, as illustrated by the presence of social problems in many neurological and developmental disorders, chronic medical and psychiatric conditions and in the context of social disadvantage, parent psychopathology or environmental deprivation. Social problems occur either directly, through disruption of a particular social or cognitive skill, or as a secondary consequence of stigma, restrictions in social participation or from paucity of social opportunities. Despite their frequency, health professionals have tended to overlook the importance of social problems for their patients, possibly because they are difficult to observe and assess in clinical contexts. Parents, also, tend to under-rate their child's problems in this domain, seeing them as of secondary importance compared to their child's health and educational status. In contrast, children rate their social skills as being of primary importance (Bohnert *et al.*, 1997).

To date, there are no global estimates of the prevalence of social problems, in children or adults, although reports suggest that 10 per cent of typically developing children are affected by social problems (Asher, 1990). Figures are much higher in '*at risk*' groups, such as survivors of early TBI, with some studies reporting rates of up to 50 per cent in the child TBI population (Catroppa *et al.*, 2009; Rutter, 1983). The lack of epidemiological data is hardly surprising given that social problems exist not only as an independent entity, but also as a symptom, or secondary consequence, of many other conditions. Even when identified as a potential difficulty, diagnosis and characterization of social problems are hindered by a lack of appropriate assessment tools and clearly defined diagnostic criteria.

The burden of social problems is undisputed. Regardless of etiology, children with poor social skills are at higher risk for delinquent or criminal behaviours in adolescence and adulthood (Hawkins *et al.*, 2005). Reduced social function is also linked with aggression and violence (Boxer *et al.*, 2005), sexual offences (Righthand & Welch, 2004), alcohol and drug use (Botvin & Kantor, 2000; Henry & Slater, 2007), conduct disorder (Hill, 2002), and bullying (Camodeca & Goossens, 2005). Poor social skills are frequently associated with neurologic and psychiatric conditions, such as TBI. The adverse social consequences of early brain injury are illustrated by the high prevalence of childhood TBI in incarcerated juveniles (35 per cent) (Kenny & Jennings, 2007) and in adult prisoners (up to 87 per cent) (Butler *et al.*, 2006; Leon-Carrion & Ramos, 2003; Slaughter *et al.*, 2003), though the nature of the link between TBI and socially maladaptive behaviours is unknown.

Social development

Social skills are characterized by protracted development, emerging gradually through infancy and childhood, and consolidating during adolescence, reflecting a dynamic interplay between the individual and his or her environment. Research examining infant behaviour demonstrates the innate bias of infants for social interaction. Newborns are uniquely sensitive to facial stimuli. By 2–3 months they display social initiatives and preferences in processing and recognition of visual and auditory stimuli (Kelly *et al.*, 2005; Rochat & Striano, 2002). By 7 months, they can integrate emotional information across modalities to recognize emotions in faces and voice (Grossmann *et al.*, 2006). Joint attention then emerges around 9 months of age as evidenced by sharing of attention between a child and an adult in reference to some third event, person or object (Carpenter *et al.*, 1998). This phase of infant social development is considered to be a precursor to complex social cognition (e.g. theory of mind), as it underpins the infant's ability to understand the thoughts and intentions of others which tends to mature around 4–5 years (Tomasello *et al.*, 2005). Essentially, the emergence of early childhood social abilities that underpin theory of mind, such as understanding of intentions and false-beliefs, provides a basis for the specialization of more complex mentalizing abilities (Flavell, 1999; Russell, 2005), which continue to mature throughout childhood and into adolescence.

Adolescence is a developmental stage of particular interest for social skills, being characterized by substantial neuro-structural change as well as environmental and biological changes that increase teenagers' exposure to social situations (Burnett *et al.*, 2012; Choudhury *et al.*, 2006). From an environmental perspective, social maturation is a function of increasing personal independence and peer group interaction and the greater importance of friendships and relationships. Concurrently, the adolescent brain undergoes marked changes in areas which have been shown to underlie social cognition, including a decrease in grey matter volume and an increase in white matter density in frontal and parietal cortices (Casey *et al.*, 2005; Giedd *et al.*, 1999; Gogtay *et al.*, 2004).

Theoretical approaches to understanding the development of social skills

Until recently, the majority of research investigating social difficulties in 'at risk' childhood populations has lacked a theoretical foundation, thus impeding progress. The emergence of 'multi-dimensional' theoretical paradigms is essential for gaining a fuller understanding of social function in the context of child development and, in particular, for contributing to clinical practices, specifically identification, diagnosis and intervention. To address this gap, Yeates and colleagues (2007) have proposed a heuristic targeted specifically at social skills in the context of TBI acquired during childhood, incorporating theoretical and empirical evidence from neuroscience, psychology and neuropsychology. These authors suggest that social skills are mediated by social-affective and cognitive-executive processes and subsumed by the social brain network, with some integration of both developmental issues and the potential impact of early disruption due to brain insult.

Similarly, the Socio-Cognitive Integration of Abilities Model (SOCIAL: Beauchamp & Anderson, 2010) defines the core dimensions of social skills and their interactions within a developmental framework founded on empirical research and clinical principles. SOCIAL acknowledges the importance of both normal and abnormal biological and environmental influences on the development of social skills and assumes that the development of intact social skills is dependent on the normal maturation of the brain, cognition and behaviour, within a supportive environmental context (i.e. a bio-psycho-social approach). Specifically, social skills are subsumed by the *'social brain network'*, and are vulnerable to environmental influences. SOCIAL (Figure 6.1) aims to provide an integrated representation of the cognitive and affective sub-skills that contribute to social function and explore how these are influenced by both internal (brain) and external (environmental) forces.

The first component of the SOCIAL model depicts factors that will shape the emergence of social function. *External factors* refer to environmental influences that may contribute to the quality and nature of social interactions, such as family environment, socioeconomic status or culture. *Internal factors* refer to components of an individual's self that impact the way in which they interact with others in social situations, such as their temperament, personality or physical attributes. *Brain development and integrity* refer to the neural underpinnings of social skills. The second element of the model incorporates neurocognitive abilities essential for intact social skills: *attention and executive functions, communication and social cognition (or socio-emotional skills)*. We propose that these processes are interrelated at both the behavioural and neural level forming a functional social system.

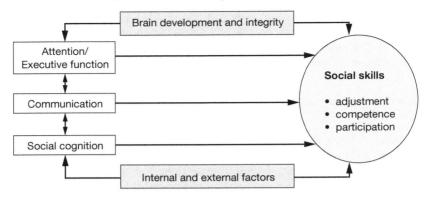

Figure 6.1 The social brain network (reprinted from Anderson & Beauchamp, 2012, with permission)

Internal and external influences

External factors

A child's social experience during early development is largely constrained to the social environment of the family. *Socioeconomic (SES) factors* have an established role for social development in typically developing children (McLoyd, 1998). Social disadvantage has been associated with poor adjustment and problematic peer interactions (Ackerman & Brown, 2006; Bulotsky-Shearer *et al.*, 2008). In the context of child TBI, where lower SES and family disadvantage are thought to be over-represented, SES has been found to be an important contributor to long-term social outcomes (Anderson *et al.*, 2004; Yeates *et al.*, 2004) with a combination of greater social disadvantage and more serious brain insult resulting in severe social problems.

Family factors are also important. Maternal attachment greatly influences the development of social skills in infancy (Bowlby, 1962; Root *et al.*, 2012). Even in adolescence, parent–child interactions predict and moderate social behaviour, with both autonomy and attachment differentially influencing the emergence of delinquency (Allen *et al.*, 2002). In the context of child TBI, family environment contributes to long-term outcomes, with family dysfunction exacerbating negative social outcomes (Anderson *et al.*, 2004; Yeates *et al.*, 2004), and family interventions resulting in improved parent mental health found to also improve child social function (Woods *et al.*, 2011).

Internal factors

Factors intrinsic to the individual, such as *temperament or personality*, are often neglected in the consideration of social outcomes, despite their potential to influence a person's social skills. Extraversion and openness are associated with proactive socialization (Wanberg & Kammeyer-Mueller, 2000), while higher levels of self-esteem predict better social and interpersonal relations (Delugach *et al.*, 1992). At a more debilitating level, social withdrawal and social phobia, frequently present in adolescent survivors of child TBI or developmental disabilities, are associated with poor social development, and therefore constitute a risk factor, with the potential to limit a child's social experience (Guralink, 1999; Rubin *et al.*, 2012). *Physical disability*, a common sequelae of child TBI, provides a source of stigmatization, negatively influencing social interactions by challenging interpersonal relationships and limiting opportunities to engage in social interactions (Major & O'Brien, 2005). For example, severe child TBI has been linked to poor social function in adulthood, with survivors demonstrating few stable relationships and a limited capacity to form new social links (Anderson *et al.*, 2010).

Neural bases of social cognition and function

The recent burgeoning of the social neurosciences reflects a growing interest in the biological bases of social function, and has established that social functions involve complex behaviours that require the efficient working of an intricate neural system. In the childhood domain, the detailed case studies published by Anderson and Eslinger (Anderson *et al.*, 2004) provide rich clinical insight into the impact of early brain insult on high level cognitive skills and social abilities. Research evidence regarding the social brain has been slower to emerge and comes primarily from studies of TBI because of the vulnerability of frontal and temporal regions which have been identified as crucial for social skills (Anderson *et al.*, 2012; Hanten *et al.*, 2012).

Rapidly evolving neuroimaging technology, such as functional magnetic resonance imaging (fMRI) and diffusor tensor imaging (DTI) (Adolphs, 2003), have also contributed to our understanding of the biological underpinnings of social function. These data emphasize that the various areas involved in specific aspects of social processing form a complex social neural network (Cunningham & Janson, 2007; Goursaud & Bachevalier, 2007; Saxe *et al.*, 2004; Van Overwalle, 2009) that develops and becomes refined through childhood and adolescence. The protracted development of social skills, and their neural substrates, reflects the multifaceted nature of underlying processes and their interactions, and highlights the system's vulnerability to dysfunction should any of the many regions involved or their connections be disrupted by biological or environmental elements. Damage or disruption involving the neural substrates of social cognition may lead to socially inappropriate behaviours (or 'function'), such as those observed in many clinical populations.

Some brain areas have been shown to be preferentially involved in basic social processing and are functional early in development. For example, face recognition emerges early in development and has been linked to the fusiform gyrus and superior temporal sulcus, while emotion perception appears to fall under the control of a widely distributed system including the amygdala, insula and ventral striatum (Adolphs, 2003; Adolphs & Spezio, 2006; Adolphs *et al.*, 2003; Phillips *et al.*, 2003). In contrast, higher-order social skills rely strongly on frontal regions, which continue to develop throughout childhood and into early adulthood. Theory of mind (mentalizing) elicits activity in the medial prefrontal cortex, as well as in the superior temporal sulcus, temporo-parietal junction and the temporal poles (Frith & Frith, 2006; Gallagher & Frith, 2003). Empathy has been linked with the mirror neuron system (Iacoboni, 2009), along with the anterior cingulate cortex, regions of the somatosensory cortex and anterior insula (Bufalari *et al.*, 2007; Cheng *et al.*, 2008; Hein & Singer, 2008; Jackson *et al.*, 2006). Moral reasoning, social judgement and social decision making appear to rely heavily on prefrontal regions such as the anterior cingulate, orbital, frontopolar and ventromedial prefrontal cortices, as well as eliciting activity from the temporo-parietal junction, amygdala, angular gyrus and posterior cingulate (Casebeer, 2003; Greene *et al.*, 2001; Moll *et al.*, 2002a; Moll *et al.*, 2003; Moll *et al.*, 2002b; Moll *et al.*, 2005).

Development, biology and environment

Social skills provide an opportunity to examine the integration of development, biology and environment. Animal work, genetics research and neuroimaging studies highlight the bidirectional influences of biology and environment on brain structure and development. Kolb and Wishaw (1998) have documented the brain's capacity to adapt both structurally and functionally to changes in experience and environment, and for these changes to translate into social behaviour. In particular, enriched environments and greater exposure to social interactions can induce experience-dependent neural changes in the rat's brain, including brain size, cortical thickness, neuron size, dendritic branching, spine density, synapses per neuron and glial number (Silasi *et al.*, 2008). Genetic influences and environmental experience may also affect the structure of the brain, and the resultant social 'phenotype' variably at different ages (Gray & Cornish, 2012; Kolb *et al.*, 1998; Raizada & Kishiyama, 2010), suggesting a complex interplay between biological and environmental dimensions, development and their implications for the emergence of social function.

Social development is also susceptible to environmental exposure and experience. Cases of maternal separation, parental loss and social isolation highlight the increased risk in children of developing indiscriminate social behaviours and social dysfunction more generally (Colvert *et al.*, 2008). As previously noted, parenting practices are also important for social development, with more rigid, unresponsive parenting associated with a greater risk of poor self-regulation and social competence (Root *et al.*, 2012). These findings suggest that, as with other sensory and cognitive systems, social development may be susceptible to adequate social stimulation during decisive developmental periods and that early nurturing is critical to socio-emotional development.

Cognitive mediators

Although it could be argued that all mental functions, from basic perceptual processes to complex cognitive functions, are necessary for social interactions to occur adequately, three higher-order cognitive domains are critical for social functioning: attention-executive, communication and social cognition. These domains each incorporate multiple sub-skills, which interact selectively and dynamically to determine social competence in varying situations.

Attention and executive skills, generally considered to be largely subsumed by frontal brain structures, are critical for efficient functioning in everyday life, and have been linked to social outcomes in the context of specific behaviours, including emotional dyscontrol, aggression, delinquency and antisocial behaviour (Hill, 2002; Jorge *et al.*, 2004). Impairments in attention and executive function are frequently reported in children as a consequence of TBI, providing a potential contribution to social skills deficits in the group (Catroppa & Anderson, 2005; Max *et al.*, 2005). Further, Muscara *et al.* (2008) describe the mediating influences of executive skills for social problem solving. Interventions focusing on attentional control have been shown to improve social competence (Greenberg, 2006; McDonald *et al.*, 2012; Riggs *et al.*, 2006).

Communication provides the basis by which we experience thought, intentions and information and thus underpins the quality of our social relationships. The evolution of communication marks important milestones in the acquisition of social skills, first evident in the appearance of social smile in the young baby, and then in the emergence of intentional imitative behaviour. The emergence of joint attention marks the transition between engaging in dyadic interactions to participating in tryadic exchanges (Grossmann & Johnson, 2007). Social skills then progress rapidly following the emergence of expressive language, but can be derailed when basic language impairments occur, disrupting the child's ability to communicate effectively with those around him/her. Subtle aspects of language processing are also essential, and are particularly vulnerable in the context of TBI where frontal brain regions, including speech and language cortex, are frequently involved. Pragmatics (conveying meaning beyond words used and without ambiguity) are fundamental for creating logical sequences and determining the burden of conversation (as in turn-taking), whereas monitoring the appropriateness of utterances provides insights into aspects of social functioning (Turkstra *et al.*, 1996). Children who are unable to decode subtle differences in prosody (pitch, loudness/intensity, intonation, rate, stress, rhythm) are at a social disadvantage (McCann *et al.*, 2007), given their importance for communicating emphasis, clarification and contradiction of word meanings. A child unable to detect the underlying meaning of ironic or deceptive messages will struggle to receive the social cues necessary to respond appropriately and may consequently breach social rules. Such difficulties have been described recently as a consequence of child TBI (Couper *et al.*, 2002; Dooley *et al.*, 2008; Walz *et al.* 2010) and are discussed further in Chapter 7.

Social cognition begins with the perception of basic aspects of face and emotion perception and extends to complex cognitive processes involving understanding mental states which modulate appropriate behaviour within social contexts.

Perception of facial expressions and emotions are equally crucial to social reciprocity (McClure, 2000), and are sometimes impaired in socio-emotional processing disorders such as autism (d'Arc & Mottron, 2012). Body language also has a role in social cognition, connecting both communication and emotion processing domains and, as with face perception, misperception of such signs can lead to poor peer relationships (de Gelder, 2006; Fujiki *et al.*, 2007).

Attribution may be seen as a mediator between basic face and emotion perception and higher-order cognitive domains such as theory of mind. It refers to the way in which people 'attribute' causes or intent to the behaviour of others (intent attribution) or to the way they ascribe lasting personality characteristics to others (trait attribution). Intentions are inferred and influence the way a person is perceived, shaping the course of social interaction (Harris *et al.*, 2005). They are also involved in social judgements of truthfulness and deception (O'Sullivan, 2003). Biases in attribution, such as a tendency to perceive intentions as hostile, can explain aggressive and antisocial behaviour (Orobio de Castro *et al.*, 2002), with obvious implications for social function. Within the TBI population, adolescents with TBI have been found to demonstrate similar patterns of intent attribution as highly aggressive youth. Specifically, when compared to their non-injured peers, adolescents with TBI are more likely to attribute hostility to others' intent during socially ambiguous situations (Dooley *et al.*, 2008).

Theory of mind (ToM) is the ability to attribute mental states (beliefs, intents, desires, pretending, knowledge) to oneself and others and to understand that others have mental states different from one's own (Frith & Frith, 2006). ToM is closely related to *empathy,* which may be defined as the emotional reaction in the observer to the affective state of another (Blair, 2005). ToM can be seen as a form of 'cognitive empathy', requiring an understanding of the mental state of another individual. Unlike cognitive perspective-taking, empathy requires the observer to be 'in an affective state', highlighting the added emotional involvement needed for empathy to occur. Not surprisingly, the consequences of impairments in ToM and empathy are profound for complex social behaviours and contribute to the development of prosocial behaviours (Walker, 2005), as is evident from the study of social disorders, such as autism (Hill & Frith, 2003).

Moral reasoning allows an individual to make decisions about right and wrong. It is closely linked to ToM, with the ability to understand and represent another person's perspective being necessary for moral behaviours. From a social cognition perspective, the moral domain is concerned with how individuals develop and understand knowledge about social events by relying on moral judgements (Arsenio & Lemerise, 2004). Impairments in moral reasoning often result in socially unacceptable actions, characteristic of antisocial, rule-breaking behaviours (Arsenio & Lemerise, 2004).

In summary, internal and external factors, shaped by biology and the environment, interact bi-directionally with the ongoing development of the brain to influence the emergence of cognitive function. For example, internal factors such as personality (Rusting, 1998) exert a direct effect on cognition and may together predispose the individual to social dysfunction, for instance, social or personality disorders (Kimbrel, 2008; Raine & Yang, 2006). External factors also influence cognitive factors directly, for example, attachment styles and family function are known to affect both cognitive and social development (Green & Goldwyn, 2002). Favourable SES is linked to better cognitive and social outcomes (Conger & Donnellan, 2007; Hackman & Farah, 2009). Cognitive and affective processes dictate an individual's ability to navigate social interactions and environments, that is, their social function and competence, and these processes exert an effect on each other. Changes in cognitive abilities can also impact back on mediators of social function (brain structure/function, biology and the environment).

Child TBI and social outcomes

Child head injury (TBI) is a frequent cause of acquired disability in childhood. The majority of such injuries are mild, with few, if any sequelae, however, children sustaining more severe TBI may suffer permanent physical, cognitive, social and behavioural impairment. These deficits will interfere with the child's ability to function effectively within his/her environment, resulting in lags in the acquisition of skills and knowledge. Secondary deficits may also emerge, relating to family stress and adjustment difficulties.

Epidemiological reports suggest that 250:100,000 children with TBI present for medical treatment each year. Of these, 85 per cent will be mild, 5–10 per cent will experience temporary and/or permanent neuropsychological impairment and around 5 per cent will sustain fatal injuries (Goldstein & Levin, 1985; Kraus *et al.*, 1986). The nature of these injuries varies with age. Infants are more likely to suffer injury due to falls or child abuse. For non-accidental injuries, 61 per cent of such injuries occur in children less than 12 months old and commonly result in more severe injury and higher mortality and morbidity than accidental injuries (Holloway *et al.*, 1994). The preschool stage is a particularly high-risk period, with the majority of injuries caused by falls and pedestrian accidents, in keeping with the greater mobility and lack of awareness of danger of this age group (Crowe *et al.*, 2010; Lehr, 1990). Older children and adolescents are more commonly victims of sporting, cycling or pedestrian accidents. In preschool children, the male to female ratio is approximately 1.5:1 (Hayes & Jackson, 1989; Horowitz *et al.*, 1983), while in the school-aged group males are more than twice as likely to suffer TBI (Kraus, 1995). The incidence of TBI increases in males through childhood and adolescence, with a contrasting decline for females over this period (Kraus *et al.*, 1986).

Child TBI occurs most frequently on holidays, weekends and afternoons, when children are involved in social and leisure pursuits, suggesting that many injuries may result from reckless behaviours, in poorly supervised environments (Chadwick *et al.*, 1981; Dalby & Obrzut, 1991). It has been suggested that child TBI is more common in socially disadvantaged families (Anderson *et al.*, 1997; Brown *et al.*, 1981; Klonoff, 1971; Rivara *et al.*, 1993; Taylor *et al.*, 1995) and in children with pre-existing learning and behavioural deficits (Asarnow *et al.*,

1991; Brown *et al.*, 1981; Craft *et al.*, 1972). Some researchers argue that post-injury sequelae, and social deficits in particular, may merely reflect premorbid cognitive, behavioural, and social disturbances. This view is not universal, and others argue that children who sustain injury cannot be differentiated from the general population (Perrott *et al.*, 1991; Prior *et al.*, 1994).

Mechanics, pathophysiology and age at insult

A range of age-specific injury mechanisms may be acting in child TBI, depending upon the maturity of the brain at the time of injury. First, as noted above, the etiology of TBI changes during childhood, with infants and toddlers more likely to be injured due to falls and older children more commonly involved in accidents associated with recreational activities or motor car accidents (Kraus, 1995), thus leading to varying injury processes. In addition, the skull and brain develop throughout childhood, resulting in different injury consequences at different developmental stages. For example, the infant has relatively weak neck muscles, which do not adequately support a proportionately large head, leading to less resistance to force of impact. Further, the infant and toddler possess a relatively thin skull, easily deformed by a direct blow and resulting in more frequent skull fractures. Studies show that more than one-third of children in this age bracket who sustain TBI will have skull fractures. In contrast, contusions, lacerations and subdural hematomas are extremely rare in infancy (Berney *et al.*, 1994; Choux, 1986; Sharma & Sharma, 1994). This may be due to the flexibility and open sutures present in the infant skull. For older children and adolescents, intra-cranial mass lesions (hematomas, contusions) are more common, although not as common as in adult samples (Berger *et al.*, 1985). Contrecoup lesions are relatively rare in all age groups, but least for young children with a gradual increase through childhood (Berney *et al.*, 1994).

The relative lack of myelination present in the brain during infancy and early childhood also leads to different consequences in response to TBI. Immature myelination causes the cerebral hemispheres to be relatively soft and pliable, enabling them to absorb the force of impact better than in an older child or adult. However, unmyelinated fibres are particularly vulnerable to shearing effects, rendering the younger child more vulnerable to diffuse axonal injury (Zimmerman & Bilaniuk, 1994). Bruce and colleagues suggest that TBI in children is more likely to result in diffuse cerebral swelling associated with vascular disruptions, with such pathology identified in one-third of the children (Bruce *et al.*, 1979; Jennett *et al.*, 1977). Outcomes are also different. Babies and toddlers lose consciousness less frequently than other age groups, however post-traumatic epilepsy is more common following early TBI (Berney *et al.*, 1994; Raimondi & Hirschauer, 1984). The implications of these age-related differences are important, arguing that pathophysiology, sequelae, recovery and outcome from childhood TBI cannot easily be extrapolated from adult findings.

Social function and child TBI

A review of the empirical literature investigating social outcomes following child TBI reveals a relative dearth of information. Various factors may contribute to this current situation. First, until recently, child health professionals have failed to recognize the importance of the social dimension for recovery and reintegration, concentrating primarily on physical and neurobehavioural domains. This is well illustrated in a study conducted by Bohnert and colleagues (1997) who report that, when asked to rank the relative importance of health, education and friendships for the injured child, health professionals and parents agreed that friendships were of least importance. In contrast, children ranked friendships as their top priority. Furthermore, in the past, social function has tended to lack a clearly defined neural substrate, consistent with a view that these skills were primarily determined by environmental factors and early experiences. Today, while the social neuroscience framework is not yet fully defined, it is clear that the CNS plays a critical role in subsuming social functions and must be considered in any formulation of social dysfunction.

More recently, research focus has turned to the social domain, however, as noted above, much of the work to date has lacked a theoretical basis and has failed to take advantage of the rich body of knowledge available from other disciplines, such as developmental psychology and developmental psychopathology. A further limitation to accumulating knowledge is the lack of reliable and psychometrically sound measurement tools. In fact, social measures with clinical applicability are rare. Most standardized tools are rating scales or questionnaires, and commonly canvas only parent or teacher perceptions. Many of these are global measures of adaptive ability, behaviour or quality of life, including a small subset of socially relevant items. A small group of measures is specific to social skills, such as relationships, social interaction, social participation and loneliness (Crowe *et al.*, 2011; Muscara & Crowe, 2012), although in general psychometric properties are limited. An even smaller selection of empirical measures is available, mostly tapping aspects of social cognition, including empathy, perspective taking and intent attribution. While many possess good face validity, few have normative data and psychometric properties are unclear. Assessment of social cognition following childhood TBI is also considered in Chapter 7.

Clinical perspectives

Child TBI occurs in the context of a rapidly developing brain where: 1) cerebral organization is likely to be incomplete; 2) neurobehavioural skills are only beginning to emerge; 3) serious damage has the potential to derail the genetic blueprint for normal CNS development; and 4) environmental factors, such as deprivation or enrichment, may have a significant influence on development.

In children, elevated risk of social dysfunction may be attributed to a number of factors. First, *brain regions and networks* important for social function might be damaged. Current understandings of the biological bases of social function suggest that many brain regions may be implicated, and linked via a distributed neural network. Of particular relevance to the developing child, many brain regions that undergo protracted development (e.g. prefrontal regions), and are thus vulnerable in the context of TBI, also contribute to social function (Adolphs, 2009; Beauchamp & Anderson, 2010; Yeates *et al.*, 2007).

Second, *medical factors* may restrict opportunities for social interaction. For example, motor co-ordination deficits will reduce the child's mobility and thus their capacity to independently interact with peers during informal play and sporting activities. Similarly, speech difficulties may lead to reduced expressive language fluency, and thus impact on opportunities for communication with peers. Seizures may cause those around the child to feel wary or anxious about the child's well-being and thus influence social interactions. Further, after the acute recovery period, child TBI may be conceptualized as a chronic illness, and is associated with ongoing medical care and health concerns, and frequent absences from school, need for special classes and additional supervision in both classroom and playground, thus limiting normal exposure to social interactions.

Third, the child's *temperament and adjustment* to their condition will contribute to their social function. It is not uncommon for children with TBI to experience reductions in self-esteem, in response to 'feeling different' from their peers, for the medical reasons noted above, or because of their psychological responses to injury-related physical and cognitive impairments, which can commonly translate into social anxiety and withdrawal. An additional symptom, common to early stages of recovery from TBI is excessive fatigue, which can severely impair the child's motivation and endurance of social interactions, further reducing social exposure. In response to these medical problems, some parents will be over-protective of their vulnerable child, potentially restricting their child's opportunities for engaging independently with peers.

Finally, the *child's environment*, and parents and family in particular, can either support or undermine social development following early TBI. Not surprisingly, in the wake of TBI, the family routine can be disrupted. Parents may need to attend hospital and outpatient appointments, and some families may experience financial hardship associated with caring for their child. The associated burden may increase stress and family dysfunction (Anderson *et al.*, 2006; Taylor *et al.*, 1995; Taylor *et al.*, 2001). A secondary impact of early TBI is the elevated risk of clinically significant stress for parents (McCarthy *et al.*, 2010), with up to one-third of parents presenting with such symptoms even six months after diagnosis. Such parent psychopathology has been shown to impact negatively on the quality of the family environment, and on the child's well-being, with recent research identifying a clear link between such factors and children's social and behavioural adjustment (Anderson *et al.*, 2006; Yeates *et al.*, 2010).

Research evidence of social outcomes

In keeping with the emergence of social neuroscience and the recognition of the debilitating and persisting impact of these problems, research has begun to describe social outcomes associated with early brain insult. The limited research available has demonstrated deficits in the cognitive skills central to social function (e.g. executive function and communication skills) (Anderson *et al.*, 2009; Catroppa & Anderson, 2005; Didus *et al.*, 1999; Hanten *et al.*, 2008; Janusz *et al.*, 2002; Long *et al.*, 2011). While not directly assessing links between these deficits and social function, these studies have provided a platform for conceptualizing the presence of social dysfunction. Only a very small number of studies have attempted to examine possible links between specific cognitive domains implicated in social function and social outcomes (Ganesalingam *et al.*, 2007a; Ganesalingam *et al.*, 2007b, 2011; Greenham *et al.*, 2010; Muscara *et al.*, 2008), with early results supporting the presence of such relationships.

By far the majority of research into social development after early insult to the CNS has focused on TBI. Children with TBI have been reported to show lower levels of self-esteem and adaptive behaviour and higher levels of loneliness and behavioural problems (Andrews *et al.*, 1998), and more difficulties in peer relationships (Bohnert *et al.*, 1997) than controls. For example, Yeates and colleagues (2004) examined social functioning in 109 children with TBI aged 6–12 and an orthopaedic injury comparison group. They showed that parents of children with moderate to severe TBI reported their child to have poor social and behavioural functioning. No substantial recovery in social function was reported over the four years post-injury, and in some cases levels of social functioning worsened. These findings are consistent with previous studies with smaller samples, which have also examined social functioning in children with TBI (Andrews *et al.*, 1998). Although only emerging as a research focus, long-term outcomes studies are also beginning to identify links between poor social function following child TBI and persisting social maladjustment and reduced quality of life (Anderson *et al.*, 2010; Cattelani *et al.*, 1998).

Social adjustment

The majority of studies examining social adjustment have done so by administering broad-band parent questionnaires, such as those tapping behavioural function, for example, the Child Behaviour Checklist (Asarnow *et al.*, 1991; Poggi *et al.*, 2005), Strengths and Difficulties Questionnaire (e.g. Tonks *et al.*, 2011) or adaptive abilities, for example, the Vineland Adaptive Behaviour Scales or the Adaptive Behaviour Assessment System (e.g. Anderson *et al.*, 2001; Fletcher *et al.*, 1990; Ganesalingam *et al.*, 2011; Sparrow *et al.*, 1984). Overall, these studies have been divided in their findings, with similar numbers reporting evidence that children and adolescents with TBI display greater social incompetence than control groups, as demonstrated by poorer parent ratings for socialization and communication skills (Fletcher *et al.*, 1990; Levin *et al.*, 2009; Max *et al.*, 1998; Poggi *et al.*, 2005) or, in contrast, no significant group differences (Anderson *et al.*, 2001; Hanten *et al.*, 2008; Papero *et al.*, 1993; Poggi *et al.*, 2005). Whether greater injury severity leads to poorer social adjustment is as yet unclear. Some studies suggest that children with severe TBI are more impaired in socialization, communication and/or social competence than children with milder injuries (Asarnow *et al.*, 1991; Fletcher *et al.*, 1990; Max *et al.*, 1998; Yeates *et al.*, 2004), but other studies failed to find these dose-response relationships (Papero *et al.*, 1993).

A smaller number of studies have incorporated findings from multiple respondents to investigate social adjustment. Ganesalingam and colleagues (Ganesalingam *et al.*, 2006; 2007a; 2007b) used both parent ratings and direct child measures, and found that children with both moderate and severe TBI were rated by parents as more socially impaired than uninjured children. Similarly, using child direct measures, survivors of child TBI reported poorer emotional and behavioural self-regulation and more frequent aggressive, avoidant or irrelevant solutions to social problems than uninjured children. These authors found no differences between children with severe and moderate TBI.

Our research team has recently conducted a study tracking 10-year functional outcomes from early TBI (age at injury < 7 years). Using parent report measures, we found differences between injury severity groups (mild, moderate, severe) for social skills and adaptive abilities, but with fewer severity effects for behavioural outcomes (Anderson, Godfrey, Rosenfeld, & Catroppa, in press), highlighting the persistence of social dysfunction in the long-term post-injury.

Social interaction

To study this aspect of social function, Bohnert and colleagues (1997) and Prigatano and Gupta (2006) each investigated friendships of children who had sustained a TBI. Bohnert *et al.* (1997) employed both children and parents as respondents, and found no differences between children with and without TBI in friendship networks or on the Friendship Quality Questionnaire (Parker & Asher, 1993). In contrast, Prigatano and Gupta (2006), using parent ratings, reported results that supported a dose-response relationship. Specifically, children with severe TBI reported less close friendships than children with moderate or mild TBI, and children with moderate TBI had less close friendships than children with mild TBI.

In an early study conducted by Andrews and colleagues (1998), a series of questionnaires, tapping various aspects of social interactions, was administered to children and parents. Findings showed that children with TBI experienced higher levels of loneliness and had a higher likelihood of aggressive or antisocial behaviours than controls. Similarly, Dooley *et al.* (2008) investigated aggressive responses in adolescents with a history of TBI, compared to a healthy control sample. These authors found that, while a frequently used broad-band measure, the Child Behaviour Checklist (Achenbach, 1991), detected no group differences in aggressive behaviour, the use of an aggression-specific measure showed greater sensitivity, showing that history of TBI was related to higher rates of both reactive and proactive aggression. Such findings suggest that, to accurately identify and characterize the social consequences of TBI, it is important to use tools sensitive to this domain.

A recent review (van Tol *et al.*, 2011) highlights the inconsistency of findings in the field of social interaction and participation after child TBI. These contradictory outcomes are difficult to interpret and are most likely explained by methodological differences including TBI definition, composition of control groups, small sample sizes and measurement tools. Van Tol *et al.* (2011) also argue for the advantages of mixed methods approaches in this domain, in order to take advantage of both qualitative and quantitative information.

In an attempt to provide some clarity around the presence of social interaction difficulties and their persistence into adulthood, we recently conducted a retrospective study and surveyed a sample of 160 survivors of child TBI, using a quality of life scale, a modified version of the Sydney Psychosocial Reintegration Scale (Tate *et al.*, 1999). Results indicated that adult survivors of severe child TBI experienced significant problems in a range of areas of their lives, including relationships and work and leisure activities. Few of these individuals reported having a stable group of friends or a life partner, and only a small number were gainfully employed. Furthermore, engagement in leisure activities, such as sports or social groups, was rare. Mild and moderate TBI was related to more normal function in social participation and other domains (Anderson *et al.*, 2010). These findings provide strong support for the lasting impact of TBI, especially severe TBI, outlining problems in social interaction, and their secondary repercussions.

Social cognition

In contrast to social adjustment and social interaction, measurement within this domain is largely based on direct child assessments, although these are currently restricted to mostly experimental tools. This domain of social function appears to have attracted the most recent attention, with a growing number of publications emerging investigating outcomes in this area following child TBI. Below, we have grouped this research into studies examining social problem solving, social communication and social information processing (incorporating theory of mind and emotion perception).

A) Social problem solving. Several recent studies have investigated social problem solving in children and adolescents post-TBI, using direct child measures. Hanten *et al.* (2008) and Janusz *et al.* (2002) both used the Interpersonal Negotiation Strategies task (INS: Yeates *et al.*, 1990), a child-based tool, to measure social problem solving. The INS consists of hypothetical interpersonal dilemmas, which involve four social-problem steps; defining the problem, generating alternative strategies, selecting and implementing a specific strategy and evaluating outcomes. Hanten *et al.* (2008) found that children with a TBI scored significantly lower on social problem solving from baseline through to one year post-TBI, with no differential improvement in performance one year after TBI in both the TBI and control groups. More recently, Hanten *et al.* (2011) later replicated these findings, using a virtual reality version of the INS task. Similarly, Janusz *et al.* (2002) reported that children with TBI scored significantly lower on social problem solving. Further, children with TBI were able to generate solutions to social problems, but had difficulty choosing the optimal solution. These authors also investigated performance differences between injury severity groups, but detected no severity effects between those with severe and moderate TBI.

Warschausky *et al.* (1997) used a similar paradigm, the Social Problem Solving Measure (Pettit *et al.*, 1988), to assess solutions to social problems in children aged 7 and 13 years. Children with TBI provided significantly less peer entry solutions in social engagement situations than control children, but the groups did not differ with regard to the number of solutions to peer provocations. In a study from our team (Muscara *et al.*, 2008) we investigated the relationship between executive function and social function ten years post-child TBI, extending the work of Yeates *et al.* (2004), which had previously proposed that social problem solving is a mediator between neurocognitive function and social skills, rather than a direct link. We identified greater executive dysfunction associated with less sophisticated social problem-solving skills and poorer social outcomes. Further, the maturity of social problem-solving skills was found to mediate the relationship between executive function and social outcomes in TBI. This provided the first empirical evidence for a link between executive and social skills in the context of childhood acquired brain injury, due to the mediating link of social problem solving.

B) Social communication. This domain of social function refers specifically to the child's ability to draw meaning from complex language. Tasks tapping these 'pragmatic language' skills include aspects of cognitive function, for example working memory and executive function, as well as abilities more commonly considered as social cognition, such as the identification of irony and sarcasm in conversation, and the ability to draw inferences from linguistic information and to distinguish truth from falsehoods (Turkstra *et al.*, 2004; Turkstra *et al.*, 2008). Using the Video Social Inference Test with a group of adolescents with TBI, Turkstra (2008) demonstrated that child TBI is associated with poorer identification of sarcasm and irony and greater difficulties interpreting inference in both photographs and stories. Dennis and colleagues have reported similar findings with younger children, showing deficits in understanding deceptive emotions, literal truth, irony and deceptive praise (Dennis *et al.*, 2001).

C) Social information processing. Studies investigating social information processing have focused primarily on theory of mind (ToM) and emotion perception in school-aged children and adolescents. For example, Turkstra *et al.* (2004; 2008) measured ToM in adolescents with TBI using a second-order belief task (i.e. requiring the ability to understand what one person thinks about another) and a pragmatic judgement test. They found that, in contrast to healthy controls, adolescents with TBI were deficient for judging whether a speaker was talking at the listener's level and for recognizing an individual monopolizing a conversation. In contrast, the TBI group performed similarly to controls on a first order belief task, identifying a good listener, as well as recognizing faux pas and understanding pragmatic inferences in the Strange Stories test.

Walz and colleagues (2010) also examined ToM in a group of children who sustained TBI between 3 and 5 years of age, and found few differences between children with TBI and controls. These authors raised the concern that, as ToM skills would only be emerging in normally developing children, at the time these children sustained their injuries, their results required follow-up. Of note, this group has recently studied a similar group of children who sustained their injuries slightly later (5–7 years) and demonstrated significant problems on ToM tasks, particularly for children with severe TBI. These studies highlight the need for a developmental perspective and the importance of taking into account both age at injury and age at assessment when interpreting study findings.

Children and adolescents with TBI have also been reported to have more difficulty recognizing emotions than controls. Tonks *et al.* (2007) found that children with a TBI were more impaired in recognizing emotions expressed in the eyes than control children, but showed equivalent competence when recognizing facial emotions, suggesting that adding context assisted social information processing.

In summary, the weight of evidence indicates that children sustaining TBI are at elevated risk of experiencing social deficits, including social adjustment, social interaction and social cognition. These problems persist long-term post-insult. Further work is needed to describe the potential impact of injury-related factors (e.g. severity, age at insult) and environmental influences on these social consequences.

Social interventions

The evidence-based literature addressing interventions for social impairment following child TBI is scarce. Maybe more surprising though is the lack of information regarding clinical management approaches for these difficulties in the context of acute or sub-acute rehabilitation. In contrast to the growing number of clinical and research publications describing physical, cognitive, behavioural and psychiatric interventions, those focusing on social rehabilitation are rare. As for the population in general, social skills appear to 'fall between the cracks' for services, with no single discipline taking ownership of this domain. This said, there are several discipline specific interventions emerging in the literature, and validated for typically developing children and adolescence, which show promise for treating social problems in the context of TBI.

Traditional social skills training models, for example, may be beneficial following child TBI. Such methods are based on behavioural principles, and usually conducted in a group context. They routinely include practice in social problem solving situations, role plays, homework tasks, positive reinforcement to encourage socially appropriate behaviours (McDonald *et al.*, 2012). While initially developed for children with developmental disabilities, these approaches have recently been trialled with adult survivors of TBI. While overall findings have been disappointing, they do suggest an improved capacity to focus on the social requirements of others, with less time spent engaged in self-focused conversation (Dalberg *et al.*, 1997; McDonald *et al.*, 2008).

Other child/adolescent evidence-based interventions have employed cognitive behaviour therapy techniques to treat social problems common to TBI survivors including social anxiety: Coping Cat (Kendall & Hedtke, 2006); Cool Kids Child and Adolescent Anxiety Program (Rapee *et al.*, 2006; Soo *et al.*, 2012); FRIENDS for life (Barrett, 2004), and Social Effectiveness Therapy for Children (Beidel *et al.*, 2004). Unfortunately, to date, no studies have systematically evaluated the effectiveness of such approaches in young TBI victims. Of note, these behavioural methods have promise, based on adult studies, commentators have argued that their assumptions (e.g. intact cognition, generalizability of learned skills) may not hold well for victims of TBI, and that future research may need to modify standard interventions to meet the specific needs of children and adolescents with TBI (Soo *et al.*, 2012).

In a review of social skills interventions for TBI, Turkstra and Burgess (2007) found that the most promising results emerged from studies which involved parents and families who were able to support positive social behaviours within the child's day-to-day environment (Bedell *et al.*, 2005; Braga *et al.*, 2005) (see also Chapter 7). Their conclusion is consistent with the view that social skills are best learned in the context in which they will be implemented. For young children, the family unit provides this natural context. In a recent study from our lab (Woods *et al.*, 2011), we found support for this family approach. We implemented an established parenting intervention ('Signposts'), based on cognitive-behavioural techniques with 48 families of children and young people with TBI. The intervention was delivered either in face-to-face mode or via telephone, and evaluated immediately post-treatment and then again at six months. Results showed significant and lasting improvements in both parent mental health and coping and children's social behaviours, for both face-to-face and telephone conditions.

Conclusions

There is growing interest in the social consequences of early brain insult, however, evidence to date is relatively scarce. Not surprisingly, the available literature does indicate that the presence of a brain injury in early life is associated with an elevated risk of social dysfunction across a range of dimensions – social adjustment, social interaction and participation, and social cognition. The way in which these domains interact with one another and with the child's other skills remains unclear, and the measures generally employed in such studies are not intended for the assessment of social skills specifically. In addition, it appears that the injury-related risk factors established as predictors of cognitive and physical outcomes from early brain insult (injury severity, lesion location, age at insult) are unable to predict social outcomes in isolation. Rather, findings suggest that environmental factors play a key role. Social context, family function, and child temperament and adjustment to brain insult are all important in determining the child's social outcome. Recent development of theoretical models of social function and early brain insult, derived largely from the social neuroscience, developmental and developmental psychopathology literatures, and from findings emerging from longitudinal studies of early brain insult show great promise, and will facilitate future research in the field.

References

Achenbach, T. M. (1991). *Manual for the Child Behavior Checklist/4–18 and 1991 profile.* Burlington: Department of Psychiatry, University of Vermont.

Ackerman, B. P. & Brown, E. D. (2006). Income poverty, poverty co-factors, and the adjustment of children in elementary school. *Advances in Child Development and Behavior, 34,* 91–129.

Adolphs, R. (2003). Investigating the cognitive neuroscience of social behavior. *Neuropsychologia, 41*(2), 119–126.

——(2009). The social brain: neural basis of social knowledge. *Annual Review of Psychology, 60,* 693–716.

Adolphs, R. & Spezio, M. (2006). Role of the amygdala in processing visual social stimuli. *Progress in Brain Research, 156,* 363–378.

Adolphs, R., Tranel, D. & Damasio, A. R. (2003). Dissociable neural systems for recognizing emotions. *Brain and Cognition, 52*(1), 61–69.

Allen, J. P., Marsh, P., McFarland, C., McElhaney, K. B., Land, D. J., Jodl, K. M. & Peck, S. D. (2002). Attachment and autonomy as predictors of the development of social skills and delinquency during mid-adolescence. *Journal of Consulting and Clinical Psychology, 70*(1), 56–66.

Anderson, V., Morse, S., Klug, G., Catroppa, C., Haritou, F., Rosenfeld, J. & Pentland, P. (1997). Predicting recovery from head injury in young children. *Journal of the International Neuropsychological Society, 3,* 568–580.

Anderson, V., Catroppa C., Morse, S., Haritou, F. & Rosenfeld, J. (2001). Outcome from mild head injury in young children: a prospective study. *Journal of Clinical and Experimental Neuropsychology, 23,* 705–717.

Anderson, V. A., Morse, S. A., Catroppa, C., Haritou, F. & Rosenfeld, J. V. (2004). Thirty month outcome from early childhood head injury: a prospective analysis of neurobehavioural recovery. *Brain, 127*(Pt 12), 2608–2620.

Anderson, V., Catroppa, C., Dudgeon, P., Morse, S., Haritou, F. & Rosenfeld, J. (2006). Understanding predictors of functional recovery and outcome thirty-months following early childhood head injury. *Neuropsychology, 20(1),* 42–57.

Anderson, V., Catroppa, C., Morse, S., Haritou, F. & Rosenfeld, J. (2009). Intellectual outcome from preschool traumatic brain injury: a 5-year prospective, longitudinal study. *Pediatrics, 124(6),* pp e1064–1071.

Anderson, V., Brown, S. & Newitt, H. (2010). What contributes to quality of life in adult survivors of childhood traumatic brain injury? *Journal of Neurotrauma, 27(5),* 863–870.

Anderson, V. & Beauchamp, M. (2012). Introduction: SOCIAL: a theoretical model of the development of social neuroscience. In V. Anderson & M. Beauchamp (Eds). *Developmental Social Neuroscience: Implications for Theory and Clinical Practice.* New York: Guilford.

Anderson, V., Godfrey, C., Rosenfeld, J. V. and Catroppa, C. (2012). 10 years outcome from childhood traumatic brain injury. *International Journal of Developmental Neuroscience,* 30(3), 217–224.

Anderson, V., Rosema, S., Gomes, A. & Catroppa, C. (2012). Impact of early brain insult on the development of social competence. In V. Anderson & M. Beauchamp (Eds), *Developmental Social Neuroscience and Childhood Brain Insult: Implications for Theory and Practice*. New York: Guilford.

Andrews, T. K., Rose F. D. & Johnson, D. A. (1998). Social and behavioural effects of traumatic brain injury in children. *Brain Injury, 12,* 133–138.

Arsenio, W. F. & Lemerise, E. A. (2004). Aggression and moral development: integrating social information processing and moral domain models. *Child Development, 75*(4), 987–1002.

Asarnow, R. F., Satz, P., Light, R., Lewis, R. & Neumann, E. (1991). Behavior problems and adaptive functioning in children with mild and severe closed head injury. *Journal of Pediatric Psychology, 16,* 543–555.

Asher, S. R. (1990). Recent advances in the study of peer rejection. In S. R. Asher & J. D. Coie (Eds), *Peer Rejection in Childhood*. Cambridge: Cambridge University Press.

Barrett, P. M. (2004). *FRIENDS for Life Group Leaders' Manual for Children*. Bowen Hills, Queensland: Australian Academic Press.

Beauchamp, M. H. & Anderson, V. (2010). SOCIAL: an integrative framework for the development of social skills. *Psychological Bulletin, 136,* 39–64.

Bedell, G. M. & Dumas, H. M. (2004). Social participation of children and youth with acquired brain injuries discharged from inpatient rehabilitation: a follow-up study. *Brain Injury, 18*(1), 65–82.

Bedell, G. M., Cohn, E. S. & Dumas, H. M. (2005). Exploring parents' use of strategies to promote social participation of school-age children with acquired brain injuries. *American Journal of Occupational Therapy, 59*(3), 273–284.

Beidel, D. C., Turner, S. M. & Morris, T. L. (2004). *Social Effectiveness Therapy for Children: A Treatment Manual*. Toronto, Canada: Multi-Health Systems.

Belsky, J. & de Haan, M. (2011). Parenting and children's brain development: the end of the beginning. *Journal of Child Psychology & Psychiatry, 52,* 409–428.

Berger, M. S., Pitts, L. H., Lovely, M., Edwards, M. S. & Bartkowsky, H. M. (1985). Outcome from severe head injury in children and adolescents. *Journal of Neurosurgery, 62,* 194–195.

Berney, J., Froidevaux, A. & Favier, J. (1994). Pediatric head trauma: influence of age and sex. II. Biochemical and anatomo-clinical observations. *Child's Nervous System, 10,* 517–523.

Blakemore, S. (2010). The developing social brain. *Neuron, 65,* 774–777.

Blair, R. J. (2005). Responding to the emotions of others: dissociating forms of empathy through the study of typical and psychiatric populations. *Consciousness and Cognition, 14*(4), 698–718.

Bohnert, A. M., Parker, J. G. & Warschausky, S. A. (1997). Friendship and social adjustment of children following a traumatic brain injury: an exploratory investigation. *Developmental Neuropsychology, 13,* 477–486.

Bos, K., Fox, N., Zeanah, C. & Nelson, C. (2009). Effects of early psychological deprivation on the development of memory and executive function. *Frontiers in Behavioural Neuroscience, 3,* 16. Do: 10.3389/neuro.08.016.2009

Botvin, G. J. & Kantor, L. W. (2000). Preventing alcohol and tobacco use through life skills training. *Alcohol Research & Health, 24*(4), 250–257.

Bowlby, J. (1962). *Deprivation of Maternal Care*. Geneva: World Health Organization.

Boxer, P., Goldstein, S. E., Musher-Eizenman, D., Dubow, E. F. & Heretick, D. (2005). Developmental issues in school-based aggression prevention from a social-cognitive perspective. *The Journal of Primary Prevention, 26*(5), 383–400.

Braga, L. W., Da Paz, A. C. & Ylvisaker, M. (2005). Direct clinician-delivered versus indirect family-supported rehabilitation of children with traumatic brain injury: a randomized controlled trial. *Brain Injury, 19*(10), 819–831.

Brown, G., Chadwick, O., Shaffer, D., Rutter, M. & Traub, M. (1981). A prospective study of children with head injuries: II. Psychiatric sequelae. *Psychological Medicine, 11(1)*, 49–62.

Bruce, D. A., Raphaely, R. C., Goldberg, A. I., Zimmerman, R. A., Bilaniuk., L. T., Schut, L. & Kuhl, D. E. (1979). Pathophysiology, treatment and outcome following severe head injury in children. *Child's Brain, 2,* 174–191.

Bufalari, I., Aprile, T., Avenanti, A., Di Russo, F. & Aglioti, S. M. (2007). Empathy for pain and touch in the human somatosensory cortex. *Cerebral Cortex, 17*(11), 2553–2561.

Bulotsky-Shearer, R., Fantuzzo, J. & McDermott, P. (2008). An investigation of classroom situational dimensions of emotional and behavioral adjustment and cognitive and social outcomes for Head Start children. *Developmental Psychology, 44,* 139–154.

Burnett, S., Sebastian, C. & Kadosh, K. (2012). Brain development and the emergence of social function. In V. Anderson & M. Beauchamp (Eds), *Developmental Social Neuroscience and Childhood Brain Insult: Implications for Theory and Practice.* New York: Guilford.

Butler, T., Andrews, G., Allnutt, S., Sakashita, C., Smith, N. E. & Basson, J. (2006). Mental disorders in Australian prisoners: a comparison with a community sample. *Australian and New Zealand Journal of Psychiatry, 40*(3), 272–276.

Cacioppo, J. (2002). Social neuroscience: understanding the pieces fosters understanding of the whole and vice versa. *American Psychologist, 57,* 819–831.

Camodeca, M. & Goossens, F. A. (2005). Aggression, social cognitions, anger and sadness in bullies and victims. *Journal of Child Psychology and Psychiatry and Allied Disciplines, 46*(2), 186–197.

Carpenter, M., Nagell, K. & Tomasello, M. (1998). Social cognition, joint attention, and communicative competence from 9 to 15 months of age. *Monographs of the Society for Research in Child Development, 63*(4), 1–143.

Casebeer, W. D. (2003). Moral cognition and its neural constituents. *Nature Reviews Neuroscience, 4*(10), 840–846.

Casey, B. J., Galvan, A. & Hare, T. A. (2005). Changes in cerebral functional organization during cognitive development. *Current Opinion in Neurobiology, 15*(2), 239–244.

Catroppa, C. & Anderson, V. (2005). A prospective study of the recovery of attention from acute to 2 years post pediatric traumatic brain injury. *Journal of the International Neuropsychological Society, 11,* 84–98.

Catroppa, C., Anderson, V., Morse, S., Haritou, F. & Rosenfeld, J. (2009). Outcome and predictors of functional recovery five years following pediatric traumatic brain injury (TBI). *Journal of Pediatric Psychology, 33(7),* 707–718.

Cattelani, R., Lombardi, R., Brianti, R. & Mazzucchi, A. (1998). Traumatic brain injury in childhood: intellectual, behavioural and social outcome in adulthood. *Brain Injury, 12,* 283–296.

Chadwick, O., Rutter, M., Brown, G., Shaffer, D. & Traub, M. (1981). A prospective study of children with head injuries: II. Cognitive sequelae. *Psychological Medicine, 11,* 49–61.

Cheng, Y., Yang, C. Y., Lin, C. P., Lee, P. L. & Decety, J. (2008). The perception of pain in others suppresses somatosensory oscillations: a magnetoencephalography study. *Neuroimage, 40*(4), 1833–1840.

Choudhury, S., Blakemore, S. J. & Charman, T. (2006). Social cognitive development during adolescence. *Social Cognitive and Affective Neuroscience, 1*(3), 165–174.

Choux, M. (1986). Incidence, diagnosis and management of skull fractures. In A. J. Raimondi, M. Choux & C. DiRocco (Eds), *Head Injuries in the New Born and Infant* (pp. 163–182). New York: Springer-Verlag.

Colvert, E., Rutter, M., Beckett, C., Castle, J., Groothues, C., Hawkins, A., Kreppner, J., O'Connor, T. G., Stevens, S. & Sonuga-Barke, E. J. S. (2008). Emotional difficulties in early adolescence following severe early deprivation: findings from the English and Romanian adoptees study. *Development and Psychopathology, 20*(2), 547–567.

Conger, R. D. & Donnellan, M. B. (2007). An interactionist perspective on the socioeconomic context of human development. *Annual Review of Psychology, 58*, 175–199.

Couper, E., Jacobs, R. & Anderson, V. (2002). Adaptive behaviour and moral reasoning in children with frontal lobe lesions. *Brain Impairment, 3*, 105–113.

Craft, A. W., Shaw, D. A. & Cartlidge, N. E. (1972). Head injuries in children. *British Medical Journal, 4*, 200–203.

Crowe, L., Anderson, V., Catroppa, C. & Babl, F. (2010). Head injuries related to sports and recreation activities in school-age children and adolescents: data from a referral centre in Victoria, Australia. *Emergency Medicine Australasia, 22*(1), 56–61.

Crowe, L. M., Beauchamp, M. H., Catroppa, C. & Anderson, V. (2011). Social function assessment tools for children and adolescents: a systematic review from 1988 to 2010. *Clinical Psychology Review, 31*, 767–785.

Cunningham, E. & Janson, C. (2007). A socioecological perspective on primate cognition, past and present. *Animal Cognition, 10*(3), 273–281.

Dahlberg, C. A., Cusick, C. P., Hawley, L. A., Newman, J. K., Morey, C. E., Harrison-Felix, C. L. & Whiteneck, G. G. (2007). Treatment efficacy of social communication skills training after traumatic brain injury: a randomized treatment and deferred treatment controlled trial. *Archives of Physical Medicine & Rehabilitation, 88 (12)*, 1561–1573.

Dalby, P. R. & Obrzut, J. E. (1991). Epidemiologic characteristics and sequelae of closed head-injured children and adolescents: a review. *Developmental Neuropsychology, 7*, 35–68.

d'Arc, F. & Mottron, L. (2012). Social cognition in autism. In V. Anderson & M. Beauchamp (Eds), *Developmental Social Neuroscience and Childhood Brain Insult: Implications for Theory and Practice.* New York: Guilford.

de Gelder, B. (2006). Towards the neurobiology of emotional body language. *Nature Reviews Neuroscience, 7*(3), 242–249.

Delugach, R. R., Bracken, B. A., Bracken, M. J. & Schicke, M. C. (1992). Self concept: multidimensional construct validation. *Psychology in the Schools, 29*, 213–223.

Dennis, M., Guger, S., Rondacin, C., Barnes, M. & Schachar, R. (2001). Attentional-inhibitory control and social-behavioral regulation after childhood closed head injury: do biological, developmental, and recovery variables predict outcome? *Journal of the International Neuropsychological Society, 7*, 683–692.

Didus, E., Anderson, V. & Catroppa, C. (1999). The development of pragmatic communication skills in head injured children. *Pediatric Rehabilitation, 3*, 177–186.

Dooley, J., Anderson, V., Hemphill, S. & Ohan, J. (2008). Aggression after pediatric traumatic brain injury: a theoretical approach. *Brain Injury, 22(11)*, 836–846.

Flavell, J. H. (1999). Cognitive development: children's knowledge about the mind. *Annual Review of Psychology, 50*, 21–45.

Fletcher, J. M., Ewing-Cobbs, L., Miner, M. E., Levin, H. S. & Eisenberg, H. M. (1990). Behavioral changes after closed head injury in children. *Journal of Consulting and Clinical Psychology, 58*, 93–98.

Frith, C. D. & Frith, U. (2006). The neural basis of mentalizing. *Neuron, 50*(4), 531–534.

Fujiki, M., Spackman, M. P., Brinton, B. & Illig, T. (2007). Ability of children with language impairment to understand emotion conveyed by prosody in a narrative passage. *International Journal of Language and Communication Disorders, 43*(3), 330–345.

Gallagher, H. L. & Frith, C. D. (2003). Functional imaging of 'theory of mind'. *Trends in Cognitive Science, 7*(2), 77–83.

Ganesalingam, K., Sanson, A., Anderson, V. & Yeates, K. O. (2006). Self-regulation and social and behavioral functioning following childhood traumatic brain injury. *Journal of the International Neuropsychological Society, 12*, 609–621.

——(2007a). Self-regulation as a mediator of the effects of childhood traumatic brain injury on social and behavioral functioning. *Journal of the International Neuropsychological Society, 13*, 298–311.

Ganesalingam, K., Yeates K.O., Sanson, A. & Anderson, V. (2007b). Social problem-solving skills following childhood traumatic brain injury and its association with self-regulation and social and behavioral functioning. *Journal of Neuropsychology, 1*, 149–170.

Ganesalingham, K, Yeates, K., Taylor, H, Wade, N., Stancin, T. & Wade, S. (2011). Executive functions and social competence in young children 6 months following traumatic brain injury. *Neuropsychology, 25*, 466–476.

Giedd, J. N., Blumenthal, J., Jeffries, N. O., Castellanos, F. X., Liu, H., Zijdenbos, A., Paus, T., Evans, A.C. & Rapoport, J. L. (1999). Brain development during childhood and adolescence: a longitudinal MRI study. *Nature Neuroscience, 2*(10), 861–863.

Gogtay, N., Giedd, J. N., Lusk, L., Hayashi, K. M., Greenstein, D., Vaituzis, A. C., Nugent, T. F., Herman, D. H., Clasen, L. S., Toga, A. W., Rapoport, J. L. & Thompson, P. M. (2004). Dynamic mapping of human cortical development during childhood through early adulthood. *Proceedings of the National Academy of Sciences of the United States of America, 101*(21), 8174–8179.

Goldstein, F.C . & Levin, H. S. (1985). Intellectual and academic outcome in children and adolescents: Research strategies and empirical findings. *Developmental Neuropsychology, 1*(3), 195–214.

Goursaud, A. P. & Bachevalier, J. (2007). Social attachment in juvenile monkeys with neonatal lesion of the hippocampus, amygdala and orbital frontal cortex. *Behavioural Brain Research, 176*(1), 75–93.

Gray, K. & Cornish, K. (2012). Genetic disorders and social problems. In V. Anderson & M. Beauchamp (Eds.), *Developmental Social Neuroscience and Childhood Brain Insult: Implications for Theory and Practice*. New York: Guilford.

Green, J. & Goldwyn, R. (2002). Annotation: attachment disorganisation and psychopathology: new findings in attachment research and their potential implications for developmental psychopathology in childhood. *Journal of Child Psychology and Psychiatry and Allied Disciplines, 43*(7), 835–846.

Greenberg, M. T. (2006). Promoting resilience in children and youth: preventive interventions and their interface with neuroscience. *Annals of the New York Academy of Sciences, 1094*, 139–150.

Greene, J. D., Sommerville, R. B., Nystrom, L. E., Darley, J. M. & Cohen, J. D. (2001). An fMRI investigation of emotional engagement in moral judgment. *Science, 293*(5537), 2105–2108.

Greenham, M., Spencer-Smith, M. M., Anderson, P. J., Coleman, L. & Anderson, V. A. (2010). Social functioning in children with brain insult. *Frontiers in Human Neuroscience, 4(22)* EPub.

Grossmann, T. & Johnson, M. H. (2007). The development of the social brain in human infancy. *European Journal of Neuroscience, 25*(4), 909–919.

Grossmann, T., Striano, T. & Friederici, A. D. (2006). Crossmodal integration of emotional information from face and voice in the infant brain. *Developmental Science, 9*(3), 309–315.

Guralink, M. (1999). Family and child influences on the peer-related social competence of young children with developmental delays. *Mental Retardation and Developmental Disabilities Research Reviews, 5,* 21–29.

Hackman, D. A. & Farah, M. J. (2009). Socioeconomic status and the developing brain. *Trends in Cognitive Science, 13*(2), 65–73.

Hanten, G., Wilde, E. A., Menefee, D. S., Li, X., Lane, S., Vasquez, C., Chu, Z., Ramos, M. A., Yallampalli, R., Swank, P., Chapman, S. B., Gamino, J., Hunter, J. V. & Levin, H. S. (2008). Correlates of social problem solving during the first year after traumatic brain injury in children. *Neuropsychology, 22,* 357–370.

Hanten, G., Cook, L., Orsten, K., Chapman, S. B., Li, X., Wilde, E. A., Schnelle, K. P. & Levin, H. S. (2011). Effects of traumatic brain injury on a virtual reality social problem solving task and relations to cortical thickness in adolescence. *Neuropsychologia 49*(3), 486–497.

Hanten, G., Levin, H., Newsome, M. & Scheibel, R. (2012). Social development and traumatic brain injury in children and adolescents. In V. Anderson & M. Beauchamp (Eds), *Developmental Social Neuroscience and Childhood Brain Insult: Implications for Theory and Practice.* New York: Guilford.

Harris, L. T., Todorov, A. & Fiske, S. T. (2005). Attributions on the brain: neuro-imaging dispositional inferences, beyond theory of mind. *Neuroimage, 28*(4), 763–769.

Hawkins, J. D., Kosterman, R., Catalano, R. F., Hill, K. G. & Abbott, R. D. (2005). Promoting positive adult functioning through social development intervention in childhood: long-term effects from the Seattle Social Development Project. *Archives of Pediatrics and Adolescent Medicine, 159*(1), 25–31.

Hayes, H. R. & Jackson, R. H. (1989). The incidence and prevention of head injuries. In D. A. Johnson, D. Uttley & M. A. Wyke (Eds), *Children's Head Injury: Who Cares?* (pp. 183–193). London: Taylor & Francis.

Hein, G. & Singer, T. (2008). I feel how you feel but not always: the empathic brain and its modulation. *Current Opinion in Neurobiology, 18*(2), 153–158.

Henry, K. L. & Slater, M. D. (2007). The contextual effect of school attachment on young adolescents' alcohol use. *Journal of School Health, 77*(2), 67–74.

Hill, E. L. & Frith, U. (2003). Understanding autism: insights from mind and brain. *Philosophical Transactions of the Royal Society of London. Series B: Biological Sciences, 358*(1430), 281–289.

Hill, J. (2002). Biological, psychological and social processes in the conduct disorders. *Journal of Child Psychology and Psychiatry and Allied Disciplines, 43*(1), 133–164.

Holloway, M., Bye, A. & Moran, K. (1994). Non-accidental head injury in children. *The Medical Journal of Australia, 160,* 786–789.

Horowitz, I., Costeff, H., Sadan, N., Abraham, E., Geyer, S. & Najenson, T. (1983). Childhood head injuries in Israel: epidemiology and outcome. *International Rehabilitation Medicine, 5,* 32–36.

Iacoboni, M. (2009). Imitation, empathy, and mirror neurons. *Annual Review of Psychology, 60,* 653–670.

Jackson, P. L., Meltzoff, A. N. & Decety, J. (2006). Neural circuits involved in imitation and perspective-taking. *Neuroimage, 31*(1), 429–439.

Janusz, J. A., Kirkwood, M. W., Yeates, K. O. & Taylor, G. (2002). Social problem-solving skills in children with traumatic brain injury: long-term outcomes and prediction of social competence. *Child Neuropsychology, 8,* 179–194.

Jennett, B., Teasdale, G., Galbraith, S., Pickard, J., Grant, H., Braakman, R., Avezaat, C., Maas, A., Minderhoud, J., Vecht, C., Heiden, J., Small, R., Caton, W. & Kurtz, T. (1977). Severe head injuries in three countries. *Journal of Neurology, Neurosurgery, and Psychiatry, 40,* 291–298.

Jorge, R. E., Robinson, R. G., Moser, D., Tateno, A., Crespo-Facorro, B. & Arndt, S. (2004). Major depression following traumatic brain injury. *Archives of General Psychiatry, 61*(1), 42–50.

Kelly, D. J., Quinn, P. C., Slater, A. M., Lee, K., Gibson, A., Smith, M., Ge, L. & Pascalis, O. (2005). Three-month-olds, but not newborns, prefer own-race faces. *Developmental Science, 8*(6), F31–36.

Kendall, P. C. & Hedtke, K. A. (2006). *Cognitive-Behavioral Therapy for Anxious Children: Therapist Manual.* Ardmore, PA: Workbook Publications.

Kenny, D. T. & Jennings, C. J. (2007). The relationship between head injury and violent offending in juvenile detainees. *Crime and Justice, 107,* 1–15.

Kimbrel, N. A. (2008). A model of the development and maintenance of generalized social phobia. *Clinical Psychology Review, 28*(4), 592–612.

Klonoff, H. (1971). Head injuries in children: predisposing factors, accident conditions, accident proneness and sequelae. *American Journal of Public Health, 61,* 2405–2417.

Kolb, B. & Whishaw, I. Q. (1998). Brain plasticity and behavior. *Annual Review of Psychology, 49,* 43–64.

Kolb, B., Forgie, M., Gibb, R., Gorny, G. & Rowntree, S. (1998). Age, experience and the changing brain. *Neuroscience and Biobehavioral Reviews, 22*(2), 143–159.

Kraus, J. F. (1995). Epidemiological features of brain injury in children. In S. H. Broman & M. E. Michel (Eds), *Traumatic Head Injury in Children* (pp. 117–146). New York: Oxford University Press.

Kraus, J. F., Fife, D., Cox, P., Ramstein, K. & Conroy, C. (1986). Incidence, severity, and external causes of pediatric brain injury. *American Journal of Epidemiology, 119,* 186–201.

Lehr, E. (1990). *Psychological Management of Traumatic Brain Injuries in Children and Adolescents.* Rockville, Maryland: Aspen.

Leon-Carrion, J. & Ramos, F. J. (2003). Blows to the head during development can predispose to violent criminal behaviour: rehabilitation of consequences of head injury is a measure for crime prevention. *Brain Injury, 17*(3), 207–216.

Levin, H. S., Hanten, G. & Li, X. (2009). The relation of cognitive control to social outcome after paediatric TBI: implications for interventions. *Developmental NeuroRehabilitation, 12,* 320–329.

Long, B., Spencer-Smith, M., Anderson, V., Jacobs, R., Mackay, M., Leventer, R. & Barnes, C. (2011). Executive function following child stroke: the impact of lesion location. *Journal of Child Neurology, 26,* 279–287.

Major, B. & O'Brien, L. T. (2005). The social psychology of stigma. *Annual Review of Psychology, 56,* 393–421.

Masten, A., Hubbard, J., Gest, S., Tellegen, A., Garmezy, N. & Ramirez, M. (1999). Competence in the context of adversity: pathways to resilience and maladaptation from childhood to late adolescence. *Development and Psychopathology, 11,* 143–169.

Max, J. E., Koele, S. L., Lindgren, S. D., Robin, D. A., Smith, W. L. Jr., Sato, Y. & Arndt, S. (1998). Adaptive functioning following traumatic brain injury and orthopedic injury: a controlled study. *Archives of Physical Medicine & Rehabilitation, 79,* 893–899.

Max, J. E., Mathews, K. K., Manes, F. F., Robertson, B. A., Fox, P. T., Lancaster, J. L. (2005). Prefrontal and executive attention netweork lesions and the development of attention-deficit/hyperactivity symptomatology. *Journal of the American Academy of Child and Adolescent Psychiatry, 44(*5), 443–450.

McCarthy, M. C., Clarke, N. E., Lin Ting, C., Conroy, R., Anderson, V. & Heath, J. A. (2010). Prevalence and predictors of parental grief and depression after the death of a child from cancer. *Journal of Palliative Medicine, 13(11),* 1321–1326.

McCann, J., Peppe, S., Gibbon, F. E., O'Hare, A. & Rutherford, M. (2007). Prosody and its relationship to language in school-aged children with high-functioning autism. *International Journal of Language and Communication Disorders, 42(6),* 1–21.

McClure, E. B. (2000). A meta-analytic review of sex differences in facial expression processing and their development in infants, children, and adolescents. *Psychological Bulletin, 126*(3), 424–453.

McDonald, S., Tate, R., Togher, L., Bornhofen, C., Long, E., Gertler, P. & Bowen, R. (2008). Social skills treatment for people with severe, chronic acquired brain injuries: a multicenter trial. *Archives of Physical Medicine & Rehabilitation, 89(9),* 1648–1659.

McDonald, S., Turkstra, L. & Togher, L. (2012). Pragmatic language impairment after brain injury: social implications and treatment models. In V. Anderson & M. Beauchamp (Eds), *Developmental Social Neuroscience and Childhood Brain Insult: Implications for Theory and Practice.* New York: Guilford.

McLoyd, V. C. (1998). Socioeconomic disadvantage and child development. *American Psychologist, 53*(2), 185–204.

Moll, J., de Oliveira-Souza, R., Bramati, I. E. & Grafman, J. (2002a). Functional networks in emotional moral and nonmoral social judgments. *Neuroimage, 16*(3 Pt 1), 696–703.

Moll, J., de Oliveira-Souza, R., Eslinger, P. J., Bramati, I. E., Mourão-Miranda, J., Andreiuolo, P. A. & Pessoa, L. (2002b). The neural correlates of moral sensitivity: a functional magnetic resonance imaging investigation of basic and moral emotions. *Journal of Neuroscience, 22*(7), 2730–2736.

Moll, J., de Oliveira-Souza, R. & Eslinger, P. J. (2003). Morals and the human brain: a working model. *Neuroreport, 14*(3), 299–305.

Moll, J., Zahn, R., de Oliveira-Souza, R., Krueger, F. & Grafman, J. (2005). Opinion: the neural basis of human moral cognition. *Nature Reviews Neuroscience, 6*(10), 799–809.

Muscara, F., Catroppa, C. & Anderson, V. (2008). Social problem-solving skills as a mediator between executive function and long-term social outcome following paediatric traumatic brain injury. *Journal of Neuropsychology, 2,* 445–461.

Muscara, F. & Crowe, L. (2012). Measuring children's social skills: questionnaires and rating scales. In V. Anderson & M. Beauchamp (Eds). *Developmental Social Neuroscience: Implications for Theory and Clinical Practice.* New York: Guilford.

O'Sullivan, M. (2003). The fundamental attribution error in detecting deception: the boy-who-cried-wolf effect. *Personality and Social Psychology Bulletin, 29*(10), 1316–1327.

Orobio de Castro, B., Veerman, J. W., Koops, W., Bosch, J. D. & Monshouwer, H. J. (2002). Hostile attribution of intent and aggressive behavior: a meta-analysis. *Child Development, 73*(3), 916–934.

Papero, P. H., Prigatano, G. P., Snyder, H. M. & Johnson, D. L. (1993). Children's adaptive behavioural competence after head injury. *Neuropsychological Rehabilitation, 3,* 321–340.

Parker, J. G. & Asher, S. R. (1993). Friendship and friendship quality in middle childhood: links with peer group acceptance and feelings of loneliness and social dissatisfaction. *Developmental Psychology, 29,* 611–621.

Perrott, S. B., Taylor, H. G. & Montes, J. L. (1991). Neuropsychological sequelae, familial stress, and environmental adaptation following pediatric head injury. *Developmental Neuropsychology, 7,* 69–86.

Pettit, G. S., Dodge, K. A. & Brown, M. M. (1988). Early family experience, social problem solving patterns, and children's social competence. *Child Development, 59,* 107–120.

Phillips, M. L., Drevets, W. C., Rauch, S. L. & Lane, R. (2003). Neurobiology of emotion perception I: The neural basis of normal emotion perception. *Biological Psychiatry, 54*(5), 504–514.

Poggi, G., Liscio, M., Adduci, A., Galbiati, S., Massimino, M., Sommovigo, M., Zettin, M., Figini, E. & Castelli, E. (2005). Psychological and adjustment problems due to acquired brain lesions in childhood: a comparison between post-traumatic patients and brain tumor survivors. *Brain Injury, 19,* 777–785.

Prigatano, G. P. & Gupta, S. (2006). Friends after traumatic brain injury in children. *Journal of Head Trauma Rehabilitation, 21,* 505–513.

Prior, M., Kinsella, G., Sawyer, M., Bryan, D. & Anderson, V. (1994). Cognitive and psychosocial outcomes after head injury in childhood. *Australian Psychologist, 29(2),* 116–123.

Raimondi, A. & Hirschauer, J. (1984). Head injury in the infant and toddler. *Child's Brain, 11,* 12–35.

Raine, A. & Yang, Y. (2006). Neural foundations to moral reasoning and antisocial behavior. *Social Cognitive and Affective Neuroscience, 1*(3), 203–213.

Raizada, R. & Kishiyama, M. (2010). Effects of socioeconomic status on brain development, and how cognitive neuroscience may contribute to levelling the playing field. *Frontiers in Human Neuroscience, 4,* 1–11, doi:10.3389/neuro 09.003.2010.

Rapee, R. M., Lyneham, H. J., Schniering, C. A., Wuthrich, V., Abbott, M. J., Hudson, J. L. & Wignall, A. (2006). *The Cool Kids Child and Adolescent Anxiety Program Therapist Manual.* Sydney: Centre for Emotional Health, Macquarie University.

Riggs, N. R., Greenberg, M. T., Kusche, C. A. & Pentz, M. A. (2006). The mediational role of neurocognition in the behavioural outcomes of a social-emotional prevention program in elementary school students: effects of the PATHS Curriculum. *Prevention Science, 7*(1), 91–102.

Righthand, S. & Welch, C. (2004). Characteristics of youth who sexually offend. *Journal of Child Sexual Abuse, 13*(3–4), 15–32.

Rivara, J. B., Jaffe, K. M., Fay, G. C., Polissar, N. L., Martin, K. M., Shurtleff, H. A. & Liao, S. (1993). Family functioning and injury severity as predictors of child functioning one year following traumatic brain injury. *Archives of Physical Medicine and Rehabilitation, 74*(10), 1047–1055.

Rochat, P. & Striano, T. (2002). Who's in the mirror? Self-other discrimination in specular images by four- and nine-month-old infants. *Child Development, 73*(1), 35–46.

Root, A., Hastings, P. & Maxwell, K. (2012). Environmental contributions to the development of social development: focus on parents. In V. Anderson & M. Beauchamp (Eds), *Developmental Social Neuroscience and Childhood Brain Insult: Implications for Theory and Practice.* New York: Guilford.

Rubin, K., Begle, A. & McDonald, K. (2012). Peer relations and social competence in childhood. In V. Anderson & M. Beauchamp (Eds), *Developmental Social Neuroscience and Childhood Brain Insult: Implications for Theory and Practice*. New York: Guilford.

Russell, J. (2005). Justifying all the fuss about false belief. *Trends in Cognitive Science, 9*(7), 307–308.

Rusting, C. L. (1998). Personality, mood, and cognitive processing of emotional information: three conceptual frameworks. *Psychological Bulletin, 124*(2), 165–196.

Rutter, M. (1983). *Developmental Neuropsychiatry*. New York: Guilford Press.

Saxe, R., Carey, S. & Kanwisher, N. (2004). Understanding other minds: linking developmental psychology and functional neuroimaging. *Annual Review of Psychology, 55*, 87–124.

Sharma, M. & Sharma, A. (1994). Mode, presentation, CT findings and outcome of pediatric head injury. *Indian Pediatrics, 31*, 733–739.

Silasi, G., Hamilton, D. A. & Kolb, B. (2008). Social instability blocks functional restitution following motor cortex stroke in rats. *Behavioural Brain Research, 188*(1), 219–226.

Slaughter, B., Fann, J. R. & Ehde, D. (2003). Traumatic brain injury in a county jail population: prevalence, neuropsychological functioning and psychiatric disorders. *Brain Injury, 17*(9), 731–741.

Soo, C., Tate, R., Rapee, R. (2012). Social anxiety and its treatment in children and adolescents with acquired brain injury. In V. Anderson & M. Beauchamp (Eds), *Developmental Social Neuroscience and Childhood Brain Insult: Implications for Theory and Practice*. New York: Guilford.

Sparrow, S., Balla, D. A. & Cicchetti, D. V. (1984). *Vineland Adaptive Behaviour Scales*. Circle Pines, Minnesota: American Guidance Service.

Tate, R., Hodgkinson, A., Veerabangsa, A. & Maggiotto, S. (1999). Measuring psychosocial recovery after traumatic brain injury: psychometric properties of a new scale. *Journal of Head Trauma Rehabilitation, 14*, 543–557.

Taylor, H. G., Drotar, D., Wade, S., Yeates, K., Stancin, T. & Klein, S. (1995). Recovery from traumatic brain injury in children: the importance of the family. In S. H. Broman & M. E. Michel (Eds). *Traumatic Head Injury in Children* (pp. 188–218). New York: Oxford University Press.

Taylor, H. G., Yeates, K. O., Wade, S. L., Drotar, D., Stancin, T. & Burant, C. (2001). Bidirectional child-family influences on outcomes of traumatic brain injury in children. *Journal of the International Neuropsychological Society, 7*, 755–767.

Tomasello, M., Carpenter, M., Call, J., Behne, T. & Moll, H. (2005). Understanding and sharing intentions: the origins of cultural cognition. *Behavioural and Brain Sciences, 28*(5), 675–691; discussion 691–735.

Tonks, J., Williams, W. H., Frampton, I., Yates, P. & Slater, A. (2007). Reading emotions after child brain injury: a comparison between children with brain injury and non-brain-injured controls. *Brain Injury, 21*, 731–739.

Tonks, J., Williams, H., Yates, P. & Slater, A. (2011). Cognitive correlates of psychosocial outcome following traumatic brain injury in early childhood: comparisons between groups of children aged under and over 10 years of age. *Clinical Child Psychology and Psychiatry, 16*, epub.

Turkstra, L. S. (2008). Conversation-based assessment of social cognition in adults with traumatic brain injury. *Brain Injury, 22*(5), 397–409.

Turkstra, L. S., McDonald, S. & Kaufmann, P. M. (1996). Assessment of pragmatic communication skills in adolescents after traumatic brain injury. *Brain Injury, 10*(5), 329–345.

Turkstra, L. S., Dixon, T. M. & Baker, K. K. (2004). Theory of Mind and social beliefs in adolescents with traumatic brain injury. *NeuroRehabilitation, 19,* 245–256.

Turkstra, L. S. & Burgess, S. (2007). Social skills intervention for adolescents with TBI. *Neurophysiology and Neurogenic Speech and Language Disorders. American Speech Language Hearing Association Special Interest Division 2 Newsletter, 17*(3), 15–19.

Turkstra, L. S., Williams, W. H., Tonks, J. & Frampton, I. (2008). Measuring social cognition in adolescents: implications for students with TBI returning to school. *NeuroRehabilitation 23,* 501–509.

Van Overwalle, F. (2009). Social cognition and the brain: a meta-analysis. *Human Brain Mapping, 30,* 829–858.

Van Tol, E., Gorter, J., Dematteo, C. & Meester-Delver, A. (2011). Participation outcomes for children with acquired brain injury: a narrative review. *Brain Injury, 23* (13–14), 1279–1287.

Walker, S. (2005). Gender differences in the relationship between young children's peer-related social competence and individual differences in theory of mind. *Journal of Genetic Psychology, 166*(3), 297–312.

Walz, N., Yeates, K., Taylor, H., Stancin, T. & Wade, S. (2010). Theory of mind skills 1 year after traumatic brain injury in 6- to 8-year-old children. *Journal of Neuropsychology, 4,* 181–195.

Wanberg, C. R. & Kammeyer-Mueller, J. D. (2000). Predictors and outcomes of proactivity in the socialization process. *Journal of Applied Psychology, 85*(3), 373–385.

Warschausky, S., Cohen, E. H., Parker, J. G., Levendosky, A. A. & Okun, A. (1997). Social problem-solving skills of children with traumatic brain injury. *Pediatric Rehabilitation, 1,* 77–81.

Woods, D. T., Catroppa, C., Barnett, P. & Anderson, V. A. (2011). Parental disciplinary practices following acquired brain injury in children. *Developmental Neurorehabilitation,* 14(5) 274–282.

Yeates, K. O., Schultz, L. H. & Selman, R. L. (1990). Bridging the gaps in child-clinical assessment: toward the application of social-cognitive development theory. *Clinical Psychology Review, 10,* 567–588.

Yeates, K. O., Swift, E., Taylor, H. G., Wade, S. L., Drotar, D., Stancin, T. & Minich, N. (2004). Short- and long-term social outcomes following pediatric traumatic brain injury. *Journal of the International Neuropsychological Society, 10,* 412–426.

Yeates, K. O., Bigler, E. D., Dennis, M., Gerhardt, C. A., Rubin, K. H., Stancin, T., Taylor, H. G. & Vannatta, K. (2007). Social outcomes in childhood brain disorder: a heuristic integration of social neuroscience and developmental psychology. *Psychological Bulletin, 133,* 535–556.

Yeates, K., Taylor, H., Walz, N., Stancin, T. & Wade, S. (2010). The family environment as a moderator of psychosocial outcome following traumatic brain injury in young children. *Neuropsychology, 24,* 345–356.

Zimmerman, R. & Bilaniuk, L. (1994). Pediatric head trauma. *Pediatric Neuroradiology,* 4, 349–366.

7 Issues in the assessment and treatment of cognitive communication disorders in children with TBI

Lindsey Byom, Kristen M. Allison and Lyn S. Turkstra

Definition of traumatic brain injury vs. acquired brain injury

According to the Centers for Disease Control and Prevention (CDC) in the U.S.A., a TBI 'is caused by a bump, blow or jolt to the head or a penetrating head injury that disrupts the normal function of the brain'. (CDC, 2012). TBI is classified either as closed head injury (i.e. due to movement of the brain within the skull, as in a car accident or fall) or open head injury in which the skull is penetrated (e.g. gun-shot wound). Causes of brain injury in children vary by age of injury, with more non-accidental injuries (child abuse) in very young children, falls in school-aged children and sports injuries, motor vehicle accidents and violence-related injuries in adolescents. As discussed in Chapter 2, TBI may result in both focal brain damage at the site of injury and widespread brain damage due to diffuse axonal injury, ischemia or other secondary effects. However, the neuropathology for child TBI differs in important ways to adult (see Chapter 6).

In addition to TBI, other causes of acquired brain injury (ABI) are particularly common in children. These include etiologies associated with loss of oxygen and widespread disruption of cell functioning, such as near drowning, brain infections (e.g. encephalitis, meningitis), congenital heart defects, chemotherapy and irradiation, and drug overdose; and also etiologies associated with focal lesions, such as brain tumours, ruptured arteriovenous malformations and strokes. This chapter will focus on describing effects of TBI; however, the information applies to other types of ABI to the extent that the neuropathology is similar.

TBI can result in complex and devastating effects at any time in life, but there are important factors to consider when injury occurs in childhood, when the brain is still developing. There are critical differences between children and adults in both clinical characteristics of ABI and trajectory of recovery and these differences have important implications for rehabilitation. In this chapter, we discuss special considerations for children and adolescents, beginning with differences in neuropathology and recovery, and then considering specific language and communication sequelae and approaches to assessment and intervention.

Mechanisms of TBI in children and adolescents

On the basis of the 'Kennard principle' (Kennard, 1936), it was widely accepted until fairly recently that an early brain injury would result in a better outcome than a similar injury sustained in adulthood. Data contradicting this notion were presented as early as the 1940s (e.g. Hebb, 1949), yet the idea that cognitive outcome is better after early injury still persists among some clinicians (Dennis, 2010). Recent research has shown that functions of the prefrontal cortex (PFC) in particular are highly vulnerable to early insult and that this region of the cortex is less 'plastic' than other brain regions (Kolb *et al.*, 2011). This is consistent with growing evidence that early damage, particularly to the PFC, can have major consequences for the continued development of cognitive functions thought to depend on PFC functions (Jacobs *et al.*, 2007), including effects on the development of personality, moral reasoning, social cognition and executive functions (Anderson *et al.*, 1999; Hanten *et al.*, 2011; Levin & Hanten, 2005; Turkstra *et al.*, 1996). In a few extreme cases adolescents who had early focal lesions never developed moral reasoning at all (Anderson *et al.*, 1999). More commonly, some cognitive functions continue to improve throughout childhood, albeit at a slower pace than those of peers, whereas other cognitive functions appear to 'stall' in their development (Gamino *et al.*, 2009), so that children who appear to function like their peers may manifest deficits many years after the initial injury. This is true for moderate-to-severe injury sustained at any time in development, as results for children with early childhood injuries (Crowe *et al.*, 2012; Ewing-Cobbs *et al.*, 1997) are similar to those of children with injuries during the school years (Fletcher & Levin, 1987), with the important exception that pre-injury skills and knowledge will vary depending on age at injury. Thus, assessment and intervention in children with TBI must consider not only the child's current status but also the potential for TBI to have derailed the development of cognitive functions that are expected to develop later in life.

Communication disorders in children and adolescents with TBI

Children and adolescents who survive a TBI frequently experience impairments in communication as well as in the cognitive processes thought to underlie it. While deficits in formal aspects of language (e.g. language syntax or morphology) may occur in children with TBI, perhaps the hallmark communication challenge faced by these children, especially as they grow up, is cognitive communication disorders (Ewing-Cobbs & Barnes, 2002). Cognitive communication disorders, as described by the American Speech-Language-Hearing Association (ASHA), are disturbances in any facet of communication (verbal or nonverbal) that are affected by cognitive disruption (ASHA, 2004). Given the broad effects of TBI on cognition, it is unsurprising that cognitive communication disorders are commonly seen in children with TBI. The following section provides a brief review of findings regarding outcomes in communication and cognition following paediatric TBI.

Cognitive impairments

The most common cognitive impairments among children and adolescents with TBI are in executive functions, working memory, declarative learning and speed of information processing. Executive functions are a set of complex cognitive functions that facilitate goal-oriented behaviour and problem solving and include updating working memory, cognitive set switching and inhibitory control (Kennedy *et al.*, 2009; Miyake *et al.*, 2000). Research on executive function subcomponents has been somewhat unclear in terms of the consequences of paediatric TBI. Some researchers have provided evidence that children and adolescents with moderate-to-severe brain injuries have lower scores than their typically developing peers on measures of cognitive flexibility (Ganesalingam *et al.*, 2011; Muscara *et al.*, 2009), inhibitory control (Ewing-Cobbs *et al.*, 2004) and goal-setting (Beauchamp *et al.*, 2011; Muscara *et al.*, 2009). Other studies, however, have reported that samples of children with TBI performed similarly to their typically developing peers on various measures of executive function component processes (Beauchamp *et al.*, 2011; Ewing-Cobbs *et al.*, 2004; Konrad *et al.*, 2000). Children and adolescents with moderate-to-severe TBI have also been reported to show executive function impairments in daily living based on parent-report measures such as the Behavior Rating Inventory of Executive Function (BRIEF; Gioia *et al.*, 2000a) (Conklin *et al.*, 2008; Ganesalingam *et al.*, 2011; Gioia *et al.*, 2003; Gioia *et al.*, 2000a, 2000b; Gioia *et al.*, 2002; Mangeot *et al.*, 2002; Proctor *et al.*, 2000). Some studies, however, have found no differences in parent-reported executive functions between children and adolescents with mild-moderate TBI and typically developing peers (Gioia *et al.*, 2002; Muscara *et al.*, 2009). These apparently incongruent findings are likely due, at least partly to differences across studies in inclusion criteria (e.g. age at injury, injury severity, time post-injury) and the measure of executive functions used.

Working memory, defined as a limited capacity system for simultaneously storing and manipulating information (Briscoe & Rankin, 2009; Just & Carpenter, 1992), has also been shown to be an area of chronic deficit for children and adolescents with moderate-to-severe TBI (Conklin *et al.*, 2008; Ewing-Cobbs *et al.*, 2004; Levin *et al.*, 2004; Moran & Gillon, 2004; Proctor *et al.*, 2000). As working memory continues to develop into adolescence (Luciana *et al.*, 2005; Luna *et al.*, 2004; Scherf *et al.*, 2006), the effect of childhood brain injury on working memory development is of particular importance. In one longitudinal study of working memory in children with TBI, all participants had improved performance on a letter-recognition n-back task over the first year post-injury; however, while those with mild or moderate injuries continued to improve during the second year after injury, the performance of children with severe TBI actually declined over the second year (Levin *et al.*, 2004). The authors hypothesized that degenerative brain changes associated with severe injury may account for this reported decline in working memory. Additional longitudinal studies that incorporate neuroimaging techniques are needed to evaluate this hypothesis.

Individuals who sustain a moderate-to-severe TBI during childhood or adolescence may also have impairments in declarative learning ability, especially for learning verbal information (Donders & Minnema, 2004; Horneman & Emanuelson, 2009; Mandalis *et al.*, 2007; Yeates *et al.*, 1995). Procedural or implicit memory, however, is typically spared in this population (Shum *et al.*, 1999; Ward *et al.*, 2002). Perhaps unsurprisingly, given the occurrence of declarative learning challenges faced by individuals with paediatric brain injury, research has shown that general intelligence may also be affected in the chronic stage after severe paediatric TBI (Anderson *et al.*, 2011; Beauchamp *et al.*, 2011; Catroppa *et al.*, 2008; Ewing-Cobbs *et al.*, 2004). Anderson and colleagues reported that a group of children who sustained a severe brain injury before the age of seven years had significantly lower full-scale, verbal and performance intelligence quotients (IQ) than did a comparison group, although IQ scores in the TBI group largely fell within the low-average range of typical scores (Anderson *et al.*, 2011).

Children and adolescents with severe TBI may also show chronic impairments in various aspects of attention (Ginstfeldt & Emanuelson, 2010). One study (Yeates *et al.*, 2005) reported that children with severe TBI had more attention problems, as reported by their parents on the Attention Problems Scale of the Child Behavior Checklist (Achenbach & Edelbrock, 1980), and performed more poorly than a group of children who had sustained orthopaedic injuries on a measure of focused attention. All aspects of attention might not be equally affected, as a study using subtests of the Test of Everyday Attention for Children (Manly *et al.*, 1998) showed that a group of children with moderate-to-severe TBI demonstrated impairments in sustained and divided attention, while focused attention was relatively spared (Anderson *et al.*, 1998). Slowed information processing speed has also been reported in children and adolescents with moderate-to-severe TBI (Anderson *et al.*, 2011; Anderson *et al.*, 2009; Beauchamp *et al.*, 2011; Konrad *et al.*, 2000), which may in turn affect both working memory and attention.

An area of cognitive deficit that has been identified relatively recently in children and adolescents with TBI is *social cognition*. Social cognition is the set of cognitive skills necessary to interact successfully in a social group (Adolphs, 1999) and is typically considered to include both emotion recognition and the ability to reason about mental states of others to predict their behaviour (i.e. theory of mind). There is emerging evidence that social cognition relies on a structurally diverse network of brain regions including the frontal lobes, amygdala and insula (for reviews see Adolphs, 1999; Adolphs, 2010; Blakemore, 2008). Given evidence that components of this social cognitive network, including the frontal lobes and connecting white matter tracts, undergo developmental changes during adolescence (Schmithorst & Yuan, 2010; Sowell *et al.*, 2001), and that social cognition undergoes major developmental changes in the first few years of life (Blakemore, 2008), it is unsurprising that social cognition is vulnerable to brain injury during childhood and adolescence. Children and adolescents with TBI may have impairments in several aspects of social cognition, including basic facial emotion recognition (Tonks *et al.*, 2007; Turkstra *et al.*, 2001), affect recognition from eyes and voices (Tonks *et al.*, 2007) and second-order theory of mind (i.e. the ability to reason about other people's thoughts) (Turkstra *et al.*, 2004). Janusz and colleagues (2002) also found that a group of children with severe TBI demonstrated less developmentally advanced social problem solving strategies than did a group of typically developing children.

The likelihood that a given child will show cognitive impairments is strongly influenced by injury and environmental factors. For example, as would be expected, children and adolescents with more severe injuries are at increased risk for more negative cognitive outcomes than those who sustain milder injuries (Anderson & Catroppa, 2005; Catroppa & Anderson, 2004; Catroppa *et al.*, 2008; Dennis *et al.*, 2001a). In addition, as noted earlier in this chapter, children who are injured earlier in childhood are at greater risk for more severe impairments in executive functions and information processing speed than those who sustain injuries later in development (Beauchamp *et al.*, 2011; Ganesalingam *et al.*, 2011; Slomine *et al.*, 2002). By contrast, there is some evidence that children injured in early adolescence (at or after age 13 years) are more at risk for long-term working memory impairments than are children injured at a younger age (Levin *et al.*, 2004), perhaps due to the protracted development of working memory. Age at injury and injury severity have also been shown to predict outcomes in relation to higher-order language and communication skills (Catroppa & Anderson, 2004; Levin *et al.*, 2001). Individual and environmental factors such as pre-injury abilities and family functioning also play an important role in cognitive and social outcomes following brain injury during childhood (Catroppa *et al.*, 2008; Crowe *et al.*, 2012).

Language impairments

Various aspects of language may be affected when a child sustains a TBI, including vocabulary, syntax, semantics and pragmatics. Research has suggested that on average, children with TBI have post-injury verbal IQ scores within the typical range, though large variability in performance has been reported (Donders & Warschausky, 2007). Children with severe TBI, however, may have lower vocabulary scores than both their peers with milder brain injuries and those with typical development (Dennis *et al.*, 2001b) and may be at risk for declines in verbal IQ over time (Jonsson *et al.*, 2004).

Children and adolescents with TBI may have impairments in syntax, with lower scores than those of peers on standardized measures of syntax comprehension (Docking *et al.*, 2000; Turkstra & Holland, 1998) and production (Docking *et al.*, 2000). There are two caveats to these findings. First, these impairments may be subclinical, i.e. standardized test scores may still be in the normal range (Docking *et al.*, 2000; Turkstra & Holland, 1998). Second, it is not clear that these impairments reflect primary impairments in syntax vs. secondary effects related to test-item construction, particularly effects of working memory load associated with complex, multi-part test questions (Turkstra & Holland,

1998). Investigations of syntax in discourse production of children and adolescents have largely failed to find group differences (Campbell & Dollaghan, 1990; Turkstra & Holland, 1998) further supporting the notion that syntax is relatively intact after TBI. This is consistent with evidence that syntax is the procedural aspect of language (Ferreira *et al.*, 2008) and that procedural memory is intact after brain injury in children (Yeates & Enrile, 2005).

Cognitive communication disorders

Communication impairments in children and adolescents with TBI typically reflect underlying cognitive impairments and thus are most evident in contexts and genres with high cognitive demands (Ewing-Cobbs & Barnes, 2002). Pragmatic language comprehension and production are especially taxing cognitively because appropriate behaviour requires multiple sensory and cognitive prerequisite skills (e.g. social cognition, working memory, implicit and explicit long-term memory, and language skills) as well as pragmatic (e.g. self and contextual awareness, behaviour option generation, selection and execution) and metapragmatic skills (e.g. strategy use and awareness of behaviour options and consequences). See Figure 7.1.

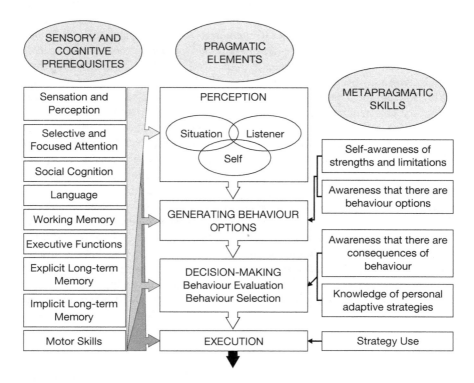

Figure 7.1 Model of pragmatic skills (reprinted from Anderson & Beauchamp, 2012, with permission)

Given the cognitive complexity associated with pragmatic language, it is unsurprising that impairment in both production and expression have been documented in children with TBI. Children and adolescents with TBI have been reported to have deficits in the comprehension of many types of pragmatic language including humour (Docking *et al.*, 2000), proverbs (Moran *et al.*, 2006), deceptive praise (Dennis *et al.*, 2001b), sarcasm (Turkstra *et al.*, 1996) and metaphors, inferences and ambiguous sentences (Dennis & Barnes, 1990).

In regard to production, findings are mixed. Two studies found no difference between children and adolescents with TBI and their typically developing peers in discourse cohesion (links among linguistic referents within a narrative) and coherence (connection of ideas to each other and the main topic) (Chapman *et al.*, 1998; Van Leer & Turkstra, 1999). Similar findings also were reported for turn-taking in conversation (Coelho *et al.*, 2002). These findings, however, should be considered carefully, as large variability in discourse performance has been reported in both children with TBI (Biddle *et al.*, 1996; Chapman *et al.*, 1998; Chapman *et al.*, 2001) and typical children and adolescents (Ciccia & Turkstra, 2002), and may obscure group differences. Consistent with the notion that pragmatic language production is impaired, there is evidence of differences between children with TBI and typical peers in the ability to organize (Chapman *et al.*, 1992; Chapman *et al.*, 2001) and maintain topics in discourse (Rousseaux *et al.*, 2010), summarize narratives (Chapman *et al.*, 2006; Chapman *et al.*, 2004), and present narrative summaries in an organized manner (Chapman *et al.*, 1998; Chapman *et al.*, 2001). It has been hypothesized that these narrative discourse impairments may be, in part, due to deficits in working memory (Chapman *et al.*, 2006). Indeed, the usefulness of summarizing and gist-based skills as the target for both assessment and treatment are explored in further detail in Chapter 9.

There is emerging evidence that impaired social cognition underlies at least some of the pragmatic communication problems of children and adolescents with TBI. For example, there is evidence that adolescents with moderate-to-severe TBI fail to recognize violations of social communication conventions (e.g. bragging) and implied meanings like sarcasm (Turkstra *et al.*, 2001), communication problems that can be clearly linked to impaired social cognition. There also is evidence that poor social cognition is associated with less talk about thoughts and feelings in conversations with peers (Stronach & Turkstra, 2008), a problem that might underlie some of the estrangement from peers that is common after paediatric TBI (Yeates *et al.*, 2007). Researchers are only beginning to examine the impact of social cognition impairments on everyday functioning in individuals with TBI, particularly in paediatrics, and this will be an important area of future study.

Assessment

Assessing language and cognitive skills in children with TBI poses unique challenges. Children with TBI are a heterogeneous group, and present with diverse and complex symptoms that interact and change over the course of recovery. The purpose of assessment also changes over the course of rehabilitation, and care must be taken to choose evaluation tools appropriate for the child's age, stage of recovery, level of functioning and purpose of assessment.

Assessment in early-stage recovery

As discussed in Chapter 2, assessment during the acute phase after TBI aims to evaluate the severity of the injury and monitor progress in coma emergence. The Glasgow Coma Scale (GCS; Jennett & Bond, 1975) is the gold standard for assessing initial injury severity in adults who have sustained brain injuries; however, there are some widely recognized problems in using this measure with young children, as it relies on verbal and motor skills that they may not have yet developed. As a result, several paediatric modifications of the GCS have been published in the literature (Durham *et al.*, 2000; Gordon, 1983; Holmes *et al.*, 2005; James & Trauner, 1985; Reilly *et al.*, 1988), but none have been widely adopted. One review of paediatric coma scales by Kirkham and colleagues showed variable sensitivity and inter-rater reliability among the measures examined, and recommended use of the Child's Glasgow Coma Scale (CGCS) (James & Trauner, 1985; Kirkham *et al.*, 2008).

Like adults, as children emerge from coma and regain consciousness, many progress through a period of disorientation and confusion referred to as post-traumatic amnesia (PTA). During this phase, a primary goal of assessment is to monitor emergence from PTA, as its duration is considered another indicator of injury severity (Russell & Smith, 1961). As expectations for orientation and memory skills of children are substantially different from those of adults progressing through PTA, paediatric measures have also been developed for this purpose. The most common of these is the Children's Orientation and Amnesia Test (COAT; Ewing-Cobbs *et al.*, 1990). The COAT is designed for evaluation of children with TBI ages 3–15 years. General orientation and memory items are administered to all ages, while temporal orientation questions are administered to children age 8 years and older. Duration of PTA is defined by the length of time until a child's COAT score reaches the cut-off for their age on two consecutive days.

The Functional Independence Measure for Children (WeeFIM, Uniform Data System for Medical Rehabilitation, Buffalo, NY) is also commonly used in paediatric hospitals to obtain a broad measure of a child's independence in mobility, self-care, communication, social interaction, memory and problem-solving skills. The WeeFIM is useful for tracking functional progress, and has been validated for evaluating functional outcomes in children with TBI (Ziviani *et al.*, 2001). In addition to measures of severity and duration of PTA, time to follow commands has also been found to be an important predictor of outcome in children with TBI (Suskauer *et al.*, 2009).

During the subacute phase, as a child progresses through PTA and becomes better able to participate in structured activities, the purpose of assessment shifts toward evaluating speech, language and cognitive skills more formally, with the goal of identifying areas for intervention. At this stage, children's skills are often continuing to change rapidly due to spontaneous recovery. As a result, scores on standardized measures may not be valid by the time the evaluation is completed and the report is written (Coelho *et al.*, 2005). Thus measures that can be administered quickly and repeated as needed, and are specifically designed to assess functional skills commonly affected by TBI, should be used. Most formal paediatric language tests, however, do not fit any of these criteria. As a result, many clinicians rely on informal testing or hospital-specific protocols to serve this purpose. While such informal testing has the advantages listed above, without normative data, interpretation of results is inherently subjective and requires in-depth knowledge of language and cognitive skills typically expected at different ages.

Standardized testing

As children progress through rehabilitation and spontaneous recovery begins to slow, a more in-depth evaluation is generally needed to fully characterize their cognitive and communication profile and plan for their return to school. The guiding framework for assessment is the World Health Organization's International Classification of Function, Disability, and Health (ICF; World Health Organization, 2001), shown in Figure 7.2.

According to this framework, a health condition may result in impairments in body structures and functions (e.g. impaired memory and executive functions), limitations in performance of activities (e.g. completing homework) and restrictions in the ability to fully participate in social roles (e.g. academic failure). Personal and environmental factors also influence outcomes, so that the link between an impairment and participation-level outcome is not linear. As recommended by both the CDC (Langlois, 2000) and the recent U.S. multi-agency task force to develop common data elements for TBI research (McCauley *et al.*, 2012), assessment of children and adolescents with TBI should address all

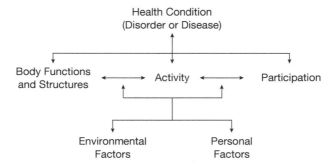

Figure 7.2 Classification of health outcomes according to the World Health Organization International Classification of Functioning, Disability, and Health (2001)

levels of the ICF framework, including not only basic functions such as cognition and language but also factors such as the child's ability to participate in age-appropriate activities, parent stress and burden, and services provided by the school.

At the level of functional impairment, all areas of language should be assessed, including vocabulary knowledge and word-finding skills, syntax, and listening and reading comprehension. Given the high likelihood of deficits in pragmatic language expression and comprehension, supralinguistic skills should also be assessed, including comprehension of figurative and ambiguous language, inference skills and use of social language. In addition, cognitive skills that have an impact on communication should be evaluated, including attention, memory, executive function and social cognition.

Using formal language tests to evaluate children and adolescents with TBI is problematic for a variety of reasons. First, there are very few standardized tests normed for use with this population. In 2005, the North American Academy of Neurologic Communication Disorders and Science (ANCDS) published a report reviewing the use of standardized language tests for assessment of cognitive communication disorders in TBI. Of over 120 tests screened in this study, only seven mentioned TBI in the test manuals or had published TBI data and met established validity and reliability criteria. Only two of these seven measures, the Test of Language Competence-Extended (TLC-E; Wiig & Secord, 1989) and the Behavior Rating Inventory of Executive Function (BRIEF; Gioia *et al.*, 2003; Gioia *et al.*, 2000a; Gioia *et al.*, 2000b), are designed for assessment of children and adolescents (Turkstra *et al.*, 2005).

As children with TBI often show relatively well-preserved syntax and vocabulary knowledge in the context of weaker pragmatic and abstract language skills, standardized assessments designed for evaluation of children with developmental language disabilities may not be sensitive to the types of deficits common in TBI. Also, many standardized language subtests rely heavily on working memory and other cognitive skills that may be affected in TBI. Thus, impaired performance on such subtests may reflect underlying cognitive deficits rather than the language impairment it purports to measure. The cognitive demands of a few common language tests have been investigated in children with TBI. A study of the Test of Adolescent Language (TOAL-3; Hammill *et al.*, 1994) showed that reducing the working memory demands of a syntax comprehension task improved the scores of adolescents with TBI, while the performance of matched controls did not change (Turkstra & Holland, 1998), suggesting that the working memory demands of the test negatively influenced performance of the TBI group. In a study of the Clinical Evaluation of Language Fundamentals – 3rd Edition (CELF-3; Semel *et al.*, 1995), the test failed to identify adolescents with TBI who had other evidence of communication problems and although results suggested underlying cognitive deficits influenced test performance, the test did not aid in the detection of these deficits (Turkstra, 1999). The Comprehensive Assessment of Spoken Language (CASL) is another language battery commonly used by paediatric speech-language pathologists. While also not designed for assessing children with TBI, this measure has many subtests that each yield a standard score and may individually be useful in identifying areas of deficit.

In recent years, some progress has been made with the development of new measures specifically designed to address cognitive communication skills in children with TBI. One such tool is the Pediatric Test of Brain Injury (Hotz *et al.*, 2010), a standardized, criterion-referenced test designed to identify cognitive communication deficits in functional skills typically mastered early in development (e.g. orientation to personal information), as well as in higher-level skills expected to be continually refined through adolescence (e.g. story-telling). The Functional Assessment of Verbal Reasoning and Executive Strategies-Adolescent (FAVRES-A) is another new standardized measure designed to assess high-level executive functioning skills using tasks designed to mimic real-world communication activities. The adult version of this test is widely used in North America and the adolescent version has recently been released (MacDonald, 2013).

Despite the paucity of standardized measures appropriate for language and cognitive communication assessment of children with TBI, speech-language pathologists often need to report standard scores for their paediatric clients. School systems often require standardized testing in order to qualify children for school-based speech-language services. Thus, as a matter of necessity, clinicians frequently turn to standardized measures designed for assessment of children with developmental communication disorders. While such language batteries may yield some valuable functional information, standard scores need to be interpreted with extreme caution, as they may either overestimate or underestimate a child's skills. Performance on each test or subtest should be interpreted in the context of the working memory, attention and other executive functioning demands of the task. See Table 7.1.

Informal testing

People with TBI are particularly affected by the cumulative cognitive demands of environmental and situational variables, and there is often a discrepancy between standardized test scores and performance in real-life settings. For children, school is a crucial functional setting and studies have shown that even brain-injured children with standardized test scores in the normal range can have marked difficulties in classroom performance (Ewing-Cobbs *et al.* 1998). Thus, nonstandard measures can be valuable in assessing performance in real-life settings, describing the cognitive and communication demands of such contexts and exploring the effects of providing modifications and supports.

The ANCDS published a report summarizing evidence and recommendations for effective use of informal cognitive communication assessment for people with TBI and found 'substantial evidence to support the assessment of communication beyond what is included in standardized aphasia or child language batteries' (Coelho *et al.*, 2005, p. 237). For nonstandard assessment of language, discourse analysis was found to be particularly sensitive to language

Table 7.1 Some common measures of paediatric language

Instrument	Nature of response	Scored by	Level of analysis	Normative information
Test of Language Competence-Extended (Wiig & Secord, 1989)	Children respond verbally and by pointing to a choice from four foils to verbally presented probe questions.	Clinician	Test is designed to assess language comprehension and use in terms of content and appropriateness for the context. Subtests evaluate semantics, syntax, and pragmatics.	Normative data collected from children aged 5 to 18 years from within the United States. Children who were receiving speech or language services were excluded from the normative sample.
Test of Adolescent and Adult Language (Hammill, et al., 1994)	Adolescents respond verbally or in written form to verbal or written test prompts.	Clinician	Subtests yield composite scores for spoken, written and general language usage. Subtests evaluate use of synonyms, antonyms, word morphology, written punctuation and the ability to combine written sentences.	Normative data available for adolescents and adults from 12:0 – 24:11 from the USA. Individuals with TBI not included in the normative sample.
Clinical Evaluation of Language Fundamentals – 4th Edition (Semel et al., 2003)	Children and adolescents respond to verbal or written probe questions and tasks either verbally or through pointing.	Clinician	Test items evaluate morphology and syntax, semantics, pragmatics, and phonological awareness to identify language strengths and challenges. Also includes subtests to address working memory ability.	Normative data available for individuals aged 5–21 years. Individuals with language disorders were included in this sample.
Pediatric Test of Brain Injury (Hotz, et al., 2010)	Children and adolescents between the ages of 6–16 years respond verbally to verbally and visually presented stimuli material.	Clinician	Evaluates cognitive, language, and literacy abilities with a focus on evaluating abilities needed for a child's return to a general education curriculum.	Criterion-reference test. Normative sample specifically based on children and adolescents with TBI.
FAVRES-Adolescent (MacDonald, 2013)	Adolescents provide written and verbal responses to four written tasks (e.g. planning an event, schedule a work day)	Clinician	Adolescents are scored on their accuracy, speed, and reasoning for each item.	Norms to be available with test publication.
Comprehensive Assessment of Spoken Language (Carrow-Woolfolk, 1999)	Participants respond verbally to spoken question prompts.	Clinician	Subtest batteries available to assess lexical/semantic, syntactic, supralinguistic, pragmatic, and core composite language abilities.	Normative data available for individuals aged 3:0 to 21:11 years from the U.S. Children receiving special education services were included, but it's unclear if children with TBI were included.

deficits in children and adolescents with TBI. A summary of recommended discourse analysis measures can be found in this ANCDS report (Coelho *et al.*, 2005) and is also described more fully in Chapter 4.

Informal assessment can also be useful for evaluating cognitive skills within real-life contexts. Substantial evidence in the TBI literature supports the use of a dynamic assessment process known as contextualized hypothesis testing to tease apart the cognitive, linguistic and environmental factors potentially affecting a youth's performance and to plan effective behavioural and contextual supports (Ylvisaker & Feeney, 1998). In addition to enabling assessment of performance in functional educational and vocational activities, this method has the benefit of encouraging input from all those involved in a child's care. Ideally, contextualized hypothesis testing involves collaboration between therapists, educators and family members to help foster common understanding of a child's disability and promote carry-over of strategies across settings (Coelho *et al.*, 2005).

Another benefit of informal assessment is that it can allow clinicians to evaluate areas for which standardized measures may not exist. As mentioned previously in this chapter, deficits in social cognition are common in children and adolescents with TBI. While there are currently few standardized tests designed to specifically measure skills in this domain, many informal and experimental tasks have been developed to evaluate social cognition skills (see Table 7.2).

Clinicians can use informal tasks to try to identify social cognition difficulties, such as asking children to recognize different emotions in facial expression. Observation of peer interactions can also provide insight into this area, for example by watching to see whether the child with TBI understands nonverbal cues and appears to react appropriately to emotions of others. In addition, selected items from some formal tests may be sensitive to deficits in social cognition, even if the test as a whole is not designed for this purpose. The paediatric version of the BRIEF contains a few items pertaining to emotion recognition. In addition, the Making Inferences subtest of the TLC-E relies on perspective taking and interpretation of social situations, which may be reflective of social cognition skills.

Overall, assessment of more subtle, higher-level cognitive skills in children and adolescents with TBI remains a challenge for clinicians and requires integration of information from performance on a variety of standardized, informal and functional tasks.

Assessment of young children

Evaluating cognitive communication skills of infants, toddlers and young children with TBI poses additional challenges, as even fewer measures exist that are targeted to the needs of this population. There are several well-established tests of early learning and development, as well as measures of social and emotional behaviour problems that have been used in studies of children with TBI (McCauley *et al.*, 2012). However, no standardized language tests have been

Table 7.2 Some paediatric measures of social cognition

Name of instrument	Nature of response	Scored by	Level of analysis
The Reading the Mind in the Eyes Test – Child Version (Baron-Cohen et al., 2001)	Children and adolescents view a series of photos of the eye regions of actors then choose the word (from 4 foils) that best describes what each actor is feeling in the picture.	Clinician	Accuracy of mental state identification is calculated.
Interpersonal Negative Strategies Task (Yeates et al., 1991)	Children and adolescents describe strategies to solve interpersonal conflicts. Probe questions ask children to infer character feelings and describe the problem as well as solutions and potential obstacles.	Clinician	Clinician rates answers to probe questions on a 4-point scale.
Pragmatic Judgment subtest of the CASL (Carrow-Woolfolk, 1999)	Children generate appropriate social responses to described social scenarios.	Clinician	Test measures the ability to generate context-appropriate responses. Standard scores can be generated.
Social Problem Solving Measure (Pettit et al., 1988)	Children are read or shown videos of peer interactions (peer entry and peer provocation) and children are asked how they would respond in the situation.	Clinician	Clinicians code child responses in terms of response type.
Social Language Development Test (Elementary and Adolescent Versions) (Bowers et al., 2010a & 2010b)	Participants are asked to explain what pictured or described characters or themselves would do in various social situations or to achieve social goals.	Clinician	Evaluates perspective taking, social problem solving, and comprehension and use of non-literal language.
Strange Stories (Happè, 1994)	Individuals hear short social stories, each accompanied by an associated picture, and are asked to decide if a statement made by a character is true or not, as well as inferring why the character made the target statement.	Clinician	Clinicians score the accuracy of individual's comprehension and mental state inferences.
Making Inferences subtest of the TLC-E (Wiig & Secord, 1989)	Children are read a short sentence about a social scenario, then the scenario's conclusion and are asked to make an inference regarding how the conclusion came about. Children choose the best inference from four foils.	Clinician	Children are scored on their ability to draw plausible inferences.
Video Social Inference Test (Turkstra, 2008)	Individuals view short video vignettes of adolescents in social interactions. Individuals are asked to make an inference regarding a target character's feelings or belief and also to predict characters' future behaviours.	Clinician	Accuracy scores for both mental state inferences and behaviour predictions can be calculated.

validated for use with young children with TBI. Furthermore, many of the previously discussed informal assessment methods may not be possible to use, as children at this age have not yet developed discourse skills and are not yet expected to perform independently in functional settings. Due to differences in amount of school experience, parenting style and exposure to pre-academic concepts, there can be a large degree of variability in the knowledge of preschool-aged children. Thus it is crucial to obtain detailed information from families about their child's premorbid knowledge and functional skills as part of any assessment. In addition, it is important to make caregivers and educators aware that emergence of deficits in higher-level language and executive functioning skills is likely as a child grows. Therefore, ongoing monitoring and future assessment of these skill areas is often warranted.

Collaboration in assessment

In recent years there has been an increased focus on interdisciplinary collaboration in health care. In many rehabilitation hospitals, speech-language pathologists and neuropsychologists are both involved in assessment and treatment of cognitive communication deficits in their TBI patients. A study involving focus groups of neuropsychologists and speech-language pathologists across several rehabilitation institutions found that neuropsychologists were relied upon for comprehensive evaluations of cognitive functions, while speech-language pathologists used more informal cognitive communication measures and were more involved in treatment of these deficits (Wertheimer *et al.*, 2008). Given the overlap in their domains, collaboration between these professionals is essential to continuity of care for brain-injured individuals. Such collaboration can help treating speech-language pathologists gain a full picture of a child's cognitive profile, which is needed to guide treatment. It also helps ensure consistency in the messages conveyed to families about their child's cognition and helps avoid duplication of testing. Based on focus group interviews, Wertheimer and colleagues concluded that, 'effective collaboration translates into better quality and access to rehabilitation services for patients who are the consumers of these services' (2008, p. 282).

In paediatric settings, special educators are often part of the interdisciplinary team and complete academic testing to assist with recommendations for school transition. All areas assessed in academic testing can be influenced by the language and cognitive deficits resulting from TBI. Thus close collaboration between educators, neuropsychologists and speech-language pathologist is necessary to integrate evaluation results and formulate cohesive recommendations. Collaboration with educators is further extended when a child with TBI returns to school. At times there can be a disconnect between the evaluation measures used by rehabilitation professionals and the standardized tests scores schools look for in order to qualify a child for school-based services. Good communication across teams can help schools understand the challenges of assessing children with TBI and the importance of considering converging information in planning supports to help maximize students' success in school.

Intervention

General framework: ICF model

The rehabilitation model for adults with communication disorders has shifted over the past two decades from a medical model, focused on remediation of impairments, to a model of social disability, in which the goal is full participation in meaningful life roles, and factors such as the person's environmental supports and beliefs about rehabilitation are considered explicitly in treatment planning. This view is embodied by the ICF framework discussed earlier in this chapter in relation to assessment. The ICF framework has begun to exert an influence in paediatric rehabilitation, which until recently was based on a developmental model in which goals were set hierarchically, based on developmental expectations.

To illustrate the difference between the traditional, medical model and the social disability model embodied by the ICF framework, consider the case of a boy, age 15 years, who sustained a severe TBI at age 3 years and now has a vocabulary of 200 words and is speaking in single-clause utterances. Goals set using a traditional approach might focus on advancing his language skills to the next developmental stage, such as using more complex syntax and an expanded vocabulary. Using the social disability model, the main goal might be to teach verbal scripts to allow him to have a conversation with peers or ask to go to the bathroom, if either of these is critical to his full participation in student life and something he is motivated to achieve.

When applying the ICF framework to children, personal factors will include pre-injury knowledge and skills, including academic language skills, as well as any premorbid conditions such as a language-based learning disability. For adolescents, motivation will be a key personal factor and social language is likely to be a high priority given the primacy of social interactions at this age (Steinberg, 2008). Critical environmental factors for children include parental support, knowledge, skills and availability, and the ability and willingness of the school system to provide appropriate academic supports. For adolescents, people may be the most important environmental factor, including peers for social communication and employers for transition to work.

The ICF framework represents a shift in the philosophy of rehabilitation from a *medical model* to a model of *social disability*, in which the clinician shares responsibility for improving life participation beyond the clinic. To date, this shift has been more evident in intervention for adults, perhaps in part because children and adolescents are thought to lack the 'perspective' (i.e. metacognitive skills) required to choose their own rehabilitation priorities, and in part because intervention for children is often based on basic-skill 'building blocks' (e.g. learning vocabulary) in the short-term, with the hope that these will ultimately benefit life participation (e.g. having a job). Even with children, however, a main question in intervention should be: *how will this goal improve life participation?* (Sohlberg & Turkstra, 2011). The answer to this question sets the stage for the entire intervention plan. The goal should be meaningful to the child or adolescent and also to third-party payers, when appropriate, as they require clear, concise goal statements that will lead to meaningful changes in everyday life functioning.

Collaborating with families and the school

The two main partners in paediatric TBI rehabilitation are families and the school. As the goal of paediatric intervention is inter-dependence with families, rather than independence as it is with adults, family members play a critical role on the rehabilitation team. TBI in childhood affects the entire family system and the response of that family system will influence outcome. As Anderson and colleagues stated (Anderson *et al.*, 2012), TBI-related cognitive impairments 'interfere with skill acquisition, causing adaptive deficits, academic failure and social and behavioural dysfunction, as well as personal and economic burden for the family and community' (p. 255). In a longitudinal study of outcome after paediatric TBI (Taylor *et al.*, 1999; Yeates *et al.*, 2010), family functioning influenced the child's adjustment, stress and even cognitive outcomes and academic achievement. Thus, education of and support for family members are important rehabilitation targets and the child's family is a critical part of the decision-making team.

Some public school systems in the U.S.A. have established integrated transition models to help make school reentry as successful as possible for students with TBI. For example, the Center for Brain Injury Research and Training (CBIRT; http://www.cbirt.org/) has partnered with the Oregon Department of Education to provide one of these model systems. In this system, educators trained by CBIRT act as local school liaisons, providing support and resources to both the family and school staff working with the child with TBI (CBIRT, 2012). In other systems, educators employed by hospitals act as liaisons by attending school meetings and communicating recommendations from the child's medical team to the school. School liaisons can play a critical role in helping schools understand how the needs of students with TBI differ from other children receiving special education services. In addition, they can help schools develop transition plans that include ongoing monitoring and reassessment of skills, as students with TBI are likely to have changing needs over time. While students with TBI may show improvement in some cognitive communication skills over time, they may also show new emerging deficits in other areas. School teams' awareness of this need for ongoing adjustment of therapy and special education services is important for the long-term academic success of students with TBI.

Special considerations for adolescents

There are many reasons for considering communication outcomes of adolescents with TBI as unique. First, existing studies suggest that social communication is important for success at home, school, work and in the community, so there is potentially a high cost to problems in this domain. Second, the adolescent brain is a 'work in progress', with significant developments ongoing until the late 20s (Ciccia *et al.*, 2009). Thus, adolescence may provide a critical window for intervention aimed at improving social functioning. Third, adolescents with severe TBI may experience what has been referred to as a 'developmental crisis' (Blazyk, 1983), from the major interruption in typical development. Fourth, and perhaps most important, the social contexts of adolescence are complex and demanding, and success in these contexts requires sophisticated communication skills: other-sex relationships are more extensive than they are in childhood (Maccoby, 1988), as romantic relationships emerge; friendships become more stable and more intimate (Berndt & Hoyle, 1985); and interaction-based groups (*cliques*) and identity-based groups (*crowds*) exercise more influence (Adler & Adler, 1998; Brown, 2004). Adolescents spend increasing amounts of time with peers (Csikszentmihalyi *et al.*, 1984; Raffaelli & Duckett, 1989) and grow more susceptible to both prosocial and antisocial peer influences (Berndt & Hoyle, 1985; Brown, 2004). Contact with and close supervision by adults diminishes (Zimmer-Gembeck & Collins, 2003) particularly in this era of electronic social communication (Subrahmanyam *et al.*, 2006). As a result, adolescents handle many of these changes without the direct guidance of adults that is typical of childhood.

To be successful in their complex communication environments, adolescents must be able to perceive social information, understand its stated and implied meaning, connect that meaning to previous experience and world knowledge, respond rapidly in a way that is appropriate to the context, evaluate their responses and modify their subsequent behaviour accordingly. The skills underlying these functions include not only basic language and cognitive skills but also social cognition, to detect rule violations and make social judgements that are congruent with the accepted behaviours of one's peer group (Turkstra, 2000), and metacognitive skills, including the ability to appraise one's own performance and make realistic predictions for one's future social behaviour. For the most part, these skills appear to be learned implicitly (Turkstra, 2005), likely influenced by parents and peers, with refinement by direct instruction (e.g. when 'job interviewing' or 'interpersonal communication' are included in a high-school school curriculum).

Studies of adolescents with moderate-to-severe TBI have revealed impairments in aspects of communication that are critical at this stage of development, including comprehension of complex syntax (Turkstra & Holland, 1998), discourse gist (Chapman *et al.*, 2006), humour (Docking *et al.*, 2000), proverbs (Moran *et al.*, 2006), deceptive praise (Dennis *et al.*, 2001b) and metaphors, implicatures and ambiguous sentences (Dennis & Barnes, 1990; Moran & Gillon, 2005; Towne & Entwisle, 1993; Turkstra *et al.*, 1996); production of well-organized discourse that is spoken (Chapman *et al.*, 1992; Ewing-Cobbs & Barnes, 2002) or written (Wilson & Proctor, 2002); expressing speech acts such as requests and hints (Turkstra *et al.*, 1996); and using appropriate thought and feeling words in conversations (Stronach & Turkstra, 2008). These communication problems are generally thought to reflect underlying cognitive impairments that are typical in adolescents with TBI, such as impairments in working memory (Chapman *et al.*, 2006; Levin *et al.*, 2002), declarative learning (Donders, 1993), executive functions (Gamino *et al.*, 2009; Hanten *et al.*, 2004; Krawczyk *et al.*, 2010; Proctor *et al.*, 2000; Wilson *et al.*, 2011) and social cognition (Schmidt *et al.*, 2010; Tonks *et al.*, 2007; Turkstra *et al.*, 2001; Turkstra *et al.*, 2008).

Adolescents with TBI have been found to be similar, on average, to their peers without brain injury in proceduralized aspects of communication such as overall amount of eye contact and production of facial expressions used in conversation (Turkstra, 2005; Turkstra *et al.*, 2006), speech fluency (Campbell & Dollaghan, 1995) and expressive grammar (Turkstra & Holland, 1998). Vocabulary may be intact in the early months after injury (Donders & Warschausky, 2007), although impairments in verbal learning and memory may lead to a lag behind peers over time (Jonsson *et al.*, 2004). It should be noted that the lack of significant between-groups differences might reflect the high within-groups variability for both typical adolescents and those with TBI.

Summary

TBI in children differs in important ways from injury in adults, including the basic causes and mechanisms of injury, interaction of injury effects with brain development, and framework and goals for assessment and intervention. Perhaps the most critical feature of TBI in children is that over time it becomes a developmental disability, as it affects the cognitive and communication foundations for later knowledge and skills. The potential for delayed emergence of cognitive and communication problems means that assessment and intervention must be ongoing and underlines the importance of collaboration with family and schools, who will be the main agents of change in the child's life.

Communication problems in children and adolescents with TBI most often are due to underlying cognitive impairments, particularly in executive functions, working memory, declarative learning, speed of information processing and social cognition. Communication problems are most evident in genres and contexts that place high demands on these cognitive functions, such as social interaction or school-based tasks that require comprehension and production of complex verbal information. While there is a growing literature describing communication problems after TBI in children and adolescents, there continue to be major gaps in the literature on how to treat these problems effectively. The ICF offers a useful overall framework for intervention, but it is clear that we have much to learn about how best to help children and adolescents with TBI achieve full participation in school, home and community life and make a successful transition to adulthood.

References

Achenbach, T. M. & Edelbrock, C. (1980). *Child Behavior Checklist*. Burlington, VT: Achenbach, T M.

Adler, P. A. & Adler, P. (1998). *Peer Power: Preadolescent Culture and Identity*. New Brunswick, NJ: Rutgers University Press.

Adolphs, R. (1999). Social cognition and the human brain. *Trends in Cognitive Sciences, 3*, 469–479.

——(2010). Conceptual challenges and directions for social neuroscience. *Neuron, 65*(6), 752–767.

American Speech-Language-Hearing Association. (2004). Knowledge and skills needed by speech-language pathologists providing services to individuals with cognitive–communication disorders. *ASHA, Supplement 24*.

Anderson, V., Fenwick, T., Manly, T. & Robertson, I. (1998). Attentional skills following traumatic brain injury in childhood: a componential analysis. *Brain Injury, 12*, 937–939.

Anderson, S. W., Bechara, A., Damasio, H., Tranel, D. & Damasio, A. R. (1999). Impairment of social and moral behavior related to early damage in human prefrontal cortex. *Nature Neuroscience, 2*(11), 1032–1037.

Anderson, V. & Catroppa, C. (2005). Recovery of executive skills following paediatric traumatic brain injury (TBI): a 2 year follow up. *Brain Injury, 19*(6), 459–470.

Anderson, V., Catroppa, C., Morse, S., Haritou, F. & Rosenfeld, J. V. (2009). Intellectual outcome from preschool traumatic brain injury: a 5-year prospective, longitudinal study. *Pediatrics, 124*(6), e1064–e1071.

Anderson, V., Brown, S., Newitt, H. & Hoile, H. (2011). Long-term outcome from childhood traumatic brain injury: intellectual ability, personality, and quality of life. *Neuropsychology, 25*(2), 176–184.

Anderson, V., Godfrey, C., Rosenfeld, J. V. & Catroppa, C. (2012). Predictors of cognitive function and recovery 10 years after traumatic brain injury in young children. *Pediatrics, 129*(2), 254–261.

Baron-Cohen, S., Wheelwright, S., Spong, A., Scahill, V. & Lawson, J. (2001). Are intuitive physics and intuitive psychology independent? A test with children with Asperger Syndrome. *Journal of Developmental & Learning Disorders, 5*, 1–58.

Beauchamp, M., Catroppa, C., Godfrey, C., Morse, S., Rosenfeld, J. V. & Anderson, V. (2011). Selective changes in executive functioning ten years after severe childhood traumatic brain injury. *Developmental Neuropsychology, 36*(5), 578–595.

Berndt, T. J. & Hoyle, S. G. (1985). Stability and change in childhood and adolescent friendships. *Developmental Psychology, 21*, 1007–1015.

Biddle, K. R., McCabe, A. & Bliss, L. S. (1996). Narrative skills following traumatic brain injury in children and adults. *Journal of Communication Disorders, 29*, 447–469.

Blakemore, S. J. (2008). The social brain in adolescence. *Nature Reviews Neuroscience, 9*(4), 267–277.

Blazyk, S. (1983). Developmental crisis in adolescents following severe head injury. *Social Work in Health Care, 8*(4), 55–67.

Bowers, L., Huisingh, R. & LoGiudice, C. (2010a). *Social Language Development Test – Adolescent Manual*. East Moline, IL: LinguiSystems, Inc.

——(2010b). *Social Language Development Test – Elementary Manual*. East Moline, IL: LinguiSystems, Inc.

Briscoe, J. & Rankin, P. M. (2009). Exploration of a 'double-jeopardy' hypothesis within working memory profiles for children with specific language impairment. *International Journal of Language & Communication Disorders, 44*(2), 236–250.

Brown, B. B. (2004). Adolescents' relationships with peers. In R. M. Lerner & L. Steinberg (Eds), *Handbook of Adolescent Psychology* (Second edn). New York: Wiley.

Campbell, T. F. & Dollaghan, C. A. (1990). Expressive language recovery in severely brain-injured children and adolescents. *Journal of Speech & Hearing Disorders, 55*(3), 567–581.

——(1995). Speaking rate, articulatory speed, and linguistic processing in children and adolescents with severe traumatic brain injury. *J Speech Hear Res, 38*(4), 864–875.

Carrow-Woolfolk, E. (1999). *Comprehensive Assessment of Spoken Language.* Circle Pines, MN: American Guidance Services, Inc.

Catroppa, C. & Anderson, V. (2004). Recovery and predictors of language skills two years following pediatric traumatic brain injury. *Brain Lang, 88*(1), 68–78.

Catroppa, C., Anderson, V. A., Morse, S. A., Haritou, F. & Rosenfeld, J. V. (2008). Outcome and predictors of functional recovery 5 years following pediatric traumatic brain injury (TBI). *Journal of Pediatric Psychology, 33*(7), 707–718.

Center on Brain Injury Research and Training (CBIRT) (2012). *School Transition & Re-Entry Program (STEP).* Retrieved May 8, 2012, from http://www.cbirt.org/our-projects/school-transition-re-entry-program-step/

Centers for Disease Control and Prevention (CDC) (2012). *Injury Prevention & Control: Traumatic Brain Injury.* Retrieved 2/9/12, from http://www.cdc.gov/Traumatic BrainInjury/

Chapman, S. B., Culhane, K. A., Levin, H. S., Harward, H., Mendelsohn, D., Ewing-Cobbs, L., Fletcher, J. M. & Bruce, D. (1992). Narrative discourse after closed head injury in children and adolescents. *Brain and Language, 43*, 42–65.

Chapman, S. B., Levin, H. S., Wanek, A., Weyauch, J. & Kufera, J. (1998). Discourse after closed head injury in young children. *Brain and Language, 61*(3), 395–419.

Chapman, S. B., McKinnon, L., Levin, H. S., Song, J., Meier, M. C. & Chiu, S. (2001). Longitudinal outcome of verbal discourse in children with traumatic brain injury: three-year follow-up. *The Journal of Head Trauma Rehabilitation, 16*(5), 441–455.

Chapman, S. B., Sparks, G., Levin, H. S., Dennis, M., Roncadin, C., Zhang, L. & Song, J. (2004). Discourse macrolevel processing after severe pediatric traumatic brain injury. *Developmental Neuropsychology, 25*(1–2), 37–60.

Chapman, S. B., Gamino, J. F., Cook, L. G., Hanten, G., Li, X. & Levin, H. S. (2006). Impaired discourse gist and working memory in children after brain injury. *Brain Lang, 97*(2), 178–188.

Ciccia, A. H. & Turkstra, L. S. (2002). Cohesion, communication burden, and response adequacy in adolescent conversations. *Advances in Speech-Language Pathology, 4*(1), 1–8.

Ciccia, A. H., Meulenbroek, P. & Turkstra, L. S. (2009). Adolescent brain and cognitive developments: implications for clinical intervention. *Topics in Language Disorders, 29*(3), 249–265.

Coelho, C., Youse, K. M. & Le, K. N. (2002). Conversational discourse in closed-head-injured and non-brain-injured adults. *Aphasiology, 16*(4–6), 659–672.

Coelho, C., Ylvisaker, M. & Turkstra, L. S. (2005). Nonstandardized assessment approaches for individuals with traumatic brain injuries. *Seminars in Speech and Language, 26*(4), 223–241.

Conklin, H. M., Salorio, C. F. & Slomine, B. S. (2008). Working memory performance following paediatric traumatic brain injury. *Brain Injury, 22*(11), 847–857.

Crowe, L. M., Catroppa, C., Babl, F. E. & Anderson, V. (2012). Intellectual, behavioral, and social outcomes of accidental traumatic brain injury in early childhood. *Pediatrics, 129*(2), e262–268.

Csikszentmihalyi, M., Larson, R. & Csikszenthi, M. (1984). *Being Adolescent: Conflict and Growth in the Teenage Years*. New York: Basic Books.

Dennis, M. (2010). Margaret Kennard (1899–1975): not a 'principle' of brain plasticity but a founding mother of developmental neuropsychology. *Cortex, 46*(8), 1043–1059.

Dennis, M. & Barnes, M. A. (1990). Knowing the meaning, getting the point, bridging the gap, and carrying the message: aspects of discourse following closed head injury in childhood and adolescence. *Brain and Language, 39*, 428–446.

Dennis, M., Guger, S., Roncadin, C., Barnes, M. & Schachar, R. (2001a). Attentional-inhibitory control and social-behavioral regulation after childhood closed head injury: do biological, developmental, and recovery variables predict outcome? *Journal of the International Neuropsychological Society, 7*(6), 683–692.

Dennis, M., Purvis, K., Barnes, M. A., Wilkinson, M. & Winner, E. (2001b). Understanding of literal truth, ironic criticism, and deceptive praise following childhood head injury. *Brain and Language, 78*(1), 1–16.

Docking, K., Murdoch, B. E. & Jordan, F. M. (2000). Interpretation and comprehension of linguistic humour by adolescents with head injury: A group analysis. *Brain Injury, 14*(1), 89–108.

Donders, J. (1993). Memory functioning after traumatic brain injury in children. *Brain Injury, 7*(5), 431–437.

Donders, J. & Minnema, M. T. (2004). Performance discrepancies on the California Verbal Learning Test-Children's Version (CVLT-C) in children with traumatic brain injury. *Journal of the International Neuropsychological Society, 10*(4), 482–488.

Donders, J. & Warschausky, S. (2007). Neurobehavioral outcomes after early versus late childhood traumatic brain injury. *Journal of Head Trauma Rehabilitation, 22*(5), 296–302.

Durham, S. R., Clancy, R. R., Leuthardt, E., Sun, P., Kamerling, S., Dominguez, T. & Duhaime, A. C. (2000). CHOP Infant Coma Scale ('Infant Face Scale'): a novel coma scale for children less than two years of age. *Journal of Neurotrauma, 17*(9), 729–737.

Ewing-Cobbs, L., Levin, H., Fletcher, J., Miner, M. & Eisenberg, H. (1990). The Children's Orientation and Amnesia Test: relationship to severity of acute head injury and to recovery of memory. *Neurosurgery, 27*, 683–691.

Ewing-Cobbs, L., Fletcher, J. M., Levin, H. S., Francis, D. J., Davidson, D. & Miner, M. E. (1997). Longitudinal neuropsychological outcome in infants and preschoolers with traumatic brain injury. *Journal of the International Neuropsychological Society, 3*, 581–591.

Ewing-Cobbs, L., Brookshire, B., Scott, M. A. & Fletcher, J. M. (1998). Children's narratives following traumatic brain injury: linguistic structure, cohesion, and thematic recall. *Brain Lang, 61*(3), 395–419.

Ewing-Cobbs, L. & Barnes, M. (2002). Linguistic outcomes following traumatic brain injury in children. *Seminars in Pediatric Neurology, 9*(3), 209–217.

Ewing-Cobbs, L., Prasad, M. R., Landry, S. H., Kramer, L. & DeLeon, R. (2004). Executive functions following traumatic brain injury in young children: a preliminary analysis. *Developmental Neuropsychology, 26*(1), 487–512.

Ferreira, V. S., Bock, K., Wilson, M. P. & Cohen, N. J. (2008). Memory for syntax despite amnesia. *Psychological Science, 19*(9), 940–946.

Fletcher, J. M. & Levin, H. S. (1987). Neurobehavioral effects of brain injury in children. In D. Routh (Ed.), *The Handbook of Pediatric Psychology* (pp. 258–298). New York: Guilford Press.

Gamino, J., Chapman, S. B. & Cook, L. G. (2009). Strategic learning in youth with traumatic brain injury: evidence for stall in higher-order cognition. *Topics in Language Disorders, 29*(3), 224–235.

Ganesalingam, K., Yeates, K. O., Taylor, H. G., Walz, N. C., Stancin, T. & Wade, S. (2011). Executive functions and social competence in young children 6 months following traumatic brain injury. *Neuropsychology, 25*(4), 466–476.

Ginstfeldt, T. & Emanuelson, I. (2010). An overview of attention deficits after paediatric traumatic brain injury. *Brain Injury, 24*(10), 1123–1134.

Gioia, G. A., Isquith, P. K., Guy, S. C. & Kenworthy, L. (2000a). *Behavior Rating Inventory of Executive Function*. Odessa, FL: Psychological Assessment Resources, Inc.

Gioia, G. A., Isquith, P. K., Guy, S. C. & Kenworthy, L. (2000b). *Behavior Rating Inventory of Executive Function: Self-report Version for Adolescents and Adults*: Unpublished.

Gioia, G. A., Isquith, P. K., Kenworthy, L. & Barton, R. M. (2002). Profiles of everyday executive function in acquired and development disorders. *Child Neuropsychology, 8*(2), 121.

Gioia, G. A., Espy, K. A. & Isquith, P. K. (2003). *Behavior Rating Inventory of Executive Function* (Preschool Version edn). Odessa, FL: Par, Inc.

Gordon, N. A., Fois, A., Jacobi, G., Minns, R. A. & Seshia, S. S. (1983). The management of the comatose child. *Neuropediatrics, 1983*(14), 3–5.

Hammill, D. D., Brown, V. L., Larsen, S. C. & Wiederholt, J. L. (1994). *Test of Adolescent and Adult Language* (Third edn). Austin, TX: Pro-Ed.

Hanten, G., Dennis, M., Zhang, L., Barnes, M., Roberson, G., Archibald, J., Song, J. & Levin, H. S. (2004). Childhood head injury and metacognitive processes in language and memory. *Developmental Neuropsychology, 25*(1&2), 85–106.

Hanten, G., Cook, L., Orsten, K., Chapman, S. B., Li, X., Wilde, E. A., Schnelle, K. P. & Levin, H. S. (2011). Effects of traumatic brain injury on a virtual reality social problem solving task and relations to cortical thickness in adolescence. *Neuropsychologia, 49*(3), 486–497.

Happé, F. (1994). An advanced test of theory of mind: understanding of story character's thoughts and feelings by able autistic, mentally handicapped, and normal children and adults. *Journal of Autism and Developmental Disorders, 24*(2), 129–154.

Hebb, D. O. (1949). *The Organization of Behaviour*. New York: Wiley.

Holmes, J. F., Palchak, M. J., MacFarlane, T. & Kuppermann, N. (2005). Performance of the pediatric Glasgow coma scale in children with blunt head trauma. *Academic Emergency Medicine, 12*(9), 814–819.

Horneman, G. & Emanuelson, I. (2009). Cognitive outcome in children and young adults who sustained severe and moderate traumatic brain injury 10 years earlier. *Brain Injury, 23*(11), 907–914.

Hotz, G., Helm-Estabrooks, N., Wolf-Nelson, N. & Plante, E. (2010). *Pediatric Test of Brain Injury*. Baltimore, MD: Brookes.

Jacobs, R., Harvey, A. S. & Anderson, V. (2007). Executive function following focal frontal lobe lesions: impact of timing of lesion on outcome. *Cortex, 43*(6), 792–805.

James, H. E. & Trauner, D. A. (1985). The Glasgow Coma Scale. In H. E. James, N. G. Anas & R. M. Perkin (Eds), *Brain Insults in Infants and Children: Pathophysiology and Management* (pp. 179–182). Orlando, FL: Grune and Stratton Inc.

Janusz, J. A., Kirkwood, M. W., Yeates, K. O. & Taylor, H. G. (2002). Social problem-solving skills in children with traumatic brain injury: long-term outcomes and prediction of social competence. *Child Neuropsychology, 8*(3), 179–194.

Jennett, B. & Bond, M. (1975). Assessment of outcome after severe brain damage: a practical scale. *Lancet, 1*, 480–484.

Jonsson, C. A., Horneman, G. R. & Emanuelson, I. (2004). Neuropsychological progress during 14 years after severe traumatic brain injury in childhood and adolescence. *Brain Injury, 18*(9), 921–934.

Just, M. A. & Carpenter, P. A. (1992) A capacity theory of comprehension: individual differences in working memory. *Psychological Review, 99*(1), 122–149.

Kennard, M. A. (1936). Age and other factors in motor recovery from precentral lesions in monkeys. *American Journal of Physiology, 115*, 138–146.

Kennedy, M. R., Wozniak, J. R., Muetzel, R. L., Mueller, B. A., Chiou, H. H., Pantekoek, K. & Lim, K. O. (2009). White matter and neurocognitive changes in adults with chronic traumatic brain injury. *Journal of the International Neuropsychological Society, 15*(1), 130–136.

Kirkham, F. J., Newton, C. R. & Whitehouse, W. (2008). Paediatric coma scales. *Developmental Medicine and Child Neurology, 50*(4), 267–274.

Kolb, B., Muhammad, A. & Gibb, R. (2011). Searching for factors underlying cerebral plasticity in the normal and injured brain. *Journal of Communication Disorders, 44*(5), 503–514.

Kolb, B., Mychasiuk, R., Williams, P. & Gibb, R. (2011). Brain plasticity and recovery from early cortical injury. *Developmental Medicine and Child Neurology, 53 Suppl 4*, 4–8.

Konrad, K., Gauggel, S., Manz, A. & Schöll, M. (2000). Inhibitory control in children with traumatic brain injury (TBI) and children with attention deficit/hyperactivity disorder (ADHD). *Brain Injury, 14*(10), 859–875.

Krawczyk, D. C., Hanten, G., Wilde, E. A., Li, X., Schnelle, K. P., Merkley, T. L., Vasquez, A. C., Cook, L. G., McClelland, M., Chapman, S. B. & Levin, H. S. (2010). Deficits in analogical reasoning in adolescents with traumatic brain injury. *Frontiers in Human Neuroscience, 4*, 1–13.

Langlois, J. A. (2000). *Traumatic Brain Injury in the United States: Assessing Outcomes in Children.* Atlanta, GA: National Center for Injury Prevention and Control of the Centers for Disease Control and Prevention.

Levin, H. S., Song, J., Ewing-Cobbs, L., Chapman, S. B. & Mendelsohn, D. (2001). Word fluency in relation to severity of closed head injury, associated frontal brain lesions, and age at injury in children. *Neuropsychologia, 39*(2), 122–131.

Levin, H. S., Hanten, G., Chang, C. C., Zhang, L., Schachar, R., Ewing-Cobbs, L. & Max, J. E. (2002). Working memory after traumatic brain injury in children. *Annals of Neurology, 52*(1), 82–88.

Levin, H. S., Hanten, G., Zhang, L., Swank, P. R., Ewing-Cobbs, L., Dennis, M. *et al.* (2004). Changes in working memory after traumatic brain injury in children. *Neuropsychology, 18*(2), 240–247.

Levin, H. S. & Hanten, G. (2005). Executive functions after traumatic brain injury in children. *Pediatric Neurology, 33*(2), 79–93.

Luciana, M., Conklin, H. M., Hooper, C. J. & Yarger, R. S. (2005). The development of nonverbal working memory and executive control processes in adolescents. *Child Development, 76*(3), 697–712.

Luna, B., Garver, K. E., Urban, T. A., Lazar, N. A. & Sweeney, J. A. (2004). Maturation of cognitive processes from late childhood to adulthood. *Child Development, 75*(5), 1357–1372.

Maccoby, E. (1988). Gender as a social category. *Developmental Psychology, 24*, 755–765.

MacDonald, S. (2013) *Functional Assessment of Verbal Reasoning and Executive Functions: Student Version (S-FAVRES).* Guelph, Ontario: CCD Publishing.

Mandalis, A., Kinsella, G., Ong, B. & Anderson, V. (2007). Working memory and new learning following pediatric traumatic brain injury. *Developmental Neuropsychology, 32*(2), 683–701.

Mangeot, S., Armstrong, K., Colvin, A. N., Yeates, K. O. & Taylor, H. G. (2002). Long-term executive function deficits in children with traumatic brain injuries: assessment using the Behavior Rating Inventory of Executive Function (BRIEF). *Child Neuropsychology, 8*(4), 271–284.

Manly, T., Robertson, I. H., Anderson, V. & Nimmo-Smith, I. (1998). *Test of Everyday Attention for Children (The TEA-CH)*. San Antonio, TX: Pearson.

McCauley, S. R., Wilde, E. A., Anderson, V. A., Bedell, G., Beers, S. R., Campbell, T. F., Chapman, S. B., Ewing-Cobbs, L., Gerring, J. P., Gioia, G. A., Levin, H. S., Michaud, L. J., Prasad, M. R., Swaine, B. R., Turkstra, L. S., Wade, S. L., Yeates, K. O. & Pediatric TBI Outcomes Workgroup (2012). Recommendations for the use of common outcome measures in pediatric traumatic brain injury research. *Journal of Head Trauma Rehabilitation, 29*(4), 678–705.

Miyake, A., Friedman, N. P., Emerson, M. J., Witzki, A. H., Howerter, A. & Wager, T. D. (2000). The unity and diversity of executive functions and their contributions to complex 'Frontal Lobe' tasks: a latent variable analysis. *Cognitive Psychology, 41*(1), 49–100.

Moran, C. & Gillon, G. (2004). Language and memory profiles of adolescents with traumatic brain injury. *Brain Injury, 18*(3), 273–288.

——(2005). Inference comprehension of adolescents with traumatic brain injury: a working memory hypothesis. *Brain Injury, 19*(10), 743–751.

Moran, C. A., Nippold, M. A. & Gillon, G. T. (2006). Working memory and proverb comprehension in adolescents with traumatic brain injury: a preliminary investigation. *Brain Injury, 20*(4), 417–423.

Muscara, F., Catroppa, C., Eren, S. & Anderson, V. (2009). The impact of injury severity on long-term social outcome following paediatric traumatic brain injury. *Neuropsychological Rehabilitation, 19*(4), 541–561.

Pettit, G. S., Dodge, K. A. & Brown, M. M. (1988). Early family experience, social problem solving patterns, and children's social competence. *Child Development, 59*(1), 107–120.

Proctor, A., Wilson, B., Sanchez, C. & Wesley, E. (2000). Executive function and verbal working memory in adolescents with closed head injury (CHI). *Brain Injury, 14*(7), 633–647.

Raffaelli, M. & Duckett, E. (1989). 'We were just talking ...': conversations in early adolescence. *Journal of Youth and Adolescence, 18*(6), 567–582.

Reilly, P. L., Simpson, D. A., Sprod, R. & Thomas, L. (1988). Assessing the conscious level in infants and young children: a paediatric version of the Glasgow Coma Scale. *Childs Nervous System, 4*, 30–33.

Rousseaux, M., Verigneaux, C. & Kozlowski, O. (2010). An analysis of communication in conversation after severe traumatic brain injury. *European Journal of Neurology, 17*(7), 922–929.

Russell, W. R. & Smith, A. (1961). Post-traumatic amnesia in closed head injury. *Archives of Neurology, 5*, 4–17.

Scherf, K. S., Sweeney, J. A. & Luna, B. (2006). Brain basis of developmental change in visuospatial working memory. *Journal of Cognitive Neuroscience, 18*(7), 1045–1058.

Schmidt, A. T., Hanten, G. R., Li, X., Orsten, K. D. & Levin, H. S. (2010). Emotion recognition following pediatric traumatic brain injury: longitudinal analysis of emotional prosody and facial emotion recognition. *Neuropsychologia, 48*(10), 2869–2877.

Schmithorst, V. J. & Yuan, W. (2010). White matter development during adolescence as shown by diffusion MRI. *Brain and Cognition, 72*(1), 16–25.

Semel, E., Wiig, E. H. & Secord, W. A. (1995). *Clinical Evaluation of Language Fundamentals* (Third edn). San Antonio, TX: The Psychological Corporation.

———(2003). *Clinical Evaluation of Language Fundamentals* (Fourth edn). San Antonio, TX: The Psychological Corporation.

Shum, D., Jamieson, E., Bahr, M. & Wallace, G. (1999). Implicit and explicit memory in children with traumatic brain injury. *Journal of Clinical and Experimental Neuropsychology, 21*(2), 149–158.

Slomine, B. S., Gerring, J. P., Grados, M. A., Vasa, R., Brady, K. D., Christensen, J. R. & Denckla, M. B. (2002). Performance on measures of 'executive function' following pediatric traumatic brain injury. *Brain Injury, 16*(9), 759–722.

Sohlberg, M. M. & Turkstra, L. S. (2011). *Optimizing Instructional Methods for Effective Cognitive Rehabilitation*. New York: Guilford Publications, Inc.

Sowell, E. R., Thompson, P. M., Tessner, K. D. & Toga, A. W. (2001). Mapping continued brain growth and gray matter density reduction in dorsal frontal cortex: inverse relationships during postadolescent brain maturation. *The Journal of Neuroscience, 21*(22), 8819–8829.

Steinberg, L. (2008). A social neuroscience perspective on adolescent risk-taking. *Developmental Review, 28*(1), 78–106.

Stronach, S. T. & Turkstra, L. S. (2008). Theory of mind and use of cognitive state terms by adolescents with traumatic brain injury. *Aphasiology, 22*(10), 1054–1070.

Subrahmanyam, K., Smahel, D. & Greenfield, P. (2006). Connecting developmental constructions to the internet: identity presentation and sexual exploration in online teen chat rooms. *Developmental Psychology, 42*(3), 395–406.

Suskauer, S. J., Slomine, B. S., Inscore, A. B., Lewelt, A. J., Kirk, J. W. & Salorio, C. F. (2009). Injury severity variables as predictors of WeeFIM scores in pediatric TBI: time to follow commands is best. *Journal of Pediatric Rehabilitation Medicine, 2*(4), 297–307.

Taylor, H. G., Yeates, K. O., Wade, S. L., Drotar, D., Klein, S. K. & Stancin, T. (1999). Influences on first-year recovery from traumatic brain injury in children. *Neuropsychology, 13*(1), 76–89.

Tonks, J., Williams, W. H., Frampton, I., Yates, P. & Slater, A. (2007). Reading emotions after child brain injury: a comparison between children with brain injury and non-injured controls. *Brain Injury, 21*(7), 731–739.

Towne, R. L. & Entwisle, L. M. (1993). Metaphoric comprehension in adolescents with traumatic brain injury and in adolescents with language learning disability. *Language, Speech and Hearing Services in Schools, 24*, 100–107.

Turkstra, L. S. (1999). Language testing in adolescents with brain injury: a consideration of the CELF-3. *Language, Speech, and Hearing Services in Schools, 30*, 132–140.

———(2000). Should my shirt be tucked in or left out? The communication context of adolescence. *Aphasiology, 14*(4), 349–364.

———(2008). Conversation-based assessment of social cognition in adults with traumatic brain injury. *Brain Injury, 22*(5), 397–409.

———(2005). Looking while listening and speaking: eye-to-face gaze in adolescents with and without traumatic brain injury. *Journal of Speech, Language and Hearing Research, 48*(6), 1429–1441.

Turkstra, L. S., McDonald, S. & Kaufmann, P. M. (1996). Assessment of pragmatic communication skills in adolescents after traumatic brain injury. *Brain Injury, 10*(5), 329–345.

Turkstra, L. S. & Holland, A. L. (1998). Assessment of syntax after adolescent brain injury: Effects of memory on test performance. *Journal of Speech, Language and Hearing Research, 41*(1), 137–149.

Turkstra, L. S., McDonald, S. & DePompei, R. (2001). Social information processing in adolescents: data from normally developing adolescents and preliminary data from their peers with traumatic brain injury. *Journal of Head Trauma Rehabilitation, 16*(5), 469–483.

Turkstra, L. S., Dixon, T. M. & Baker, K. K. (2004). Theory of Mind and social beliefs in adolescents with traumatic brain injury. *NeuroRehabilitation, 19*(3), 245–256.

Turkstra, L., Ylvisaker, M., Coehlo, C., Kennedy, M., Sohlberg, M. M. & Avery, J. (2005). Practice guidelines for standardized assessment for persons with traumatic brain injury. *Journal of Medical Speech-Language Pathology, 13*(2), ix–xxviii.

Turkstra, L. S., Brehm, S. E. & Montgomery, E. B. J. (2006). Analysing conversational discourse after traumatic brain injury: isn't it about time? *Brain Impairment, 7*(3), 234–245.

Turkstra, L. S., Williams, W. H., Tonks, J. & Frampton, I. (2008). Measuring social cognition in adolescents: implications for students with TBI returning to school. *NeuroRehabilitation, 23*, 1–9.

Van Leer, E. & Turkstra, L. (1999). The effect of elicitation task on discourse coherence and cohesion in adolescents with brain injury. *Journal of Communication Disorders, 32*(5), 327–349.

Ward, H., Shum, D., Wallace, G. & Boon, J. (2002). Pediatric traumatic brain injury and procedural memory. *Journal of Clinical and Experimental Neuropsychology, 24*(4), 458–470.

Wertheimer, J. C., Roebuck-Spencer, T. M., Constantinidou, F., Turkstra, L., Pavol, M. & Paul, D. (2008). Collaboration between neuropsychologists and speech-language pathologists in rehabilitation settings. *Journal of Head Trauma Rehabilitation, 23*(5), 273–285.

Wiig, E. & Secord, W. (1989). *Test of Language Competence* (Expanded edn). San Antonio, TX: Psychological Corporation.

Wilson, B. M. & Proctor, A. (2002). Written discourse of adolescents with closed head injury. *Brain Injury, 16*(11), 1011–1024.

Wilson, K. R., Donders, J. & Nguyen, L. (2011). Self and parent ratings of executive functioning after adolescent traumatic brain injury. *Rehabilitation Psychology, 56*(2), 100–106.

World Health Organization (2001). *International Classification of Functioning, Disability and Health* (Report). Geneva: Switzerland.

Yeates, K. O. & Enrile, B. G. (2005). Implicit and explicit memory in children with congenital and acquired brain disorder. *Neuropsychology, 19*(5), 618–628.

Yeates, K. O., Schultz, L. H. & Selman, R. L. (1991). The development of interpersonal negotiation strategies in thought and action: a social-cognitive link to behavioral adjustment and social status. *Merrill-Palmer Quarterly, 37*(3), 369–405.

Yeates, K. O., Blumenstein, E., Patterson, C. M. & Delis, D. C. (1995). Verbal learning and memory following pediatric closed-head injury. *Journal of the International Neuropsychological Society, 1*, 78–87.

Yeates, K. O., Armstrong, K., Janusz, J., Taylor, H. G., Wade, S., Stancin, T. & Drotar, D. (2005). Long-term attention problems in children with traumatic brain injury. *Journal of the American Academy of Child and Adolescent Psychiatry, 44*(6), 574–584.

Yeates, K. O., Bigler, E. D., Dennis, M., Gerhardt, C. A., Rubin, K. H., Stancin, T., Taylor, H. G. & Vannatta, K. (2007). Social outcomes in childhood brain disorder: a heuristic integration of social neuroscience and developmental psychology. *Psychological Bulletin, 133*(3), 535–556.

Yeates, K. O., Taylor, H. G., Walz, N. C., Stancin, T. & Wade, S. L. (2010). The family environment as a moderator of psychosocial outcomes following traumatic brain injury in young children. *Neuropsychology, 24(3)*, 345–356.

Ylvisaker, M. & Feeney, T. J. (1998). *Collaborative Brain Injury Intervention: Positive Everyday Routines*. San Diego, CA: Singular Publishing Group, Inc.

Zimmer-Gembeck, M. J. & Collins, W. A. (2003). Autonomy development during adolescence. In G. R. Adams & M. Berzonsky (Eds), *Handbook of Adolescent Development* (pp. 175–204). London: Blackwell.

Ziviani, J., Ottenbacher, K. J., Shephard, K., Foreman, S., Astbury, W. & Ireland, P. (2001). Concurrent validity of the Functional Independence Measure for Children (WeeFIM) and the Pediatric Evaluation of Disabilities Inventory in children with developmental disabilities and acquired brain injuries. *Physical & Occupational Therapy in Pediatrics, 21*(2–3), 91–101.

8 Dysarthria in children and adults with TBI

Angela Morgan

Introduction

Dysarthria has been defined as 'a collective name for a group of related speech disorders that are due to disturbances in muscular control of the speech mechanisms resulting from impairment of any of the basic motor processes involved in the execution of speech' (Darley *et al.*, 1975, p. 2). According to this definition, the term 'dysarthria' is restricted to those speech disorders which have a neurogenic origin (i.e. those speech disorders that result from damage to the central or peripheral nervous system), and does not include those speech disorders associated with either somatic structural defects (e.g. cleft palate, malocclusion, etc.) or psychological disorders (e.g. psychogenic aphonia).

Dysarthria constitutes one of the most persistent sequelae of traumatic brain injury (TBI), often remaining beyond the resolution of any concomitant language disorder (Najenson *et al.*, 1978; Sarno and Levin, 1985). Despite this recognition, the literature relating to the prevalence of post-TBI dysarthria is unclear. Estimates of the prevalence of dysarthria following TBI in adults have been found to vary from 6–53 per cent, see Table 8.1. The wide range of reported prevalence is due to methodological issues of study design such as the speech assessment measures used, the stage post-injury when the measures were taken, the way the population was sampled and the injury severity of the population studied. Similar methodological issues plague the literature on childhood dysarthria prevalence after TBI, again resulting in a wide range of reported prevalence figures dependent upon study design, i.e. 4.5 to 47 per cent (Table 8.1).

Similarly to the lack of clarity around prevalence figures, data on the natural course and recovery versus persistence of dysarthria associated with TBI sustained in childhood or adulthood is also unclear. Yet there is sufficient evidence to suggest the chronic nature of dysarthria that may persist for as long as 5 to 15 years following the initial injury (Table 8.1). Olver *et al.* (1996) reported that motor speech problems were evident in 34 per cent of their 103 participants with severe TBI at 5 years post-injury. In a follow-up study of 40 severe TBI cases, Thomsen (1984) reported that all 15 subjects who exhibited dysarthria in the acute stage (approximately 4 months post-injury) continued to demonstrate

Table 8.1 Reported prevalence of dysarthria associated with traumatic brain injury in children and adults

Author	Age range (years)	Study design	Time post-injury (years)	Severity of TBI	% with dysarthria
Boyer & Edwards, 1991	6 months–21 yrs	Prospective	1	Severe	17 (31/178)^
Brink et al., 1970	2–18	Prospective	1–7	Severe	43 (20/46)*
Costeff et al., 1990	3–15	Prospective	5–11	Severe	47 (14/30)
Dresser et al., 1973	22.7 (average)	NA	15	NA	25 (217/864)
Groher, 1977	31.1 (average)	Prospective	Approximately 2–3 weeks	NA	93 (13/14) (initial examination) 50 (7/14) (4 months)
Morgan et al., 2010	3–17	Retrospective	Acute inpatient phase (<4 months)	Severe Moderate Mild	20 (17/83) 4.5 (1/23) 4.5 (2/44)
Najenson et al., 1978	19–61	Prospective	1 month–2 years	Severe	60 (9/15)
Olver et al., 1996	11–69	Prospective	5	Mild–severe	34 (35/103)#
Rusk et al., 1969	13–79	NA	5–15	Severe	52 (15/29)
Safaz et al., 2008	6–70	Retrospective	0–3 months, 4–12 months, >1 yr	Moderate, Severe	19 (9/47) (0–3 months) 38 (13/34) (4–12 months) 37 (13/35) (>1 yr) 30 (35/116) (overall)
Thomsen, 1984	15–44	Prospective	4.5 months, 2.5 years, 10–15 years	Severe	38 (15/40) (for all three examination periods)
Toyoshima et al., 2011	16–36	Prospective	11–40 months	Severe	6 (8/140)#
Sarno et al., 1986	14–78	Prospective	45 weeks (average)	Severe	34 (43/125)

^A further 5 had "other voice disorder" and 24 were non-speaking (i.e. anarthria or apraxia); *Used term 'articulation defects'; #Motor speech disorder diagnosis noted without distinction between dysarthria or apraxia; NA: data missing or not clear in original text.

dysarthria 10–15 years later. Rusk *et al.* (1969) noted that of their original 29 TBI subjects diagnosed as dysarthric, half of those subjects remained unimproved 5–15 years later. In terms of the persistence of dysarthria after injury sustained in childhood, two separate long-term follow-up studies of children who had suffered severe TBI indicated that 10 per cent of children and 8 per cent of adolescents were unintelligible (Ylvisaker, 1986). Such findings suggest that the prognosis for complete resolution of the dysarthric speech disturbance in individuals with severe TBI is poor. Despite the often persistent and resilient nature of dysarthria post-TBI, however, the findings of several studies suggest that restoration of functional verbal communication is possible in TBI cases many years post-injury, and certainly long after the accepted period of 'neurological recovery' has passed (Beukelman & Garrett, 1988; Workinger & Netsell, 1992).

The presence of a persistent dysarthria has important implications for the long-term quality of life of survivors of severe TBI. As pointed out by Beukelman and Yorkston (1991), the presence of such a disorder reduces the individual's ability to function in communication situations that require understandable, efficient and natural sounding speech (e.g. public speaking, vocational positions that require independent interaction with the public, etc.). In its most severe form, the dysarthria may necessitate the use of alternative and/or augmentative communication systems to bypass the impaired speech production apparatus. Put simply, the presence of a dysarthria may impede the successful return of the affected TBI patient to study, work or general social activities, leading to loss of vocational standing and social isolation.

A diverse range of dysarthric subtypes has been observed in individuals subsequent to TBI (Theodoros *et al.*, 2001) and within these subtypes reported levels of motor speech dysfunction have been reported to vary from mild articulatory imprecision, to non-functional speech intelligibility (Sarno *et al.*, 1986). The precise nature of the dysarthria that manifests as a consequence of TBI is governed by the location and scope of neural damage endured (Theodoros *et al.*, 2001). The inherently diffuse nature of TBI, however, typically accommodates potential disruption at exponential loci along the neural axis, implicating upper as well as lower motor neuron systems. Indeed, classifications of spastic (Groher, 1977), hyperkinetic/hypokinetic (Kent *et al.*, 1975; Lehiste, 1965), flaccid (Netsell & Daniel, 1979; von Cramon, 1981), ataxic (Simmons, 1983; Yorkston & Beukelman, 1981; Yorkston *et al.*, 1984) and mixed (Groher, 1977; Theodoros *et al.*, 1994) dysarthria have been reported within TBI literature (Marquardt *et al.*, 1990), however, spastic (Marquardt *et al.*, 1990) and more recently mixed (i.e. spastic-ataxic) (Theodoros *et al.*, 1994) subtypes have been highlighted as the most prevalent motor speech disturbances in this population. This motor speech profile is consistent with diffuse bilateral hemispheric damage following TBI, potentially implicating terminal loci of the neural fulcrum, such as the frontal lobes (Langfitt *et al.*, 1986; Netsell & Lefkowitz, 1992; Wilson *et al.*, 1992) and cerebellum, as the neuropathological substrates of the dysarthria of TBI.

The aforementioned neuroanatomical classification of dysarthric subtypes based on the Mayo Clinic classification system largely relates to motor speech anomalies acquired in adulthood or at neurodevelopmentally stable life stages. Historically, this taxonomy has been adopted as a frame of reference to classify dysarthria resulting from TBI in childhood, however, not without recognized limitations (Cahill *et al.*, 2001; Morgan & Liégeois, 2010; Murdoch & Hudson-Tennent, 1994). Previously, it has been assumed that the physiologic impairment underlying dysarthria in children is the same as in adults and consequently the adult classification of dysarthria correlating with the pathophysiology of the motor systems has usually been applied to describe childhood dysarthria. More recently, it has been suggested that acquired dysarthria occurring in children requires its own classification system (Morgan & Liégeois, 2010; Murdoch, 2011), given that there are a number of reasons why the physiologic manifestation of dysarthria in children with TBI may differ from that in adults with TBI. Indeed, TBI in childhood has been documented to recover more rapidly than that endured in adulthood, as a consequence of distinctive neuroplasticity mechanisms. Furthermore, children have been reported to predominantly endure brain injuries as a result of low speed motor vehicle accidents or falls, in opposition to adolescents and adults, commonly involved in high-speed collisions (Morgan & Liégeois, 2010; Murdoch, 2011). These factors suggest that the mechanisms of child versus adult TBI may be incongruent, with greater rotational acceleration effects and consequently more diffuse brain damage expected in adult populations (Cahill *et al.*, 2001; Morgan & Liégeois, 2010).

Neural bases of dysarthria associated with TBI

In peacetime, dysarthria is most commonly associated with non-penetrating or closed head injury. Consequently, the proceeding discussion of the neural bases of dysarthria will focus on the neuropathophysiology of TBI associated with closed rather than open (penetrating) head injury. The neuropathophysiology of TBI is complex, encompassing a heterogeneous group of intracranial injuries that result from both primary physical trauma incurred at the time of impact as well as deleterious cascade of secondary biochemical/physiological perturbations often combining both diffuse and focal brain damage.

Primary neuropathophysiological effects of TBI

Diffuse cerebral injury, in the form of widespread damage to the axons in the white matter of the brain, produced at the moment of impact is widely considered to be the primary mechanism of brain damage in individuals with closed head injury, and a more important factor in determining outcome than the presence of focal lesions. This pathological state, referred to as diffuse axonal injury (DAI), is caused at the time of impact by rotational acceleration which occurs when the head receives a force which does not pass through its centre of gravity. This results in the head assuming an angular acceleration and rotating around its own centre of gravity resulting in a twisting motion between the brain and the skull causing shear-strain or distortion of the brain tissue. Such distortion of the brain tissue results in the permanent stretching or rupturing of neuronal fibres that interconnect different brain regions, including potentially the descending motor pathways involved in regulation of the speech production muscles. DAI was first described by Strich (1956) who concluded the severe neurological deficit subsequent to TBI is primarily the result of axonal damage produced by mechanical forces shearing the fibres at the moment of impact. DAI is now recognized as one of the most important causes of neurological dysfunction post-TBI and most likely represents the major factor underlying the occurrence of dysarthria in people with TBI.

A number of different areas of the brain have been reported to be commonly affected by DAI subsequent to traumatic head injury, including the subcortical white matter of the cerebral hemispheres, the upper brainstem, the superior cerebellar peduncles and the basal ganglia, all of which have been identified as sites where lesions could potentially lead to the variety of dysarthria reported in TBI. In their review of the neural bases of motor speech impairment in childhood, Liégeois and Morgan (2012) similarly found that children with dysarthria after TBI had typically diffuse and bilateral white matter injuries of the cerebral hemispheres and the internal capsule as well as damage to the corpus callosum. The interface between the grey and white matter is also commonly involved after TBI due to shearing between the different tissue types. Magnetic resonance imaging has also identified DAI in the brainstem, hippocampus, corpus callosum and at interfaces between the brain and dura mater (Guthrie *et al.*, 1999).

The concept proposed by Strich (1956) that DAI is an immediate effect of a closed head injury has often been challenged. Although agreeing that one aetiological factor of DAI is mechanical damage to the nerve fibres, several authors have suggested that vascular, oedematous and anoxic damage to the cerebral cortex and basal ganglia may also play a significant role in the pathogenesis of white matter changes (Bramlett & Dietrich, 2004; Letarte, 1999). According to the latter authors, the majority of axons that will eventually suffer damage remain in continuity immediately after injury, and that it is not until around six hours post-injury that the neurofilaments are destroyed and axotomy occurs. This proposal differs to the immediate, irreversible mechanism described by many earlier researchers and implies that the deterioration in patients post-injury may be due to this progressive secondary injury and raises the possibility of developing medical strategies to intervene in this progressive degeneration of axons. (Mechanisms of secondary injury that may contribute to dysarthria are discussed further below.)

In addition to DAI, symptoms of dysarthria may also develop as a consequence of primary focal lesions. For example, a linear impact on the skull may result in transient distortion and inbending of the bone near the point of impact causing compression of adjacent brain tissue and bruising of the brain in an area directly below the area of impact. Such contusions which occur at the point of impact are termed 'coup' contusions. In addition to causing lesions at this site, the impact may cause the brain to strike the skull at a point opposite to the point of trauma, thereby resulting in additional vascular disruption and bruising at this latter site. Contusions of the latter type are termed 'contre-coup' contusions. Both coup and contre-coup lesions may cause specific and localizable behavioural alterations that accompany closed head injury. The symptoms produced by a brain contusion depend on the size and location of the contusion, and may include speech, language and swallowing disorders.

A severe closed head injury can cause dysfunction of a variety of cranial nerves, either by damaging the cranial nerve nuclei in the brainstem or disrupting the nerves themselves in either their intracranial or extracranial course. Contusions of the brainstem can damage the cranial nerve nuclei leading to flaccid paralysis of the muscles innervated by the affected nerves. In particular, should these affected muscles include the muscles supplied by cranial nerves V, VII, X or XII, speech disorders in the form of flaccid dysarthria may result. The most common cause of damage to the cranial nerves in their intracranial course is fracture of the base of the skull. The facial nerve (VII) is most commonly affected by this condition leading to flaccid paralysis of the muscles of facial expression. Branches of the facial (VII) and trigeminal (V) nerves may be damaged extracranially by trauma to the face. In general traumatic cranial nerve palsies are permanent, the exceptions being those resulting from contusions of extracranial branches of the nerves.

Secondary neuropathophysiological effects of TBI

Secondary neuropathological changes in the brain that may be associated with the occurrence of dysarthria post-TBI include cerebral oedema, intracranial haemorrhage, ischaemic brain damage, pathological changes associated with increased intracranial pressure (ICP), cerebral atrophy and ventricular enlargement. Cerebral oedema, involving an increase in brain volume due to an accumulation of excess water in the brain tissue, is the most common secondary effect of TBI. Oedema resulting from TBI is most commonly vasogenic and results from an increase in the permeability of brain capillaries which allows water and other solutes to exude out into the extracellular spaces within the brain tissue. Various neuropathological changes may occur as a result of sustained cerebral oedema, including stretching and tearing of axonal fibres, compression of brain tissue resulting in cell loss, compression of blood vessels with subsequent infarction of brain tissue, and herniation of the brain.

Elevated ICP is also a common finding after closed head injury, most frequently due to the development of extradural, subdural or intracerebral haematomas or generalized cerebral oedema. Uncontrolled increases in ICP may cause herniation (e.g. transtentorial herniation) and can also impede cerebral blood flow resulting in ischaemic brain damage. Ischaemic brain damage subsequent to TBI ranges from focal necrosis to wide areas of infarction. Cortical atrophy is also a frequent sequelae of TBI and reportedly most frequently involves the frontal and temporal lobes.

Clinical features of dysarthria associated with TBI

Clinical features of dysarthria are heterogeneously expressed across the TBI population, consistent with the profile of diffuse and variable brain injury outlined in the previous section. Perceptually detected impairments may be seen across any or all aspects of speech production including prosody, resonance, phonation and articulation. With moves towards a need for more objective approaches to assessment, there has also been a growing body of literature using instrumental techniques to pinpoint the underlying physiological bases of perceptually observed symptoms of dysarthria. Here we provide the reader with an overview of the key perceptual symptoms and physiologically based deficits associated with dysarthria after TBI, with a view to informing our clinical observation, assessment and treatment goal planning for this patient population.

Perceptually detected clinical impairments of dysarthria after TBI

Only a handful of studies have provided detailed reports on perceptually measured clinical features of dysarthria in children (e.g. Cahill *et al.*, 2002; Morgan *et al.*, 2007; Theodoros *et al.*, 1998; Vitorino, 2009) and adults (e.g. Jaeger *et al.*, 2000; Pilon *et al.*, 1998; Vitorino, 2009; Ziegler *et al.*, 1988), see Table 8.2 for examples of key studies in this field. Findings are similar across the lifespan with the majority of participants within these studies presenting with deficits across the speech sub-domains of respiration, phonation, articulation, resonance and prosody. A common respiratory issue is reduced or altered breath support for speech (Cahill *et al.*, 2002; Morgan *et al.*, 2010; Theodoros *et al.*, 1998), having obvious impacts on the ability to generate a sufficient pressurized air stream for achieving phonation and hence speech production. Deficits in phonation are commonly characterized as glottal fry (Cahill *et al.*, 2002; Theodoros *et al.*, 1998; Vitorino, 2009) or harsh, hoarse or breathy vocal quality (Morgan *et al.*, 2010; Ziegler *et al.*, 1988). Prosodic deficits are frequently manifest as disruptions in pitch and loudness variation, reduced stress, reduced length of phrases and alterations in speech rate, with a slower rate of speech most commonly perceived (Cahill *et al.*, 2002; Morgan *et al.*, 2010; Pilon *et al.*, 1998; Theodoros *et al.*, 1998). Hypernasality is the most common disturbance of resonance reported across both child (Cahill *et al.*, 2002; Morgan *et al.*, 2010; Theodoros *et al.*, 1998) and adult populations (e.g. Jaeger *et al.*, 2000; Pilon *et al.*, 1998). Articulatory deficits are also frequently reported, with an overall perception of imprecision or lack of distinction of consonants and vowels (Cahill *et al.*, 2002; Jaeger *et al.*, 2000; Morgan *et al.*, 2010; Pilon *et al.*, 1998; Theodoros *et al.*, 1998; Ziegler *et al.*, 1988) and some reports of perceived increased length of phonemes (Cahill *et al.*, 2002; Jaeger *et al.*, 2000; Theodoros *et al.*, 1998).

Until recently, the clinical features of dysarthria resulting from TBI in childhood have been relatively unexplored (Morgan & Liégeois , 2010; Murdoch, 2011). Contemporary research, however, has revealed similar dysarthric profiles in children as compared to adults following TBI (Cahill *et al.*, 2001; van Mourik

Table 8.2 Perceptually detected clinical features of dysarthria associated with traumatic brain injury in children and adults

Authors	Age range (years)	No. participants	Injury severity	Time post-injury	Speech domain	Perceptual speech deficit
Cahill et al., 2002	5–18 yrs	16	Moderate–severe	6 months	Respiration	Reduced breath support for speech
					Phonation	Glottal fry
					Articulation	Imprecise consonants; imprecise vowels; increased length of phonemes
					Resonance	Hypernasality
					Prosody	Reduced rate of speech; decreased pitch variation; impaired general stress pattern; impaired phrase length; impaired variation of loudness
Jaeger et al., 2000	21–58 yrs	10	Severe	NA	Articulation	Imprecise consonants; imprecise vowels; increased length of vowels
					Resonance	Hypernasality
					Prosody	Mild slowness of articulator mobility
Morgan et al., 2010	3–17 yrs	22	Mild–severe	Acute inpatient period	Respiration	Reduced breath support for speech
					Phonation	Hoarse, harsh or breathy voice
					Articulation	Imprecise consonants
					Resonance	Hypernasality
					Prosody	Decreased pitch variation, impaired variation of loudness
Pilon et al., 1998	23–44 yrs	3	NA	12–24 months	Articulation	Imprecise articulation; irregular breakdowns; laboured
					Resonance	Hypernasality; distorted
					Prosody	Reduced rate of speech; decreased pitch variation; impaired general stress pattern; impaired variation of loudness

Table 8.2 continued

Authors	Age range (years)	No. participants	Injury severity	Time post-injury	Speech domain	Perceptual speech deficit
Theodoros et al., 1998	14 yrs	1	Severe	12 months	Respiration	Reduced breath support for speech
					Phonation	Glottal fry
					Articulation	Imprecise consonants; imprecise vowels; increased length of phonemes
					Resonance	Hypernasality
					Prosody	Reduced rate of speech; decreased pitch variation; impaired general stress pattern; impaired phrase length; impaired variation of loudness
Vitorino, 2009	8–16 yrs	15	Moderate–severe	6 months–6 years	Phonation	Glottal fry; harsh voice
	21–55 yrs	15	Moderate–severe	1–12 yrs	Phonation	Glottal fry; wetness; strained-strangled; harsh voice
Ziegler et al., 1988	18–35 yrs	6	NA	5 months–14 years	Respiration	Shortened expirations, increased inspiration frequency
					Phonation	Reduced volume; rough; breathy; tense; reduced intensity
					Articulation	Loss of vowel-consonant distinction Imprecise consonants and vowels)
					Prosody	Increased rate of speech

NA: data missing or unclear in original article.

et al., 1997; Morgan & Liégeois, 2010). Despite these clinical parallels, future research investigating the nature of interactions between developmental and acquired factors is considered critical to the better elucidation of mechanisms underpinning dysarthrias contracted in childhood (Murdoch & Hudson-Tennent, 1994). In particular, resultant motor speech impairments may represent a maturation-sensitive consequence of head injury, within the context of developmental neurological systems. As such, longitudinal monitoring of motor speech abilities in children with TBI is considered pivotal to the prompt identification and remediation of speech deficits that may potentially manifest at any point during the course of motor development.

Overall however, whilst there is some diversity of clinical symptom presentation across individual participants and potentially across the lifespan dependent upon age at injury, it is clear to see a cluster of similar clinical patterns here. Specifically, as for most populations with dysarthria, there is a reduction in the respiratory-phonatory support for speech and further impairments 'up stream' in relation to finer aspects of speech motor control at the level of the velopharynx and articulators. An understanding of the clinical perceptual presentation of dysarthria after TBI is clearly critical to help inform assessment goals and the identification of treatment targets during evaluation of patients. It is also necessary to have an understanding of how these perceptually detected symptoms are correlated with underlying physiological deficits. In order to have a greater understanding of physiological disruption, it is arguably necessary to look to more objective measurement of the speech sub-systems, i.e. to take an instrumental approach (see section on Perceptual Assessment of dysarthria later in this chapter for further discussion of the benefits and limitations of a perceptual approach). The following section provides a discussion of key findings from the instrumental literature in this field.

Instrumentally detected clinical impairments of dysarthria after TBI

A detailed description of instrumental or physiological approaches to assessment is outlined in the following section. Here we focus on some of the key instrumental findings on physiological deficits associated with dysarthria after TBI with respect to each of the speech sub-systems. Arguably because of the wider variety of techniques available, the majority of instrumental studies in this field have been conducted in the area of articulation, with approaches of electromagnetic articulography (EMA) (Bartle *et al.*, 2006; Goozée *et al.*, 2000; Kuruvilla *et al.*, 2007), electropalatography (EPG) (Kuruvilla *et al.*, 2008), lip and tongue miniature pressure transducers (Barlow & Burton, 1990; Goozée *et al.*, 2001; Goozée *et al.*, 2002; Theodoros *et al.*, 1995; Theodoros *et al.*, 1998), and acoustic analyses (e.g. Ziegler & von Cramon, 1983a, 1983b). Key findings across the articulatory sub-system have been that participants with TBI show difficulty with spatial and temporal articulatory control, with common findings of 'over' or 'under'-shooting of lip and tongue placement and difficulty with tongue–jaw co-ordination for the production of sound targets. These physiological findings are thought to have a perceptual correlate of articulatory imprecision. Articulatory-prosodic studies using acoustic analyses have revealed reduced speech rates that are also in line with the perceptually derived symptoms of slower speech rates in children and adults with TBI, as discussed in the previous section. Significant reductions in lip and tongue strength, endurance and rate of repetitive movements have also been reported based on lip and tongue transduction systems, but the correlation between these physiological oral-motor function limitations and speech function or intelligibility has been variably reported across studies.

Respiratory function has been evaluated using spirometric and kinematic techniques to demonstrate that adults with dysarthria following severe TBI typically demonstrate reduced vital capacities, lower expiratory volumes and impaired co-ordination of the rib-cage and abdomen during speech tasks (Murdoch *et al.*, 1993). These physiological findings are thought to correlate with the perceptual symptoms of reduced breath support for speech and incoordination of breath support for phonation.

A final area of physiological or instrumental focus has been the use of computerized accelerometry techniques to measure velopharyngeal function and oral/nasal resonance (e.g. McHenry *et al.*, 1998; Theodoros *et al.*, 1998). Reduced velopharyngeal resistance or dysfunction has been reported in this group and is thought to have a perceptual correlate of hypernasality. For example, McHenry and colleagues (1998) found that approximately 50 per cent of a selected sample of n = 83 adult participants with severe TBI had reduced velopharyngeal airway resistance and that the severity of this deficit was clearly associated with perceived hypernasality. They also noted that velopharyngeal deficits were much less likely in cases with absent or mild dysarthria.

Assessment of dysarthria in TBI

Techniques available for assessing dysarthric speech for the purposes of differential diagnosis and determination of treatment priorities can be broadly divided into four major categories. These include: perceptual techniques – these assessments are based on the clinician's impression of the auditory-perceptual attributes of the speech; acoustic techniques – assessments in this category are based on the study of generation, transmission and modification of sound waves emitted from the vocal tract; physiological techniques – these methods are based on instrumental assessment of the functioning of the various sub-systems of the speech production apparatus in terms of their movements, muscular contractions, biomechanical activities and so on; neuradiological/brain stimulation techniques – assessments in this category include methods based on magnetic resonance imaging (MRI) and brain stimulation methods such as transcranial magnetic stimulation (TMS). The reader is also referred to 'Considering the impact of dysarthria on activity, participation and quality of life' in the treatment section for a newly emerging assessment approach, focused around the evaluation of conversational interaction. It is beyond the scope of this chapter to provide a comprehensive description of this technique because it is early in its development and has not yet been applied to the evaluation of individuals with TBI, but further detail and readings in this area are provided later in the treatment section.

Conventionally, perceptual speech analysis has provided the mainstay of dysarthria assessment. Despite offering qualitative insights into the audible deviations apparent in dysarthric speech, these methods proffer little with respect to empirically identifying the neuromuscular locus or neurophysiological basis of the presenting deficits. Recently, advancements in technology have catalysed the development of more objective motor speech assessment tools, affording the compilation of quantitative acoustic and physiological profiles by way of state-of-the-art instrumentation. Notwithstanding the value of the data generated via instrumental assessments, speech is by its very nature an audible entity, its 'normalcy' considered by some to be most efficiently judged by the human ear. To this end, perceptual and instrumental techniques combined have been recommended as the most effective means of evaluating motor speech dysfunction (Cahill *et al.*, 2001), taking into consideration relevant pathophysiological substrates as well as deviant perceptual features impacting upon functional communication proficiency. The proceeding summary of assessment methods utilized in the evaluation of dysarthria is largely applicable to both adult and paediatric populations. Recommendations have been made, however, with respect to the screening of developmental articulatory/phonological processes in children.

Perceptual assessment

In past years, perceptual analysis of dysarthric speech has been the 'gold standard' and preferred method by which clinicians made differential diagnosis and defined treatment programmes for their dysarthric clients. In fact, many clinicians have relied almost exclusively on auditory-perceptual judgements of speech intelligibility, articulatory accuracy or subjective ratings of various speech dimensions on which to base their diagnosis of dysarthric speech and plan their intervention. Darley *et al.* (1969a, 1969b, 1975) pioneered the use of auditory-perceptual assessments to characterize deviant speech features that are found to be associated with a specific overall type of dysarthria. As indicated earlier, it was from the findings of their auditory-perceptual studies of dysarthria that the system of classification of dysarthria most frequently used in clinical settings and discussed throughout the present chapter was developed. Darley *et al.* (1969a, 1969b) assessed speech samples taken from 212 dysarthric speakers with a variety of neurological conditions on 38 speech dimensions which fell into seven categories: pitch, loudness, voice quality (including both laryngeal and resonatory dysfunction), respiration, prosody, articulation and two summary dimensions relating to intelligibility and bizarreness. A key component of their research was the application of the 'equal-appearing intervals scale of severity', which used a seven-part scale of severity. In addition to rating scales, other perceptual assessments used to investigate dysarthric speech include application of intelligibility measures, phonetic transcription studies and articulation inventories. A full description of these methods is beyond the scope of the present chapter; however, Table 8.3 provides a summary of specific perceptual assessments applicable to TBI.

The major advantages of perceptual assessment are those that have led to its preferred use as the tool for characterizing and diagnosing dysarthric speech. Perceptual assessments are readily available and require only limited financial outlay. In addition, all students of speech-language pathology are taught how to test for and identify perceptual symptoms. Enderby (1983) reported good discrimination ability (90 per cent accuracy) of the perceptual dimensions rated in the Frenchay Dysarthria Assessment when differentiating subgroups of dysarthria. Finally, perceptual assessments are useful for monitoring the effects of treatment on speech intelligibility and the adequacy of communication.

Clinicians need to be aware, however, that there are a number of inherent inadequacies with perceptual assessment that may limit their use in determining treatment priorities. First, accurate reliable judgements are often difficult to achieve as they can be influenced by a number of factors including the skill and experience of the clinician and the sensitivity of the assessment (Chenery, 1998).

Second, perceptual assessments are difficult to standardize both in relation to the client being rated and the environment in which the speech samples are recorded. Patient variability over time and across different settings prevents maintenance of adequate intra- and inter-rater reliability. Further, the symptoms may be present in certain conditions and not in others. This variability is also found in the patients themselves such that characteristics of the person being rated (for example, their age, premorbid medical history and social history) may influence speech as well as the neurological problem itself.

A third factor that limits reliance on perceptual assessments is that certain speech symptoms may influence the perception of others. This confound has been well reported in relation to the perception of resonatory disorders, articulatory deficits and prosodic disturbances.

Probably the major concern of perceptual assessments, particularly as they relate to treatment planning, is that they have restricted power for determining which sub-systems of the speech motor system are affected. In other words, perceptual assessments are unable to accurately identify the pathophysiological basis of the speech disorder manifest in various types of dysarthria. It is possible that a number of different physiological deficits can form the basis of perceptually identified features, and that different patterns of interaction within a patient's overall symptom complex can result in a similar perceptual deviation (for example, distorted consonants can result from reduced respiratory support for speech, from inadequate velopharyngeal functioning or from weak tongue musculature). When crucial decisions are required in relation to optimum therapeutic planning, an over-reliance on only perceptual assessments may lead to a number of questionable therapy directions.

Table 8.3 Comprehensive perceptual motor speech assessment battery applicable to TBI

Name of instrument	Relevance to dysarthria and TBI
Assessment of Intelligibility of Dysarthric Speech (Yorkston & Beukelman, 1981)	• standardized assessment of severity of dysarthric speech • incorporates measures of speech intelligibility at both single word and sentential levels, overall speech rate, rate of intelligible speech and a ratio of communication efficiency
Frenchay Dysarthria Assessment (Enderby, 1983)	• standardized assessment of neuromuscular systems associated with motor speech production, including: reflexive, respiratory, articulatory, resonatory and phonatory mechanisms • provides composite profile relative to status of motor speech sub-system functioning
Speech feature analysis (FitzGerald et al., 1987)	• following reading aloud of a standard citation such as 'The Grandfather Passage' or in the case of children who may not be able to read, an oral picture description task, speech samples are analysed and rated according to the presence and severity of 33 possible deviant speech dimensions • relevant dimensions encompass five domains of speech production, namely: prosody (i.e. pitch, loudness, phrasing, rate, stress); respiration (i.e. breath support for speech); resonance (i.e. nasality); phonation (i.e. vocal quality) and; articulation (i.e. consonant precision, length of phonemes, precision of vowels) • also provides an overall rating of speech intelligibility • this approach can be applied to both children and adults (e.g. Cahill *et al.*, 2002; Morgan *et al.*, 2007; Liégeois *et al.*, 2010; Morgan *et al.*, 2011)
Goldman-Fristoe Test of Articulation II (Goldman & Fristoe, 2000) and Diagnostic Evaluation of Articulation and Phonology (Dodd et al., 2006)	• *relevant to childhood TBI*, these assessments provide a measure of articulation or phonological abilities within the context of development.
Verbal Motor Production Assessment for Children (VMPAC; Hayden & Square, 1999)	• *relevant to childhood TBI*, the VMPAC assesses aspects of oral motor and speech motor functioning in children aged three to 12 years. The VMPAC includes subtests examining Global Motor Control, Focal Motor Control, Sequencing, Speech Characteristics and Connected Speech.
Children's Speech Intelligibility Measure (CSIM; Wilcox & Morris, 1999) and the recent Test of Children's Speech Plus – Sentence Measure (TOCS+ SM; Hodge, 2008).	• *relevant to childhood TBI*, the CSIM assesses intelligibility at a single word level, whereas the TOCS+ SM evaluates sentence-level intelligibility.

Acoustic assessment

Acoustic assessment is specifically dedicated to the evaluation of voice, providing measures of frequency, amplitude, perturbation and signal noise, as well as temporally constrained aspects of phonation (e.g. maximum phonation time and voice onset time) (Theodoros & Murdoch, 2001) and is certainly applicable to TBI populations. A number of acoustic analysis systems are available commercially, including the Computerised Speech Lab® (CSL) (Kay Elemetrics Corp.), VisiPitch® (Kay Elemetrics Corp.), CSpeech®, the Canadian Speech Research Environment® (CSRE), MacSpeech Lab II® and Dr. Speech Science for Windows® (Tiger Electronics) (Colton & Casper, 1996; Thompson-Ward & Theodoros, 1998). The CSL and VisiPitch, however, represent the most commonly employed acoustic analysis programs, rated as user friendly via the provision of real-time visual displays of acoustic parameters and the facility to store and analyse data (Theodoros & Murdoch, 2001).

Physiological assessment

Physiological assessments represent a corpus of instrumentation dedicated to the evaluation of the neuromuscular control mechanisms underlying speech. Available physiological apparatus not only evaluate phonatory aspects of speech production, but also extend to the assessment of articulation, resonance and respiration, including devices such as the laryngograph, Electromagnetic Articulograph, Nasometer and Respitrace. Table 8.4 provides a summary of physiological instrumentation that may be utilized in the assessment of individuals with TBI.

Table 8.4 Physiological instrumentation utilized in the assessment of dysarthria following TBI

Physiological function	Instrumental equipment
Laryngeal Function	• electroglottographic assessment (Laryngograph®)
	• aerodynamic assessment (Aerophone II®)
Respiratory Function	• spirometric assessment
	• kinematic assessment (Respitrace®)
	• aerodynamic assessment (Aerophone II®)
Articulatory Function	• lip and tongue pressure transduction systems
	• electropalatography (EPG)
	• electromagnetic articulography (EMA)
Velopharyngeal Function	• Nasometer® (Kay Elemetrics)
	• accelerometric assessment

Physiological measures of laryngeal function

In relation to the physiological assessment of laryngeal function, electroglottography (EGG) and measures of laryngeal aerodynamics represent two of the most commonly applied physiological tools in the clinical assessment of voice (Theodoros & Murdoch, 2001). EGG provides a means of representing vocal fold vibratory patterns (Colton & Conture, 1990) and aerodynamic measures generate information pertaining to the interaction of various phonatory parameters. Waveforms generated via electroglottographic methods (e.g. Fourcin® Laryngograph) correspond to the opening and closing phases of the glottal cycle, and the velocity at which the vocal folds adduct (Colton & Casper, 1996). Measures of laryngeal aerodynamics such as the Aerophone II® (see Figure 8.1), provide indices relating to the interplay of various laryngeal mechanisms in the production of voice, such as subglottal pressure, phonatory airflow, sound pressure level and laryngeal airway resistance (Theodoros & Murdoch, 2001). In addition to the parameters mentioned above, the Aerophone II® is also capable of measuring vocal fold adduction-abduction rates (Theodoros & Murdoch, 1994). Of note, high variability rates in performance have been reported in studies of aerodynamic laryngeal function (Theodoros & Murdoch, 2001). In order to counteract these variability effects, it has been recommended that the average of at least five repetitive samples should be established as a representative illustration of laryngeal function on such measures (Hammen & Yorkston, 1994). Within the context of TBI, however, fatigue effects as a result of effortful or repetitive physiological assessment tasks must also be considered in the interpretation of such data (Theodoros & Murdoch, 2001).

Physiological measures of respiratory function

Assessments of laryngeal function routinely co-occur with an evaluation of respiratory mechanisms underlying speech production (Theodoros & Murdoch, 2001). Physiological measures of speech breathing may be divided into two broad categories: 1) spirometric (i.e. direct measures of lung volume and capacity); and 2) kinematic (i.e. indirect measures of lung function by way of monitoring chest wall activity during breathing cycles and speech production tasks). Dry spirometers (see Figure 8.2) provide a means of measuring a range of respiratory parameters including: vital capacity, inspiratory capacity, expiratory and inspiratory reserve volumes, forced expiratory volume, respiration rate, tidal volume and volume/flow relationships. Furthermore, each of the parameters obtained may be compared to predicted age, height and sex-based values by way of formulae weighted for age and/or height.

Kinematic measures of speech breathing provide independent yet simultaneous recordings of alterations in ribcage and abdomen volumes during speech and non-speech tasks. A range of kinematic instrumentation has been applied to the study of speech breathing in neurologically impaired populations (Theodoros & Murdoch, 1994), including magnetometers, strain-gauge belt pneumographs and

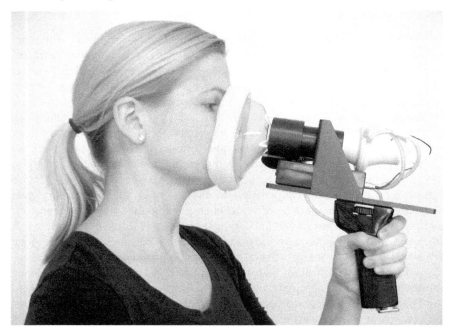

Figure 8.1 Aerophone II airflow measurement system

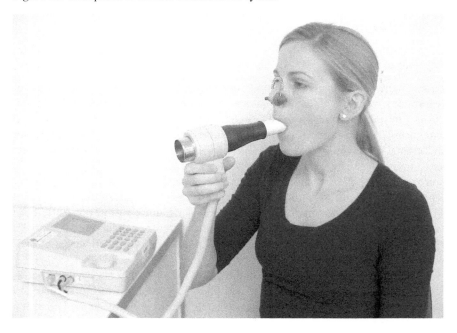

Figure 8.2 Respiratory spirometer

inductance plethysomography (Solomon & Hixon, 1993; Stathopoulos & Sapienza, 1993). Respitrace® (see Figure 8.3), an inductance plethysomographic measure of respiratory function, is the instrument of choice in our research laboratory. This instrument monitors changes in chest wall circumference via electrical inductance. Wires contained within elasticized straps placed around the chest and abdomen register dimensional alterations during specified tasks. A visual display signal is generated for analysis purposes and may also function as a biofeedback tool during therapy.

Figure 8.3 Respitrace system for kinematic assessment of speech breathing

Physiological measures of articulatory function

In relation to the evaluation of articulatory function, pressure transduction systems are commonly employed to measure lip and tongue strength, endurance, velocity of movement and fine force control. As an example, within our research laboratory a miniaturized pressure transducer (Entran Flatline®, Entran Devices Inc., Model EPL 20001-10) with factory calibration, mounted upon an aluminium strip, is used to measure interlabial pressures during speech and non-speech tasks, resembling that initially described by Hinton and Luschei (1992). Similarly a rubber-bulb pressure transduction system is utilized to evaluate tongue function (Murdoch *et al.*, 1995).

Electropalatography (EPG) and electromagnetic articulography (EMA) represent measures of dynamic articulatory function. More specifically, EPG provides a means of evaluating the positioning and timing of tongue to hard palate contacts during speech via a thin acrylic palate studded with miniature sensory electrodes, fitted within a subject's oral cavity (see Figure 8.4). Contact patterns during speech are subsequently acquired and stored in an external processing unit for analysis. By way of transmitter and receiver coil systems generating electromagnetic fields, the Electromagnetic Articulograph® (EMA) AG-500 (Carstens Medizinelektronic, Germany) provides a three-dimensional representation of articulatory movements (Murdoch, 2011) (see Figure 8.5). More specifically, the EMA has the capacity to generate kinematic articulatory parameters, including trajectory, velocity, duration and acceleration, via the tracking of displacement relative to receiver coils positioned on the tongue, upper and lower lips, velum and mandible.

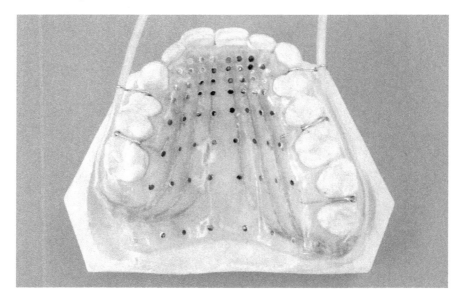

Figure 8.4 Acrylic electropalatography plate with imbedded touch sensors

Figure 8.5 Client fitted with AG500 system

Physiological measures of velopharyngeal function

Measures of nasal airflow, air pressure, vibration and oro-nasal acoustic output offer non-invasive, clinically viable methods of assessing velopharyngeal competence. Nasal accelerometry and measures of oro-nasal acoustic output ratios represent the assessments of velopharyngeal function utilized routinely within our research laboratory. Nasal accelerometry involves the placement of miniature, vibration sensitive accelerometers upon the lateral nasal cartilage and thyroid lamina, which detect nasal and laryngeal vibrations during speech. The magnitudes of vibration detected are then used to calculate a ratio of nasal to laryngeal vibration, providing an index of nasality, the Horri Oral Nasal Coupling (HONC) index (Horri, 1983). High HONC indices are considered representative of velopharyngeal incompetence.

The Nasometer® (Kay Elemetrics) (see Figure 8.6) offers a measure of nasality via the generation of oro-nasal acoustic output ratios (Dalston & Seaver, 1992). Two directional microphones separated by a sound-separating plate are positioned anterior to the nose and mouth which record acoustic output signals. Accompanying software calculates nasalance scores which effectively represent nasal to oral acoustic output ratios during various speech tasks. High scores are considered representative of velopharyngeal dysfunction.

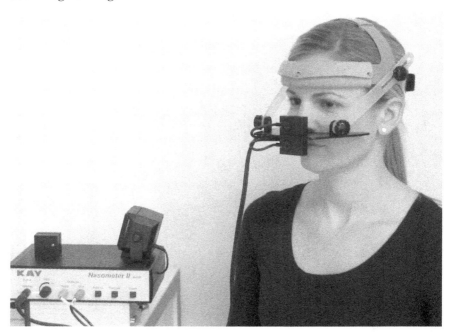

Figure 8.6 Nasometer

Neuroradiological/brain stimulation assessment

In addition to the perceptual, acoustic and physiological assessments outlined above, recently introduced neuroradiological and brain stimulation techniques also have added to the battery of procedures available to determine the pathophysiological basis of communication impairments seen in individuals post-TBI. Communication deficits subsequent to TBI are the products of induced brain pathologies, in particular, diffuse axonal injury (DAI) (Murdoch, 2010). DAI disrupts fibre tracts connecting different parts of the brain leading to the production of speech and language deficits. A powerful emerging advanced MR neuroimaging technique to visualize white matter integrity and any axonal damage sustained is the acquisition of diffusion magnetic resonance images based on tensor or higher-order models and the subsequent tractography analysis of white matter pathways (diffusion MRI tractography). This technique allows the virtual *in vivo* dissection of white matter fasciculi in the brain providing measures of location and integrity of speech fibre tracts (Glasser & Rilling, 2008). Recent studies relating measures of fibre integrity in the brain to neurobehavioural outcomes following TBI consistently report high correlations between the two and emphasize the higher sensitivity for DAI detection for tractography procedures as compared to computed tomography (CT) or conventional MRI (Ewing-Cobbs *et al.*,

2008; Levin *et al.*, 2008; Wilde *et al.*, 2006). Further, diffusion MRI tractography findings have been reported to be instructive to the prognosis in persons with TBI, predicting not only coma duration, but also long-term motor and cognitive deficits leading some authors to suggest that diffusion MRI tractography should be included in MR imaging protocols used for the evaluation of persons with TBI (Gasparetto *et al.*, 2011).

Transcranial magnetic stimulation (TMS) is a non-invasive form of brain stimulation that can be used to modulate the activity of specific regions of the cerebral cortex. The technique involves the application of rapidly changing magnetic fields to the scalp via a copper wire coil connected to a magnetic stimulator. These brief pulsed magnetic fields of 1 to 4 Tesla pass through the skull and create electric currents in discrete brain regions. Two types of TMS can be administered, a single pulse or a repetitive train of pulses (rTMS). Of the two types, single pulse TMS has the most immediate application to the assessment of the functional integrity of the motor system involved in the control of speech production. As the name suggests, in single pulse TMS the magnetic stimuli are delivered individually and not coupled with another pulse. Single pulse TMS can be used to measure aspects of cortico-motor excitation and inhibition. It can be used to map cortical representation (Wassermann *et al.*, 1992), examine central motor conduction time (Rossini & Rossi, 1998), or probe cortical movement encoding (Classen *et al.*, 1998). In these circumstances, responses to TMS (motor evoked potentials [MEPs]) are recorded peripherally using electromyography. The size and latency of the MEP provide information regarding the integrity of the cortico-motor pathway (e.g. corticobulbar tracts) to the target muscle (e.g. tongue). Single pulse TMS therefore has the potential to be used to test the integrity of the corticobulbar and corticospinal tracts in persons with dysarthria associated with a variety of neurological conditions such as stroke, multiple sclerosis, Parkinson's disease, etc.

Treatment of dysarthria associated with TBI

Approaches to dysarthria treatment for individuals with TBI have been many and varied, perhaps speaking to the heterogeneous clinical profile associated with this population. As with many areas of communication, there is an encouraging growth of literature in this field, but no randomized controlled trials. As such, we acknowledge that there are methodological limitations of treatment studies discussed in this section. It is not within the scope of the chapter to appraise existing literature in this field. The reader is referred elsewhere for detailed and constantly updated paediatric (Morgan & Vogel, 2008, updated review in progress) and adult-based (Sellars *et al.*, 2005, updated 2009) Cochrane reviews of treatment for dysarthria associated with acquired brain injury and the speechBITE website (www.speechbite.com/) for detailed methodological appraisal of studies. Furthermore, given the relative youth of this research field, we understand little about treatment parameters such as the optimal dose, level of specificity and intensity of treatment. It is beyond the scope of this chapter to provide a detailed discussion of these issues. The reader is referred elsewhere for a detailed discussion of important principles of treatment neuroplasticity (Kleim & Jones, 2008; Ludlow *et al.*, 2008).

Here we provide an overview of approaches applied to the treatment of dysarthria associated with TBI in adults and children. Traditionally, an emphasis has been placed on treating at the impairment level in dysarthria. As such, many of the existing studies mentioned here fit within this traditional approach. In recent times however, in keeping with the World Health Organization's International Classification of Functioning, Disability and Health (ICF; World Health Organization, 2001), there is increasing recognition for the need to consider and where possible modify how dysarthria impacts on activity and participation in daily life. We conclude this chapter by discussing important new data on the correlation between speech intelligibility and daily life participation and its implications for clinical management in individuals with dysarthria after TBI.

Overview of treatment approaches for dysarthria

The majority of approaches for treating dysarthria after TBI are aimed at improving underlying physiological impairments to effect a common end goal, i.e. to improve speaker intelligibility. Hodge and Wellman (1999) have suggested that the source-filter theory of speech production (Kent & Read, 2002) provides a possible working model for consideration of key principles of dysarthria treatment. The 'source' component of source-filter theory acknowledges a need to create sufficient breath support for sustaining a pressurized airstream and vibration of the vocal folds (vocalization) along with the ability to control or stop this airstream to vary the manner of articulation (e.g. to result in a plosive versus a fricative). As a second step, once breath support is established, these 'sources' are 'filtered' through the resonant properties of the vocal tract and movements of the articulators to result in the consonants and vowels of our language (Hodge, 2010; Kent & Read, 2002). Treatments for dysarthria typically focus on improving functioning of the speech sub-system(s) of respiration, phonation, velopharyngeal function and/or articulation. Clearly, using this model, respiratory- and phonation-based treatments are source-based approaches, and velopharyngeal and articulatory-based treatments are filter-based approaches. The following section outlines specific interventions that have been applied to manage dysarthria after TBI.

The majority of studies on treating dysarthria after TBI have attempted to improve respiration and phonation as a core focus of intervention (e.g. Bellaire *et al.*, 1986; Murdoch *et al.*, 1999; Solomon *et al.*, 2001; Solomon *et al.*, 2004; Wenke *et al.*, 2008; Wenke *et al.*, 2010), see Table 8.5. Four of these six studies utilized the Lee Silverman Voice Treatment (LSVT®, see http://www. lsvtglobal.com/ for specific details of this program) and reported favourable results immediately post-treatment, with more variability in outcomes at longer-term follow-up. The largest of these trials examined efficacy of the

LSVT in a group of seven adults who presented with a variety of dysarthria sub-types after TBI (Wenke *et al.*, 2008). Participants received 1 hour of treatment four days per week over four weeks for a total of 16 hours of therapy. Significant post-treatment improvements were noted immediately after therapy and included increases in loudness and articulatory precision and word- and sentence-level intelligibility. At 6 months follow-up, articulatory precision was maintained but word and sentence level intelligibility was not. Importantly, significant improvements in activity, participation and wellbeing/distress were also maintained at follow-up.

Studies of treatments attempting to modify the articulatory speech sub-system are the next most common approach in the field of interventions for dysarthria after TBI (e.g. Hartelius *et al.*, 2005; Morgan *et al.*, 2007; Nordness *et al.*, 2010). A range of methods have been applied, including electropalatography (see section on physiological assessment of dysarthria earlier in this chapter for further description of this technique) as examined in one adult case aged 30 years and approximately 7;5 years post-injury (Hartelius *et al.*, 2005) and in a case series of three children aged between 14 and 15 years and between 2;3 to 5 years post-injury (Morgan *et al.*, 2007). Promise was shown for EPG in both studies, with improvements detected across cases at the single sound, single word and/or sentence level, yet there was no evaluation of the impact of EPG therapy on activity and participation in daily life in these early preliminary studies. The additional visual feedback provided by EPG and other similar interventions may be particularly beneficial for patients with brain injury because of co-morbid difficulties with understanding verbal or auditory instructions, approaches traditionally relied upon by clinicians in remediation programmes (Morgan & Vogel, 2008). Visual biofeedback techniques may provide a more tangible or concrete example of the patient's speech pattern for remediation, avoiding the need for complex instructions (Morgan & Vogel, 2008).

Given the well-acknowledged feature of altered speech rate in dysarthric patients (see earlier section on clinical features of dysarthria associated with TBI), another approach to articulatory sub-system treatments for dysarthria are interventions based around directly or indirectly modifying rate of speech. These approaches include pacing boards, cueing and pacing strategies, delayed auditory feedback and alphabet board supplementation (see Blanchet & Snyder 2010, for review). A recent evaluation examined the use of alphabet supplementation (AS) in ten adults presenting with varied dysarthria sub-types between 6 months and 12 years post-injury (Nordness *et al.*, 2010). Use of an alphabet supplementation approach was found to be associated with significantly slower speaking rate, greater pause time, greater total speaking time and increased speaking intelligibility. There was no evaluation of the impact of this treatment on aspects of activity or participation.

Table 8.5 Example approaches for treatment of dysarthria associated with traumatic brain injury in children and adults

Study	Participants	Intervention type	Intervention dose	Outcome measures	Timing of outcome measures	Summary of key outcomes
Bellaire et al., 1986	20 yr old M with mild dysarthria at 9 months post-injury	Treatment programme focused on breath patterning	NA	Respiratory control during speech and perceptual ratings of speech naturalness	Pre- and post-treatment	• Increase in mean length of breath groups • Reduction in pauses • Improved speech naturalness
Cahill et al., 2004	Three participants (2M, 1F) aged 24–30 years with moderate-severe and severe flaccid dysarthria at 7–30 months post-severe injury	Continuous positive airway pressure (CPAP)	4 weeks, four sessions per week lasting 10–24 minutes	Perceptual ratings of resonance, articulation and speech intelligibility, and instrumental assessment of velopharyngeal competency	Pre-treatment, at week 3 of treatment, immediately and 1 month post-treatment	• At 1 month post-treatment: Reduction in nasalance scores (n=3) • Improved speech intelligibility (n=2)
Hartelius et al., 2005	30 yr old M 7 years, 7 months post severe TBI Moderate spastic-ataxic dysarthria	Electropalatography (EPG)	5 weeks, three sessions per week lasting 45 minutes	Perceptual ratings of articulation and speech intelligibility, and EPG measures (timing, spatial palatal, contactgrams, variability)	Pre-treatment EPG measures: end of wks 2 through to 5 Perceptual measures: end of wks 3 and 5	• 10% improvement in word and sentence level intelligibility • Reduction in lingual consonant error patterns • Significantly longer consonant durations • Increased variability during /s/ and 'sh' productions

Study	Participants	Intervention	Frequency	Outcome measures	Assessment	Findings
Honda et al., 2007	31 yr old M with severe TBI, dysarthria and apraxia of speech	Palatal lift prosthesis	NA	Degree of nasal resonance (instrumental and perceptual) and speech intelligibility	Pre-treatment and during treatment (1 week, 2 months and 1 yr following therapy commencement)	• Reduced nasality scores for sentences containing velar plosive and fricative sounds (no differences for vowels) • Reduction in degree of perceived hypernasality • Significant improvement in speech intelligibility
McGhee et al., 2006	Two adults with severe TBI Subject 1: M aged 45 years, 95 days post-onset with a moderate flaccid-ataxic dysarthria Subject 2: F aged 33 years, 54 days post-onset with a mild flaccid-ataxic dysarthria	Behavioural management of dysarthria	Ten sessions per week (twice daily) lasting 15 minutes	Oromotor ability, respiratory-phonatory control, vocal quality and speech intelligibility. Perceptual ratings of the speech sub-systems	Pre-treatment and following emergence from PTA	*Subject 1:* • Dysarthria severity improved to mild • Improvements in speech intelligibility • Increased sustained phonation • Improved respiratory-phonatory control • Improvements in respiratory, laryngeal and articulatory speech sub-systems • Improvements in voluntary movements of lips and tongue *Subject 2:* • No change in dysarthria severity. • Improvements in mandibular and tongue movements

Table 8.5 continued

Study	Participants	Intervention type	Intervention dose	Outcome measures	Timing of outcome measures	Summary of key outcomes
						• Improvements in respiratory, laryngeal and articulatory speech sub-systems • Improvements in general stress pattern • Improvements in speech intelligibility
Morgan et al., 2007	Three children (2M, 1F) aged 14–15, 2.5–5 years post severe TBI. One mild spastic, one moderate spastic and one severe mixed spastic-ataxic	EPG	Ten sessions lasting 45 minutes per week	Perceptual ratings of articulation and speech intelligibility (raters blinded), and EPG spatial and durational measures	Immediately pre- and post-treatment	• Perceptual improvements in phoneme precision and length (n=3) and vowel distortion (n=1) • Improvements in speech intelligibility at word (n=2) and sentence level (n=3) • Minimal functional speech intelligibility improvements (n=2) • Increased accuracy and reduced variability of phoneme production

Study	Participants	Intervention	Outcome measures	Therapy details	Assessment	Results
Murdoch et al., 1999	12 yr old M 2.5 years post severe TBI with mixed spastic-ataxic-flaccid dysarthria	Traditional therapy and physiological biofeedback therapy for speech breathing	Perceptual and instrumental measures of respiratory support for speech	Traditional therapy provided over eight sessions lasting 30–45 minutes over two weeks. Biofeedback therapy commenced following ten weeks of no treatment. Biofeedback therapy provided over eight sessions lasting 30 minutes over 2 weeks.	Pre-treatment, during treatment, withdrawal phase, immediately post-treatment	• Improvements in speech breathing patterns compared to traditional therapy techniques e.g. improved coordination of expiration and phonation, increased depth of inspiration, reduction in voice onset latency and increased phonation time • Perceptual improvements following biofeedback therapy mixed (and no improvements following traditional therapy) • No improvements in vital capacity or forced expiratory volume following both therapies
Nordness et al., 2010	Ten adults (eight M, two F) 0.6–12 years post TBI. Four mixed spastic-ataxic. Five mixed spastic-flaccid. One mixed spastic-ataxic-flaccid	Alphabet supplementation (AS) compared to habitual speech	Speech and pause temporal characteristics	NA	NA	• Significantly slower speaking rate • Significantly greater pause time • Significantly greater total speaking time • Increased intelligibility

Table 8.5 continued

Study	Participants	Intervention type	Intervention dose	Outcome measures	Timing of outcome measures	Summary of key outcomes
Solomon et al., 2001	Adult M 20 months post severe TBI (injury sustained at 20 years of age) Hypokinetic-spastic dysarthria	LSVT and LSVT combined with respiration treatment and physical therapy. Combination treatment commenced after a 1 week break following LSVT. Combination treatment involved one day of LSVT and three days of LSVT with respiration treatment per week	LSVT: 1 hr sessions, 4 days per week over 4 weeks Combined treatment: 1 hr sessions, 4 days per week over 6 weeks Follow-up treatment: 1 hr per week over 10 weeks (post combination treatment)	Breathing and speech function Chest-wall kinematics, laryngeal aerodynamic, acoustic measurements, and speech intelligibility	Pre-treatment, post-LSVT, post-combination treatment, post follow-up treatment, and 3 months post-treatment	*After LSVT:* • Increased sound pressure level and loudness • Reduced breathiness *After combination treatment:* • Further increase in sound pressure level • Marked increase in speech intelligibility • Increased lung volume levels for speech
Solomon et al., 2004	58 yr old M 10 months post TBI with hypokinetic-spastic dysarthria	Treatment phase 1: Breathing-for-Speech Treatment (BST; including physical therapy and LSVT-type tasks) Treatment phase 2: LSVT	BST: 11 1 hr sessions over 6 weeks (max of four sessions per week) LSVT: Four 1 hr sessions per week over 4 weeks	Self-perceived Voice Handicap Index (VHI), speech breathing and perceptual ratings of articulation, breathiness, severity and sentence intelligibility	Twice prior to initiating treatment (2 months apart); immediately following trial therapy; day following BST completion; day following LSVT completion; and at follow-up (1 and 4 months post-treatment)	• Speech intelligibility improved only following LSVT • Improvements in speech breathing, articulatory precision and breathiness following both treatments • VHI score reduced to minimal disability following LSVT but returned to severe at follow-up

Study	Participants	Intervention	Dosage/Design	Measures	Assessment	Outcomes
Thompson-Ward et al., 1997	66 yr old M 15 years post TBI with moderate spastic dysarthria	Biofeedback therapy of: i) chest wall excursions; and ii) breath control during phonation	Both interventions provided over five sessions lasting 45 minutes within 1 week	Perceptual ratings of intelligibility, respiratory support for speech, phrase length and rate of speech. Circumferential changes in the rib cage and abdomen	Pre-treatment and following each therapy session	• Increased lung volumes and increased excursion of abdominal muscles • Improved 'offset coordination and phonation times'
Wenke et al., 2008	Seven adults (four M, three F) aged 19–42 years with TBI, 6–46 months post-onset 1 flaccid 1 spastic 1 flaccid-spastic 2 spastic-flaccid 1 ataxic 1 spastic-ataxic	LSVT	1 hr sessions, 4 days per week over 4 weeks	Perceptual ratings of articulation, loudness and speech intelligibility Acoustic measures (duration of sustained vowel, sound pressure level, fundamental frequency) Everyday communication (activity, participation and wellbeing/distress) Raters blind to treatment type and assessment session	Pre- and post-treatment, and 6 months post-treatment	• Post-treatment increases in loudness and articulatory precision (significant improvements in articulation maintained at follow-up), and in word and sentence intelligibility (not maintained at follow-up) • Increases in sustained vowel duration, fundamental frequency, and loudness during sustained phonation and conversational speech (all maintained at follow-up except loudness of conversational speech) • Improvements in activity, participation and wellbeing/distress post-treatment that were maintained at follow-up

Table 8.5 continued

Study	Participants	Intervention type	Intervention dose	Outcome measures	Timing of outcome measures	Summary of key outcomes
Wenke, et al., 2010	Five M adults aged 19–40 years with TBI, 9 months to 12 years post-onset time 1 spastic-ataxic 2 spastic-flaccid 1 spastic-hypokinetic 1 spastic	Participants randomly allocated to receive either traditional dysarthria (n=2) therapy or LSVT (n=3)	Both treatments provided over 16 1 hr sessions, 4 days per week over 4 weeks	Perceptual ratings of hypernasality and degree of nasalance	Pre-treatment, immediately post-treatment and 6 months post-treatment	• Reduced perceived hypernasality maintained at follow-up by 1/3 receiving LSVT • No clear reductions following traditional therapy • Decrease in nasalance scores of LSVT group that was maintained at follow-up (2/3) • No significant decrease in nasalance scores post-traditional therapy

NA: not reported or unclear in original manuscript.

A final group of treatment approaches for dysarthria are based around modifying the velopharyngeal sub-system of speech (e.g. Cahill *et al.*, 2004; Honda *et al.*, 2007). One particular treatment approach that has been gaining wide appeal to manage velopharyngeal deficits is continuous positive airway pressure (CPAP). Cahill and colleagues (2004) examined the efficacy of using CPAP in a case series of three participants aged 24–30 years who presented with moderate to severe and severe flaccid dysarthria with a key impairment in nasal resonance at between 7 and 30 months post-severe TBI. Participants took part in 4 weeks of treatment for four sessions per week, with each session lasting between 10 and 24 minutes. At one month post-treatment a reduction in nasalance scores was noted for all participants and two of the three individuals also demonstrated improved speech intelligibility. Further trials examining the efficacy of this 'filter'-based approach are required.

Considering the impact of dysarthria on activity, participation and quality of life

Whilst the existing treatments for dysarthria reported earlier in this section have focused on improving speech intelligibility, recent studies examining daily life interactions or activity and participation for individuals with dysarthria have highlighted potential limitations of this approach. It appears there is not a straightforward positive correlation between speech intelligibility and success in tasks of daily life. McAuliffe *et al.* (2010) examined perceived communication effectiveness between a group of eight participants with chronic dysarthria after TBI and their nominated communication partners. The authors found that there was no significant correlation between conversation level speech intelligibility and perceived communicative effectiveness as rated by either the individuals with TBI or their partners. This finding highlights that there are other complex factors at play regarding dysarthria and successful daily life communication interactions beyond speech intelligibility. As the authors highlighted, there is a need for careful examination of activity and participation when identifying goals for management in this population. Similar findings were reported by Guo and Togher (2008) who compared the everyday communication of five participants with mild and five with moderate dysarthria following TBI. Specifically, the authors recorded and analysed telephone conversations regarding service enquiries with bus timetable call centre operators. Listener comfort ratings (a proxy measure of intelligibility) were also recorded. Whilst participants with moderate dysarthria were given poorer listener comfort ratings, this finding did not affect the way information was exchanged with the call centre operators. This provided further evidence that there is not a simple 1:1 relationship between speech intelligibility (or listener comfort) and success in tasks of daily life. In this instance, the authors unpacked the possible factors that may have been contributing to success of the interactions beyond speech intelligibility to include the amount of disability awareness training and experience held by call centre operators, the highly structured nature of bus timetable enquiries and the powerful interactional role of TBI participants as customers.

Further research groups have emphasized the importance of assessing conversational interactions between people with dysarthria and their communication partners to identify sources of communication breakdown and explore effective repair strategies (Bloch & Wilkinson, 2009; Bloch & Wilkinson, 2011). In their study of two adults with dysarthria communicating with their spouses, Bloch and Wilkinson (2011) concluded that conversational problems resulting from dysarthria can require extensive repair work involving *both* parties. The authors highlighted that the communication activities of both the speaker with dysarthria and their partner should be considered during assessment and treatment planning to promote strategies for both communication participants. Whilst this more functional approach to treatment has been used increasingly for people with aphasia, it is a relatively new and exciting field for future research and clinical practice in the management of dysarthria. For further discussion of communication partner training, see Chapter 12.

Summary

Dysarthria is an often debilitating communication disorder associated with TBI. Prognosis is arguably poor for affected individuals, with long-term reports of dysarthria persisting for up to 15 years post-TBI (e.g. Rusk *et al.*, 1969; Thomsen 1984). Key features of dysarthria typically include reduced breath support for speech, prosodic deficits, articulatory imprecision, deficits in voice quality and altered resonance, typically hypernasality. At a functional level, these deficits are associated with poor speech intelligibility and conversational breakdown for the affected individual, with potentially devastating impacts on their daily activities and participation in life. Encouragingly, there is a steadily growing evidence base for dysarthria treatment, occurring in parallel with a growing appreciation for the need to evaluate and modify the impact of dysarthria on an individual's activity and participation, and not only the physiological impairment. Future research treatment directions include working together with the families, friends and other communication partners of individuals with TBI to improve awareness of strategies that will result in more positive communicative interactions and more successful participation in daily life.

Acknowledgement

Thank you to Ms Cristina Mei, Murdoch Children's Research Institute for invaluable assistance with performing literature searches and generating tables for this chapter.

References

Barlow, S. M. & Burton, M. K. (1990). Ramp-and-hold force control in the upper and lower lips: developing new neuromotor assessment applications in traumatically brain injured adults. *Journal of Speech and Hearing Research, 33,* 660–675.

Bartle, C. J., Goozée, J. V., Scott, D., Murdoch, B. E. & Kuruvilla, M. (2006). EMA assessment of tongue-jaw co-ordination during speech in dysarthria following traumatic brain injury. *Brain Injury, 20*(5), 529–545.

Bellaire, K., Yorkston, K. M. & Beukelman, D. R. (1986). Modification of breath patterning to increase naturalness of a mildly dysarthric speaker. *Journal of Communication disorders, 19*(4), 271–280.

Beukelman, D. R. & Garrett, K. (1988). Augmentative and alternative communication for adults with acquired severe communication disorders. *Augmentative and Alternative Communication, 4,* 104–121.

Beukelman, D. R. & Yorkston, K. M. (1991). Traumatic brain injury changes the way we live. In D. R. Beukelman & K. M. Yorkston (Eds), *Communication Disorders Following Traumatic Brain Injury* (pp. 1–13). Austin, TX: PRO-ED.

Blanchet, P. G. & Snyder, G. J. (2010). Speech rate treatments for individuals with dysarthria: a tutorial. *Perceptual Motor Skills, 10,* 965–982.

Bloch, S. & Wilkinson, R. (2009). Acquired dysarthria in conversation: identifying sources of understandability problems. *International Journal of Language and Communication Disorder, 44*(5), 769–783.

——(2011). Acquired dysarthria in conversation: methods of resolving understandability problems. *International Journal of Language and Communication Disorder, 46*(5), 510–523.

Boyer, M. G. & Edwards, P. (1991) Outcome 1 to 3 years after severe traumatic brain injury in children and adolescents. *Injury: The British Journal of Accident Surgery, 22,* 315–320.

Bramlett, H. M. & Dietrich, W. D. (2004). Pathology of cerebral ischemia and brain trauma: similarities and differences. *Journal of Cerebral Blood Flow Metabolism, 24,* 133–150.

Brink, J. D., Garrett, A. L., Hale, W. R., Woo-Sam, J. & Nickel, V. L. (1970) Recovery of motor and intellectual function in children sustaining severe head injuries. *Developmental Medicine and Child Neurology, 12,* 565–571.

Cahill, L., Murdoch, B. E. & Theodoros, D. G. (2001). Dysarthria following traumatic brain injury in childhood. In B. E. Murdoch & D. G. Theodoros (Eds), *Traumatic Brain Injury: Associated Speech, Language and Swallowing Disorders* (pp. 121–153). San Diego, CA: Singular Thompson Learning.

Cahill, L. M., Murdoch, B. E. & Theodoros, D. G. (2002). Perceptual analysis of speech following traumatic brain injury in childhood. *Brain Injury, 16*(5), 415–446.

Cahill, L. M., Turner, A. B., Stabler, P. A., Addis, P. E., Theodoros, D. G. & Murdoch, B. E. (2004). An evaluation of continuous positive airway pressure (CPAP) therapy in the treatment of hypernasality following traumatic brain injury: a report of 3 cases. *Journal of Head Trauma Rehabilitation, 19*(3), 241–253.

Chenery, H. J. (1998). Perceptual analysis of dysarthric speech. In B. E. Murdoch (Ed.), *Dysarthria: A Physiological Approach to Assessment and Treatment* (pp. 36–67). Cheltenham, UK: Stanley Thornes.

Classen, J., Liepert, J., Wise, S. P., Hallett, M. & Cohen, L. G. (1998). Rapid plasticity of human cortical movement representation induced by practice. *Journal of Neurophysiology, 79,* 1117–1123.

Colton, R. & Conture, E. G. (1990). Problems and pitfalls in electroglottography. *Journal of Voice, 4,* 10–24.

Colton, R. & Casper, J. K. (1996). The voice: history, examination and testing. In R. Colton & J. K. Casper (Eds), *Understanding Voice Problems: A Physiological Perspective for Diagnosis and Treatment* (2nd edn, pp. 186–240). Baltimore, MD: Williams and Williams.

Costeff, H., Groswasser, Z. & Goldstein, R. (1990) Long-term follow-up review of 31 children with severe closed head trauma. *Journal of Neurosurgery, 73,* 684–687.

Dalston, R. M. & Seaver, E. J. (1992). Relative values of various standardised passages in nasometric assessment of patients with velopharyngeal impairment. *Cleft Palate and Craniofacial Journal, 29,* 17–21.

Darley, F. L., Aronson, A. E. & Brown, J. R. (1969a). Differential diagnostic patterns of dysarthria. *Journal of Speech and Hearing Research, 12,* 246–269.

——(1969b). Cluster of deviant speech dimensions in the dysarthrias. *Journal of Speech and Hearing Research, 12,* 462–496.

——(1975). *Motor Speech Disorders.* Philadelphia, PA: W. B. Saunders.

Dodd, B., Hua, Z., Crosbie, S., Holm, A. & Ozanne, A. (2006). *Diagnostic Evaluation of Articulation and Phonology.* San Antonio, TX: Pearson.

Dresser, A. C., Meirowsky, A. M., Weiss, G. J., McNeel, M. L., Simon, G. A. & Caveness, W. F. (1973). Gainful employment following head injury: prognostic factors. *Archives of Neurology, 29,* 111–116.

Enderby, P. (1983). *Frenchay Dysarthria Assessment.* San Diego, CA: College Hill Press.

Ewing-Cobbs, L, Prasad, M. R., Swank, P., Kramer, L., Cox, C. S., Fletcher, J. M., Barnes, M., Zhang, X. & Hasan, K. M. (2008). Arrested development and disrupted callosal microstructure following pediatric outcome. *Neuroimage, 42,* 1305–1315.

FitzGerald, F. J., Murdoch, B. E. & Chenery, H. J. (1987). Multiple sclerosis: associated speech and language disorders. *Australian Journal of Human Communication Disorders, 15,* 15–33.

Gasparetto, E. L., Rueda Lopes, F. C., Domingues, R. C. & Domingues, R. C. (2011). Diffusion imaging in traumatic brain injury. *Neuroimaging Clinics of North America, 21,* 115–125.

Glasser, M. F. & Rilling, J. K. (2008). DTI tractography of the human brain's language pathways. *Cerebral Cortex, 18,* 2471–2482.

Goldman, R. & Fristoe, M. (2000). *Goldman Fristoe Test of Articulation* (2nd Edn). San Antonio, TX: Pearson.

Goozée, J. V., Murdoch, B. E., Theodoros, D. G. & Stokes, P. D. (2000). Kinematic analysis of tongue movements in dysarthria following traumatic brain injury using electromagnetic articulography. *Brain Injury, 14*(2), 153–174.

Goozée, J. V., Murdoch, B. E. & Theodoros, D. G. (2001). Physiological assessment of tongue function in dysarthria following traumatic brain injury. *Logopedics, Phoniatrics, Vocology, 26*(2), 51–65.

——(2002). Interlabial contact pressures exhibited in dysarthria following traumatic brain injury during speech and nonspeech tasks. *Folia Phoniatrica et Logopedica, 54*(4), 177–189.

Groher, M. (1977). Language and memory disorders following closed head trauma. *Journal of Speech and Hearing Research, 20,* 212–222.

Guo, Y. E. & Togher, L. (2008). The impact of dysarthria on everyday communication after traumatic brain injury: a pilot study. *Brain Injury, 22*(1), 83–97.

Guthrie, E., Mast, J., Richards, P., McQuaid, M. & Pavlakis, S. (1999). Traumatic brain injury in children and adolescents. *Child and Adolescent Psychiatric Clinics of North America, 8,* 807–826.

Hammen, V. & Yorkston, K. M. (1994). Effect of instruction on selected aerodynamic parameters in subjects with dysarthria and control subjects. In J. A. Till, K. M. Yorkston & D. R. Beukelman (Eds), *Motor Speech Disorders: Advances in Assessment and Treatment* (pp. 161–173). Baltimore, MD: Paul H. Brooks.

Hartelius, L., Theodoros, D. & Murdoch, B. (2005). Use of electropalatography in the treatment of disordered articulation following traumatic brain injury: a case study. *Journal of Medical Speech-Language Pathology, 13*(3), 189–204.

Hayden, D. & Square, P. (1999). *Verbal Motor Production Assessment for Children.* San Antonio, TX: Pearson.

Hinton, V. A. & Luschei, E. S. (1992). Validation of a modern miniature transducer for measurement of interlabial pressure during speech. *Journal of Speech and Hearing Research, 35,* 245–251.

Hodge, M. (2008). *Test of children's speech plus (TOCS+).* Version 5.3. Alberta, CA: University of Alberta.

——(2010). Developmental dysarthria interventions. In A. L. Williams, S. McLeod & R. J. McCauley, *Interventions for Speech Sound Disorders* (pp. 557–578). London: Paul H. Brookes.

Hodge, M. & Wellman, L. (1999). Management of children with dysarthria. In A. Caruso & E. Strand (Eds), *Clinical Management of Motor Speech Disorders in Children* (pp. 209–280). New York: Thieme.

Honda, K., Urade, M. & Kandori, Y. (2007). Application of a specially designed palatal lift prosthesis to a patient with velopharyngeal incompetence due to severe brain injury. *Quintessence International, 38*(6), e316–320.

Horri, Y. (1983). An accelerometric measure as a physical correlate of perceived hypernasality in speech. *Journal of Speech and Hearing Research, 26,* 476–480.

Jaeger, M., Hertrich, I., Stattrop, U., Schonle, P. W. & Ackermann, H. (2000). Speech disorders following severe traumatic brain injury: kinematic analysis of syllable repetitions using electromagnetic articulography. *Folia Phoniatrica et Logopedica, 52*(4), 187–196.

Kent, R. D. & Read, C. (2002). *The Acoustic Analysis of Speech* (2nd edn). Clifton Park, NY: Thomson Delmar Learning.

Kent, R. D., Netsell, R. & Bauer, L. (1975). Cineradiographic assessment of articulatory mobility in the dysarthrias. *Journal of Speech and Hearing Disorders, 40,* 467–480.

Kleim, J. A. & Jones, T. A. (2008). Principles of experience-dependent neural plasticity: implications for rehabilitation after brain damage. *Journal of Speech, Language and Hearing Research,* 51(1), S225–239.

Kuruvilla, M., Murdoch, B. & Goozée, J. (2007). Electromagnetic articulography assessment of articulatory function in adults with dysarthria following traumatic brain injury. *Brain Injury, 21*(6), 601–613.

——(2008). Electropalatographic (EPG) assessment of tongue-to-palate contacts in dysarthric speakers following TBI. *Clinical Linguistics & Phonetics, 22*(9), 703–725.

Langfitt, T. W., Obrist, W. D., Alavi, A., Grossman, R. I., Zimmerman, R., Jaggi, J., Uzzell, B., Reivich, M. & Patton, D. R. (1986). Computerized tomography, magnetic resonance imaging, and positron emission tomography in the study of head trauma. Preliminary observations. *Journal of Neurosurgery, 64,* 760–767.

254   *Angela Morgan*

Lehiste, I. (1965). Some acoustic characteristics of dysarthric speech. *Biblotheca Phonetica, 2,* 1–124.
Letarte, P. B. (1999). Neurotrauma care in the new millennium. *Surgical Clinics of North America, 79,* 1449–1470.
Levin, H. S., Wilde, E. A., Chu, Z., Yallampalli, R., Hanten, G. R., Li, X., Chia, J., Vasquez, A. C. & Hunter, J. V. (2008). Diffusion tensor imaging in relation to cognitive and functional outcome of traumatic brain injury in children. *Journal of Head Trauma Rehabilitation, 23,* 197–208.
Liégeois, F. J. & Morgan, A. T. (2012). Neural bases of childhood speech disorders: lateralization and plasticity for speech functions during development. *Neuroscience & Biobehavioural Reviews, 36(*1), 439–458.
Liégeois, F., Morgan, A. T., Stewart, L. H., Cross, J. H., Vogel, A.P., Vargha-Khadem, F. (2010). Speech and oral motor profile after childhood hemispherectomy. *Brain & Language, 114*(2), 126–134.
Ludlow, C. L., Hoit, J., Kent, R., Ramig, L. O., Shrivastav, R., Strand, E., Yorkston, K. & Sapiennza, C. M. (2008). Translating principles of neural plasticity into research on speech motor control recovery and rehabilitation. *Journal of Speech, Language and Hearing Research, 51*(1), S240–58.
Marquardt, T. P., Stoll, J. & Sussman, H. (1990). Disorders of communication in traumatic brain injury. In E. D. Bigler (Ed.), *Traumatic Brain Injury: Mechanisms of Damage, Assessment, Intervention and Outcome* (pp. 181–205). Austin, TX: PRO-ED.
McAuliffe, M. J., Carpenter, S. & Moran, C. (2010). Speech intelligibility and perceptions of communication effectiveness by speakers with dysarthria following traumatic brain injury and their communication partners. *Brain Injury, 24*(12), 1408–1415.
McGhee, H., Cornwell, P., Addis, P. & Jarman, C. (2006). Treating dysarthria following traumatic brain injury: investigating the benefits of commencing treatment during post-traumatic amnesia in two participants. *Brain Injury, 20*(12), 1307–1319.
McHenry, M. A. (1998). Velopharyngeal airway resistance disorders after traumatic brain injury. *Archives of Physical Medicine & Rehabilitation, 79*(5), 545–549.
Morgan, A. T. & Vogel, A. P. (2008). Intervention for dysarthria associated with acquired brain injury in children and adolescents. *Cochrane Database of Systematic Reviews 2008,* Issue 3. Art. No.: CD006279. DOI: 10.1002/14651858.CD006279.pub2.
Morgan, A. T. & Liégeois, F. (2010). Re-thinking diagnostic classification of the dysarthrias: a developmental perspective. *Folia Phoniatrica et Logopaedica, 62,* 120–126.
Morgan, A. T., Liegéois , F. & Occomore, L. (2007). Electropalatography treatment for articulation impairment in children with dysarthria post-traumatic brain injury. *Brain Injury, 21*(11), 1183–1193.
Morgan, A. T., Mageandran, S. D. & Mei, C. (2010). Incidence and clinical presentation of dysarthria and dysphagia in the acute setting following paediatric traumatic brain injury. *Child: Care, Health & Development, 36*(1), 44–53.
Morgan, A. T., Liégeois, F., Liederkerke, C., Vogel, A. P., Hayward, R., Harkness, W., Chong. K. & Vargha-Khadem, F. (2011). Role of cerebellum in fine speech control in childhood: persistent dysarthria after surgical treatment for posterior fossa tumour. *Brain & Language, 117*(2), 69–76.
Murdoch, B. E. (2010). *Acquired Speech and Language Disorders: A Neuroanatomical and Functional Neurological Approach* (2nd edn). Oxford, UK: Wiley-Blackwell.
——(2011). *Handbook of Acquired Communication Disorders in Childhood.* San Diego, CA: Plural Publishing.

Murdoch, B. E. & Hudson-Tennent, L. J. (1994). Speech disorders in children treated for posterior fossa tumours: ataxic and developmental features. *European Journal of Disorders of Communication, 29,* 379–397.

Murdoch, B. E., Theodoros, D. G., Stokes, P. D. & Chenery, H. J. (1993). Abnormal patterns of speech breathing in dysarthric speakers following severe closed head injury. *Brain injury, 7*(4), 295–308.

Murdoch, B. E., Attard, M. D., Ozanne, A. E. & Stokes, P. D. (1995). Impaired tongue strength and endurance in developmental verbal dyspraxia: a physiological analysis. *European Journal of Disorders of Communication, 30,* 51–64.

Murdoch, B. E., Pitt, G., Theodoros, D. G. & Ward, E. C. (1999). Real-time continuous visual biofeedback in the treatment of speech breathing disorders following childhood traumatic brain injury: report of one case. *Pediatric Rehabilitation, 3*(1), 5–20.

Najenson, T., Sazbon, L., Fiselzon, J., Becker, E. & Schecter, I. (1978). Recovery of communicative functions after prolonged traumatic coma. *Scandinavian Journal of Rehabilitation Medicine, 10,* 15–21.

Netsell, R. & Daniel, B. (1979). Dysarthria in adults: physiologic approach in rehabilitation. *Archives of Physical Medicine and Rehabilitation, 60,* 502–508.

Netsell, R. & Lefkowitz, D. (1992). Speech production following traumatic brain injury: clinical and research implications. *American Speech-Language-Hearing Association Special Interests Division: Neurophysiology and Neurogenic Speech and Language Disorders, 2,* 1–8.

Nordness, A. S., Beukelman, D. R. & Ullman, C. (2010). Impact of alphabet supplementation on speech and pause durations of dysarthric speakers with traumatic brain injury: a research note. *Journal of Medical Speech-Language Pathology, 18*(2), 35–43.

Olver, J. H., Ponsford, J. L. & Curran, C. A. (1996). Outcome following traumatic brain injury: a comparison between 2 and 5 years after injury. *Brain Injury, 10,* 841–848.

Pilon, M. A., McIntosh, K. W. & Thaut, M. H. (1998). Auditory vs visual speech timing cues as external rate control to enhance verbal intelligibility in mixed spastic-ataxic dysarthric speakers: a pilot study. *Brain Injury, 12*(9), 793–803.

Rossini, P. M. & Rossi, S. (1998). Clinical applications of motor evoked potentials. *Electroencephalography & Clinical Neurophysiology, 106,* 180–194.

Rusk, H., Block, J. & Lowmann, E. (1969). Rehabilitation of the brain-injured patient: a report of 157 cases with long-term follow-up of 118. In E. Walker, W. Caveness & M. Critchley (Eds), *The Late Effects of Head Injury* (pp. 327–332). Springfield, IL: Charles C. Thomas.

Safaz, I., Alaca, R., Yasar, E., Tok, F. & Yilmaz, B. (2008). Medical complications, physical function and communication skills in patients with traumatic brain injury: a single centre 5-year experience. *Brain Injury, 22*(10), 733–739.

Sarno, M. T. & Levin, H. S. (1985). Speech and language disorders after closed head injury. In J. K. Darby (Ed.), *Speech and Language Evaluation in Neurology: Adult Disorders* (pp. 323–339). New York, NY: Grune & Stratton.

Sarno, M. T., Buonaguro, A. & Levita, E. (1986). Characteristics of verbal impairment in closed head injured patients. *Archives of Physical Medicine and Rehabilitation, 67,* 400–405.

Sellars, C., Hughes, T. & Langhorne, P. (2005). Speech and language therapy for dysarthria due to non-progressive brain damage. *Cochrane Database of Systematic Reviews* 2005, Issue 3. Art. No.: CD002088. DOI: 10.1002/14651858.CD002088.pub2. (Online update 2009).

Simmons, N. (1983). Acoustic analysis of ataxic dysarthria: an approach to monitoring treatment. In W. Berry (Ed.), *Clinical Dysarthria* (pp. 283–294). San Diego, CA: College Hill Press.

Solomon, N. & Hixon, T. J. (1993). Speech breathing in Parkinson's disease. *Journal of Speech and Hearing Research, 36,* 294–310.

Solomon, N. P., McKee, A. S. & Garcia-Barry, S. (2001). Intensive voice treatment and respiration treatment for hypokinetic-spastic dysarthria after traumatic brain injury. *American Journal of Speech-Language Pathology, 10*(1), 51–64.

Solomon, N. P., Makashay, M. J., Kessler, L. S. & Sullivan, K. W. (2004). Speech-breathing treatment and LSVT for a patient with hypokinetic-spastic dysarthria after TBI. *Journal of Medical Speech-Language Pathology, 12*(4), 213–219.

Stathopoulos, E. T. & Sapienza, C. (1993). Respiratory and laryngeal function of women and men during vocal intensity variation. *Journal of Speech and Hearing Research, 36,* 64–75.

Strich, S. J. (1956). Diffuse degeneration of the cerebral white matter in severe dementia following head injury. *Journal of Neurology, Neurosurgery, and Psychiatry, 19,* 163–185.

Theodoros, D. G. & Murdoch, B. E. (1994). Laryngeal dysfunction in dysarthric speakers following severe closed head injury. *Brain Injury, 8,* 667–684.

——(2001). Laryngeal dysfunction following traumatic brain injury. In B. E. Murdoch & D. G. Theodoros (Eds), *Traumatic Brain Injury: Associated Speech, Language and Swallowing Disorders* (pp. 89–109). San Diego, CA: Singular Thomson Learning.

Theodoros, D. G., Murdoch, B. E. & Chenery, H. J. (1994). Perceptual speech characteristics of dysarthric speakers following severe closed head injury. *Brain Injury, 8,* 101–124.

Theodoros, D. G., Murdoch, B. E. & Stokes, P. (1995). A physiological analysis of articulatory dysfunction in dysarthric speakers following severe closed-head injury. *Brain Injury, 9*(3), 237–254.

Theodoros, D. G., Shrapnel, N. & Murdoch, B. E. (1998). Motor speech impairment following traumatic brain injury in childhood: a physiological and perceptual analysis of one case. *Pediatric Rehabilitation, 2*(3), 107–122.

Theodoros, D. G., Murdoch, B. E. & Goozée, J. V. (2001). Dysarthria following traumatic brain injury: incidence, recovery and perceptual features. In B. E. Murdoch & D. G. Theodoros (Eds), *Traumatic Brain Injury: Associated Speech, Language and Swallowing Disorders* (pp. 27–52). San Diego, CA: Singular Thomson Learning.

Thompson-Ward, E. C. & Theodoros, D. G. (1998). Acoustic analysis of dysarthric speech. In B. E. Murdoch (Ed.), *Dysarthria: A Physiological Approach to Assessment and Treatment* (pp. 102–129). Cheltenham, UK: Stanley Thornes.

Thompson-Ward, E. C., Murdoch, B. E. & Stokes, P. D. (1997). Biofeedback rehabilitation of speech breathing for an individual with dysarthria. *Journal of Medical Speech-Language Pathology, 5*(4), 277–288.

Thomsen, I. V. (1984). Late outcome of severe blunt head injury: a ten to fifteen year second follow-up. *Journal of Neurology, Neurosurgery, and Psychiatry, 47,* 260–268.

van Mourik, M., Catsman-Berrevoets, C. E., Paquier, P. F., Yousef-Bak, E. & van Dongen, H. R. (1997). Acquired childhood dysarthria: review of its clinical presentation. *Pediatric Neurology, 17,* 299–307.

von Cramon, D. (1981). Traumatic mutism and the subsequent reorganization of speech functions. *Neuropsychologie, 19,* 801–805.

Vitorino, J. (2009). Laryngeal function: a comparative analysis between children and adults subsequent to traumatic brain injury. *Journal of Head Trauma Rehabilitation, 24*(5), 374–383.

Wassermann, E. M., McShane, L. M., Hallett, M. & Cohen, L. G. (1992). Noninvasive mapping of muscle representations in human motor cortex. *Electroencephalography & Clinical Neurophysiology, 85,* 1–8.

Wenke, R. J., Theodoros, D. & Cornwell, P. (2008). The short- and long-term effectiveness of the LSVT for dysarthria following TBI and stroke. *Brain Injury, 22*(4), 339–352.

——(2010). Effectiveness of Lee Silverman Voice Treatment (LSVT)® on hypernasality in non-progressive dysarthria: the need for further research. *International Journal of Language & Communication Disorders, 45*(1), 31–46.

Wilcox, K. & Morris, S. (1999). *Children's Speech Intelligibility Measure*. San Antonio, TX: The Psychological Corporation.

Wilde, E. A., Chu, Z., Bigler, E. D., Hunter, J. V., Fearing, M. A., Hanten, G., Newsome, M. R., Scheibel, R. S., Li, X. & Levin, H. S. (2006). Diffusion tensor imaging in the corpus callosum in children after moderate to severe traumatic brain injury. *Journal of Neurotrauma, 23,* 1412–1426.

Wilson, J. T. L., Hadley, D. M., Weidmann, K. D. & Teasdale, G. M. (1992). Intercorrelations of lesions detected by magnetic resonance imaging after closed head injury. *Brain Injury, 6,* 391–399.

Workinger, M. & Netsell, R. (1992). Restoration of intelligible speech 13 years post-head injury. *Brain Injury, 6,* 183–187.

World Health Organization (2001). *International Classification of Functioning, Disability and Health*. Geneva: World Health Organization.

Ylvisaker, M. (1986). Language and communication disorders following pediatric head injury. *Journal of Head Trauma Rehabilitation, 1,* 48–56.

Yorkston, K. M. & Beukelman, D. R. (1981). *Assessment of Intelligibility of Dysarthric Speech*. Austin, TX: PRO-ED.

Yorkston, K. M., Beukelman, D. R., Minifie, F. & Sapir, S. (1984). Assessment of stress patterning in dysarthric speakers. In M. McNeil, A. Aronson & J. Rosenbek (Eds), *The Dysarthrias: Physiology, Acoustics, Perception, Management* (pp. 131–162). San Diego, CA: College Hill Press.

Ziegler, W. & von Cramon, D. (1983a). Vowel distortion in traumatic dysarthria: a formant study. *Phonetica, 40*(1), 63–78.

——(1983b). Vowel distortion in traumatic dysarthria: lip rounding versus tongue advancement. *Phonetica, 40*(4), 312–322.

Ziegler, W., Hartmann, H. E. & von Cramon, D. (1988). Accelerated speech in dysarthria after acquired brain injury: acoustic correlates. *British Journal of Disorders of Communication. 23,* 21s–228.

9 Higher-level cognitive–communication approaches in chronic TBI to harness brain plasticity

Lori G. Cook, Asha Vas and Sandra B. Chapman

Traumatic brain injury (TBI) continues to be one of the major causes of long-term disability for individuals worldwide (Langlois *et al.*, 2006). However, emerging research regarding neuroplasticity provides evidence-based promise for recovery, particularly at chronic stages post-injury. This new evidence has compelled professionals involved in the research, diagnoses and/or treatment of cognitive–communication impairments in TBI to seek effective methodologies and follow-up monitoring to advance long-term recovery and higher brain performance levels.

The need to provide regular monitoring is particularly true in the paediatric realm, as younger age-at-injury has been widely shown to have a detrimental effect on cognitive-linguistic recovery from TBI (e.g. Chapman, 2006; Chapman *et al.*, 2004; Ewing-Cobbs *et al.*, 2003). Typically, children with TBI, especially those with moderate to severe injuries, are well treated during the acute period of care while still in the hospital system, whether it be in an inpatient or outpatient rehabilitation setting. However, upon discharge, families rarely receive specific direction regarding how to effectively facilitate the child's reintegration and continued success in school and social activities. As a result, the majority of children with TBI end up 'falling through the cracks' of what should rightly be a continuous system of care. In particular, failure to provide ongoing monitoring and follow-up care over the ensuing years after sustaining an injury increases the probability of poorer long-term outcomes due to the perturbation of a developing brain (Blosser & DePompei, 2003; Chapman, 2006; DePompei, 2010; Savage *et al.*, 2005). Mitigating the risk of later emerging deficits could be realized by application of timely, evidence-based monitoring protocols and interventions which promote both neural and functional recovery and continued achievement of cognitive milestones such as advanced reasoning abilities.

In this chapter, we review recent evidence that motivates efforts to address deficits in cognitive–communication skills years after sustaining a TBI, particularly in the domain of higher-order cognitive discourse abilities such as gist reasoning. Focus on higher-level cognitive skills which engage the frontal regions of the brain along with integrated neural networks is key to ameliorating the long-term effects of brain injury on daily life functioning. First, we briefly discuss the primary symptom domains associated with long-term outcome of TBI in children and adults and introduce complex language metrics to detect, characterize and monitor the long-term sequelae associated with chronic TBI. Second, we review typical pathology of TBI and associated cognitive implications as well as developmental considerations. Also, we consider the neurobiological evidence motivating use of higher-order strategy-based versus specific process-based approaches to cognitive–communication remediation. Third, we describe the clinical utility of cognitive strategy training. Paediatric and adult examples are included to illustrate application of a gist-based reasoning intervention to mitigate impairments in higher-order cognitive–communication skills and enhance functional learning efficiency across the lifespan. Finally, we offer attainable challenges to transform long-term outcomes in TBI.

Characterizing chronic-stage cognitive–communication deficits

Neurocognitive stall

The long-term effects of sustaining a TBI cross over several different domains, including deficits in language, cognition, behaviour, motor skills, psychosocial function and learning (e.g. Ewing-Cobbs *et al.*, 2004; Levin & Hanten, 2005; Max *et al.*, 2006; Savage *et al.*, 2005, Ylvisaker *et al.*, 2005). Extant longitudinal research in cognitive outcomes from brain injury has effectively negated the once widely held view that with a younger age at injury comes a better long-term prognosis. What increasing evidence continues to reinforce is that good recovery of *old* (i.e. previously learned) skills is often quite attainable following brain injury, whereas the ability to engage *new* skills (i.e. new learning) is negatively affected. In effect, earlier brain injury is, in fact, more detrimental to cognitive recovery in the long term due to the paucity of learning and development that has yet occurred at the time of injury (Chapman & McKinnon, 2000; Chapman *et al.*, 2004; Cook *et al.*, 2007). Essentially, a child with brain injury must recover again each time he or she reaches a new stage in development. As a result, often it is common to see marked recovery of pre-existing basic intellectual function and adaptive skills for a child with TBI, particularly within the first year post-injury, but then witness signs of difficulties in higher-level cognitive skills that emerge years after the initial injury. This 'neurocognitive stall', defined as a failure or lag in achieving subsequent cognitive milestones, as described by Chapman (2006), is characterized largely by an increasing 'gap' in cognitive–communication, social and educational domains relative to typically developing, non-injured peers over time. Ongoing monitoring throughout this latent stage (i.e. from one year post-injury through age 25) in children and adolescents with TBI is crucial for preventing a continued increase in this gap over time. Providing timely identification and characterization of functional cognitive–communication deficits can facilitate getting these children back 'on track' with their expected developmental course until they reach adulthood.

Cognitive–communication difficulties associated with neurocognitive stall include aspects such as disorganized language output, word retrieval difficulties, concrete thinking, inefficient study skills and impulsive and/or context-insensitive social interactions (Blosser & DePompei, 2003; Cook *et al.*, 2011; Turkstra *et al.*, 2008; Ylvisaker *et al.*, 2005). These are all aspects which are crucial for success in many different real-life contexts and areas which a rehabilitation professional should proactively assess and remediate, given the appropriate tools.

In most cases, typical standardized measures are not sensitive to the cognitive–communication deficits described above. For example, evidence indicates that achievement tests which provide a benchmark of academic skills (e.g. grade-level reading and maths) largely assess basic abilities that are typically either overlearned or automatic. Such skills tend to be relatively spared in brain injury, especially when considering recovery in the long term, so these assessments, in effect, do not reflect the skills that are contributing to academic difficulty (e.g. Ewing-Cobbs *et al.*, 1998, 2004). Ewing-Cobbs and colleagues' (1998) study, for one, well exemplifies this notion, as they reported average academic achievement test performance in children with TBI two years post-injury. Nonetheless, these same children demonstrated significant ongoing struggles in academic settings necessitating grade retention and/or special education intervention. As such, standardized achievement tests failed to reflect deficits that affect learning at chronic stages post-TBI.

In general, specific cognitive–communication deficits after TBI have been largely assessed by means of standardized language batteries. Until recently, there has not been a standardized cognitive assessment designed specifically for the paediatric brain injury population. The new screening tool, *The Pediatric Test of Brain Injury* (PTBI; Hotz *et al.*, 2010), helps fill the void by providing a mechanism for elucidating potential long-term issues in education and cognitive–communication domains after brain injury and offers a general understanding of how an individual child uses language to learn (Hotz *et al.*, 2001; Hotz *et al.*, 2009). The criterion-referenced assessment focuses on skills needed to adequately function in the school environment and provides a profile of strengths and weaknesses in different cognitive areas to guide general recommendations for intervention. However, because it is a screening measure, the PTBI does not provide the clinician with an in-depth interpretation of a child's functioning in any one particular area for more targeted remediation.

Complex language metrics

When evaluating the effectiveness of standard language and aphasia batteries in characterizing persistent cognitive–communication impairments in brain injury across the age range, they largely fall short. The primary reason is that such batteries focus on more basic language competency such as fluency, recall, naming, repetition, complexity of syntax and categorizing (Armstrong, 2005; Caplan *et al.*, 1996; Miceli *et al.*, 1981) and tend to employ measures on an isolated word or sentence level rather than on a discourse (i.e. connected language) level. In general, survivors of brain injury demonstrate relatively good recovery of these lower-level language skills (Brookshire *et al.*, 2000; Coelho *et al.*, 1991; McDonald, 2000), contributing to the view that specific language abilities are rarely persistently impaired in all but the most severe cases of TBI. For example, formal aspects of expressive language (such as phonology, syntax and semantics) have been shown to improve very early in recovery (i.e. as early as three months post-injury) from childhood brain injury (Ewing-Cobbs *et al.*, 1998, 2004). On the other hand, existing evidence indicates that many children with TBI, even though performing within normal limits on traditional expressive language measures such as use of complex syntax, demonstrate persistent difficulties with conveying their ideas in connected language, i.e. discourse (Chapman *et al.*, 2006; Chapman *et al.*, 1995a; Chapman *et al.*, 1995b). Likewise, chronic adult TBI patients have been reported to persistently struggle with absorbing and applying complex information, skills that draw upon proficiency in higher-order language function (Cannizzaro & Coelho, 2002; Galski *et al.*, 1998; Ylvisaker, 1992). Furthermore, measures of basic language ability demonstrate little to no correspondence with everyday functional tasks such as engaging in new learning, social functioning and job performance. In contrast, measures of discourse are fundamental to academic success, development of social skills and later functional independence (e.g. Chapman *et al.*, 1995a; Chapman *et al.*, 2001; Vas *et al.*, in press).

Additionally, much of the previous research in cognitive–communication functioning after brain injury has focused on characterizing the general cognitive sequelae and, in particular, executive function impairments, at the expense of elucidating language-based difficulties. Again, this diminished focus on linguistic outcomes was largely due to the predominant characterization of language as primarily the lexicon and syntax used for verbal expression. More recent work has reinforced the idea that utilizing assessment of higher-order discourse abilities over that of more basic or low levels of language is more likely to be sensitive to the persistent cognitive-linguistic impairments typically seen in children and adults with brain injury which impact success in many different settings (e.g. Coelho *et al.*, 2005; Ewing-Cobbs *et al.*, 2004; Gamino *et al.*, 2009a; Vas *et al.*, 2009, 2011). Increasingly, evidence supports the view of a dynamic interdependence between performance on measures of executive function and performance on higher-order discourse tasks (Anand *et al.*, 2011; Brookshire *et al.*, 2000; Chapman *et al.*, 2006; Gamino *et al.*, 2009a; Vas *et al.*, 2011).

In sum, much of the current momentum in language-based TBI clinical research is in utilizing discourse metrics as a tool for detecting, characterizing and treating the residual cognitive-linguistic effects of brain injury (e.g. Chapman *et al.*, 2006; Gamino *et al.*, 2009a; Vas *et al.*, 2011). Application of these more complex language metrics provides not only enhanced diagnostic sensitivity over traditional measures of basic language function but also an improved functional basis for treatment planning, as they are central to everyday life communication functions.

The discourse metrics typically used with the TBI population fall into two distinct categories: conversational discourse, often used to target social pragmatics (e.g. McDonald & Flanagan, 2004; Togher *et al.*, 2004) and monologues (e.g. Coelho, 2007; Jorgensen & Togher, 2009). Monologues encompass tasks eliciting procedural, descriptive, narrative or expository discourse. For example, procedural discourse may be elicited by having the patient explain the series of steps involved in making scrambled eggs (Chapman *et al.*, 2005). Eliciting descriptive discourse might involve asking the individual to provide a description of his or her family or the appearance of the family home (Hough & Barrow, 2003). Narrative discourse has most typically been assessed through elicitation of a straightforward retell (e.g. Chapman, 1997; Chapman *et al.*, 2001) or, more recently, by means of a more complex summarization of a story or text (e.g. Chapman *et al.*, 2006; Gamino *et al.*, 2009a; Vas *et al.*, 2009, 2011). Retells are often used as recall measures (i.e. to assess how many explicit facts/details were remembered from the original text). They can also be used to assess organization, as a retell should adhere to a standard discourse structure, including an initiating event (i.e. setting), character actions and a conclusion (i.e. resolution). A summary, on the other hand, requires not only conveying important information in an organized manner but also higher-order aspects such as condensing and synthesizing information to form abstracted meanings, or gist-based concepts, with less focus on detail-level information.

In terms of TBI, the majority of individuals demonstrate relatively preserved ability to apply linguistic knowledge during discourse output by using appropriate vocabulary and amount of language and formulating complex sentences, particularly in the spoken modality. In effect, the casual listener may not perceive any overt disruption in language structure and assume a lack of communication deficits requiring remediation (Cook *et al.*, 2007). However, use of discourse measures of information content and organization has revealed measurable and persistent deficits in children with TBI (Chapman *et al.*, 1997; Chapman *et al.*, 1995b). In sum, children with TBI were noted to express very little of importance or substance and were more likely to employ poor organization than their typically developing peers, even though they demonstrated comparable amounts of language output. Specifically, discourse impairments in paediatric TBI have been characterized by conveyance of fewer key ideas, poor organization and difficulty comprehending and/or conveying the central message of a text (Chapman *et al.*, 1992, 1995b, 1997, 2006). The overall communicative ability of individuals with brain injury can be affected by increased demand on cognitive processes required for synthesizing, organizing and abstracting meaning from large amounts of information, i.e. discourse (Cook & Chapman, in press; Gamino *et al.*, 2009a).

Although several different discourse procedures have been utilized with the TBI population, for the purposes of this chapter, we will focus on one promising discourse metric which evaluates gist reasoning, or the ability to strategically comprehend and convey generalized, core meaning(s) from complex information. The ability to abstract meaning has been shown to be a persistent and debilitating consequence of brain injury across age and severity ranges and has been associated with performance on executive control measures (Brookshire *et al.*, 2000; Chapman *et al.*, 2004, 2006; Gamino *et al.*, 2009a; Vas *et al.*, 2011). Each of us is daily flooded with massive amounts of information from which we must derive useful meaning(s) (Gabrieli, 2004), whether it be for purposes such as new learning or even job performance. In essence, the human brain is continually required to disregard or inhibit a majority of incoming data and to extrapolate global meanings from what is most relevant (Anand *et al.*, 2011; Ulatowska & Chapman, 1994; Vas *et al.*, in press). This process is conceptualized as *strategic learning*, or implementing a strategic approach to learning by: (1) extracting important information while inhibiting unimportant information; (2) holding key ideas in working memory; and (3) synthesizing information to form abstracted gist-based meanings through complex reasoning (Gamino *et al.*, 2009a; Gamino *et al.*, 2010).

Research in cognitive science continues to reinforce the idea that the human brain is designed for efficiency when it comes to learning, i.e. one is most effective at abstracting meaning and much less proficient at recalling large quantities of specific details (e.g. Brainerd & Reyna, 1998; Gabrieli, 2004). Therefore, the focus of learning should not be on how many facts or ideas an individual retains. Rather, the aim should be directed toward how effectively one can hone in on the major points or central message while excluding irrelevant information. As a result, vital memory manipulation and storage capacities are less likely to be exhausted (Gamino *et al.*, 2009a; Gamino *et al.*, 2010). Seeking higher-level meaning allows one to extract the 'gist' or core essence of information, a deeper-level meaning that is more long lasting and resilient to decay than detail-level meaning (Gabrieli, 2004).

In order to evaluate strategic learning ability through the metric of gist reasoning, Chapman and colleagues developed a discourse-based assessment entitled the *Scale of Advanced Reasoning* (SOAR; Chapman *et al.*, under review-b) based on more than 20 years of research following cognitive-linguistic recovery after paediatric brain injury (e.g. Chapman *et al.*, 1992, 1997, 2001, 2004, 2006; Gamino *et al.*, 2009a). The SOAR is a criterion-referenced, discourse-based assessment which evaluates skills encompassing different levels of complexity. These include: summary production (i.e. paraphrasing, inferencing, organizing, abstracting gist), generating an overall interpretative statement/'take-home' message (i.e. generalized analysis and application of text information to a real-life context), memory for explicitly stated and implicit content (i.e. recalling and inferring key ideas) and judgement of important versus unimportant content. The assessment calls upon the cognitive processes which are fundamental to learning ability, including inhibition, selection and integration of information (Gamino *et al.*, 2010).

The most recent study using the SOAR to assess gist reasoning ability in youth with TBI at least one year post-injury revealed significant impairment relative to typically developing peers in the ability to abstract gist-based meanings (Gamino *et al.*, 2009a). This added to our previous findings in paediatric TBI populations, as the measure has demonstrated sensitivity to higher-order cognitive-linguistic impairments at chronic stages, including: (1) difficulty constructing generalized interpretive statements (Chapman *et al.*, 2004); (2) stall at immature developmental level of 'copy-delete' approach to information reduction (Chapman *et al.*, 2006); (3) tendency to express more verbatim-level content than novelly constructed gist concepts (Chapman *et al.*, 2006). The overarching conclusion reached is that, when faced with the challenge of learning large amounts of information, children/adolescents with TBI persistently struggle with effectively combining details into bigger gist ideas. In general, children with TBI may opt to simply condense (i.e. delete) and retell (i.e. copy) the explicit detail-level information rather than constructing higher-order, abstracted meanings. This is in stark contrast to typically developing children, who are generally able to spontaneously abstract gist meanings, demonstrating integration of knowledge and synthesis of ideas, beginning in late childhood/early adolescence (Gamino *et al.*, 2009a; Gamino *et al.*, 2010).

The implications for memory functioning are evident as well, as Gamino and colleagues' (2009) study also found that the post-TBI gist reasoning impairment was present even though ability to recall detail information from the texts was preserved (Gamino *et al.*, 2009a). A similar disparity – good ability to recall details versus poor ability to abstract gist meanings – was revealed in their earlier 2006 study. Specifically, the youth with TBI demonstrated gist reasoning impairments but performed comparably to typically developing children in performance on an immediate memory word-list measure (Chapman *et al.*, 2006). Moreover, that same study revealed a significant positive correlation between gist reasoning ability and performance on a working memory measure, in contrast with no significant correlation for basic memory span (Chapman *et al.*, 2006). Taken together, the implication is that using working memory to synthesize details into larger abstracted meanings is a more strategic, top-down approach to processing information than relying solely on immediate memory to retain a series of disconnected details. The latter, bottom-up approach to absorbing content is likely to overwhelm cognitive resources.

The underlying reasons for the gist reasoning difficulties observed in children with TBI may be twofold. First, they may tend to 'over-select' when faced with learning new information. That is, they may have impaired inhibition mechanisms (i.e. ability to filter less relevant information in order to facilitate focus on important information). Second, they may predominantly rely on a less sophisticated 'bottom-up' approach to information processing, as demonstrated by good recovery of straightforward information recall and poor recovery of higher-order functions required to strategically learn new information, including difficulty deriving abstract meaning from details (e.g. Chapman *et al.*, 2004, 2006; Gamino *et al.*, 2009a; Hanten *et al.*, 2004). The observed 'stall' in gist reasoning ability associated with paediatric TBI, particularly during adolescence, can hinder cognitive–communication as required for academic success. Moreover, this stall may also detrimentally impact the long-term prognosis for succeeding in post-secondary education or even obtaining and holding down a job.

Frontal networks and gist: neurobiological evidence

Pathology and implications for cognition

Most instances of moderate to severe traumatic brain injury entail a combination of focal injury and diffuse injury, indicating more serious widespread damage than less severe injuries (Ewing-Cobbs *et al.*, 2003). Historically, the most common lesions observed in magnetic resonance imaging (MRI) studies of children with moderate-severe TBI are frontal and anterior temporal contusions (e.g,. Levin *et al.*, 1993; Mendelsohn *et al.*, 1992). Additional evidence suggests that children with severe TBI regularly present with tissue loss in prefrontal areas, even in the absence of focal brain lesions in the region (Berryhill *et al.*, 1995). In general, the relationship between injury severity and cognitive performance is increased by the size of frontal lobe lesions (Levin *et al.*, 1993). For example, children with relatively large frontal lobe injuries evident on MRI have been shown to exhibit significantly greater deficits than other children with severe, extra-frontal-lobe injuries when asked to retell a story (Chapman *et al.*, 1992). In particular, children with frontal lesions struggled with organizing information, manifested largely by omission of critical setting and action information, in addition to demonstrating decreased ability to retain the gist of the story (Chapman *et al.*, 1992).

The utility of discourse metrics in TBI populations is motivated by a neurobiological framework representing two dimensions that distinguish brain-behaviour relations proposed by Chen and colleagues (2006). Specifically, the two domains are labelled and defined as: (1) *functional specialization* – conceptualized as basic cognitive functions that are localized to specific cortical regions; and (2) *functional integration* – conceptualized as the dynamic interaction of complex networks across brain regions engaged during complex cognitive processing. With regard to language function, the domain of functional specialization would entail the capacity to use basic language functions such as semantics, syntax and retrieval of simple, explicitly stated facts. Studies have revealed specific brain lesions associated with impaired semantics, typically areas in the left temporal region, whereas specific brain lesions in Broca's area are associated with impaired syntax. In contrast to these more localized functions, functional integration is represented by processes with complex neuronal activation patterns which are widely distributed across brain regions. For example, evidence suggests that gist reasoning engages the frontal cortex, which integrates neuronal activity from temporal and parietal cortices (Anand *et al.*, 2009; Nichelli *et al.*, 1995; Wong *et al.*, 2006). Thus, complex language competence, manifested by synthesizing higher-order meaning through gist reasoning, involves functional integration across brain neural networks. The frontal cortices and precuneus play a central role in the integration of neuronal activity across multiple brain regions in abstracting meaning from complex information (Anand *et al.*, 2009; Wong *et al.*, 2006).

Brain-behaviour relations are being expanded by integrating neural and theoretical evidence. By engaging frontal networks to modulate distributed neuronal activity, functional integration facilitates processes that are relevant to internal goals while simultaneously suppressing processes that are not relevant via a top-down approach (Curtis & D'Esposito, 2003; Fuster, 2000; Miller & Cohen, 2001). Top-down cognitive control processes are characterized as goal-oriented, internally driven and voluntary operations that allow focused attention on task-relevant stimuli while ignoring irrelevant distractions (Kane & Engle, 2002). From a neurobiological perspective, top-down modulation involves bidirectional operations. That is, both the enhancement and suppression of neural activity in cortical regions may be warranted depending upon the relevance to ongoing goals. Functional imaging data increasingly support the primary role of prefrontal cortices in top-down modulatory tasks. The functional integration framework is particularly relevant to characterizing cognitive performance following a TBI, as frontal lobe damage and diffuse neuropathology of distributed cortical and subcortical networks are often indicated (Chen *et al.*, 2006).

Developmental considerations

In order to fully characterize cognitive–communication impairment after brain injury, one must take into account the nature of the developing brain, namely, frontal lobe development. The frontal lobes and their subsequent connections are the final neural systems to reach maturity, with imaging evidence indicating a protracted rate of development and rapid growth from ages 13 to 25 years (Giedd *et al.*, 1999). Injuries to this area prior to full maturation may be particularly detrimental. The complex neural pathways associated with the frontal lobes can be prematurely disconnected as a result of injury in childhood or adolescence (Chapman & McKinnon, 2000), affecting frontal circuitry which is undergoing elaboration and myelination (Giedd *et al.*, 1999). Additionally, diffuse axonal injury or shearing of white matter, a common occurrence in brain injury, may disrupt the long-term brain maturation process of the frontal-striatal-temporal-cerebellum neural networks in the developing brain. Therefore, a neurocognitive stall may appear more evident when the functions of this complex neural network are first emerging during and after adolescence. Moreover, children with marked brain injury to frontal networks may work hard to compensate for initial deficits in lower level skills, such as immediate memory, thereby strengthening the neural network supporting this skill. At the same time, the neural networks mediating more complex cognitive functions (e.g. working memory, gist abilities) may either lag behind in recovery, become weakened, or fail to develop at all (Chapman, 2006; Chapman *et al.*, 2006).

Chapman and colleagues' longitudinal and retrospective studies provided some of the first evidence of gist reasoning impairments in youth who have sustained a TBI, elucidating a distinction between higher-order versus lower-order cognitive–communication functions (Chapman, 2006; Chapman *et al.*, 2004, 2006; Gamino *et al.*, 2009a). Gist reasoning is a developmental phenomenon that continues to evolve from lower-level verbatim, fact-based learning to a more advanced and sophisticated gist-based learning (Reyna & Kiernan, 1994). This transition begins in early school years (as early as 5 years of age) and is refined through adolescence into young adulthood (college age), with further expansion possible into late life (e.g. Anand *et al.*, 2011; Brown & Day, 1983; Chapman *et al.*, 2006; Cook *et al.*, 2007). An important question continues to surface as to whether a TBI occurring prior to the full development of frontal networks will disrupt later maturation of frontal functions, leading to neurocognitive stall. The most compelling evidence for problems in later developing frontal lobe skills is derived from behavioural studies documenting a failure to develop higher-order language skills of gist reasoning.

Counter to the widely held view that younger brains show greater resilience, children with earlier age at injury have demonstrated lower gist reasoning performance when compared to children injured at an older age (e.g. Chapman *et al.*, 2004). Specifically, children injured before 8 years of age demonstrated lower performance than those injured after 8 years of age, despite similar injury severity and comparable recovery period. This disparity in development of higher-order cognitive skills as a result of a TBI at an earlier age could be attributed to the disruption in the developing frontal brain network, since rapid maturation is taking place with elaborate myelination and pruning during adolescence (Chapman *et al.*, 2001, 2004; Chapman *et al.*, 1995b; Giedd *et al.*, 1999; Levin, 2003). Thus, sustaining a brain injury in childhood or adolescence may alter or impede subsequent acquisition of higher-order language due to perturbation of developing brain networks (Dennis, 2000; Gamino *et al.*, 2009a).

Neural differences motivating strategy versus detail-based training

Distinct neural support for complex/integrated language functions versus basic/isolated skills comes from imaging studies that indicate a significant role of frontal networks in processing gist. Several functional brain imaging studies have examined the underlying neural differences in processing abstracted, gist-based information versus detail-based information (e.g. Anand *et al.*, 2009; Nichelli *et al.*, 1995; Robertson *et al.*, 2000; Wong *et al.*, 2006). For example, Nichelli and colleagues (1995) found activation in the right prefrontal cortex corresponding with abstracting gist-based meaning from discourse. Researchers have also documented brain regions to be differentially active during encoding of details versus gist. Plante and colleagues (2006) reported that encoding of details recruited a large area in the superior temporal gyrus in the left hemisphere and extended into the superior temporal sulcus and middle temporal gyrus. Encoding of gist was largely associated with frontal activation, specifically, in the region centred over the right precentral sulcus (Plante *et al.*, 2006). Positive correlation between perfusion in right frontal regions and proficient gist reasoning abilities was also reported in a SPECT study of youth with TBI (Wong *et al.*, 2006).

Most recently, a study employing a strategy-based gist reasoning training with healthy older adults (Chapman *et al.*, under review-a) revealed several significant cognitive and brain changes linked to the training, including increases in global and regional cerebral blood flow, increased connectivity and increased white matter integrity. They proposed that strategy-based cognitive training which integrates multiple neural networks rather than process-based training focused on single skills and, in effect, isolated brain areas, can improve not only trained and untrained cognitive domains but also enhance overall brain function.

Evidence-based neurocognitive interventions

High-order cognitive strategy training

Recent research discoveries regarding neuroplasticity, i.e. the brain's inherent capacity to change, reorganize and heal – generate new neurons, strengthen existing neural connections, form new pathways – has motivated creation of novel intervention applications to remediate the residual cognitive–communication effects of brain injury. The overarching goal of many clinical researchers who work with this population is to develop effective, evidence-based cognitive interventions which promote both neural and functional recovery, even at chronic stages post-injury.

Discourse-level applications have heretofore focused primarily on conversational discourse methods, targeting verbal communication skills and social pragmatics that play a role in daily life interactions (e.g. Coelho *et al.*, 2005; Helffenstein & Wechsler, 1982; Jorgensen & Togher, 2009; McDonald & Flanagan, 2004; Thomas-Stonell *et al.*, 1994). Specific goals include improvements in awareness of social rules and metacognitive aspects such as monitoring appropriateness of verbal communication. Additionally, aspects of discourse output, including logical and coherent expression of ideas, are often targeted (e.g. Jorgensen & Togher, 2009). Typical strategies to address these targets include methods such as modelling, role-playing, feedback, self-monitoring, behavioural rehearsal and social reinforcement.

Various researchers have employed these strategies by different means, all with the goal of improving communication performance in functionally relevant contexts. For example, Helffenstein and Wechsler's (1982) social skill training, or interpersonal process recall, utilized review of videotaped interactions. The training encompassed a total of 20 hours of videotaping relevant interpersonal exchanges followed by replay and review, with collaborative feedback provided by the therapist, the conversation partner and the individual with TBI. Other more recent conversational discourse approaches have incorporated more context-specific strategies. Thomas-Stonell and colleagues (1994) focused on the communicative context of the classroom for students with TBI and provided a computer-based programme targeting classroom-based communication skills. Teachers played an active role in providing guidance for aspects such as conversation initiation, turn-taking and topic maintenance. Coelho and colleagues' Communication Awareness Training (Coelho *et al.*, 2005) teaches increased awareness of disrupted conversational discourse, providing a three-step technique for specific contexts as well as practice for novel situations.

Research in discourse-level interventions in TBI beyond the realm of verbal communication and social pragmatics has been considerably more scarce and reported primarily at the individual patient, or case study, level. One representative example is a small-sample study (one adult with TBI and three non-injured, healthy adults) by Cannizzaro & Coelho (2002), which successfully utilized discourse organization training. The strategies focused on producing cohesive narratives, including the required story grammar elements of an initiating event which prompts a goal-directed action, the important action sequence and the consequence (whether the goal was attained or not). Another discourse-level application is an intervention approach called Strategies of Observed Learning Outcomes (SOLO; Biggs & Collis, 1982), designed to improve discourse comprehension abilities. The programme entailed training five increasingly difficult levels of text comprehension over 15 treatment sessions, ranging from prestructural (e.g. no relation between question and answer) to elaboration of learning to other situations. After training, the individual with TBI demonstrated not only improved accuracy in answering questions about the texts but also improved integration of information and self-monitoring abilities. Overall, evidence indicates that functional improvements in cognitive–communication impairments can be achieved through discourse-level interventions. Certain conversational and narrative discourse applications have been shown to yield immediate benefits, although long-term benefits and generalization beyond trained domains are either limited or unknown.

Our own work in assessment of gist reasoning with the paediatric TBI population has provided insight into some potential contributors to functional difficulties experienced by children in the long term, pointing to clear targets for discourse-level, strategy-based remediation. Evidence by Hanten and colleagues (2002, 2004) using selective learning paradigms suggests that children with TBI often 'over-select' information rather than strategically blocking or filtering incoming information, perhaps overwhelming already-taxed memory resources. This, coupled with neurobiological evidence of low efficiency of prefrontal neural connections, suggests that youth with TBI may be more prone to utilize a predominantly bottom-up approach to information processing. They are likely to demonstrate relatively good recovery of straightforward information recall, such as in being able to relay a list of facts back to you. However, the more top-down, or higher-order cognitive functions involved in creating new knowledge, or strategically learning new information, may pose a continued challenge. As such, we employed a top-down complex reasoning approach to remediate strategic learning using gist reasoning. Gist reasoning incorporates aspects which are pivotal for acquiring new meaning. These include strategic attention as well as aspects of integrated reasoning, such as drawing upon pre-existing knowledge, and elaborated reasoning, or generalizing new insights to create innovative solutions. Moreover, focus on gist reasoning abilities facilitates transition from classroom-based skills to functional/social aspects because of its utility across many different real-life domains.

The intervention programme developed by Chapman and colleagues is entitled *Strategic Memory Advanced Reasoning Training* (SMART; copyright) and is designed to target gist reasoning ability, as revealed by performance on the *Scale of Advanced Reasoning* (SOAR). The primary objective of SMART is improvement in the ability to abstract gist-based meaning from complex information. The programme can be adapted for use with either adults or older children/adolescents. In general, for the younger populations, training is broken down into 8–10 intensive 45-minute sessions carried out over a four- to five-week period, typically meeting two times per week. The programme is strategy-based rather than content-based, but does utilize predominantly text-based materials as well as some of the child's own schoolwork for immediate application/reinforcement when possible. Additionally, strategies are addressed hierarchically, with each one building upon the next and being reinforced at the next level, with an emphasis on generalization to other contexts/modalities (e.g. social scenarios, television or movie-viewing, etc.). Each stage aims to block the use of immature detail-based learning by reinforcing the global idea of transforming concrete details into abstracted, generalized meanings to create novel ideas. Key ideas of the SMART programme include: eliminating unimportant information, abstracting information in your own words, coming up with your own questions, generating multiple interpretations and 'take-home' messages, raising the information to a new level of understanding and creating new knowledge to apply to your own life in other contexts. Each strategy is given a child-friendly name (e.g. Link it!) to promote memory for the strategy and the cognitive process(es) associated with it. From the very first strategy (i.e. Bounce it!) up to the final steps (i.e. Step it up! and Live it!), the child is increasingly challenged to use top-down strategies of gist-based learning rather than the bottom-up approach of verbatim information recall.

The efficacy of the SMART programme was initially evaluated with children with Attention Deficit Hyperactivity Disorder (ADHD). In their 2009 study, Gamino and colleagues demonstrated significant gains in ability to abstract gist-based meanings by children and adolescents with ADHD who completed SMART. In contrast, those who completed an alternative intervention focused on basic attention and inhibition skills demonstrated no significant gains in advanced reasoning (Gamino *et al.*, 2009b). Thus, the implication is that solely attending better does not enable a person to abstract complex meaning more effectively. The SMART programme has also been effectively implemented in a group-based classroom setting, yielding significant gist-reasoning gains and corresponding improvements in standardized academic testing for typically developing, economically disadvantaged middle-school students (Gamino *et al.*, 2010).

In a recent study by Vas *et al.* (2011), the SMART programme was employed with adults with TBI (ages 20–65 years) who were at least one year post-injury. After SMART training, participants demonstrated significantly improved gist reasoning ability (nearly 30 per cent gain), with their responses improving from being comprised of mostly copied or paraphrased ideas to inclusion of more abstracted, generalized meanings. Moreover, observed benefits of training generalized to untrained domains including performance on executive function measures of inhibition, working memory and cognitive flexibility as well as measures of daily life functioning. Importantly, the improvements in performance (across trained and untrained domains) were maintained even at 6 months post-training. In comparison, individuals who completed an equally engaging training programme that focused on information dissemination about TBI and brain health in general did not demonstrate significant gains in these areas.

These studies motivated application of the gist reasoning training to remediate higher-order cognitive deficits associated with neurocognitive stall in youth with TBI. Preliminary results from an ongoing pilot study employing the SMART training with 10 adolescents (ages 12–20 years) with chronic-stage TBI reveal significantly improved gist reasoning performance after completing SMART coupled with improved ability to provide generalized interpretive statements as well as gains in ability to recall details from texts (see Figure 9.1). For a control group receiving a fact-based rote memory strategy training, preliminary findings indicate no significant gains in any of these areas. Overall, the implication is that a top-down complex reasoning approach is effective in remediating higher-order cognitive deficits in adolescents with chronic-stage traumatic brain injury. Further, top-down modulation of information has a positive impact on bottom-up processes such as recall of details.

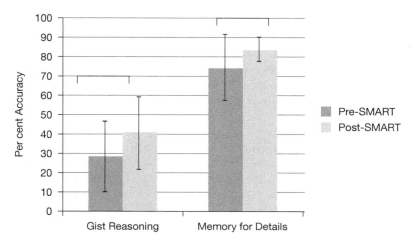

Figure 9.1 Preliminary findings for adolescent TBI group mean scores for gist reasoning and memory for text details before and after SMART training

Additionally, similar to the adult TBI study, the primary study group (SMART) demonstrated significant improvement in untrained measures of executive function, namely those of working memory and inhibition. Again, for the memory training control group, preliminary findings indicate no significant gains in any of these untrained domains.

SMART gist reasoning training: case illustrations

Children/adolescents with TBI

In order to illustrate the improvements in gist reasoning ability for the adolescents with TBI who underwent the SMART training, the following represent excerpts from summary responses, both before and after training. Responses were elicited by asking participants to provide a high-level summary (i.e. convey the important information and high-level ideas in their own words) of a 575-word text about a man's life (which reads like a history lesson).

> *Participant 1 – Summary excerpt from* before *training:*
> John *graduated from college.* He *became a teacher but was too easy on his students.* Then he *became a lawyer and was too soft with his clients and wouldn't take high paying cases.* He then opened a store but his prices were too low. He tried to be a minister but his thoughts on slavery weren't right at the time. During the war he volunteered in a group but *he had to resign because of his health. For the last five years of his life he worked as a clerk.* He had a hard time finding a job that he liked all his life, so *he died as a failure, but he is remembered for the song Jingle Bells.*

> *Participant 1 – Summary excerpt from* after *training:*
> John Pierpont was this man who **tried to see what's in life that best fits him.** He went through all kinds of [work] **just to be told that he was not cut out for that.** He **failed at every job he tried because he was too generous.** *When he died, he felt as though he accomplished nothing.* When **in reality, he led an incredible life of remembered generosity.** He **became a good man, endowed society.**

> *Participant 2 – Summary excerpt from* before *training:*
> John's life to him was a failure. He *failed at everything he did* because he was too nice or had a different opinion towards important things that made him either be fired or have to quit. He lived his whole life and died thinking that he was a failure and could never finish anything that he started. Little did John know *he wasn't a failure.* Now *John is seen as a very successful man* that *changed lots of ways that needed to be changed, like the law, credit, slavery* and many more things.

Participant 2 – Summary excerpt from after *training:*
John and everyone else might have seen him as a failure, but really he wasn't. He accomplished so many things because he was a **very socially involved person**. *He left the world with a gift of service* and **how important it is to give back to your community**. He gave our society the gift of well service to one another. **With his kind heart, others benefited from him and learned from him, which is the best gift of all.**

In the excerpts, the italic portions represent phrases that are almost verbatim pieces from the original story. In contrast, the portions in bold represent phrases that convey abstracted ideas from the story. Before training, both participants demonstrated little to no interpretation or abstracting of ideas but rather expressed a serial account of the details or a few basic main idea statements (i.e. essentially a low-level 'copy and delete' strategy). After training, we see inclusion of several gist-based, abstracted, novel ideas that go beyond the surface-level details to incorporate the 'bigger picture' or central theme of the story, which involves standing up for one's moral values or putting service to others above personal gain.

Practical applications

Possible suggestions for practical applications based on the SMART strategies within school or home environments might include the following:

1. Have the child practice identifying unimportant information when studying difficult reading material and preparing for class assignments. The child can eliminate irrelevant, repeated and/or distracting information by means of crossing out/covering up (think of this as using a 'black marker' instead of a 'yellow highlighter') and making an outline of just the important information to be learned. Not every detail is important, so the ones that are critical are worth pulling out and documenting, especially when having to juggle many different readings.
2. Encourage the child to be strategic within other everyday-life modalities as well (e.g. lectures, videos, conversations). Rather than attempting to hold on to every piece of incoming information, identify what is important to keep in mind while disregarding irrelevant content and synthesize a 'take-home message'. This makes more efficient use of cognitive resources and frees one from carrying out needless loads of mental work.
3. Help the child with organization strategies for class note-taking by creating an outline, during class or after, including only the most important information and overall gist for the lesson. Encourage him/her to listen first, then to write ideas/impressions in his/her own words. It is particularly important to hone in on the central point from all the information, as disconnected ideas are more likely to become less substantive over time.
4. Have the child summarize information as he/she studies, putting the important information to be learned in his/her own words, then combining

the information to create a summary of what was studied. Also encourage generating multiple interpretations and 'take-home' messages. Convey that research reinforces that we are able to learn things in a more lasting way when we make information our own (i.e. abstract information in our own words) rather than getting bogged down in the word-for-word details.

5. Assist the child in finding a way to group or find relationships between information to be learned, such as when having to memorize things for schoolwork (for example, memorizing the periodic table of elements for chemistry class). It is easier to store and remember information in 'chunks' rather than in individual pieces. Find commonalities in meaning among content in order to commit more efficient, organized chunks to memory.

6. When studying for a test, have the child set up a schedule which allows him/her to practise over a number of days rather than trying to 'cram' everything into a short time period.

7. Help the child facilitate a tactical approach to a multi-step task (such as a term-long project or paper). Help him or her formulate the overall goal first and then reasonably consider what the most important first step should be. Once the more foundational groundwork is laid, the smaller steps are less overwhelming. Focus on one step at a time, regarding the highest priority first. Establish small deadlines along the way for maintaining constant progress rather than trying to get the entire project done at once for the final deadline.

8. Motivate the child to decrease the amount of time spent multitasking by organizing his/her time in a way that allows focus on a single task at a time and minimizes potential distractions. For example, if the child is to write a paper at his/her computer, encourage making sure that the internet browser is closed, the television is off and the child's phone is silenced. Productivity and quality of output will be enhanced by focusing on one task at a time and decreasing multitasking may also help relieve some pressure of 'information overload'.

Adults with TBI: example application and real-life remarks

To illustrate the application of the SMART strategies for a more adult context, the following is an example using a real-life task of writing a resume: the first step of *strategic attention* (i.e. strategy of filter) involves deleting information that would not be relevant to include in the individual's resume. That is, the individual has to identify the most important information related to his/her own skills and strengths. The second step of *integration* (i.e. strategies of zoom in and zoom out) involves categorizing the individual's skills and strengths into academic accomplishments, leadership qualities, professional or personal characteristics and work experience, including volunteer work that relates to the job he/she is applying for. These categories are supported with relevant details to help the employer/interviewer capture the breadth and depth of earlier experiences and expertise. The third principle of *innovation* (i.e. strategies of flexibility and perspectives) involves summarizing the qualifications and abilities at a higher/broader level into two or three succinct statements to provide the resume 'objective' statement. Innovation also involves flexibility in preparing the resume in multiple formats and revising the objectives statements to adapt to the different employers' needs and job requirements. Application of SMART strategies to other daily life tasks such as planning an event, learning from a lecture, or discussion of a movie are also discussed in the training sessions.

The benefits of the SMART training for adults were best exemplified by the participants' testimonies as to the relevance of the strategies in their daily lives, even at a year after completion of the training. A 22-year old participant, Sally, expressed the usefulness of the strategies in her academics: *'It just really feels good to actually make an "A" (97%) in a class.'* A parent of a 25-year-old participant, Brian, observed a similar improvement in her son. *'When he went back to school for the next semester, he was able to focus better, keep up with his classes and do all that needs to be done as a college student ... He got all As in his fall semester, even with the addition of another class.'* She also noted spillover benefits beyond just academics, stating, *'Not only did the SMART programme help [Brian] in his academic life, but his social skills have improved a lot as well.'* Another adult participant (Roger, 41 years old) appeared to get the most out of the strategies at his workplace. He stated, *'I am still using the skills you taught us and am enjoying the productivity that comes with finishing tasks. I was offered a 35% pay increase. Thanks for giving me the tools to do that.'* Patient Matt (30 years old) credited the use of the SMART strategies in helping him get his life in order, which allowed him to more easily pursue his life goals. *'I am going to school and loving being married. It has been very good for my wife and me. I still struggle with organization and money management and follow through, but it is so much better now than a year ago.'* His family member summed it up best, saying, *'I see maturity in him, which is a blessing and with focus on the things he has learned and applying them, he will continue to be successful.'*

Attainable challenges to transform TBI outcomes

Currently, researchers and healthcare professionals are poised at an exciting stage for generating positive change in the clinical management of TBI across the lifespan. Research over the past decade, in particular, has afforded a better understanding of proactive approaches for overcoming the current challenges faced by individuals with TBI, their families and the professionals who help guide their recovery. Specifically, clinical professionals must consider the possibility that, as a whole, the way that we have traditionally detected and treated TBI is essentially 'upside-down and backwards'. We must align our efforts toward three attainable challenges that are essential to systematically advance methods for improving long-term outcomes in TBI.

First, clinical researchers and care providers must embrace the brain's inherent ongoing neuroplasticity and focus on promoting brain repair even at later stages after injury. As one parent of a child with brain injury so astutely pointed out, *'We were surrounded by help when the brain was undergoing spontaneous recovery. There was NO help when we and our child's brain needed treatment the most ... years later.'* Unfortunately, the majority of the targeted treatment for individuals with TBI is during the acute phase, when they are more likely to receive intensive rehabilitation and multifaceted support, and there is often good recovery of previously acquired skills and general functionality. However, there is very little, if any, focus on providing monitoring and treatment at long-term intervals, either to target later-emerging difficulties, particularly in the developing child, or to help mitigate the occurrence of substantial issues down the road (e.g. school dropout/loss of employment, psychosocial dysfunction, etc.). Consider the model example represented by standard protocols for managing an individual diagnosed with leukaemia. Intensive treatment is typically provided upon detection of the disease and, once successful, ongoing monitoring is mandated to ensure remission and provide for detection of reoccurrence(s) so that timely interventions can be applied. Clinical management of TBI should follow a similar pattern, with chronic-stage monitoring and intervention being just as crucial to recovery as acute-stage rehabilitation.

Second, researchers and clinical professionals must work to improve provision of evidence-based, top-down approaches to assessment and treatment rather than perseverating less effective, bottom-up approaches to remediation. Recent evidence indicates that addressing higher-level, integrated cognitive processes can have a more comprehensive and rapid benefit to functional outcomes and even enhance overall brain reorganization, in contrast to targeting of lower-level, isolated skills. The significance for higher-order cognitive metrics, in general, and gist reasoning, in particular, to enhance long-term outcomes is suggested by: (1) diagnostic sensitivity of gist reasoning to the long-term cognitive–communication deficits in TBI; (2) ecological validity of gist reasoning in characterizing the complex cognitive functions necessary to achieve personal educational and occupational goals; (3) spillover of gist reasoning training benefits to other cognitive control functions; and (4) emerging evidence suggesting that gist reasoning training can improve not only trained and untrained cognitive domains but also enhance overall brain function (Anand *et al.*, 2011; Chapman *et al.*, under review-a; Chapman *et al.*, 2004, 2006; Cook & Chapman, in press; Gamino *et al.*, 2009a; Gamino *et al.*, 2010; Vas *et al.*, 2011).

Third, both healthcare providers and brain injury communities alike must champion the capacity for individuals with TBI to become or return to being productive members of society without having to lose access to valuable support at later stages. In many medical systems, rehabilitation services are only covered during the acute phase and it is very difficult for individuals to obtain insurance coverage for services needed later down the road. Further, in order to receive continuing financial support, an individual must often be designated as disabled, or unable to work. As a result, many individuals with TBI may feel unmotivated or held back from ever entering or rejoining the work force for fear of losing his or her benefits. On the other hand, others may not want to be labelled as disabled or to be enabled by disability benefits. Rather, they want to perform at their highest level of potential and independence, both physically and cognitively. Being empowered and engaged in meaningful activities is one of the most valuable contributors to recovery and resilience, and gainful employment and access to services which maximize one's potential are often key to facilitating such lasting success.

In closing, traumatic brain injury remains one of the major causes of long-term disability, but we are becoming more keenly aware of the detrimental effect of TBI on multiple aspects of brain health and to the dramatic increase from high-impact contexts such as extensive combat and sports participation. Recently, public awareness of the lasting impact of TBI has greatly increased across the globe. In particular, those traditionally considered to be on the mild end of the spectrum, such as combat-related head injuries and concussions incurred during play of high-impact sports, have been widely publicized due to associations with long-term risk factors such as dementia or depression. Increasingly, clinical professionals are recognizing the vital need to implement follow-up assessments at regular intervals and offer short-term intensive treatment throughout recovery. Such ongoing monitoring and timely cognitive training would serve to keep the cumulative effects of TBI in 'remission', helping to stave off later-emerging or worsening deficits.

Rehabilitation and brain performance training for TBI should harness the brain's remarkable capacity for plasticity at every stage by utilizing top-down treatment approaches. Rapidly advancing the field of brain repair in TBI has never been more vital to enhancing functional outcomes for the millions of children and adults who suffer 'invisible' but life-altering injuries.

Acknowledgements

This work was supported by the National Institute of Neurological Disorders and Stroke (NINDS) Grant 2R01 NS 21889-16, the National Institute of Child Health and Human Development (NICHD) Grant R21-HD062835, as well the Horizon Foundation.

References

Anand, R., Motes, M. A. Maguire, M. J., Moore, P. S., Chapman, S. B. & Hart, J. (2009). Neural basis of abstracted meaning. Poster presented at Neurobiology of Language, Chicago, IL.

Anand, R., Chapman, S. B., Rackley, A., Keebler, M., Zientz, J. & Hart, J. (2011). Gist reasoning training in cognitively normal seniors. *International Journal of Geriatric Psychiatry, 26*, 961–968.

Armstrong, E. (2005). Language disorder: a functional linguistic perspective. *Clinical Linguistics & Phonetics, 19*(3), 137–153.

Berryhill, P., Lilly, M. A., Levin, H. S., Hillman, G. R., Mendelsohn, D., Brunder, D. G., Fletcher, J. M., Kufera, J., Kent, T. A. & Yeakley, J. (1995). Frontal lobe changes after severe diffuse closed head injury in children: a volumetric study of magnetic resonance imaging. *Neurosurgery, 37*, 392–400.

Biggs, J. B. & Collis, K. F. (1982). *Evaluating the Quality of Learning: The SOLO Taxonomy.* New York: Academic Press.

Blosser, J. & DePompei, R. (2003). *Pediatric Traumatic Brain Injury: Proactive Intervention.* (2nd edn). Albany, NY: Delmar Publishing/Thompson Learning.

Brainerd, C. J. & Reyna, V. F. (1998). Fuzzy-trace theory and children's false memories. *Journal of Experimental Child Psychology, 71,* 81–129.

Brookshire, B. L., Chapman, S. B., Song, J. & Levin, H. S. (2000). Cognitive and linguistic correlates of children's discourse after closed head injury: a three-year follow-up. *Journal of the International Neuropsychological Society, 6*(7), 741–751.

Brown, A. L. & Day, J. D. (1983). Macrorules for summarizing texts: the development of Expertise. *Journal of Verbal Learning and Verbal Behavior, 22,* 1–14.

Cannizzaro, M. S. & Coelho, C. A. (2002). Treatment of story grammar following traumatic brain injury: a pilot study. *Brain Injury, 16*(12), 1065–1073.

Caplan, D., Hildebrandt, N. & Makris, N. (1996). Location of lesions in stroke patients with deficits in syntactic processing in sentence comprehension. *Brain,* 119(3), 933–949.

Chapman, S. B. (1997). Cognitive–communication abilities in children with closed head injury. *American Journal of Speech-Language Pathology, 6,* 50–58.

——(2006). Neurocognitive stall, a paradox in long term recovery from pediatric brain injury. *Brain Injury Professional, 3*(4), 10–13.

Chapman, S. B. & Mckinnon, L. (2000). Discussion of developmental plasticity: factors affecting cognitive outcome after pediatric traumatic brain injury. *Journal of Communication Disorders, 33*(4), 333–344.

Chapman, S. B., Culhane, K. A., Levin, H. S., Harward, H., Mendelsohn, D., Ewing-Cobbs, L., Fletcher, J. M. & Bruce, D. (1992). Narrative discourse after closed head injury in children and adolescents. *Brain and Language, 43,* 42–65.

Chapman, S. B., Levin, H. S. & Culhane, K. (1995a). Language impairment in closed head injury. In H. Kirschner (Ed.), *Handbook of Neurological Speech and Language Disorders* (pp. 387–414). New York: Marcel-Dekker.

Chapman, S. B., Levin, H. S., Matejka, J., Harward, H. & Kufera, J. A. (1995b). Discourse ability in children with brain injury: correlations with psychosocial, linguistic, and cognitive factors. *Journal of Head Trauma Rehabilitation, 10,* 36–54.

Chapman, S. B., Watkins, R., Gustafson, C., Moore, S., Levin, H. S. & Kufera, J. A. (1997). Narrative discourse in children with closed head injury, children with language impairment, and typically developing children. *American Journal of Speech-Language Pathology, 6,* 66–76.

Chapman, S. B., McKinnon, L., Levin, H. S., Song, J., Meier, M. C. & Chiu, S. (2001). Longitudinal outcome of verbal discourse in children with traumatic brain injury: three year follow-up. *Journal of Head Trauma Rehabilitation, 16,* 441–455.

Chapman, S. B., Sparks, G., Levin, H. S., Dennis, M., Roncadin, C., Zhang, L. & Song, J. (2004). Discourse macrolevel processing after severe pediatric traumatic brain injury. *Developmental Neuropsychology, 25,* 37–61.

Chapman, S. B., Bonte, F. J., Chiu Wong, S. B., Zientz, J. N., Hynan, L. S., Harris, T. S., Gorman, A. R., Roney, C. A. & Lipton, A. M. (2005). *Alzheimer Disease and Associated Disorders, 19,* 202–213.

Chapman, S. B., Gamino, J. F., Cook, L. G., Hanten, G., Li, X. & Levin, H. S. (2006). Impaired discourse gist and working memory in children after brain injury. *Brain and Language, 97,* 178–188.

Chapman, S. B., Aslan, S., Hart, J. J., Bartz, E. K., Mudar, R. A., Keebler, M. W., Gardner, C. M., DeFina, L. F. & Lu, H. (under review-a). Neural mechanisms of brain plasticity with complex cognitive training in healthy seniors.

Chapman, S. B., Gamino, J. F. & Cook, L. G. (under review-b). *Scale of Advanced Reasoning.*

Chen, A. J. W., Abrams, G. M. & D'Esposito, M. (2006). Functional reintegration of prefrontal neural networks for enhancing recovery after brain injury. *Journal of Head Trauma Rehabilitation, 21*(2), 107.

Coelho, C. A. (2007). Management of discourse deficits following traumatic brain injury: progress, caveats, and needs. *Seminars in Speech and Language, 28,* 122–135.

Coelho, C. A., Liles, B. Z. & Duffy, R. J. (1991). Discourse analyses with closed head injured adults: evidence for differing patterns of deficits. *Archives of Physical Medicine and Rehabilitation, 72*(7), 465–468.

Coelho, C. A., Grela, B., Corso, M., Gamble, A. & Feinn, R. (2005). Microlinguistic deficits in the narrative discourse of adults with traumatic brain injury. *Brain Injury,* 19(13), 1139–1146.

Coelho, C., Ylvisaker, M. & Turkstra, L. S. (2005). Nonstandardized assessment approaches for individuals with traumatic brain injuries. *Seminars in Speech and Language, 26*(4), 223–41.

Cook, L. G. & Chapman, S. B. (in press). Neurocognitive stall in pediatric TBI: new directions for preventing later emerging deficits. *Journal of Medical Speech-Language Pathology.*

Cook, L. G., Chapman, S. B. & Gamino, J. F. (2007). Impaired discourse gist in pediatric brain injury: missing the forest for the trees. In K. Cain and J. Oakhill (Eds), *Children's Comprehension Problems in Oral and Written Language: A Cognitive Perspective* (pp. 218–243). New York: Guilford Publications, Inc.

Cook, L. G., DePompei, R. & Chapman, S. B. (2011). Cognitive communication challenges in TBI: assessment and intervention in the long term. *Perspectives on Neurophysiology and Neurogenic Speech and Language Disorders, 21,* 33–42.

Curtis, C. E. & D'Esposito, M. (2003). Persistent activity in the prefrontal cortex during working memory. *Trends in Cognitive Sciences, 7*(9), 415–423.

Dennis, M. (2000). Developmental plasticity in children: the role of biological risk, development, time, and reserve. *Journal of Communication Disorders, 33*(4), 321–332.

DePompei, R. (November 2, 2010). Traumatic brain injury: where do we go from here? *ASHA Leader* (pp. 17–20). Washington, DC: ASHA.

Ewing-Cobbs, L., Fletcher, J. M., Levin, H. S., Iovino, I. & Miner, M. E. (1998). Academic achievement and academic placement following traumatic brain injury in children and adolescents: a two-year longitudinal study. *Journal of Clinical and Experimental Neuropsychology, 20,* 769–781.

Ewing-Cobbs, L., Barnes, M. A. & Fletcher, J. M. (2003). Early brain injury in children: development and reorganization of cognitive function. *Developmental Neuropsychology, 24,* 669–704.

Ewing-Cobbs, L., Barnes, M., Fletcher, J. M., Levin, H. S., Swank, P. R. & Song, J. (2004). Modeling of longitudinal academic achievement scores after pediatric traumatic brain injury. *Developmental Neuropsychology, 25,* 107–133.

Fuster, J. M. (2000). Executive frontal functions. *Experimental Brain Research, 133*(1), 66–70.

Gabrieli, J. D. E. (2004). Memory: Pandora's hippocampus? *Cerebrum, 6,* 39–48.

Galski, T., Tompkins, C. & Johnston, M. V. (1998). Competence in discourse as a measure of social integration and quality of life in persons with traumatic brain injury. *Brain Injury, 12*(9), 769–782.

Gamino, J. F., Chapman, S. B. & Cook, L. G. (2009a). Strategic learning in youth with traumatic brain injury: evidence for stall in higher-order cognition. *Topics in Language Disorders, 29*(3), 224–235.

Gamino, J. F., Chapman, S. B., Hart, J. & Vanegas, S. (2009b). Improved reasoning in children with ADHD after strategic memory and reasoning training: a novel intervention for strategic learning impairment. Abstract presented at the International Neuropsychological Society Annual Meeting in Atlanta, Georgia.

Gamino, J. F., Chapman, S. B., Hull, E. L. & Lyon, R. (2010). Effects of higher-order cognitive strategy training on gist reasoning and fact learning in adolescents. *Frontiers in Educational Psychology, 1*, 1–16. doi:10.3389/fpsyg.2010.00188

Giedd, J. N., Blumenthal, J., Jeffries, N. O., Castellanos, F. X., Liu, H., Zijdenbos, A. & Rapoport, J. L. (1999). Brain development during childhood and adolescence: a longitudinal MRI study. *Nature Neuroscience, 2*(10), 861–863.

Hanten, G., Zhang, L. & Levin, H. S. (2002). Selective learning in children after traumatic brain injury: a preliminary study. *Child Neuropsychology, 8*, 107–120.

Hanten, G., Chapman, S. B., Gamino, J. F., Zhang, L., Benton, S. B., Stallings-Roberson, G., Hunter, J. V. & Levin, H. S. (2004). Verbal selective learning after traumatic brain injury in children. *Annals of Neurology, 56*(6), 847–853.

Helffenstein, D. A. & Wechsler, F. S. (1982). The use of interpersonal process recall (IPR) in the remediation of interpersonal and communication skill deficits in the newly brain-injured. *Clinical Neuropsychology, 4*, 139–142.

Hotz, G., Helm-Estabrooks, N. & Nelson, N. (2001). Development of the pediatric test of brain injury. *Journal of Head Trauma Rehabilitation, 16*(5), 426–440.

Hotz, G., Helm-Estabrooks, N., Nelson, N. & Plante, E. (2009). The pediatric test of brain injury: development and interpretation. *Topics in Language Disorders, 29*(3), 207–223.

——(2010). *Pediatric Test of Brain Injury.* Baltimore, MD: Paul H. Brookes Publishing Co.

Hough, M. S. & Barrow, I. (2003). Descriptive discourse abilities of traumatic brain-injured adults. *Aphasiology, 17*(2), 183–191.

Jorgensen, M. & Togher, L. (2009). Narrative after traumatic brain injury: a comparison of monologic and jointly-produced discourse. *Brain Injury, 23*(9), 727–740.

Kane, M. J. & Engle, R. W. (2002). The role of prefrontal cortex in working-memory capacity, executive attention, and general fluid intelligence: an individual-differences perspective. *Psychonomic Bulletin & Review, 9*(4), 637–671.

Langlois, J. A., Rutland-Brown, W. & Thomas, K. E. (2006). *Traumatic Brain Injury in the United States: Emergency Department Visits, Hospitalizations, and Deaths.* Atlanta, GA: Centers for Disease Control and Prevention, National Center for Injury Prevention and Control.

Levin, H. S. (2003). Neuroplasticity following non-penetrating traumatic brain injury. *Brain Injury, 17*(8), 665–674.

Levin, H. S. & Hanten, G. (2005). Executive functions after traumatic brain injury in children. *Pediatric Neurology, 33*, 79–93.

Levin, H. S., Culhane, K. A., Mendelsohn, D., Lilly, M. A., Bruce, D., Fletcher, J. M., Chapman, S. B., Harward, H. & Eisenberg, H. M. (1993). Cognition in relation to magnetic resonance imaging in head-injured children and adolescents. *Archives of Neurology, 50*, 897–905.

Max, J. E., Levin, H. S., Schachar, R. J., Landis, J., Saunders, A. E., Ewing-Cobbs, L., Chapman, S. B. & Dennis, M. (2006). Predictors of personality change due to traumatic brain injury in children and adolescents six to twenty-four months after injury. *Journal of Neuropsychiatry and Clinical Neuroscience, 18*, 21–32.

McDonald, S. (2000). Putting communication disorders in context after traumatic brain injury, *Aphasiology, 14*(4), 339–347.

McDonald, S. & Flanagan, S. (2004). Social perception deficits after traumatic brain injury: interaction between emotion recognition, mentalizing ability, and social communication. *Neuropsychology, 18*(3), 572–579.

Mendelsohn, D., Levin, H. S., Bruce, D., Lilly, M., Harward, H., Culhane, K. A. & Eisenberg, H. M. (1992). Late MRI after head injury in children: relationship to clinical features and outcome. *Child's Nervous System, 8*, 445–452.

Miceli, G., Caltagirone, C., Gainotti, G., Masullo, C. & Silveri, M. (1981). Neuropsychological correlates of localized cerebral lesions in nonaphasic brain damaged patients. *Journal of Clinical Neuropsychology, 3*, 53–63.

Miller, E. K. & Cohen, J. D. (2001). An integrative theory of prefrontal cortex function. *Annual Review of Neuroscience, 24*(1), 167–202.

Nichelli, P., Grafman, J., Pietrini, P., Clark, K., Lee, K. Y. & Miletich, R. (1995). Where the brain appreciates the moral of a story. *Neuroreport, 6*(17), 2309–2313.

Plante, E., Ramage, A. E. & Magloire, J. (2006). Processing narratives for verbatim and gist information by adults with language learning disabilities: a functional neuroimaging study. *Learning Disabilities Research & Practice, 21*(1), 61–76.

Reyna, V. F. & Kiernan, B. (1994). Development of gist versus verbatim memory in sentence recognition: effects of lexical familiarity, semantic content, encoding instructions, and retention interval. *Developmental Psychology, 30*(2), 178–191.

Robertson, D. A., Gernsbacher, M. A., Guidotti, S. J., Robertson, R. R., Irwin, W., Mock, B. J. & Campana, M. E. (2000). Functional neuroanatomy of the cognitive process of mapping during discourse comprehension. *Psychological Science, 11*(3), 255–260.

Savage, R., DePompei, R., Lash, M. & Tyler, J. P. (2005). Pediatric traumatic brain injury: review of pertinent issues. *Pediatric Rehabilitation, 8*(2), 92–103.

Thomas-Stonell, N., Johnson, P., Schuller, R. & Jutai, J. (1994). Evaluation of a computer-based program for remediation of cognitive–communication skills. *Journal of Head Trauma Rehabilitation, 9*(4), 25–37.

Togher, L., McDonald, S., Code, C. & Grant, S. (2004). Training communication partners of people with traumatic brain injury: a randomised controlled trial. *Aphasiology, 18*(4), 313–335.

Turkstra, L. S., Williams, W. H., Tonks, J. & Frampton, I. (2008). Measuring social cognition in adolescents: implications for students with TBI returning to school. *NeuroRehabilitation, 23*, 501–509.

Ulatowska, H. K. & Chapman, S. B. (1994). Discourse macrostructure in aphasia. In R. L. Bloom, L. K. Obler, S. DeSanti & J. S. Ehrlich (Eds), *Discourse Analysis and Applications* (pp. 29–46). Hillsdale, NJ: Lawrence Erlbaum Associates.

Vas, A. K., Keebler, M. & Krishnan, K. (2009). Neuroscience to neurorehabilitation: new frontiers. Poster presentation at the Third International Conference, Vocational Outcomes in Traumatic Brain Injury, in Vancouver, Canada.

Vas, A. K., Chapman, S. B., Cook, L. G., Elliott, A. C. & Keebler, M. (2011). Higher-order reasoning training years after traumatic brain injury in adults. *Journal of Head Trauma Rehabilitation, 26*(3), 224–239.

Vas, A. K., Chapman, S. B. & Cook, L. G. (in press). Language impairments in traumatic brain injury: a window into complex cognitive performance. In J. H. Grafman & A. M. Salazar (Eds), *Handbook of Clinical Neurology (Traumatic Brain Injury)*.

Wong, S. B. C., Chapman, S. B., Cook, L. G., Anand, R., Gamino, J. F. & Devous, M. D. (2006). A SPECT study of language and brain reorganization three years after pediatric brain injury. In A. R. Moller (Ed.), *Reprogramming the Brain: Progress in Brain Research* (vol. 157, pp. 173–185). Amsterdam: Elsevier.

Ylvisaker, M. (1992). Communication outcome following traumatic brain injury. *Seminars in Speech and Language, 13*, 239–250.

Ylvisaker, M., Adetson, P. D., Braga, L. W., Burnett, S. M., Glang, A., Feeney, T., Moore, W., Rumney, P. & Todis, B. (2005). Rehabilitation and ongoing support after pediatric TBI: twenty years of progress. *Journal of Head Trauma Rehabilitation, 20*, 95–109.

10 Evidence-based practice and cognitive rehabilitation therapy

Mary R.T. Kennedy

Evidence-based practice and cognitive rehabilitation therapy

Imagine the following scenario. A speech-language pathologist (SLP) has three years of experience working with adults with acquired brain injury (ABI) who have cognitive and communication disorders. Her hospital-based caseload consisted of inpatients on a rehabilitation unit with medical diagnoses of stroke, degenerative diseases and traumatic brain injury (TBI). The hospital has created an outpatient, interdisciplinary programme to support individuals with TBI as they transition back into the community and the SLP has recently joined this team of professionals. While some of her clinical experience with acute recovery TBI patients will be useful, she needs to expand her knowledge and skills in order to evaluate, treat and support individuals who are at a more chronic phase of recovery. How will she gain the knowledge and skills to make evidence-based practice (EBP) decisions with a sample of the population for whom she has little experience? In short, how will she become an EBP clinician with this chronic, transitioning population?

The purpose of this chapter is to provide an overview of EBP and how clinicians can become informed, critical consumers of 'the evidence', using cognitive rehabilitation therapy (CRT) after TBI as an example. This chapter begins with a conceptual model of EBP. Accessing and interpreting the scientific evidence for CRT is then described. Resources for accessing and interpreting CRT evidence are presented and examples of systematic reviews and recommendations are provided so that readers can see how and why reviews differ in their conclusions. This chapter concludes with a discussion of how to apply the evidence that reflects 'best-practices' and when and how to rely upon practical clinical decision-making.

Evidence-based practice

Although clinicians have historically looked to research evidence to inform their clinical decision making, it has only been in the past 20 years that the terms 'evidence-based practice' or 'evidence-based medicine' have been used to describe this process. There are numerous definitions of EBP (e.g. Sackett *et al.*,

1997). Muir Gray (1997) described EBP as 'an approach to decision making in which the clinician uses the best evidence available, in consultation with the patient, to decide upon the option that suits that patient best'. In all definitions of EBP, there are three common features: 1) current scientific evidence including published systematic reviews, meta-analyses, randomized controlled trials, case reports and expert opinion; 2) clients' abilities, disabilities, goals and values; and 3) clinicians' expertise and decision-making skills (American Speech, Language, and Hearing Association, www.asha.cnet/maps).

A model of EBP is depicted in Figure 10.1 where therapeutic context influences four features rather than the three outlined above. The influence of 'context' is described immediately below followed by a discussion of two specific factors, 'practice-based evidence' and 'clinician expertise'. The other two factors, 'client abilities and goals' and 'scientific evidence' are described within the framework of cognitive rehabilitation therapy with an emphasis on the tools clinicians need to access, interpret and apply the scientific evidence that is currently available.

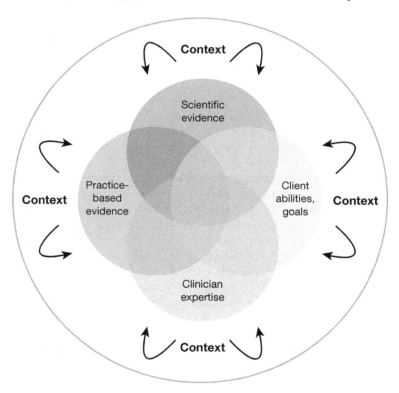

Figure 10.1 Evidence-based practice (EBP) represented in a Venn diagram of four overlapping features considered within a therapeutic context

The *therapeutic context*, be it a hospital, outpatient clinic, transitional programme, home, work or school setting, impacts clinical decisions about evaluation procedures, goals and intervention. There are several reasons for considering the impact of context on EBP (McCauley & Fey, 2006). First, environments provide fertile ground for determining if strategies taught in a clinic room will generalize or transfer to the environment where they are used. For example, using a planner is a practical skill on an in-patient rehabilitation unit and one that will also be needed as the patient transitions to home. Secondly, goals and strategies are more easily understood by clients when the need is obvious to them as a function of their involvement in activities and situations that occur in their everyday context. A young adult with impaired learning and executive functions problems (and his clinicians) may not know if the goal to return to college is a realistic goal early in his recovery phase; it is only later, when both clinicians and clients see how much recovery has occurred that these kinds of goals can be considered. It is in the later context that instructing the client in encoding strategies for learning would be especially relevant – when the client experiences the need for the strategy. Thus, the context has important functional relevance; the context provides reasons for using strategies by demonstrating the 'value added' to the client and family.

Thirdly, contexts can alter or even constrain the kinds of intervention that can be realistically delivered. For example, working with someone who has returned to work does not necessarily allow the time for repetitive practice and drill work espoused for individuals with severe memory impairments; however, the functional work setting provides a natural schedule with which to practice a new skill. For example, practice may occur naturally and regularly throughout the day as that skill is needed (e.g. Kennedy & Krause, 2011).

Finally, it may be that context and third party payers are related. Most payers are interested in functional outcomes that lead to cost containment, i.e. improved self-reliance and independence that leads to a reduction in burden of care and lower costs. When clinicians create intervention plans within the natural community context (e.g. home, school, work), the plans will more likely reflect practical and functional outcomes needed in those settings. When clinicians create intervention plans within a hospital context, the plans will more likely reflect foundational skills that can be built on later as one transitions in the community, and skills needed to reduce the burden of care upon discharge. '*Practice-based evidence*' (PBE) is one of four features of the model in Figure 10.1. PBE is often missing in depictions of EBP even though clinicians engage in it regularly. PBE is the ongoing evaluation process in which clinicians determine the benefits of therapy by carefully tracking progress (in the form of data) that clients make during therapy while considering the other factors that could account for improved performance (Wambaugh, 2007). When available, the scientific evidence (EBP) taken together with PBE allows clinicians to determine if their particular client is benefiting from a specific, validated intervention. In CRT, as in many areas of rehabilitation, there are more therapy approaches available to clinicians than there is scientific evidence to support their use. This means that clinicians must use their 'best clinical judgement' when selecting a therapy and, based on PBE, evaluate the ongoing outcomes. Sohlberg and Tursktra (2011) described a PBE approach to therapeutic decision making in their Plan (P), Implement (I), and Evaluate (E) model (PIE). Here clinicians carefully and systematically collect data as they implement the therapy plan, evaluate the outcomes, modify the plan if needed and implement the modified plan.

'*Clinician expertise*' is a fourth factor of EBP that intersects with the other three in several ways. This includes the experience clinicians have working with: various populations of clients, e.g. brain injury; various levels of severity and types of deficits in cognitive, speech, language and social communication deficits; various contexts, such as hospitals, clinics, home, schools, etc.; various intervention approaches typically recommended for clients with that severity of deficit; and various kinds of outcomes and goals that lead to functional outcomes. Importantly, expertise includes clinicians' knowledge of the scientific evidence and how to weigh the evidence in light of individual clients' abilities, disabilities, goals and the context. Indeed, the intent of this chapter is to enhance clinicians' understanding of EBP within CRT.

What is cognitive rehabilitation therapy (CRT)?

CRT is an 'umbrella' term that refers to a wide variety of interventions that are intended to restore or compensate for cognitive and communication deficits after TBI (e.g. Katz *et al.*, 2006; Harley *et al.*, 1992). It is not a single intervention, but a collection of interventions; a more accurate term would be 'cognitive rehabilitation therap*ies*'. As such, it is:

> a systematic, functionally oriented service of therapeutic cognitive activities, based on an assessment and understanding of the person's brain-behaviour deficits. Services are directed to achieve functional changes by 1) reinforcing, strengthening, or reestablishing previously learned patterns of behavior, or 2) establishing new patterns of cognitive activity or compensatory mechanisms for impaired neurological systems.
>
> (Harley *et al.*, 1992, p. 63).

A more recent description emphasizes the impact of CRT 'on social, communication, behaviour, and academic/vocational performance' and the kinds of instruction clinicians engage in when delivering CRT, including 'modeling, guided practice, distributed practice, errorless learning, direct instruction with feedback, paper-and-pencil tasks, communication skills, computer-assisted retraining programs, and use of memory aids' (Benedict *et al.*, 2010, p. 62).

Regardless of the definition, there are several common features in definitions of CRT:

1.   CRT can restore cognition and communication and/or can compensate for deficits in cognition and communication. Many have argued that nearly all

of CRT strategies compensate for a former way of thinking or behaving. Indeed, neuroscience evidence is showing that brain connections and structures change with repetitive behavioural routines, creating new perhaps compensatory, neural networks.

2. Modular and/or comprehensive approaches are used. Modular CRT approaches assume that underlying processes can be isolated and targeted in therapy and therefore focus on improving a specific cognitive process (e.g. selective attention through direct attention training). Comprehensive approaches assume that cognitive processes are difficult to isolate in context; these approaches are typically provided during acute recovery stages shortly after injury or at chronic recovery stages for those with pervasive cognitive and/or psychosocial deficits. In reality, both approaches are often used but at different recovery stages depending on individuals' needs (Sohlberg & Mateer, 2000).

3. CRT must be individualized and tailored to clients' specific abilities, disabilities, goals, preferences, values and context. While this highly specific approach of CRT has individualized benefits, this is a challenge to researchers who attempt to determine its effectiveness to groups of individuals. The Chair of the Committee on Cognitive Rehabilitation Therapy for Traumatic Brain Injury from the Institute of Medicine (Washington, DC, USA) observed that

> CRT seems to be tailored to each individual patient, so that it is challenging to identify the unifying elements or ingredients that can be applied to most individuals with cognitive deficits after TBI. We have a different challenge in other areas of therapeutics where we are faced with the need to individualize and personalize treatments that appear to benefit broad groups of patients.
>
> (Personal communication, Ira Shoulson, MD, Neurology, 2011)

Client abilities, disabilities and goals with CRT

Evaluating *clients' abilities, disabilities and understanding their own goals* is a critical feature of EBP (Figure 10.1) and weighs heavily into clinicians' decisions about which therapy approach should be used. 'SLPs assess and treat the underlying cognitive processes (e.g. attention, memory, self-monitoring, executive function) as they interact and are manifest in communication behaviour, broadly understood (listening, reading, writing, speaking, gesturing) at all levels of language (phonological, morphologic, syntactic, semantic, pragmatic)' (Kennedy *et al.*, 2002, p. x).' Using the World Health Organization's International Classification Framework of Enablement (2001), SLPs have traditionally focused much of their evaluation on identifying the underlying cognitive and communication *impairments*, including various attentional, memory, organizational and executive function processes. Turkstra *et al.* (2005) surveyed SLPs about their evaluation practices with individuals with TBI. The vast majority of clinicians reported using impairment-based tests, even though their psychometric strength varied greatly. Few had, what is called 'ecological validity', which means that the test is related to other measures of everyday functioning. For example, in February 2012, a clinician sent out a request on a list serve for recommendations of tests for a high level professional who had a TBI, but had recovered well with lingering high-level cognitive deficits. Responses were numerous; the tests that were recommended targeted the impairment level of the WHO ICF model, with the exception of one test, *The Functional Assessment of Verbal Reasoning* (MacDonald, 2005: see Chapter 4 for more details), which targets functional, everyday activities. No questionnaires, surveys or interview tools that capture activities and participation information were recommended. Standardized, impairment-level test performance does not necessarily provide a roadmap for determining functional, practical and contextualized goals (Turkstra *et al.*; Wilson, 1993). It does however, assist clinicians when considering types of strategies that would be beneficial and when considering the kinds of instructional approaches used to teach clients practical strategies at later and chronic stages of recovery.

Although most cognitive and communication assessment tools target the impairment level of WHO ICF, there are increasing numbers of questionnaires, surveys and structured interviews, techniques that capture the client's, family's and careprovider's perspectives and desired outcomes. These standardized tools and procedures provide clinicians with a way to measure this perspective and understand how the client views their daily activities and participation at home, school, work and community. Examples of these tools include the Behavior Rating Inventory of Executive Function (Children & Adults versions) (Gioia *et al.*, 2000), the College Survey for Students with Brain Injury (CSS-BI) (Kennedy & Krause, 2009), the La Trobe Communication Questionnaire (Douglas *et al.*, 2000) and Mayo-Portland Adaptability Inventory-4 (Malec & Lezak, 2005).

These kinds of self-reported outcomes predict functional outcomes and participation at chronic recovery stages. For example, Sveen and colleagues (2008) found that the cognitive and interpersonal factors on the Patient Competency Rating Scale (Hart, 2000) predicted community participation at 3 and 12 months post-injury. However, these self-reported tools should not be used alone. A combination of self-reported (and/or family reported) perception and goals and clinical observation can lead to functional goals and strategies to achieve those goals. When considered together, activity and participation level information help clinicians to structure goals into an overall treatment plan whereas impairment level information helps clinicians identify instructional approaches that are likely to be useful when teaching strategies. Readers are referred to other sources for lists of evaluation tools of impairment, activity and participation, such as Constantinidou & Kennedy (2011) and Stiers *et al.* (2012).

Accessing and understanding the scientific evidence

In the scenario at the beginning of this chapter, the SLP finds herself working with a new population in a new context, so she needs to be educated on best practices for working with individuals at a chronic recovery stage. Most likely she will first consult with her colleagues who have more experience than her and who know what the job responsibilities entail. When clinicians are asked 'What is the first thing you do when you are unsure how to proceed with a particular client?', the most common answer is 'Ask a clinician who has more experience than I do'. That is, they consult with colleagues who have more experience with this kind of client, treatment and outcomes. When asked, 'What is the second most likely way for you to figure out how to work with this client?', the most common response is to 'Look at the scientific evidence published in journals'. Even though reviews of evidence are readily available on-line, the order of these answers is unlikely to change. Why? Clinicians explain that they have little time to search for, find and read publications and it is more efficient to ask colleagues. After all, through brief conversations with colleagues, clinicians can quickly determine if their clients are a good fit for a particular kind of intervention. However, there could be an additional reason for this. Research conducted on how to persuade people's opinions, beliefs and behaviour suggests that anecdotal evidence, especially in the form of stories, is more persuasive than trying to change an opinion based on the 'facts'. So consider this – experienced clinicians have years of anecdotal evidence in their biographical clinical memories which may make it difficult for them to change their practice when scientific evidence conflicts with their clinical experiences (Baldoni, 2011).

While getting input from colleagues is valuable, the SLP needs to be able to access the scientific literature of intervention studies, systematic reviews and best practice clinical recommendations that have targeted this sample of the TBI population. If she has access to university library databases, she can search for these publications using keywords. Knowing which keywords to use is critical – many relevant studies do not use the term 'cognitive rehabilitation therapy', so she needs to start with numerous terms and narrow her search from there. For example, if wanting to search for studies verifying the benefits of compensatory external cognitive aids, she would need to use various combinations of the following keywords (but not limited to):

- Population: 'brain injury', 'traumatic brain injury', 'acquired brain injury', 'adults', 'children', 'paediatrics'
- Therapeutic strategy: 'cognitive rehabilitation', 'cognitive aids', 'memory aids', 'internal' or 'external memory strategies', 'metacognitive strategies', 'cognitive orthotics', 'planners', 'technology', 'smart phones', 'assistive technology', etc.
- To target the kind of publication narrow the identifier search to case study, case series, controlled trial, randomized controlled trial, systematic review and/or meta-analysis.

Many internet browsers have a specific category dedicated to scholarly publications which saves time and narrows the search quickly (e.g. Google Scholar). But accessing publications can be challenging if clinicians are not affiliated with a college or university. Fortunately 'open access' journals are becoming more commonplace and as the scientific integrity of these journals improves, clinicians will soon have assurance that these publications have gone through the rigour of peer review.

What kinds of publications should clinicians target when first starting a search? Many would start by searching for the results specific to randomized controlled clinical (RCT) trials. However, an important consideration is how *bias* can confound the search and selection process. Since clinicians often go to colleagues for advice first, it is likely that colleagues will recommend a study that reported results based on *their own bias*. Additionally, clinicians who select a single study to review without examining other studies on the topic run the risk of ignoring studies that may have found dissimilar results. For this reason, it is best that *clinicians first search for systematic reviews.* The assumption here is that the authors of peer-reviewed systematic reviews engaged in methodological processes that protected against their own biases.

In addition to finding scholarly publications, there are many websites that are dedicated to, or have a webpage dedicated to the scientific evidence of CRT, including assessment and intervention studies, systematic reviews, meta-analyses and summaries of clinical recommendations. The following are examples of organizations and websites that provide direct access to a variety of evidence resources, listed alphabetically.

- The *Academy of Communication Disorders and Sciences* (ANCDS; www. ancds.org/) provides direct access to published systematic reviews, clinical recommendations, tables of evidence, and opinion pieces on CRT.
- *The Center for Reviews and Dissemination* (http://www.crd.york.ac.uk/ CRDWeb/ResultsPage.asp) contains summaries and critiques of systematic reviews.
- *Evidence-Based Review of Moderate To Severe Acquired Brain Injury* (ERABI: http://www.abiebr.com/) contains educational modules for clinicians to learn about the evidence in specific areas of CRT.
- *Global Evidence Mapping (GEM) Initiative* (Bragge *et al.*, 2011, National Trauma Research, www.evidencemap.org) created maps of the research evidence for the care of individuals with spinal cord injury and traumatic brain injury.
- The *National Center for Evidence-based Practice* (American Speech, Language and Hearing Association, NCEP; http://www.ncep.org/) contains 'evidence maps' which has organized access to references on the assessment and treatment of individuals with cognitive, speech or language impairments after TBI.
- The *Psychological Database for Brain Impairment Treatment Efficacy* (psycBITE; www.psycbite.com) provides searching capabilities of over 400 intervention studies, reviews and clinical recommendations of CRT for individuals with brain injury.

- *SpeechBITE, a Database for Brain Impairment Treatment Efficacy* (speechBITE; http://www.speechbite.com/) provides similar searching capabilities as PsycBITE for publications that pertain to speech, language and/or communication disorders.

Understanding and interpreting published scientific evidence

Before clinicians can interpret the CRT evidence they need to understand the evolution of intervention research (Golper, *et al.*, 2001; Robey & Schultz, 1998). Initially, when researchers have hypotheses about the benefits of a particular intervention, they engage in what is called 'discovery' or 'efficacy' studies where the feasibility and initial testing of that intervention are conducted under ideal conditions that are carefully controlled, e.g. quiet clinic rooms delivered in large dosages over a long period of time. These studies range from single case studies, non-randomized group cohort studies, to fully randomized and controlled clinical trials (RCTs). Efficacy studies typically compare an experimental treatment to no treatment or treatment that is unrelated to the experimental treatment. Most of the research conducted on CRT after TBI remains at the efficacy or 'discovery' phase.

Once treatment efficacy is established researchers embark on studies of 'comparative effectiveness'. These studies involve comparing the experimental intervention to another intervention, often one that reflects conventional practice that is hypothesized to produce very different results. This second phase of research can also compare an intervention under ideal conditions, to the same intervention delivered under 'typical conditions', e.g. delivering the intervention at home versus the clinic. However, in order to conduct effectiveness studies, researchers need published or publically available 'manuals', as has been done for other complex interventions, such as for cognitive behavioural therapy. Additionally, comparative effectiveness research requires large samples of the population to have sufficient statistical power to determine that one treatment is more beneficial (or benefits differing outcomes) than the other (IOM, 2011; Vickery, 2012). This is especially important since presumably there will be 'some' benefit to receiving the alternative treatment, but that benefit should be smaller than the benefit of the experimental treatment. Finally, researchers need validated outcomes that improve the 'ability to carry out important daily activities in the person's physical and social environment' and which, in turn, result in changes in the person's participation in society (e.g. employment, role at home, return to school, caregiver's) and quality of life (IOM, 2011, p. 274). 'Cost effectiveness' studies of CRT have not been conducted, although there are some comparative effectiveness studies.

The final stage of intervention research, called 'efficiency' research, is typically conducted after a treatment protocol has been found to be effective with real-life outcomes in comparative effectiveness studies. Here, researchers want to determine the precise dosage of intervention that is needed to obtain the desired outcomes, or which parts of the intervention package are critical in order to obtain the desired outcomes. It is unfortunate that most of the CRT literature ends after the efficacy stage. This means that the active ingredients that result in intervention effects in CRT and the cost benefit of CRT are yet to be determined.

Interpreting individual intervention studies

Once clinicians have access to individual intervention studies and/or systematic reviews, they need to know how to interpret them. Individual intervention studies are typically ranked using a hierarchy that places randomized, controlled trials (RCT) and n-of-1 trials as the strongest form of evidence. There are additional grades of evidence within RCTs and also for studies that compare groups that are not randomized. Grades of evidence are summarized in Table 10.1.

It seems logical that clinicians should be assured that the intervention study they are reading is of high methodological quality. Yet it is too simplistic to assume that all group studies including RCTs automatically deserve a higher

Table 10.1 Levels of evidence, clinical recommendations and evidence requirements for recommendations as specified by the American Academy of Neurology (AAN) (2004, 2011)

Level of evidence	Clinical recommendations	Requirements of the evidence
Class I evidence: randomized controlled trials (RCT) with masked outcome assessment in a representative population with qualifiers.	**Practice Standard** is a Level A recommendation 2004 – 'it should be done' 2011 – 'it must be done'	At least 2 Class I (studies), established as effective, useful, in a specified population.
Class II evidence: prospective matched group cohort studies in a representative population with masked outcome assessment that meets Class I criteria or a randomized controlled trial that lacks one criterion for Class I.	**Practice Guideline** is a Level B recommendation 2004 – 'it should be considered' 2011 – 'it should be done'	At least 1 Class I study or 2 consistent Class II studies probably effective for a given condition in the specified population.
Class III evidence: controlled studies including natural history control or patients serves as their own controls and outcomes are independent of treatment.	**Practice Option** is a Level C recommendation 2004 – 'it may be considered' 2011 – 'it may be done'	At least 1 Class II or 2 Class III studies which determine that treatment is possibly effective.
Class IV evidence: uncontrolled studies, case series, case reports, or expert opinion.	Level U, 'no recommendation'	Data is inadequate or conflicting; current knowledge, treatment is unproven.

ranking than carefully controlled single-subject multiple baseline designs. RCTs and single-subject studies have different purposes and methodologies and are therefore difficult to compare to each other. It has been argued that while the intent of group treatment studies is to determine *the group* benefits from treatment, it is also true that the treatment benefit *to individuals* can be lost when outcomes are averaged across study participants. There are several challenges that CRT researchers face when attempting to conduct RCTs that meet the traditional criteria used to rate study quality. For example, one of the biggest methodological issues is the blinding of participants to the purpose of the intervention and the expected outcomes. With the focus of CRT moving towards person-centred intervention and outcomes, where the individual plays an integral role in identifying their own goals (to the extent that they are able to do so) and the steps needed to attain these goals, ensuring that the person is 'not aware' of the purpose or outcomes of the intervention is not feasible or even encouraged. This research practice of 'blinding' study participants is important particularly for guarding against a placebo effect and is standard practice in drug studies, but is impractical in intervention studies where changes in complex behaviours are being targeted, such as in CRT for individuals with TBI (Kennedy & Turkstra, 2006). An advantage that single-subject multiple baseline studies have over group studies is the tight experimental control that the researcher has in the intervention process as they respond to each individual's progress. However, the degree to which the outcomes of studies employing small numbers of individuals can be generalized to a larger sample is a valid concern.

There are numerous evaluation tools available that are used to rate or rank how well the researchers controlled for bias in an individual study, i.e. to what extent are the results due to the therapy that was provided rather than internal and external factors that may or may not have been experimentally controlled. Two such tools are the PEDro-P and SCED scales. The PEDro-P scale (http://www. psycbite.com/docs/The_PEDro-P_Scale.pdf) has 11 criteria that are used to evaluate RCT and non-RCT group comparison studies. 'The first item relates to the external validity (specifically the participant selection criteria). The remaining 10 items (criteria 2–11) assess the internal validity of each trial and whether the trial contains sufficient statistical information to make it interpretable. Thus, the internal validity of each trial is ranked based on a total score out of 10 (i.e. excluding criterion 1)' (www.psycbite.com, accessed on June 6, 2012). Maher and colleagues (2003) found that the original PEDro scale on which the PEDro-P scale is based was stable and reliable in rating RCTs.

The SCED scale (http://www.psycbite.com/docs/The_SCED_Scale.pdf) provides criteria for rating single-subject designed studies and its reliability has been published by Tate *et al.* (2008). Eleven elements are rated by the SCED and as such provide Level 1 evidence according to the Oxford Centre for Evidence-Based Medicine (http://www.cebm.net/index.aspx?o=5653): 1) Clinical history is provided, including age, gender, aetiology and severity; 2) Target behaviours are repeatable and measured; 3) There are three phases, either A-B-A or multiple baseline; 4) Pre-treatment baseline is established with sufficient sampling; 5)

The treatment phase is characterized with sufficient sampling; 6) Raw data points are recorded and reported; 7) Inter-rater reliability is established for at least one of the target behaviours; 8) Evaluation is completed by independent assessors; 9) Statistical analysis is included; 10) Replication is present either across subjects, therapists or settings; and 11) There is evidence of generalization. The SCED scale has since been revised as the Risk of Bias in N-of-1 Trials (RoBiN-T) Scale which has finer grained items assessing both internal and external validity. See Chapter 13 for further details.

Interpreting systematic reviews

Published systematic reviews are extremely useful to clinicians who are looking for scientific evidence, though they vary in purpose and method (Kennedy, 2007). Some reviews are conducted in order to assess the benefits of a type of CRT, whereas other reviews focus on various kinds of outcomes (e.g. participation outcomes versus impairment test score outcomes). Reviews may or may not include a meta-analysis, which is a statistical procedure used to analyse the magnitude of the treatment effect or the size of outcome effects across several studies. Unfortunately, the terms 'systematic review' and 'meta-analysis' are sometime used interchangeably, even in databases where clinicians and researchers search for studies, e.g. PsychInfo database. In CRT, there are numerous systematic reviews but very few meta-analyses. Indeed, because CRT is an umbrella term for a collection of therapies meant to compensate or restore cognition, finding studies that employ the same therapy in the same manner is challenging. Furthermore, it is challenging to identify to what extent the therapeutic elements or ingredients are sufficiently similar across therapies, which would allow treatment effects to be grouped, commonly done in meta-analyses.

Regardless of the purpose, systematic reviews follow careful procedures to locate, identify, select, rate the quality of the selected studies and evaluate the outcomes in an effort to control for bias and provide methodological transparency (American Academy of Neurology, AAN, 2011). Indeed, published reviews should list all of the databases that were searched and keywords used in the search. If the search was narrowed by excluding certain databases, then the careful consumer would know that it is possible that some studies were missed. For example, when searching for CRT studies, it is important to include not only health and medical databases (e.g. PubMed, Medline), but also educational and vocational rehabilitation databases (e.g. ERIC) since some of CRT takes place outside the medical model. Similar to understanding the methods of a sole intervention study, consumers of systematic reviews need to know how each decision was made, so that they can choose to apply (or not apply) the evidence to their individual client within the existing therapeutic context.

Systematic reviews synthesize the research evidence into hierarchies based on the methodological rigour of the studies. There are numerous 'levels of evidence' available to researchers who conduct systematic reviews. A clinically useful hierarchy comes from the American Academy of Neurology (AAN, 2011) where levels of evidence are directly 'translated' into clinical practice recommendations. Table 10.2 provides readers with the language and definitions. Level A, the strongest recommendation has been revised to use the helping verb 'must' use, Level B recommendations now use 'should' and Level C now use 'may'. They explain that

> *Must* recommendations are rare, as they are based on the high confidence in the evidence and require both a high magnitude of benefit and low risk … *Should* recommendations tend to be more common, as the requirements are less stringent but still based on the evidence and benefit-risk profile.
>
> (AAN, 2011, p. 20)

Two other commonly used hierarchies of evidence are the Oxford Centre for Evidence Based Medicine, 2.1 (2011) and the National Health and Medical Research Council (NHMRC, 2000). The former hierarchy includes five levels of evidence with additional subdivisions, whereas the latter one includes six levels of evidence that map nicely onto PEDro scale scores for RCTs, and the SCED scores for controlled single-subject design studies (see Table 10.2). Regardless of the hierarchy, stronger evidence results in stronger language used to describe the practice recommendation.

Table 10.2 Levels of evidence, requirements of the evidence as specified by National Health and Medical Research Council (NHMRC, 1999) using PEDro-P scores (PsycBITE; www.psycbite.com) to rate the evidence from group trials

Level of evidence	Requirements of the evidence	Maximum PEDro Scale score
I	Evidence obtained from a systematic review of all relevant randomized controlled trials.	Not rated on PsycBITE
II	Evidence obtained from at least one properly designed randomized controlled trial.	10
III-1	Evidence obtained from well-designed pseudo-randomized controlled trials (alternate allocation or some other method).	8
III-2	Evidence obtained from comparative studies (including systematic reviews of such studies) with concurrent controls and allocation not randomized, cohort studies, case-control studies, or interrupted time series with a control group.	8
III-3	Evidence obtained from comparative studies with historical control, two or more single arm studies, or interrupted time series without a parallel control group.	8
IV	Evidence obtained from case series, either post-test or pretest/post-test.	Not rated on PsycBITE

A summary of the scientific CRT evidence

A critical feature of EBP is the strength of the scientific evidence. For over 20 years, systematic reviews have been published that describe the evidence of CRT. There are two kinds of systematic reviews; those with and those without clinical recommendations. The reviews summarized here are examples of the different kinds of reviews and are not intended to be inclusive of all of the available reviews of CRT.

CRT reviews with practice recommendations

Several reviews have targeted a range of CRT interventions and populations and are organized by the cognitive domain that is the intended intervention target. Table 10.3 lists the reviews and practice standards and guidelines that emerged from these reviews. Readers are directed to the publications themselves to obtain a list of practice options.

Table 10.3 A summary of practice standards and guidelines made by authors of CRT systematic reviews and organized by cognitive domain

Review	Practice Standard – should be done	Practice Guideline – should be considered
Cicerone et al., 2011 (multiple cognitive domains)	1. Direct attention and metacognitive training to develop strategies that are applicable to real world activities. 2. Visual scanning training for left neglect after stroke in the right hemisphere. 3. Gestural or strategy training for apraxia during acute recovery after left hemisphere stroke. 4. Language therapy during acute and postacute recovery for language impairments after lesions in the left hemisphere. 5. Functional communication therapy, including pragmatics for social communication skills. 6. Memory strategy training for mild memory impairment after TBI, including internal and external compensations. 7. Metacognitive strategy training for executive dysfunction after TBI, including emotional self-regulation and as components of attention, neglect and memory therapy.	1. Isolated computer exercises for left neglect after stroke are not effective and not recommended. 2. Cognitive intervention for aphasia (e.g. reading comprehension, language expression) after left hemisphere stroke or TBI. 3. Treatment intensity is a key factor for language intervention after left hemisphere stroke. 4. External memory aids as compensation when directly linked to functional activities for individuals with severe memory impairments after stroke or TBI. 5. Problem-solving strategy training applied to everyday, functional activities during post-acute recovery from TBI.

Table 10.3 continued

Review	Practice Standard – should be done	Practice Guideline – should be considered
Cicerone et al., 2011 continued	8. Comprehensive-holistic neuropsychological rehabilitation during postacute recovery to reduce cognitive and functional disability after moderate or severe TBI.	
Sohlberg et al., 2003 (attention training)		*Candidacy* 1. Those with intact vigilance and awareness of inattention. 2. Those in the post-acute recovery phase. *Intervention* 1. Direct Attention Training (DAT) programmes need to be individualized 2. Training more than 1 time weekly 3. Use with metacognitive strategy instruction (self-monitoring/ assessment, strategy selection, evaluate performance, etc.) 4. Use on complex attention tasks *Outcomes* 1. Impairment level outcomes 2. Attention problems in specific skills and tasks
Sohlberg et al., 2007 (external memory aids)		*Candidacy* 1. Those with significant memory impairment that affects every day functioning *Intervention* 1. Aids can include technology, planners, lists, etc. 2. Training methods are unspecified *Outcomes* 1. Everyday functional activities and participation by compensating for memory and/or cognitive impairments.
Kennedy et al., 2008 (executive functions)	*Candidacy* 1. Young and middle aged adults 2. Those in the post-acute recovery phase 3. Those with some 'self-awareness' *Intervention* 1. Step-by-step metacognitive strategy instruction	

Review	Practice Standard – should be done	Practice Guideline – should be considered
Kennedy et al., 2008 continued	Outcomes 1. Functional, personally relevant activities, problem situations, complex tasks with the likelihood of maintenance	
Ylvisaker et al., 2007 (Social and challenging behaviour)		*Candidacy* 1. Children and adults with severe brain injury 2. Individuals in the acute or post-acute recovery phase *Intervention* 1. Systematic behavioural therapy that is individualized. 2. Use positive behavioural supports and/or contingency management, depending on individual response to intervention. *Outcomes* 1. Observed challenging behaviours and routines in specific activities and everyday functioning in context (i.e. participation). 2. Others reports of behavioural changes.

The Task Force of the American Congress of Rehabilitation Medicine, Brain Injury Interdisciplinary Special Interest Group (Cicerone *et al.*, 2000, 2005 & 2011) published a series of reviews that combined CRT studies for both stroke and TBI populations. They reviewed intervention studies for attention, visuospatial and praxic deficits, language and communication (including aphasia), memory and executive functioning. They also reviewed the evidence for comprehensive-integrated neuropsychological rehabilitation. To evaluate individual studies, they use the Oxford Centre of Evidence Based Medicine hierarchy and to evaluate the strength of the evidence, they used the AAN levels of recommendations (1999) (practice standards, guidelines, options). In total, they reviewed 370 studies, ranging from RCTs to single subject and case reports. In the most recent update (Cicerone *et al.*, 2011), eight practice standards, five guidelines, and 11 options emerged as clinical recommendations.

A group of SLPs, supported by the *Academy of Neurologic Communication Disorders and Sciences* (ANCDS) (http://www.ancds.org/index.php?option= com_content&view=article&id=9&Itemid=9#TBI) have reviewed specific domains within CRT. Inclusion criteria were more narrowly defined than criteria used by Cicerone *et al.*; studies had to include individuals with TBI, i.e. studies of only stroke or other kinds of acquired brain injury were excluded. Four such reviews have been published to date.

Sohlberg *et al.* (2003) provided an update of the evidence on direct attention training (DAT) using the AAN's (Miller *et al.*, 1999) three classification levels of evidence. This resulted in several guidelines but no practice standards. In 2007, Sohlberg *et al.* reviewed the published evidence on the effectiveness of external memory aids (planners, technology, etc.) to compensate for cognitive and memory impairment after brain injury. Twenty-one studies were reviewed: one class I (RCT), ten class II and ten class III. The absence of detailed descriptions of how individuals were taught to use the aids precluded reviewers from recommending the use of external aids as a practice standard. Kennedy *et al.* (2008) reviewed the evidence for interventions for executive dysfunction, including goal setting, problem solving, planning and organization. Fifteen studies were included in this review: five class I (RCTs), three class II and seven class III. Eleven studies used 'metacognitive strategy training/instruction' (MSI) and/or 'direct instruction' approaches. In a meta-analysis, MSI/direct instruction and 'control' intervention resulted in improved impairment level outcomes, whereas the MSI/direct intervention resulted in larger benefits to functional outcomes compared to 'control' intervention. This led to practice standards and guidelines. Finally, Ylvisaker *et al.* (2007) reviewed interventions for challenging and social behaviour after TBI. Sixty-five studies were reviewed: two class I, two class II, 36 class III and 25 class IV. Interventions included contingency management (traditional behavioural therapy), positive behavioural intervention and supports, and a combination of the two types. Methodological issues precluded recommendations at the level of practice standards, although several practice guidelines were generated.

Reviews without clinical recommendations

Some reviews summarize the evidence but do not attempt to translate the evidence into practice recommendations when there is little evidence or when studies vary so much that common features are difficult to identify. Five recent examples from the CRT literature are provided here.

The Institute of Medicine (IOM, 2011) conducted the most recent review of CRT where an emphasis was placed on 'patient-centred outcomes' (activity or participation levels) for civilians and service military with TBI in the US. Stricter inclusion criteria were applied here than used by Cicerone *et al.* (2011) or the ANCDS reviews, by limiting studies to those where TBI participants made up the majority of the total participants in the study. Furthermore, studies were organized by severity of injury (mild, moderate/severe) and stage of recovery (subacute, chronic). Ninety studies met inclusion criteria and were reviewed, of which 37 were RCTs. Interventions that targeted deficits in attention, memory, language and communication, executive functions and visual-spatial processing were included, as well as CRT delivered in comprehensive/holistic programmes and telemedicine. Evidence was graded as not informative, limited, modest or strong. The highest level of evidence achieved was modest and this was as follows:

1. Treating social communication problems resulted in immediate treatment benefits for individuals with moderate/severe impairments at the chronic recovery phase.
2. Using internal *and* external memory strategies resulted in immediate treatment benefits for individuals with moderate/severe impairments at the chronic recovery phase.
3. Using external memory strategies resulted in patient centred benefits for individuals with moderate/severe impairments at the chronic recovery phase.

There were 'no' or 'limited' levels of evidence to support the long-term benefit of treatment intended to improve or compensate for attention, language and communication, memory impairments and executive functions. Even though modest evidence was found in just a few areas of CRT, reviewers stressed that this should not be interpreted as evidence against various forms of CRT, but rather as an indication of the amount and quality of the current evidence available.

> The committee emphasizes that conclusions based on the limited evidence regarding the effectiveness of CRT does not indicate that the effectiveness of CRT treatments are 'limited;' the limitations of the evidence do not rule out meaningful benefit. *In fact, the committee supports the ongoing clinical application of CRT interventions for individuals with cognitive and behavioral deficits due to TBI.*
>
> (IOM, 2011, p. 201).

Two reviews on the use of assistive technology (AT) in CRT are illustrative of how quickly the evidence can change. deJoode and colleagues (2010) reviewed the AT literature up until early 2009. This resulted in only 26 studies, of which only one was a RCT. In general, reviewers found that while the use of AT results in positive changes in functional activities, most studies had very small numbers of participants and few described how the intervention was provided. Gillespie, Best & O'Neill (2012) conducted a more recent review of AT that extended through to April 2011. Their search revealed 91 studies, including three RCTs. Between 2006 and 2010, 34 studies on the use of AT were published, more than double the number of studies published between 1996 and 2000. Not only were more studies included in this review, but reviewers also analysed the use or intent of the AT by cognitive domain: high-level cognitive functions, memory, emotion regulation, calculation, self and time functions, and other functions. In summary, they found that attention was managed by alerting systems, self-orientation and time was managed using GPS, high-cognitive functions of time management and organization were managed through PDAs and smart phone applications, and episodic memory was managed using devices that store and display information.

Lastly, two reviews have been published that describe the evidence for using instructional technical practices while delivering CRT. Instructional practices are the methods by which clinicians teach individuals to use strategies, follow instructions, restore memory, establish routines, use AT, etc. (Sohlberg, Ehlhardt & Kennedy, 2005). Ehlhardt *et al.* (2008) reviewed 51 studies of instructional practices across three populations (ABI, dementia, and schizophrenia) and intervention targets. Of the 38 studies on adults with ABI, none were RCTs. They concluded that the instructional literature *suggests* that individuals with impaired learning benefit from explicit targets and careful systematic teaching and provided six recommendations for clinicians: 1) identify valid therapy targets; 2) use task analyses when training multi-step procedures; 3) constrain errors; 4) provide sufficient practice that is distributed or spaced; 5) vary the stimuli; and 6) promote effortful, deep processing. However, these recommendations do not have unanimous agreement. A recent review of errorless instruction concluded that its use runs the risk of eliminating opportunities for effortful or difficult retrieval practice, something that both individuals with aphasia and individuals with brain injury need (Middleton & Schwartz, 2012).

Why do conclusions vary across reviews?

Variable conclusions across reviews can be traced to different inclusion criteria used to select studies for the review. Reviewers decide a priori on inclusion and exclusion criteria and these criteria vary substantially across reviews of CRT. Reviewers make decisions around whether to include studies with participants with a variety of ABI and to what extent. For example, the Cicerone reviews (Cicerone *et al.* 2000, 2005, 2011) included studies of any kind of ABI, the ANCDS reviewers required that studies have participants with TBI, and the IOM reviewers required that studies have a majority of TBI participants to be included.

Inclusion criteria can differ based on the hierarchy or level evidence that is used to rate the evidence as well. Some reviewers have restricted studies to only RCTs (e.g. ECRI, 2009). Others have included only group studies (RCTs and other group designs) (Solhberg *et al.*, 2003), whereas others have included all kinds of studies including case studies (e.g. Cicerone *et al.*, 2011; Kennedy *et al.*, 2008). It is easy to understand then why reviews with narrower or stricter inclusion criteria find fewer studies to include and end up with lower clinical recommendations or conclusions.

Applying evidence to make clinical decisions

Once the evidence has been accessed and read, what are the steps that clinicians go through to make clinical decisions for an individual client? Guyatt (2000) and others (McCauley & Fey, 2006) provide a list of steps that clinicians should go through as they select treatment options for individual clients. First, clinicians formulate questions about the treatment and the individual client. The PICO process of Patient or Population (P), Intervention (I), Comparison (C) and

Outcomes (O) ensures that clinicians are considering all aspects of the EBP when making these decisions (Sackett *et al.*, 1997).

- P = What sample of the population with TBI does this client belong to (age, severity of injury, severity of impairment)? What are the major limitations or restrictions? How should these characteristics influence my search of the scientific evidence?
- I = What intervention should be considered?
- C = Are there alternative or additional interventions that I should consider given the specific characteristics and/or needs of the client?
- O = What specific outcomes are valid? What are the client's desired outcomes? Are there interventions that result in these specific outcomes? Should other outcomes be considered?

Secondly, clinicians search and then evaluate the evidence (systematic reviews, and/or individual studies) as described earlier in this chapter, looking for validated interventions, client characteristics and outcomes that match those of the individual client. Having obtained the evidence, clinicians then integrate the findings and recommendations with the client-specific information (including goals and values) to select the optimal treatment approach. To do this, clinicians can ask themselves: are these the most desirable outcomes for this client? Are these outcomes ones that the client desires? Is there the time and funding to implement this kind of intervention? Once a decision is made and the intervention begins, clinicians track the performance, using practice-based evidence (PBE), described at the beginning of this chapter. This data collection phase informs the clinician about intervention effects and is critical to determining whether or not the intervention approach is useful for obtaining the desired outcomes.

What can clinicians do when the scientific evidence does not match the client or their goals? This happens more often than not, but fortunately there are several options available (Fey & Justice, 2007). First, clinicians have the option of proceeding with the therapy while being aware of the mismatch. Typically, clinicians reconcile this with a logical rationale. For example, perhaps the client has many of the same symptoms and the same severity as the population that has shown benefit, even though the medical diagnosis differs. The clinician may decide to use that intervention approach for a client who is at the chronic recovery stage but not for clients in acute recovery, i.e. when illness or disease remains active. Secondly, clinicians can modify the approach to meet the functional goals of clients, thereby 'individualizing' the intervention. Even though this is often done, clinicians should be mindful that once an intervention is altered, it may or may not change the likelihood of it being effective. Finally, if clients are reluctant to engage with the intervention for some reason, clinicians can educate clients on the rationale and probable outcomes, and initiate the intervention approach while 'data' is collected so that the client can experience the benefits of this treatment approach.

Future of evidence-based practice in CRT

Perhaps in all areas of rehabilitation, it is not especially useful to simply state that more research is needed. That is certainly the case in CRT. In particular, studies that go beyond the efficacy or discovery phase are needed to advance the science of CRT so that the active ingredients in intervention packages can be identified (Whyte, 2006). This can only be done through studies of effectiveness and studies that replicate initial, preliminary results (IOM, 2011). Furthermore, CRT outcomes studies across levels of the WHO ICF (impairments, limitations, restrictions) are needed; these will be accomplished as researchers integrate person- or patient-centred outcomes into experimental designs that embrace both quantitative and qualitative outcomes (Kennedy *et al.*, 2012). Finally, cost effectiveness studies are needed and models of these can be obtained by looking to other complex intervention and populations. For example, Gitlin *et al.* (2010) showed that an Environmental Skill Building Program delivered by occupational therapists in a government-funded programme resulted in reducing the caregiver burden on families of individuals with dementia and was cost effective.

In the more immediate future though, clinicians can expect to see dissemination and knowledge translation efforts come to fruition. Several groups around the world are working on projects that will provide guidance to clinicians when making key clinical decisions that consider the desired outcomes, characteristics of individuals with TBI who would benefit from specific interventions and availability of manuals to instruct clinicians in how to teach strategies, e.g. MacDonald & Wiseman-Hakes (2010) and the National Center for the Dissemination of Disability Research (http://www.ncddr.org). Regardless of these efforts, clinicians will always have to rely heavily on the client-specific abilities, disabilities, goals and values, and on their therapeutic relationship with the client, when making decisions about intervention approaches.

References

American Academy of Neurology (AAN) (2011). *Clinical Practice Guideline Process Manual, 2011 Edn.* St. Paul, MN: The American Academy of Neurology. http://tools.aan.com/globals/axon/assets/9023.pdf (accessed 3 April 2012).

Baldoni, J. (2011). Using stories to persuade. *The Harvard Business Review Blog Network*, 24 March 2011. http://blogs.hbr.org/cs/2011/03/using_stories_as_a_tool_of_per.html, (accessed 3 April 2012).

Benedict, S. M., Belanger, H. G., Ceperich, S. D., Cifu, D. X., Cornis-Pop, M., Lew, H. L. & Meyer, K. (2010). *Veterans Health Initiative on Traumatic Brain Injury.* U.S. Department of Veterans Affairs. http://www.publichealth.va.gov/docs/vhi/traumatic-brain-injury-vhi.pdf (accessed 19 November 2012).

Bragge, P., Clavisi, O., Turner, T., Tavender, E., Collie, A. & Gruen, R. L. (2011). The global evidence mapping initiative: scoping research in broad topic areas, *BMC Medical Research Methodology*, 11, 92.

Cicerone, K. D., Dahlberg, C., Kalmar, K., Langenbahn, D. M., Malec, J. F., Bergquist, T. F., Felicetti, T., Giacino, J. T., Harley, J. P., Harrington, D. E., Herzog, J., Kneipp, S., Laatsch,

L. & Morse, P. A. (2000). Evidence-based cognitive rehabilitation: recommendations for clinical practice. *Archives of Physical Medicine and Rehabilitation, 81,* 1596–1615.

Cicerone, K. D., Dahlberg, C., Malec, J. F., Langenbahn, D. M., Felicetti, T., Kneipp, S., Ellmo, W., Kalmar, K., Giacino, J. T., Harley, J. P., Laatsch, L., Morse, P. A. & Catanese, J. (2005). Evidence-based cognitive rehabilitation: updated review of the literature from 1998 through 2002. *Archives of Physical Medicine and Rehabilitation, 86,* 1681–1692.

Cicerone, K. D., Langenbahn, D. M., Braden, C., Malec, J. F., Kalmar, K., Fraas, M., Felicetti, T., Laatsch, L., Harley, J. P., Bergquist, T., Azulay, J., Cantor, J. & Ashman, T. (2011). Evidence-based cognitive rehabilitation: updated review of the literature from 2003 through 2008. *Archives of Physical Medicine and Rehabilitation, 92,* 519–530.

Constantinidou, F. & Kennedy, M. R. T. (2011). Traumatic brain injury. In I. Papathanasiou, P. Coppens & C. Potagas (Eds), *Aphasia and Related Disorders* (pp. 365–396). Burlington, MA: Jones & Bartlett.

Douglas, J., O'Flaherty, C. & Snow, P. (2000). Measuring perception of communicative ability: the development and evaluation of the La Trobe communication questionnaire. *Aphasiology,* 14, 251–268.

ECRI (2009). *Cognitive Rehabilitation for the Treatment of Traumatic Brain Injury.* Plymouth Meeting, PA: ECRI Institute.

Edlund, W., Gronseth, G., So, Y. & Franklin. G. (2005). *Clinical Practice Guidelines Process Manual,* 2004 Edition. St. Paul, MN: The American Academy of Neurology.

Ehlhardt, L. A., Sohlberg, M. M., Kennedy, M., Coelho, C., Ylvisaker, M., Turkstra, L. & Yorkston, K. (2008). Evidence-based practice guidelines for instructing individuals with acquired memory impairments: what have we learned in the past 20 years? *Neuropsychological Rehabilitation,* 18, 300–342.

Fey, M. E. & Justice, L. M. (2007). Evidence-based decision making in communication intervention. In R. Paul and P. W. Cascella (Eds), *Introduction to Clinical Methods in Communication Disorders,* 2nd Edition (pp. 179–202), Baltimore: Brookes Publishing.

Gillespie, A., Best, C. & O'Neill, B. O. (2012). Cognitive function and assistive technology for cognition: a systematic review. *Journal of the International Neuropsychological Society,* 18, 1–19.

Gioia, G. A., Isquith, P.K., Guy, S. C. & Kenworthy, L. (2000). *Behavior Rating Inventory of Executive Function.* Odessa, FL: Psychological Assessment Resources, Inc.

Golper, L., Wertz, R. T., Frattali, C., Yorkston, K., Myers, P., Katz, R., Beeson, P., Kennedy, M., Bayles, K. & Wambaugh, J. (2001). Evidence-based practice guidelines for the management of communication disorders in neurologically impaired individuals: project introduction. *Academy of Neurologic Communication Disorders and Sciences (ANCDS).* www.ancds.org/PracticeGuidelines (accessed 1 April 2010).

Harley, J. P., Allen, C., Braciszewski, T. L., Cicerone, K. D., Dahlberg, C., Evans, S., Foto, M., Gordon, W. A., Harrington, D., Levin, W., Malec, J. F., Millis, S., Morris, J., Muir, C., Richert, J., Salazar, E., Schiavone, D. A. & Smigelski, J. S. (1992). Guidelines for cognitive rehabilitation. *NeuroRehabilitation* 2(3), 62–67.

Hart, T. (2000). *The Patient Competency Rating Scale.* http://www.tbims.org/combi/pcrs (accessed April 14, 2010).

Institute of Medicine (IOM) (2011). *Cognitive Rehabilitation Therapy for Traumatic Brain Injury.* Institute of Medicine/National Academy of Sciences, Washington, DC: The National Academies Press.

Katz, D. I., Ashley, M., O'Shanick, G. J. & Connors, S. H. (2006). *Cognitive Rehabilitation: The Evidence, Funding, and Case for Advocacy in Brain Injury.* Brain Injury Association of America. http://www.biausa.org/biaa-position-papers.htm (accessed 13 May 2011).

Kennedy, M. R. T. (2007). Evidence-based reviews of cognitive rehabilitation for individuals with traumatic brain injury: what clinical questions do they answer? *Evidence BRIEF, 1*(4), 69–80.

Kennedy, M. R. T. & Tursktra, L. (2006). Group intervention studies in the cognitive rehabilitation of individuals with traumatic brain injury: challenges faced by researchers. *Neuropsychology Review, 16,* 151–159.

Kennedy, M. R. T. & Krause, M. O. (2009). *College Survey for Students with Brain Injury.* http://neurocognitivelab.com/wp-content/uploads/2011/12/College-Survey-for-Students-with-Brain-Injury.pdf (accessed on May 30, 2012).

Kennedy, M. R., Avery, J., Coelho, C., Sohlberg, M., Turkstra, L. & Ylvisaker, M. (2002). Evidence-based practice guidelines for cognitive–communication disorders after traumatic brain injury: initial committee report. *Journal of Medical Speech-Language Pathology, 10*(2), ix–xiii.

Kennedy, M. R., Coelho, C., Turkstra, L., Ylvisaker, M., Moore Sohlberg, M., Yorkston, K., Chiou, H. H. & Kan, P. F. (2008). Intervention for executive functions after traumatic brain injury: a systematic review, meta-analysis and clinical recommendations. *Neuropsychological Rehabilitation, 18,* 257–299.

Kennedy, M. R. T., Krause, M. O. & Turkstra, L. (2008). An electronic survey about college experiences after traumatic brain injury. *NeuroRehabilitation, 23,* 511–520.

Kennedy, M. R. T., O'Brien, K. H. & Krause, M. O. (2012). Bridging person-centered outcomes and therapeutic processes for clients with traumatic brain injury. *Perspectives on Neurophysiology and Neurogenic Speech and Language Disorders, 22,* 143–151.

MacDonald, S. (2005). *Functional Assessment of Verbal Reasoning and Executive Strategies,* CCD Publishing: Ontario, CN.

MacDonald, S. & Wiseman-Hakes, C. (2010). Knowledge translation in ABI rehabilitation: a model for consolidating and applying the evidence for cognitive–communication interventions. *Brain Injury, 24,* 486–508.

Maher, C. G., Sherrington, C., Herbert, R. D., Moseley, A. M. & Elkins, M. (2003). Reliability of the PEDro scale for rating quality of randomized controlled trials. *Physical Therapy, 83,* 713–721.

Malec, J. F. & Lezak, M. (2005). *Mayo-Portland Adaptability Index – 4.* Available at *The Center for Outcome Measurement in Brain Injury.* http://www.tbims.org/combi/chart (accessed July 2, 2012).

McCauley, R. J. & Fey, M. E. (2006). Introduction to treatment of language disorders in children. In R. J. McCauley and M. E. Fey (Eds), *Treatment of Language Disorders in Children* (pp. 1–17), Baltimore: Brookes Publishing.

Miller, R. G., Rosenberg, J. A., Gelinas, D. F., Mitsumoto, H., Newman, D., Sufit, R., Borasio, G. D., Bradley, W. G., Bromberg, M. B., Brooks, B. R., Kasarskis, E. J., Munsat, T. L. & Oppenheimer, E. A. (1999). Practice parameter: the care of the patient with amyotrophic lateral sclerosis (an evidence-based review): Report of the Quality Standards Subcommittee of the American Academy of Neurology. *Neurology, 52,* 1311–1325.

Muir Gray, J. A. (1997). *Evidence-Based Healthcare: How to Make Health Policy and Management Decisions.* London: Churchill Livingstone.

NHMRC (National Health and Medical Research Council) (2000). How to use the evidence: assessment and application of scientific evidence. Handbook series on preparing clinical practice guidelines, http://www.nhmrc.gov.au/_files_nhmrc/publications/attachments/cp69.pdf (accessed on 7 July 2013).

Oxford Centre for Evidence-Based Medicine (2011) *The Oxford 2011 Levels of Evidence.* http://www.cebm.net/index.aspx?o=5653 (accessed 24 July 2012)

Robey, R. R. & Schultz, M. C. (1998). A model for conducting clinical-outcome research: an adaptation of the standard protocol for use in aphasiology. *Aphasiology*, 12, 787–810.

Sackett, D. L., Richardson, W. S., Rosenberg, W. & Haynes, R. B. (1997). *Evidence-based Medicine: How to Practice and Teach EBM.* New York: Churchill Livingston.

Sohlberg, M. M. & Mateer, C. (2000). *Cognitive Rehabilitation.* New York: The Guilford Press.

Sohlberg, M. M. & Turkstra, L. S. (2011). *Optimizing Cognitive Rehabilitation: Effective Instructional Methods.* New York: The Guilford Press.

Sohlberg, M., Avery, J., Kennedy, M. R. T., Coelho, C., Ylvisaker, M., Turkstra, L. & Yorkston, K. (2003). Practice guidelines for direct attention training. *Journal of Medical Speech-Language Pathology, 11*, 3, xix–xxxix.

Sohlberg, M. M., Ehlhardt, L. & Kennedy, M. (2005). Instructional techniques in cognitive rehabilitation: a preliminary report. *Seminars in Speech and Language, 26,* 268–279.

Sohlberg, M. M., Kennedy, M., Avery, J., Coelho, C., Turkstra, L., Ylvisaker, M. & Yorkston, K. (2007). Evidence based practice for the use of external aids as a memory rehabilitation technique. *Journal of Medical Speech Pathology*, 15(1), xv–li.

Stiers, W., Carlozzi, N., Cernich, A., Velozo, C., Pape, T., Hart, T., Gulliver, S., Rogers, M., Villarreal, E., Gordon, S., Gordon, W. & Whiteneck, G. (2012). Measurement of social participation outcomes in rehabilitation of veterans with traumatic brain injury. *Journal of Rehabilitation and Research Development, 49,* 139–154.

Sveen, U., Mongs, M., Røe, C., Sandvik, L. & Bautz-Holter, E. (2008). Self-rated competency in activities predicts functioning and participation one year after traumatic brain injury. *Clinical Rehabilitation*, 22, 45–55.

Tate, R., McDonald, S., Perdices, M., Togher, L., Schultz, R. & Savage, S. (2008). Rating the methodological quality of single-subject designs and n-of-1 trials: introducing the Single-Case Experimental Design (SCED) Scale. *Neuropsychological Rehabilitation,*18, 385–401.

Turkstra, L., Ylvisaker, M., Coelho, C., Kennedy, M., Sohlberg, M. M. & Avery, J. (2005). Practice guidelines for standardized assessment for persons with traumatic brain injury. *Journal of Medical Speech-Language Pathology, 13*(2), ix–xxxviii.

Vickery, B. G., Hirtz, D., Waddy, S., Cheng, E. M. & Johnston, C. S. (2012). Comparative effectiveness and implementation research: directions for neurology. *Annals of Neurology, 71,* 732–742.

Wambaugh, J. L. (2007). The evidence-based practice and practice-based evidence nexus. *Perspectives on Neurophysiology and Neurogenic Speech and Language Disorders* 17, 1, 14–18 (doi:10.1044/nnsld17.1.14).

Whyte, J. (2006). Using treatment theories to refine the designs of brain injury rehabilitation treatment effectiveness studies. *Journal of Head Trauma Rehabilitation,* 21, 99–106.

Whyte, J. & Barrett, A. M. (2012). Advancing the evidence base of rehabilitation treatments: a developmental approach. *Archives of Physical Medicine and Rehabilitation, 93,* S101–110.

Wilson, B. A. (1993). Ecological validity of neuropsychological assessment: do neuropsychological indices predict performance in everyday activities. *Applied and Preventive Psychology, 2,* 209–215.

World Health Organization (2001). *International classification of functioning, disability and health* (Report). Geneva: Switzerland. http://www.who.int/classifications/icf/en/, (accessed on 20 June 2012).

Ylvisaker, M., Coelho, C., Kennedy, M., Sohlberg, M. M., Turkstra, L., Avery, J. & Yorkston, K. (2002). Reflections on evidence-based practice and rational clinical decision making. *Journal of Medical Speech-Language Pathology, 10*(3), xxv–xxxiii.

Ylvisaker, M., Turkstra, L., Coelho, C., Kennedy, M. R. T., Sohlberg, M. M. & Yorkston, K. M. (2007). Behavioral interventions for individuals with behavior disorders after traumatic brain injury: A systematic review. *Brain Injury, 21*(8), 769–805.

11 Communication and social skills training

Cynthia Braden

Introduction

This chapter will review the research related to social skills training for persons with traumatic brain injury (TBI), abstract the specific treatment information from these studies and translate the interventions described in the research into recommendations for clinical practice. This evidence-based review comes from the Brain Injury Special Interest Group (BI-SIG) of the American Congress of Rehabilitation Medicine (ACRM), who conducted evidence-based reviews of the literature regarding cognitive rehabilitation for persons with TBI or stroke, leading to specific recommendations for clinical practice. The search strategies and classification ratings used for the three evidence-based review articles are described in detail in Cicerone *et al.* (2000, 2005, 2011). The first publication reviewed articles identified in the literature search published through the year 1997 (Cicerone *et al.*, 2000); the second publication updated the review for evidence-based articles published from 1998 through 2002 (Cicerone *et al.*, 2005), and the third update covered research published from 2003 to 2008 (Cicerone *et al.*, 2011). Well-designed, prospective, randomized controlled trials were considered Class I evidence; studies using a prospective design with 'quasi-randomized' assignment to treatment conditions were designated as Class Ia studies. Given the inherent difficulty in blinding rehabilitation interventions, blinding of assessments was not considered as criterion for Class I or Ia studies, consistent with all the BI-SIG reviews. Class II studies consisted of prospective, non-randomized cohort studies; retrospective, non-randomized case-control studies; or multiple-baseline studies that permitted a direct comparison of treatment conditions. Clinical series without concurrent controls, or single-subject designs with adequate quantification and analysis were considered Class III evidence (Cicerone *et al.*, 2011). See Chapter 10 for further discussion of these levels of evidence.

Following the review of the research evidence, the ACRM group determined practice standards, guidelines and options. *Practice standards* were based on at least one, well-designed Class I study with an adequate sample, with support from Class II or Class III evidence that directly addressed the effectiveness of the treatment in question, and provided substantive evidence of effectiveness to support a recommendation that the treatment be specifically considered for people with acquired brain injury (TBI and stroke). *Practice guidelines* were based on one or more Class I studies with methodological limitations, or well-designed Class II studies with adequate samples, which directly addressed the effectiveness of the treatment in question, providing evidence of probable effectiveness to support a recommendation that the treatment be specifically considered for people with acquired brain injury. *Practice options* were based upon Class II or Class III studies that directly addressed the effectiveness of the treatment in question, providing evidence of possible effectiveness to support a recommendation that the treatment be specifically considered for people with acquired brain injury (Cicerone *et al.*, 2000, 2005, 2011).

The final recommendations from ACRM's BI-SIG regarding treatment of social communication skills were based on the combined review of Class I and Class III studies. There were no Class II studies identified on this topic. One practice standard and one practice option were recommended as follows:

- Practice Standard: Specific interventions for functional communication deficits, including pragmatic conversational skills are recommended after traumatic brain injury (TBI) – (Cicerone *et al.*, 2000, 2005, 2011).
- Practice Option: Group based interventions may be considered for remediation of social communication deficits after TBI (Cicerone *et al.*, 2011).

This chapter will focus on how the evidence is translated into specific recommendations for clinicians to provide treatment for social communication disorders. However, it is important to remember that the absence of evidence does not mean a specific treatment is not effective, but indicates there is a lack of research conducted and published to evaluate a particular treatment.

Terminology

Over the years, there have been a number of terms in the literature which seem to describe overlapping or similar social communication problems. Terms related to 'social skills' include: functional communication, pragmatics, social communication, social competence, and social and emotional perception. Those clinicians experienced in treatment of persons with TBI may easily recognize the type of cognitive–communication problems that these terms encompass, and understand that social communication involves a complex hierarchy of verbal and nonverbal language skills influenced by social and cultural conversational rules.

A theoretical model of social behaviours was described by Trower, Bryant, Argyle and Marzillier (1978). These authors noted that nonverbal elements of facial expression, gestures, eye gaze, appearance and body positioning convey information in a social exchange. Nonverbal speech aspects such as tone of voice and prosody provide meaning. The verbal elements of social communication include speech acts such as instructions, directions, questions, comments, social routines and informal exchanges. Nonverbal communications influence interpersonal relationships, whereas the verbal elements provide for information exchange. Verbal and nonverbal elements are then part of a conversation with others following rules for back and forth exchange, speaking and listening, and feedback. Furthermore, there are expectations for different social situations, as well as cultural variations within a conversational exchange.

Pragmatics is another term used to describe the rules of using language to communicate within a social context which varies across cultures and within cultures. Pragmatics involves using language for different purposes, such as greetings, information, requesting; changing language to meet the needs of the listener or situation and following rules for conversations. Rules in conversation include taking turns, introducing topics, listening, speaking and providing feedback. Milton, Prutting and Binder (1984, p. 114) use the term pragmatics broadly, referring to 'behaviors which have the potential, if used inappropriately, to disrupt or penalize conversational interchanges'. Prutting and Kirchner (1987) defined specific verbal, nonverbal and speech related parameters in their pragmatic protocol.

Social perception includes the interpretation of others' emotional expression and feelings, understanding conversational inferences and determining others' intentions and beliefs in conversational exchange (McDonald *et al.*, 2003). Social competence encompasses the complex interactions of social skills, language, pragmatics, emotions and cognitive skills involved in social interactions (McDonald *et al.*, 2008; Hawley & Newman, 2010). More simply, Prutting (1982, p. 129) described social competence as 'appropriate communication'.

In reviewing the terms as provided above, several thoughts come to mind. First, there are many areas to focus social skills treatment, from specific pragmatic skills to communication competence to overall aspects of social competence which include emotions and cognitive abilities. Secondly, the terms overlap and in the remainder of this chapter, the terms social communication or social skills will be primarily utilized to encompass how people interact in a conversation exchange. Finally, most clinicians experienced in assessment and treatment of persons with TBI are able to identify the types of subtle and not-so-subtle communication problems that are defined above. Based on a review of the research evidence in this area, both individual and group interventions have shown efficacy for treatment of some aspects of social communication. However, there is a greater number of evidence-based research studies published on group intervention versus individual treatment for improving social communication, and the more recent research has been focused on group interventions.

Importance of treating social skills

From a clinical perspective, Milton *et al.* (1984) expressed that after TBI, persons 'talk' better than they communicate (p. 114) which leads to problems with social and work interactions, relationships with friends and family, and social isolation and loneliness (Ylvisaker & Feeney, 2001; Brooks *et al.*, 1987; Thomsen, 1984; Koskinen, 1998). Furthermore, persons with TBI have identified social integration as the most important aspect of overall community integration (McColl *et al.*, 1998). The relationship between social communication abilities and participation outcomes was examined in studies by Struchen and colleagues (Struchen *et al.*, 2008; Struchen *et al.*, 2011) who found that social communication skills were related to both social integration and occupational participation outcomes, after accounting for executive functioning and demographics measures. The authors noted there was a modest correlation between executive functioning abilities and social communication, but that social communication abilities had a significant and unique relationship with participation outcomes of occupational and social integration. Facial affect perception was reported as a significant predictor of occupational outcomes, and self-rating of communication abilities was a predictor for social integration (Struchen *et al.*, 2008). These findings support the importance of clinical assessment of social skills, including aspects of emotional perception and self-rating of social communication skills. Treatment may then be tailored to the social communication skill deficits identified and associated with outcomes of improved specific social skills and overall social integration for persons with TBI.

Assessment of social communication skills prior to treatment

The following measures: the Profile of Pragmatic Impairment in Communication (PPIC), the Behaviorally Referenced Rating System of Intermediate Social Skills – Revised (BRISS-R), the LaTrobe Communication Questionnaire (LCQ), the Goal Attainment Scale (GAS) and The Awareness of Social Inferences Test (TASIT) may be useful to the clinician to identify social communication deficits in persons with TBI. Although many other measures have been cited and may be available, those presented here have been developed for use in persons with TBI, have established validity and reliability, and have been used in evidence-based studies as measures of social communication. Details of the PPIC, the BRISS-R, the LCQ and TASIT can also be found in Chapter 4.

The Profile of Functional Impairment in Communication (PFIC) was developed as a tool to measure communication impairments following TBI and has demonstrated good inter-rater reliability with high concurrent validity (Linscott *et al.*, 1996). This tool was renamed the *Profile of Pragmatic Impairment in Communication (PPIC)* in later publications by the author, but the test itself was not altered with the name change as confirmed through personal communication with the author (Linscott, 2010). The PPIC is based on principles of social communication and the specific impairments seen in TBI. The person with TBI is videotaped with an unfamiliar partner, and after introductions, the instructions are along the lines of 'Get to know one another'. The conversational partner has been instructed not to lead or dominate the conversation. The 10–15 minute videotape is then rated using the PPIC scale, which includes 84 behaviour items to assess the frequency and severity of specific communication impairments.

These 84 items are categorized into ten subscales: (1) Logical Content – use of logical, understandable and coherent language; (2) General Participation – participation in conversation in a manner which is organized and sensitive to the other's interests; (3) Quantity – information provided is the appropriate amount given the other's needs or understanding; (4) Quality – subject contributes information that appears honest and factual; (5) Internal Relation – as a speaker, the subject's ideas are clear, cohesive, relevant and related; (6) External Relation – as a listener, the subject relates their own comments to the other's preceding contributions; (7) Clarity of Expression – ideas are presented clearly and concisely; (8) Social Style – use of appropriate social style given the context and background of the conversation; (9) Subject Matter – subject adheres to socially, culturally or morally appropriate subject matter in conversation; and (10) Aesthetics – speech characteristics of loudness, rate, affect, articulation, phoneme stress, and other aesthetic features of communication.

Each of the ten PPIC subscales has an overall summary scale rating: 0–normal; 1–very mildly impaired; 2–mildly impaired; 3–moderately impaired; 4–severely impaired; and 5–very severely impaired. Thus, lower scores on the PPIC indicate better functional communication skills (Linscott *et al.*, 1996). For one study, a PPIC summary score was computed by summing the ten subscale 0–5 ratings in order to provide one overall measure of a subject's performance in a social conversation (Braden *et al.*, 2010). Clinically, the time and resources to obtain the videotape and complete the PPIC rating may seem to be somewhat excessive for therapists primarily engaged in direct treatment, but the PPIC provides an objective rating of a person's communication abilities and is detailed enough to identify specific areas for treatment. Above and beyond using the videotape for the PPIC rating, the video may be useful in treatment as a self-assessment to help the client identify social communication goals. Use of videotape feedback during treatment will be discussed later in this chapter.

Another rating scale that may be used to rate a videotaped conversation is the *Behaviorally Referenced Rating System of Intermediate Social Skills – Revised (BRISS-R)* (Wallender *et al.*, 1985; Farrell *et al.*, 1985; Flanagan *et al.*, 1995, Marsh & Knight 1991). The BRISS-R is a measure of verbal and nonverbal aspects of social competence. Subjects are videotaped in a social interaction and then the conversation is rated using the BRISS-R scales. The scenario for the videotape involves an interaction with an opposite-sex stranger who introduces themselves, and asks 'How has everything been going this morning?' and proceeds with a 10-minute conversation. Reasonable discriminate and concurrent validity and internal consistency has been reported (Wallander *et al.*, 1985, Flanagan *et al.*, 1995; Farrell *et al.*, 1985). The BRISS-R consists of six subscales: (1) Language – quality and appropriateness of vocabulary, grammar and syntax; (2) Speech Delivery – fluency, rate, quality and mannerism of speech delivery; (3) Conversational Structure – silences, asking questions, topic change; (4) Conversational Content – topic interest and substance; (5) Personal Conversational Style – amount and appropriateness of self-disclosure, use of humour and social manners; and (6) Partner Directed Behaviour – use of reinforcers and attention towards partner, self-centred behaviour and sensitivity to the partner. The BRISS-R subscales are rated on a seven point Likert scale from one (very inappropriate), four (normal) to seven (very appropriate). A BRISS-R rating of less than four is considered 'below normal' (Flanagan *et al.*, 1995; Marsh & Knight, 1991). Scale five (Personal Conversational Style) is particularly relevant and sensitive to communication difficulties following TBI (Flanagan *et al.*, 1995), and scale six (Partner Directed Behaviour) was sensitive to identifying change post-treatment in a study by McDonald and colleagues (McDonald *et al.*, 2008). After videotaping a 10-minute conversation with an unknown person, clinicians could use either the PPIC or the BRISS-R or both as an assessment tool.

A communication skills self or other rating scale that has been used in the research literature is the *LaTrobe Communication Questionnaire (LCQ)* (Douglas *et al.*, 2007), a 30-item questionnaire that measures cognitive–communication ability. The tool was developed to obtain information from various sources (e.g. self-rating by the individual with TBI or rating by their support person). Individuals are asked whether or not a particular communication behaviour is a change since injury (happens more, about the same, or less) in addition to rating the frequency of the communication behaviour problem such as 'When talking to others do you leave out important details?' on a four point scale ranging from '1=never or rarely', '2=sometimes', '3=often' and '4=usually or always'. A total score is obtained by summing ratings across 30 items, and higher scores reflect the rater's perception of greater communication difficulties. A psychometric evaluation of the LCQ with adults who had sustained severe TBI and their 'close others' was conducted and showed adequate internal consistency and test–retest reliability, and that the LCQ was sensitive to the effect of injury severity (Douglas *et al.*, 2007). A recent article noted the LCQ had discriminative validity comparing those with TBI to non-injured matched controls (Struchen *et al.*, 2008).

The Goal Attainment Scale (GAS) (Kiresuk *et al.*, 1994) has been used with persons with TBI (Malec *et al.*, 1991; Malec *et al.*, 1993; Malec, 1999; Dahlberg *et al.*, 2007; Braden *et al.*, 2010). The GAS is a flexible system of measuring outcome goals, based on a five point scale. Levels of goal attainment are expressed objectively in terms of concrete behaviours that can be observed and recorded. Goals and goal scaling are developed collaboratively with clinicians and persons with TBI, and the goal setting process itself encourages the client's self-assessment and self-awareness. The current level of communication function for each particular goal is usually assigned as the second step of the scale, to allow for a one step decline on a particular goal, and three steps for improvement on the five point scale. In two published studies on a group intervention for social communication, the GAS documented improvement in individual social communication goals (Dahlberg *et al.*, 2007; Braden *et al.*, 2010) and goal attainment continued to improve up to six months after treatment ended. The GAS is reported to be more sensitive to change than other outcome measures, and correlates moderately with other rehabilitation outcome measures (Malec, 1999; Turner-Stokes *et al.*, 2009). Therapy participants and family members are asked to rate the participant's current functioning on individual goals, and then periodically throughout an intervention. Clinicians can also rate the participant on the GAS. For those in longer term treatment, new goals can be added as established goals are achieved. An example of concrete and objective goal scaling is as follows (Dahlberg *et al.*, 2007):

GOAL: *I will ask more questions in conversations.*

1. I will ask questions in 10 per cent or less of conversations.
2. I will ask questions in 30 per cent of conversations.
3. I will ask questions in 50 per cent of conversations.
4. I will ask questions in 70 per cent of conversations.
5. I will ask questions in 90 per cent or more of conversations.

GOAL: *I will interrupt less during a 15-minute conversation.*

1. I will interrupt four or more times during a 15-minute conversation, with one prompt.
2. I will interrupt less than 4 times during a 15-minute conversation.
3. I will interrupt less than 2 times during a 15-minute conversation.
4. I will interrupt only one time during a 15-minute conversation.
5. I will not interrupt during a 15-minute conversation.

GOAL: *I will visit new social settings where I could make new friends.*

1. I will think of one new social setting where I could make new friends.
2. I will think of three new social settings where I could make new friends.
3. I will visit a new social setting where I could make new friends.
4. I will visit two new social settings where I could make new friends.
5. I will visit three new social settings where I could make new friends.

For clinicians, the GAS provides a valuable addition to other assessments for very little investment of effort (Turner-Stokes *et al.*, 2009). The person-centred goals defined by the GAS may not be captured in standardized measures and provide useful information about the participant's priorities in treatment. The GAS is an adjunct to other, more objective standardized measures, and is clinically very useful to help the clinician, client and significant others focus on individual goals. Progress on those personal social communication goals can be concretely measured by change on the GAS five point scale. However, using the GAS change score in research is somewhat controversial. Turner-Stokes *et al.* (2009) noted that large-scale studies on inter-rater reliability are lacking; the mathematical concepts underlying the tool are non-linear, there is lack of uni-dimensionality of the goals, and the scores are not interval. Kiresuk *et al.* (1994) recommends the GAS score be converted to a t-score, as change over time is built into the way the GAS scores are derived. The t-score avoids some of the problems of computing change scores. That being said, using the GAS scaling is a useful clinical tool for participants to self-assess and identify personalized goals, then self-monitor and measure change on the goals.

Two evidence-based treatment research articles (Bornhofen & McDonald, 2008a, 2008b) have utilized *The Awareness of Social Inferences Test (TASIT)* (McDonald *et al.*, 2003) to measure social perception following TBI. The TASIT has three sections; part one presents 28 brief video vignettes to evaluate the person's ability to identify six basic emotions commonly recognized across cultures from a list of seven choices: happiness, sadness, anger, surprise, disgust, fear, or no particular emotion. Judgements must be made on nonverbal facial, vocal and body language cues. Parts two and three of TASIT assess the ability to understand social inferences as sincere or sarcastic on the basis of emotional expression or nonverbal cues in 15 video vignettes (part two) and 16 video vignettes (part three) to distinguish between sarcasm and lies. The authors of the TASIT developed the test to enhance assessment of social perception in persons with TBI and help with planning treatment goals (McDonald *et al.*, 2003). See Chapter 4 for further detail.

Any clinician embarking on treatment of social communication problems could consider a combination of these assessments; including videotaped rating of conversation (PPIC and/or the BRISS-R), social perception ability (TASIT), self and other ratings of social communication skills (LCQ) and goal setting (GAS) during treatment. These assessments help identify therapy treatment goals. They may also be used to increase the client's self-awareness of communication skills, enhance the participation of a family member in assisting with goal achievement, and measure progress, all important for the client's continued motivation in a treatment programme.

Class I evidence for treatment of social communication skills

The strongest evidence for improving social communication skills has been presented in five randomized control trials (RCTs). A sixth Class I study by Braverman *et al.* (1999) included a pragmatics group as part of a comprehensive treatment programme for military personnel with TBI. However, this study did not measure the specific treatment effects of the pragmatics group, only broad outcomes of return to work, active duty or school. Thus, this study cannot be directly used as evidence for efficacy of a social skills treatment. In order to determine the clinical implications and social communication outcomes, the specific treatments as described in the research studies will be reviewed here. A summary of the clinical implications of all the evidence-based research studies for treatment of social communication problems used in the development of this chapter are presented in Table 11.2.

Interpersonal Process Recall (IPR)

Helffenstein and Wechsler (1982) compared the effectiveness of an interpersonal communication skills training named Interpersonal Process Recall (IPR) for 16 subjects with TBI in a randomized, controlled design comparing IPR to alternate non-specific treatment. The eight members of the experimental group underwent 20 hours of individual treatment with frequent, immediate and exact visual and auditory videotape feedback from a conversation partner and an objective observer. Specific skills were modelled by the clinicians and practised by the subject during the treatment sessions. Dependent measures of self-perceived change in skills, ratings of anxiety, self-concept, an independent observer rating scale, and independent videotape analysis demonstrated that the treatment facilitated improved interpersonal and communication skills when compared to the alternate treatment group, and maintenance of the treatment effect was reported at one month follow-up. Of note, the participants' self-ratings of communication skills did not show improvement.

The IPR treatment included a videotape of a 10–15-minute interaction between the participant with TBI and a staff member. Following the videotaped conversation, the participant, conversational partner and a therapist spent the next 45–50 minutes reviewing the tape and identifying deficient skills. More adaptive and appropriate means of interaction were discussed, and new skills were rehearsed with the participant. Professionals providing treatment included counsellors, psychologists and a speech pathologist. The IPR treatment over 20 sessions reportedly resulted in reduced anxiety, and improved social self-concept and interpersonal and communications skills. These skills generalized to improved interpersonal communication in non-therapy settings. The authors noted that feedback appeared to be the greatest strength of the treatment approach (Helffenstein & Wechsler, 1982). This original study design using IPR to treat interpersonal and communication skills is being replicated by The Institute for Rehabilitation and Research (TIRR Memorial Hermann) in Houston, Texas for the TBI Model Systems of the National Institute on Disability and Rehabilitation Research (NIDRR) of the US Department of Education.

Manualized group treatment for social communication was efficacious in improving individual communication goals, self-rated communication abilities and videotaped conversation skills in a randomized control trial waitlist design with 52 subjects (Dahlberg *et al.*, 2007). The intervention used in this study was Group Interactive Structured Treatment (GIST) (Hawley & Newman, 2008). GIST is a publicly available manualized programme consisting of a workbook with 13 hour and a half sessions addressing self-assessment, goal setting, starting conversations, conversation strategies and using feedback, being assertive and solving problems, positive self-talk, social boundaries, videotape feedback and conflict resolution. This group treatment emphasizes self-awareness and self-assessment of social competence leading to individual goal setting, and using the group process to facilitate interactions, feedback, problem solving and social support. Family involvement and weekly practice in the home and community are important aspects of the GIST treatment (Hawley & Newman, 2008). This treatment was developed by a speech pathologist and a clinical social worker, who served as the group therapists in the randomized control trial. The GIST manual provides information for group leaders and materials for participants to discuss each week. The programme is designed for six to eight participants with TBI in the group with two group facilitators. The specific topics for each of the sessions are listed in Table 11.1. The GIST model was developed to sequentially develop a participant's engagement, awareness, goal setting, skill mastery and generalization to improve social competence. The study showed significant benefits on self-ratings of communication skills and aspects of functional communication using the PPIC blind objective ratings. The authors concluded that the social communication skills training improved specific individual social communication deficits for individuals with TBI as measured by the GAS from the subject, family and clinician perspective. The subjects in the study averaged almost ten years post-injury, and gains were maintained on six month follow-up. Overall life satisfaction also significantly improved and was maintained at six months post-treatment.

The third class I study was an RCT by McDonald and colleagues (McDonald *et al.*, 2008). This included 51 participants randomized to the experimental treatment, a general social group, or a waitlist. Treatment included 12 weekly group sessions of three hours with three to five participants and two therapists, a speech pathologist and a psychologist. In addition, each participant attended an hour weekly session with a clinical psychologist. Two hours per session focused on training a different facet of social behaviour using a manual; topics were greetings, introductions, listening, giving compliments, starting a conversation, topic selection, being assertive and coping with disagreements. Individual goals were identified for each client. Sessions included warm-up games, review of homework, introduction of a target skill, discussion of issues and solutions, therapist modelling of appropriate and inappropriate behaviour and role playing. Social reinforcement aided confidence and motivation. Immediate feedback and

Table 11.1 Topics for treatment sessions during Group Interactive Structured Treatment (GIST)

Session	Gist Topic
1	Group Orientation
2	Telling "My Story"
3	Defining successful social skills
4	Self-assessment – strengths and challenges
5	Setting realistic social communication goals
6	Conversations – start, maintain, end
7	Recognize and respond to social cues
8	Being assertive and social problem solving
9	Practice in the community
10	Developing social confidence through positive self-talk
11	Videotaping and social problem solving
12	Conflict resolution
13	Closure and celebration

repetition aided learning and memory. The treatment emphasized positive feedback. A specific problem solving strategy 'WSTC' was used to help achieve goals: What am I doing? What is the best Strategy? Try it. Check it out.

One hour was focused on social perceptions and social inferences, following a manualized approach (Bornhofen & McDonald, 2008a) although some participants in the study did not have deficits in social perception. The study concluded that direct assessment of behavioural skills was the most effective means of measuring change, using the Partner Directed Behavior Scale of the BRISS-R. Clients were less inclined to talk about themselves and more inclined to encourage their conversational partner to contribute to the conversation following treatment. The authors noted that poor social skills related to poor executive function did appear to be amenable to treatment. They concluded that group social communication skills training improved participants' social behaviour with modest reduction of self-centred behaviour and greater effort to involve the conversational partner.

Emotional perception and affect recognition have been shown to be essential skills for successful interpersonal interactions (McDonald, 2005; McDonald & Flanagan, 2004; Radice-Neuman *et al.*, 2007). Thus, it is important for clinicians to evaluate emotional perceptive abilities and consider treatment for these deficits to improve overall social functioning in persons with TBI. Emotional perception can be assessed using TASIT, as described earlier in this chapter. Two class I studies from the same authors have presented treatment strategies for emotional perception deficits.

Bornhofen & McDonald (2008a) provided group treatment for 25 hours across eight weeks for one and a half hour sessions for 12 persons with severe and chronic TBI, randomized into treatment and waitlist control. The groups included up to six participants and one therapist. The treatment is described as 'graduated practice of increasingly complex, guided tasks relevant to perception of static and dynamic emotion cues. Greater independence was promoted as ability improved. Task requirements included group activities, notebook maintenance, and home practice tasks' (p. 29). Treatment activities were presented in a game format to allow for repetition of skills and increase participant motivation. The hierarchy of tasks started with interpretation of conventional emotional contexts, then judging static visual emotional drawings and photographs. The next step was judging dynamic emotional cues presented in various modalities singly and then simultaneously (e.g. visual, vocal, modelling, video). The final step involved making social inferences using situational and emotional cues. Treatment techniques included concepts of errorless learning, self-instruction training, distributed and massed practice of emotional discrimination tasks, rehearsal of different modes of expression, positive reinforcement, immediate feedback and review of materials both within and outside of the sessions. Participants in the treatment programme showed improved recognition of emotional expressions in video vignettes of happiness, sadness, anger, fear, disgust and surprise (Bornhofen & McDonald, 2008a).

The second Class I study by Bornhofen & McDonald (2008b) compared the efficacy of an errorless learning strategy to self-instructional training for emotional perception deficits in 18 adults with TBI in a waitlist control design. The treatment involved a total of 25 hours across ten weeks in two and a half hour sessions with either the errorless learning or self-instructional treatment, using the group treatment strategies as described in the first study (Bornhofen & McDonald, 2008a). The same therapist provided both treatments. The authors noted that the treatment programme is manualized with graduated practice of tasks relevant to perception of static and dynamic emotions and available from the authors. Both groups experienced modest improvements in judging facial expressions and drawing inferences, with limited evidence that the self-instruction strategy may be more efficacious than errorless learning, and the authors recommended the need for further study (Bornhofen & McDonald, 2008b).

Class III evidence for treatment of social communication skills

As mentioned above, there were no Class II studies examining social communication disorders in people with TBI. There were, however, three additional Class III studies, including case reviews, pre-post-treatment assessments and multiple-baseline studies that contributed information on treatment strategies that were reviewed as part of the evidence for treatment of social communication skills in TBI. These studies are summarized in Table 11.2, including the number of participants in the study, average age, severity of injury, time post-onset, treatment findings and clinical implications. The following discussion reviews social communication skills training that encompasses both Class I and Class III studies, in order to provide additional recommendations for clinicians wishing to implement evidence-based treatment programmes for their clients with social communication skills deficits. These studies are grouped into approaches that use group training, those that use individualized training and those that have trained communication skills and evaluated these within a broader rehabilitation programme.

The evidence for group treatment of social communication skills

There were 12 studies (Class I and Class III) that analysed efficacy of a group format for treatment of social communication skills with a total of 251 persons with TBI (Dahlberg *et al.*, 2007; McDonald *et al.*, 2008; Bornhofen & McDonald, 2008a, 2008b; Braden *et al.*, 2010; Ehrlich & Sipes, 1985; Gajar *et al.*, 1984; Goldblum *et al.*, 2001; Johnson & Newton, 1978; Ownsworth *et al.*, 2000, 2008; Wiseman-Hakes *et al.*, 1988). Details of these studies and specific treatments, clinical measures and findings with clinical implications are described in Table 11.2. The conclusions that can be drawn from review of these studies are that group treatment improved functional communication skills, including pragmatic language skills, social communication skills and aspects of social competence.

Groups provide a more natural environment and give participants practice in spoken and non-spoken communication and social skills, improve awareness and self-monitoring of communication and give participants real life practice. Strategies included discussion, role playing, self-evaluation, goal setting, rehearsal and peer feedback.

Specific factors of evidence-based treatment can be synthesized from review of the studies presented. The size of the group ranged from two to 13 participants with traumatic brain injury; and most commonly the groups had three to eight participants. The group members were as young as 14 years to age 64 but were generally in the age range typical for persons with TBI, from 20–45 years. Most participants were a year or more post-injury, and many were a number of years post-injury, which is encouraging to clinicians and clients with TBI, as improvements in social skills can be experienced for persons with chronic TBI. A promising finding is that persons with severe TBI may benefit from a group treatment, as most studies were conducted with participants with severe TBI. The group leaders for social communication skills groups had various clinical backgrounds, including speech pathology, clinical social work, psychology, counselling and occupational therapy. Two leaders were frequently used to facilitate the group, sometimes just one. The frequency of holding the group ranged from one to four times per week, and sessions ranged from one to three hours. The total duration of the groups varied; some completed a curriculum in six to 16 weeks, others were ongoing a year or more.

Manualized treatment programmes using a workbook were reported in five studies and proved to be efficacious (Dahlberg *et al.*, 2007; Braden *et al.*, 2010; Bornhofen & McDonald, 2008a, 2008b; Wiseman-Hakes *et al.*, 1998). The three workbooks used in the evidence-based studies are publically available and provide activities for improving functional communication skills. Two of these treatment manuals, *Group Interactive Structured Treatment-GIST for Social Competence* (Hawley & Newman, 2008) and *Improving First Impressions: A Step-by-Step Social Skills Program* (McDonald *et al.,* 2008), were reviewed earlier in this chapter. The third manual, *Improving Pragmatic Skills in Persons with Head Injury* (Sohlberg *et al.*, 1992) was used in the research study by Wiseman-Hakes *et al.* (1988). Two other workbooks are commercially available but have not been used in the evidence-based research studies reviewed here, *Building Functional Social Skills Group Activities for Adults* (Dikengil & Kaye, 1992) and *Behavior Functional Rehabilitation Activity Manual* (Messenger & Ziarnek, 2004). Clinicians wanting to provide group treatment for social skills are advised to review the above manuals and determine which of them best meet the needs of their clients. Those manuals with evidence of efficacy would be more highly recommended.

Common group treatment strategies were abstracted from the review of the research studies on treatment of social skills in persons with TBI. Most studies reported that the group leaders emphasized self-awareness and self-assessment. Group leaders helped participants set individualized communication goals. The group format encouraged self-monitoring to improve conversational behaviours.

Problem solving strategies to achieve goals were frequently part of the group content. Use of videotape feedback was reported as a powerful strategy to increase awareness and self-monitoring, as well as peer feedback. Social support from the group members enhanced group cohesion and participant motivation. Homework assignments and community exercises were common to provide extended practice. In addition, friends and family members were utilized to provide feedback regarding individualized treatment goals and support generalization of skills.

Outcomes of the group intervention reported in these studies included increased social activity at one year (Johnson & Newton, 1987), and improved pragmatic and social communication skills (Wiseman-Hakes *et al.*, 1988; Dahlberg *et al.*, 2007; Braden *et al.*, 2010; Brotherton *et al.*, 1988; Ehrlich & Sipes, 1985; Gajar *et al.*, 1984; McDonald *et al.*, 2008; Ownsworth *et al.*, 2000; Ownsworth *et al.*, 2008) which were maintained after treatment ended (Braden *et al.*, 2010 ; Dahlberg *et al.*, 2007; Brotherton *et al.*, 1988, Wiseman-Hakes *et al.*, 1988). Improved social and emotional perception (Bornhofen & McDonald, 2008a, 2008b) and individual goal attainment were achieved (Braden *et al.*, 2010; Dahlberg *et al.*, 2007; Malec, 2001). Improved life satisfaction (Dahlberg *et al.*, 2007) and quality of life (Goldblum *et al.*, 2001) were reported following the social skills group treatment.

Although the majority of the evidence on treatment of social communication skills is conducted as a group treatment, there are several articles describing individual treatment approaches. For the clinician who is unable to provide a group setting for treatment of these deficits, the evidence-based options in the literature for one-on-one treatment are next described.

Individual treatments for social communication skills

Based on the literature review regarding treatment of social communication skills, it would appear that individual treatment has been less recently and less frequently studied, and the more current published evidence supports a group intervention. However, it is interesting to examine the studies describing individual treatment, as clinicians may need to provide one-to-one treatment of social skills in persons with TBI. These studies were published in the 1980s, quite a number of years ago, and describe individual interventions (Helffenstein & Wechsler, 1982; Lewis *et al.*, 1988; Brotherton *et al.*, 1988; Giles *et al.*, 1988; Milton, 1988). The summary of these five studies on individual treatment of social communication have a total of 23 treated subjects and are detailed in Table 11.2.

Individual therapy for persons with traumatic brain injury typically used direct feedback to improve communication skills in the five studies. The only Class I individual treatment study by Helffenstein & Wechsler (1982) was previously described in detail. The authors noted that feedback from the videotaping of conversation appeared to be the greatest strength of the treatment approach (Helffenstein & Wechsler, 1982).

Table 11.2 Evidence for treatment of social communication, pragmatics, social skills impairments in TBI

Reference/ study	Class 1 level of evidence	N TBI severity	Time post onset – age	Treatment focus	Social communication measures and findings – clinical implications
Helffenstein & Wechsler, 1982	Class I RCT	16 severity not specified	~2+ years post 17–35 years old	Effectiveness of individual intervention to improve interpersonal communication vs. non-therapeutic attention. Participants randomly assigned to experimental treatment, which received feedback on 20 hours of videotaped communication interactions; and control group, who received 20 hours of individual therapy without feedback on interpersonal communication skills. Conversational partner and therapist worked individually with participant.	Measures: State-Trait Anxiety Scale, Tennessee Self-Concept Scale, Interpersonal Communication Inventory, Interpersonal Relationship Rating Scale, Independent Observer Report Scale, Videotape analysis. Those in experimental treatment demonstrated reduction in anxiety, improved self-concept, others' ratings of interpersonal and communication skills, and observed frequency of specific behaviours related to effected interpersonal communication in non-therapeutic social settings. Gains maintained on one month follow-up
Dahlberg et al., 2007	Class I RCT	52 severe	avg. 10 years post ~41 avg. age	Group Treatment; Used 2 therapists SLP and social worker. Manualized workbook topics in 12 1.5 hour sessions included self-assessment, goal setting, starting conversations, conversation strategies and using feedback, being assertive and solving problems, positive self-talk, social boundaries, videotape feedback, conflict resolution. The group treatment emphasized self-awareness and self-assessment of social competence leading to individual goal setting, and using the group process to build interactions, feedback, problem solving, and social support. To generalize skills, family involvement and weekly practice in the home and community were emphasized.	Measures included the PPIC, GAS and self and other rated social communication skills. Group treatment in social communication skills was efficacious in improving individual communication goals; self-rated communication abilities, and videotaped conversation skills. Satisfaction with life improved. Most gains maintained on six month follow-up.

Table 11.2 continued

Reference/ study	Class I level of evidence	N TBI severity	Time post onset – age	Treatment focus	Social communication measures and findings – clinical implications
McDonald, et al., 2008	Class Ia RCT (violation of the initial randomization)	51 severe	avg. ~4.6 years post 34 years avg. age	Group treatment to address social behaviour, social perception and emotional adjustment (anxiety, depression) for clients referred for deficits in social skills. Treatment included 3 hour sessions 1x/wk for 12 weeks with 3–5 participants and 2 therapists. In addition, each participant attended an hour weekly session with a clinical psychologist. Two hours per session focused on training a different facet of social behaviour using a manual; topics were greetings, introductions, listening, giving compliments, starting a conversation, topic selection, being assertive, and coping with disagreements. Individual goals were identified for each client. Sessions included warm-up games, review of homework, introduction of target skill, discussion of issues and solutions, therapist modelling of appropriate and inappropriate behaviour, role playing. One hour was devoted to social perception training. Social reinforcement aided confidence and motivation. Immediate feedback and repetition aided learning and memory. Focus on positive feedback.	BRISS-R, TASIT, LCQ Treatment effects modest; direct measures of social behaviour improved (BRISS-R partner-directed behaviour scale). Clients were less inclined to talk about themselves and more inclined to encourage their conversational partner to contribute to the conversation. Poor social skills related to poor executive function did appear amenable to treatment. No follow-up was reported.
Bornhofen & McDonald, 2008a	Class I RCT	12 severe	avg. ~8 years post ~37 avg. age	Group treatment to improve recognition of emotional expressions with 2–3 participants and a therapist; 1.5 hours – 2x/wk for 8 weeks (24 hours total). Tasks included. Visual or auditory presentations of happiness, sadness, anger, fear, disgust, surprise; static and dynamic emotional cues, making social inferences.	TASIT Improved recognition of basic emotions, and drawing inferences. Gains were maintained at one month follow-up

Study	Design	N	Severity	Time post / age	Treatment	Outcome
Bornhofen & McDonald, 2008b	Class I RCT	18	severe	avg. ~8 years post ~37 avg. age	Group treatment with 2–3 participants and a therapist. Sessions were 2.5 hours 1x/wk for 10 weeks. Manualized programme with graduated practice of tasks relevant to perception of emotions.	TASIT Modest improvements in judging facial expressions and drawing inferences. Self-instruction training was more efficacious. Follow-up data not reported.
Braverman et al., 1999	Treatment arm of a Class I RCT (Salazar *et al.* 2000)	67	mod to severe	38 days avg. post ~25 avg. age	Comprehensive 8 week treatment programme for military, included a Pragmatic group led by 2 SLPs. Group size ranged from 1–7; Efficacy of multidisciplinary TBI cognitive rehab for military members vs. home rehab. Milieu-based programme with focus on goal oriented employment-type work tasks and individualized treatment sessions. Groups included: planning/organizing (30–40 minutes – 4x/wk) facilitated by OT/SLP used videotaping; Cognitive skills group (50 minutes – 5x/wk) facilitated by OT/SLP; Pragmatic group (60 m – 1x/wk) 2 SLPs; Milieu (30 m – 3x/wk) patients and entire team; Community re-entry group outing (2+ hr – 2x/mo) OT/SLP; Group psychotherapy (2x/wk) neuropsychologist; medication group (45 m – 1x/wk) psych RN; Individual sessions: Speech Tx (50 m – 2x/wk); OT (50 m – 1–2x/wk); Work Tx (2–3 hrs – 4x/wk). After 8-wk programme a follow-up cognitive battery was administered and if team deemed the patient 'ready' they began 6 month trial of duty.	At one year follow-up 64/67 participants (96%) were employed or enrolled in college and 44/67 (66%) remained 'active duty' or 'fit for active duty'. Scores on pre- and post-treatment cognitive batteries or statistical analysis was provided. No difference in treatment groups; however a subgroup analysis of those with severe injuries showed more improvement than those in the home programme arm.

Table 11.2 continued

Reference/ study	Class I level of evidence	N	TBI severity	Time post onset – age	Treatment focus	Social communication measures and findings – clinical implications
Braden et al., 2010	Class III – pre-post testing	30	severe	avg. ~8 years post ~42 avg. age	Group Treatment: 7–8 participants in group; 2 group leaders Manualized workbook topics in 13 1.5 hour sessions included self-assessment, goal setting, starting conversations, conversation strategies and using feedback, being assertive and solving problems, positive self-talk, social boundaries, videotape feedback, conflict resolution. The group treatment emphasized self-awareness and self-assessment of social competence leading to individual goal setting, and using the group process to build interactions, feedback, problem solving, and social support. To generalize skills, family involvement and weekly practice in the home and community were emphasized.	PPIC, GAS, LCQ Results: Group treatment in social communication skills was efficacious in improving individual communication goals; self-rated communication abilities, and positive trend on videotaped conversation skills. Satisfaction with life improved. Gains maintained on 6 month follow-up.
Brotherton et al., 1988	Class III- Multiple baseline	4	severe	avg. ~6 years post ~24 avg. age	Individual social skills training programme consisted of: 1. modifying target behaviours; 2. modelling correct behaviours; 3. behaviour rehearsal; 4. video feedback; 5. social reinforcement. Baselines session were conducted 3x/wk for 40 minutes each for 2–3 weeks. Treatment sessions were conducted 2x/wk for 60 minutes to criterion for up to 32 baseline and treatment sessions.	Video feedback alone was reported as an effective intervention. Three of 4 subjects with residual cognitive impairment (e.g. memory deficits) showed improved social skills and were maintained over a period of one year post-treatment.

Study	Design	N	Severity	Time post	Age	Intervention	Outcome
Ehrlich & Sipes, 1985	Class III- Pre-post test	6	severity not indicated	1 year+ post	~25 avg. age	Pragmatics Group – Used 2 SLPs in one hour sessions 3x/wk for 12 weeks. Generation of individual and group goals. Multiple types of feedback from both therapists and group members, including verbal and gestural cues and videotaped feedback were used. This feedback helped facilitate the client's self-evaluation and monitoring. Therapists used positive social and verbal reinforcement. Four modules included: nonverbal communication, communication in context, message repair, and cohesiveness of narrative. Therapists role played appropriate and inappropriate examples of the target behaviour. Videotaping was instrumental and reviewed by the group. Clients were encouraged to relate daily life experiences relevant to the group topic.	Communication performance scale with pragmatic and linguistic skills. Clients made improvements in pragmatics: topic maintenance, initiation of conversation, syntax, cohesiveness and repair. The group was a natural environment for training interpersonal skills, with practice, feedback from members and a supportive atmosphere. No follow-up reported.
Gajar et al., 1984	Class III- multiple baseline	2	severity not indicated	1.5 years post	22 years old	Group of 4 TBI (data collected on 2 participants) and facilitator (SLP) 20 sessions – used a red or green light to provide feedback on positive or negative conversational behaviour – group members asked to explain why red or green light was activated. Then the lights were activated by group members, identifying positive or negative behaviours.	Feedback and self-monitoring had a positive effect on conversational behaviours of two clients; rates of positive social interactions were higher; treatment gains had a therapeutic influence in less structured group situations.

Table 11.2 continued

Reference/ study	Class I level of evidence	N	TBI severity	Time post onset – age	Treatment focus	Social communication measures and findings – clinical implications
Giles et al., 1988	Class III-Case study	1	severe	Time post injury not reported 27 years old	Person with TBI used inappropriate attention-seeking circumlocutory conversational style. Half hour sessions, 5x/wk for one month – reinforcement with social attention and praise, negative behaviour was 'timed out on the spot' (i.e., no reinforcement for 20 seconds), prompted to give short answers. Treatment included teaching, practice and reinforcement of appropriate responses, cognitive over learning of what was appropriate, alternative strategies for delayed information processing.	Verbal performance improved and was maintained. Authors conclude relatively simple methods can be effective in remediating social interactional deficits.
Goldblum et al., 2001	Class III-Pre-post test	6	severe (coma duration 18 days–7 mo)	Time post injury not specified, most are post acute 26 years old	6 TBI clients attended the group for two years (others were in group); 2 facilitators (SLP students, supervised by instructor) met once weekly for 1.5 hours; 6–8 in group at any one time. Group goals were to improve pragmatic skills and quality of life by practising communication strategies in the group, facilitating acceptance of functional cognitive–communication deficits and impact on interaction with others, instilling a sense of empowerment to take responsibility and control of their daily lives. Phase 1: pragmatics focusing on individual cognitive–communication needs, planning, insight, social skills, conflict management, self-confidence, assertiveness. Phase 2: quality of life – regular outings. Phase 3: re-entry to life and work, community service project and regular outings. Used the inherent power of groups in perceived increase in self-confidence, assertiveness, acceptance and overall life participation.	Pragmatic Protocol and Quality of Life Scale. Treatment in a conversation group resulted in perceived improvements in social-communicative competence and quality of life. Pragmatic competence plateaued, group members and family reported improvement in quality of life dimensions and social-communicative competence.

Author/Year	Design	N / Severity	Time post / Age	Description	Results
Johnson & Newton, 1987	Class III-Pre-post testing	10 severe	avg. ~5 years post; ~35 years avg. age	Social skills training in severe TBI population; group met 1.5 hours – 1x/wk for a year; group leadership not specified. Group focus on individual social performance, introductions, starting a conversation, asking questions, listening, nonverbal aspects, maintaining a conversation, self-evaluation, social activities, dealing with anger using review, practice, discussion, feedback, generalization.	Social performance rating from videotape. Group changes not significant; trend toward improvement in social performance and reduction in social anxiety. Subjects did have increased social activities at one year as reported by an other.
Lewis et al., 1988	Class III-Case study	1 severe – from cardiac arrest	2+ years post; 21 years old	Goal was to reduce inappropriate talk and increase socially appropriate comments. 5x/day, 4 days/wk, 3 therapists initiated a 2 minute conversation (total of 15 – two minute conversations per treatment day). Three forms of feedback provided during a conversation in a natural setting – attention and interest, systematic ignoring and correction.	Correction was more effective that ignoring in reducing inappropriate remarks. Attention and interest exacerbated the problem and demonstrated that a high rate of inappropriate talk observed in the natural environment was likely maintained by social reinforcement.
Malec, 2001	Class III-Pre-post test	96 TBI: 7% mild 7% mod 82% severe 4% unknown	avg. ~4.6 years post; 34 years avg. age	Examined impact of comprehensive day treatment (CDT) on societal participation using multidisciplinary group leaders; included daily programs for orientation, cognition, social awareness, communication, and life skills. Weekly groups included health education and vocation; monthly patient/family group. Used peer, staff and videotape feedback. Average time in programme ~27 weeks.	Outcome measures included vocational independence scale, Independent Living Scale, GAS, and Mayo-Portland Adaptability Inventory (MPAI-22). Significant goal achievement (GAS) was exhibited; as was a significant improvement in functional abilities (MPAI-22). CDT improved social participation, independent living and vocational status.

Table 11.2 continued

Reference/ study	Class I level of evidence	N	TBI severity	Time post onset – age	Treatment focus	Social communication measures and findings – clinical implications
Milton, 1988	Class III-Case study	1	severe	9 months post 35 years old	7 mo treatment; 135 hours of home and vocational programme; specific skills and compensatory strategies were developed to improve cognition and communication. One aspect of vocational treatment involved improving conversations with work personnel. Treatment was based on observation at work, development of a detailed performance evaluation, joint identification of problem areas, joint development of possible solutions, development of strategy, mass practice and refinement.	Outcome described as 'successful cognitive communication and vocational rehabilitation' no test data or specific treatment goals for communication presented in article; more detail on improved memo writing.
Ownsworth et al., 2000	Class III-Pre-post	21 14% mild 9% mod 76% sev	avg 8.6 years post ~34 years avg. age	16 week group programme for self-awareness and self-regulation to improve psychosocial functioning (facilitator manual available) – Groups met for 90 mins 1x/wk – 2 groups, 8 and 13 participants – leader not specified. Topics included cognition, communication and relationships, emotions, stress, motivation and goals, work, social life, and self-confidence and assertiveness. Specific techniques included problem solving, self-reflection, role plays, compensatory strategies, and practice of new behaviours.	Measures of self-awareness, self-regulation and psychosocial functioning. Greater levels of social interaction, emotional behaviour and communication skills, improved self-regulation skills, 6 month follow-up gains maintained.

Study	Design	N	Time post injury / age	Treatment	Outcomes
Ownsworth et al., 2008	Class III- RCT without statistical comparison of groups	35 (included TBI, stroke) severity not specified	avg 5.3 years post injury ~44 years avg. age	3 hours/week for 8 weeks comparing three types: (1) group treatment (5–6 participants) led by psychologist with focus on cognition, social skills and communication, emotions, coping, goals. (2) Individual treatment focused on client centred goals – OT provided treatment. (3) Combined group (with psychologist) and individual (with OT) for development of meta-cognitive skills in home and community with social supports.	Patient Competency Rating Scale, other outcome measures. Individual intervention contributed to goal attainment but was not maintained; combined intervention was associated with maintained gains in performance and satisfaction with goal attainment. Overall gains were variable but supported the efficacy of brief intervention formats. 3 month follow-up.
Wiseman-Hakes et al., 1998	Class III pre-post test	6	3 mo to 9 years post injury Avg. age ~15 years	Group treatment for pragmatic communication skills. Sessions were 1 hour, 4x/week for 6 weeks, (24 sessions) group size 4; led by SLP. Adolescents used a workbook 'Improving Pragmatic Skills in Persons with Head Injury' with modifications. Topics included initiation of conversation, topic maintenance, turn taking, active listening. Hierarchical treatment emphasized awareness, skill practice, and generalization. Videotape feedback was used in practice and generalization.	Pragmatic communication skills ratings. Mean scores on communication performance scales significantly improved and were maintained on follow-up at 6 months.

Well-designed, prospective, randomized controlled trials were considered Class I evidence; studies using a prospective design with 'quasi-randomized' assignment to treatment conditions were designated as Class Ia studies. Class II studies consisted of prospective, non-randomized cohort studies; retrospective, non-randomized case-control studies; or multiple-baseline studies that permitted a direct comparison of treatment conditions. Clinical series without concurrent controls, or single-subject designs with adequate quantification and analysis were considered Class III evidence (Cicerone *et al.* 2011).

BRISS-R – Behaviourally Referenced Rating System of Intermediate Social Skills – Revised; GAS – Goal Attainment Scaling; LCQ – LaTrobe Communication Questionnaire; OT – Occupational Therapist; PPIC – Profile of Pragmatic Impairment in Communication; RN – registered nurse; SLP – Speech Language Pathologist; TASIT – The Awareness of Social Inferences Test; TX – treatment.

One case study in a person who sustained anoxic brain injury showed direct correction of inappropriate communication was more efficacious than ignoring inappropriate comments. In addition, attention and interest to inappropriate talk exacerbated the problem, leading the authors to conclude that a high rate of inappropriate talk observed in the natural environment was likely maintained by social reinforcement. Treatment consisted of all staff on the unit providing correction in response to inappropriate remarks (Lewis *et al.*, 1988). Another case study (Giles *et al.*, 1988) provided direct feedback to use clear, concise statements in social interactions. Positive and intermittent reinforcement for appropriate conversation, as well as a 'time out' for unwanted verbal behaviour led to improved conversation in a case study. These gains were maintained at two month follow-up.

Brotherton *et al.* (1988) reported that participants with TBI were treated twice weekly in individual one hour sessions. Interventions included verbal instruction, modelling, behavioural rehearsal, videotape feedback and social reinforcement to improve social skills. Participants were given homework and family members were instructed to reinforce changes in target behaviours. Those behaviours that improved with training showed good maintenance a year after training. The authors noted that video feedback alone was a potent intervention for modifying social behaviour. In a case study by Milton (1988) specific cognitive and communication strategies were applied in the home and worksite, including on-site behavioural observation, feedback and reinforcement over 135 hours and seven months of treatment. The client improved specific skills in conversing with work personnel, among other goals that were required for a successful vocational reintegration.

Communication groups in comprehensive treatment programmes

Two studies described comprehensive treatment programmes that addressed multiple skills; one Class I hospital based (Braverman *et al.*, 1999), the other a Class III community-based programme (Malec, 2001). In the hospital based treatment study, therapists from different disciplines (e.g. occupational therapy, speech therapy and neuropsychology) worked together to address the goals of the individual. Treatments were provided in both group and one-on-one therapy sessions. Communication groups were a component of the larger treatment programme and focused on improved self-awareness of communication skills and setting individual goals. Descriptions of the groups addressing functional communication included a Pragmatics Group which met once weekly for eight weeks to improve problem solving and decision-making in various communication settings and increase awareness of interactions in different settings. Specific goals and tasks were dependent on the needs and deficits of the group participants. General outcomes were reported as return to active duty, employed or enrolled in college. Outcome measures did not include specific assessment of social communication (Braverman *et al.*, 1999). In the study by Malec (2001) participants with TBI averaged six months in a comprehensive programme, which included a communication group that met each day to develop verbal and nonverbal skills and enhance effective interpersonal communication. Treatment strategies included discussion, role-playing and social skills training, self-monitoring of communication and feedback. The overall programme demonstrated achievement of goals and increased societal participation after six months (Malec 2001). Neither of these studies of comprehensive treatment programmes measured the unique contributions of social communication groups in the outcome measures reported.

Social communication groups as part of a comprehensive programme are typically provided as part of inpatient or outpatient rehabilitation programmes. In these settings, persons with TBI are usually more recently injured, as compared to the other group and individual studies cited here. There is not definitive evidence that these groups are efficacious during the acute and rehabilitation stage post-TBI, but as stated earlier, lack of evidence just means that the research has not been done.

Conclusions

In summary, based on the review of the evidence in the literature and evidence-based treatment programmes the following recommendations for treatment of social communication skills in persons with TBI are provided. First, evidence supported treatment for persons in the chronic, post-acute stage post-TBI. No studies reported treatment efficacy in the acute stage post-injury. Persons with TBI selected for treatment should have some impairment in social communication skills. It is highly recommended to assess the client's social communication skills using one or several of the measures described in this chapter to determine the specific social communication skill deficits and help guide treatment. The clinician or clinicians providing treatment could come from various backgrounds, such as speech pathology, clinical social work, psychology or occupational therapy, and preferably would be experienced in treatment strategies for persons with TBI. Group treatment is recommended for social skills deficits and several studies recommended two facilitators to conduct the group treatment. The group size is optimally three to eight participants with social communication skill deficits. The frequency of group sessions, the length of sessions and duration of the treatment would need to be determined and communicated to the participants. The literature review would suggest meeting one to four times weekly, in sessions lasting from one to three hours, extending the duration of the group from six to 16 weeks. It is recommended that the group leaders select an evidence-based manualized treatment workbook (Hawley & Newman, 2008; McDonald *et al.*, 2008) to guide the treatment sessions. During the treatment, there is strong evidence that direct feedback from facilitators and group peers, as well as video feedback, improves self-monitoring and self-awareness which leads to improved social communication skills. Specifically, group leaders should provide positive feedback and reinforcement for desired behaviours and encourage peer feedback.

A main focus of group treatment is to help the participants in the group identify individual communication goals. The initial assessments can help identify goals, as well as observations in the group; goals can then be scaled using the GAS to measure progress. Problem solving strategies such as the 'WSTC' as steps toward achieving goals are recommended. The literature suggests the involvement of family and friends for reinforcement and generalization of the new social communication skills. Community outings are important to generalize skills practised in a real-life setting. Repetition, practice and homework throughout the group sessions are critical to establish improved communication skills. If a group format is not possible, consider one-to-one treatment using video and direct feedback, goal setting, and involvement of friends and family in the community. The publicly available manuals may be modified for individual treatment sessions.

The body of evidence reviewed in this chapter supports the efficacy of group and individual treatment of social communication skills for persons with TBI, as recommended by Cicerone *et al.* (2011). Not only can individualized social skills and goals be attained through treatment, improvements in social communication skills are then associated with greater social integration in the community, quality of life and life satisfaction.

References

Bornhofen, C. & McDonald, S. (2008a). Treating deficits in emotion perception following traumatic brain injury. *Neuropsychological Rehabilitation*, 18, 22–44.

——(2008b). Comparing strategies for treating emotion perception deficits in traumatic brain injury. *Journal of Head Trauma Rehabilitation*, 23, 103–115.

Braden, C., Hawley, L., Newman, J., Morey, C., Gerber, D. & Harrison-Felix, C. (2010). Social communication skills group treatment: a feasibility study for persons with traumatic brain injury and comorbid conditions. *Brain Injury*, 24(11), 1298–1310.

Braverman, S. E., Spector, J., Warden, D. L., Wilson, B. C., Ellis, T. E., Bamdad, M. J. & Salazar, A. M. (1999). A multidisciplinary TBI inpatient rehabilitation programme for active duty service members as part of a randomized clinical trial. *Brain Injury*, 13(6), 405–415.

Brooks, N., McKinlay, W., Symington, C., Beattie, A. & Campsie, L. (1987). Return to work within the first seven years of severe head injury. *Brain Injury*, 1, 5–19.

Brotherton, F. A., Thomas, L. L., Wisotzek, I. E. & Milan, M. A. (1988). Social skills training in the rehabilitation of patients with traumatic closed head injury. *Archives of Physical Medicine and Rehabilitation,* 69 (10), 827–832.

Cicerone, K. D., Dahlberg, C., Kalmar, K., Langenbahn, D. M., Malec, J. F., Bergquist, T. F., Felicetti, T., Giacino, J. T., Harley, J. P., Harrington, D. E., Herzog, J., Kneipp, S., Laatsch, L. & Morse, P. A. (2000). Evidence-based cognitive rehabilitation: recommendations for clinical practice. *Archives of Physical Medicine and Rehabilitation,* 81, 1596–1615.

Cicerone, K. D., Dahlberg, C., Malec, J. F., Langenbahn, D. M., Felicetti, T., Kneipp, S., Ellmo, W., Kalmar, K., Giacino, J. T., Harley, J. P., Laatsch, L., Morse, P. A. & Catanese, J. (2005). Evidence-based cognitive rehabilitation: updated review of the literature 1998–2002. *Archives of Physical Medicine and Rehabilitation,* 86, 1681–1692.

Cicerone, K. D., Langenbahn, D. M., Braden, C., Malec, J. F., Kalmar, K., Fraas, M., Felicetti, T., Laatsch, L., Harley, J. P., Bergquist, T., Azulay, J., Cantor, J. & Ashman, T. (2011). Evidence-based cognitive rehabilitation: updated review of the literature from 2003 through 2008. *Archives of Physical Medicine and Rehabilitation*, 92, 519–530.

Dahlberg, C. A., Cusick, C. P., Hawley, L. A., Newman, J. K., Morey, C. E., Harrison-Felix, C. L. & Whiteneck, G. G. (2007). Treatment efficacy of social communication skills training after traumatic brain injury: a randomized treatment and deferred treatment controlled trial. *Archives of Physical Medicine and Rehabilitation*, 88, 1561–1573.

Dikengil, A. T. & Kaye, M. E. (1992). *Building Functional Social Skills Group Activities for Adults*. Tucson: Therapy Skill Builders.

Douglas, J. M., Bracy, C. A. & Snow, P. C. (2007). Measuring perceived communicative ability after traumatic brain injury: reliability and validity of the La Trobe Communication Questionnaire. *Journal of Head Trauma Rehabilitation*, 22(1), 31–38.

Ehrlich, J. & Sipes, A. (1985). Group treatment of communication skills for head trauma patients. *Cognitive Rehabilitation*, 3, 32–37.

Flanagan, S., McDonald, S. & Togher, L. (1995). Evaluating social skills following traumatic brain injury: the BRISS as a clinical tool. *Brain Injury*, 9(4), 321–338.

Farrell, A. D., Rabinowitz, J. A., Wallander, J. L. & Curran, J. P. (1985). An evaluation of two forms of the intermediate level assessment of social skills. *Behavioral Assessment*, 7, 155–171.

Gajar, A., Schloss, P. J., Schloss, C. N. & Thompson, C. K. (1984). Effects of feedback and self-monitoring on head trauma youths' conversational skills. *Journal of Applied Behavioral Analysis*, 17, 353–358.

Giles, G. M., Fussey, I. & Burgess, P. (1988). The behavioral treatment of verbal interaction skills following severe head injury: a single case study. *Brain Injury*, 2, 75–77.

Goldblum, G., Mulder, M. & von Gruenewaldt, A. (2001). An examination of the impact of participation in a conversation group for individuals with a closed head injury. *The South African Journal of Communication Disorders*, 48, 3–20.

Hawley, L. & Newman, J. (2008). *Group Interactive Structured Treatment – GIST: For Social Competence*. Denver, CO; previously titled *Social Skills and Traumatic Brain Injury: A Workbook for Group Treatment* (2006); *Social Problem Solving Group* (2003).

——(2010). Group Interactive Structured Treatment (GIST): a social competence intervention for individuals with brain injury. *Brain Injury*, 24(11), 1292–1297.

Helffenstein, D. & Wechsler, R. (1982). The use of interpersonal process recall (IPR) in the remediation of interpersonal and communication skill deficits in the newly brain injured. *Clinical Neuropsychology*, 4, 139–143.

Johnson, D. A. & Newton, A. (1987). Social adjustment and interaction after severe head injury: II. Rationale and basis for intervention. *British Journal of Clinical Psychology*, 26, 289–298.

Kiresuk, T. J., Smith, A. & Cardillo, J. E. (eds) (1994). *Goal Attainment Scaling: Applications, Theory, and Measurement*. New Jersey: Lawrence Erlbaum Associates.

Koskinen, S. (1998). Quality of life 10 years after a very severe traumatic brain injury (TBI): the perspective of the injured and the closest relative. *Brain Injury*, 12, 631–648.

Lewis, F. D., Nelson, J., Nelson, C. & Reusink, P. (1988). Effects of three feedback contingencies on the socially inappropriate talk of a brain injured adult. *Behavior Therapy*, 19, 203–211.

Linscott, R. J. (2010). Personal communication.

Linscott, R. J., Knight, R. G. & Godfrey, H. P. (1996). The Profile of Functional Impairment in Communication (PFIC): a measure of communication impairment for clinical use. *Brain Injury*, 10, 397–412.

Malec, J. (1999). Goal attainment scaling in rehabilitation. *Neuropsychological Rehabilitation*, 9(3/4), 253–275.

Malec, J. F. (2001). Impact of comprehensive day treatment on societal participation for persons with acquired brain injury. *Archives of Physical Medicine and Rehabilitation*, 82(7), 885–895.

Malec, J., Smigielski, J. & DePompolo, R. (1991). Goal attainment scaling and outcome measurement in postacute brain injury rehabilitation. *Archives of Physical Medicine and Rehabilitation*, 72, 138–143.

Malec, J. F., Smigielski, J. S., DePompolo, R. W. & Thompson, J. M. (1993). Outcome evaluation and prediction in a comprehensive-integrated post-acute outpatient brain injury rehabilitation programme. *Brain Injury*, 7, 15–29.

Marsh, N. V. & Knight, R. (1991). Behavioral assessment of social competence following severe head injury. *Journal of Clinical and Experimental Neuropsychology*, 13(5), 729–740.

McColl, M. A., Carlson, P., Johnston, J., Minnes, P., Shue, K., Davies, D. & Karlovits, T. (1998). The definition of community integration: perspectives of people with brain injuries. *Brain Injury*, 12, 15–30.

McDonald, S. (2005). Are you crying or laughing? Emotion recognition deficits after severe traumatic brain injury. *Brain Impairment*, 6, 56–67.

McDonald, S. & Flanagan, S. (2004). Social perception deficits after traumatic brain injury: interaction between emotion recognition, mentalizing ability, and social communication. *Neuropsychology* 18, 572–579.

McDonald, S., Flanagan, S., Rollins, J. & Kinch, J. (2003). A new clinical tool for assessing social perception after traumatic brain injury. *Journal of Head Trauma Rehabilitation* 18(3), 219–238.

McDonald, S., Tate, R., Togher, L., Bornhofen, C., Long, E., Gertler, P. & Bowen, R. (2008). Social skills treatment for people with severe, chronic acquired brain injuries: a multicenter trial. *Archives of Physical Medicine and Rehabilitation*, 89(9), 1648–1659.

Messenger, B. & Ziarnek, N. (2004). *Behavior Functional Rehabilitation Activity Manual.* Wake Forest: Lash and Associates Publishing/Training.

Milton, S. B. (1988). Management of subtle communication deficits. *Journal of Head Trauma Rehabilitation*, 3, 1–11.

Milton, S., Prutting, C. & Binder, G. (1984). Appraisal of communicative competence in head injured adults. In *Clinical Aphasiology Conference Proceedings*, Minneapolis, MN, pp. 114–123.

Ownsworth, T. L., McFarland, K. & Young, R. M. D. (2000). Self-awareness and psychosocial functioning following acquired brain injury: an evaluation of a group support programme. *Neuropsychological Rehabilitation*, 10(5), 465–484.

Ownsworth, T. L., Fleming, J., Shum, D., Kuipers, P. & Strong, J. (2008). Comparison of individual, group and combined intervention formats in a randomized controlled trial for facilitating goal attainment and improving psychosocial function following acquired brain injury. *Journal of Rehabilitation Medicine*, 40, 81–88.

Prutting, C. A. (1982). Pragmatics as social competence. *Journal of Speech and Hearing Disorders*, 47, 123–134.

Prutting, C. A. & Kirchner, D. M. (1987). A clinical appraisal of the pragmatic aspects of language. *Journal of Speech and Hearing Disorders*, 52, 105–119.

Radice-Neumann, D., Zupan, B., Babbage, D. R. & Willer, B. (2007). Overview of impaired facial affect recognition in persons with traumatic brain injury. *Brain Injury,* 21, 807–816.

Sohlberg, M. M., Perlewitz, P. G., Johansen, A., Schultz, J., Johnson, L. & Hartry, A. (1992). *Improving Pragmatic Skills in Persons with Head Injury.* Tucson: Communication Skill Builders.

Struchen, M. A., Clark, A. N., Sander, A. M., Mills, M. R., Evans, G. & Kurtz, D. (2008) Relation of executive functioning and social communication to outcomes. *NeuroRehabilitation,* 23, 185–198.

Struchen, M. A., Pappadis, M. R., Mazzei, K., Clark, A. N., Davis, L. C. & Sander, A. M. (2008). Perceptions of communication abilities for persons with traumatic brain injury: validity of the LaTrobe Communication Questionnaire. *Brain Injury,* 22, 940–951.

Struchen, M. A., Pappadis, M. R., Sander, A. M., Burrows, C. S. & Myszka, K. A. (2011). Examining the contribution of social communication abilities and affective/behavioral functioning to social integration outcomes for adults with traumatic brain injury. *Journal of Head Trauma Rehabilitation,* 26, 130–142.

Thomsen, I. V. (1984). Late outcome of very severe blunt head trauma: a 10–15 year second follow-up. *Journal of Neurology, Neurosurgery and Psychiatry,* 47, 260–268.

Trower, P., Bryant, B., Argyle, M. & Marzillier, J. (1978). *Social Skills and Mental Health.* Pittsburgh: University of Pittsburgh Press.

Turner-Stokes, L., Williams, H. & Johnson, J. (2009). Goal attainment scaling: does it provide added value as a person-centered measure for evaluation of outcome in neurorehabilitation following acquired brain injury? *Journal of Rehabilitation Medicine,* 41, 528–535.

Wallander, J. L., Conger, A. J. & Conger, J. C. (1985). Development and evaluation of a behaviorally referenced rating system for heterosocial skills. *Behavioral Assessment,* 7(2), 137–153.

Wiseman-Hakes, C., Stewart, M. L., Wasserman, R. & Schuller, R. (1998). Peer group training of pragmatic skills in adolescents with acquired brain injury. *Journal of Head Trauma Rehabilitation,* 13(6), 23–38.

Ylvisaker, M. & Feeney, T. (2001). What I really want is a girlfriend: meaningful social interaction after traumatic brain injury. *Brain Injury Source,* 12–17.

12 Training communication partners of people with TBI

Communication really is a two way process

Leanne Togher

Traumatic brain injury can lead to profound interactional difficulties, which most communication partners find challenging, sometimes embarrassing, and even exhausting to deal with during everyday social encounters. The effect of these difficulties is often compounded by the realization that they may be entrenched and therefore difficult to modify in the long term. Those for whom the person with TBI predominately interacts include family members, wives, husbands, mothers and children and therefore it is for these people that communication problems can be the most difficult to deal with on a daily basis. The person with TBI will also have contact with people in the community including shop assistants, service providers, people who work for government agencies and, in some cases, law and justice personnel. Until recently, there has been a paucity of research investigating how to improve the knowledge, skills and confidence of communication partners to deal with difficult conversational behaviours. This chapter describes our programme of research, which has: (1) investigated novel ways to evaluate the interactions of people with TBI; and (2) studied the effectiveness of education and training for communication partners including police officers (Togher *et al.*, 2004), family members (Togher *et al.*, 2013) and paid caregivers (Behn *et al.*, 2012).

Assessing interactions of people with TBI: the communication partner matters

The theoretical basis of including the communication partner of people with TBI during the assessment and treatment process extends beyond mere common sense. Involving communication partners has arisen from extensive work evaluating the effect of communication partners on the everyday exchanges of people with TBI. This chapter will describe the underlying theoretical basis for this course of study, which will necessarily involve a description of the analyses used. These analyses which derive from a sociolinguistic perspective called Systemic Functional Linguistics (Halliday, 1994) have enabled a clearer picture of the nature of interaction for people with TBI and their partners. While traditional assessment methods have been described in Chapters 1 and 4 in this volume, a brief summary is provided here.

Traditionally, communication impairment following TBI has been viewed as a range of deficits, which are identified from assessments administered in clinical settings. These difficulties have been described in terms of phonological, lexical, syntactic and other more global impairments. Frequently, the testing process fails to include interlocutors other than the therapist and the person with the TBI. Tasks are often monologic (i.e. the person with TBI is evaluated on their performance during tasks such as telling a story or describing the procedure underlying simple everyday activities). Procedural and narrative tasks provide valuable information regarding particular linguistic parameters such as story structure or cohesion, however they cannot be extrapolated to the wider strata of everyday interactions. The ability of the person with TBI to converse is typically judged on their interactions with the clinician or at best with a family member who might be present at the time of the assessment. What does this type of an assessment tell us about how the person with TBI manages once they leave the clinic environment? How representative are such 'discourse' samples? The way a person interacts is determined by a number of complex factors, which vary immensely from one interaction to the next. Such factors include the relationship between the interactants, the situation, the purpose of the interactions and the way language is used during the interaction. This chapter will discuss the importance of approaching communication following TBI as a two-way process, and therefore will emphasize the need to consider the communication partner's influence within interactions of the person with TBI. The chapter will describe the use of systemic functional linguistics as a framework for examining two-way language use following TBI.

Defining conversation

Conversation is a two way process, where information sharing takes place as an interactionally negotiated achievement (McTear & King, 1991). Conversation is one of many genres we use each day including procedural (i.e. describing the steps in how to carry out an activity), expository (i.e. giving an opinion) and narrative (i.e. recounting a story about an event or retelling a story) discourse types. Unfortunately, the term conversation has been used with abandon with some studies examining any kind of connected speech above the level of the sentence, and terming these tasks conversational (Ehrlich & Sipes, 1985; Parsons *et al.*, 1989). Some of these so-called conversational tasks include picture description, and describing routine activities, such as changing a tyre. Describing the steps one needs to take to change a tyre cannot be considered a conversational task when the patient is asked to produce this discourse as a separate monologue speaking task. As it is a monologue rather than a dialogue, it therefore does not involve the communication partner in the same way that a conversation would. Unfortunately, some studies have made assumptions regarding conversational skills of people with TBI from completion of tasks which were in no sense interactional (Ehrlich & Sipes, 1985; Parsons *et al.*, 1989). Such assumptions are falsely based and conclusions from these studies need to be carefully considered.

To characterize conversation or social interactions in a meaningful way, and to contrast them with other discourse types (such as narrative and procedural) requires a coherent model which captures the complexity of the genre. What has been lacking is a theoretical model to account for the changing communicative environments that we are faced with when conversing on a daily basis. The concept of context has been taken up as a starting point to describe the characteristics of a communicative situation. Hartley (1992) identified three categories of context; (a) participants, (b) setting and (c) medium or code. 'Speakers select words, sentence structures, and modes of communication based on their knowledge of the cognitive and social status of the communication partner, of the physical context or setting of the communication, and of the linguistic and non-linguistic context' (Hartley, 1992, p. 265). This way of viewing communication was driven by the pragmatics literature and while valuable, it failed to elaborate on how different contextual variables may influence the way the words, sentences and modes of communication are selected. The pragmatic categories that are described vary according to context and are not part of a cohesive theory.

So, while early TBI researchers were starting to recognize the importance of viewing communication in a dialogic interactive setting (Hartley, 1992; Ylvisaker *et al.*, 1992) a further conceptualization of communication in context was necessary. This led me to the theory of Systemic Functional Linguistics (SFL) (Halliday, 1994) which provided a coherent model of the interconnectedness of context with language use for people with TBI and their partners. The remainder of this section examines a range of genres in TBI using SFL, providing short examples of each.

Systemic Functional Linguistics

Systemic Functional Linguistics (SFL) is a theory of language use developed by Halliday (1994) who was concerned with the practical use of language which he described as a system of choices. Each time we speak we make a choice (which is usually unconscious) about what we are going to say and how we are going to say it which, in turn, is influenced by whom we are speaking to and the situation we are in. All language characteristics are described in terms of the functions they perform in conveying meanings. Halliday described three primary functions of language which reflect three different types of meanings (Halliday, 1994). These meanings are understood to occur simultaneously. Briefly these are:

1. Ideational meanings which express the processes, events, actions, states and/ or ideas. Analyses within this area of meaning examine the types of words used to express processes (or verbs) and participants (or what the text is about). These analyses investigate how speakers choose to represent their experiences through the types of processes and participants they use.
2. Textual meanings, which ensure that what is said is relevant and relates to its context. Analyses of textual meaning examine how clauses are structured in

relation to each other. One of the analyses used here is cohesion analysis. This analysis describes the connections between words in a piece of discourse. It is described in greater detail in Chapter 4.

3. Interpersonal meanings are concerned with the interaction and how this is achieved. Analyses therefore focus on the speaker and the hearer and how they negotiate the interaction, e.g. who initiates an interaction and how this occurs. Interpersonal meanings are very useful to analyse the discourse of TBI as they capture the problems people experience within their interactions. Being able to provide information credibly, asking for clarification of information given by others and adhering to the appropriate sequence of events during a telephone enquiry all require an ability to manipulate interpersonal meanings. People with TBI, however, have difficulty with these 'interactional' skills. We have used some of the analyses from within the interpersonal function to describe interactional difficulties of people with TBI and a range of communication partners.

Context

SFL explores the dimensions of, and the manner in which, context influences language use. Eggins (1994, p. 9), building on Halliday's notion of context, suggests that SFL has described:

1. exactly what dimensions of context have an impact on language use. Since clearly not every aspect of context makes a difference to language use ... just what bits of the context do get 'into' the text? And

2. which aspects of language use appear to be affected by particular dimensions of the context. For example, if we contrast texts in which the interactants are friends with texts where the interactants are strangers, can we specify where in the language they use this contextual difference?

Halliday and Hasan conceptualized context as a combination of three important dimensions termed field, mode and tenor (Halliday & Hasan, 1985). Field refers to what is happening, to the nature of the social interaction that is taking place, e.g. a lecture, casual conversation. The ideational function relates to the field. The mode of the discourse refers to the part that the language is playing in the interaction in terms of the channel through which it is being transmitted (e.g. oral vs. written). The textual function relates to the mode of discourse. The tenor refers to who is taking part, to the nature of the participants, their status and roles, e.g. lecturer–student, two friends, salesperson–customer. The interpersonal metafunction relates to the tenor. These three dimensions have a significant and predictable impact on language use.

Let's look at an example of this thinking. If you ring your local pizza shop to order a pizza, the context could be described as in Table 12.1.

Table 12.1 Contextual dimensions for a service encounter (ordering pizza over the phone)

Contextual variable	Description
Field	a verbal service encounter over the telephone
Tenor	unfamiliar participants, unequal status between participants, customer – superordinate, information provider – subordinate
Mode	spoken, but may refer to written material

Genre

The concept of genre describes the impact of the context of culture on language by identifying the staged, step-by-step structure that cultures institutionalize as ways of achieving goals (Eggins, 1994; Eggins & Slade, 1997). That is, our day-to-day activities are composed of a series of different generic structures, consisting of a series of goal-oriented steps that unfold according to the situation we are in. If, for example, you were telling a funny story to a friend on the way to work, you would probably follow a sequence of steps, such as providing the setting information, the time, the place, who told the story in the first place, the introduction to the story, the complicating action, the punch line and the summary. These steps fall into what is generally known as the structure of a narrative. The important difference when viewing this structure from the SFL framework is that the language choices made are intertwined with the generic structure as well as the context (i.e. the field, tenor and mode).

Ideology

SFL emphasizes the importance of ideology on the way we interact (Martin, 1992). This represents the impact of our biases, values, upbringing, life experience or personal perspectives. Many of these influences may be quite unconscious or inherent in the speaker's makeup (e.g. gender, ethnicity, religious orientation, class and generation). Our ideological background determines the types of words we are likely to use, the genres to which we have access and our position within various discourse interactions. Such issues must be taken into account when examining how a person interacts across different situations. This broad perspective places SFL in sharp contrast to traditional or generative grammars. SFL differs from traditional grammar in that it conceptualizes function as driving the form of language rather than the form of the language determining the functions. Language is not viewed as a set of rules, but rather as a set of linguistic resources. Each utterance we produce actualizes all three metafunctions concurrently. That is, we don't just produce an utterance with interpersonal meanings or textual meanings or ideational meanings, but all three happen simultaneously. This notion shows the complexity of language use in everyday interactions.

Given the reported difficulty people with TBI show during interactions, it is not surprising that it is the interpersonal function of language that presents the greatest challenge. Analyses of interpersonal functions focus on the interaction between the speaker and the hearer by examining which language structures are used to establish and maintain interactions.

Two interpersonal analyses from SFL will be described in this chapter as they have particular sensitivity in revealing the difficulties experienced by people with TBI AND their communication partners. In order to illustrate these let us take the earlier example of an interaction where someone is making a request for information to the bus timetable information service on the telephone. This is an example of the service encounter genre. The interpersonal analysis of genre is *generic structure potential analysis*, which outlines the overall structure of the interaction (Halliday & Hasan, 1985). Another discourse analysis of interest to TBI researchers is the way people with TBI exchange information (Berry, 1981; Coelho *et al.*, 1991b). In SFL, this can be examined using *exchange structure analysis* which addresses who has the knowledge in an interaction and how that knowledge is transferred. The context of the situation (i.e. field, mode and tenor) has an impact on the way requests for information are made. For example, the type of request made between two people of equal status will be very different to one made by a superior to a subordinate. Example 1 shows a request for information between two people of equal status.

Example 1. Request for information between communication partners of equal status

Customer:	What time would I need to be at Strathfield station to catch a bus to Macquarie Shopping Centre and be there by 12.30?
Call center operator:	We don't have a service that does that.

Using this example we can now illustrate each of the above types of analysis. Starting with the genre level, this request would form part of the Service Request (SR) element in the Generic Structure Potential (GSP) analysis. The Service Request (SR) element is one of the obligatory elements in the GSP analysis. It is usually followed by a Service Compliance (SC) where the answer to the SR is provided. At the discourse semantics level, exchange structure analysis would enable us to code the customer as a secondary knower (K2), i.e. someone who doesn't have some information and who is requesting it from the bus timetable person who is the primary knower (K1). The degree to which a person is a primary knower has been associated with the degree of power they have in an interaction. This request is 'congruently formed'. That is, it conforms to all the features one would expect when fulfilling the task of requesting information.

Sometimes, however, requests are not congruently formed. This can be seen in Example 2.

Example 2. Request for information from superior to subordinate

Superior: Show me where the timetables are.
Employee: They're over on the table (pointing).

In this example the superior is requesting information from a subordinate. This is no longer a service encounter at the genre level and would more likely be part of a different generic structure potential such as workplace procedural discourse text. The superior's request for information would be marked in exchange structure analysis terms as a request for action. When requesting someone to do an action, you are said to be a secondary actor (A2) who requests an action from the primary actor (A1). Therefore this request for information has now become a request for action. Thus, at all levels the different status of the participants is reflected in the language structures used. If people are in a position of unequal status their language use will reflect this from the tone they use through to the way information is requested and received and all these levels relate to the activity that is occurring at the time. This brief example demonstrates the depth and complexity of some of the analyses within the SFL framework. It shows promise as a way of analysing communicative interactions between TBI and a range of communication partners. The following section describes a series of studies we have completed to examine TBI interactions using exchange structure analysis and generic structure analysis.

Exchange structure of TBI interactions

Exchange structure analysis has been a useful way to measure the performance of people with TBI on a range of functional day-to-day tasks including telephone service encounters, casual conversations, joint narrative storytelling, chatroom discourse and conversations with family members. This has helped to establish how their communication impairments influence their ability to assume the social roles of patient, child, spouse, friend and enquirer in service encounters with members of the public. We have examined whether people with TBI and matched control participants change their communication behaviour with different conversational partners who vary according to familiarity (i.e. social distance) and power relationships. Exchange structure analysis examines who has the knowledge in an interaction and how this knowledge is conveyed from one communication partner to another. If the participants are of unequal power (e.g. in a doctor–patient interaction), the dominant communication partner is more likely to be a primary knower (K1) or the person who is giving the information. The subordinate is more likely to be a secondary knower (K2) or the one who does not have the information and wants to gain it from the primary knower. Using this analysis, it is possible to examine how often a person is given the opportunity to be a primary knower in different interactions. This will vary according to the communicative task (field) and the people involved (tenor).

Exchange structure analysis taps into how information and goods and services are exchanged. All interactions are based on the demanding and giving of information or goods and services. The exchange is made up of moves, which are the basic units of analysis. A move is a unit of information and an exchange is composed of a sequence of moves. When involved in an exchange, one is either: (a) requesting or providing information; or (b) requesting or providing action. Exchange analysis has two types of moves: *synoptic* moves and *dynamic* moves. When analysing conversational exchanges the abbreviations K1 and K2 are used to refer to the exchange of this information. Exchanges can be initiated by either interlocutor. Therefore, subjects and their communication partners can be both primary (K1) and secondary knowers (K2) during different exchanges. Synoptic moves are denoted by brackets and dynamic moves are marked with arrows. The following example shows an exchange consisting of a request for information (K2) by the control subject and provision of information (K1) by the bus timetable person, ending with a follow up move (K2f).

Example 3. Control subject 3 – bus timetable condition

Moves 117–119
S = Subject B = Bus timetable person

117 K2 S: So I really suppose it wouldn't be more than two dollars?
118 K1 B: Well your bus is going to cost them a dollar twenty each way.
119 K2f S: Right.

Exchanges of information are rarely this smooth, so to facilitate the exchange speakers use dynamic moves which perform the function of negotiating meanings such as checking or clarification. In Example 4 we have two exchanges of information which are made up of an information giving exchange (moves 19–22); and an information requesting exchange (moves 23–29). Dynamic moves of confirmation (cf) and responses to confirmation (rcf) are also used, possibly to assist the subject to remember the information being given to him or her, as well as backchannelling (bch) which is another kind of dynamic move which is important for the flow of information during telephone calls.

Example 4. Control subject 4 – police condition

Moves 19–29
S = Subject P = Policeman

19 K1 P: I mean if you contact their head office at Rosebery
20 cf S: Head office at Rosebery, yeah
21 rcf P: Yeah mate
22 K1 P: they'd be able to give you all the info you'd need
23 K2 S: Alright could I get that phone number?
24 K1 P: Mate I haven't got it unfortunately
25 cf S: Oh you haven't got it
26 K1 P: If you look them up under the Roads and Traffic Authority, you'll come up with their head office mate down at Rosebery
27 bch S: yeah
28 K1 P: And they'll be able to give you a hand from there
29 K2f S: Alright then

Synoptic moves consist of K1, K2, K1f and K2f moves during exchanges of information. If the request or receipt of action is occurring, the exchanges are made up of the synoptic moves of A1, A2, A1f and A2f (see Table 12.2 for examples). The interactions which were the subject of interest in this study were primarily exchanges of information, therefore K1, K2 and the follow up moves of K1f and K2f were the primary synoptic units of analysis.

K1 moves

The K1 move serves to provide information to the other person. When making a K1 move, one is termed the 'primary knower'. The primary knower is 'someone who already knows the information' (Berry, 1981). The tasks in this study required the communication partner in the interaction (e.g. the bus timetable person or the therapist) to assume this role, as they were being asked for information. Being the primary knower frequently during an interaction has been associated with being in a more powerful position in that interaction (Poynton, 1985). The primary knower must make a contribution (that is, it is an obligatory element of the exchange structure) if an exchange is to occur (Berry, 1981). Thus, the K1 slot is where the primary knower indicates that they know the information and where they confer the information with a 'kind of a stamp of authority' (Berry, 1981).

K2 moves

The 'secondary knower' (i.e. K2) in an interaction is 'someone to whom the information is imparted' (Berry, 1981). Interactants are in the K2 role either because they are directly requesting information or because they are receiving information. It is the former K2 role that is of interest. The subjects (both TBI and normal) were required in the tasks set for them to assume the K2 role to request specific information. This provides a measure of success in requesting information. Being placed in the K2 role has been described as being in a less powerful position (Poynton, 1985); however, the ability to ask questions has also been described by others as a powerful conversational strategy (Cameron *et al.*, 1989; O'Barr & Atkins, 1987). Analysis of K2 moves therefore needs to take account of the context in which they occur.

The teaching exchange

The teaching exchange occurs when a person asks a question to which they already know the answer. In exchange structure parlance this is referred to as a dK1 led exchange. The 'd' stands for a delayed K1 move, as the K1 move does not occur until the end of the exchange. This is typical of teaching and therapy interactions, although it was also noted during conversations between mothers of people with TBI and their sons. For example:

Example 5. TBI subject 1 – mother condition

Moves 15–17
M = Mother S = Subject

15 dK1 M: and what did you do on Mondays?
16 K2 S: Wasn't that the day, that afternoon we went to the swimming pool?
17 K1 M: Yes ... That's right

Dynamic moves

Dynamic moves are used to facilitate the negotiation of meaning, either actively (such as clarification or checking) or by giving feedback that the information has been conveyed successfully (by confirmation or backchannelling). Dynamic moves are used when the information exchange process is challenged or when people misunderstand each other.

Table 12.2 provides some further examples of different types of exchanges.

As conditions were varied according to social distance and power imbalance, it was hypothesized that the person with TBI would be less able to adapt to this variation. This hypothesis was based on evidence regarding the impaired adaptive executive functions reported to follow TBI (Ylvisaker & Szekeres, 1994: see also

Table 12.2 Examples of exchange types

Types of moves		Examples	
Information requesting exchange			
K2	= secondary knower, who does not have the information	K2	How do I get my licence back?
K1	= primary knower, who already knows the information	K1	You go to the registry
K2f	= a follow up move by the secondary knower to finish the exchange	K2f	Oh
The teaching exchange			
dK1	= primary knower asking a question to which they know the answer	dK1	Where did we go?
		K2	To the beach
		K1	That's right!
Information seeking exchange			
cfrq	= dynamic move which asks for confirmation	K2	Do you know where the registry is?
		cfrq	Where?
rcfrq	= response to confirmation	rcfrq	The registry
		K1	Yeah it's at Rosebery
Information giving exchange			
bch	= backchannelling move	K1	I'm here with Leanne at the moment
		bch	Ah ha
		K1	at Lidcombe
		K2f	OK

Chapter 3). It was also hypothesized that the person with TBI would be less able to request information and would ultimately receive less information on the basis of previous research implicating such difficulties (Coelho *et al.*, 1991a; Mentis & Thompson, 1991). By examining K1 moves, K2 moves and dynamic moves, social distance and power imbalance could be investigated.

In a study of telephone conversations where TBI participants requested information from a range of communication partners (e.g. therapists, mothers, police officers and call centre service providers), they were asked for and were given less information than matched control participants (who were brothers of the TBI participants) (Togher *et al.*, 1996, 1997a, 1997b). Therapists and mothers never asked people with TBI questions to which they did not already know the answer. Additionally, TBI participants were more frequently questioned regarding the accuracy of their contributions and contributions were followed up less often than matched control participants. This was in contrast to the control interactions, where participants were asked for unknown information, encouraged to elaborate, did not have their contributions checked frequently and had their contributions followed up. In the following example, a young man with a brain injury was meant to be discussing his occupational therapy goals with his clinician. At this point in the conversation, they were talking about going shopping; however, the person with TBI, who we will call John, was taking the opportunity to suggest that he did not feel like he belonged in the brain injury unit (Example 6).

Example 6. John talking with his therapist about shopping goals

Moves 67–82
S = John, T = Therapist, [= overlap, XX = unintelligible

67 S: I'm not used to being with a group like this
68 T: Mm I know it can be difficult, but [I think that
69 S: [What's going to happen when I'm not here any more?
70 T: [I guess it'll be a good goal to work on
71 S: [There'll be no groups like this around
72 S: I'm in a protected environment
73 T: Mm
74 S: It's weird
75 T: It is [quite difficult
76 S: [and XX all the ways like this
77 T: a protected environment, but if you're sitting down,
78 T: if you've planned to meet someone, you don't just get up and leave them in the middle of [talking to them
79 S: [I do
80 T: while they're in the middle of coffee
81 S: I do
82 T: But it wouldn't seem a good idea to do that

In this example, John's information giving overlapped with the therapist's attempts to provide information regarding his goals. John's attempt to give information was ignored by the therapist who continued with her conversational intention which was to give John information (moves 77–78). He challenged her information giving more directly (moves 79, 81). The conflict seen here resulted from John attempting to give information at a time where the therapist was also giving information. Notably she did not respond to his concerns at all during this conversation.

This data suggested that for some people with brain injury, their impaired communication led to the circumstance where they were being talked down to, where the accuracy of their conversational contributions were questioned and where they had lost control over the most basic aspects of their life. In cases where people with TBI attempted to assert control, they were described as 'non-compliant', or more subtly, as I found in interactions between clinicians and people with TBI, they didn't have a chance to speak.

This disturbing discovery led to the question of whether this situation could be improved by manipulating the context of the communication situation. The next stage of our research found that was indeed possible. For example, when people with TBI were placed in a powerful information-giving role, e.g. as a guest speaker talking with school students and speaking about the experience of having a serious injury, their communication approximated matched control participants (who had a spinal injury) (Togher, 2000; Togher & Hand, 1999). Thus, when provided with a facilitative context, such as an equal communicative opportunity, TBI participants were primed to match the performance of control participants. These results suggested that greater opportunities and increased conversational competence could be created for the person with TBI.

Generic structure analysis

The theory of SFL allows a clear description of how the context is realized in the text. We completed a study which attempted to answer a small part of one of the questions posed by Eggins (1994): namely, which aspects of language use appear to be affected by particular dimensions of the context following TBI (Togher *et al.*, 1997a). The richness of this approach is that, as well as analysing at the level of discourse semantics (i.e. exchange structure analysis), it is also possible to take the same data and analyse it at the level of genre (i.e. generic structure analysis).

Generic structure analysis examines oral texts as genre (Hasan, 1984; Martin, 1992; Ventola, 1987). Each social process is seen as unfolding step by step, according to the context of the situation (i.e. field, tenor and mode) and also according to the core structural elements that would be expected in that particular type of interaction. The bus and police telephone data were analysed using this approach as they both represented service encounters (Togher *et al.*, 1997b). Normal service encounters have been previously well described (Halliday & Hasan, 1985; Ventola, 1987). The texts were divided into key structural elements (see Table 12.3 and Appendix 2 for further detail) which have been described as typifying a service encounter. An example of a simple service encounter is:

Greeting A:	Hello, this is Sarah from Zonta Hair Salon
Service initiation A:	Can I help you?
Greeting B:	Hello
Service request B:	Do you have any appointments available for Saturday morning?
Service enquiry A:	Do you mean this weekend?
B:	Yes
Service compliance A:	Well we could see you at 10am or 11.30
B:	I'll take the 10am appointment then
A:	What's your name?
B:	My name is Maria
A:	OK then well we'll see you at 10am this Saturday morning Maria!
Close B:	OK thanks very much
Goodbye A:	No problem
A:	Bye

Table 12.3 Elements of service encounters according to generic structure analysis

Element	Description
Greeting (GR)	Caller and information service provider greet each other
Address (AD)	Caller and information service provider identify selves or ask for identification e.g. 'What's your name?'
Service initiation (SI)	'Can I help you?'
Service request (SR)	Makes primary request for information known to service provider
Service enquiry (SE)	Seeks further information or detail regarding initial SR. Can be made by either party
Service compliance (SC)	Response to request for information and invitation for further requests
Close (CL)	Closing remarks – usually interpersonally oriented, e.g. 'Is that OK? Thanks very much'
Goodbye (GB)	Final goodbye 'Bye, bye'
Call for attention (CALL)	Call for attention from either speaker, either due to lack of response, or because speaker was returning to the phone after suspending conversation
Action (ACT)	Statements of action e.g. 'I'll just write that down'
Incomplete/inappropriate (*)	Inappropriate or incomplete elements either because of delayed responding or a lack of response
Unrelated (UNR)	Comments or enquiries which are unrelated to the task at hand
Personal comment (PERSONAL)	Comments of a personal nature which, while not directly relevant to the information seeking task, appear to fulfil an interpersonal function e.g. 'You're not nervous about driving are you?'
Repetition (rpt)	Elements which are repeated due to misunderstanding; failure to take in information or forgetting of information

A more thorough description of this analysis can be found in Togher, Hand and Code (1997b), but for the purpose of this chapter it is useful to look at one aspect of this analysis to demonstrate its value. We found that the generic structural elements in the TBI service encounters were of a different length and composition to those of the control interactions. There were difficulties with the opening sequences of TBI interactions, as well as with the main *service request*. Repeated and inappropriate elements were present in TBI samples, whereas they did not occur in the control samples. There were also significant differences between the bus timetable condition and the police interactions. In the control–police interactions, the *greeting* sequences were short and quickly followed by a clear succinct service request and the *close/goodbye* sequences were significantly longer than in the bus condition. In contrast, the TBI participant–police interactions evidenced long greeting sequences and short close/goodbye elements. Opening and closing elements reflect the development of interpersonal relationships, by initially establishing credibility and finally, by confirming the success of the encounter, as well as encouraging future contact. In all control interactions, the police officer encouraged participants to call again. The interpersonal relationship was therefore reinforced by a longer closure than in the TBI interactions.

The description of the macrostructure identified potentially problematic features for both the person with TBI and their partners. For example, once the service request was found to be problematic, one can focus on this element, examine why it is breaking down, model the use of service requests using cues, and practice these in different situations with different levels of difficulty.

Training communication partners of people with TBI

In a similar vein to the work done in aphasia (Simmons-Mackie *et al.*, 2010; Turner & Whitworth, 2006), training programmes are now beginning to emerge to help families and other caregivers deal with the ongoing problems that can follow TBI (Carnevale, 1996; Holland & Shigaki, 1998; Ylvisaker *et al.*, 1993). Ylvisaker *et al.* (1993) described the importance of providing a positive communication culture within the rehabilitation context. They suggest that role-playing and modelling combined with ongoing coaching and support in vivo are appropriate methods to facilitate training for communication partners of people with TBI. Further work is needed, however, to develop such training programmes to address individual communication profiles in collaboration with the family and peer network of the person with TBI. Importantly, there are few communication training programmes for community groups who interact with people with TBI. Thus, although community reintegration is frequently suggested as the primary objective of TBI rehabilitation (Ylvisaker *et al.*, 2005), there are few documented cases where community agencies have been assisted to encourage more appropriate participation for these clients. This is despite the fact that there are now a number of studies that have clearly documented the nature of social interaction difficulties that commonly occur when people with TBI communicate in everyday settings.

To examine this question our research team developed and evaluated a communication-training programme for police officers, as members of a service industry who are likely to encounter people with TBI. We trained the police officers to manage specific service encounters with people with TBI who they had not previously met. This was evaluated in a randomized controlled trial (Togher *et al.*, 2004). The TBI speakers rang the police to ask their advice both before and after the police had been trained. Training resulted in more efficient, focused interactions. In other words, this study confirmed that training communication partners improved the competence of people with TBI.

One of the key ramifications of training police officers was that a well-trained communication partner could improve the communication of people with TBI. Taken to its natural conclusion, this study asked the question whether training family members could lead to improved communication for the person with TBI. In order to address this, in a non-randomized clinical trial, 44 people with chronic severe traumatic brain injury and their chosen communication partners were allocated to one of the three groups, the TBI only group, where only the person with TBI was trained, the JOINT group where both the communication partner and person with TBI were trained together, and a delayed treatment control condition. Tests, questionnaires and ratings of video conversations were used to evaluate outcomes for communication, as well as measures of social skills, carer burden and self-esteem (Togher *et al.*, 2009). The training programme was entitled TBI Express and the contents are described below.

TBI Express: a communication training programme for people with TBI and their everyday communication partners

The aim of TBI Express was to teach the communication partner how to facilitate interactions with their family member or friend with a TBI (Togher *et al.*, 2011). The content was based on the findings from our previous research in combination with the findings of the considerable body of work by Ylvisaker, Feeney and colleagues (Ylvisaker, 1996; Ylvisaker & Feeney, 2000; Ylvisaker *et al.*, 1993; Ylvisaker *et al.*, 2008; Ylvisaker *et al.*, 2005). Specifically, participants were taught to ask questions in a positive, non-demanding manner; encourage discussion of opinions in conversations; and work through difficult communication situations collaboratively. The training manual, called *TBI Express*, has been published and a free website has been launched which has demonstration videos of some of the positive techniques we taught to communication partners, as well as other resources. The website can be found at: http://sydney.edu.au/health_sciences/disability_community/tbi_express/.

The communication partner-training programme was divided into ten modules run over ten weeks. Each person with TBI and their communication partner attended a two and a half hour group session with three to four other pairs as well as a one hour individual session. The training programme consisted of an introductory session where the aims of training, group guidelines and home practice expectations were established. Session 2 contained an educational component on TBI and communication. Both session 3 and 4 explored communication roles and rules in society as well as some general communication strategies.

Collaborative conversation techniques were the focus of session 5. The aim of this module was to help conversations to be a collaborative process where both the 'feel' and information exchange are more equal, shared and organized. For example, the following example of collaboration is an excerpt from the manual:

Collaborative Communication – Problem Solving

Difficult communication situation: _____

> **"I'm with you – it's OK"**
> Communicate emotional support about the situation.
> This may be all that is needed in some situations.

Emotional support: _____

> **"We're doing this together"**
> Discuss the communication options _____ has in the situation
> Help to identify the consequences of each option
> Support them in thinking through their options

> **"What can help make this easier?"**
> Use cognitive supports (i.e., diary, timeline, paint a picture)
> Work out together the best communication option
> Work out a script

> **Script (practice this and role play):**

> **Catchphrase or reminder you both agree to use:**

Continue to problem solve and refine use of strategies as necessary.

Figure 12.1 Example of communication problem solving form from *TBI Express* for working through difficult communication situations

Collaboration

'We are doing this together, as a cooperative project'
When in conversation, this means that we intend to convey this message to the other person. That is, we take turns, each having a go and helping the other person. Conversation is more about shared meaning than whether content is right or wrong alone. Collaboration is a way of 'sharing the floor' in a conversation, making sure that each person contributes as much as they can in the situation, supporting the person with brain injury to participate as much as possible.

We are here to provide you with the tools into the future to maximize conversation. As brain injury affects conversation due to cognitive communication difficulties, the communication partner has a special role to help make communication flow as best as possible.

To achieve collaboration we need 5 key ingredients (Table 12.4).

Table 12.4 Ingredients for successful collaboration in conversation

For real collaboration we need:		This means we need to convey:
• Collaborative intent	→	*'We're doing this together'*
• Cognitive support	→	*'What can help make this easier?'*
• Emotional support	→	*'I'm with you, it's OK'*
• Positive question style	→	*'I'm interested in what you have to say'*
• Collaborative turn taking	→	*'I'm interested in sharing conversation'*

Learning how to collaborate within a conversation is a key ingredient to the training. The elements contributing to a positive collaborative style (from (Ylvisaker *et al.*, 1998) are listed in Table 12.5.

In session 6, participants learned about the concept of 'keeping conversations going' (Elaboration) with techniques that help to organize and link both simple and more complex topics, with the use of both questions and comments. Similar to the concept of collaboration, the use of positive elaboration is encouraged and practised during the training (Table 12.6).

Session 7 explored the use of questions with particular attention on how to use helpful questions. It also provided methods to avoid using negative, or 'testing' questions where communication partners asked for information when they already knew the answer. This was the focus of homework tasks (see Example 7).

Table 12.5 Types of collaboration

A positive collaborative style:	*A non-collaborative style:*
Collaborative intent	*Non-collaborative*
<ul><li>Shares information</li><li>Use collaborative talk *'Let's think about it'*</li><li>Shows understanding of what was said</li><li>Invites partner to evaluate their contribution</li><li>Confirms partner's contribution</li><li>Shows enthusiasm for contributions</li><li>Establishes equal leadership roles</li></ul>	<ul><li>Demands information</li><li>Talks as teacher or examiner</li><li>Fails to show understanding of what was said</li><li>Fails to invite partner to evaluate contribution</li><li>Fails to confirm partner's contribution</li><li>Expresses lack of enthusiasm</li><li>Takes leadership role only</li></ul>
Cognitive support	*Lack of cognitive support*
<ul><li>Gives information when needed</li><li>Uses memory, organization supports (*calendars, photos, diaries, books, notes*)</li><li>Gives cues in a conversational manner</li><li>Responds to errors by giving correct information in a non-punitive manner</li></ul>	<ul><li>Doesn't give information when needed; instead quizzes</li><li>Fails to use or encourage cognitive supports at appropriate times</li><li>Fails to give cues</li><li>Corrects in a punishing manner and considers accuracy more important than the message</li></ul>
Emotional support	*Lack of emotional support*
<ul><li>Communicates respect for other's concerns, perspectives and abilities</li><li>Acknowledges difficulties (*It's hard to get all these things in order isn't it?*)</li></ul>	<ul><li>Fails to communicate respect for other's concerns, perspectives and abilities</li><li>Fails to acknowledge difficulty of the task and continues despite difficulties</li></ul>
Questions: positive style	*Questions: negative style*
<ul><li>Questions in a non-demanding manner</li><li>Questions in a supportive manner (*What do you need to do that?*)</li></ul>	<ul><li>Questions in a demanding manner (*quiz like*)</li><li>Questions in a non-supportive manner (*How are you going to do that?*)</li></ul>
Collaborative turn taking	*Non-collaborative turn taking*
<ul><li>Takes appropriate conversational turns</li><li>Helps partner express thoughts when struggle occurs (*word finding difficulties*)</li></ul>	<ul><li>Interrupts in a way that disrupts the partner's thought processes and statements</li><li>Fails to help partner when struggling occurs</li></ul>

Table 12.6 Examples of exchange types

Elaboration is about extending and organizing thinking and conversation.

Positive elaborative style:	Non-elaborative style:
Elaboration of the topics	*Non-elaboration of topics*
• Introduce and initiate topics of interest which can go further.	• Introduces topics of marginal interest, with little potential for elaboration.
• Maintain the topic for many turns — Partner contributes many pieces of information to the topic. — Partner invites elaboration (e.g. open ended questions).	• Changes topic frequently • Partner fails to add adequate information to the topic • Partner fails to invite the other person to add information
Elaborative organization	*Non-elaborative organization*
• Organizes information in the conversation as clearly as possible: — Sequential order (e.g. first we ... then we ...) — Physical causality (e.g. the radio's not working because ... — Psychological cause (e.g. maybe you feel that because ...) — Similarity & difference (e.g. yes, they're similar / different because) — Association (e.g. that reminds me of ... that's like ...) • Make connections when topics change • Make connections among day to day conversational themes • Reviews organization of information	• Fails to organize information • Fails to review organization of information • Fails to make connections clear when topics change • Fails to make connections among day to day conversational themes. Meaning is vague

---

Example 7. Questioning homework task from *TBI Express*

Conversation 1: Using follow-up questions and dynamic questions

- After a period of time (an afternoon, day or weekend) which you spent apart, have a conversation about what the other person did (e.g. What have you been doing this afternoon?)
- Aim to use follow-up questions to keep the topic going for as long as possible, rather than changing the topic rapidly.
- Aim to use dynamic questions to keep the conversation progressing smoothly.

Conversation 2: Avoiding 'testing' questions

- Have a look together at one or two articles from a newspaper or magazine. One of you might read it out loud, or just read it through silently together.
- Aim to have a conversation using 'true' questions or comments, rather than 'testing' questions (that you already know the answer to).

Conversation 3: General question practice

- Use any conversational situation you are in this week.
- Aim mainly to use the following question types in your conversation.
  - Balance of open and closed questions as appropriate.
  - Simple and short questions (rather than long and complex).
  - Follow-up questions and dynamic questions (keep the conversation going).
  - True questions (rather than testing questions).

Sessions 8–10 then revised the information and practised each technique learnt in previous sessions with more intensive conversational practice. Every group session contained session handouts, a mix of role-plays, information content and conversational practice. Additionally, each pair was encouraged to play recorded home practice tapes to enable peer problem solving of conversational difficulties as well as peer support for good use of techniques or successful conversations. The programme taught communication partners how to help the person with TBI actively engage in conversations in everyday life and so the strategies were immediately applicable in everyday situations.

The primary finding was that the communication partner training led to greater improvements in the communication of the person with brain injury compared to the other two conditions (Togher *et al.*, 2013). In addition to our quantitative data analysis, we collected data from our participants about the experiences of the training (Togher *et al.*, 2012). This comment from one pair illustrates their experience with the training programme:

> Participant with TBI: *'My communication after the programme is very good with my three kids, I communicate better with them, especially my kids, they're older now and I just communicate a lot better, a lot better'.* His communication partner said: *'And they actually want to socialize with us whereas before they just walked away. Now we'll never get rid of them (laughs). They want to sit and have a conversation with him but they used to only talk to me'.*

The training programme for communication partners consisted of a series of central components that we believe have been keys to successful interactions with their relative or friend with TBI. We encouraged both the communication partner and the person with TBI to approach their interactions with an improved awareness of how BOTH participants were contributing to the topic. In many cases we found that the communication partners, who were frequently mothers and wives in our study, were not consciously aware of how they were communicating. Once this awareness had been raised, they were able to change some communication behaviours that interfered with a successful interaction.

Key strategies for communication partners in developing positive communication skills

1. *Approach conversations with the goal of collaborating with each other to reach a common understanding or decision.* Conversations need a balance of asking questions, listening and understanding, and sharing information about your own ideas and experiences. One participant said: 'I realized I just asked questions all the time like "Did you enjoy the holiday, and what did we do?". Now I use comments and give her time to spark her own memory from what I say rather than from nothing at all. I say, "It was a great holiday, my favourite day was the zoo and the white tiger, he was amazing". When I give her a little bit of information she can build on it'.

2. *Use conversations as a way of introducing new and more complex information and ideas (elaboration).* People with traumatic brain injury may have a limited range of topics they can talk about. By talking about new topics in daily conversations, people with TBI can expand their knowledge of the world and have more interesting things to talk about with other people. One of our participants found that by introducing her son to other topics in the world and exploring those more, he was able to provide many opinions she thought he wasn't capable of expressing. He also reduced the amount of time he spent on the same topic and subsequently, also the frustration his family experienced with his repetition.

3. *Use supports for thinking as part of daily conversations.* For example, make reference to a diary when planning for the future, look back at photos when talking about past events; use a written organizer with headings (e.g. who, what, where, when) when talking about planning for an event. One participant remarked that over the last 8 years, she had organized all her son's events, but in using this technique she realized with 'back-up support' he could do most of it himself.

4. *Avoid asking questions to which you already know the answer.* Instead, try to use real questions, which explore ideas, feelings and opinions. This creates a more natural, adult conversation and gives more confidence to the person with TBI in front of others. One participant said; 'He went to the movies and I knew what he saw. Before the course I would have asked him, did he remember what it was called and who went with him. How boring! I was like a teacher correcting him. Now I ask him, what was the best bit of the movie, or did he prefer the other *Die Hard* movies or this one, how were they

different? It's amazing what he remembers then. It's not perfect but wouldn't you rather talk about that … I would!'
5. *Give specific, positive feedback when you have a successful conversation* with the person with TBI, or when you notice the person having a successful conversation with someone else!

Conclusion

Addressing the communication needs of partners of people with TBI offers new direction in the field of rehabilitation for these individuals. There are many advantages to working with communication partners, not least that they are typically interacting with the person with brain injury on a regular basis, thus offering numerous opportunities to practice positive communication strategies. It is important to note here that I am not suggesting the communication partner become a therapist. It is critical that family members retain their roles as wives, parents, husbands and children, first and foremost, without feeling the burden of needing to be 'the therapist' as well. Rather, the idea is that communication partners may benefit from learning communication strategies which provide positive supports for their relative or friend with TBI, as well as helping to make interactions fun, interesting and pleasurable. After all, the goal of interacting with our family and friends is to maintain and even deepen our relationships, to facilitate our social identity and solidarity and to provide feelings of well-being and happiness. Speech pathologists have a critical role in facilitating this process.

References

Behn, N., Togher, L., Power, E. & Heard, R. (2012). Evaluating communication training for paid carers of people with traumatic brain injury. *Brain Injury,* 26, 1702–1715.
Berry, M. (1981). Systemic linguistics and discourse analysis: a multi-layered approached to exchange structure. In C. Coulthard & M. Montgomery (Eds), *Studies in Discourse Analysis* (pp. 120–145). London: Routledge and Kegan Paul.
Cameron, D., McAlinden, F. & O'Leary, K. (1989). Lakoff in context: the social and linguistic functions of tag questions. In J. Coates & D. Cameron (Eds), *Women in Their Speech Communities* (pp. 74–93). London: Longman.
Carnevale, G. (1996). Natural-setting behavior management for individuals with traumatic brain injury: results of a three-year caregiver training program. *Journal of Head Trauma Rehabilitation,* 11(1), 27–38.
Coelho, C., Liles, B. Z. & Duffy, R. J. (1991a). Discourse analysis with closed head injured adults: evidence for differing patterns of deficits. *Archives of Physical Medicine and Rehabilitation,* 72, 465–468.
——(1991b). The use of discourse analyses for the evaluation of higher level traumatically brain-injured adults. *Brain Injury,* 5(4), 381–392.
Eggins, S. (1994). *An Introduction to Systemic Functional Linguistics.* London: Pinter.
Eggins, S. & Slade, D. (1997). *Analysing Casual Conversation.* London: Cassell.
Ehrlich, J. S. & Sipes, A. L. (1985). Group treatment of communication skills for head trauma patients. *Cognitive Rehabilitation,* Jan/Feb, 32–37.

Halliday, M. A. K. (1994). *An Introduction to Functional Grammar* (2nd edn). London: Edward Arnold.

Halliday, M. A. K. & Hasan, R. (1985). *Language, Context, and Text: Aspects of Language in a Social-semiotic Perspective*. Victoria: Deakin University Press.

Hartley, L. L. (1992). Assessment of functional communication. *Seminars in Speech and Language*, 13, 264–279.

Hasan, R. (1984). The nursery tale as a genre. *Nottingham Linguistic Circular*, 13 (Special Issue on Systemic Linguistics), 71–102.

Holland, D. & Shigaki, C. (1998). Educating families and caretakers of traumatically brain injured patients in the new health care environment: a three phase model and bibliography. *Brain Injury*, 12(12), 993–1009.

Martin, J. R. (1992). *English Text. System and Structure*. Amsterdam: Benjamins.

McTear, M. F. & King, F. (1991). Miscommunication in clinical contexts: the speech therapy interview. In N. Coupland, H. Giles & J. M. Wiemann (Eds), *'Miscommunication' and Problematic Talk* (pp. 195–214). Newbury Park, CA: Sage.

Mentis, M. & Thompson, S. A. (1991). Discourse: a means for understanding normal and disordered language. *Pragmatics of Language: Clinical Practice Issues* (pp. 199–227). San Diego, CA: Singular.

O'Barr, W. M. & Atkins, B. K. (1987). 'Women's language' or 'powerless language'? In B. M. Mayor & A. K. Pugh (Eds), *Language, Communication and Education* (pp. 205–217). London: Croom Helm.

Parsons, C. L., Snow, P., Couch, D. & Mooney, L. (1989). Conversational skills in closed head injury: part 1. *Australian Journal of Human Communication Disorders*, 17, 37–46.

Poynton, C. (1985). *Language and Gender: Making the Difference*. Victoria: Deakin University Press.

Simmons-Mackie, N., Raymer, A., Armstrong, E., Holland, A. & Cherney, L. R. (2010). Communication partner training in Aphasia: a systematic review. *Archives of Physical Medicine and Rehabilitation*, 91(12), 1814–1837.

Togher, L. (2000). Giving information: the importance of context on communicative opportunity for people with traumatic brain injury. *Aphasiology*, 14(4), 365–390.

Togher, L. & Hand, L. (1999). The macrostructure of the interview: are traumatic brain injury interactions structured differently to control interactions? *Aphasiology*, 13 (9–11), 709–723.

Togher, L., Hand, L. & Code, C. (1996). A new perspective in the relationship between communication impairment and disempowerment following head injury in information exchanges. *Disability and Rehabilitation*, 18 (11), 559–566.

——(1997a). Analysing discourse in the traumatic brain injury population: telephone interactions with different communication partners. *Brain Injury*, 11 (3), 169–189.

——(1997b). Measuring service encounters in the traumatic brain injury population. *Aphasiology*, 11 (4/5), 491–504.

Togher, L., McDonald, S., Code, C. & Grant, S. (2004). Training communication partners of people with traumatic brain injury: a randomised controlled trial. *Aphasiology*, 18(4), 313–335.

Togher, L., McDonald, S., Tate, R., Power, E. & Rietdijk, R. (2009). Training communication partners of people with traumatic brain injury: reporting the protocol for a clinical trial. *Brain Impairment*, 10 (2), 188–204.

Togher, L., McDonald, S., Tate, R., Power, E., Ylvisaker, M. & Riedijk, R. (2011). *TBI Express: A Social Communication Training Manual for People with TBI and Thier Communication Partners*. Sydney: Australian Society for the Study of Brain Impairment.

Togher, L., Power, E., Riedijk, R., McDonald, S. & Tate, R. (2012). An exploration of participant experience of communication training programs for people with traumatic brain injury and their communication partners. *Disability and Rehabilitation*, 34(18), 1562–1574.

Togher, L., McDonald, S., Tate, R., Power, E. & Rietdijk, R. (2013). Training communication partners of people with severe traumatic brain injury improves everyday conversations: a multicenter single blind clinical trial. *Journal of Rehabilitation Medicine*, 45, 637–645.

Turner, S. & Whitworth, A. (2006). Conversational partner training programmes in aphasia: A review of key themes and participants' roles. *Aphasiology* 20(7), 616–643.

Ventola, E. (1987). *The Structure of Social Interaction: A Systemic Approach to the Semiotics of Service Encounters.* London: Pinter.

Ylvisaker, M. (1996). Socially co-constructed narratives: competencies associated with an elaborative/collaborative interactive style. In M. Ylvisaker (Ed.), *Head Injury Rehabilitation: Children and Adolescents* (Revised Edition). Newton, MA: Butterworth-Heinemann.

Ylvisaker, M. & Szekeres, S. F. (1994). Communication disorders associated with closed head injury. In R. Chapey (Ed.), *Language Intervention Strategies in Adult Aphasia* (3rd edn, pp. 546–568). Baltimore, Maryland: Williams & Wilkins.

Ylvisaker, M. & Feeney, T. (2000). Reconstruction of identity after brain injury. *Brain Impairment*, 1(1), 12–28.

Ylvisaker, M., Urbanczyk, B. & Feeney, T. J. (1992). Social skills following traumatic brain injury. *Seminars in Speech and Language*, 13, 308–321.

Ylvisaker, M., Feeney, T. J. & Urbanczyk, B. (1993). Developing a positive communication culture for rehabilitation: communication training for staff and family members. In C. J. Durgin, N. D. Schmidt & L. J. Fryer (Eds), *Staff Development and Clinical Intervention in Brain Injury Rehabilitation* (pp. 57–81). Gaithersburg, MD: Aspen.

Ylvisaker, M., Sellars, C. & Edelman, L. (1998). Rehabilitation after traumatic brain injury in preschoolers. In M. Ylvisaker (Ed.), *Traumatic Brain Injury Rehabilitation. Children and Adolescents* (pp. 303–329). Newton, MA: Butterworth-Heinemann.

Ylvisaker, M., Turkstra, L. S. & Coelho, C. (2005). Behavioral and social interventions for individuals with traumatic brain injury: a summary of the research with clinical implications. *Seminars in Speech & Language*, 26(4), 256–267.

Ylvisaker, M., McPherson, K., Kayes, N. & Pellett, E. (2008). Metaphoric identity mapping: facilitating goal setting and engagement in rehabilitation after traumatic brain injury. *Neuropsychological Rehabilitation*, 18(5), 713–741.

13 Using single-case methodology to treat social–pragmatic communication disorders

Robyn L. Tate, Vanessa Aird and Christine Taylor

This chapter addresses social–pragmatic communication disorders after traumatic brain injury (TBI), these being classified in the broader category of cognitive–communication disorders (also known as nonaphasic neurogenic communication disorders). The more specific term, social–pragmatic communication disorder, reflects the predominant feature, social interaction skills. Nomenclature and terminology of the nonaphasic neurogenic communication disorders has lacked clarity and agreement (Body & Perkins, 2006) and to this end we adopt the definition of Dahlberg *et al.* (2007, p. 1564) regarding social communication skills:

> a combination of pragmatic language skills, social behaviours, and cognitive abilities that are required in successful social interactions and relationships. Social communication skills include: communicating needs and thoughts; listening and understanding others; giving and interpreting nonverbal communication; regulating emotions in social interactions; following social boundaries and rules; working with others to solve tasks; and being assertive.

Social–pragmatic communication disorders may or may not involve the use of augmentation communication systems to facilitate language in conversational exchanges for the purpose of social interaction. We draw a distinction, however, between treatments for social–pragmatic communication disorders and those interventions that are focused on the acquisition and/or improvement of functional language for transactional purposes (e.g. yes/no responding, identifying/labelling objects, sentence construction); the latter treatments are not in the scope of this chapter.

In Part 1 of the chapter we review the evidence base of interventions for social–pragmatic communication disorders from systematic reviews, clinical trials and other group-based studies, as well as single-case reports. A rich variety of specific target behaviours and a wide range of treatment alternatives are provided in the single-case reports, and it is argued that their content provides a valuable contribution to the evidence base that is not furnished by group studies. Yet currently there are vital and contentious issues involved in single-case research. Consequently, in Part 2 of the chapter we address methodological and clinical issues in using single-case designs by (a) providing guidance on the classification of the variety and evidence standards of single-case designs, (b) critically evaluating the single-case literature on interventions for social–pragmatic communication disorders, and (c) describing a model for the application of single-case methodology in clinical practice.

Part 1: the evidence base of interventions for social–pragmatic communication disorders

Evidence from group studies

We conducted searches of the PsycBITE (http://www.psycbite.com) and speechBITE (http://www.speechbite.com)[1] databases (last accessed 13 January 2012) for systematic reviews and randomized controlled trials (RCTs), as representing robust research designs for demonstrating treatment effect. In terms of group designs, searches revealed only three systematic reviews and six RCTs of interventions for social–pragmatic communication disorders following TBI.

Two of the three systematic reviews were not relevant to the present chapter in that these included primary studies focused on children (Laatsch *et al.*, 2007) or moderate to severe aphasia after stroke (Simmons-Mackie *et al.*, 2010). The systematic review of Rispoli, Machalicek and Lang (2010) examined a range of communication functions, including social–pragmatic communication disorders. The review is particularly pertinent to this chapter in that it included single-case reports. An important feature of this review, which is lacking from many systematic reviews, is that the authors applied rigorous criteria to evaluate the certainty of the evidence, which went beyond classification of level of evidence. They applied a two-stage process: first, the study had to employ an experimental design; then meet four criteria: (i) provide a convincing demonstration of treatment effect, (ii) report adequate inter-rater agreement on measures of the target behaviour, (iii) operationally define the target behaviours and interventions, and (iv) adequately describe procedures to enable replication.

Rispoli *et al.* (2010) identified 356 studies, of which 21 met selection criteria, with a small number (n=4) addressing social–pragmatic communication disorders after TBI, three of which used single-case methodology. The targeted communication skills in the group study were increasing initiations and verbal exchanges, and improving single topic maintenance, turn-taking and active listening (Wiseman-Hakes *et al.*, 1998). Rispoli *et al.* classified the evidence from this study as inconclusive, because it did not have experimental control.

The six RCTs identified from the searches (none of which were included in the systematic review of Rispoli *et al.*, 2010) examined a disparate set of interventions, including interpersonal and social skills training (Dahlberg *et al.*, 2007; Helffenstein & Wechsler, 1982; McDonald *et al.*, 2008), remediation of emotion perception deficits (Bornhofen & McDonald, 2008a), communication partner training (Togher *et al.*, 2004), and social mentoring by peers who had also previously sustained TBI (Struchen *et al.*, 2011).

Interpersonal and social skills training is one of the standard approaches to improve skills in social communication after TBI and has been classified as a practice standard (Cicerone *et al.*, 2011). The first published study was that of Helffenstein and Wechsler (1982) who demonstrated that 20 sessions (1 hour per session) of training in interpersonal interactions (using feedback from the participant's videotaped social interactions, along with modelling and role play) improved *inter alia* communication skills. The Dahlberg *et al.* (2007) social communication programme ran for 12 sessions (1.5 hours per session) over 3 months. Components of the group-based, manualized programme focused on self-awareness, self-assessment and personal goal setting, feedback on interactions, problem-solving, social support and skill generalization. Improvements in the trained group were documented on objective measures of communication skills. McDonald *et al.* (2008) trained social skills in a mix of individual and group-based sessions over 3 months: 12 group sessions (3 hours per session) and 12 individual sessions (1 hour per session), using their previously developed manualized programme (Flanagan *et al.*, 1995). The programme targeted three broad areas: social behaviour, social perception and emotional adjustment. Group sessions were conducted thematically in which selected skill areas were targeted in each session (e.g. starting conversations, listening skills), using techniques such as group discussion of potential problems and solutions, therapist modelling of appropriate and inappropriate behaviours, participant practice and role play with feedback, and so forth. Improvements in the trained group were documented on objective measures of social behaviour (specifically, behaviours reliant on self-awareness, along with sensitivity and capacity to adapt to and involve the communication partner). The studies of Dahlberg *et al.* (2007) and McDonald *et al.* (2008) were methodologically adequate, scoring 7/10 and 6/10 respectively on the PEDro scale for rating method quality of RCTs (Maher *et al.*, 2003) that is used on the PsycBITE and speechBITE databases. The Helffenstein and Wechsler (1982) study was subject to greater risk of bias, scoring 4/10.

In the remaining three clinical trials, Bornhofen and McDonald (2008a) used a cognitive rehabilitation programme to improve emotion perception, arguing that treating underlying deficits in reading social cues may hold the key to improving social communication and behaviours. They developed an intervention, conducted in 16 sessions (1.5 hours per session) over 2 months, in which people with TBI were trained to recognize emotions by attending to facial features, tone of voice, body posture and movement, and so forth. Significant between-group interactions were found for judging dynamic emotional cues and making social inferences. The study was methodologically sound, scoring 7/10 on the PEDro scale. A second study by Bornhofen and McDonald (2008b) compared instructional method for treating emotion perception deficits (errorless learning versus self-instructional training), finding some support for the superiority of the latter procedure. Further details of the specific techniques in these studies are reported in Chapter 11.

Togher and colleagues (2004) focused their intervention on communication partners rather than the person with TBI, on the premise that improving communication skills of the partner will enhance the communication environment, which in turn will facilitate optimal communication behaviours of people with TBI. Communication partner training was conducted over six 2-hour sessions and included techniques such as analysis of spoken scripts to identify problem areas, suggestions for responses to difficult situations, role-plays and practice of new communication behaviours. Between-group comparisons showed significant improvements in communication efficiency in the trained group of partners. The study scored 7/10 on the PEDro scale. A second controlled (but nonrandomized) trial extending the communication-partner paradigm was also shown to be efficacious (Togher *et al.*, 2012, Togher *et al.*, 2013), along with a further successful RCT from their group (Behn, Togher & Power, 2012).

The method of training the communication partner was also adopted by Struchen *et al.* (2011), in this case peers who had previously sustained TBI and achieved good social outcomes. The peers received two training sessions of 2 hours each to serve as mentors of more recently injured people with TBI, with the aim of increasing social activities and participation over a 3-month period. No treatment effects, however, were demonstrated on the primary outcome measures for increasing social network size, social activity levels or social integration, as measured by standardized instruments. Their study had a low score on the PEDro scale (3/10). Further details of communication partner training can be found in Chapter 12.

In summary, as the foregoing demonstrates, there is only a small body of evidence from methodologically adequate clinical trials to guide the clinician in treatments for social–pragmatic communication disorders. Training in interpersonal and social skills has proved effective in the three clinical trials reviewed above and, as noted, is classified as a practice standard. Training communication partners has also shown promise as an alternative treatment approach to improve communication efficiency (Togher *et al.*, 2004; 2012; 2013; Behn *et al.*, 2012), although at this stage replication by independent research groups would be advantageous. In treating people with TBI themselves, use of cognitive therapies for treating emotion perception deficits (Bornhofen & McDonald, 2008a) is a treatment option, but will require replication before it could be recommended as a practice guideline or a practice standard.

In the clinical setting, however, it is difficult to determine from treatments that contain multiple components precisely which components are the active ingredients that lead to treatment success. Moreover, manualized treatment packages, which are the subject of the above clinical trials, may not always be the most appropriate form of therapy in clinical practice for the particular patient at hand, who may require focused and sustained intervention of a specific target behaviour (e.g. topic maintenance). Arguably, specific impairment(s) would be better treated by intensive intervention of the specific deficit, rather than, for example, a general social skills training package. Yet, there is no evidence from controlled group studies (e.g. a clinical trial on the treatment of topic maintenance) to guide clinical practice. An answer to the dilemma of a limited evidence base is the application of single-case experimental methodology.

Evidence from single-case studies

We also searched the PsycBITE and speechBITE databases (last accessed 13 January 2012) to identify single-case reports for the treatment of social–pragmatic communication disorders after TBI, and supplemented this with hand searching of reference lists. The searches yielded 13 reports and Table 13.1 provides a detailed description of the studies, in terms of the participant characteristics, problem area, specific target behaviours to be treated, description of the intervention and its effectiveness. The studies are also mapped to a standard framework for assessing pragmatic communication disorders, the Prutting and Kirchner (1987) Pragmatic Protocol. This inventory covers three areas of pragmatic communication (verbal linguistic, paralinguistic and nonverbal communication behaviours) and contains 30 separate communicative acts within seven domains. Detailed descriptors for each communicative act are provided.

An advantage of these single-case reports is that information is provided on the intensive study of isolated and specified target behaviour(s), as opposed to outcome of a general therapeutic treatment package, such as a social skills training programme. With reference to the Pragmatic Protocol, 17 of the 30 communicative acts were addressed by the single-case reports, covering six of the seven domains (the exception being the 'style variations' domain): (i) speech acts (Brotherton *et al.*, 1988; Gajar *et al.*, 1984; Schloss *et al.*, 1985; Youse & Coelho, 2009); (ii) topic (Cannizzaro & Coelho, 2002; Carlson & Buckwald, 1993; Dixon *et al.*, 2004; Gajar *et al.*, 1984; Grochmal-Bach *et al.*, 2009); (iii) turn-taking (Carlson & Buckwald, 1993; Gajar *et al.*, 1984; Giles *et al.*, 1988; Kirsch *et al.*, 2004; Sohlberg *et al.*, 1988; Youse & Coelho, 2009); (iv) lexical selection (Bellon & Rees, 2006); (v) intelligibility (Bellon & Rees, 2006; Brotherton *et al.*, 1988; Carlson & Buckwald, 1993; Stringer, 1996); and (vi) nonverbal (Brotherton *et al.*, 1988; Sohlberg *et al.*, 1988; Stringer, 1996). There was considerable variability in method quality of the single-case reports, but seven of the 13 studies used single-case experimental designs suggesting that their results are reliable and these studies are described below.

The study of Brotherton *et al.* (1988) provides a heuristic of how a social skills training package can be adapted for use in a single-case experiment. Their training program contained five components (instruction in a rationale for changing the behaviour, modelling by the therapist, rehearsal, video feedback and social reinforcement) using eight to ten scenarios of social interactions. A multiple baseline design across behaviours and subjects (n=4) was used. Six target behaviours based on the protocol of Kolko and Milan (1985), (e.g. positive statements, reinforcing feedback) mapped to three domains of the Pragmatic Protocol – see Table 13.1) and treatment was introduced sequentially for each of the behaviours as appropriate. For example, four of the six behaviours were targeted for Patient 1, a 27 year old male with severe TBI (coma of 10 days) who was 8 years post-trauma. The experiment consisted of nine baseline sessions (40-minute sessions, three times per week) followed by training sessions (60-minute sessions, twice per week), with independent observers rating the patient's

Table 13.1 Summary of single-case studies on interventions for social–pragmatic communication disorders

Author/s	Sample characteristics	Problems identified	Target behaviour identified	Area/s of pragmatic protocol addressed	Description of intervention	Methodology	Did it work?	MATE level	RoBINT total Scores (max.30)
Bellon & Rees (2006)	4 participants all with severe brain injury Female, age 24 yrs, some yrs post-injury; Male, age 38 yrs, 4.7 yrs post-injury; Male, age 42 yrs, 6 mths post-injury; Female, age 35 yrs, 8 mths post-injury	Language and communication skills in interactions	Rating on language and communication scales based on observed communication behaviours related to successful / unsuccessful meaning, fluency and language appropriateness.	F:23 intelligibility and prosodies: fluency D:16 / 17 Lexical selection across speech acts: accuracy and cohesion B:3 topic: selection	Sessions with mentors providing cueing, regular conversation, modelling, structured activities *Total duration of intervention, including baseline:* 3 mths, 3 days + follow-up	Described as ABCA design (baseline, intervention x 2 phases, follow up)	Better ratings during intervention phases	2	7
Brotherton et al. (1988)	4 participants, all with severe brain injury from MVA Male, age 27 yrs, 8 yrs post-injury Male, age 22 yrs, 5 yrs post-injury Male, age 25 yrs, 7 yrs post-injury Female, age 20 yrs, 3 yrs post- injury	Social interaction difficulties	Six target behaviours: Self manipulation, Posture, Speech dysfluencies, Personal attention, Reinforcing feedback, Positive statements (Kolko & Milan).	G:26 Kenesics and proxemics: body posture F:23 intelligibility and prosodies: fluency A:2 Speech acts: variety of speech acts	Verbal instruction modelling, behavioural rehearsal, videotaped feedback, social reinforcement. 40 minute baseline session 3x/wk Training session 1 hour 2x/wk *Total duration of intervention, including baseline:* 32 sessions + follow-up	Multiple baseline design across behaviours	Effective in 3/4 cases	6	16

Study	Participant	Deficit	Measures	Topic	Intervention	Design	Outcomes		
Cannizzaro & Coelho (2002)	Male, age 39 yrs, with severe TBI, 12 years post-injury	Discourse production deficits, specifically story grammar	1. Story generation condition: number of complete and incomplete episodes in each session (including initiating event, action and direct consequence). 2. story retell condition: percentage of episodes and components accurately identified.	B:5 Topic: maintenance	1 hour 3x/wk training sessions training story re-telling and story generation using a scaffold, prompting and modelling, using picture description. *Total duration of intervention, including baseline:* 23 sessions over 8 weeks + follow-up	A-B design (baseline, treatment), with age, gender and educational matched controls	Improvement noted during treatment phase but not maintained at follow-up. While number of complete episodes improved, the story quality was poor.	5	11
Carlson & Buckward (1993)	Male, age 24 yrs, TBI with significant residual disability, 4 yrs post-injury	Impulsivity, diminished speech intelligibility, decreased organizational and comprehension skills (frequent interruptions) Difficulties problem-solving, planning and executing productive interpersonal communications	Not defined; used no formal pre & post measures	B:5 Topic: maintenance C:11 Turn-taking: Interruption/overlap F:19 Intelligibility and prosodics: intelligibility	Case illustration of a patient who participated in their Vocational Communication group with 6–8 other participants. *Total duration of intervention:* 26 sessions over 12 weeks	Case description	No. Descriptive improvement noted but no data provided to support reported outcomes	1	2

Table 13.1 continued

Author/s	Sample characteristics	Problems identified	Target behaviour identified	Area/s of pragmatic protocol addressed	Description of intervention	Methodology	Did it work?	MATE level	RoBINT total Scores (max.30)
Dixon et al. (2004)	4 males with severe TBI, in a residential, inpatient setting P.1: age 21 yrs, P.2: age 20 yrs, P.3: age 48 yrs, P.4: age 61 yrs	Inappropriate verbal behaviours	Frequency of: — negative self-statements — vocally aggressive behaviours — verbal outbursts that were sexually inappropriate/ aggressive — negative self-statements, profanities and threats	B:3 topic selection	Assessed on various conditions that provided different responses to the inappropriate behaviour (functional analysis). Condition eliciting the highest no. of inappropriate behaviours served as 'control' condition for treatment. Intervention used: Differential Reinforcement of Alternative behaviour (DRA) with no attention given to inappropriate verbal utterances *Total duration of intervention:* baseline of 16 sessions for behavioural analysis; intervention of 5 sessions + follow-up	BAB design (treatment, baseline, treatment) with baseline functional analysis to identify the condition that maintained the negative behaviours	DRA condition resulted in reduced frequency of inappropriate utterances	5	12

Study	Participants	Presenting problem	Outcome measures	Measures	Intervention	Design	Outcome		
Gajar et al. (1984)	2 males, age 22 yrs, with severe TBI following, 18 mths post-injury	Confabulation, unable to stay on topic, perseverative responses, self disclosures, interruptions and inappropriate laughter.	% of positive communication behaviours (relevant statement, agreed or disagreed with rationale, asked relevant question, % of negative communication behaviours (i.e. silent following another participants Qu or statement, expressed 3 words or less, off topic, mumbled, joked or interrupted).	A:2 Speech acts: variety of speech acts C:10 Turn-taking: pause time B:5 Topic: maintenance C:11 Turn-taking: interruption / overlap	Training, self-monitoring and feedback of positive and negative communication behaviours in context of conversation *Total duration of intervention, including baseline*: 20 sessions	ABCACB design (baseline, treatment 1, treatment 2, baseline, treatment 2, treatment 1)	Yes positive effects of therapy bringing client performance within performance range of age-matched peers.	6	16
Giles et al. (1988)	Male, age 27 yrs, with severe TBI, 2 yrs post-injury	Inappropriate attention seeking circumlocutory conversational style.	Mean words per minute across sentence types	C:15 turn-taking: quantity/conciseness	Baselines transcribed from recordings of 3x 5-minute conversations. Utilized 'TOOTS' method to extinguish lengthy utterances. Measures were taken pre-treatment, post treatment and at follow-up *Total duration of intervention, including baseline*: ~20 sessions over 1 month	'Pre-test/ post-test'	While session data showed reduction in mean number of words per minute the authors state that it is not possible to ascribe any particular proportion of the improvements to the programme.	2	8

Table 13.1 continued

Author/s	Sample characteristics	Problems identified	Target behaviour identified	Area/s of pragmatic protocol addressed	Description of intervention	Methodology	Did it work?	MATE level	RoBINT total Scores (max. 30)
Grochmal-Bach et al. (2009)	Female, age 22 yrs, with severe TBI, 7 yrs post-injury	Lack of logical connections in story retell and erroneous conclusions.	No specified target behaviour	B:5 Topic: maintenance	Descriptive case study based on analysis of story retell of 'the giving tree'. Based on microgenetic theory directed at reducing symptoms over a 3-month period followed by 'text therapy'. *Total duration of intervention, including baseline:* 3 months	Case description	No, unable to demonstrate efficacy because there was no pre and post assessment using the same data points. No operationally defined behaviours.	2	3
Kirsch et al. (2004)	Male, age mid 30s, with severe TBI, 1 yr post-injury, premorbid severe alcohol abuse	Verbosity	Number of utterances and total utterance time	C:15 Turn-taking: quantity, conciseness	Recorded message to "be brief" played every 15 minutes from client's PDA during group sessions. Client rated on utterance duration and total number of utterances. During baseline, client was reminded to be brief but the cueing via PDA was turned off. *Total duration of intervention:* 18 sessions (excluding several weeks of clinical observation prior to treatment)	BAB design (treatment, withdrawal, treatment)	Total utterance time was improved in cueing treatment condition.	6	12

| Schloss et al. (1985) | Male, age 20 yrs, with severe TBI, 2 yrs post-injury Male, age 21 yrs, with severe TBI, 1 yr post-injury | Both had difficulties establishing and maintaining social interactions – excessive talk of themselves and minimal requests or acknowledgement of information from conversational partners – especially when talking with females | Frequency counts of the following behaviours: 1. Complimenting others (statements directed to confederate about a positive feature of the other person). 2. Asking others questions about themselves (questions that elicit information from the confederate – usually included the pronoun 'you'). 3. Telling others about self (each statement that disclosed information – usually contained personal pronouns I, me and we). | A:2 Speech acts: variety of speech acts | Self-monitoring training – conditions varied instructing the subject to self-monitor one of the 3 target behaviours during the 5 minute interaction. Subjects were given; a) instructions to self-monitor; or b) no instructions to self-monitor prior to the conversational interaction. 5 minute interactions between males and unfamiliar females of similar age were recorded. *Total duration of intervention, including baseline:* 28 sessions (5 sessions per week) over 6 weeks | Multiple baseline design across behaviours, with an embedded alternating treatment design | Yes | Instructions to self-monitor resulted in higher frequency or compliments and questions and slightly lower frequency of self-disclosure than in the condition of no instructions to self-monitor. |

Table 13.1 continued

Author/s	Sample characteristics	Problems identified	Target behaviour identified	Area/s of pragmatic protocol addressed	Description of intervention	Methodology	Did it work?	MATE level	RoBINT total Scores (max.30)
Sohlberg, Sprunk & Mezelaar (1988)	Male, age 38 yrs, severe TBI, 13 mths post-injury	Rarely initiates conversation or any spontaneous body movement in conversational interaction (adynamic) but tends to perseverate on head nodding.	Verbal initiation of conversation in 30 minute period Response acknowledgement (eye contact with speaker, smiling contingent upon another's verbal behaviour, body oriented towards speaker, nodding 3 times or less in response to speaker) in 30 minute period	C:7 Turn-taking: initiation G:26 Kenesics and proxemics: body posture G:28 Kinesics and proxemics: gestures	Context of routine morning and afternoon group therapy sessions. Used external cueing to train each target behaviour. Role play and demonstration by therapist. Self-monitoring training – client was provided with cue card at set intervals to prompt either 'am I initiating conversation?' or 'am I acknowledging?' Education of importance of these behaviours *Total duration of intervention, including baseline:* 34 sessions, 2 per day	Multiple baseline across behaviours design.	Treatment was successful immediately post-therapy but gains were not maintained once external cues were removed.	6	15

Study	Participants	Communication deficit	Outcome measures	Intervention	Design	Outcome		
Stringer (1996)	Female, age 36 yrs, severe TBI, 11 mths post-injury, premorbid history of previous TBI with seizure disorder	Monotone voice and minimal facial expression	1. Pitch variation 2. Tone of voice and facial expression for target emotions	F:22 Intelligibility and prosodics: Prosody G:29 Kinesics and Proxemics: Facial expression	Biofeedback for pitch using visipitch (24 sessions, each 15 mins). Training expression of emotions using mirror feedback and explicit instruction (e.g. how to move eyebrows) using modelling, practice and feedback *Total duration of intervention:* 2 months + follow-up	'Pre-test/ post-test'	Some slight improvements noted on visipitch instrument, and on the Affective Communication Test	2	10
Youse & Coelho (2009)	Male, age 43 yrs, with severe TBI, 16 yrs post-injury Male, age 25 yrs, with severe TBI, 7 yrs post-injury	Reduced attention and poor conversational discourse performance	Speaker initiations: obliges – defined as utterances containing explicit requirements for a response, comments – defined as utterances not containing an explicit demand for a response Speaker responses: adequate – defined as utterances that appropriately met the initiator's verbalization adequate plus – defined as utterances that are relevant and elaborate on the theme, providing more information than was requested. Measured during 6 minute sample.	A:1 Speech acts: pair analysis C:14 Turn-taking: contingency	Compared two training packages: Attention Process Training and Interpersonal Process Recall *Total duration of intervention, including baseline:* 22 sessions over 17 weeks + follow-up	ABACA design (baseline, treatment 1, baseline, treatment 2, baseline)	No. Only minimal change from baseline	5	12

interactions with the Kolko and Milan protocol throughout all sessions. Onset of training sessions for subsequent target behaviours commenced after notable improvement occurred in the current target behaviour (or it was clear that no improvement was occurring). The entire experiment was conducted over 32 sessions, with maintenance of treatment evaluated at a 1-year follow-up. Improvements in all four target behaviours occurred in Patient 1 when training was initiated.

Schloss *et al.* (1985) specifically focused on 'speech acts' of the Pragmatic Protocol. They stipulated more specific target behaviours than the Brotherton *et al.* (1988) study, aiming to improve conversational skills by having the participant increase the frequency of three behaviours: giving compliments, asking questions and making self-disclosures. The investigators were also interested in determining whether instructions to self-monitor would result in improved performance in comparison with sessions where no such instructions were provided and, to this end, they used an alternating treatment design embedded within a multiple baseline design across behaviours and participants (n=2). Training occurred in 30-minute sessions three times per week. The participant was informed that the purpose of the session was to learn and practise recording one of the target behaviours, which was then operationally defined, and examples of conversational behaviours meeting criteria were provided. After this, the participant practiced using a hand tally counter to record occurrences of the target behaviour from audiotaped conversations, followed by feedback. The experiment was conducted over 28 sessions, in each of which a 5-minute recording of a conversation with an unknown and unfamiliar female confederate (a different confederate for each session) was made. Two male patients were used, the first of whom was aged 20 years, sustained a severe TBI (coma of 1 month) and was 2 years post-trauma. Improvements were observed in the first two (but not the third) target behaviours when treatment was introduced: giving compliments increased from M=0 during baseline to M=1.33 during the treatment phase and asking questions increased from M=0.7 to M=6.0 respectively. The authors reported that sessions with instructions to self-monitor resulted in improved performance.

Multiple treatments were also compared in the study of Youse *et al.* (2009), which addressed 'turn-taking' of the Pragmatic Protocol. The hypothesis of their experiment was that training attention (with Attention Process Training) would improve not only attention, but also conversational skills, whereas training in social skills (with Interpersonal Process Recall) would only improve conversational skills. They used an A-B-A-C-A design over 22 sessions, and the two treatment conditions, examined in two participants, were evaluated in the B and C phases. The participants were 7 and 16 years post-trauma, and severely disabled, both living in supervised accommodation. Neither of these standard and well-validated treatments improved conversational skills or attentional abilities in either of the participants beyond baseline levels.

A classic study by Sohlberg *et al.* (1988) provided a single-case experiment within the context of a group therapy setting. Specific and intensive treatment of two target behaviours (mapping to 'turn-taking' and 'nonverbal' areas of the

Pragmatic Protocol) was undertaken. JK was a 38 year-old man, who sustained severe TBI as a result of a road traffic accident. He was 13 months post-trauma at the time of the study. The target behaviours were treated in a multiple-baseline across behaviours design over 40 sessions of a group treatment programme. The two problem behaviours targeted for treatment were poor initiation of conversation and lack of acknowledgement of other people's communicative acts. Treatment comprised training in self-monitoring skills using an external cuing procedure with therapist role-play and demonstration. During group sessions, JK was intermittently (on average every 5 minutes) handed a card with a star on it, which prompted him to ask himself the question ('am I initiating conversation?'), along with other, similar techniques described by the authors. For the second target behaviour, JK was also intermittently (on average every 6 minutes) handed a card during group sessions, which had a circle drawn on it, which acted as a cue to ask himself the question ('am I acknowledging other people talking?'). The frequency of verbal initiations and response acknowledgements showed immediate increase contingent on the introduction of the treatment.

Whereas Sohlberg *et al.* (1988) aimed to increase behaviours, Dixon *et al.* (2004) focused on decreasing inappropriate verbal behaviours. There are no RCTs that address this problem, and thus there is no evidence on which to base a treatment. Dixon and colleagues addressed the area of 'topic selection' of the Pragmatic Protocol. Tommy was a 21 year-old male with TBI after a fall. He made negative self-statements in relation to physical pain and the effect of the brain injury on his life (e.g. 'I just want to die'). A functional analysis of behaviour occurred over 16 sessions, followed by implementation of a B-A-B withdrawal design, in which treatment consisted of the Differential Reinforcement of Alternative behaviour (DRA). Examiner attention and response was made to any of Tommy's comments or questions that were relevant and appropriate to the speaker and context (e.g. 'I would like to have pizza for lunch today') and no attention was given to negative self-statements. The number of inappropriate verbal utterances was substantially less during the DRA experimental condition than during the baseline phase. Treatment efficacy was demonstrated in five sessions with the DRA paradigm. The same DRA treatment was replicated in another three patients with problematic verbal behaviours: Matt with vocally aggressive behaviour to staff, Chaz with sexually inappropriate vocalizations to staff and Eddie with verbal outbursts and threats to staff.

Kirsch *et al.* (2004) also addressed a gap in the literature in that there are no RCTs of the use of assistive technology to treat verbose speech. Moreover, their patient, VP, had severe impairments, as well as a long history of severe alcohol abuse, and is thus likely to have been the type of patient who would be excluded from clinical trials on the basis of: (a) the severity of his condition; and (b) his comorbidities. Yet, such a patient is commonly encountered in the clinical setting. The study addressed the area of 'turn-taking' in the Pragmatic Protocol. VP was a man in his mid-thirties who sustained severe TBI as the result of an assault. Following unsuccessful attempts to treat his verbose communication, a software program was developed using the Visor Neo calendar with audible alarms. The phrase 'be brief' was delivered (via earphones) every 15 minutes during group treatment sessions. Using a BAB design over 18 sessions, total utterance length was substantially shorter when the software program was used.

Like Kirsch *et al.* (2004), Gajar and colleagues (1984) used assistive technology and a withdrawal design (A-B-C-A-C-B) over a 20-session experiment. Target behaviours were six negative conversational behaviours (confabulation, perseverative responding, poor topic maintenance, excessive self-disclosures, interruptions and inappropriate laughter), which map to 'speech acts' and 'topic maintenance' of the Pragmatic Protocol. Trainers role-played simple conversations in which at least one example of each of the six target behaviours was used and feedback provided. Training involved a feedback device, in which a red light was illuminated whenever any of the target behaviours occurred in conversations in group therapy; a green light was illuminated when the participant's response was appropriate. One of the two participants involved in the experiment was a 22 year-old male who was 18 months post-trauma. The baseline phase showed that appropriate responding was more than 1 standard deviation below the level of a comparison group (less than 40 per cent), but after experiencing feedback from the device (B phase) appropriate behaviours increased to 58 per cent. Introduction of a self-monitoring condition with the device (C phase) further increased appropriate behaviours to 73 per cent, but when the feedback device was withdrawn appropriate behaviours returned to baseline levels. Reinstatement of the self-monitoring condition saw improved performance to 67 per cent.

In summary, the single-case experimental studies described in the text above add to the evidence base provided by group studies of interventions for social–pragmatic communication disorders. By virtue of their methodology, they provide intensive treatment and documentation of performance in selected areas including improvement in fluency, initiating, asking questions, giving compliments, response acknowledgements, reinforcing feedback and positive statements, attention to communication partner; decrease of excessive self-disclosures, confabulation, interruptions, verbose speech, perseverative responding, excess body movements unrelated to speech, body posture and inappropriate laughter. Thus, single-case methodology in the field of social–pragmatic communication disorders after TBI has a lot to recommend it, not only as a research tool, particularly when there are insufficient patients at hand to mount a clinical trial, but also its potential application in providing a gold standard for best practice in the clinical setting with individual patients. Yet, these possibilities are hampered by methodological issues which are discussed in the following section.

Part 2: issues in using single-case methodology in research and clinical practice

The 13 single-case reports reviewed in Table 13.1 demonstrated considerable variability in methodological rigour. At a general level, some single-case reports, like the group-based RCT, are very rigorous in methodology and able to demonstrate cause–effect relationships; other single-case reports, like the group-based case series, are essentially clinical case descriptions, without experimental control and consequently are of questionable value in making a contribution to the evidence base.

This variability in methodological rigour is likely responsible for the contentious position that single-case research has occupied within the medical model, these designs usually being absent from traditional tables of levels of evidence. The methodology is generally (but erroneously) regarded as weak, in spite of the long and well-established history in clinical psychology (e.g. Hersen & Barlow, 1976), special education (e.g. Kratochwill, 1978), speech pathology (e.g. McReynolds & Kearns, 1983), as well as medicine (e.g. Guyatt *et al.*, 1986, 1988). Guyatt and colleagues (2002) from McMaster University are strong advocates of the value of the single-case experimental design (which, in medicine, is referred to as the 'n-of-1 trial'). Indeed, they proposed that for treatment decision purposes the randomized n-of-1 trial should be considered Level 1 evidence, comparable to systematic reviews of multiple RCTs. In 2011, the Oxford Centre for Evidence-based Medicine posted a revised table of levels of evidence on their website, entitled 'Levels of Evidence 2', in which the n-of-1 trial was ranked as Level 1 evidence for treatment decision purposes, alongside systematic reviews of multiple RCTs. The single RCT was ranked as Level 2 evidence (Howick *et al.*, 2011). These developments provide a fertile foundation for the growth of single-case research.

Method design and quality of single-case reports

Part of the reason for the difficulty in recognizing the value of single-case methodology within the medical field may lie in confusion as to what exactly constitutes an n-of-1 trial/single-case experimental design. In essence, single-case experimental methodology refers to an intervention that is delivered in a planned, prospective and systematic manner to a patient who serves as his or her own control. Perdices and Tate (2009) surveyed articles using a single participant published in *Neuropsychological Rehabilitation* from inception to 2008 and identified a range of methodological designs, which they ranked in a loose hierarchy in terms of methodological rigour for demonstrating treatment effect. The four types are described below, and there is agreement in the literature that only the first type, multi-phase designs, meet criteria for an n-of-1 trial/single-case experimental design (Barlow *et al.*, 2009; Horner *et al.*, 2005; Kazdin, 2011; Kratochwill *et al.*, 2010, 2013).

(1) *multi-phase designs* (e.g. withdrawal/reversal; multiple baseline across patients, therapists or settings; alternating treatment; changing criterion) provide the most rigorous test of cause–effect relationships in the individual patient and meet criteria for a single-case experimental design. The basic elements of a single-case experimental design involve the following: (i) the intervention component (independent variable) has a series of discrete

phases in which the treatment is systematically manipulated (e.g. treatment vs no treatment; treatment 1 vs treatment 2); and (ii) the repeated and frequent measurement of the behaviour being treated (dependent variable) is conducted during all phases. These two conditions thus provide the basis for a controlled experiment and sufficient data points to demonstrate whether the dependent variable (target behaviour) changes in accordance with the phase of treatment. In the *Neuropsychological Rehabilitation* survey, 43 per cent of single-case reports involved multi-phase designs.

(2) *simple A-B designs* with repeated measures of the target behaviour (dependent variable) in the A (baseline) and B (treatment) phases. These designs are not true experiments because there is no experimental manipulation of the independent (treatment) variable. Although they do provide sufficient data to demonstrate if there has been a change in the dependent variable (target behaviour) between the A and B phases, it is not possible to attribute such change to the treatment *per se* in the absence of the control of other extraneous variables (e.g. the passage of time, spontaneous recovery, practice effects, environmental changes). In the *Neuropsychological Rehabilitation* survey, 10 per cent of single-case reports involved A-B designs and 7 per cent were single B-phase training studies.

(3) *designs which may be described as 'pre-test/post-test'*. These designs do not meet criteria for single-case methodology because: (i) they do not systematically manipulate the independent (treatment) variable in a series of phases; and (ii) the target behaviour (which generally differs from standardized outcome measures) is not measured repeatedly and frequently in all phases (particularly before and during the intervention). The *same* measure of the target behaviour must be used in all phases. These designs may be considered the equivalent of a case description with data. In the *Neuropsychological Rehabilitation* survey, 28 per cent of reports with a single participant involved 'pre-test/post-test' designs.

(4) *the clinical case report or description* is a simple description in which any therapy introduced is conducted in a scientifically uncontrolled fashion and assessment may or may not occur. As noted, if evaluation is conducted both prior to and following the intervention, such a report may be classified in the above group of a 'pre-test/post-test' design. In the *Neuropsychological Rehabilitation* survey, 12 per cent of single-case reports involved case descriptions.

Apart from the design of the single-case study, one of the questions that arise about these (and other) designs relates to their methodological rigour in terms of features ensuring high internal and external validity. Kratochwill *et al.* (2010, 2013) have published rigorous design and evidence standards for single-case experimental designs recommending, for example, that withdrawal designs have a minimum of four phases (i.e. A-B-A-B) and multiple baseline designs have a minimum of six phases, that a minimum of five data points are taken per phase and so forth. Rating scales are also available for evaluating risk of bias. The first published psychometric scale of method quality designed for reports using single-case designs was the Single-Case Experimental Design (SCED) Scale (Tate *et al.*, 2008), which has since been revised as the Risk of Bias in N-of-1 Trials (RoBiNT) Scale (Tate *et al.*, in press). The revised scale has items which are divided into two subscales internal validity (e.g. use of randomization, blinding, evaluation of inter-rater reliability of target behaviours) and external validity/interpretation (e.g. generalization, replication, data analysis). Requirements for meeting criteria on the RoBiNT Scale items are stringent.

The 13 single-case reports on interventions for social–pragmatic communication disorders described in the preceding section were rated on the RoBiNT Scale. The results (see Table 13.1) demonstrate extreme variability in method quality score, with the total score ranging from 2 to 23 out of a possible 30. Only four of the 13 reports scored at least 15/30. These results suggest that the majority of single-case reports published to date on social–pragmatic communication disorders are subject to risk of bias. It is acknowledged that tools to guide the construct of methodologically robust single-case designs have only recently appeared in the literature, which puts previously published work at distinct disadvantage. It is expected that the availability of these resources will, however, benefit the field in the future because they explicitly describe the features that need to be considered in designing a single-case study, as well as the minimum standards for design and evidence.

In summary, single-case methodology, and specifically multi-phase design, involves true experiments that are able to demonstrate cause–effect relationships. By contrast, simple A-B designs, 'pre-test/post-test' studies and clinical case descriptions do not manipulate the independent (treatment) variable in any manner and consequently it is not possible to attribute any change in the behaviour that is targeted for treatment (dependent variable) to the intervention itself, as opposed to other extraneous variables. Yet it also needs to be borne in mind that just as the gold standard of group designs, the RCT, varies in methodological quality (Moseley *et al.*, 2000; Perdices *et al.*, 2006), so too does the single-case experimental design. Consequently, the major sources of risk of bias need to be addressed when planning and implementing a single-case experimental design. Design and evidence standards such as those provided by Kratochwill *et al.* (2010, 2013) and other resources such as the RoBiNT Scale are helpful in this regard. We have drawn upon single-case methodology in developing the model for assessing treatment effect (MATE; Tate *et al.*, 2012, 2013), which is described below.

A clinical model for assessing treatment effect (MATE) was designed to bridge the gap between research methodologies and clinical practice, by bringing single-case methodology into the clinic (Tate *et al.*, 2012, 2013). It incorporates the taxonomy of the International Classification of Functioning, Disability and Health (ICF; WHO, 2001) and elements of single-case methodology, thereby guiding both the measurement and treatment planning process in individual patients. The model derives from our observations over many years of the way in which therapy is typically delivered in TBI rehabilitation settings and ways in which it could be improved. We have data (manuscript in preparation) to support our impression that in clinical practice the control of extraneous variables in the delivery of therapy is not done and formal assessment to determine whether therapy has been effective is rarely conducted; at the most, a pre-treatment assessment using standardized instruments is used and therapy is delivered in a scientifically uncontrolled fashion.

We intentionally designed the MATE to apply to many types of interventions including physical, cognitive, behavioural and psychosocial therapies delivered by a range of disciplines, including speech-language pathology, physical and occupational therapy, psychology, psychiatry and social work, and rehabilitation medicine. It also applies throughout the rehabilitation continuum, including inpatient rehabilitation and community settings. The model addresses the range of single-case designs, as described previously in this chapter, in acknowledgement of the clinical reality that it is not always possible to implement the gold standard experimental design in the typical clinical setting. As a result of all these features, the MATE has potential application for benchmarking a clinical programme with respect to the calibre of its service delivery.

The MATE is a 7-level hierarchical model, ranging from the lowest level (Level 0) where therapy is not conducted, through to the highest level (Level 6) in which a multi-phase, single-case experimental design is implemented. Lesser levels of single-case designs occupy lower levels of the model. The levels of the MATE, as depicted in Figure 13.1 reproduced from the MATE Manual, are described below (see also Tate *et al.*, 2012, for an easy to follow decision tree for classification on the MATE).

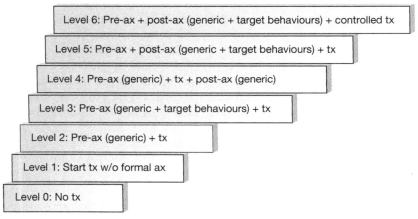

Level 6: Pre-ax + post-ax (generic + target behaviours) + controlled tx

Level 5: Pre-ax + post-ax (generic + target behaviours) + tx

Level 4: Pre-ax (generic) + tx + post-ax (generic)

Level 3: Pre-ax (generic + target behaviours) + tx

Level 2: Pre-ax (generic) + tx

Level 1: Start tx w/o formal ax

Level 0: No tx

Note: tx=therapy, ax=assessment; Colour gradations within cells: dark grey=therapy at the Impairment level; pale grey=therapy at the Activities/Participation level; white=therapy at the Environmental level

Figure 13.1 Schematic representation of the Model for Assessing Treat Effect (MATE)

Level 0 is used to indicate that therapy has not taken place. This may occur in situations where, for example, admission to a rehabilitation unit is solely for the purpose of assessment, or a patient with a very low level of functioning does not have opportunity to engage in a therapy programme.

Level 1: Therapy proceeds in the absence of formal or standardized assessment by the treating clinician(s). This may occur in situations where, for example, the behaviour needs urgent intervention with respect to patient safety and formal pre-intervention assessment is not feasible.

Level 2: A formal pre-intervention assessment is conducted prior to the implementation of therapy. As we describe elsewhere (Tate *et al.*, 2012, 2013), formal assessment, which can be quantitative or qualitative, usually involves the administration of: (i) standardized performance-based tests, rating scales, questionnaires; (ii) structured observations with a quantitative record; or (iii) measures specific to the target behaviour. A case description which provides a formal pre-treatment assessment may be classified at Level 2.

Level 3: Assessment at this level involves the specific behaviour to be targeted in therapy (as opposed to general constructs such as 'communication', 'language' etc). Selection of the measure of the target behaviour needs to ensure that it is operationalized, observable, quantifiable, measurable, and repeatable (Kazdin, 2011). When such measures have not been subject to formal psychometric evaluation, their inter-rater reliability needs to be established. The wide variety of measures of the target behaviour typically fall into the following categories: evaluation of successful performance (e.g. object naming), time taken to complete a task (e.g. reading a passage), ratings of internalized (e.g. feeling states) and externalized (e.g. social interactions) function, tallies or checklists of frequencies of behaviours (e.g. number of occasions of turn-taking in conversations).

As described earlier, the crucial feature of measures used in single-case methodology is the frequent and repeated measurement of the target behaviour throughout all phases. Consequently, measures need to be selected (or, where not available, developed tailor-made for the target behaviour) with the capacity to make frequent administrations without being subject to practice effects. Although, it is possible to conduct a high quality single-case experiment using the specific measures of the target behaviour alone, without necessarily administering any other standardized instruments, we advocate the procedure of administering a standardized pre-intervention assessment in clinical practice to understand the broader context of the patient's strengths and weaknesses. Assessments using standardized tools also assist in communicating features of the patients that will enable comparison among cases. The B-phase training study (containing at least three occasions of measurement of the target behaviour during the treatment phase) may be eligible for Level 3 ranking, as long as it provides a formal pre-intervention assessment (see Level 2).

Level 4: Post-therapy evaluation enables the clinician to know whether the behaviour targeted by the treatment has changed. This can be achieved by re-administration of the same instruments as at pre-intervention so that a direct comparison can be made. A 'pre-test/post-test' study in an individual patient/

client may qualify for Level 4 ranking, if at least three occasions of measurement of the target behaviour are taken either before or during the treatment phase. A caveat to this level is that, in order to demonstrate treatment effect in single-case methodology, administration of standardized, generic assessments is not as important as the repeated and frequent measurement of the specific target behaviour throughout all phases (see Level 3), and therefore post-therapy evaluation with standardized instruments is not necessary if a single-case methodology is used, as in Levels 5 and 6.

Level 5: Evaluation concerns repeated and frequent measurement of the specific target behaviours as described in Level 3 during *all* phases. A-B designs in which at least three measurement occasions of the target behaviour are taken during the baseline (A) and intervention (B) phases qualify for Level 5 ranking, because it is possible to demonstrate between-phase change statistically. Yet, simple A-B designs do not qualify for Level 6 ranking because they do not control for extraneous variables which makes it impossible to attribute change in behaviour directly to the intervention.

Level 6: The intervention used comprises one of the multi-phase, single-case experimental designs described earlier in this chapter, such as well-designed withdrawal/reversal, multiple baseline, alternating treatment, changing criterion, all of which are described in standard texts (Barlow *et al.*, 2009; Kazdin, 2011; McReynolds & Kearns, 1983). Because of the requirement in single-case methodology to measure the target behaviour repeatedly and frequently throughout all phases, those studies in which: (a) assessment is conducted only before and after an intervention; or (b) where one set of standardized, generic measures is administered before and after the intervention, with a *different* measure taken exclusively during the intervention phase do not qualify as a single-case methodology.

Two of the authors (RT and VA) made consensus ratings of the MATE level of each of the 13 single-case reports described in Table 13.1. Thirty-eight per cent (5/13) of the single-case reports were rated at MATE Level 6, and the remainder of reports spanned the mid ranges of the MATE: Level 1 (n=1), Level 2 (n=4), Level 5 (n=3). Studies at MATE Level 6 (n=5) provided a controlled evaluation of treatment effect without major design flaws and were less subject to risk of bias than reports with a ranking less than MATE Level 6, scoring significantly higher on the RoBiNT Scale (MATE Level 6 reports: M=16.4/30, SD=4.04; Mdn=16.0 vs MATE <Level 6 reports: M=8.13/30, SD=3.91, Mdn=9.0; z=–2.80, p=0.003), as well as both the internal validity (z=–2.69, p=0.006) and external validity/interpretation (z=–2.30, p=0.019) subscales. The correlation coefficient between MATE Level and RoBiNT total score was high $r_s=0.94$, as were coefficients for the internal validity ($r_s=0.83$) and external validity/interpretation ($r_s=0.84$) subscales.

In conclusion, we advocate the application of single-case methodology in clinical practice as a means to adopt an evidence-based approach to treatment in the clinical setting, for four primary reasons.

First and foremost, clinicians need to know whether the treatments they are delivering to individual patients are effective and whether there is a change in the target behaviour (Sohlberg *et al.*, 1988). Even when treatments are based on firm evidence from multiple RCTs, as is the case for social skills treatments for social–pragmatic communication disorders after TBI, for example, it cannot be assumed that the treatment will be effective for the individual patient at hand, because generally not all patients who participate in a clinical trial improve. For example, no information was provided in the Dahlberg *et al.* (2007), Helffenstein and Wechsler (1982), or McDonald *et al.* (2008) trials regarding the number of participants from the sample who actually improved – only group descriptive data were provided. Thus we argue that clinicians need to evaluate the effect of their therapy, even those therapies that have a sound evidence base (e.g. social skills training programmes); single-case methodology and the MATE provide guidance for this process. The Youse *et al.* (2009) study, for example, used treatment packages that have been well validated and recommended as practice standards, yet measures of the target behaviours indicated that neither of their two patients improved beyond baseline levels.

Moreover, the results of a clinical trial do not generalize beyond the characteristics of the participant sample. It is often the case that the selection criteria of RCTs are very narrow. For example, in the Dahlberg *et al.* (2007) trial of their social skills treatment programme, patients were excluded if they did not speak English; had significant premorbid or co-morbid psychiatric, psychological, substance use, or behavioural disorders; experienced severe cognitive deficits; significant motor disorder precluding ease of speech; or had need for physical assistance in a group setting. Helffenstein and Wechsler (1982) and McDonald *et al.* (2008) reported similar exclusion criteria, albeit fewer in number and less restrictive. In clinical practice, however, patients with such backgrounds may well be appropriate candidates for social skills training. On this point, Sackett and colleagues (2000) advocate a fairly lenient interpretation, and they suggest that the clinician should ask: is my patient so very different from this sample that the results will not apply? They do, however, cite co-morbidities as an example of such a significant difference. The study of Kirsch *et al.* (2004) provides an example of using single-case methods in a patient with co-morbid severe alcohol abuse, such patients usually being excluded from clinical trials.

In addition, there is often a mismatch between a particular intervention (e.g. a social communication skills training programme) and the individual patient's deficit pattern, whereby the patient may require more focused and intensive treatment of a specific target behaviour (e.g. turn taking, speech acts) than is addressed in the general social skills programme. The Sohlberg *et al.* (1988) study provides an example of a specific behaviour (initiation of conversation) treated over 40 sessions; similarly, Schloss *et al.* (1985) targeted the behaviours of giving compliments, asking questions and making self-disclosures which were treated in 30-minute sessions three times per week over 28 sessions. Single-case methodology also enables demonstration of the efficacy of a specific treatment for a specific target behaviour, which can thereby assist in identifying the active ingredients of a multi-component treatment package.

Finally, there is also the matter of the quantum of available evidence. An accepted protocol for delineating the cognate areas of social–pragmatic communication disorders is that of Prutting and Kirchner (1987). They identify 30 separate communicative acts within seven domains, yet there is no evidence from RCTs for many of the problem areas. Single-case methodology has the capacity to address each of the communicative acts, and thus with replication the evidence base can be increased, whereas mounting RCTs is difficult and costly. The studies of Dixon *et al.* (2004) and Kirsch *et al.* (2004) provide examples of using single-case methodology to treat a behaviour (negative self-statements and verbose speech respectively) in situations where there is no evidence from a clinical trial to guide choice of intervention.

Perhaps most profoundly for clinicians, single-case methodology is the research method most closely resembling operations in clinical practice. That is, clinicians assess clients and devise individualized goals and treatment strategies. The MATE offers considerable assistance to clinicians to enhance this process and transform their clinical practice into a more scientifically rigorous and rewarding application, as we have demonstrated with some of our clinical cases (see Tate *et al.*, 2013).

In spite of the promise and potential of single-case methodology, the current single-case literature in TBI, including interventions for social–pragmatic communication disorders, is variable and the field will only be advanced if the very best designs and methods are used. There is a ground swell of current activity to raise the profile, use and quality of single-case reports, including two international groups developing reporting guidelines for single-case reports in the CONSORT tradition: the CONSORT Extension for N-of-1 Trials (CENT; personal communication, S. Vohra, 26 April 2013) for the medical n-of-1 trial, and the Single-Case Reporting guideline In BEhavioural interventions (SCRIBE; Tate *et al.*, in preparation) for the behavioural sciences. In addition, as noted Kratochwill *et al.* (2010, 2013) have published design and evidence standards for single-case designs and method quality rating scales such as the RoBiNT Scale also assist in discriminating among the rigour of reports. These developments will provide clear criteria for the evaluation and reporting of single-case designs and have the potential to improve their conduct.

Note

1. PsycBITE and speechBITE are databases that archive all of the published literature on, *inter alia*, cognitive and communication impairments after TBI. Their content is drawn from six databases: AMED, CINAHL, Cochrane Library, EMBASE, Medline, PsycINFO. Search terms used in PsycBITE and speechBITE for the present chapter were as follows: traumatic brain injury, pragmatics/social communication, systematic review, randomized controlled trial, single-participant design.

References

Barlow, D. H., Nock, M. K. & Hersen, M. (2009). *Single Case Experimental Designs. Strategies for Studying Behaviour Change.* 3rd edn. Boston: Pearson.

Behn, N., Togher, L., Power, E. & Heard, R. (2012) Evaluating communication training for paid carers of people with traumatic brain injury. *Brain Injury, 26*(13–14), 1702–1715.

Bellon, M. L. & Rees, R. J. (2006). The effect of context on communication: a study of the language and communication skills of adults with acquired brain injury. *Brain Injury, 20*(10), 1069–1078.

Body, R. & Perkins, M. R. (2006). Terminology and methodology in the assessment of cognitive-linguistic disorders. *Brain Impairment, 7*(3), 212–222.

Bornhofen, C. & McDonald, S. (2008a). Treating deficits in emotion perception following traumatic brain injury. *Neuropsychological Rehabilitation, 18*(1), 22–44.

——(2008b). Comparing strategies for treating emotion perception deficits in traumatic brain injury. *Journal of Head Trauma Rehabilitation, 23*(2), 103–115.

Brotherton, F. A., Thomas, L. L., Wisotzek, I. E. & Milan, M. A. (1988). Social skills training in the rehabilitation of patients with traumatic closed head injury. *Archives of Physical Medicine and Rehabilitation, 69*(10), 827–832.

Cannizzaro, M. S. & Coelho, C. A. (2002). Treatment of story grammar following traumatic brain injury: a pilot study. *Brain Injury, 16*(12), 1065–1073.

Carlson, H. B. & Buckwald, M. B. W. (1993). Vocational communication group treatment in an outpatient head injury facility. *Brain Injury, 7*(2), 183–187.

Cicerone, K. D., Langenbahn, D. M., Braden, C., Malec, J. M., Kalmar, K., Fraas, M., Felicetti, T., Laatsch, L., Harley, J. P., Bergquist, T., Azulay, J., Cantor, J. & Ashman, T. (2011). Evidence-based cognitive rehabilitation: updated review of the literature from 2003 through 2008. *Archives of Physical Medicine and Rehabilitation, 92*, 519–530.

Dahlberg, C. A., Cusick, C. P., Hawley, L. A., Newman, J. K., Morey, C. E., Harrison-Felix, C. L. & Whiteneck, G. G. (2007). Treatment efficacy of social communication skills training after traumatic brain injury: a randomized treatment and deferred treatment controlled trial. *Archives of Physical Medicine and Rehabilitation, 88*, 1561–1573.

Dixon, M. R., Guercio, J., Falcomata, T., Horner, M. J., Root, S., Newell, C. & Zlomke, K. (2004). Exploring the utility of functional analysis methodology to assess and treat problematic verbal behavior in persons with acquired brain injury. *Behavioral Interventions, 19*(2), 91–102.

Flanagan, S., McDonald, S. & Togher, L. (1995). Evaluation of the BRISS as a measure of social skills in the traumatically brain injured. *Brain Injury, 9*, 321–338.

Gajar, A., Schloss, P. J., Schloss, C. N. & Thompson, C. K. (1984). Effects of feedback and self-monitoring on head trauma youths' conversation skills. *Journal of Applied Behavior Analysis, 17*(3), 353–358.

Giles, G. M., Fussey, I. & Burgess, P. (1988). The behavioural treatment of verbal interaction skills following severe head injury: a single case study. *Brain Injury, 2*(1), 75–79.

Grochmal-Bach, B., Pachalska, M., Markiewicz, K., Tomaszewski, W., Olszewski, H. & Pufal, A. (2009). Rehabilitation of a patient with aphasia due to severe traumatic brain injury. *Medical Science Monitor, 15*(4), CS67–CS76.

Guyatt, G., Sackett, D., Taylor, D. W., Chong, J., Roberts, R. & Pugsley, S. (1986). Determining optimal therapy – randomized trials in individual patients. *New England Journal of Medicine, 314*(14), 889–892.

Guyatt, G., Sackett, D., Adachi, J., Roberts, R., Chong, J., Rosenbloom, D. & Keller, J. (1988). A clinician's guide for conducting randomized trials in individual patients. *CMAJ (Canadian Medical Association Journal), 139,* 497–503.

Guyatt, G., Jaeschke, R. & McGinn, T. (2002). N-of-1 randomized controlled trials. In: G. Guyatt, D. Rennie, M. O. Meade & D. J. Cook (Eds) *User's Guide to the Medical Literature: A Manual for Evidence-based Clinical Practice.* 2nd edn. New York: McGraw Hill and AMA, pp. 179–192.

Helffenstein, D. A. & Wechsler, F. S. (1982). The use of interpersonal process recall (IPR) in the remediation of interpersonal and communication skill deficits in the newly brain-injured. *Clinical Neuropsychology, IV*(3), 139–143.

Hersen, M. & Barlow, D. H. (1976). *Single-case Experimental Designs. Strategies for Studying Behaviour Change.* New York: Pergamon.

Horner, R. H., Carr, E. G., Halle, J., McGee, G., Odom, S. & Wolery, M. (2005). The use of single-subject research to identify evidence-based practice in special education. *Exceptional Children, 71*(2), 165–179.

Howick, J., Chalmers, I., Glasziou, P., Greenhaigh, T., Heneghan, C., Liberati, A., Moschetti, I., Phillips, B. & Thornton, H. (2011). *The 2011 Oxford CEBM Evidence Table (Introductory Document).* Oxford Centre for Evidence-Based Medicine, http://www.cebm.net/index.aspx?o=5653 (accessed 21 June 2013).

Kazdin, A. E. (2011) *Single-case Research Designs. Methods for Clinical and Applied Settings.* 2nd edn. New York: Oxford University Press.

Kirsch, N. L., Shenton, M., Spirl, E., Simpson, R., LoPresti, E. & Schreckenghost, D. (2004). An assistive-technology intervention for verbose speech after traumatic brain injury: a single case study. *Journal of Head Trauma Rehabilitation, 19*(5), 366–377.

Kolko, D. J. & Milan, M. A. (1985). A women's heterosocial skill observational rating system. Behavior-analytic development and validation. *Behavior Modification, 9,* 165–192.

Kratochwill, T. R. (Ed.) (1978). *Single Subject Research: Strategies for Evaluating Change.* New York: Academic Press.

Kratochwill, T. R., Hitchcock, J., Horner, R. H., Levin, J. R., Odom, S. L., Rindskopf, D. M. & Shadish, W. R. (2010). Single-case designs technical documentation. Retrieved from *What Works Clearinghouse* website: http://ies.ed.gov/ncee/wwc/pdf/wwc_scd.pdf (accessed 1 July 2013).

Kratochwill, T. R., Hitchcock, J. H., Horner, R. H., Levin, J. R., Odom, S. L., Rindskopf, D. M. & Shadish, W. R. (2013). Single-case intervention research design standards. *Remedial and Special Education, 34*(1), 26–38.

Laatsch, L., Harrington, D., Hotz, G., Marcantuono, J., Mozzoni, M. P., Walsh, V. & Hersey, K. P. (2007). An evidence-based review of cognitive and behavioral rehabilitation treatment studies in children with acquired brain injury. *Journal of Head Trauma Rehabilitation, 22*(4), 248–256.

Maher, C. G., Sherrington, C., Herbert, R. D., Moseley, A. M. & Elkins, M. (2003). Reliability of the PEDro scale for rating quality of RCTs. *Physical Therapy, 83,* 713–721.

McDonald, S., Tate, R., Togher, L., Bornhofen, C., Long, E., Gertler, P. & Bowen, R. (2008). Social skills treatment for people with severe, chronic acquired brain injuries: a multicentre trial. *Archives of Physical Medicine and Rehabilitation, 89,* 1648–1659.

McReynolds, L. V. & Kearns, K. P. (1983). *Single-subject Experimental Designs in Communicative Disorders.* Baltimore: University Park Press.

Moseley, A., Sherrington, C., Herbert, R. & Maher, C. (2000). The extent and quality of evidence in neurological physiotherapy: an analysis of the Physiotherapy Evidence Database (PEDro). *Brain Impairment, 1*(2), 130–140.

Perdices, M. & Tate, R. L. (2009). Single-subject designs as a tool for evidence-based clinical practice: are they unrecognised and undervalued? *Neuropsychological Rehabilitation, 19*(6), 904–927.

Perdices, M., Schultz, R., Tate, R., McDonald, S., Togher, L., Savage, S., Winders, K. & Smith, K. (2006). The evidence base of neuropsychological rehabilitation in acquired brain impairment (ABI): how good is the research? *Brain Impairment, 7*(2), 119–132.

Prutting, C. A. & Kirchner, D. M. (1987). A clinical appraisal of the pragmatic aspects of language. *Journal of Speech and Hearing Disorders, 52,* 105–119.

Rispoli, M. J., Machalicek, W. & Lang, R. (2010). Communication interventions for individuals with acquired brain injury. *Developmental Neurorehabilitation, 13*(2), 141–151.

Sackett, D. L., Straus, S. E., Richardson, W. S., Rosenberg, W. & Haynes, R. B. (2000). *Evidence-based Medicine. How to Practise and Teach EBM,* 2nd edn. Edinburgh: Churchill-Livingstone.

Schloss, P. J., Thompson, C. K., Gajar, A. H. & Schloss, C. N. (1985). Influence of self-monitoring on heterosexual conversational behaviors of head trauma youth. *Applied Research in Mental Retardation, 6*(3), 269–282.

Simmons-Mackie, N., Raymer, A., Armstrong, E., Holland, A. & Cherney, L. R. (2010). Communication partner training in aphasia: a systematic review. *Archives of Physical Medicine and Rehabilitation, 91,* 1814–1837.

Sohlberg, M. M., Sprunk, H. & Metzelaar, K. (1988). Efficacy of an external cuing system in an individual with severe frontal lobe damage. *Cognitive Rehabilitation, 6*(4), 36–41.

Stringer, A. Y. (1996). Treatment of motor aprosodia with pitch biofeedback and expression modelling. *Brain Injury, 10*(8), 583–590.

Struchen, M. A., Davis, L. C., Bogaards, J. A., Hudler-Hull, T., Clark, A. N., Mazzei, D. M., Sander, A. M. & Caroselli, J. S. (2011). Making connections after brain injury: development and evaluation of a social peer-mentoring program for persons with traumatic brain injury. *Journal of Head Trauma Rehabilitation, 26*(1), 4–19.

Tate, R. L., McDonald, S., Perdices, M., Togher, L., Schultz, R. & Savage, S. (2008). Rating the methodological quality of single-subject designs and n-of-1 trials: introducing the Single-case Experimental Design (SCED) Scale. *Neuropsychological Rehabilitation, 18*(4), 385–401.

Tate, R. L., Aird, V. & Taylor, C. (2012). Bringing single-case methodology into the clinic to enhance evidence-based practices. *Brain Impairment, 13*(3), 347–359.

Tate, R. L., Taylor, C. & Aird, V. (2013). Applying empirical methods in clinical practice: introducing the Model for Assessing Treatment Effect (MATE). *Journal of Head Trauma Rehabilitation, 28*(2), 77–88.

Tate, R.L., Perdices, M., Rosenkoetter, U., Wakim, D., Godbee, K., Togher, L. & McDonald, S. (in press). Revision of a method quality rating scale for single case experimental designs and n-of-1 trials: the 15-item Risk of Bias in N-of-1 Trials (RoBiNT) Scale. *Neuropsychological Rehabilitation.*

Tate *et al.* (in preparation). The Single-Case Reporting guideline In BEhavioural interventions (SCRIBE): Explanation and elaboration.

Togher, L., McDonald S., Code, C. & Grant, S. (2004). Training communication partners of people with traumatic brain injury: a randomised controlled trial. *Aphasiology, 18*(4), 313–335.

Togher, L., Power, E., Rietdijk, R., McDonald, S. & Tate, R. (2012) An exploration of participant experience of communication training programs for people with traumatic brain injury and their communication partners. *Disability and Rehabilitation, 34*(18), 1562–1574.

Togher, L., McDonald, S., Tate, R., Power, E. & Rietdijk, R. (2013) Training communication partners of people with severe traumatic brain injury improves everyday conversations: A multicenter single blind clinical trial. *Journal of Rehabilitation Medicine, 45*, 637–645.

Wiseman-Hakes, C., Stewart, M. L., Wasserman, R. & Schuller, R. (1998). Peer group training of pragmatic skills in adolescents with acquired brain injury. *Journal of Head Trauma Rehabilitation, 13*(6), 23–38.

World Health Organization. (2001). *International Classification of Functioning, Disability and Health.* Geneva: World Health Organization.

Youse, K. M. & Coelho, C. A. (2009). Treating underlying attention deficits as a means for improving conversational discourse in individuals with closed head injury: a preliminary study. *NeuroRehabilitation, 24*(4), 355–364.

Subject index

academics 275
adolescence 113, 192, 193, 194, 200, 207, 264, 266, 267
adolescents 8–10, 38, 39, 40, 92, 97, 109, 127, 134–135, 206, 209, 210, 215, 216, 260, 264, 270, 271, 272–274; in dysathria 200, 221
adynamia 137, 140, 141
age at injury 37, 40, 174, 177, 191, 192, 227, 259, 267
altered consciousness 2, 30, 31–34
amnesia *see also* memory 31, 33, 55, 197; post-traumatic amnesia (PTA) 31, 33, 34, 35, 37, 55, 197, 243; retrograde amnesia 55, 80, 81, 82
aphasia 1, 2, 3–8, 13, 14, 40, 73, 89, 200, 250, 260, 295, 297, 300, 350, 362; incidence of 38–39
arousal 12, 52, 53, 67, 68, 69, 71, 121, 122, 140
aspontaneity 137
assessment 2, 3–5, 6, 7–9, 10, 12, 13, 26, 38, 48, 53, 54, 59, 64, 79, 81, 82, 83, 84, 86, 91, 100, 105, 106, 109, 110, 127, 128, 141, 145, 162, 177, 191, 196, 197, 198, 199, 200, 202, 204, 205, 208, 218, 224, 227, 228, 229, 230, 231, 232, 233, 235, 238, 239, 242, 247, 250, 260, 261, 263, 269, 276, 285, 287, 289, 291, 296, 309, 310, 312, 314, 315, 317, 330, 336, 337, 370, 378, 380, 381, 382, 385; *see also* language assessment
assistive technology 220, 288, 299, 375, 376
attention 5, 6, 36, 38, 48–54, 56, 58, 61, 62, 102, 120, 125, 127, 130, 131, 133, 140, 162, 163, 167, 193, 199, 200, 266, 270, 286, 295, 296, 297, 298, 299, 312, 321, 326, 327, 330, 349, 353, 366, 368, 369, 373, 374, 375, 376; Attention Process Training 373, 374; strategic attention 269
augmentative systems *see* assistive technology

Behavior Rating Inventory of Executive Function – Adult version (BRIEF-A) 192, 199, 202

Behaviorally Referenced Rating System of Intermediate Social Skills – Revised (BRISS-R) *see* social skills
blunt head injury 20, 76, 256
brain repair 275, 277
brain stimulation 228, 238, 239

child TBI 161, 164, 165, 167, 169, 170–177, 190
children 4, 8, 9, 10, 11, 13, 36, 38, 39, 95, 97, 124, 129, 218, 219, 220, 221, 222, 223, 224, 225, 227, 228, 229, 231, 233, 235, 237, 239, 240, 241, 242, 244, 249, 258, 259, 260, 261, 262, 264, 265, 266, 267, 269, 270, 288, 336, 362
clinical features 30, 224, 225, 241; of attention deficits 48; of executive function impairments 60; of memory impairments 55
closed head injury *see also* open head injury *and* penetration head injury 2, 19, 97, 190, 221, 222, 223
cognitive communication disorders 6, 12, 13, 14, 15, 17, 114, 190, 361; *see also* nonaphasic neurogenic communication disorder
cognitive control 136, 185, 266, 276
cognitive empathy 124–125, 127, 129–131, 132, 135, 141, 168
cognitive processes 6, 11, 49, 51, 61, 62, 63, 65, 71, 102, 119, 125, 136, 160, 167, 191, 262, 263, 276, 286
cognitive rehabilitation therapy *see* therapy
cognitive sequelae 105, 261
coherence: global 91, 92, 95; local 92, 94, 95
cohesion analysis 8, 93
collaboration 59, 202, 204, 208, 350, 351, 353, 354
coma *see also* Glasgow Coma Scale 4, 30, 31, 32, 33, 34, 37, 45, 197, 239, 326, 365, 374
communication goals 311, 312, 313, 315, 316, 319, 321, 324, 332
communication partner 9, 10, 12, 15, 90, 98, 99, 106, 108, 110, 249, 250, 362, 363, 364, 376
communication partner training 15, 108, 250, 251, 350–358, 362, 364

complex language 176, 259, 260–261, 265
context 4, 9, 12, 13, 49, 56, 57, 89, 93, 97, 98, 99, 100, 119, 130, 161, 163, 164, 167, 171, 172, 176, 177, 178, 195, 199, 200, 201, 202, 207, 227, 231, 260, 263, 268, 274, 280, 283, 284, 286, 287, 293, 297, 309, 311, 325, 338, 339, 340, 341, 345, 347, 348, 350, 369, 372, 374, 375, 381
contra-coup 28, 29, 170, 223; *see also* coup
control *see also* disorders of control 4, 6, 9, 10, 11, 36, 38, 39, 50, 51, 52, 54, 60, 61, 62, 63, 64, 65, 67, 68, 70, 71, 72, 73, 90, 93, 94, 95, 96, 99, 102, 103, 104, 107, 109, 123, 128, 129, 133, 135, 136, 137, 139, 140, 141, 142, 143, 165, 167, 173, 174, 175, 176, 177, 192, 213, 218, 227, 232, 236, 239, 240, 242, 243, 247, 263, 271, 272, 291, 292, 293, 294, 298, 314, 315, 317, 318, 321, 326, 342, 343, 346, 347, 348, 349, 350, 351, 362, 368, 377, 378, 380
contusions 29, 170, 222, 223, 265
conversation 6, 8, 10, 11, 15, 32, 38, 48, 55, 66, 91, 92, 95, 96, 98, 102, 106–107, 108, 124, 127, 167, 176, 177, 196, 205, 208, 247, 249, 268, 269, 308, 309, 310, 311, 312, 313, 314, 315, 316, 317, 320, 321–329, 330, 337–338, 339, 345, 346, 347, 351, 353, 355–356, 357, 366, 369–373, 374, 375
coup *see also* contra-coup 28, 29, 222, 223

depression 3, 12, 17, 67, 68, 71, 72, 140, 277, 322
diffuse axonal injury 26, 51, 53, 119, 122, 136, 170, 190, 221, 238, 266
diffusion tensor imaging 26, 27, 51
discourse 3, 7, 8, 9, 11, 18, 19, 76, 78, 80, 86, 89, 90, 91, 92, 93, 94, 95, 96, 97, 98, 99, 101, 102, 103, 104, 105, 110, 112, 113, 114, 116, 117, 118, 127, 195, 196, 200, 202, 204, 207, 210, 211, 258, 261, 262, 265, 267, 268, 269, 337, 338, 339, 340, 341, 342, 348, 358, 373; procedural genre 8, 20, 57, 91, 94, 95, 102, 195, 208, 262, 337, 338, 342; propositional analysis 92
discourse analysis 3, 8, 9, 90–93, 110, 200, 202, 341; microlinguistic structure in 8, 91, 110
disinhibition *see* inhibition
disorders of control 61, 68, 123, 132, 136
disorders of drive 61, 64, 68, 137, 140, 141
dysarthria 12, 38; articulatory function in 236, 239; assessment of 232, 240–241; incidence of 38; clinical features of 224; laryngeal function 229, 232, 233, 243–246, 337; perceptual assessment of 227, 229–230; physiological assessment of 232–237, 238, 241; prevalence of 218, 219; respiratory function in 30, 228, 232, 233–235; severity of 50; treatment for 38, 228, 229, 230,

239–249; velopharyngeal function in 228, 230, 237, 240

early brain insult 160, 165, 173, 178, 179
ecologically valid measures 131
effectiveness 178, 249, 260, 286, 290, 298, 299, 307, 308, 314, 321, 365
efficacious 315, 318, 319, 321–324, 330, 331, 364
efficacy 241, 249, 270, 289–290, 291, 302, 309, 314, 317, 318, 319, 323, 329, 331, 332, 370, 375, 383
efficiency 92, 104, 107, 231, 259, 263, 269, 290, 364
elaboration 266, 269, 353, 355, 357
emotion 2, 5, 11–12, 13, 14, 37, 63, 68, 70, 71–72, 105, 106, 109, 111, 119, 120–124, 125, 126, 127–129, 131, 132, 133–135, 136, 137, 139, 141–144, 145, 162, 163, 165, 167, 168, 175, 176, 177, 193, 194, 202, 295, 299, 308, 310, 314, 317, 318, 320, 322, 323, 328–329, 352, 353, 354, 361, 362, 363, 364, 373; assessment of 127–129; emotion perception 11, 13, 14, 17, 109, 119, 120, 121, 122–123, 126, 127, 128, 131, 151, 165, 167, 168, 175, 176, 362, 363, 364; emotion regulation 11–12, 68, 70, 71, 123–124, 136, 141, 145, 299; emotional empathy 123–124, 131–132, 135; emotional perception 123, 308, 310, 317, 318, 320; negative emotions 121–122, 123; vocal emotion 120–121
environmental factors 161, 171, 178, 194, 198, 202, 205
exchange structure analysis 91, 92, 341–343, 348; dynamic moves 92, 343, 345–346; synoptic moves 343, 344
executive functions 6, 7, 12, 40, 48, 54, 56, 57, 60–66, 71, 102–104, 107, 109, 110, 125, 127, 136, 143, 163, 164, 167, 173, 176, 191, 192, 194, 195, 198, 199, 200, 204, 208, 216, 271, 272, 284, 286, 287, 296, 297, 298, 299, 310, 317, 322, 345; clinical features 60
external validity 292, 293, 378, 379, 382

family 3, 10, 12, 17, 59, 66, 67, 89, 108, 132, 163, 164, 169, 172, 178, 194, 202, 206, 208, 262, 284, 309, 312, 314, 315, 316, 320, 321, 324, 326, 327, 330, 332, 336, 337, 342, 350, 351, 357, 358
faux pas 124, 130, 133, 176
frontal lobe 6, 7, 28, 52, 57, 59, 63, 64, 65, 66, 70, 119, 136, 148, 149, 193, 220, 265, 266, 267; frontal function 121, 267; frontal networks 265–268
functional communication 10, 229, 295, 308, 311, 316, 318, 319, 330
Functional Independence Measure for Children (WeeFIM) 197

generalization 91, 270, 320, 327, 329, 332, 363, 379
generic structure analysis 91, 93, 98–99, 342, 348; generic structure potential analysis 92, 341–342, 349; superstructural 91, 92, 98, 110
genetics 166, 171
genre 8, 9, 90–91, 93, 98, 195, 208, 337, 338, 340, 341, 342, 348
gist 7, 14, 196, 207, 258, 259, 262, 263, 264, 265–268, 269, 270, 271, 272–273, 276
Glasgow Coma Scale (GCS) *see also* coma 27, 31, 32, 34, 197
Goal Attainment Scale (GAS), 310, 312–314, 316, 321, 324, 327, 329, 332
Group Interactive Structured Treatment (GIST) 315–316, 319, 333

hints 127, 207
humour 74, 106, 108, 121, 124, 126, 196, 207, 311

incidence (of TBI) 1, 26, 35–36, 37, 39, 48, 67, 169; of personality change 67, 71, 72, 73; of social dysfunction 127
indifference 137–138, 142
information processing 4, 175–177, 264, 269; speed of 36, 39, 48–54, 103, 104, 109, 136, 192, 193, 194, 208, 326
inhibition 11, 39, 50, 51, 61, 64, 65, 71, 102, 103, 123, 132, 136, 137, 140, 141, 142, 143, 239, 263, 264, 270, 274
inhibitory control 50–51, 54, 136, 140, 192
initiation 6, 71, 99, 136, 139, 143, 269, 325, 329, 348, 349, 362, 372–373, 375, 383
integration 3, 40, 72, 119, 121, 137, 163, 166, 171, 175, 202, 258, 263, 264, 265–266, 269, 274, 310, 330, 332, 350, 364
intelligibility 220, 228, 229, 230, 231, 239, 240, 241, 242, 243, 244, 245, 246, 247, 249, 250, 365, 366, 367, 373
interference control 51, 54, 56, 61, 136, 141
internal validity 292, 379, 382
International Classification of Functioning, Disability and Health (ICF) 13, 14, 15, 198, 199, 205–206, 208, 240, 287, 302, 379
Interpersonal Process Recall (IPR) 268, 314–318, 373, 374
Interpersonal Reactivity Index (IRI) 132, 135
interpersonal skills 3, 16, 132, 325
intervention *see also* therapy 14, 15, 29, 90, 161, 163, 164, 167, 177–178, 190, 191, 198, 205–208, 229, 239, 252, 258, 259, 260, 268–277, 284, 285, 288, 289–293, 295, 296, 297, 298, 299, 300–301, 302, 303, 304, 307, 309, 312, 313, 315, 320, 321, 324, 329, 330–331; social intervention in child TBI 177–178, 205–208

Iowa Gambling Task (IGT) 138, 141
ischemia 27, 29, 190

lack of insight 3, 69–70, 71, 72, 326
language assessment 3–5, 7–12
LaTrobe Communication Questionnaire (LCQ) 7, 103, 110, 310, 312, 314, 322, 324, 329
learning (and impairments of) *see also* new learning 6, 33, 39, 40, 48, 55, 56–57, 58, 59, 60, 72, 89, 104–105, 125, 134, 139, 169, 192, 193, 202, 205, 208, 259, 260, 261, 263, 264, 267, 269, 270, 275, 284, 285, 300, 317, 318, 322, 326, 358, 363; errorless learning 285, 300, 317–318, 363; procedural learning 57, 60
lexical selection 92, 201, 365, 366
linguistics, 8, 9, 116, 337

macrostructure 103, 350
magnetic resonance imaging (MRI) 28, 30, 165, 222, 228, 238, 239, 265
medical factors (effects of) 172, 230, 282, 293, 301
memory *see also* amnesia 5, 6, 30, 33, 36, 38, 39, 40, 48, 51, 52, 53, 55–60, 62, 69, 74, 89, 102, 104–105, 109, 125, 127, 129, 131, 138, 139, 143, 176, 192, 193, 194, 195, 196, 198, 199, 200, 208, 257, 263, 264, 266, 269 270, 271, 274, 284, 285, 286, 288, 295, 296, 297, 298, 299, 300, 317, 322, 324, 354; autobiographical memory 55–56; assessment of 59–60; prospective memory 57–58, 59, 60; working memory 40, 49–56, 57, 58, 62, 74, 79, 89, 102, 104, 105, 109, 125, 127, 131, 143, 176, 192, 193, 194, 195, 196, 199, 200, 201, 208, 263, 264, 266, 271, 272
meta-analysis 120, 288, 293, 298
metacognition 61, 62
method quality 363, 365, 379, 384
metrics 259, 260–262, 265
Model for Assessing Treatment Effect (MATE) 366, 368, 370, 372, 379, 380, 382, 383, 384
MRI tractography 238, 239
multiple baseline designs 16, 292, 307, 318, 324, 325, 329, 365, 366, 371, 372, 374, 375, 377, 378, 382

naming *see also* word finding 4, 5, 6, 38, 128, 129, 134, 260, 381
narrative 8, 91, 92, 94, 95, 98, 102, 104, 196, 262, 269, 325, 337, 338, 340, 342
neuroplasticity *see also* brain repair *and* plasticity 5, 221, 240, 258, 268, 275
neuropsychological sequelae 39, 60
new learning *see also* learning 33, 55, 89, 104–105, 259, 261, 263

nonaphasic neurogenic communication
   disorder 361
nonverbal communication 124, 309, 325, 361,
   365

open head injury 190
outcomes 3, 13, 14, 15, 17, 26, 31, 34, 35, 36–39,
   40, 48, 68, 70, 72, 73, 101, 108, 138, 157,
   161, 164, 167, 169, 170, 171, 172, 173, 174,
   175, 176, 178, 191, 194, 197, 198, 206, 221,
   238, 241, 242, 244, 246, 248, 258, 259, 261,
   269, 275, 276, 277, 278, 280, 281, 284, 285,
   287, 288, 290, 291, 292, 293, 296, 297, 298,
   301, 302, 310, 312, 314, 320, 327, 328, 329,
   330, 331, 335, 351, 364, 365, 367, 378

parents 37, 109, 161, 171, 172, 173, 174, 178,
   193, 207, 358
participation 8, 12, 13, 15, 90, 106, 107, 108,
   160, 161, 164, 171, 175, 178, 198, 205, 208,
   228, 240, 241, 247, 249, 250, 277, 287, 290,
   293, 296, 297, 298, 310, 311, 314, 326, 327,
   331, 350, 364, 380
Pediatric Test of Brain Injury (PTBI) 200, 201,
   260
penetrating head injuries (PHI) *see also* open
   head injury 1, 2, 7, 97, 190, 221
personality change 11, 37, 48, 66–73, 158, 163,
   164, 169, 191; premorbid personality 12, 67,
   72–73, 168
plasticity *see also* neuroplasticity 14, 30,
   258–277
practice-based evidence 283, 284
pragmatics 3, 9, 89–111, 167, 194, 201, 262,
   268, 269, 295, 308, 309, 314, 321, 325, 326,
   330, 338, 384; indirect language in 102;
   Pragmatic Protocol 105, 107, 309, 326, 365,
   366–372, 374–375, 376; Profile of Pragmatic
   Impairment in Communication (PPIC)
   310–311, 312, 314, 316, 321, 324, 329;
   sarcasm 9, 11, 102, 104, 106, 126, 135, 176,
   196, 314; speech acts 9, 11, 99–100, 101, 207,
   309, 365, 366, 369, 371, 374, 376, 383
prevalence of TBI 35–36, 66, 68, 160, 161, 162
problem solving 6, 48, 61, 64, 98, 102, 103, 105,
   167, 175–176, 177, 192, 194, 203, 295, 298,
   315, 316, 317, 320, 321, 324, 328, 330, 332,
   352, 356, 363, 367; problem solving strategy
   194, 295, 317, 332
PsycBITE *see also* speechBITE 16, 289, 290,
   292, 294, 362, 363, 365, 384
psychological reactions 71
psychosocial 2, 3, 12, 17, 36, 37, 39, 40, 48–74,
   175, 259, 276, 286, 328, 380; psychosocial
   outcome 2, 3, 37–38, 48, 73

quality of life 35, 160, 171, 173, 175, 220, 228,
   249, 290, 320, 326, 332

randomized controlled trial (RCT) 15, 16, 239,
   283, 288, 289, 290, 291, 292, 294, 297, 298,
   299, 300, 307, 314, 316, 321, 322, 323, 329,
   350, 362, 363, 375, 376, 377, 379, 384
rating scales 10, 89, 105, 171, 229, 378, 381, 384
reasoning 6, 10, 14, 65, 104, 107, 110, 124, 125,
   126, 166, 168, 191, 200, 201, 258, 259, 262,
   263, 264, 265, 266, 267, 268, 269, 270, 271,
   272, 276, 287
recovery 3, 14, 30, 31, 32, 35, 37, 38, 40, 170,
   171, 172, 173, 190, 197, 198, 218, 220, 258,
   259, 260, 261, 263, 264, 266, 267, 268, 269,
   275, 276, 277, 282, 284, 286, 287, 288, 295,
   296, 297, 298, 299, 301, 378
rehabilitation *see also* intervention,
   rehabilitation, remediation, therapy,
   treatment 5, 13–17, 31, 35, 38, 40, 60, 72,
   177, 190, 197, 198, 204, 205, 206, 258, 260,
   276, 277, 307, 312, 318, 319, 328, 331, 350,
   358, 363, 377, 378, 379, 380, 381
remediation *see also* intervention,
   rehabilitation, therapy, treatment 2, 5, 7, 12,
   13–17, 26, 74, 105, 161, 205, 227, 241, 259,
   260, 262, 269, 276, 308, 362
Risk of Bias in N-of-1 Trials (RoBiN-T) Scale
   16, 293, 366, 367, 368, 372, 379, 382, 384

secondary effects 29, 190, 194
self-esteem 139, 160, 172, 173, 351
self-monitoring 103, 132, 143, 269, 286, 296,
   319, 320, 325, 331, 371, 372, 375, 376
self-regulation 69, 123, 166, 174, 295, 328
service encounters 91, 98, 99, 103, 340, 341,
   342, 348, 349, 350
severity 1, 4, 26, 27, 37, 38, 39, 48, 52, 57, 60,
   61, 63, 64, 65, 67, 70, 71, 138, 144, 173, 174,
   176, 177, 178, 192, 194, 197, 218, 219, 225,
   226, 228, 229, 231, 243, 246, 263, 265, 267,
   285, 292, 298, 301, 310, 312, 318, 321, 322,
   324, 325, 326, 328, 329, 375; assessing
   severity 31–35
simulation 51, 122–123
single-case experimental design 16, 361–384
single-case methodology *see* single-case
   experimental design
skin conductance 122, 123, 137, 138, 140
skull fractures 27, 33, 170
social adjustment 72, 73, 161, 173, 174, 175,
   177, 178
social brain network 163–164
social cognition 11, 13, 48, 66, 69, 71, 105, 109,
   111, 119–145, 160, 162, 163–164, 165, 167,
   168, 171, 175–177, 178, 191, 193, 194, 195,
   196, 199, 202, 203, 207, 208; neural basis of
   165–167
social communication skills *see also* social
   skills 12, 124, 175, 196, 205, 206, 207, 285,
   295, 299, 307–332, 361, 363, 383

social interaction 90, 105, 124, 125–126, 138, 140, 160, 161, 162, 163, 165, 166, 168, 169, 171, 172, 174, 175–176, 177, 178, 197, 203, 205, 208, 260, 309, 311, 325, 326, 328, 330, 338, 339, 350, 361, 363, 365, 371, 372, 381
social knowledge 125, 138, 139
social participation 15, 90, 161, 171, 175, 327
social perception 109, 129, 131, 134, 314, 309, 314, 317, 322, 363
social problem solving 167, 175–177, 194, 203, 316
social skills 3, 10, 13, 14–15, 55, 66, 72, 89, 105–108, 160, 161–164, 165, 166, 167, 171, 174, 176, 177, 178, 261, 275, 307–331, 351, 362, 363, 364, 365, 374, 383; Behaviorally Referenced Rating System of Intermediate Social Skills – Revised (BRISS-R) 10, 105–108, 310, 311, 312, 314, 317, 322, 329
sociolinguistics 3, 9, 99
speechBITE *see also* psychBITE 16, 240, 290, 362, 363, 365, 384
Strategic Memory Advanced Reasoning Training (SMART) 270–275
systematic review 15, 16, 282, 283, 288, 289, 291, 293–295, 301, 361, 362, 377, 384
Systemic Functional Linguistics (SFL) 9, 336, 337, 338, 339, 340, 341–350

T-units 91, 104
talkativeness 2, 6, 11
target behaviours 292–293, 324, 330, 361, 362, 365, 366, 371, 374–376, 379, 380, 382–383, 392, 393
TBI Express 351, 352, 355, 359
temperament 163, 164, 172, 178
tenor 9, 339, 340, 341, 343, 348
Test of Language Competence-Extended (TLC-E) 7, 199, 201, 202, 203
The Awareness of Social Inferences Test (TASIT) 10, 106, 109, 131, 135, 310, 314, 317, 322, 323, 329
The Social Decision Making Task (SDMT) 139–141
Theory of Mind (ToM) 11, 106, 120, 124–125, 162, 166, 168, 175–176, 193, 194

therapy *see also* intervention, rehabilitation, treatment 13–17, 31, 48, 178, 190–208, 230, 235, 242–248, 290, 292, 293, 295, 297, 298, 300, 301, 307–335, 336–360, 364, 369, 370, 372, 374, 376, 378, 379, 380, 381, 383; cognitive rehabilitation therapy (CRT) 282–301
topic 8, 73, 91, 92, 93, 95, 96, 107, 124, 127, 196, 269, 309, 311, 316, 321–329, 353, 355, 357, 362, 364, 365, 366–370, 375, 376; analysis of topic 95–96; topic maintenance 92, 95, 96, 196, 269, 325, 329, 362, 364, 376; topic selection 107, 316, 322, 366, 368, 375
training 14–15, 90, 249, 259, 267–268, 269–277, 286, 295, 296, 298, 300, 305, 307–331, 364, 365, 367, 371–373, 374, 375, 378, 381; social skills training 177, 307–331, 362–363, 365, 383; training communication partners 108, 250, 336–358, 364
treatment *see also* intervention, rehabilitation, therapy 1, 4, 7–8, 13, 15, 16, 105, 190–208, 224, 227, 228, 229, 258, 261, 269, 275–276, 277, 286, 288, 289–290, 291–293, 295, 299, 300–302, 307, 308, 309, 310, 311, 312, 313, 314, 315, 316, 317–331, 336, 361, 362, 364, 365, 366–373, 374, 375, 376, 377, 378, 379, 381, 382, 383, 384; for aphasia 14–15; information processing approach to 4
treatment *see also* intervention, therapy, training, rehabilitation: for dysarthria *see* dysarthria; individual treatment 309, 315, 320, 329, 332; group treatment 16, 292, 315, 317, 318–320, 321, 322–329, 330–331, 332, 375, 376; manualized treatment 315, 317, 318, 319, 321, 323, 324, 331, 363, 364
turn-taking 90, 167, 269, 362, 365, 369–373, 374, 375, 381

video feedback 324, 330, 331, 365

Wallerian degeneration 29, 119
white matter 26, 27, 36, 51, 52, 58, 63, 119, 163, 193, 221, 222, 238, 266, 268
withdrawal design 375, 376, 378, 382
word finding 2, 4, 6, 38, 103, 199, 354
WSTC 317, 332

Name index

Abbott, M. J. 187
Abbott, R. D. 184
Abell, F, 129.145
Abelson, R. 8, 23
Abraham, E. 184
Abrams, G. M. 278
Abutalebi, J. 24, 78, 150
Achenbach, T. M. 174, 179, 208
Ackerman, B. P. 164, 179
Ackermann, H. 253
Acosta-Cabronero, J. 153
Adachi, J. 386
Adamovich, B. L. B. 4, 17
Adams, G. R. 217
Adams, J. H. 42, 145, 119
Adams, R. L. 43, 47
Addis, P.E. 251, 254
Adduci, A, 187
Adelman, P. 122, 145
Adler, P., 207, 209
Adler, P. A., 207, 209
Adolphs, R, 119, 120, 121, 122, 126, 145, 146,
    151, 152, 153, 165, 172, 179, 193, 209
Agar, N., 75, 77
Aglioti, S. M., 181
Agranov, E. 20
Aharon-Peretz, J, 117, 157
Aird, V., 387
Alaca, R. 44, 255
Alavi, A. 253
Alcott, S. 147
Alderman, N. 88, 159
Aldich, F. K, 80
Alessandrini, F. 46
Alessandro, D. 42
Alexander, M. P. 63, 71, 74, 86
Allain, P. 151
Allen, C. 303
Allen, J. P. 164, 179
Allen, T. T, 152
Allison, C, 132, 146
Allnutt, S., 181

Altman, D.G. 22.
Altman, I. W. 70, 71, 84
Anand, R. 261, 263, 265, 266, 267, 276, 277,
    281
Anderson, C. V. 63, 74
Anderson, E. 155
Anderson, J. W. 58, 74
Anderson, P. J. 184
Anderson, S.W. 75, 147, 191, 209
Anderson, T. 43, 74, 146
Anderson, V. 12, 18, 50, 58, 143, 160, 161, 163,
    164, 165, 167, 169, 172, 173, 174, 175, 179,
    180, 181, 182, 183, 184, 185, 186, 187, 188,
    189, 191, 193, 194, 195, 206, 209, 210, 212,
    214
Andrade, J. 85, 146
Andreiuolo, P. A. 186
Andrew, C. M., 156
Andrewes, D. 71, 74, 136, 137, 146
Andrews, G. 181
Andrews, T. k, 173, 174, 180, 181
Angeleri, R. 95, 102, 111
Angrilli, A. 122, 146
Annarita, A. 42
Annoni, J. M, 139, 146
Ansaldo, A-I. 24
Anson, K. 17
Appemzeller, T. 57, 83
Aprile, T, 181
Arango-Lasprilla, J. C. 44
Archibald, J. 212
Argyle, M. 308, 335
Armonda, R. A. 18, 40
Armstrong, E. 8, 17, 92, 111, 260, 277, 359, 387
Armstrong, K. 214, 217
Arndt, S. 80, 185, 186
Arnett, P. A. 76
Arnold, R. 153
Aron, A. R., 51, 75
Aronson, A. E. 252, 257
Arsenio, W. F. 168, 180
Asarnow, R.F. 169, 173, 174, 180

Asher, S. R. 180, 187
Ashkanazi, G, 80
Ashley, M, 303
Ashman, T. A. 52, 75, 303, 333, 385
Ashton, R. 78
Aslan, S. 278
Asloun, S. 50, 75
Astbury, W. 217
Atkins, B. K. 345, 359
Attard, M. D. 255
Audy, J. 84
Avenanti, A, 181
Avery, J, 216, 304, 305, 306
Avezaat, C. 185
Azouvi, P. 75, 77
Azulay, J. 303, 333, 385

Babbage, D. R. 11, 18, 120, 146, 335
Babl, F. 182, 210
Bachevalier, J. 165, 183
Baddeley, A. 49, 55, 56, 57, 62, 74, 75, 81, 88
Baddeley, B. T. 85
Baguley, I. J. 46, 78, 87, 150
Bahr, M. 215
Bain, J. 85
Baird, A. 42
Baird, J. A. 78
Bakchine, S. 157
Baker, J. 23
Baker, K. K. 158, 189, 216
Baldoni, J. 288, 302
Balla, D. A. 188
Bamdad, M. J. 332
Bara, B. G. 111, 146
Barat, M. 116, 155
Barber, J. 76
Barbizet, J. 55, 75
Bargallo, N. 84
Baribeau, J. M. C. 5, 18
Barker, L. A. 126, 146
Barker, S. L. 44
Barlow, D. H. 377, 382, 385, 386
Barlow, S. M. 227, 251
Barnes, C. 185
Barnes, M. A. 101, 104, 111, 113, 182, 191, 195, 196, 207, 211, 212, 252, 279
Barnett, S. D. 44, 189
Baron-Cohen, S. 120, 129, 130, 132, 133, 135, 146, 147, 152, 157, 158, 203, 209
Barrow, I. 94, 114, 262, 280
Barry, P. 8, 19, 95, 113
Barry, R.J. 140, 147, 157
Bartels, M., 158
Barth, J. 44, 85
Bartkowsky, H. M. 180
Bartle, C. J. 227, 251
Bartz, E. K. 278
Baruah, S. 80

Bassili, J. N. 120, 147
Basso, A. 38, 40
Basson, J. 181
Batchelor, J. 45
Battista, D. 43
Bauder, H. 21
Bauer, L. 253
Bauer, R. 147
Baum, k. M. 129, 147
Bautz-Holter, E, 305
Bayen, U. J. 58, 86
Bayles, K. 303
Beattie, A. 41, 76, 147, 332
Beauchamp, M. 12, 18, 160, 161, 163, 164, 172, 179, 180, 181, 182, 183, 184, 186, 187, 188, 192, 193, 194, 195, 209
Bechara, A. 63, 75, 137, 138, 147, 158, 209
Becker, E., 255
Beckett, C, 182
Bedell, G. M., 180
Beer, S. 146
Beers, S. R. 214
Begle, A., 188
Behn, N. 108, 111, 336, 358, 364, 385
Behne, T. 188
Belanger, H. G. 302
Beldarrain, M. G. 57, 75
Bell, I. 86
Bell, M.D. 150
Bell, R.S. 2, 18, 21, 36, 40
Bellaire, K. 240, 242, 251
Bellon, M.L. 365, 366, 385
Bellugi, U. 152
Belmont, A. 52, 75
Belsky, J. 160, 180
Benedict, S. M. 285,302
Benson, D.F. 57, 71, 74, 86, 140, 147
Benton, A. L. 4, 5, 7, 18, 21, 23, 43, 64, 75, 77, 79, 81, 84, 149
Benton, S.B. 280
Berger, M. S. 170, 180
Bergquist, T. 302, 303, 332, 333, 385
Berlin, L. J. 97, 111
Berndt, T. J. 207, 209
Berney, J. 170, 180
Bernicot, J, 112
Berrol, S. 43
Berry, M. 341, 344, 345, 358
Berry, W. 256
Berryhill, P. 265, 277
Berzonsky, M., 217
Best, C. 299, 303
Beukelman, D.R. 20, 38, 40, 220, 231, 251, 253, 255, 257
Bibby, H. 66, 75, 124, 125, 127, 131, 147
Biddle, K.R. 92, 111, 196, 209
Biederman, J. 76
Biester, R.C. 40

Biggs, J. B., 269, 277
Bigler, E.D. 26, 27, 28, 29, 40, 46, 71, 74, 75,
    119, 147, 189, 217, 254, 257
Bilaniuk, L. T. 170, 181, 189
Binder, G. 83, 116, 309, 334
Binder, L. M. 44
Bishara, S. N, 79, 114, 117
Bishop, D. V. M. 7, 18
Bishop, N. 44
Black, M. A. 43
Black, S. E. 43, 79, 81, 150, 153
Blackstein, H. 56, 75
Blair, R. J. R. 66, 75, 119, 121, 122, 126, 147,
    168, 180
Blairy, S, 122, 123, 147, 149, 152
Blakemore, S. 160, 180, 182, 193, 209
Blanchet, P. G., 241, 251
Blank, M. 97, 111
Blanton, P.D. 42
Blatter, D. D., 74
Blazyk, S. 207, 209
Bliss, L. S. 111, 209
Bloch, S. 250, 251
Block, J., 255
Blonder, L. X. 147
Blosser, J. 258, 260, 277
Blumenstein, E, 216
Blumenthal, J. 183, 280
Blumer, D. 140, 147
Bly, B. M. 148
Boake, C. 70, 76, 88
Bock, K. 211
Body, R. 92, 102, 111, 361, 385
Bogaards, J. A, 387
Bogner, J. 24, 72, 87
Bohnen, N. I. 36, 40
Bohnert, A. M. 161, 171, 173, 174, 180
Bolis, L., 46
Bombardier, C. H. 72, 76
Bond, F. 3, 10, 18, 90, 111
Bond, M. 37, 41, 42, 70, 72, 76, 80, 83, 155,
    197, 212
Bonnelle, V. 81
Bonnier, C. 40, 41
Bonte, F. J. 278
Boon, J. 216
Borasio, G. D. 304
Borg, J. 41
Borgaro, S. 23, 120, 147
Bornhofen, C. 14, 18, 116, 153, 154, 186, 314,
    317, 318, 319, 320, 322, 323, 332, 334, 362,
    363, 364, 385, 386
Bos, K. 160, 180
Bosch, J. D. 186
Bosco, F. M, 111
Boss, M. R. 90, 95, 113
Bottenberg, D. E. 8, 18
Botvin, G. J. 162, 180

Bouamra, I. 44
Bourgeois, M. 57, 87
Bowen, A. 71, 72, 76
Bowen, R. 116, 186, 334, 386
Bowers, D. 128, 134, 147
Bowers, L. 203, 209, 147
Bowers, S. 43
Bowlby, J. 160, 164, 180
Bowler, D. M. 124, 147
Boxer, P. 162, 180
Boyer, M. G. 219, 251
Braakman, R. 185
Braciszewski, T. L. 303
Bracy, C. A. 113, 333
Braden, C. 303, 311, 312, 318, 319, 320, 324,
    332, 333, 385
Bradley, V.A, 80
Bradley, W.G. 304
Brady, k. D. 215
Braga, L. W. 178, 181, 281
Bragge, P, 289, 302
Brainerd, C. J. 263, 278
Bramati, I. E., 186
Bramham, J, 152
Bramlett, H. M. 222, 251
Brammer, M. J, 156
Bratton, S. L. 39, 43
Brauer, M. 155
Braun, C. M. 5, 18, 77
Braverman, S .E. 314, 323, 330, 332
Brehm, S. E. 216
Breneiser, J. 82
Brewer, M. B. 150
Brianti, R. 181
Briggs, L. M. 42
Briggs, R. W. 156
Brink, J. D. 219, 251
Brinton, B. 183
Briscoe, J. 192, 209
Broe, G. A. 23, 45, 137, 158
Broglio, S. P. 45, 46
Broman, S. H. 185, 188
Bromberg, M. B. 304
Brooks, B. R. 304
Brooks, D. N. 11, 18, 31, 37, 41, 42, 66, 67, 68,
    70, 72, 76, 80, 83, 132, 147, 155
Brooks, N. 76, 310, 332
Brookshire, R. 7, 17, 18, 20, 42, 80, 83, 92, 94,
    95, 102, 103, 104, 116, 261
Brookshire, B. L. 111, 211, 261, 263, 278
Brossart, S. 21
Brotherton, F. A. 320, 324, 330, 332, 365, 366,
    374, 385
Brouwer, W. H. 50, 51, 52, 53, 62, 74, 76, 87
Brown, A. L. 267, 278
Brown, A.W. 34, 35, 41, 82, 85
Brown, B. B. 207, 209
Brown, E. D. 164, 169, 170, 179

Brown, G. 169, 170, 181
Brown, J. R. 19, 252
Brown, M. M. 187, 214
Brown, P. 100, 111
Brown, S. 179, 209
Brown, V. L. 212
Brownell, H. 116, 151
Bruce, D. 18, 76, 112, 170, 181, 210, 278, 280
Brum, C. 87
Brunder, D. G. 277
Bryan, K. L. 7, 18
Bryan, D. 187
Bryant, B. 308, 335
Bryant, R. 83
Buckle, L, 86
Buckwald, M. B. W. 365, 385
Buelow, M. T, 138, 148
Bufalari, I. 166, 181
Bullmore, E. T, 156
Bullock, P. 152
Bullock, R. 43
Bulotsky-Shearer, R. 164, 181
Bunning, S. 152
Buonaguro, 18, 255
Burant, C. 188
Burdon-Cooper, C. 80
Burgess, P. 133, 385
Burgess, P. W. 61, 64, 65, 66, 69, 85, 87, 88, 159
Burgess, S. 178, 189, 333
Burnett, 162, 181, 281
Burnett, S, 181, 281
Burns, C. T, 81, 151
Burrows, C. S. 23, 157, 335
Burrows, E. H. 80
Burt, D. 156
Burton, M. k. 227, 251
Bush, G. 51 76
Butler, T. 162, 181
Buttsworth, D. L. 114
Bye, A. 184
Byom, L. J. 148

Cabeza, R. 51, 76, 81
Cacioppo, 160, 181
Cahill, L. 221, 224, 225, 229, 231, 242, 249, 251
Cain, K., 279
Calabrese, P. 82
Calder, A, 159
Call, J. 188
Callahan, B. L. 121, 148
Caltagirone, C. 281
Cameron, D. 345, 358
Cameron, I. D. 46, 87
Camodeca, M. 162, 181
Campana, M. E., 281
Campbell, T. F. 195, 208, 210, 214
Campbell, A, 81, 153
Campsie, L. 41, 76, 147, 332

Canavan, A. 63, 76
Cannito, M. P. 154
Cannizzaro, M. S. 93, 111, 261, 269, 278, 365, 367, 385
Cannon, A. 20
Cannon, B. J. 142, 148
Cantagallo, A. 146, 150
Cantor, J. 75, 303, 333, 385
Caplan, D. 260, 278
Cappa, S. 22, 24, 82
Cardillo, J. E., 333
Carey, S. 188
Carlomagno, S, 94, 111, 115
Carlozzi, N. 305
Carlson, H. B. 365, 367, 385
Carlson, P. 334
Carlson, R. A. 76
Carnevale, G. 350, 358
Caroselli, J. S. 387
Carpenter, M. 162, 181, 188
Carpenter, P. A. 192, 213
Carpenter, S. 254
Carr, E.G. 386
Carr, L. 122, 148
Carr, T. H. 153
Carroll, L. J. 41
Carrow-Woolfolk, E. 201, 203, 210
Cartlidge, N. E. 182
Carton, J. 135, 156
Carton, S. 83
Caruso, A. 253
Caruso, D. R. 129, 154
Cascella, P. W. 303
Casebeer, W. D. 166, 181
Casewood, B. 84, 116
Casey, B. J. 163, 181
Casper, J. K. 232, 233, 252
Cassidy, J. D. 35, 41
Casson, I. R. 46, 158
Castellanos, F. X. 183, 280
Castelli, E. 187
Castle, J. 182
Catalano, R. 184
Catanese, J. 303, 332
Caton, W. 185
Catroppa, C. 161, 167, 173, 174, 179, 180, 181, 182, 186, 189, 193, 194, 209, 210, 214
Catsman-Berrevoets, C. E. 256
Cattelani, R. 173, 181
Cattran, C. J. 68, 76
Caughlin, B. P. 43, 81
Cautela, J. R. 142, 153
Cavallucci, C. 88
Caveness, W. 252, 255
Cenni, P. 45
Ceperich, S. D. 302
Cernich, A. 305
Chadwick, O. 169, 181

Chalmers, I, 386
Chamberlain, A., 76
Chan, R. C. K. 86
Chan, W. 84
Chang, C. C. 213
Chang, E. F. 29, 41
Channon, S. 66, 76, 102, 104, 105, 111, 112, 124, 125, 127, 148
Chapey, R. 25, 360
Chapman, S. B. 7, 8, 18, 19, 24, 42, 73, 76, 90, 92, 93, 95, 97, 98, 101, 103, 111, 112, 118, 152, 184, 196, 207, 208, 210, 211, 212, 213, 214, 258, 259, 261, 262, 263, 264, 265, 266, 267, 268, 270, 276, 277, 278, 279, 280, 281
Charbonneau, S, 84
Charman, T. 182
Chartrand, T. L. 139, 153
Chaytor, N. 141, 148
Chelune, G. J. 80
Chen, A. J. W. 265, 266, 278
Chen, T. 46
Chenery, H. J. 230, 251, 252, 255, 256
Cheng, E. M. 305
Cheng, X-M. 46
Cheng, Y. 166, 181
Cherney, L. R. 359, 387
Chetelat-Mabillard, D. 21
Cheung, C. K. 159
Cheung, G. 81, 153
Chevignard, M. 112
Chia, J. 46, 254
Chiale, D. 156
Chiou, K. S. 61, 76
Chiou, H. H. 213, 304
Chiu, S. 210, 278
Chiu Wong, S. B. 278
Choi, D. W. 29, 41
Choi, W. 159
Chong, J. 386
Chong. k. 254
Cho-Reyes, S. 5, 18
Choudhury, S. 162, 182
Choux, M. 182
Christensen, J. R. 215
Christensen, B. k. 87
Christodoulou, C. 136, 148
Chu, Z. 46, 184, 254, 257
Cicchetti, D. V. 188
Ciccia, A. H. 196, 207, 210
Cicerone, K. D. 43, 119, 124, 148, 295, 296, 297, 298, 300, 302, 303, 307, 308, 329, 332, 333, 363, 385
Cifu, D. X. 41, 302
Cipolotti, L. 66, 75, 119, 122, 126, 147
Clancy, R. R. 211
Clare, L. 84, 88
Clark, K. 281
Clark, A. N. 157, 335, 387

Clark, H. H. 100, 112
Clarke, N. E. 186
Clarke, A. R. 147
Clasen, L. S. 183
Classen, J. 239, 251
Clavisi, o, 302
Cleary, J. 7, 8, 22
Clement, P. 77, 80
Clinchot, D. 24
Coates J. 358
Cockburn, J. 88
Code, C. 4, 18, 22, 24, 117, 281, 349,359, 388
Coelho, C. A. 8, 10, 18, 21, 25, 90, 91, 92, 93, 94, 95, 97, 102, 103, 104, 111, 112, 113, 114, 115, 116, 118, 196, 198, 200, 202, 210, 216, 261, 262, 268, 269, 278, 279, 303, 304, 305, 306, 341, 346, 358, 360, 365, 367, 373, 385, 388
Cohen, E. H. 189
Cohen, J. D. 183, 266, 281
Cohen, L G. 155, 251, 257
Cohen, N. J. 211
Cohn, E. S. 180
Coie, J. D. 180
Cole, M. A. 156
Cole, P. 19, 114
Coleman, L. 184
Colle, L. 111
Collie, A.,302
Collins, W. A. 207, 217
Collis, K. F. 269, 277
Coltheart, M. 4, 18, 20, 23, 84
Colton, R. 232, 233, 252
Colvert, E. 166, 182
Colvin, A. N. 214
Condon, B. 151
Conger, A. J. 335
Conger, J. C. 335
Conger, R. D. 169, 182
Conklin, H. M. 192, 210, 213
Connors, S. H. 303
Conroy, C. 185
Conroy, R. 186
Constantinidou, F. 216, 287, 303
Conture, E. G. 233, 252
Conzen, M. 31, 41
Cook, L. G. 19, 24, 42, 184, 210, 211, 212, 213, 259, 260, 262, 267, 276, 278, 279
Cook, D. J. 386
Cooke, D. L. 57, 76
Cooper, D. B. 77
Cooper, D. J. 44
Cooper, G. 146
Cooper, K. D. 36, 41
Coppens, P. 38, 41, 303
Corcoran, R. 131, 134, 148
Cornelissen, K. 14, 19
Cornish, k. 166, 183

Cornis-Pop, M. 302
Cornwell, P. 254, 257
Coronado, V. G. 41, 42
Corrigan, J. 24, 34, 35, 41, 72, 77, 139, 144, 145, 148
Corrigan, P. W. 148
Corso, M. 112, 279
Cosentino, S. A. 76
Coslett, H. B. 88
Costa, D. 146
Coste, C. 56, 77
Costeff, H. 184, 219, 252
Couch, D. 86, 359
Coughlan, T. 22, 44, 84
Couillet, J. 75
Counsell, S. J. 81
Couper, E. 167, 182
Coupland, N.. 359
Courville, C. B. 119, 148
Cox, C. F. 252
Cox, P, 185
Craft, A. W. 170, 182
Craig, A. 82
Craik, F. I. M. 76
Crawford, J. R. 65, 77, 83, 88, 151, 152, 155
Crawford, S. 102, 112, 124, 125, 148
Cremonini, A. M. 45
Crespo-Facorro, B. 185
Crinean, J. 82
Cristofori, L. 46
Critchley, M. 255
Critchley, H. D, 140, 148, 156
Croker, V. 120, 121, 122, 128, 148
Crosbie, S. 252
Cross, J. H. 254
Crossen, B. 70, 72, 73, 74, 77, 87
Crosson, B. 100, 112, 124, 148
Crowe, L. 169, 171, 182, 186, 191, 194, 210
Crowe, S. F. 140, 148
Csikszenthi, M. 211
Csikszentmihalyi, M. 207, 211
Culbertson, J. L. 47
Culhane, K. A. 18, 76, 112, 210, 278, 280
Cullum, C. M. 152
Cummings, J. L 82, 140, 149
Cunningham, W. A., 159
Curran, C. 44, 255
Curran, J. P. 19, 113, 333
Currie, D. 152, 155
Curtis, C. E. 266, 279
Curtiss, G. 80
Cushman, F. 153
Cusick, C. P, 112, 182, 333, 385
Cutica, I. 146
Cutter, N. 147

d'Arc, F. 168, 182
D'Elia, L. 156

D'Esposito, M. 266, 278, 279
Da Paz, A. C. 181
Dagenbach, D. 153
Dahlberg, C. 43, 105, 112, 182, 302, 303, 312, 313, 315, 318, 319, 320, 321, 332, 333, 361, 362, 363, 383, 385
Daigneault, S. 62, 77
Dalby, P. R., 182
Dalston, R. M., 237, 252
Damasio, A. 63, 65, 70, 75, 77, 78, 85, 119, 137, 138, 146, 147, 149, 150, 151, 153, 179, 209
Damasio, H. 75, 77, 146, 147, 149, 151, 209
Daniel, B. 220, 255
Danna, M. 24
Darby, D. 71, 71, 77, 102, 112, 125, 136, 137, 149
Darby, J. K. 255
Dardier, V. 95, 112
Darley, F. L. 19, 218, 229, 252
Darley, J. M. 183
Davidson, D. 211
Davidson, G. 83
Davies, D. 334
Davis, P. K. 15, 20
Davis, G. 92, 93, 94, 102, 113
Davis, L. M. 335, 387
Davis, M. H. 132, 135, 149
Day, J. D. 267, 278
de Gelder, B. 168, 182
de Haan, M. 160, 180
de la Plata, C. D. M . 58, 77, 87, 122, 149
de Lacy Costello, A. 87
de oliveira-Souza, R. 186
de Sousa, A. 22, 69, 77, 122, 123, 124, 132, 135, 137, 149, 154, 155
Dearden, M. 45
DeBoa, J. 87
Decety, J. 119, 123, 149, 181, 185
DeFillipis, N. A. 64, 77
DeFina, L. F. 278
Dehaene, S. 155
DeJong, J. 56, 77
Del Bolgia, F. 46
Delanov, A. 112
DeLeon, R. 211
Delis, D.C. 7, 19, 23, 59, 64, 77, 216
Delis, D. E. 77
Della Rocchetta, A. I. 59, 77
DeLuca, J. 57, 59, 70, 77, 148
Demakis, G. J. 44, 66, 67, 71, 72, 77, 78
Dematteo, C. 189
Demery, J. A. 156
Denburg, N. L. 158
Denckla, M. B. 215
Denmark, J. 68, 78
Dennis, M. 101, 102, 104, 111, 112, 113, 125, 149, 176, 182, 189, 191, 194, 196, 207, 210, 211, 212, 213, 217, 267, 278, 279, 280

Depino, A. 43
DePompei, R. 216, 258, 260, 277, 279, 281
DePompolo, R 334
DeRuyter, F. 5, 20
Deser, T. 8, 19, 92, 93, 94, 113
Desgranges, B. 84
Dethier, M. 123, 149
Deutsch, G. K. 23
Devereux, R. 21
Devinsky, O.151
Devous, M. D. 77, 87, 281
DeWitt, D. S. 21
Di Russo, F. 181
Diamond, B. J. 57, 59, 70, 77
Diaz-Arrastia, R. 77, 87, 149
DiCocco, M. 158
Didehbani, N. 152
Didus, E. 173, 182
Diehl, N. 41
Dietrich, W. D. 222, 251
Dijkers, M. 75
Dikengil, A. T. 319, 333
Dikmen, S. S. 36, 37, 39, 41, 48, 67, 76, 78, 79, 151
Dillon, J. D. 23
Dimberg, U. 122, 149
Dimoska, A. 22, 51, 77, 78, 120, 121, 136, 140, 149, 150, 154, 155
DiRocco, C. 182
Dixit, N. k.156
Dixon, M. R. 365, 368, 375, 384, 385
Dixon, T. M.,158, 189, 216
Docking, K. 194, 196, 207, 211
Dockree, P. 83, 85
Dodd, B. 231, 252
Dodge, k. A. 187, 214
Dolan, R. J, 147, 148, 152, 156, 159
Dollaghan, C. A. 195, 208, 210
Domingues, R. C. 252
Dominguez, T. 211
Donders, J. 23, 56, 77, 193, 194, 208, 211, 216
Donnellan, M. B. 169, 182
Donovick, P. 159
Dooley, J. 167, 168, 174, 182
Douglas, J. M 7, 10, 19, 23, 94, 102, 103, 107, 110, 113, 117, 118, 120, 121, 126, 127, 153, 158, 287, 303, 312, 333
Doyle, D. 42, 145
Draper, K. 36, 37, 41, 48, 78
Drebing, C. 156
Dresser, A. C. 219, 252
Drevets, W. C. 84, 156, 187
Drewe, E.A. 63, 78
Drotar, D. 188, 189, 215, 217
Drummond, S. S. 90, 95, 113
Dubeau, M.-C. 148
Dubois, B. 112
Dubow, E. F. 180

Duckett, E. 207, 214
Dudgeon, P. 179
Duffy, J. D. 80
Duffy, R. J. 18, 21, 95, 112, 115, 279, 358
Duhaime, A. C. 211
Duke, M. P. 135, 156
Dumas, H. 161, 180
Dumas, J. 158
Duncan, C. C. 50, 62, 78
Duncan, J. 78
Dunne, J. R. 18, 40
Durgin, C. J. 360
Durham, M. S. 42
Durham, S. R. 197, 211
Durwen, H. F. 82
Dywan, J. 152, 158

Eames, P. 31, 41, 71, 78
Ebel, N. 41
Edelaar, M. J. A. 46
Edelbrock, C. 193, 208
Edlund, W. 303
Edwards, k. E. 76
Edwards, M. S 180
Edwards, P. 219, 251
Egan, G. 153
Egan, M. 75
Eggins, S. 339, 340, 348, 358
Ehde, D. 188
Ehlhardt, L. A. 300, 303, 305
Ehrle, N. 157
Ehrlich, J. 8, 19, 73, 78, 95, 113, 281, 318, 320, 325, 333, 337, 358
Einstein, G. O. 58, 82
Eisenberg, H. M. 19, 75, 77, 79, 81, 84, 87, 149, 183, 211, 280
Ekman, P. 127, 128, 133, 150, 153, 159
Eleftheriou, E. 155
Elkins, M. 304, 386
Ell, P. 146
Elliott, A. C. 24, 281
Ellis, C. 4, 19, 92, 93, 113
Ellis , T. E. 332
Elsass, L. 3, 11, 19, 68, 70, 78, 142, 150
Ely, T. A. 153
Emanuelson, I. 193, 212, 213
Emerson, M. J. 214
Emslie, H. 88, 159
Enderby, P. 38, 41, 230, 231, 252
Englander, J. 41, 79
Engle, R. W. 266, 280
Engmann, C. 75
Enrico, C. 42
Enrile, B. G. 195, 216
Ensenat-Cantallops, A. 150
Entwisle, L. M. 207, 215
Erb, M. 158
Erlich, J. S. 93, 95, 101, 113

Eslinger, P. J. 63, 65, 69, 71, 78, 119, 124, 136, 137, 141, 150, 151, 165, 186
Espir, M. L. E. 2, 23
Espy, k. A. 212
Esselman, P. C. 34, 42, 76
Etcharry-Bouyx, F. 151
Eustache, F. 84
Evans, A. C. 183
Evans, G. 157, 335
Evans, J. 79, 88, 159
Evans, S. 303
Ewing-Cobbs, L. 92, 113, 183, 191, 192, 193, 195, 197, 200, 207, 211, 213, 214, 238, 252, 258, 259, 260, 261, 265, 278, 279, 280

Fabiano, R. J. 143, 151
Fadiga, L 122. 150
Fairbanks, L. A. 82
Falcomata, T. 385
Fann, J. R. 76, 188
Fantuzzo, J. 181
Farah, M. J. 51, 62, 63, 78, 80, 138, 150, 169, 184
Farrell, A. D. 10, 19, 43, 105, 106, 113, 311, 333
Faul, M. 39, 42
Favier, J. 180
Fay, G. C. 187
Fayada, C. 112
Fazio, F. 22, 82
Fearing, M. A. 257
Featherstone, 148
Featherstone, E. 148
Feeney, T. J. 202, 217, 281, 310, 335, 351, 360
Feinberg, T. 147
Feiner, C. 41
Feinn, R. 112, 279
Felicetti, T. 302, 303, 332, 333, 385
Fellows, L. K. 63, 78, 138, 150
Felmingham, k. L. 51, 78, 136, 150
Fenelon, B. 45, 86, 158
Fenwick, T. 209
Fergusson, D. M. 44
Fernandez-Duque, D. 61, 78
Fernandez-Espejo, D. 84
Ferraro, M. 150
Ferreira, V. S. 195, 211
Ferstl, E. 104, 113
Ferstl, R. 79
Fey, M. E. 284, 300, 301, 303, 304
Fife, D. 185
Figini, E. 187
Finfer, S. R. 44
Fischer, R. 79
Fiselzon, J. 255
Fiske, S. T. 184
Fiszdon, J. M. 131, 150
FitzGerald, F. J. 231, 252
Flanagan, S. 22, 69, 74, 75, 78, 90, 102, 108, 109, 113, 115, 116, 124, 125, 127, 150, 154,

262, 268, 280, 311, 312, 317, 333, 334, 363, 385
Flashman, L. A. 154
Flavell, J. H. 162, 182
Fleming, J. M. 70, 78, 84, 334
Fleming, M. 88
Fleminger, S. 71, 72, 79
Fletcher, J. M. 18, 76, 113, 173, 174, 183, 191, 210, 211, 252, 277, 278, 279, 280
Flood, J. 114
Floris, R. 46
Foerster, A. F. 22
Fogassi, L. 150
Fois, A. 212
Foley, J. 88
Fonez, J. 86
Forbes, M. M. 17
Ford, B. 81
Ford, I. 145
Fordyce, D. J. 22, 70, 79, 84, 85, 116
Foreman, S. 217
Forgie, M. 185
Fortuny, 33, 42
Foto, M,.303
Fox, A. M, 150
Fox, N. 180
Fox , P. T. 186
Foxe, J. J. 85
Fraas, M. 303, 333, 385
Frampton, I. 158, 188, 189, 215, 216, 281
Francis, D. J. 211
Frank, A. 22
Frank , E. 120, 129, 157
Frankle, B. C. 42
Franklin, G. 303
Franklin, M. 87
Frattali, C. 303
Frazier, J. A. 76
Freedle, R. 117
Freedman, H. 51, 62, 79
Freelands, J. C. 76
French, L. M. 24
Frenchmen, K. A. 136, 150
Friederici, A. D. 184
Friedman, N. P. 214
Friesen, W. 127, 128, 150, 153
Frings-Dresen, M. H. W. 46
Frith, U. 124, 145, 151, 152, 166, 168, 183, 184
Frith, C. 147, 148, 152, 166, 168, 183
Froidevaux, A. 180
Frost, B. G. 45
Fryer, L. J. 360
Fuchs, S. 83, 84, 155
Fugate, L. 24
Fujiki, M. 168, 183
Fujiwara, E. 63, 79, 138, 150
Fussey, I. 333, 385
Fuster, J. M. 62, 79, 266, 279

Gabrieli, J. D. 23, 263, 279
Gainotti, G. 281
Gajar, A. 318, 320, 325, 333, 365, 369, 376, 385, 387
Galanaud, D. 155
Galas, J. 159
Galbiati, S. 187
Galbraith, S. 185
Galera, C. 116, 155
Galetto, V,.115
Gallagher, H. L. 166, 183
Galski, T. 94, 95, 102, 113, 261, 279
Galvan, A. 181
Gamble, A. 112, 279
Gamino, J. F. 7, 19, 40, 42, 184, 191, 208, 210, 211, 261, 262, 263, 264, 267, 270, 276, 278, 279, 280, 281
Ganesalingam, K. 173, 174, 183, 192, 194, 212
Gantz, C. 88
Gao, F. 43, 79, 150
Garavan, H. 85
Garces, J. 77, 149
Garcia-Barry, S. 256
Garcia-Molina, A. 150
Garcia-Monco, J. C. 75
Gardner, C. 153
Gardner . C. M. 278
Gardner, W. L. 139
Garmezy, N. 186
Garrett, A. L. 251
Garrett, K. 220, 251
Garver, k. E. 213
Gasparetto, E. L. 239, 252
Gauggel, S. 213
Ge, L.. 185
Geary, E. k. 82
Gehlen, W. 82
Gelinas, D. F. 304
Geneinhardt, M. 68, 78
Gennarelli, T. A. 145
Gentry, L. R. 119, 150
Geraci, A. 124, 125, 150
Geraldina, P. 40, 42
Gerber, D. 43, 332
Gerhardt, C. A. 189, 217
Gernsbacher, M. A. 281
Gerring, J. P. 214, 215
Gertler, P. 116, 186, 334, 386
Geschwind, N. 20, 42, 114
Gest, S. 186
Geyer, S. 184
Ghajar, J. 29, 42
Giacino, J. T. 32, 40, 42, 302, 303, 332
Giampietro, V. 156
Giannotti, S. 111
Gibb, R. 185, 213
Gibbon, F. E. 186
Gibbs, R.W. 11, 19

Gibson, A. 185
Gideon, D. A, 153
Giedd, J. N. 163, 183, 266, 267, 280
Giguère, J. F. 84
Gilbert, S. J. 87
Giles, G. M. 320, 326, 330, 333, 365, 369, 385
Giles, H. 359
Gillespie, A. 299, 303
Gillon, G. 192, 207, 214
Ginsberg, A. 75
Ginstfeldt, T. 193, 212
Gioia, G. A. 156, 192, 199, 212, 214, 287, 303
Giordani, B. 44, 85
Giovannetti, T. 79
Girgis, M. 70, 79
Giroire, J. M. 75
Giuliani, G. 45
Giza, C. C. 39, 42
Glang, A. 281
Glasser, M. F. 238, 252
Glasziou, P. 386
Glenn, C. G. 96, 117
Glisky, E. L. 58, 83
Glosser, G. 8, 19, 92, 93, 94, 113
Godbee, k. 387
Godersky, J. C. 150
Godfrey, C. 174, 179, 209
Godfrey, H. P. D. 3, 10, 18, 21, 70, 72, 79, 90, 95, 111, 114, 115, 117, 334
Goebel, S. 64, 79
Gogtay, N. 163, 183
Goka, R. 43
Goldberg, A. I. 181
Goldblum, G. 318, 320, 326, 333
Goldman, A. I. 122, 151
Goldman, R. 231, 252
Goldman-Rakic, P. 51, 62, 79
Goldstein, K. 1, 19
Goldstein, F. C. 81, 169, 183
Goldstein, R. 252
Goldstein, S. E. 180
Goldwyn, R. 169, 183
Golper, L. 290, 303
Gomes, A. 180
Gonen-Yaacovi, G. 87
Goodglass, H. 5, 19, 20
Goodwin, G. M. 151
Goossens, F. A. 162, 181
Goozée, J. V. 227, 251, 252, 253, 256
Goran, D. A. 143, 151
Gordon, N. A. 197, 212
Gordon, W. A. 24, 75, 303, 305
Gordon , S. 305
Gorelick, P. B. 82
Gorman, A. R. 278
Gorny, G. 185
Gorter, J. 189
Gould, K. R. 72, 79, 85

Gourley, E. 81
Goursaud, A. P. 165, 183
Gouvier, W. D. 32, 42
Gow, C. A. 86, 157
Grace , J. 141, 142, 151
Grace, R. C. 44
Graciarena, M. 43
Grados, M. A. 215
Grady, C. L. 76
Grafman, J. H. 1, 2, 19, 23, 75, 79, 87, 112, 114, 116, 126, 155, 186, 281
Graham, D. I. 27, 42, 121, 145
Graham, R. 151
Gramling, S. E. 43
Grant, H. 185
Grant, J. 152, 281, 359
Grant, S. 114, 281, 359, 388
Grassi, F. 22, 82
Grattan, L. M. 69, 78, 124, 141, 150, 151
Gray, k. 166, 183
Green, A. M. 78, 120, 122, 150
Green, J. 169, 183
Green, K. M. 150
Green, R. E. 87, 151
Greenberg, M. T. 167, 183, 187
Greene, J. D. 166, 183
Greenfield, P. 215
Greenfield, E. 88
Greenhaigh, T. 386
Greenham, M. 173, 184
Greenstein, D. 183
Greenwood, R. 81
Greig, T. 131, 150, 151
Grela, B. 112, 279
Grice, H. P. 9, 10, 19, 101, 102, 103, 105, 107, 110, 114, 127
Grieb-Neff, P. 88
Grill, R. J. 21
Grimes, J. 8, 19
Grinnan, J. 77, 149
Grochmal-Bach, B. 365, 385
Groher, M. 3, 4, 19, 219, 220, 252
Gronseth, G. 303
Gronwall, D. 36, 42, 50, 52, 53, 79
Groot, Y. 88
Groothues, C. 182
Gross , D. 122, 158
Gross, J. J. 159
Gross, Y. 83, 116
Grossman, R. G. 21, 43, 81, 114, 153
Grossman, R. I. 253
Grossmann, T. 162, 167, 184
Grosswasser, Z. 38, 42
Groswasser, Z. 252
Gruen, A.K. 38, 42
Gruen, R. L. 302
Guercio, J. 385
Guerin, S. J. 154

Guger, S. 113, 182, 211
Guichart-Gomez, E, 155
Guidotti, S. J, 281
Guiller y-Girard, B. 77
Gulliver, S. 305
Gumperz, J. J. 20
Guo, Y. E. 249, 252
Gupta, S. 174, 187
Guralink, M. 165, 184
Gustafson, C. 278
Guthke, T. 113
Guthrie, E. 222, 253
Guy, S. C. 212, 303
Guyatt, G. 300, 377, 386
Guynn, M. J. 82

Haak, N. J. 116
Habert, M.-O. 155
Hackman, D. A. 169, 184
Hadley, D. M. 119, 151, 257
Hagan, C. 3, 5, 19, 32, 42, 56, 73, 79, 81, 101, 114
Halberstadt, J. B. 155
Hale, W. R. 251
Hall, K. 72, 73, 79
Halle, J. 386
Hallett, M. 251, 257
Halliday, M. A. K. 9, 19, 89, 91, 92, 93, 114, 336, 338, 339, 341, 348, 359
Halpern, H. 3, 19
Halson, D. 152
Hamilton, D. 188
Hamilton, M. 112
Hammen, V. 233, 253
Hammill, D. D. 199, 201, 212
Hammond, F. 40, 44, 46, 77, 78
Hamsher, K. 18
Hand, L. 24, 93, 101, 117, 348, 349, 359
Hanks, R. A. 3, 20, 44, 68, 79, 132, 151
Hanna, J. 46
Hanten, G. R. 46, 165, 173, 175, 184, 185, 191, 208, 210, 212, 213, 214, 254, 257, 259, 264, 269, 278, 280
Happè, F. 124, 130, 133, 145, 151, 157, 203, 212
Harari, H. 130, 151
Hare, T. A. 181
Haritou, F. 179, 181, 209, 210
Harkness, W. 254
Harley, P. 43
Harley , J. P. 285, 302, 303, 332, 333, 385
Harmer, C. J. 121, 151
Harper, C. 87
Harradine, P. G. 46, 87
Harrington, 43, 302, 303, 332, 386
Harris, B. S. H. 43
Harris , R. D. 46, 87
Harris , J. 75, 81
Harris, L. T. 168, 184

Harris, T. S. 278
Harrison- Felix, C. L 112, 182, 332, 333, 385
Hart, T. 44, 61, 79, 85, 287, 303, 305
Hart, J. 277, 278, 279
Hartelius, L 253
Hartley, L. L. 6, 8, 9, 15, 20, 73, 80, 92, 93, 94,
    98, 101, 104, 114, 338, 359
Hartmann, H. E.. 257
Hartry, A. 335
Harvey, A. S. 212
Harward, H. 18, 76, 112, 210, 278, 280
Hasan, R. 91, 92, 93, 98, 114, 252, 339, 341,
    348, 359
Hastings, P. 187
Haupts, M. 82
Hauser, A. 41
Hauser, M. 153
Haut, M. W. 56, 80
Havet-Thomassin, V. 125, 130, 151
Havill, J. H. 80, 154
Hawkins, A. 182
Hawkins, J. D. 162, 184
Hawkins, K. 88
Hawkins, P. C. 81
Hawley, L. 112, 182, 309, 315, 319, 331, 332,
    333, 385
Hayashi, k. M. 183
Hayden, D. 231, 253
Hayden, M. E. 81
Hayes, R. L. 21
Hayes, H. R. 169, 184
Haynes, 116, 305, 387
Haynes, W, 116
Hayward, R. 254
He, Z. 30, 45
Heard, R. 111, 358, 385
Heath, J. A. 186
Heaton, R. K. 64, 80
Hebb, D. O. 191, 212
Heberlein, A. S. 126, 151
Hedberg, N. L. 18
Hedtke, K. A. 178, 185
Heiden, J. 185
Heilman, K. M. 3, 4, 20, 38, 42, 89, 114, 140,
    147, 151
Hein, G. 166, 184
Heled, E. 20
Helffenstein, D. A. 268, 280, 314, 315, 320, 321,
    333, 362, 363, 383, 386
Helm-Estabrooks, N. 212, 280
Helmick, K. M. 24
Hemphill, S. 182
Henderson, J. A. 4, 17
Heneghan, C. 386
Henry, A. 157
Henry, J. D. 123, 125, 128, 130, 133, 151, 154,
    157, 162
Henry, K. L. 184

Henschel, M. 22
Herbert, R. D. 304, 386, 387
Heretick, D. 180
Herman, D. H. 183
Herrera, P. 147
Hersen, M. 377, 385, 386
Hersey, k. P. 386
Hertrich, I. 253
Herzog, H. 21
Herzog, J. 302, 332
Hess, U. 122, 123, 147, 152
Hessol, N. 43
Hetherington, C. 86, 157
Hexum, C. 80
High, W. M. Jr. 181
Higlett, T. 44
Hildebrandt, N. 278
Hill, E. L. 162, 167, 168
Hill, K. G. 184
Hill, J. 146, 184
Hillary, F. G. 76
Hillbom, M. 47
Hillis, A. E. 4, 20
Hillman, G. R. 277
Hilt, J. 43
Himanen, L 153
Hinkka, S. 153
Hinton, V. A. 236, 253
Hirschauer, J. 170, 187
Hitch, G. 75
Hitchcock, J. 386
Hixon, T. J. 235, 256
Hodge, M. 231, 240, 253
Hodges, J. R., 153
Hoffman, J. F. 153
Hoile, H. 209
Hoit, J. 254
Holland, A. L. 4, 5, 9, 17, 19, 20, 38, 42, 73, 79,
    80, 114, 194, 195, 199, 207, 208, 216, 359,
    387
Holland, D. 350, 359
Holland, M. 41
Holloway, M. 169, 184
Holm, A. 252
Holm, L. 41
Holmes, J. F. 197, 212
Holtel, C. 21
Honda, K. 243, 249, 253
Honkalampi, k. 153
Hoofien, D. 75
Hooper, C. J. 213
Hopkins, M. J. 121, 122, 137, 152
Horn, L. 43
Hornak, J. 120, 121, 122, 152
Horneman, G. 193, 212, 213
Horner, M. J, 377, 385
Horner , R. H. 386

Horowitz, I. 169, 184
Horri, Y. 237, 253
Horwood, L. J. 44
Hotz, G. 200, 201, 212, 260, 280, 386
Hough, M. S. 94, 114, 262, 280
Houle, S. 76
Howerter, A., 214
Howick, J. 377, 386
Howieson, D. B. 21
Hoyle, S. G. 207, 209
Hua, Z. 252
Hubbard, J. 186
Hudson, J. L., 187
Hudson-Tennent, L. J. 221, 227, 255
Hugenholtz, H. 86
Hughes, T. 255
Huisingh, R. 209
Hull, E. L. 280, 287
Humphrey, M. 70, 83
Humphreys, M. S. 85
Hunkin, N. M. 56, 80
Hunt, 91, 114
Hunt, C. 154
Hunt, k, 114
Hunter, J. V. 46, 184, 254, 257, 280
Hunter, M. 45, 86, 158
Huntzinger, C. D., 158
Hymes, D. 8, 20
Hynes, C. D. 123, 124, 152

Iacoboni, M. 148, 166, 185
Iannotti, F. 45
Ietswaart, M. 120, 121, 128, 151, 152, 155
Illig, T. 183
Innes-ker, Å. H. 155
Inscore, A. B. 215
Iovino, I. 279
Ireland, P.. 217
Irwin, W. 281
Isgrò, E. 46
Ishai, A. 126, 152
Isoniemi, H. 153
Isquith, P. K. 156, 212, 303
Ivins, B. 23, 45

Jackson, H. F. 11, 20, 120, 121, 152
Jackson, P. L. 166, 185
Jackson , R. H. 169, 184
Jacobi, G. 212
Jacobs, R. 182, 185, 191, 212
Jaeger, M. 224, 225, 253
Jaervensivu, T. 19
Jaeschke, R. 386
Jaffe, k. M. 187
Jaggi, J. 253
James, C. 22, 77, 149, 150, 154, 155
James , H. E. 197, 212
Jamieson, E. 215

Jane, J. 44, 85
Janota, I. 76
Janowsky, J. S. 59, 80, 85
Jansain, A. 80
Jansen, A. 22
Janusz, J. A. 173, 175, 185, 194, 212, 217
Jarman, C. 254
Jarvie, H. F. 73, 80
Jeffries, N. O. 183, 280
Jenike, M. A. 76
Jenkins, D. 22, 44, 46, 84, 88, 151
Jennett, B. 27, 31, 33, 34, 35, 36, 42, 46, 66, 80,
    170, 185, 197, 212
Jennings, C. J. 162, 185
Jennings, J. M. 76
Jensen, P. J. 8, 20, 73, 80, 92, 93, 94, 98, 101,
    104, 114
Joanette, Y. 24, 116
Job, R. 18, 23
Jodl, K. M. 179
Johansen, 335
Johansen, A. 335
Johanson, C. 30, 42
Johns, D. F. 46
Johns , L. C. 156
Johnson, C. J. 10, 21, 107, 110, 115
Johnson, D. A. 90, 116, 180, 184, 318, 320, 327,
    333
Johnson, D. L. 187
Johnson, J. 335
Johnson, K. 15, 20
Johnson, L. 335
Johnson, M. H. 167, 184
Johnson, N. S. 8, 21
Johnson, P. 281
Johnson, S. C. 154
Johnston, C. S. 305, 334
Johnston, J. 334
Johnston, L. 79, 85, 88, 127, 130, 152
Johnston, M. V. 113, 279
Johnstone, B. 60, 80
Johnstone, E. 153
Johnstone, L. 79
Johnstone, S. 78, 150
Jokelainen, J. 47
Jokic, C. 84
Jolles, J. 40
Jolliffe, T. 146
Jones, T. A. 5, 20, 240, 253
Jones , D. 44
Jonides, J. 87
Jonsson, C. A. 194, 208, 213
Jordan, F. M. 4, 20, 94, 95, 114, 211
Jorge, R. E. 72, 80, 167, 185
Jorgensen, M. 92, 94, 114, 262, 268, 280
Joseph, J. 82
Joseph, P. A. 75, 116, 155
Joukamaa, M. 153

Junque, C. 84
Just, M. A. 192, 213
Justice, L. M. 301, 303
Jutai, J. 281

Kadosh, K. 181
Kaelin, D. 40
Kagan, A. 24, 118
Kaipio, M. L. 80
Kaitaro, T. 67, 68, 80
Kaland, N. 124, 152
Kalmar, K. 40, 42, 302, 303, 332, 333, 385
Kalsbeek, W. D. 36, 43
Kamerling, S. 211
Kammeyer-Mueller, J. D. 164, 189
Kampe, 126, 152
Kampe, k. K. W.152
Kan, P. F. 304
Kandalaft, M. R. 129, 152
Kandori, Y. 253
Kane, M. J. 266, 280
Kantor, L. W. 162, 180
Kanwisher, N. 188
Kaplan, E. 5, 7, 19, 20, 77
Kaplan, S. P. 31, 43
Kapur, S. 76
Karafin, M. S. 126, 152
Karimi, A. 45
Karlovits, T. 334
Karmiloff-Smith, A. 119, 152
Karzmark, P. 79
Kasarskis, E. J. 304
Kato, M. 87
Katz, 6, 20, 40, 151, 285, 303
Katz, R, 303
Kaufmann, P. M.118, 188, 216
Kauslen, D. H. 57, 76
Kave, G. 7, 20
Kay, G. G. 80
Kay, J. 5, 20
Kay, T. 34, 43
Kaye, M. E. 319, 333
Kayes, N. 360
Kazdin, A. E. 377, 381, 382, 386
Kean, J. 40
Kearns, K. P. 377, 382, 387
Keebler, M. 24, 277, 278, 281
Keenan, H. T. 39, 43
Keller, J. 386
Kellett, D. 152
Kelly , D. J. 162, 185
Kelly, G. 144, 145,152
Kelly , M. 78, 139, 150, 152
Kelly, P. J. 21, 43
Kelso, L. A. 152
Kendall, E. 124, 152
Kendall, P. 178, 185
Kennard, M. 191, 211, 213

Kennedy, J. 50, 77, 80
Kennedy, M. R. T. 5, 20, 192, 213, 216, 284, 286, 287, 292, 293, 298, 300, 302, 303, 304, 305, 306
Kenny, D. T. 162, 185
Kent, R. D. 220, 240, 253, 254
Kent, T. A. 277
Kenworthy, L. 212, 303
Kerr, C. 4, 20
Kersel, D. A. 72, 80, 154
Kertesz, A. 5, 20
Kesselring, J. 146
Kessler, L. S. 256
Ketchum, J. M. 46
Kiernan, B. 267, 281
Kilov, A. M. 98, 114
Kilts, C. D. 122, 153
Kim, S. H. 68, 80
Kimberg, D. 51, 62, 80
Kimbrel, N. A. 169, 185
Kime, S. K. 57, 80
Kinch, J. 22, 58, 80, 115, 154, 334
King, A. I. 46, 158
King, C. 46
King, F. 337, 359
Kinnunen, K. M. 58, 63, 81
Kinsella, G. 3, 11, 19, 20, 37, 43, 49, 50, 52, 67, 68, 70, 72, 74, 78, 81, 84, 123, 132, 136, 142, 150, 153, 156, 187, 214
Kintsch, W. 95, 114, 118
Kipps, C. M. 127, 153
Kirchner, D. M. 102, 105, 116, 309, 334, 365, 384, 387
Kiresuk, T. J. 312, 313, 333
Kirk, J. W. 215
Kirkham, F. J. 197, 213
Kirkwood, M. W, 185, 212
Kirsch, N. L. 365, 370, 375, 376, 383, 384, 386
Kishiyama, M. 166, 187
Kleim, J. A. 5, 20, 240, 253
Klein, S. 188, 215
Kleinmann, A. E, 159
Klima, E. 152
Klonoff, H. 169, 185
Klug, G. 179
Knecht, S. 22
Kneipp, S. 302, 303, 332
Knight, R. 3, 21, 50, 52, 56, 69, 74, 79, 81, 82, 90, 114, 115, 117, 143, 146, 157, 311, 312, 334
Knight, R. T. 52, 81
Knotts, A. 77, 78
Knowlton, S. 43
Knox, L. 120, 121, 127, 153
Koele, S. L. 186
Koenigs, M. 126, 153
Kojori, E. S. 77, 149
Kolb, B. 166, 185, 188, 191, 213
Kolko, D. J. 365, 366, 374, 386

Konrad, K. 192, 193, 213
Koops, W. 186
Kopelman, M. 59, 81
Koponen, S. 123, 153
Kosier, T. 80
Koskinen, S. 80, 310, 333
Kosmidis, M. H. 78
Kosterman, R. 184
Kovacevic, N. 117, 214
Kramer, J. H. 19, 77, 211
Kramer, L. 211, 252
Kratochwill, T. R. 377, 378, 379, 384, 386
Kraus, M. F. 35, 36, 41, 63, 81, 82
Kraus, J. 35, 41, 43, 169, 170, 185
Krause, M. O. 284, 287, 304
Krawczyk, D. C. 152, 208, 213
Kremer, P. 152
Kreppner, J. 182
Kreutzer, J. S. 24, 43, 72, 73, 81
Krishnan, K. 77, 149, 281
Krueger, F. 112, 114, 116, 186
Kubota, Y. 157
Kufera, J. A. 112, 210, 277, 278
Kuhl, D. E. 181
Kuppermann, N. 212
Kurki, T. 153
Kurosaki, Y. 87
Kurtz , D. 157, 335
Kurtz, J. E. 67, 72, 73, 81
Kurtz, T. 185
Kuruvilla, M. 227, 251, 253
Kusche, C. A. 187
Kwasnica, C 147

Laatsch, L. 302, 303, 332, 333, 363, 385, 386
Labov, W. 8, 21
Lacey, S. C. 87
Laganaro, M. 21
Lah, S. 85
Laine, M. 19
Lakin, J. L. 153
Lamb, D. 80
Lambier, J. 86
Lancaster, J. L. 186
Land, D. J, 179
Landry, S. H. 211
Lane, R. D. 84, 151, 156, 187
Lane, S. 184
Lane-Brown, A. T. 46, 68, 81
Lang, R., 387
Lange, G. 148
Langenbahn, D. M. 302, 303, 332, 333, 385
Langfitt, T. W. 220, 253
Langhinrichsen-Rohling, J. 44
Langhorne, P. 255
Langlois, J. A. 44, 198, 213, 258, 280
Lapierre, F. 45
LaPorte, K. K. 42

LaRochelle, S. 86
Larrabee, G. J. 44
Larsen, S. C. 212
Larson, M. J. 156
Larson, R. 211
Lash, M. 281
Law, S.-P. 5, 25
Lawrie, S. 153
Lawson, J. 209
Lazar, N. A. 213
Lazzarino, G. 46
Le, k. N, 95, 97, 98, 103, 104, 112, 114, 116, 210
Leber, W. 87
Lecky, F. 44
Lee, K. 185
Lee , K. Y. 281
Lee, P. L. 181
Leech, R. 81
Leemann, B. 5, 21
Lefebvre, H. 3, 21
Leggett, J. A. 66, 67, 88
Lehiste, I. 220, 254
Lehmkuhl, D. 43
Lehr, E. 169, 185
Lehtilahti, M. 47
Leininger, B. E. 36, 43
Lemerise, E. A. 168, 180
Lemme, M. L. 18
Lenzi, G. L 148
Leon-Carrion, J. 11, 21, 162, 185
Lerner, R. M. 209
Lesser, R. 20
Letarte, P. B. 222, 254
Leuthardt, E. 211
Levendosky, A. A. 189
Levenson, R. W. 122, 153
Leventer, R. 185
Levert, M. J. 3, 21
Levick, W. R. 45
Levin, H. S. 3, 4, 17, 18, 19, 21, 29, 31, 33, 38, 43, 46, 55, 56, 69, 70, 72, 75, 77, 79, 81, 84, 86, 87, 89, 111, 112, 114, 124, 149, 153, 169, 173, 183, 184, 185, 191, 192, 194, 208, 210, 211, 212, 213, 214, 218, 238, 254, 255, 257, 259, 265, 267, 277, 278, 279, 280, 303, 386
Levin, J. R. 386
Levine, B. 36, 43, 56, 59, 63, 79, 81, 138, 150, 153
Levine, H. S. 18, 76
Levinson, S. C. 9, 21, 100, 111
Levita, E. 4, 18, 23, 38, 45, 89, 117, 255
Levkovitz, Y. 151
Levy, M. L. 68, 82
Lew, H. L. 302
Lewelt, A. J. 215
Lewis, F. D. 320, 327, 330, 333
Lewis, R. 180
Ley, P. 43

Lezak, M. D. 6, 11, 21, 31, 43, 52, 57, 60, 64, 68, 69, 70, 82, 119, 132, 140, 153, 287, 304
Li, S. 22, 149, 154, 155
Li, S.-C. 46
Li, X. 184, 185, 210, 212, 213, 214, 254, 257, 278
Liao, S. 187
Liberati, A. 386
Liégeois, F. 221, 222, 224, 227, 231, 254
Liepert, J. 14, 21, 251
Liess, J. 82
Light, D, 159
Light, R. 180
Liles, B. 8, 18, 21, 92, 93, 94, 95, 97, 112, 115, 279, 358
Lilly, M. A. 277, 280
Lim, k. o. 213
Lin, C. P, 181
Lindgren, S. D. 186
Ling, J. 132, 155
Linscott, R. J. 105, 107, 115, 310, 311, 333, 334
Lin Ting, C. 186
Liossi, C. 24, 88, 159
Lipton, A. M. 278
Liscio, M. 187
Lishman, W. A. 69, 70, 73, 82
Little, D. M. 43, 81, 82
Liu, H. 183, 280
Logan, G. D. 50, 51, 82, 136, 153
LoGiudice, C. 209
Lohman, T. 4, 21
Lombardi, R. 181
Long, B. 185
Long, E. 26, 116, 142, 153, 154, 186, 334, 386
Longoni, F. 14, 21
Lopes, F. C. 252
LoPresti, E. 386
Loring, D. W. 21
Lovely, M. 180
Lowe, M. R. 142, 153
Lowmann, E. 255
Lu, H. 278
Lu, W. C. 24
Luciana, M. 192, 213
Ludlow, C. 23, 240, 254
Lulham, J. 23, 45, 46
Luna, B. 192, 213, 214
Lundquist, L.-O 122, 149
Luria, A. R. 2, 21, 63, 71, 76, 82, 136, 137, 140, 153
Luschei, E. S. 236, 253
Lusk, L 183
Luukinen, H. 47
Lyerly, S. B. 6, 20
Lyketsos, C. 136, 156
Lyneham, H. J. 187
Lyon, R. 280

Maas, A. I. 26, 27, 29, 30, 43, 44, 185
Maas, A. J. 45
Macaluso-Haynes, S. 24
Maccoby, E. 207, 213
MacDonald, S. 10, 21, 107, 110, 115, 200, 201, 213, 287, 302, 304
MacFarlane, M. R. 44
MacFarlane, T. 212
Machalicek, W. 362, 387
Machamen, J.E. 41, 78, 79, 151
Mackay, M.185
MacPherson, P. 151
Madden, C. 77
Madigan, N. k. 148
Madikians, A. 42
Mageandran, S. D. 44, 254
Maggiotto, S. 188
Magloire, J. 281
Maguire, M. J. 277
Maher, C. G. 292, 304, 363, 386, 387
Maia, T. V. 138, 153
Maietti, A. 146
Major, B. 165, 185
Makashay, M. J. 256
Makris, N. 278
Malec, J. F. 41, 43, 72, 82, 85, 287, 302, 303, 304, 312, 320, 327, 330, 331, 332, 333, 334
Malec, J. M. 385
Malkmus, D. 14, 21, 42
Malloy, P. F. 141, 142, 151
Mamourian, A. C. 154
Mandalis, A. 193, 214
Mandler, J. A. 8, 21
Manes, F. 80, 186
Mangeot, S. 192, 214
Manly, T. 85, 193, 209, 214
Manning, M. 45, 86, 158
Manz, A. 213
Mar, R. 97, 115
Marcantuono, J. 386
Mariarosaria, L. 42
Marien, P. 78, 150
Marini, A. 94, 101, 102, 111, 115
Marique, P. 41
Marjoram, D. 131, 153
Markiewicz, K. 385
Markowitsch, H. J. 56, 59, 82
Marosseky, J. E. 45
Marquardt, T. P. 120, 154, 220, 254
Marsh, N. V. 69, 80, 82, 90, 114, 115, 139, 154, 311, 312, 334
Marsh, P. 179
Marshall, L. 43
Marshall, M. M. 83, 155
Martin, C. 152
Martin, I. 11, 104, 115, 154, 187
Martin, J. R. 104, 115, 340, 348, 359
Martin, K. M. 187

Martin, N. 19
Martinage, D. P. 83, 155
Martínez-Selva, J. M. 157
Martin-Rodriguez, J. F. 11, 21
Marwitz, J. H. 46, 81
Marziale, S. 46
Marzillier, J. 308, 335
Masel, B. E. 2, 21
Massimino, M. 187
Mast, J. 253
Masten, A. 160, 186
Masterman, D. 82
Masullo, C. 281
Mateer, C. A. 38, 45, 57, 82, 286, 305
Matejka, J. 112, 278
Mathews, k. k. 186
Mathias, C. J. 148
Mathias, J. L 50, 52, 74, 82, 136, 82, 154
Mathieu, P. 30, 43
Mattioli, F. 55, 59, 82
Max, J. E. 167, 173, 174, 186, 213, 259, 280
Maxwell, K. 187
Maxwell, W. L. 26, 29, 40
Maxzziotta, J. C. 148
Mayberry, M. T. 150
Mayer, J. D. 129, 154
Mayor, B. M. 359
Mazaux, J.-M. 75, 116, 155
Mazzei, D. M. 335, 387
Mazzucchi, A. 181
McAlinden, F. 358
McAllister, T. W. 136, 154
McArthur, D. L. 35, 43
McAuliffe, M. J. 249, 254
McAvinue, L. 62, 82
McCabe, A. 111, 209
McCampbell, E. 77
McCann, J. 167, 186
McCarthy, M. C. 172, 186
McCarthy, R. 147
McCauley, R. J. 253, 284, 300, 304
McCauley, S. R. 46, 198, 202, 214
McClelland, J. L. 138, 153
McClelland, M. 213
McClelland, R. L. 41
McClure, E. B. 168, 186
McColl, M. A. 310, 334
McColl, R. 77
McDaniel, M. A. 58, 82
McDermott, P. 181
McDonald, S. 8, 10, 12, 14, 15, 18, 21, 22, 23, 24, 46, 58, 66, 73, 74, 75, 77, 78, 80, 82, 83, 84, 90, 93, 94, 95, 98, 101, 102, 103, 104, 105, 106, 108, 109, 113, 115, 116, 118, 120, 121, 122, 123, 124, 125, 126, 127, 128, 131, 135, 137, 139, 140, 141, 147, 148, 149, 150, 152, 153, 154, 155, 157, 167, 177, 186, 188, 216, 261, 262, 268, 280, 281, 305, 309, 312, 314, 316, 317, 318, 319, 320, 322, 323, 331, 332, 333, 334, 359, 360, 362, 363, 364, 383, 385, 386, 387, 388
McFall, R. M. 89, 116
McFarland, C. 179
McFarland, C. P. 58, 83
McFarland, K. 85, 334
McGee, G. 386
McGhee, H. 243, 254
McGinn, T. 386
McHenry, M. A. 228, 254
McIntosh, A. R. 76, 81
McIntosh , D. N. 123, 155
McIntosh, T. K. 46
McIntosh, K. W. 255
Mckinlay, W. 11, 18, 35, 36, 41, 70, 76, 83, 147, 155, 332
Mckinlay , A. 35, 36, 44, 48, 66, 68, 70, 76, 132, 152
Mckinnon, A. 152, 210, 259, 266, 278
Mckinnon, L. 210, 278
McLauren, R. 43
McLean, A. 41
McLellan, D. R. 145
McLeod, S. 253
McLoyd, V. C. 164, 186
McMackin, D. 82
McMillan, T. M. 71, 83
McMordie, W. R. 37, 44
McNeel, M. L. 252
McNeil, M. R. 5, 22, 257
McPherson, K. 360
Mcquaid, M. 253
McReynolds, L. V. 377, 382, 387
McTear, M. F. 337, 359
Meade, M. O. 386
Meeker, M. 41
Meester-Delver, A. 189
Mehdorn, H. M. 79
Mehrabian, A. 131, 135, 155
Mei, C. 44, 250, 254
Meier, M. C. 210, 278
Meirowsky, A. M. 252
Mellink, R. 40
Melmed, R. N. 148
Meltzoff, A. N. 185
Mendelsohn, D. 18, 76, 112, 210, 213, 265, 277, 278, 280
Mendez, M. F. 126, 155
Menefee, D. S. 184
Menon, D. K. 30, 44
Mentis, M. 8, 9, 10, 22, 92, 93, 94, 95, 96, 116, 346, 359
Mercer, G. 148
Merckelbach, H. 155
Merkley, T. L. 213
Mersch, P. P. 155
Merzenich, M. M. 23

Messenger, B. 319, 334
Mesulam, M. M. 63, 83
Metham, L. 88
Metzelaar, k. 387
Meulenbroek, P. 210
Meyer, M. 119, 123, 149, 302
Meyer, K. 302
Meyers, C. A. 81
Meythaler, J. 46, 155
Miceli, G. 260, 281
Michel, M. E. 185, 188
Michela, S. 42
Milan, M. A. 332, 365, 366, 374, 385, 386
Milders, M. 66, 83, 120, 121, 124, 125, 126,
    128, 130, 131, 133, 152, 155
Milders, M. V. 157
Miles, L.152
Miletich, R. 281
Miller , B. L. 82
Miller. E. K. 266, 281
Miller, G. A. 124, 156
Miller, J. D. 43
Miller, L. A. 85, 124
Miller, P. 281
Miller, R. G. 298, 304
Mille. S. L. 23
Millis, 56, 83, 303
Millis, S. R, 83
Mills, M. R. 157, 335
Milne, E. 126, 155
Milner, B. 59, 77, 83
Miltner, W. H. 21
Milton, S. B. 73, 74, 83, 95, 100, 101, 116, 309,
    320, 328, 330, 334
Minderhoud, J. 185
Miner, M. E. 183, 211, 279
Minich, N. 189
Minifie, F. 257
Mink, R. B. 42
Minnema, M. T. 193, 211
Minnes, P. 334
Minns, R. A.. 212
Mirsky, A. F. 78
Mishkin, M. 57, 83
Mitsumoto, H. 304
Miyahara, Y. 87
Miyake, A. 192, 214
Mock, B. J. 281
Moessner, A. M. 82, 85
Moffatt, N. J. 11, 20, 121
Moher, D. 16, 22
Moir, J. F. 76
Molina-Holgado, E. 29, 30, 44
Molina-Holgado, F. 29, 30, 44
Moll, J. 166, 186
Moll, H. 188
Moloney, P. 83
Mongs, M. 305

Monshouwer, H. J. 186
Montes, J. L. 187
Montgomery, E. B. J. 216
Montgomery, M. W, 79, 358
Mooney, L. 86, 359
Mooney, M. 44
Moore, C. 77, 87
Moore, P. S. 277
Moore, S. 278
Moore, W. 281, 304
Moore Sohlberg, M. 304
Moran, C. 81, 192, 196, 214, 254
Moran, K. 184, 207
Morey, C. 112, 182, 332, 333, 385
Morgan, A. T. 38, 44, 219, 221, 222, 224, 225,
    227, 231, 239, 241, 244, 254
Morgan, J. 19. 114
Moriarty, J. 146
Moroney, B. 114
Morris, J. S, 147, 303
Morris, R. 152
Morris, S. 231, 257
Morris, T. L. 180
Morse, P. A. 303, 332
Morse, S, 179, 181, 209, 210
Mortensen, L. 95, 116
Mortensen, E. L. 152
Mortimore, C. 146
Moschetti, I. 386
Moseley, A. M. 304, 379, 386, 387
Moser, D. 185
Mossop, C. 18, 40 .
Motes, M. A. 277
Mottron, L. 168, 182
Mozeiko, J. 95, 103, 112, 114, 116
Mozzoni, M. P. 386
Mudar, R. A. 278
Mueller. B. A. 213
Mueller, R. A. 11, 19
Muhammad, A. 213
Muir, C. 303
Muir Gray, J. A. 283, 304
Mukherjee, P. 36, 44
Mulder, M. 333
Muller, F. 105, 116, 125, 127, 130, 132, 155
Muncer, S. J. 132, 146, 155
Munsat, T. L 304
Murai, T. 148, 157
Murdoch, B. E. 20, 38, 46, 114, 211, 221, 224,
    227, 228, 232, 233, 236, 238, 240, 245, 251,
    252, 253, 254, 255, 256
Murray, G. D. 45
Murre, J. M. J. 14, 23
Muscara, F. 186, 214
Musher-Eizenman, D. 180
Myburgh, J. A. 36, 44
Mychasiuk, R. 213
Myers, P. 303

Myles, B. M. 46, 87
Mysiw, W. 24
Myszka, K. A. 23, 157, 335

Naccache, L. 138, 155
Nadel, L. 151
Nagell, k. 181
Najenson, T. 42, 184, 218, 219, 255
Nakase-Richardson, R. 34, 35, 37, 44
Nance, M. L. 76
Nasi, M. T. 45
Neal, C. J. 18, 40
Nee, D. E. 87
Neidenthal, P. M. 122, 155
Nelson, C. 180
Nelson, J. 333
Nelson, L. 142, 156
Nelson, N. 280
Nepomuceno, C. 42
Nespoulous, J-L. 95, 16
Nestor, P. J. 153
Netsell, R. 220, 253, 255, 257
Neulinger, k. 116, 154
Neumann, D. 18, 146
Neumann, E. 180
Neumann, V. 76
Newcombe, F. 42
Newell, C. 385
Newitt, H. 179, 209
Newman, D. 304
Newman, J. 112, 182, 309, 315, 319, 331,332, 333, 385
Newsome, M. 184, 257
Newton, A. 90, 116, 318, 320, 327, 333
Newton, C. R. 213
Nguyen, L. 216
Ni, A. C. 148
Nica, E. 43
Nichelli, P. 265, 267, 281
Nicholls, S. S. 151
Nick, T. G. 45, 85
Nickel, V. L. 251
Nickels, L. 92, 116
Nicolas, V. 22
Nigg, J. T. 50, 83, 136, 156
Nimmo-Smith, I. 214
Niogi, S. N. 36, 44
Nippold, M. A. 214
Nixon, S. J. 47
Nock, M. k., 385
Nordness, A. S. 241, 245, 255
Norman, D. 49, 62, 83
North, A. J. 24
North , P. 84
Novack, T. A.155
Nowicki, S. 128, 129, 135, 147, 156
Nugent, T. F. 183
Nyberg, L. 76

Nystrom, L. E. 183

O'Barr, W. M. 345, 359
O'Brien, K. H. 304
O'Brien, L. T., 185
O'Connor, T. G. 182
O'Doherty, J. 152, 156, 159
O'Donnell, V. M. 43
O'Flaherty, C. A. 19, 113, 303
O'Hare, A. 186
O'Hare, P. 79
O'keeffe, F. 61, 82, 83
O'Leary, K. 358
O'Mara, S. M. 85
O'Neill, B. O. 299, 303
O'Shanick, G. J. 303
O'Toole, C. 81, 153
Oakhill, J. 279
Obrist, W. D. 253
Obrzut, J. E. 169, 182
Occomore, L. 254
Oddy, M. 17, 22, 31, 44, 46, 48, 66, 68, 70, 76, 83, 84, 88
Odhuba, R. A. 137, 156
Odom, S. 386
Ogden, J. A. 14, 22
Ohan, J. 182
Ohman, J. 45
Okada, T. 157
Okun, A. 189
Oliver, D. L. 79
Olszewski, H. 385
Olver, J. 20, 23, 43, 44, 81, 153, 218, 255
Ong, B. 214
Oppel, F. 41
Oppenheimer, E. A. 304
Orman, J. A. L. 41
Orobio De Castro, B. 186
Orsten, K. 184, 212, 214
Osterrieth, P. 59, 64, 65, 84
Ottenbacher, K. J. 217
Overmeyer, S. 156
Ownsworth, T. 70, 84, 318, 320, 334
Ozanne, A. E. 20, 252, 255
Ozonoff, S. 124, 156

Pachalska, M. 385
Packer, S. 20, 43, 81, 153
Page, N. 86
Palacios, E. M. 51, 84
Palchak, M. J. 212
Palomba, D.146
Palumbo, C. L. 86
Pantekoek, k.. 213
Paolo, T. M. 44
Paolucci, S. 22
Pape, T. L. 40, 305
Papero, P. H. 173, 174, 187

Pappadis, M. R. 23, 157, 335
Paquier, P. F. 256
Parker, J. G. 102, 174, 180, 187, 189
Parkin, A.J. 80
Parson, C. 86
Parsons, C. L. 337, 359
Parsons, J. L. 47
Partridge, F. M. 79
Pascalis, O. 185
Pascual-Leone, A. 75
Pasini, A. 123, 156
Patel, M. C. 81
Patry, R. 95, 116
Patterson, C. M. 216
Patterson, J. 151
Patton, D. R. 253
Paul, D. 216
Paul, R. 303
Paulesu, E. 22
Paulsen, J. S. 82
Paus, T. 183
Pavawalla, S. P. 58, 84
Pavesi, G. 150
Pavlakis, S. 253
Pavol, M. 216
Peach, R. 4, 19, 92, 93, 113
Pearce, S, 74, 83, 84, 95, 98, 101, 102, 103, 115, 120, 124, 126, 141,154
Peck, E. A. 43
Peck, S. D. 179
Peduzzi, J. D. 155
Pell, M. C. 150
Pellett, E. 360
Pellijeff, A. 112, 148
Pellman, E. J. 46, 158
Peloso, P. M. 41
Pena-Casanova, J. 150
Penn, C. 7, 8, 22
Penny, k. 45
Pentland, P. 179
Pentz, M. A. 187
Peppe, S. 186
Pepper, C. 159
Pepping, M. 84, 116
Perani, D. 22, 24, 82
Perdices, M. 16, 22, 23, 305, 377, 379, 387
Perel, P. 27, 44
Perkin, R. M. 212
Perkins, M. R. 92, 102, 111, 361, 385
Perlewitz, P. G.,335
Perlstein, W. M. 136, 156
Perret, D. 159
Perrett, D. I. 147, 156
Perrott, S. B. 170, 187
Persson, L. 45
Pessoa, L. 186
Petitfour, E. 77
Petrides, M. 59, 84

Petterson, M. 122, 149
Pettit, G. S. 176, 187, 203, 214
Pfaff, A. 23, 45, 46
Pfister, H. P. 45
Phillips, B. 386
Phillips, L. H. 151
Phillips, M. L. 71, 84, 119, 121, 136, 140, 156, 165, 187
Pickard, J. 185
Pickett, C. L. 150
Pico-Azanza, N. 150
Picton, T. 86
Pidikiti, R. 77, 149
Pierce, R. S. 21, 24, 118
Pilon, M A. 224, 225, 255
Pimentel, J. I. 117
Piolino, P. 56, 77, 84
Pitossi, F. 43
Pitt, G. 255
Pitterman, H. 129, 156
Pitts, L. H. 180
Pivik J. 86
Pizzamiglio, L. 14, 22
Plamondon, A. 148
Plante, E. 212, 280, 281
Pleger, B. 14, 22
Pliskin, N. 82
Ploetz, D. M. 44
Plumb, I. 146
Poggi, G. 173, 187
Pogue, J. 86
Poirier, C. 86
Poirier, C. A. 86
Polansky, M. 88
Poldrack, R. A. 23, 51, 75
Polissar, N. L. 187
Polkey, C. 152
Ponsford, M. 23
Ponsford, J. 17, 22, 23, 36, 37, 39, 41, 44, 45, 49, 50, 52, 53, 61, 72, 73, 74, 78, 79, 81, 84, 85, 86, 88, 117, 136, 156, 255
Porch, B. E. 4, 22
Portin, R. 153
Posner, M. I,.78
Potagas, C. 303
Potelle, D. 41
Potter, S. 47
Potvin, M. J. 58, 84
Pouk, J. A. 86, 157
Powell, J. H. 81
Power, E. 24, 111, 118, 358, 359, 360, 364, 385, 388
Poynton, C. 344, 345, 359
Prasad, M. R. 211, 214, 252
Prescott, T. E. 5, 22
Pribram, K. H. 11, 22, 120, 121, 156
Prigatano, G. P. 3, 6, 7, 11, 22, 23, 70, 71, 73, 74, 79, 84, 85, 100, 101, 116, 120, 121, 147, 156, 174, 187

Prince, S. 102, 116
Prior, M. 170, 187
Proctor, A. 118, 192, 207, 208, 214, 216
Prutting, C. A. 8, 9, 10, 22, 83, 92, 93, 94, 95, 96, 102, 105, 107, 116, 309, 334, 365, 384, 387
Pufal, A. 385
Pugh, A. K. 359
Pugsley, S. 386
Purvis, K. 113, 211
Putnam, S. H. 81

Quinette, P. 77
Quinn, P. C. 185

Rabinowitz, J. A. 19, 113, 333
Rackley, A. 277
Radel, M. 84
Radford, K. A. 59, 85
Radice-Neumann, D. 335
Raffaelli, M. 207, 214
Rahman Q. 157
Raimondi, A. J. 170, 182, 187
Raine, A. 169, 187
Raizada, R. 166, 187
Ramage, A. E. 281
Ramig, L. O. 254
Ramirez, M. 186
Ramos, F. J. 162, 185
Ramos, M. A. 184
Ramstein, K. 185
Rankin, P. M. 192, 209
Rao, V. 136, 156
Rapee, R. M. 178, 187, 188
Raphaely, R. C. 181
Rapoport, J. L. 183, 280
Rapport, L. J. 20
Rasband, M. N. 21
Raskin, S. 85
Raste, Y. 146
Ratcliffe, G. 42
Rauch, S. L. 76, 84, 156, 187
Ravid, M. 151
Raymer, A. 359, 387
Read, C. 240, 253
Rees, R. J. 385
Reilly, P. L. 197, 214
Reitan, R. M. 23, 53, 85
Reivich, M. 253
Rempel, R. 24
Rennie, D. 386
Retzlaff, P. 87
Reusink, P. 333
Reviriego, E. 116, 155
Reyna, V. F. 263, 267, 278, 281
Ria, A. 46
Ribbers, G. M. 46
Richard, M. 86

Richards, P. 253
Richardson, R. 150, 157
Richardson, W. S. 305, 387
Richburg, T. 154
Richert, J. 303
Ricken, J. H. 56, 83
Ricker, J. H. 148
Ridder, E. M. 44
Ridgeway, V. 85
Rietdijk, R. 24, 118, 359, 360, 388
Riggs, N. R. 167, 187
Righthand, S. 162, 187
Rilling, J. K. 238, 252
Rimel, R. 34, 44, 72, 85
Rindskopf, D. M. 386
Ring, H. 146
Ringholz, G. M. 76
Rios-Brown, M. 154
Rispoli, M. J. 362, 387
Ritch, J. L. 158
Ritzel, D. V. 21
Rivara, J. B. 169, 187
Rizzolati, G. 150
Roberson, G. 212
Roberts, I. 44
Roberts, R. 18, 40, 386
Robertson, B. A. 186
Robertson, D. A. 267, 281
Robertson, I. H. 14, 23, 50, 54, 82, 83, 85, 209, 214
Robertson, M. 146
Robertson, R. R. 281
Robey, R. R. 290, 305
Robin, D. A. 186
Robinson, R. G. 80, 185
Roca, V. 43
Rochat, P. 162, 187
Roche, R. A. 50, 85
Røe, C. 305
Roebuck-Spencer, T. M. 216
Rogers, M. 305
Rogers, P. 77
Rohling, M. L. 36, 44
Roig-Rovira, T. 150
Roig, T, 84
Rokaw, W. 43
Rollins, J. 22, 115, 116, 154, 334
Rolls, E, 152
Román, F., 157
Romanowski, C. A. J, 146
Roncadin, C, 112, 113, 149, 210, 211, 278
Rondacin, C, 182
Roney, C. A., 278
Root, 164, 166, 187, 385
Root, A, 187
Rose, D. 90, 115
Rose, F. D. 180
Rose, J. E. 21, 43, 90, 114. 153

Rose, S. 97, 111
Rosema, S, 180
Rosen, B. R., 76
Rosenbaum, A. M. 40
Rosenbek, J. 257
Rosenberg, H. 149
Rosenberg, J. A. 304
Rosenberg. W. 305, 387
Rosenbloom, D. 386
Rosenfeld, J. V. 174, 179, 181, 209, 210
Rosenkoetter, U, 387
Rosenthal, M. 24
Ross, E. 3, 24
Rossi, S. 239, 255
Rossini, P. M. 239, 255
Roth, R. M. 143, 156
Rothwell, J. C. 151
Roueche, J. R. 22, 70, 79, 85, 116
Roueche, M. 84, 116
Rouleau, I. 84
Rourke, B. P. 88
Rousseaux, M. 90, 117, 196, 214
Rowan, J. o. 151
Rowntree, S. 185
Rubia, k.136, 156
Rubin, K. H. 165, 188, 189, 217
Rueda, A. 58, 85
Rueda Lopes, F. C. 252
Rueda, A. 85
Rule, A. 112, 148
Rumney, P., 281
Rush, B. K. 67, 70, 71, 72, 85
Rushby, J. 22, 77, 140, 147, 149, 154, 155, 157
Rusk, H. 219, 220, 250, 255
Russell, 2, 23, 33, 34, 44, 86, 131, 133, 146, 156, 157, 162, 188, 197, 214
Rusting, C. L., 168, 188
Rutherford, M., 186
Rutter, M. 161, 181, 182, 188
Ryan, C. 159
Ryan, L. M.24
Ryland, H. 47

Saad, A., 155
Sacco, k, 111
Sackett, 282, 301, 305, 383, 386, 387
Sackett, D. 305, 386, 387
Sadan, N. 184
Safaz, I. 38, 44, 219, 255
Safran, A. 20, 42, 114
Sakashita, C. 181
Sakata, D. 148
Salazar, A. M. 1, 2, 19, 23, 281, 323, 332
Salazar, E. 303
Salmelin, R. 19
Salorio, C. F. 210, 215
Salovey, P. 129, 154
Sampson, H. 50, 79

Sanchez, C. 214
Sanchez-Carrion, R. 84, 150
Sánchez-Navarro, J.P. 122, 137, 157
Sandanam, J. 45
Sander, A. M. 23, 44, 157, 335, 387
Sandra, S. 42
Sandvik, L. 305
Sanson, A. 183
Santoro, J. M. 86, 157
Sapiennza, C. M. 254
Sapienza, C. 235, 256
Sapir, S. 257
Sarno, M. T. 4, 5, 6, 23, 38, 45, 89, 117, 218, 219, 220, 255
Sartori, G. 18, 23
Sarwar, M. 21
Sato, W. 121, 157
Sato, Y. 186
Satz, P. 156, 180
Saunders , A. E. 280
Saunders, C. 115, 116, 154
Saunders, J. C. 109, 115, 120, 121, 122, 137, 154, 157
Savage, R. 258, 259, 281
Savage, S. 22, 23, 305, 387
Saver, J. L. 65, 70, 85
Sawyer, M.187
Sawyer, T. 77
Saxe, R. 165, 188
Say, M. J. 85
Sayer, L. 86
Saykin, A. J. 154
Sazbon, L. 255
Scahill, V. 209
Scarpa, M. T. 38, 40
Schaal, B. 157
Schachar, R. 113, 182, 211, 213, 280
Schank, R. 8, 23
Schecter, I. 255
Schecter, L. 42, 255
Scheibel, R. 184, 257
Scherf, k. S. 192, 214
Schiavone, D. A., 303
Schinka, J. A. 87
Schloss, C. N., 333, 385, 387
Schloss, P. J. 333, 365, 371, 374, 383, 385, 387
Schmidt, A. T. 208, 214, 360
Schmidt, N. D. 360
Schmidt, U. 157
Schmithorst, V. J. 193, 215
Schmitter-Edgecombe, M. 74, 84, 85, 148
Schmitz, B. 146
Schneider, R. 49, 85
Schnelle, k. P. 184, 212, 213
Schnider, A. 21
Schniering, C. A. 187
Schoenberg, B. S. 46
Schöll, M. 213

Schönberger, M. 17, 22, 23, 45, 72, 78, 79, 85, 88
Schonle, P. W. 253
Schreckenghost, D. 386
Schuller, R. 281, 335, 388
Schultz, J. 335
Schultz, L. H. 189, 216
Schultz, M. C. 290, 305
Schultz, R. 22, 23, 387
Schulz, K. F. 22
Schunk, D. H. 100, 112
Schurr, P. H. 76
Schut, L. 181
Schwab, K. A. 23, 24, 44, 45
Schwartz, G. 83
Schwartz. M. F. 79
Schwartz, M. L . 43, 79, 81, 150, 153, 300
Schwartz , R. 42
Schwenkreis, P. 22
Scott, C. L. 152
Scott, D. 251
Scott, J. G. 47
Scott, M. A. 113, 211
Searle, J. 89, 117
Seaver, E. J. 237, 252
Sebastian, C. 181
Secord, W. 7, 24, 199, 201, 203, 215, 216
Seel, R. T. 40, 44, 81
Segal, O. 20
Segalowitz, S. J. 152
Seibert, L. k. 154
Seidman, L. J. 76
Seignourel, P. J. 156
Selassie, A. W. 41
Selikowitz, M. 147
Sellars, C. 240, 255, 360
Selman, R. L. 189, 216
Semel, E. M. 7, 24, 199, 201, 215
Senathi-Raja, D. 37, 38, 45
Sengoku, A. 157
Ser vadei, F. 45
Serpia, S. 156
Servadei, F. 29, 45
Seshia, S. S. 212
Shadish, W. R. 386
Shaffer, D. 181
Shallice, T. 4, 23, 49, 61, 62, 64, 65, 66, 69, 83, 85
Shamay, S. G. 157
Shamay-Tsoory, S. G. 102, 104, 117, 126, 127, 151, 157
Shapira, J. S. 155
Shapiro, D. 83
Sharma, A. 170, 188
Sharma, H. 42
Sharma, M. 170, 188
Sharma, T. 156
Sharp, D. J. 81
Shaw, D. A. 182
Shenton, M. 386

Shephard, k. 217
Sherer, M. 34, 40, 44, 45, 46, 70, 85, 88
Sherrington, C. 304, 386, 387
Shiel, A. 88
Shiffrin, R. 49, 85
Shigaki, C. 350, 359
Shimamura, A. P. 59, 80, 85
Shores, A. 45
Shrapnel, N. 256
Shrivastav, R. 254
Shue, k. 334
Shulman, K. 41
Shum, D, 50, 57, 58, 85, 86, 116, 152, 154, 193, 215, 216, 334
Shurtleff, H. A. 187
Signoretti, S. 46
Silasi, G. 166, 188
Silveri, M. 281
Silverman, L. 257
Simion, A,.116, 155
Simmons, A. 156
Simmons, N. 220, 256
Simmons-Mackie, N. 350, 359, 362, 387
Simon, G. A., 252
Simpson, D. A. 214
Simpson, G. k. 72, 86, 152
Simpson. R. 386
Singer, T. 184
Sipes, A. L. 318, 320, 325, 333, 337, 358
Sivan, A. B. 18
Skreczek, W. 41
Slade, D. 340, 358
Slater, A.M. 185, 188, 215
Slater, M. D. 162, 184
Sleigh, J. W. 80, 154
Sloan, S. 61, 84, 86
Slomine, B. S. 194, 210, 215
Sluiter, J. K. 46
Smahel, D. 215
Small, R. 185
Smigelski, J. S. 303
Smigielski, J. 334
Smith, A. 33, 34, 44,197, 214, 333
Smith, K. 22, , 58, 119, 387
Smith, L. 152
Smith, M. 185
Smith, N. E. 181, 184
Smith, R. E. 84, 85, 86
Smith, W. L. 186, 387
Snoek, J. 42, 80
Snow, P. C. 2, 11, 19, 23, 73, 84, 86, 94, 95, 102, 113, 117, 303, 333, 359
Snyder, G.J. 241, 251
Snyder, H. M., 187
So, Y. 303
Sohlberg, M. M. 38, 45, 82, 205, 215, 216, 285, 286, 296, 298, 300, 303, 304, 305, 306, 319, 335, 365, 372, 374, 375, 383, 387

Solomon, N. P. 235, 240, 246, 256
Sommer, k. L. 139, 159
Sommerville, R. B. 183
Sommovigo, M. 187
Song, J. 18, 111, 112, 210, 212, 213, 278, 279
Sonuga-Barke, E.J. S. 182
Soo, C. 178, 188
Sopena, S. 88
Sorge, R. 46
Soury, S. 75
Soussignan, R. 122, 137, 157
Sowell, E. R. 193, 215
Spackman, M. P. 183
Sparks, G. 112, 210, 278
Sparling, M. B. 154
Sparrow, S. 173, 188
Specht, K. 21
Spector, J. 332
Spell, L. A. 120, 129, 157
Spence, J, 77, 87
Spence, S. 90, 117
Spencer-Smith, M. M. 184, 185
Spettell, C. 33, 45
Spezio, M. 165, 179
Spielman, L. 75
Spiers, M. V. 69, 86, 124, 157
Spikman, J. M. 124, 125, 157
Spirl, E. 386
Spong, A. 209
Spreen, O. 7, 23
Sprengelmeyer, R. 159
Sprod, R. 214
Sprunk, H. 372, 387
Square, P. 253
Squire, L. R. 55, 57, 59, 80, 85, 86
Sripada, C. S. 122, 151
Stabler, P. A. 251
Stallings-Roberson, G. 280
Stam, H. J. 46
Stancin, T. 183, 188, 189, 212, 215, 217
Stathopoulos, E. T. 235, 256
Stattrop, U. 253
Stegagno, L. 146
Stein, N. L. 96, 117
Stein, S. C. 33, 45
Steinberg, L. 205, 209, 215
Stern, M. J. 42
Stethem, L. L. 86
Stevens, M. 79
Stevens, S. 182
Stewart, M. L. 335, 388
Stewart, L. H. 254
Stiers, W. 287, 305
Stocchetti, N. 43, 45
Stokes, P. D., 252, 255, 256
Stoll, J. 254
Stone, M. H. 146
Stone, V. 124, 130, 133, 152, 157

Stone, C, 81
Stopa, E. 42
Stout, C. E. 92, 93, 117
Strand, E. 253, 254
Strange, B. A. 159, 203
Straus, S. 387
Strettles, B. 23, 45
Striano, T.,184, 187
Strich, S. J. 222, 256
Stringer, A. Y. 365, 373, 387
Stronach, S. T. 127, 157, 196, 207, 215
Strong, C-A. H. 7, 23
Strong, J. 78, 84, 334
Struchen, M. A. 15, 23, 45, 127, 139, 157, 310, 312, 335, 362, 364, 387
Sturm, W. 21
Stuss, D. T. 50, 57, 59, 71, 74, 81, 86, 136, 137, 157
Subrahmanyam, K. 207, 215
Sufit, R. 304
Suhr, 138, 148
Suhr, J. A, 148
Sui, D. 158
Sullivan, C. 43
Sullivan, K. W. 256
Summers, C. F. 2, 23, 36, 45
Summers, F. 151
Sun, F. 30, 45
Sun, P. 211
Sunderland, A. 75
Surian, L. 124, 150, 158
Susanna, G. 42
Suskauer, S. J. 197, 215
Susmaras, T. 43, 81, 82
Sussman, H. 254
Sutherland, D. 77
Sveen, U. 287, 305
Swaine, B. 214
Swank, P. 184, 213, 252, 279
Swart, E. 41
Sweeney, J. A. 43, 81, 213, 214
Swift, E. 189
Sylvester, C.-Y. 87
Symington, C. 41, 76, 147, 332
Szekeres, S. F. 6, 25, 345, 360

Tabaddor, K. 41
Taiminen, T. 153
Tallal, P. 23
Talley, J. L. 80
Tamminga, C. A. 152
Tanenbaum, L. N. 119, 124, 148
Tarkiainen, A. 19
Tate, R. L. 3, 16, 17, 22, 23, 24, 32, 33, 35, 36, 37, 39, 45, 46, 48, 61, 67, 68, 72, 73, 78, 81, 86, 87, 88, 116, 118, 123, 132, 136, 137, 142, 145, 150, 153, 154, 158, 175, 186, 188, 292, 305, 334, 359, 360, 377, 379, 380, 381, 384, 386, 387, 388

Tateno, A. 185
Taub, E. 21
Tavazzi, B. 46
Tavender, E. 302
Taylor, C. 387
Taylor, D. W. 386
Taylor, E. M, 59, 87, 156
Taylor, G. S. 45, 185
Taylor, H. G. 169, 172, 183, 187, 188, 189, 206, 212, 214, 215, 217
Tchanturia, K. 157
Teasdale, G. M. 21, 31, 43, 45, 46, 114, 151, 153, 185, 257
Tegenthoff, M. 22
Teh, M. 152
Tellegen, A. 186
Temkin, N. R. 41, 76, 78, 79, 151
Temple, E. 14, 23
Tennant, A. 76
Tenovuo, O. 153
Terasawa, Y. 87
Tessner, k. D. 215
Tettamanti, M. 24
Thaut, M. H. 255
Theodoros, D. G. 38, 46, 220, 224, 226, 227, 228, 232, 233, 251, 252, 253, 255, 256, 257
Theodorou, G. 151
Thilo, k. V. 151
Thomas, C. 42
Thomas, K. E. 44, 214, 280, 332
Thomas, L. L. 214, 332, 385
Thomas-Stonell, N. 268, 281
Thompson, C. K. 5, 18, 24, 333, 346, 385, 387
Thompson, B. 150
Thompson, J. M. 334
Thompson, P. M. 183, 215
Thompson, S. A. 359
Thompson, W. F. 151
Thompson-Ward, E. C. 232, 247, 256
Thomsen, I. V. 3, 4, 11, 24, 31, 36, 37, 38, 46, 66, 67, 68, 70, 74, 87, 89, 117, 132, 158, 218, 219, 250, 256, 310, 335
Thornton, H. 386
Thunberg, M. 122, 149
Tiesma, D. 23
Tigno, J.18, 40
Till, C. 66, 67, 87
Till, J. A. 253
Timmerman, M. E. 157
Ting, C, 186
Tirassa, M. 146
Todd, J. 152
Todis, B. 281
Todorov, A. 184
Toga, A. W. 183, 215
Togher, L. 10, 15, 22, 23, 24, 78, 90, 92, 93, 94, 98, 99, 101, 106, 108, 111, 113, 114, 116, 117, 118, 150, 153, 155, 186, 249, 252, 262, 268,

280, 281, 305, 333, 334, 336, 346, 348, 349, 350, 351, 356, 358, 359, 360, 362, 363, 364, 385, 386, 387, 388
Tok, F. 44, 255
Tomasello, M. 162, 181, 188
Tomaszewski, W. 385
Tomer, R. 117, 157
Tomita, 18, 146
Tompkins, C. 113, 279
Tonks, J. 158, 173, 177, 188, 189, 194, 208, 215, 216, 281
Tormos, J. M. 84
Toth, J. P. 81
Toussaint, L. 135, 158
Towne, R. L. 207, 215
Tranel, D. 75, 77, 119, 121, 146, 147, 149, 151, 152, 153, 158, 179, 209
Traub, M. 181
Trauner, D. A. 197, 212
Trexler, L. E. 19, 52, 87
Trojanowski, T. 45
Trower, P. 308, 335
Troyanskaya, M. 46
Tulving, E. 76, 81
Turkstra, L. S. 25, 57, 87, 94, 95, 102, 118, 124, 125, 127, 148, 157, 158, 167, 176, 178, 186, 188, 189, 191, 194, 195, 196, 199, 203, 205, 207, 208, 210, 214, 215, 216, 260, 279, 281, 285, 286, 287, 292, 303, 304, 305, 306, 360
Turner, A. B. 251
Turner, G. R. 151
Turner, S. 350, 360
Turner, S. M. 180
Turner, T. 302
Turner-Stokes, L. 312, 313, 335
Twijnstra, A. 40
Tyerman, A. 22, 44, 84
Tyler, E. 112
Tyler, J. P. 281

Uchiyama, C. L. 156
Ueda, k. 148
Ulatowska, H. 7, 8, 24, 90, 118, 263, 281
Ullman, C. 255
Umeda, S. 59, 87
Unterberg, A. 45
Uomoto, 34, 42
Urade, M. 253
Urban, T. A. 213
Urbanczyk, B. 360
Uttley, D. 83, 184
Uzzell, B. P. 83, 116, 253

Vagnozzi, R. 36, 46
Vaituzis, A. C. 183
Vakil, E. 20
Valkil, E. 75
Vallar, G. 22

van den Hout, M. A. 155
van Hout, W. 155
van Bennekom, C. A. M. 46
van den Broek, M.D. 156
van der Naalt, J. 157
van Dijk, T.A. 8, 24, 95, 114, 118
van Dongen, H.R. 256
Van Hout, A. 41
Van Hout, W. 155
Van Leer, E. 94, 95, 118, 196, 216
van Mourik, M. 224, 256
Van overwalle, F. 165, 189
Van Sommers, 73, 74, 83, 101, 115, 124, 154
Van Sommers, P, 83
Van Tol, E. 175, 189
van Velzen, J. M. 37, 46
Van Wolffelaar, P. C. 52, 76
van Zomeren, A. H. 48, 50, 51, 52, 53, 62, 74, 87
Vanberten, M. 112
Vance, S. C. 23
Vanderploeg, R. 57, 87
Vanegas, S. 279
Vangel, S. 20
Vannatta, K. 189, 217
Vargha-khadem, F. 254
Vas, 7, 14, 24, 261, 262, 263, 271, 276, 281
Vasa, R. 215
Vasquez, C. 184, 213, 254
Vecht, C. 185
Veenstra, W. S. 157
Veerabangsa, A. 188
Veerman, J. W, 186
Velikonja, D. 66, 67, 71, 72, 87, 88
Velligan, D. I. 141, 158
Velozo, C. 305
Vendrell, P. 84
Venkatesh, B. 44
Ventola, E. 98, 118, 348, 360
Verhagen, A. P., 46
Verigneaux, C. 117, 214
Viano, D. C. 26, 46, 119, 158
Vickery, B. G. 290, 305
Viinamäki, H. 153
Villarreal, E. 305
Vitali, 5, 24
Vitorino, 224, 226, 257
Vitorino, J. 257
Vo, A. H. 18, 40
Vogel, A. P. 239, 241, 254
Volle, E. 58, 87
Cramon, D.Y. 113, 220, 227, 256, 257
von Gruenewaldt, A. 333
von Holst, H. 41
Von Laufen, A. 81
Vorano, L. 111, 115
Vrana, S. R.. 158

Wade, C. 21
Wade, D. 152
Wade, N. 183
Wade, S. 183, 188, 189, 212, 214, 215, 217
Wager, T. D. 51, 87, 214
Wakim, D. 387
Wald, 42
Walker, C. J. 43, 81
Walker, E. 255
Walker, S. 168, 189
Walker, W. C. 34, 35, 44, 46
Wallace, C. 3, 24, 72, 87
Wallace, G. 215, 216
Wallander, J. L. 19, 113, 311, 333, 335
Walsh, k. W. 57, 62, 64, 69, 71, 77, 87, 102, 112, 125, 136, 137, 140, 149, 158
Walsh, V. 386
Walz, N. 189, 212, 217
Wambaugh, J. L. 5, 24, 284, 303, 305
Wanberg, C. R. 189
Wanek, A. 210
Wang, C.-C. 35, 36, 46
Wang, J. Y. 87
Wang, Y. 45
Wang, Z. J. 46
Ward, E.C. 255
Ward, H. 193, 216, 247
Ward, T. 85
Warden, D. L. 2, 24, 332
Warner, M. A. 63, 87
Warriner, E. M. 67, 71, 87, 88
Warschausky, S. A. 176, 180, 189, 194, 208, 211
Wasserman, R. 335, 388
Wassermann, E. 239, 257
Watkins, R. 278
Watson, M. 45
Watson, P. 88
Watts, A. J. 110, 118, 121, 126, 127, 158
Watts, C. 110
Watts, k. P. 75
Watts , M. 66, 76, 102, 104, 105, 111
Webb, J. R. 135, 158
Wechsler, D. 6, 7, 24, 53, 54, 59, 60, 64, 65, 88, 152
Wechsler, F. S. 268, 280, 314, 315, 320, 321, 333, 362, 363, 383, 386
Wedcliffe, T. 3, 24
Weddell, R. 37, 46, 66, 67, 88
Wehlman, P. H. 81
Weidmann, k. D. 257
Weiller, C. 21
Weingarter, H. 23
Weintraub, S. 20
Weis, S. 21
Weiss, G. J. 252
Welch, C. 162, 187
Wellman, L. 240, 253
Wells, R. 124, 125, 158

Wenke, R. J. 241, 247, 248, 257
Wertheimer, J. C. 204, 216
Wertz, R.T. 38, 46, 73, 74, 83, 100, 116, 303
Wesley, E. 214
Wethe, J. 23
Wexler, B. E. 151
Weyauch, J. 210
Whalen, P. J. 76
Wheaton, P. 50, 52, 74, 82, 136, 154
Wheelwright, S. S. J. 132, 135, 146, 147, 209
Whelan-Goodinson, R. 72, 84, 88
Whishaw, I. Q. 185
Whitaker, H. A. 77
Whitehouse, W. 213
Whiteneck, G. G. 182, 333, 385
Whitworth, A. 350, 360
Whyte, J. 40, 42, 52, 85, 88, 302, 305
Widdig, W. 22
Wiederholt, J. L. 212
Wiemann , J. M.. 359
Wignall, A. 187
Wiig, E. H. 7, 24, 199, 201, 203, 215, 216
Wijen, G. 40
Wilcox, K. 231, 257
Wilcox, M. J. 24, 118
Wild, B. 122, 158
Wilde, E. A. 36, 46, 184, 212, 213, 214, 254, 257
Wilde, M. C. 56, 88
Wilkinson, M. 113, 211
Wilkinson, R. 250, 251
Willemse-van Son, A. H. P. 46
Willer, B. 17, 18, 24, 146, 335
Willer, J.-C. 155
Williams, A. L. 253
William, C. 66, 88, 123, 132 135,159
Williams, D. H. 81
Williams, K. D. 139, 159
Williams, K. R. 123, 159
Williams, P. 213
Williams, S. C. 156
Williams, W. H. 36, 47, 79, 83, 139, 158, 188, 189, 215, 216, 281, 335
Williamson, D. J. G. 47
Wilson, B. A. 59, 66, 75, 81, 88, 143, 159, 207, 208, 211, 214, 216, 287, 305
Wilson, B. C. 332
Wilson, B. M. 80, 93, 94, 118, 207, 214, 216
Wilson, K. R. 208, 216
Wilson, M. 81, 211
Wilson, J. T. L. 220, 257
Winders, K. 22, 387
Winn, H. 41, 78
Winner, E. 113, 151, 211
Winqvist, S. 35, 47
Winstanley, J. B. 46, 87
Winston, J. 126, 156, 159
Wise, S. P. 251

Wiseman-Hakes, C. 302, 304, 318, 319, 320, 335, 362, 388
Wisotzek, I. E. 332, 385
Witol, A. D. 81
Witzki, A. H. 214
Wolery, M. 386
Wolf-Nelson, N. 212
Wong, S. B. 265, 266, 267, 268, 278, 281
Wood, L. 24, 88, 159
Wood, R. L. 24, 41, 66, 68, 76, 78, 88, 123, 132, 135, 159
Woodford, M. 44
Woods, D. T. 164, 178, 189
Woo-Sam, J. 251
Workinger, M. 220, 257
Wozniak, J. R. 213
Wright, S. 5, 24
Wright, D. W. 44
Wright, J. 79
Wuthrich, V. 187
Wyke, M. A. 184

Xi, Y. L. 44
Xu, L. 42

Yablon, S. A. 44, 45, 85
Yallampalli, R. 46, 184, 254
Yang, K. H. 46, 158
Yang , Y. 169, 187
Yang, Y.-C. 46, 181
Yanofsky, N. 154
Yarger, R. S. 213
Yasar, E. 44, 255
Yates, P. 188, 215
Yeakley, J. 277
Yeates, K. O. 163, 164, 172, 173, 174, 175, 176, 183, 185, 188, 189, 193, 195, 196, 203, 206, 212, 214, 215, 216, 217
Yeung, O. 5, 25
Yiend, J. 85
Yilmaz, B. 44, 255
Yim, J. 18, 146
Ylvisaker, M. 6, 15, 25, 181, 202, 210, 216, 217, 220, 257, 259, 260, 261, 279, 281, 297, 298, 303, 304, 305, 306, 310, 335, 338, 345, 350, 351, 353, 359, 360
Yorkston, K. 20, 38, 40, 117, 220, 231, 233, 251, 253, 254, 257, 303, 304, 305, 306
Yoshikawa, S. 157
Young, A. 128, 133, 153, 159, 296
Young, H. F. 81
Young, R. L. D. 334
Youse, K. M. 92, 104, 112, 118, 210, 365, 373, 374, 383, 388
Yousef-Bak, E. 256
Yuan, W. 193, 215

Zafonte, R. 40

Zahn, R. 186
Zajonc, R. 122, 145
Zalagens, M. R. 21, 115
Zampieri, E. 115
Zappala, G. 52, 87
Zappi, D. 45
Zasler, N. 40
Zeanah, C. 180
Zeiner, J. R. 84, 116
Zelazo, P. D. 136, 159
Zettin, M. 111, 115, 187
Zhang, E. J. 46, 158
Zhang, L. 112, 210, 212, 213, 278, 280
Zhang, X. 252

Zhou, X. J. 82
Ziarnek, N. 319, 334
Ziegler, W. 224, 226, 227, 257
Zientz, J. 277, 278
Ziggas, D. 21
Ziino, C. 52, 88
Zijdenbos, A. 183, 280
Zimmer-Gembeck, M. J. 217
Zimmerman, R. 170, 181, 189, 253
Ziviani, J. 197, 217
Zlomke, k. 385
Zoccatelli, G. 46
Zupan, B. 18, 146, 335

CPSIA information can be obtained
at www.ICGtesting.com
Printed in the USA
LVHW082117171118
597504LV00001B/4/P

9 781848 721357